The Amendments to the Constitution

The Amendments to the Constitution

A COMMENTARY

George Anastaplo

The Johns Hopkins University Press

BALTIMORE AND LONDON

04   03   02   01   00   99   98   97   96   95   5   4   3   2   1

The Johns Hopkins University Press
2715 North Charles Street
Baltimore, Maryland 21218-4319
The Johns Hopkins Press Ltd., London

ISBN 0-8018-4959-4
ISBN 0-8018-4960-8 (pbk.)

Library of Congress Cataloging-in-Publication Data

Anastaplo, George, 1925–
    The amendments to the Constitution : a commentary /
George Anastaplo.
        p.   cm.
    Includes bibliographical references and index.
    ISBN 0-8018-4959-4 (hc).—ISBN 0-8018-4960-8 (pbk.)
    1. United States—Constitutional law—Amendments.
I. Title.
    KF4557.A53   1995
    342.73'03—dc20
    [347.3023]   94-25199
                                                            CIP

A catalog record for this book is available from the British Library.

TO
MY BROTHERS
who,
not without considerable personal sacrifice,
have for decades honored
that ancient republican faith
which is grounded in the integrity of the family

"There again," [Euthydemus] cried, "you really must stop adding these qualifications." "But," [Socrates] said, "I am so afraid this word 'always' may bring us to grief."

—PLATO

And as they bound him with thongs, Paul said to the centurion who stood by, "Is it lawful for you to scourge a man who is a Roman, and uncondemned?" When the centurion heard that, he went and told the commander, saying, "Take care what you do, for this man is a Roman." . . . Then immediately those who were about to examine him withdrew from him; and the commander was also afraid after he found out that he was a Roman, and because he had bound him.

—ACTS OF THE APOSTLES

The appeal to the rights of man, which had been made in the United States, was taken up by France, first of the European nations. From her, the spirit has spread over those of the South. The tyrants of the North have allied indeed against it; but it is irresistible. Their opposition will only multiply its millions of human victims; their own satellites will catch it, and the condition of man through the civilized world will be finally and greatly ameliorated. This is a wonderful instance of great events from small causes. So inscrutable is the arrangement of causes and consequences in this world, that a two-penny duty on tea, unjustly imposed in a sequestered part of [the world], changes the condition of all its inhabitants.

—THOMAS JEFFERSON

I am not one of those who say that everybody should be equal, but what I do say is that no one should have anything unless everybody has something.

—WINSTON S. CHURCHILL

Nor is it implausible to say that the supreme guarantor of Right can not be simply subject to Right, but must have his hands free.

—LEO STRAUSS

A state without the means of some change is without the means of its conservation.

—EDMUND BURKE

It is significant that the seceding States of the South, in 1861, did not appeal to the right of revolution. They appealed—however speciously—to the right to secession as a constitutional right. They went to great lengths to avoid appealing to a right whose exercise would obviously apply far more to their slaves than to themselves.

—HARRY V. JAFFA

When I went into the house [at Appomattox Court House] I found General Lee. We greeted each other, and after shaking hands took our seats. . . . What General Lee's feelings were I do not know. As he was a man of much dignity, with an impassible face, it was impossible to say whether he felt inwardly glad that the end had finally come, or felt sad over the result, and was too manly to show it. Whatever his feelings, they were entirely concealed from my observation; but my own feelings, which had been quite jubilant on the receipt of his letter [offering to surrender his army], were sad and depressed. I felt like anything rather than rejoicing at the downfall of a foe who had fought so long and valiantly, and had suffered so much for a cause, though that cause was, I believe, one of the worst for which a people ever fought, and one for which there was the least excuse. I do not question, however, the sincerity of the great mass of those who were opposed to us. . . . I feel that we are on the eve of a new era, when there is to be great harmony between the Federal and Confederate. I cannot stay to be a living witness to the correctness of this prophecy; but I feel it within me that it is to be so.

—ULYSSES S. GRANT

We must not be afraid to be free.

—HUGO LAFAYETTE BLACK

Contents

Preface   xv

1. The Intentions of the Federal Convention of 1787   1
2. The Federal Convention and a Bill of Rights   11
3. Predecessors to the American Bill of Rights   22
4. The Purposes and Effects of the Bill of Rights of 1791   33
5. Amendment I   47
6. Amendments II, III, and IV   59
7. Amendments V, VI, VII, and VIII   77
8. Amendments IX, X, XI, and XII   92
9. Education in the New Republic   107
10. The Confederate Constitution of 1861   125
11. The Emancipation Proclamation of 1862–1863   135
12. Amendments XIII, XIV, and XV   168
13. Amendments XVI, XVII, and XIX   186
14. Amendments XVIII and XXI   195
15. Amendments XX, XXII, XXIII, and XXV   207
16. Amendments XXIII, XXIV, XXVI, and XXVII   217
17. The Constitution in the Twenty-first Century   228

APPENDIXES AND SOURCES   239
A. Magna Carta (1215)   244

B. Thomas More's Petition to Henry VIII on
Parliamentary Freedom of Speech (1521)   256

C. The Petition of Right (1628)   259

D. The English Bill of Rights (1689)   263

E. Declarations by American Congresses (1765–1776)
E-1. Declarations of Rights & Grievances by the
Stamp Act Congress (1765)   269
E-2. Declaration and Resolves by the First Continental
Congress (1774)   271
E-3. The Declaration of Independence (1776)   276

F. Declarations of Rights (1776–1780)
F-1. Virginia Declaration of Rights (1776)   281
F-2. Massachusetts Declaration of Rights (1780)   283

G. Virginia Statute of Religious Liberty (1785)   291

H. The Principal Bill of Rights Discussions in James
Madison's *Notes of Debates in the Federal Convention*
(1787)
H-1. Monday, August 20, 1787   293
H-2. Wednesday, September 12, 1787   294
H-3. Saturday, September 15, 1787   295

I. Amendment Proposals by the Last States to Ratify the
Constitution before Its Initial Implementation (1788)
I-1. Virginia Ratification Convention (June 26–27, 1788)   298
I-2. New York Ratification Convention (July 26, 1788)   305

J. Stages of the Bill of Rights in the First Congress and in
the State Legislatures (1789–1791)
J-1. James Madison's Proposals in the House of
Representatives (June 8, 1789)   315
J-2. Amendments Reported by a House of
Representatives Committee (July 28, 1789)   320
J-3. Amendments Passed by the House of Representatives
(August 24, 1789)   323
J-4. Amendments Passed by the Senate (September 9,
1789)   325
J-5. Amendments Proposed by Congress for Ratification
by the States (September 25, 1789)   326

Contents

J-6. Ratification Returns from the States
(November 20, 1789–December 15, 1791) 329

K. Letters Exchanged by Thomas Jefferson and
John Adams (1814)
K-1. Letter from Thomas Jefferson to John Adams
(July 5, 1814) 330
K-2. Letter from John Adams to Thomas Jefferson
(July 16, 1814) 335

L. Anglo-American Responses to Slavery (1771–1863)
L-1. Somerset's Case (1771–1772) 341
L-2. The Constitution of the Confederate States
of America (1861) 344
L-3. The Emancipation Proclamation (1862–1863) 362

M. The Constitution of 1787 with Amendments
(1787–1992)
M-1. The Constitution of 1787 (1787) 363
M-2. Amendments to the Constitution of 1787
(1791–1992) 375

Notes 385
Index 455

Preface

Thus says the Lord of hosts, the God of Israel, "Amend your ways
and your doings, and I will let you dwell in this place. Do not trust in
these deceptive words: 'This is the temple of the Lord, the temple of
the Lord, the temple of the Lord.' For if you truly amend your ways
and your doings, if you truly execute justice one with another, if you
do not oppress the alien, the fatherless or the widow, or shed innocent blood in this place, and if you do not go after other gods to your
own hurt, then I will let you dwell in this place, in the land that I
gave of old to your fathers for ever."
—Jeremiah 7: 3–7

I was not surprised to confirm, upon preparing these lectures for
publication, that there is readily available much more material bearing upon the amendments to the United States Constitution than
it would be useful for anyone to try to notice in a Commentary devoted (as this one is) primarily to the texts of those twenty-seven
amendments. We can appropriate for our response to this abundant
and often useful amendments-related material, both official and
scholarly, an observation made by Abraham Lincoln about a book
he was once asked to comment upon, "People who like this sort of
thing will find this the sort of thing they like."

The reader interested only in the texts of the amendments may
want to skip, in a first reading of this Commentary, the first four
lectures as well as Lectures No. 9, No. 10, and No. 11. There are
things said in my opening lectures that are likely to seem much
more plausible once the reader begins to get a sense of this Commentary as a whole. The reader who is particularly interested in
how the fateful accommodations to slavery in the Constitution of

1787 have been dealt with since the Founding Period should perhaps begin with Lectures No. 10, No. 11, and No. 12. Such a reader is also referred to Sections VI–IX of Lecture No. 13 of the companion volume to this Commentary on the Amendments. (That companion volume, my Commentary on the Constitution of 1787, was published in 1989.)

Almost all of the lectures upon which this Commentary is based were prepared for audiences made up of the students and faculty of Lenoir-Rhyne College and the townspeople of Hickory, North Carolina. Those lectures were delivered between September 1990 and April 1991, combining thereby a centennial celebration of the College with a bicentennial celebration of the Bill of Rights. My work with and on the Constitution, for more than four decades now, has been designed to redeem the story of this Country in such a way as to contribute (despite the corrosive effects of our Cold War follies) both to the edification of this generation of my fellow citizens and to the education of the teachers of future generations. (These efforts had their patriotic and hence fortunate beginning in November 1950 when I was a twenty-five-year-old would-be lawyer. An earlier, more conventional, and less chance-driven beginning of my constitutional efforts had been in the fall of 1943 when I, as a seventeen-year-old, set out to enlist in the Air Cadet program of the Army Air Corps.) One exasperating, if not even dangerous, consequence of American restlessness is a widespread insistence upon more and more change, almost for its own sake, so much so as to keep all too many of us from acknowledging and enjoying the many good things we do happen to have in our households and in our communities. We would all do well to take to heart the counsel once offered to Xerxes about "how evil it is to teach the soul always to seek to have more than it has at the moment."

My Commentary on the Constitution of 1787 (published in law-journal form in 1987 and in book form in 1989) had been based upon lectures given in 1985–1986 at the Rochester Institute of Technology, in Rochester, New York. I observed, in the preface to that Commentary, that in journeying to New York to deliver those Rochester lectures anticipating the bicentennial of the Constitution I had felt a certain kinship with the James Madison of *The Federalist*, who also made use of the opportunity provided him in that State to explain the Constitution. The appropriateness, in turn, of a North Carolina venue for my 1990–1991 Lenoir-Rhyne lectures on the amendments is suggested by the recollection that that State had withheld its assent to the Constitution of 1787 until the First Congress had submitted a bill of rights to the States for their ratification. It proved an attractive coincidence that the editor primarily responsible for the initial publication of these amendments lectures (in the Summer 1992 issue of the *Loyola University of Chicago Law Journal*) should herself be a descendant of Charles Pinckney, the *South* Carolina delegate in the Federal Convention of 1787 who was eager to prepare a bill of rights for the Constitution. Another connection I have with the Carolinas is through my wife's family, which was partly responsible for the founding of Davidson College in 1837.

These Centennial Lectures were arranged by President John E. Trainer of Lenoir-Rhyne College, who was assisted by J. Larry Yoder, Marianne Yoder, and Joseph S. Mancos of the College faculty. Critical to the despatch with which the Hickory lectures were developed for law journal and subsequent book publication were the efforts of two most reliable secretaries, Beverly R. Hefner of Lenoir-Rhyne College and Janice K. Haddon of the Loyola School of Law. The very useful Loyola law-journal publication benefited from the help of Virginia Thomas of the Loyola law library research staff and from the contributions of sympathetic student editors: Laura Banks Hardwicke, Thomas Cargie, Lori Griess, Paul A. Sheldon, Allan Jay Spellberg, and Stephanie Rae Williams. Stephen J. Vanderslice, of Louisiana State University at Alexandria, made many useful suggestions prior to law-journal publication.

I have had the benefit also of comments and suggestions by readers of the law-journal version of this Commentary as I have prepared it for publication in book form. These readers include Laurence Berns of St. John's College, Keith Cleveland of Columbia College, Leo Paul S. de Alvarez of the University of Dallas, Jules Gleicher of Rockford College, Daniel N. Hoffman of Johnson C. Smith University, Andrew J. Majeske of the Illinois bar, John A. Murley of the Rochester Institute of Technology, Andrew Patner of the Chicago press and radio, Robert L. Stone of Oklahoma City University, and Stephen J. Vanderslice of Louisiana State University. J. Kent Calder of the Indiana Historical Society was once again very helpful as copy editor.

I have benefited as well, in preparing Lecture No. 9 (on a pivotal exchange in 1814 between Thomas Jefferson and John Adams bearing upon the education of the American people), from the suggestions and work of John Alvis of the University of Dallas, Larry E. Arnhart of Northern Illinois University, Laurence Berns of St. John's College, David Bevington of the University of Chicago, William T. Braithwaite of Loyola University of Chicago, Eva T. H. Brann of St. John's College, Christopher A. Colmo of Rosary College, Thomas Engeman of Loyola University of Chicago, Don E. Fehrenbacher of Stanford University, Harry V. Jaffa of Claremont McKenna College, John Van Doren of the Institute for Philosophical Research, Bernard Weisberg of the United States District Court in the Northern District of Illinois, and Thomas G. West of the University of Dallas. I have been encouraged in these and other efforts by the good will of John A. Murley, William T. Braithwaite, and Robert L. Stone in preparing an instructive *festschrift* in my honor, *Law and Philosophy: The Practice of Theory*, a two-volume collection of remarkably instructive essays upon which I repeatedly draw in the notes of this Commentary. I have been encouraged as well by a generous John C. Fitzgerald Faculty Research Award by the Loyola School of Law.

Most of the notes in this Commentary (which can be skimmed, if not even skipped, during one's first reading of the text) have been prepared since the Lenoir-Rhyne lectures were originally given, although some of the material in the notes was originally in the lectures. (One's discussions of the many rights associated with the amendments tend to be—perhaps, indeed, should be—more "personal" than do one's discussions of the Constitution of 1787. Modern individualism asserts itself in various ways.) Appendixes have been added for this book, including various constitutional documents drawn upon in my Commentary. The reader will discover that the materials in the Appendixes provide many more instances than it is useful for me to point out in detail (except in the Index for this book) of predecessors to key elements both in the Constitution of 1787 and in its twenty-seven amendments down to our day.

I hope that the reader will also discover that the materials in the Appendixes are illuminated by this Commentary. Preparation of the Appendixes was aided by the collection of documents I assembled for the 1991 volume of *Great Ideas Today* in celebration of the bicentennial of the Bill of Rights. I have had, for a decade now, a most productive association with Mortimer J. Adler and John Van

Doren, the editors of that invaluable *Encyclopedia Britannica* annual, *Great Ideas Today*. (I have published under their thoughtful supervision a series of introductions to non-Western thought in *Great Ideas Today*, beginning in 1984 with Confucian thought. Such explorations of other ways of life should help us see ourselves better.)

The original lecture format, despite the occasional repetitions that it requires, has been retained here for several reasons. This Commentary is directed to the general reader, even as it keeps in mind the training of judges, legislators, and scholars. I have published elsewhere considerably more detailed discussions than there can be in this Commentary of a variety of constitutional and legal matters, a sample of which is provided in Lecture No. 11. (I have adapted that lecture on Lincoln's Emancipation Proclamation, as is indicated in its first note, from earlier lectures and publications.) Another sample of much more detailed discussion is my 1971 treatise, *The Constitutionalist: Notes on the First Amendment*. Lest I be suspected of skirting troublesome issues, I take the liberty on this occasion of citing extensively my previously published discussions of many points that I can do no more than touch upon in this Commentary.

My lecture format should put the reader on notice that comprehensiveness, despite extensive citations to other work of mine, is not to be expected in this Commentary. But I trust that enough is said in these explorations to suggest three critical objectives in the development of the Constitutional amendments we now have: the confirmation and deepening of the traditional rights of the English-speaking peoples, the ever-widening application of the equality principle in American constitutionalism, and the related opening to liberty seen in such things as the prohibition of slavery (thereby liberating masters as well as slaves) and the steady expansion of suffrage in this Country. (Connected to this expansion of suffrage is the concern that equality-minded Americans have always had about the proper mode of supplying the Presidency. In addition, the centuries-long opening to liberty in this Country finds sometimes-bizarre expression these days in our ever-growing concern about the right to privacy.) The equality we treasure looks to justice and the common good; the liberty we exercise looks to self-preservation and excellence—and all this depends upon and should contribute further to a decent and happy community that is both confident of its merits and willing to face up to its shortcomings. (The dedication of Americans to both liberty and equality is such that it is generally believed that the rights considered fundamental to equality and liberty should be respected by all governments in this Country, however controversial the scope of judicial authority in protecting these rights may be.)

Just as this Commentary on the texts of the amendments presupposes my Commentary on the text of the Constitution of 1787, so does this preface presuppose what is said in the preface to that earlier volume. (That other Commentary, as is indicated in its Index, includes preliminary discussions of many of the amendments to the Constitution, most of which discussions I do not cite to here.) In both volumes of commentary an attempt is made to work principally from the original texts of the Constitutional documents considered. The mountain of secondary material here, piled up over two centuries, can sometimes block one's view of the vital texts upon which the necessary integrity of our people depends. It may be only by relying primarily upon fundamental texts that the people of the United States (continually rejuvenated and nourished, as well as intermittently threatened, by immigrants from all over the world) can retain that commonsensical grasp of their Constitutional system that is needed if they are to remain reasonably united and truly self-governing.

The counsel here of the Declaration of Rights issued in 1776 by Thomas Jefferson's Virginia is salutary: "[N]o free government, or the blessings of liberty, can be preserved to any people, but by a firm adherence to justice, moderation, temperance, frugality, and virtue, and by frequent recurrence to fundamental principles." Or, as this counsel was elaborated by John Adams in the Massahusetts Declaration of Rights of 1780, "A frequent recurrence to the fundamental principles of the constitution, and a constant adherence to those of piety, justice, moderation, temperance, industry, and frugality, are absolutely necessary to preserve the advantages of liberty, and to maintain a free government." Thus, illustrious patriots both North and South could substantially agree, from the beginning of this Republic, on the character of the people that is needed for the enduring well-being of a nation that was "conceived in Liberty, and dedicated to the proposition that all men are created equal."

The Amendments to the Constitution

1. The Intentions of the Federal Convention of 1787

I

The greatest wars fought by the American people have been civil wars. The first was the struggle between Patriots and Loyalists from 1774 to 1784; the second was the struggle between Northerners and Southerners from 1857 to 1865.[1]

The victors in both wars suppressed far-reaching claims by their rivals. No later British monarch ever plausibly aspired to the power in the British Empire that George III and his Ministers tried to exercise on this continent between 1774 and 1781. No later State government ever again aspired to the power in the American Union that the Confederate States tried to exercise on this continent between 1860 and 1865. In each case the overreaching aspirants were confronted by armed responses rooted in the constitutional history of a people.

Civil wars tend to be exceptionally destructive, partly because the cost for each victory is paid twice over: the victor suffers not only his own casualties but those of his fraternal opponent as well. The Patriots could refer, as in the 1776 Declaration of Independence, to their "British Brethren." And in the 1863 Gettysburg Address, the reference to the "brave men, living and dead, who struggled here" unites the desperate enemies of that battlefield.[2]

Desperate circumstances are very much in evidence in civil wars, so much so that people are often obliged to resort to constitutional irregularities in making the supreme efforts to which they dedicate themselves. Rules tend to be flexible in such extremities, with war seeming to dictate a "logic" of its own. This may be seen even in

1

military build-ups, short of war, in troubled times. Such magnification of the national power can be difficult to reverse, however much the military forces of a country may be trimmed from time to time.

In both of the great North American civil wars the long-established principles of the victors asserted themselves, whatever the formal constitution and laws of the day provided. And in both cases formal constitutional developments thereafter ratified what had been achieved by war. These constitutional developments included a determination not to permit everyday life to be governed routinely by the measures that may have to be resorted to in extreme cases.

Two particularly dramatic constitutional developments among Americans have come in the aftermath of their great civil wars: the emergence of the Constitution and its Bill of Rights after the first civil war on this continent and the emergence of the Thirteenth, Fourteenth, and Fifteenth Amendments after the second civil war. In neither case should these developments endure as disappointments for any of the parties engaged in those struggles. The people of Great Britain had their own liberties confirmed by the check placed upon ambitious royal power in North America; the people of the American South were liberated from crippling institutions that they had been saddled with by their imprudent ancestors centuries before.

II

We must set aside until Lecture No. 10 of this Commentary our effort to explain what happened, and did not happen, after 1857 in this Country. It is what happened, and did not happen, after 1774 that is our immediate concern.

The traditional, as well as the natural, rights and liberties of Englishmen were regularly invoked on this side of the Atlantic by the men and women who made the American Revolution. Those prerogatives of a self-governing people were enshrined in such constitutional testimonials as Magna Carta (in 1215), the Petition of Right (in 1628), and the English Bill of Rights (in 1689).[3] In this sense, then, the American Revolution was a deeply conservative movement, however radical it has since been in its effects upon the rest of the world. The Declaration of Independence could be invoked by Vietnamese patriots against French colonialists in the 1940s and by university students in Tiananmen Square against Chinese despots in the 1980s.

We can, for our immediate purposes, begin the story of the Constitution of 1787 and its amendments with standard accounts of what happened in the 1770s and thereafter. "On September 5, 1774," we are told,

> delegates from the [American] colonies convened in Philadelphia in a "Continental" Congress, so called to differentiate it from local or provincial congresses. The First Continental Congress adopted a Declaration and Resolves to protest British measures and promote American rights; it also adopted the [Continental] Association.[4]

The Continental Association was the agreement "created by the First Continental Congress on October 18, 1774":·

> It was "a non-importation, non-consumption, and non-exportation agreement" undertaken to obtain redress of American grievances against the British Crown and Parliament. The Articles of Association were signed on October 20 by the representatives of twelve colonies, solemnly binding themselves and their constituents to its terms.
>
> The Articles listed the most pressing American grievances (taxation without representation, extension of admiralty court jurisdiction, denial of trial by jury in tax cases), enumerated the measures to be taken (cessation of commercial ties to Britain), prescribed the penalty for noncompliance (a total breaking off of communication with offenders), and established the machinery for enforcement (through committees of correspondence).[5]

A knowledgeable scholar recently observed,

> The Association was a major step toward the creation of a federal union of American states. It was the first prescriptive act of a national Congress to be binding directly on individuals, and the efforts at enforcement of or compliance with its terms certainly contributed to the formation of a national identity.[6]

This scholar concluded, "With but little exaggeration [it has been said], 'The signature of the Association [in 1774] may be considered as the commencement of the American union.'"[7]

The First Continental Congress dissolved four days after the signing of the Articles of Association, "having decided that the colonies should meet again if necessary on May 10, 1775. By that time, the colonies and Great Britain were at war."[8] We conclude our reliance upon standard accounts of the Continental Congress with this report:

> The Second Continental Congress adopted a Declaration of the Causes and Necessity of Taking Up Arms on July 6, 1775, and the Declaration of Independence a year later. The Congress appointed George Washington as commander-in-chief of its armies, directed the war, managed foreign affairs, and adopted a plan of union designated as the Articles of Confederation. After the thirteenth state ratified the Articles in 1781, the official governing body of the United States became known as "the Congress of the Confederation," but it was a continuation of the Continental Congress and was not reconstituted until 1789, when a Congress elected under the Constitution of the United States took office.[9]

Voting in the Continental Congress, as later in the Confederation Congress, was by Colonies (or States), with each of the thirteen having one vote.

III

It is difficult to exaggerate the constitutional implications of the Declaration of Independence, which has long been set forth in the United States Statutes as the first of "the organic laws of the United States of America." Indicative of the fundamental character of this document is the practice in the United States of dating official papers from July 4, 1776.[10] This mode of dating may be seen as well in the opening words of the Gettysburg Address, "Four score and seven years ago," with a Nation or Country (not just a mere alliance, association, confederation, or even union) having firmly taken root in July 1776.

Much of the constitutional system that we have long been accustomed to is already taken for granted in the Declaration of Independence, where grievances and remedies are routinely put in terms of the principles and history of the English-speaking peoples. The ends of government are indicated; the significance of the consent of the governed is affirmed. Various of the rights and liberties protected in our Constitution and its Bill of Rights are drawn upon in

4

the grievances collected in the Continental Association, in the Declaration of Independence, and elsewhere.

The form of government implied in the Declaration of Independence assumes a qualified separation of powers, reliance upon representative assemblies, and access to independent courts. An executive power is recognized as legitimate, but only if kept within constitutional bounds that respect the prerogatives of legislatures in the making of laws. The supervisory authority of a national government is also recognized, but again only if kept within constitutional bounds that respect the prerogatives of local governments and ultimately of the people.

It should again be noticed that the Declaration of Independence does not purport to devise or invent new principles and forms. Rather, it confirms and uses long-established principles in identifying accumulated grievances and in responding to intolerable conditions.

The Declaration of Independence also leaves various questions open, such as the character that a people should have in order to make the best use of the rights and liberties it invokes. The Declaration of Independence does not address, in a systematic way, the perennial question of the political, social, and other arrangements that are most likely, in a variety of circumstances, to secure the enduring happiness that human beings are naturally bound to pursue.[11]

IV

Vital to the affirmations of the Declaration of Independence is the self-evident truth that "all Men are created equal." The meaning and application of this principle have been major concerns of the American people for more than two centuries now. Precisely how the equality principle should be interpreted and applied depends on circumstances. At times it can mean that all States (as the agents of diverse communities of human beings) should be treated the same, and at other times it can mean that all persons should be treated the same.

That aspect of the equality of "all Men" which is expressed through the States may be seen in the Articles of Confederation, in which the States had equal votes. It may still be seen in, among other places, the Senate of the United States under the Constitution of 1787. This expression of equality through the States is further seen in the uniformity of Constitutional obligations and restrictions imposed upon both the United States and the States in dealing with one another. That aspect of the equality of "all Men" which is expressed on behalf of persons may be seen, for example, in the extension of the vote to eighteen-year-olds by the Twenty-sixth Amendment. It may be seen as well in the divergent efforts made to extend constitutional protection both to fetuses virtually from the moment of conception and to pregnant women desiring abortions, to say nothing of efforts made to minister to those desperate people who want to relieve their intense suffering by ending what they take to be their hopeless lives. It should be evident that the contending applications of the powerful equality principle have to be accommodated on the basis of an even higher principle, a principle of excellence grounded in liberty that finds just and sustained expression through the dictates of prudence. Prudence, with its dependence on nature, is an underlying concern of these lectures, as it is of my lectures on the Constitution of 1787.[12]

Prudence may be seen in the practices that a people resorts to as well as in the principles that it is guided by. Although the Articles of Confederation (first drafted in the Continental Congress in 1776) were not fully ratified until 1781, the Country was governed and a war was fought pursuant to the Articles well before their ratification. The Articles of Confederation formalized, from 1776 on, much of what had been the practice of the Continental Congress even before Independence. The Articles, as the name suggests, had features of a treaty relationship, with the law of nations influential in guiding the States in providing for their dealings with one another.

But the Articles of Confederation were somewhat irregular: they were never in conformity with the best constitutional thought of the day. The Constitution of 1787 is much closer to what a natural constitutionalism (if it may be so designated) called for. This is testified to by what was done by the Confederation Congress sitting in New York while the Federal Convention was sitting in Philadelphia. That Congress produced the Northwest Ordinance, which provides, for a territory comparable in size to the original thirteen States, a constitutional system much closer in form and in spirit to that found in the Constitution of 1787 than to that found in the Articles of Confederation.

The Confederation Congress was better able in the Northwest Ordinance than the Federal Convention proved to be in the Constitution to apply the equality principle to a critical issue of that day: slavery. Congress provided in its Ordinance of 1787 that there should be "neither slavery nor involuntary servitude in [the Northwest Territory] otherwise than in punishment of crimes whereof the party shall have been duly convicted."

It was this recourse to the equality principle in the Northwest Ordinance that may have been decisive to the fate of the Nation in the Civil War seven decades later. Because of that dramatic military vindication of the equality principle, on which the rule of law and hence both our personal liberties and our rights to property depend, there were only victors, and no permanent losers, in the American Civil War.

V

Problems with the Articles of Confederation were recognized from the outset, but the need to get on with the Revolutionary War precluded the political efforts and the extended deliberations needed to move beyond this treaty-like arrangement. That something would have to be done eventually was implicitly recognized by the insistence in the Articles that the Union being provided for was "perpetual." It must have been obvious to most thoughtful observers from 1776 on that, however "perpetual" the Union itself might be, the cumbersome constitutional arrangements that had had to be settled for during the war could not last long.

The complaints that accumulated about the Articles of Confederation (such as about how difficult it had become for the American people to be governed properly) began to rival in scope, although not in moral intensity, those that had been collected in the Declaration of Independence. The General Government, under the Articles, had no direct control over citizens, no source of substantial revenues of its own, no independent executive, only one house in its legislature, no national judicial system, limited legislative powers (especially with respect to the commerce, or economy, of the Country), and no way of formally amending the Articles of Confederation without the consent of all thirteen States. Repeated efforts to make modest changes in the Articles of Confederation fell afoul of this unanimity rule. That led in turn to the 1787 Federal Convention with its proposal of a comprehensive reworking of the form of government so as to make it conform to generally recognized republican principles, not least with respect to the mode of ratification of a constitution and thereafter of its amendments.

One of the things that the fettered Confederation Congress could manage to do was to call a Federal Convention to consider changes for the Articles of Confederation. This call led to that grand (however irregular) meeting in Philadelphia between May and September of 1787 which produced the Constitution we now have.

VI

To speak as we sometimes do of "the intentions of the Federal Convention" suggests that that body had an overall purpose or plan. An overall plan tends to be lost sight of by those who emphasize the compromises, if not even the chance aspects, in the drafting of the Constitution of 1787.

Whether or not one considers the Constitution well crafted affects how one attempts to read it and whether it makes sense to try to read it at all. My own efforts to read the Constitution have been described as "based primarily on analysis of the original text of the Constitution itself."[13]

What, then, were the intentions of the Federal Convention? If the more perceptive of the Framers knew what they were doing, and if they were pretty much able to get their way, then their intentions were to produce substantially the document that came out of the Convention on September 17, 1787. Three departments, or branches, of government are set forth, with the Congress clearly in charge; plenary powers are provided the General Government with respect to commerce, war, and the foreign affairs of the Country; adequate revenue powers are also provided; significant restraints are placed upon the States, with a supervisory power entrusted to the General Government with respect to both the creation and the conduct of States.

The Framers were particularly concerned that there be a pervasive rule of law in the United States. This concern is reflected not only in the superiority assigned by them to the legislative branch, but even more in the genuine reliance by a people upon a constitution. Congress itself is restrained in critical respects, especially with a view to insuring that it is primarily by laws that Congress exerts itself, as may be seen in the detailed provisions about how a law is enacted and in the prohibitions upon ex post facto laws and bills of attainder.

This approach to the Constitution looks to an overall constitutional development that should continue to work its way out, if things go well, until the promises of the Declaration of Independence are substantially realized for the "new nation" there "brought forth." We will be obliged to consider, as we review the twenty-seven Amendments that have been added thus far to the Constitution of 1787, what remains to be changed either informally through adaptations in practices or formally through the amendatory processes prescribed in Article V of the Constitution. (Article V is discussed in Lecture No. 14 of my Commentary on the Constitution of 1787.)

VII

Before we turn to the background and development of the amendments to the Constitution known as the Bill of Rights, it is important to recognize that the talented men who arranged for and finally controlled the Federal Convention of 1787 managed thereafter to get the Constitution ratified in the States. They then managed to secure control not only of the Presidency but also of the First Congress in which the Bill of Rights was drafted. It should not surprise us, therefore, that the drafters of the Bill of Rights of 1791 accepted both the understanding of the Union and the extent of the General Government's powers evident in the Constitution of 1787. The Articles of Confederation substantially confirmed the arrangements by which the delegates to the Continental Congresses had been conducting their affairs since 1774. (It took Americans of the 1770s a decade to get enough over their British-engendered hostility to a central government to prepare a national constitution.) Its scope of powers, it was generally understood, would eventually have to resemble that usually available to decent and competent Western governments. Even so, Americans have always tended to misunderstand what is required for government to help provide them the things they are accustomed to. For example, Americans probably pay less in taxes and yet complain more about taxes than any other people among the Western industrialized countries.

It is generally known that the First Congress refused, in the amendment now known as the Tenth, to limit the Government of the United States only to powers that had been "expressly delegated" to it. That amendment reads, "The powers not delegated to the United States by the Constitution, nor prohibited by it to the States, are reserved to the States respectively, or to the people." The term *expressly* had been used in like circumstances in Article II of the Articles of Confederation, where it is provided, "Each state retains its sovereignty, freedom, and independence, and every Power, Jurisdiction and right, which is not by this confederation expressly delegated to the United States, in Congress assembled." Instead of such a limitation, the Constitution of 1787 provides, in Section 8 of Article I, that Congress has power to "make all Laws which shall be necessary and proper for carrying into Execution the foregoing Powers, and all other Powers vested by this Constitution in the Government of the United States, or in any Department or Officer thereof." The efforts made by a lively minority in the First Congress to curtail the implied powers of Congress were soundly defeated. This, as I have said, is generally known.

What is not generally known is that although the Articles of Confederation had identified the powers of the General Government as coming from the States, the Constitution of 1787 assumes that those powers come not from separate and somehow independent States, but rather from the People of the United States. The "perpetual Union" of the States of that People is made "more perfect" by the Constitution of 1787. We shall see in Lecture No. 8 of this Commentary that the authority of the "one People," recognized both at the outset of the Declaration of Independence and at the outset of the Preamble to the Constitution of 1787, is further recognized in the Tenth Amendment, something that comes as a surprise to the typical States' Rights advocate.

In these matters, however, the major surprises lie not in the information that is made use of by students of the Constitution, but rather in how that information is interpreted. After all, the documents and other materials from which relevant information about the Constitution is drawn have long been known to students of American constitutional developments. Also once known, but largely lost sight of these days, is the usefulness of a proper assessment of the information long available about our remarkable constitutional system.

2. The Federal Convention and a Bill of Rights

I

Proposals were made from time to time during the Federal Convention of 1787 for a systematic protection of rights to be included in the instrument that was being prepared.

Some individual rights are provided for in the Constitution that came out of that Convention. Affirmations of those rights are usually required in the Constitution of 1787 because of powers granted therein to the Government of the United States. Thus, in Article I, limitations are placed upon the power that a national legislature might traditionally have had to suspend the privilege of the writ of habeas corpus. Also, in Article III, limitations are placed upon the power that courts had traditionally had to punish the crime of treason.

It was argued, however, that there was no need to provide assurances for additional rights, since the powers of the proposed Congress did not extend to putting those rights in jeopardy. For example, it was said during the Ratification Campaign that explicitly provisions for liberty of the press were unnecessary because Congress was not given any power to regulate the press.[14]

Even so, there are numerous rights recognized in the Constitution of 1787, in addition to those found in the habeas corpus and treason guarantees. These include assurances with respect to elections, the relation of the military to civilian authority, bills of attainder, ex post facto laws, legislative immunity, impeachment of civil officers, trial by jury in criminal cases, and life tenure for judges. Overarching all of these are the explicit guarantee by the National Government of a republican form of government in each

11

State and the obvious provision of a republican form of government for the Country as a whole. Critical to such republican government are the elections of legislative and executive officers for fixed terms and the understanding that there cannot be any taxation without adequate representation.

II

There was considerable demand during the Ratification Campaign of 1787–1788 for a Bill of Rights. Perhaps the demand would have been moderated if the dozen or so traditional guarantees in the body of the Constitution had been collected by the Convention in one place rather than left scattered throughout the document. But this would have obscured the instructive organization of the Constitution, an organization that is reflected in the placements therein of various rights.

The demand for a Bill of Rights was anticipated, although rather casually, during the Federal Convention itself. There were only three occasions, so far as we know, on which something substantial was said about including a bill of rights in the constitution that was being prepared that summer. These occasions were on August 20, September 12, and September 15.[15]

The most systematic effort recorded with respect to a bill of rights was that made by Charles Pinckney of South Carolina on August 20. Bill-of-rights proposals were included by him among the dozen propositions he submitted to the Convention on that occasion.[16] Or, as Madison first put it in his *Notes* for that date (the expanded version of this account in Appendix H-1 of this Commentary is taken from the *Journal* of the Convention):

> Mr. Pinkney submitted sundry propositions—1. authorizing the Legislature to imprison for insult. 2. to require opinion of the Judges. 3. securing the benefit of the habeas corpus. 4. preserving the liberty of the press. 5. guarding agst billeting of soldiers. 6. agst. raising troops without the consent of the Legislature. 7. rendering the great officers of the Union incapable of other offices either under the Genl Govt. or the State Govts. 8. forbidding religious tests. 9. declaring the U. States to be a body politic and corporate. 10. providing a great seal to be affixed to laws &c. 11. extending the jurisdiction of the Judiciary to controversies between the United States & States or individuals.[17]

Madison adds that "these were referred to the Committee of detail for consideration & report."[18]

Various of these propositions, such as the habeas corpus guarantee, may be found in the Constitution, but the Pinckney collection as such was not (so far as we know) reported back to the Convention by the Committee of Detail. Elsewhere, Pinckney refers to three rights (two of them in his list of August 20) as "essential in Free Governments": "the privilege of the Writ of Habeas Corpus—The Trial by Jury in all cases, Criminal as well as Civil—The Freedom of the Press."[19] A fourth provision (also in his list), "the prevention of Religious Tests, as qualifications to Offices of Trust or Emolument," he speaks of as "a provision the world will expect from [the Federal Convention], in the establishment of a System founded on Republican Principles, and in an age so liberal and enlightened as the present."[20]

There is no discussion of the Pinckney propositions recorded in the entry for August 20 or for any other session during the life of the Convention.

III

Not mentioned by Pinckney on August 20, but returned to by the Convention on September 12, is the right to trial by jury in civil cases (for the most part in suits at common law). By this time, the Constitution included a guarantee of trial by jury in criminal cases.

Madison's *Notes* for September 12 include this exchange prompted by the suggestion that civil juries be guaranteed:

Mr. Williamson, observed to the House that no provision was yet made for juries in Civil cases and suggested the necessity of it.

Mr. Gorham. It is not possible to discriminate equity cases from those in which juries are proper. The Representatives of the people may be safely trusted in this matter.

Mr. Gerry urged the necessity of Juries to guard against corrupt Judges. He proposed that the Committee last appointed should be directed to provide a clause for securing the trial by Juries.

Col: Mason perceived the difficulty mentioned by Mr. Gorham. The jury cases can not be specified. A general principle laid down on this and some other points would be sufficient. He wishes the plan [the Constitution] had been prefaced with a Bill of Rights, & would second a Motion if made for the purpose—It would give great quiet to the people; and with the aid of the State declarations, a bill might be prepared in a few hours.

Mr. Gerry concurred in the idea & moved for a Committee to prepare a Bill of Rights. Col: Mason 2ded the motion.[21]

Thereafter, the Bill of Rights proposal was voted down, 10-0, with no vote recorded for Gerry's Massachusetts.[22]

Juries were looked to in civil as well as in criminal cases as a guard against corrupt judges. The people, acting in part through juries, were depended upon to help keep the judges in line. George Washington, in a letter to the marquis de La Fayette the following April, recalled this reason why the civil-jury guarantee was not provided by the Convention:

[I]t was only the difficulty of establishing a mode which should not interfere with the fixed modes of any of the States, that induced the Convention to leave it, as a matter of future adjustment [that is, by the Legislature].[23]

What is the significance of variations from State to State in these matters? It seems that the determination of rights always depended, in part, on local practices and hence did not rely exclusively on an understanding of natural right or something developed by reason alone. What people are accustomed to does matter and can vary from place to place, especially if there are no supervisory legislatures and courts to assess local variations. The Framers of the Constitution appear to have agreed that variations with respect to civil-trial practice made it prudent to allow the new government room to experiment with these matters, rather than to settle permanently upon a single mode in the Constitution.

There were those who preferred to allow local variations to develop as they would, altogether free from any interference by the General Government. The courts provided for by the Constitution threatened to interfere so much with State judicial practices that George Mason could protest in the Convention on September 15:

The Judiciary of the United States is so constructed and extended, as to absorb and destroy the judiciaries of the several States; thereby rendering law as tedious, intricate and expensive, and justice as unattainable, by a great part of the community, as in England, and enabling the rich to oppress and ruin the poor.[24]

Even so, the Convention (but not Mason) went on, two days later, to sign the proposed Constitution, imperial judiciary and all.

IV

We have seen that the raising of the civil-jury issue on September 12 led to George Mason's expressing the wish for a bill of rights. We have also seen that Elbridge Gerry concurred and moved that a committee be assigned to prepare a bill of rights. We have seen as well that not a single State delegation voted on September 12 to establish such a committee. So far along were the proceedings by this time that a draft of the Constitution was reported that day by the Committee of Style, a draft that looks much like the Constitution that was finally approved. (These futile efforts to get a bill of rights were by two of the three delegates, present in the Convention at the end, who were to refuse their signatures for the Constitution the following week.) This September 12 action seems to have been the only direct vote in the Convention on the question of a bill of rights.

Roger Sherman, arguing against recourse to a bill of rights, said that he too "was for securing the rights of the people where requisite." But he added, "The State Declarations of Rights are not repealed by this Constitution; and being in force are sufficient." Mason replied to Sherman, "The Laws of the U.S. are to be paramount to State Bills of Rights."[25]

It was insisted upon again and again, even more during the Ratification Campaign than during the Convention, that the rights of the people were not in jeopardy and hence no bill of rights was needed. What are we to make of Sherman's suggestion that the States' recognition of these rights sufficed? He seemed to believe that the States' bills of rights were not to be treated simply as laws; if that was how they were to be regarded, then Mason's response would probably have been decisive. Rather, the Sherman approach indicates, the States' declarations served primarily to recall and thereby to reaffirm the rights that the English-speaking peoples had long had and were still developing. (The term *declaration*, which was often used here, may itself be revealing.) It was also pointed out during the Ratification Campaign that the security of these rights in the States themselves did not depend upon bills of rights, since half of the States had no such bills in their own constitutions.

We have noticed that the great rights of the English-speaking peoples are not simply natural rights, however much they may be influenced by natural-rights doctrines. They depend, for their precise forms and effects, upon historical (or accidental) developments from place to place or from time to time. This suggests that these rights, except for those directing judicial proceedings, do not necessarily depend upon the Courts for their enforcement against the Legislature and the Executive.

The important thing here, Sherman seems to say, is that these rights be recognized by the American people, not that they be added to the Constitution of the United States. In fact, it can be argued, their being added to the Constitution in the form of the Bill of Rights in 1791 tended to eclipse the State bills of rights, obscuring from view some of the rights found there but not in the 1791 Bill of Rights. This development may also have obscured the traditional basis of all such rights.

V

On September 15, the next-to-last meeting of the Convention, the delegates dealt with various odds and ends in the draft constitution. Gouverneur Morris, for example, was concerned that the pardoning power not be lodged with the legislature.

Pinckney and Gerry took the opportunity of this final review of the draft constitution to suggest that the following provision be added to the Judiciary Article: "And a trial by jury shall be preserved as usual in civil cases." It was again argued in response, "The constitution of Juries is different in different States and the trial is *usual* in different cases in different States."[26] The proposal was voted down once again. But this approach bore fruit eventually, since it was used, but without the "usual," in the Seventh Amendment.

Further on, Madison warned that if any special provisos were permitted in this final stage of the proceedings, "every State will insist on them, for their boundaries, exports &c."[27] The three dissenters (Elbridge Gerry, George Mason, and Edmund Randolph) made a last-ditch effort to have a second convention called at which delegates could review the responses of the people to the constitution that had been prepared. The last major comment recorded on this occasion was that made by one of the three holdouts, a delegate from Massachusetts:

> Mr. Gerry, stated the objections which determined him to withhold his name from the Constitution. 1. the duration and re-eligibility of the Senate. 2. the power of the House of Representatives to conceal their journals. 3—the power of Congress over the places of election. 4. the unlimited power of Congress over their own compensations. 5. Massachusetts has not a due share of Representatives allotted to her. 6. 3/5 of the Blacks are to be represented as if they were freemen. 7. *under* the power over commerce, monopolies may be established. 8. The vice president being made head of the Senate. He could however he said get over all these, if the rights of the Citizens were not rendered insecure 1. by the general power of the Legislature to make what laws they may please to call necessary and proper. 2. raise armies and money without limit. 3. to establish a tribunal without juries, which will be a Star-chamber as to Civil cases. Under such a view of the Constitution, the best that could be done he conceived was to provide for a second general Convention.[28]

Gerry expressed a concern about the lack of protection for "the rights of the Citizens." The problem of no bill of rights was again alluded to, even though only three bill of rights matters are listed thereafter, concluding with the lack of a guarantee of trial by jury in civil cases, which Gerry saw as permitting "a Star-chamber as to Civil cases."

We should notice another concern, expressed again and again not only by those who lamented the lack of a bill of rights—the concern lest the military (or the Executive as Commander in Chief) get out of control. Several provisions in the Constitution, including the grant to Congress exclusively of the power to declare war, speak to this concern. This problem is still with us, as we could see in the free hand that the President insisted upon during the 1990–1991 Persian Gulf War despite Constitutional provisions that seem to provide for his ultimate subordination in such matters to Congress. The traditional concern about proper political supervision of the military may be seen in how our Persian Gulf allies took all this: they insisted upon directions from the United Nations Security

Council before force was resorted to by the United States and its allies against Iraq. Thus, a political or legislative judgment was to be relied upon more than our President was inclined to recognize. It was a curious state of affairs that found the Russians and others urging upon us models of constitutional propriety and hence moderation.

VI

One of the changes proposed and accepted on September 15, 1787, dealt with the sensitive issue of slavery. The Fugitive Slave provision in Article IV now reads:

> No Person held to Service or Labour in one State, under the Laws thereof, escaping into another, shall, in Consequence of any Law or Regulation therein, be discharged from such Service or Labour, but shall be delivered up on Claim of the Party to whom such Service or Labour may be due.

We are told by Madison that on September 15 "the term 'legally' was struck out, and 'under the Laws thereof' inserted [after the word 'State,'] in compliance with the wish of some who thought the term ['legal'] equivocal, and favoring the idea that slavery was legal in a moral view."[29]

We can see here, as elsewhere, an awareness of the moral and political principles upon which the proposed constitutional system depends. This awareness is reflected in, among other places, the common law that serves as a major part of the foundation of the system. However important morality was taken to be, certain proposed efforts on its behalf were more drastic than the Convention wished to write into the Constitution. Consider the concern about the kind of character that republican institutions require. Plutarch, for example, tells us that Mark Antony was criticized, in a troubled Rome that still had republican aspirations, for his impudent luxury.[30] It was in this spirit, perhaps, that Mason proposed on August 20 that Congress be empowered to enact sumptuary laws. Three State delegations (Delaware, Maryland, and Georgia) supported him after a discussion that is recorded in this fashion:

> Mr. Mason moved to enable Congress "to enact sumptuary laws."
> No Government can be maintained unless the manners be made

18

consonant to it. Such a discretionary power may do good and can do no harm. A proper regulation of excises & of trade may do a great deal but it is best to have an express provision. It was objected to sumptuary laws that they were contrary to nature. This was a vulgar error. The love of distinction it is true is natural; but the object of sumptuary laws is not to extinguish this principle but to give it a proper direction.

Mr. Elseworth, The best remedy is to enforce taxes & debts. As far as the regulation of eating & drinking can be reasonable, it is provided for in the power of taxation.

Mr. Govr. Morris argued that sumptuary laws tended to create a landed Nobility, by fixing in the great-landholders and their posterity their present possessions.

Mr. Gerry, the law of necessity is the best sumptuary law.[31]

The sumptuary-laws issue was returned to by Mason on September 13:

Col. Mason—He had [on August 20] moved without success for a power to make sumptuary regulations. He had not yet lost sight of his object. After descanting on the extravagance of our manners, the excessive consumption of foreign superfluities, and the necessity of restricting it, as well with economical as republican views, he moved that a Committee be appointed to report articles of Association for encouraging by the advice the influence and the example of the members of the Convention, economy frugality and american manufactures.

Docr. Johnson 2ded the motion which was without debate agreed to, nem: con: and a Committee appointed, consisting of Col: Mason, Docr. Franklin, Mr. Dickenson, Docr. Johnson, and Mr. Livingston.[32]

This committee of the more elderly delegates to which the Mason proposal was assigned is not recorded as ever having returned to the Convention with a report. Perhaps we should consider the question of the appropriate republican character still open, especially as we see among us today more and more luxury and a perhaps related increasing privatization of everyday life.

It seems to have been recognized in the exchange on August 20 that the commerce power and the taxation power could properly be used to advance ends having to do with the moral character of the people, something to be kept in mind when we hear it argued either that moral standards are "relative" or that morality cannot or should not be legislated. Whatever reservations the Convention may have had about the more rigorous Mason approach, it evidently did not believe that moral training was beyond either the scope or the competence of American legislatures (and perhaps also executives and judges), especially if the people were to be able to continue to use sensibly the rights to which they had long been accustomed.

VII

We must wonder, then, about the level of moral character required to make the Constitution work, especially if enforcement of and respect for rights depend upon the people's vigilance (as distinguished from the people's paranoia). What the people can do when rights are perceived to be threatened may be seen in the 1980s experience in Great Britain with the "poll tax." The principal measures resorted to by opponents of that tax were political, not judicial. Conjuring up something old and feared, or detested, those opponents developed a formidable (and evidently successful) resistance, whether or not justified. (There may still be seen in Great Britain what was once generally accepted in the United States, that authoritative interpretations of the Constitution would be provided by the national legislature.)

Another initiative of August 20 with respect to morality came from Pinckney and the hardheaded Morris. They suggested that the duties of the Chief Justice should include recommending "such alterations of and additions to the laws of the U.S. as may in his opinion be necessary to the due administration of Justice, and such as may promote useful learning and inculcate sound morality throughout the Union."[33] Thus, morality was not considered only a State-by-State concern but rather was national in scope.

Fundamental to a proper inculcation and preservation of morality, the Framers obviously believed, was the establishment and perpetuation of a proper national government for the people of the United States. Effective government means, by the way, that ex post facto laws might have to be resorted to in civil matters, something that Mason believed the Constitution should not forbid, lest the impossibility of complying with such an absolute prohibition lead to the habit of disregarding the Constitution.[34] (We see, in Section II of Lecture No. 17 of this Commentary, that much the same can be said about the proposed balanced-budget amendment today. The terms of the proposed amendment of January 1995 may be found in Section IX of Lecture No. 14 of this Commentary.)

Proper government requires, among other things, an enduring rule of law, which in turn depends upon and promotes liberty and the rights of citizens, such rights as a people might seek to protect by a bill of rights. It could therefore be maintained during the Ratification Campaign of 1787–1788, as in *Federalist* No. 84, that the Constitution itself was a bill of rights. Proper government also presupposes a general understanding of what constitutes the Country with which a government should be concerned.

The South's Civil War attempt to redefine the basis of the Country began, it will be recalled, in South Carolina in 1860, if not before. But it should also be recalled that the bill of rights and other propositions submitted to the Convention on August 20, 1787, by a South Carolinian, Charles Pinckney, included this provision: "The U.S. shall be for ever considered as one Body corporate and politic in law, and entitled to all the rights privileges and immunities, which to Bodies corporate do or ought to appertain."[35] We hear echoes here of the opening and closing lines of the Declaration of Independence. We hear also a reaffirmation, as in the Declaration and later in the statements of Abraham Lincoln, of the united people from whom all powers flow and to whom various rights belong, whether or not those powers and rights happen to be acknowledged for the moment by any particular document.

3. Predecessors to the American Bill of Rights

I

The Bill of Rights of 1791 and the agitation for it in 1787–1789 did not come out of nothing. For one thing, it is vital for an effective bill of rights that the rule of law already be established in a community. A bill of rights may guide and refine that rule of law; it cannot create or do without it.

Whether there is an adequate rule-of-law background affects what can be done with declarations of rights in a variety of regimes all over the world. Without a proper rule of law there is not likely to be either the secure civil liberties that a people yearn for or the reliable economic and other social conditions that stable government depends on. All this bears upon both whether our civil liberties can be exported and whether the many economic and social bills of rights of the twentieth century make much sense as constitutional guarantees.

If there is an established rule of law it is awkward for a government to be as oppressive toward minorities as it might like to be. A rule of law tends toward a respect for general principles, which means that a government cannot easily, or openly, harm a minority without running the risk of at least inconveniencing the majority. On the other hand, exceptions to the general rule of law may take the form of affirmative action on behalf of a minority with a view to remedying old abuses or their consequences.

Underlying the rule of law in the United States is the common law of England which was established on this continent in Colonial days. The common law, as originally understood, is critical to the rule of law for the English-speaking peoples, reflecting and reinforcing as it does a general constitutional system.[36]

The common law, with its application of reason to the implementation of generally accepted moral standards in a variety of circumstances, provides much of the legal underpinning of the Constitution of 1787. Most of the guarantees found in the Bill of Rights of 1791 had been developed by and incorporated in the common-law system in England long before American independence. This system was grounded in a modern natural-rights, if not in the traditional natural-right, tradition.

The people who demanded a bill of rights for the Constitution of 1787 drew upon an approach to these matters that had been more or less established for centuries. Their demands were voiced, as we have seen, in the Federal Convention that drafted the Constitution. It should be instructive to review, however briefly, some of the predecessors to the Bill of Rights that was drafted by Congress in 1789 and ratified by the States in 1789–1791.

II

A plausible place to begin any inventory of predecessors to our Bill of Rights is Magna Carta, the Great Charter exacted from King John in 1215 by the barons at Runnymede, "sword in hand" (as *Federalist* No. 84 and many others put it). This charter, revised repeatedly during subsequent reigns, stands for an affirmation of the principle that even the King is bound by the law of the land.

A number (if not all) of the rights referred to in Magna Carta, especially with respect to property, were already familiar enough to be invoked in 1215. This particular charter was preceded by such instruments as the Constitutions of Clarendon.[37] The fourth version of Magna Carta, issued in 1225 during the reign of Henry III, is said to be still the law of England, except as it has been repealed.[38] We are told that "it now stands on the statute books of common law jurisdiction [as] a sober, practical, and highly technical document."[39]

Magna Carta (called, in the 1628 Petition of Right, "The great Charter of the Liberties of England") began its glorious career as an effort on the part of the barons to assert their rights. But it is hard to state principles on one's own behalf without allowing them to be extended to others eventually. This may be a natural tendency, reflecting a sense of natural justice among a people. Positions advanced only for partisan purposes have a way of meaning more than was originally anticipated. This can be seen closer to home by Americans who appreciate how the *created equal* language subscribed to by embattled slaveholders in the Declaration of Independence eventually helped to undermine the long-established system of chattel slavery in this Country. (Consider, also, the discussion of the Fourteenth Amendment in Sections VII and XII of Lecture No. 12 of this Commentary.)

Fundamental to Magna Carta is the respect seen throughout that instrument for family relations. Much of the property of the day was linked to inherited establishments; changes in the allocations or uses of property often followed upon changes in family circumstances. The King, in licensing the barons to take corrective measures against him in the event of default on his part, exempts in Magna Carta his own family from their measures: "saving harmless our person, and the persons of our Queen and children."

It has been said that "the whole of English constitutional history is a commentary upon the Great Charter."[40] It has also been said that there may be something mythical, however salutary, in the place now accorded to the Great Charter. But it is no myth that the Great Charter taught people how important such documents can be. Nor is it a myth that there are provisions in the Great Charter of 1215 that have come ringing across the seven centuries since, such as the famous assurance: "No freeman shall be seized, or imprisoned, or dispossessed, or outlawed, or exiled, or in any way destroyed; nor will we condemn him, nor will we commit him to prison, excepting by the legal judgment of his peers, or by the law of the land."[41]

III

The next great document in our selective inventory appeared four centuries later in the form of the Petition of Right issued by Parliament in 1628. (It may be found in Appendix C of this Commentary.) In the meantime, of course, the common law of England had been steadily developed by the judges in collaboration with Parliament.

Various long-familiar rights of the English people were reaffirmed

24

in the Petition of Right, including the potent "law of the land" guarantee from Magna Carta. These rights were, for the most part, well enough established by 1628 to be invoked as they were here.

Among the complaints registered in the 1628 Petition of Right were those that spoke of royal usurpations with respect to the mode of taxation, the basis for imprisonment, the quartering of soldiers in private homes, and the use of martial law against civilians. (All of these became critical in the American Colonies in the 1770s.) These and other complaints are reflected in the summary prayers by Parliament with which this petition of 1628 ends:

They doe therefore humblie pray your most Excellent Majestie, that no man hereafter be compelled to make or yeild any Guift Loane Benevolence Taxe or such like Charge without common consent by Act of Parliament, And that none be called to make aunswere or take such Oath or to give attendance or be confined or otherwise molested or disquieted concerning the same or for refusall thereof. And that no freeman in any such manner as is before mencioned be imprisoned or deteined. And that your Majestie would be pleased to remove the said Souldiers and Mariners and that your people may not be soe burthened in tyme to come. And that the aforesaid Commissions for proceeding by Martiall Lawe may be revoked and annulled. And that hereafter no Commissions of like nature may issue forth to any person or persons whatsoever to be executed as aforesaid, lest by colour of them any of your Majesties Subjects be destroyed or put to death contrary to the Lawes and Franchise of the Land.

All which they most humblie pray of your most Excellent Majestie as their Rights and Liberties according to the Lawes and Statutes of this Realme, And that your Majestie would alsoe vouchsafe to declare that the Awards doings and proceedings to the prejudice of your people in any of the premisses shall not be drawne hereafter into consequence or example. And that your Majestie would be also graciouslie pleased for the further comfort and safetie of your people to declare your Royall will and pleasure, That in the things aforesaid all your Officers and Ministers shall serve you according to the Lawes and Statutes of this Realme as they tender the Honor of your Majestie and the prosperitie of this Kingdome.

It was important on this occasion that there be an insistence that the writ of habeas corpus be respected by the King, his subordinates, and the courts. Habeas corpus means that government, among others, must justify holding someone with an explanation grounded in some law whenever a challenge to a detention is made in an appropriate court by anyone. Here is how this complaint reads in the 1628 Petition of Right:

> And where alsoe by the Statute called The great Charter of the Liberties of England [Magna Carta], It is declared and enacted [in Chapter 39], That no Freeman may be taken or imprisoned or be disseised of his Freehold or Liberties or his free Customes or be outlawed or exiled or in any manner destroyed, but by the lawful Judgment of his Peeres or by the Law of the Land.
>
> And in the eight and twentith yeere of the raigne of King Edward the third it was declared and enacted by authoritie of Parliament, that no man of what estate or condicion that he be, should be put out of his Land or Tenements nor taken nor imprisoned nor disherited nor put to death without being brought to aunswere by due processe of Lawe.
>
> Nevertheless against the tenor of the said Statutes and other the good Lawes and Statutes of your Realme to that end provided, divers of your Subjects have of late been imprisoned without any cause shewed: And when for their deliverance they were brought before your Justices by your Majesties Writts of Habeas corpus there to undergoe and receive as the Court should order, and their Keepers commaunded to certifie the causes of their detayner, no cause was certified, but that they were deteined by your Majesties speciall commaund signified by the Lords of your Privie Councill, and yet were returned backe to severall prisons without being charged with any thing to which they might make aunswere according to the Lawe.

The right of habeas corpus was reinforced by the Habeas Corpus Act of 1679.[42] This act confirmed what the judges had developed and what the Petition of Right and other statements had insisted upon.[43] All of this became part of the common-law and constitutional system inherited by the Americans.

In the meantime, however, England underwent a series of bloody revolutions. Charles I, only three years on the throne in 1628 (he was born in 1600), had been obliged to consent to the Petition of Right. But from 1629 to 1640, he contrived to rule without calling a Parliament. This usurpation eventually led to the Civil War, the climax of which was the execution of the king in 1649. There were then eleven years of Republican rule, ending with the Restoration and Charles II in 1660. But things were never to be the same there-after in the constitutional arrangements of England.[44]

IV

A legal historian has described in this way what happened after the restoration of the monarchy in 1660:

> The reign of Charles II saw the re-establishment in a harsher form of the Church of England, and the short reign of James II witnessed a rapid crisis. The determination of that monarch [James II] to pursue a religious policy which was contrary to that solemnly laid down by Parliament in a long series of statutes was the immediate cause of his fall. It may have been that his project of complete toleration for Roman Catholics as well as Dissenters was intrinsically an advance upon the partisanship of the Church [of England] as represented in Parliament. But it is impossible to discuss the merits of the policy when the methods of its promotion were so drastic and so completely contrary to the spirit of contemporary institutions. James II claimed that by his prerogative he could dispense individual cases from the operation of a statute; more than that, he even endeavoured to suspend entirely the operation of certain of the religious laws. Upon this clear issue the conflict was fought out. After an ineffective show of military force James II retired to France, William III of Holland was invited by Parliament to become joint ruler with his wife, Mary II, James's daughter, and so "the great and glorious revolution" was accomplished. The terms of the settlement were embodied in *the last great constitutional documents in English history,* the Bill of Rights (1689) and the Act of Settlement (1701).[45]

We shall consider the Bill of Rights of 1689 after this brief notice of the Act of Settlement of 1701:[46]

> After the death of Queen Mary (1694), William III ruled alone, until he in turn was succeeded by her sister, Anne (1702–1714), who was therefore the last of the reigning Stuarts; in order to secure the succession, the Act of Settlement was passed . . . which not only limited the descent of the Crown (in accordance with which the present royal family reigns) but also added a few constitutional provisions supplementary to those of the Bill of Rights.[47]

The English speak of "the great and glorious revolution" which culminated in the "abdication" of James II and the installation of

William and Mary (James's daughter and her husband) according to the terms of the Bill of Rights of 1689. That Bill of Rights (found in Appendix D of this Commentary) is not simply a collection of guarantees of rights, which is how Americans usually understand bills of rights today. Rather, it is even more important in that it confirms the rule of law and the general constitutional system by which the English are to be governed.

The demand for a bill of rights to be added to the Constitution, which was heard in the United States during the 1787–1788 Ratification Campaign, was in some ways curious. The Constitution of 1787, which recognized various rights, was similar in critical respects to the English Bill of Rights of 1689 in that both documents defined a new constitutional order. But the very name, *Bill of Rights*, had become potent by that time, and so a separate document was called for, something that had already been supplied (as a list of rights guaranteed) for some of the State Constitutions before 1787. The demand for a bill of rights depended, at least in part, upon a misunderstanding in this Country of what the English Bill of Rights was and did. Calls can be heard in Great Britain today for an American-style bill of rights. These are calls for a more elaborate collection of guarantees of rights than are found, say, in the 1689 Bill of Rights. In political matters, we should thereby be reminded, public opinion can be decisive or at least has to be reckoned with, however limited it may be in its understanding.

V

When the First Congress came to draft a national bill of rights in 1789, it had not only venerable English predecessors to draw upon but also many American instruments and the experience of the Federal Convention of 1787. I have already referred to several State bills of rights, which had been preceded by Colonial guarantees in charters and statutes. Perhaps the most illustrious of the State bills of rights of that period was the Virginia Declaration of Rights of 1776 (found in Appendix F-1 of this Commentary).

Innumerable speeches had also helped shape American opinion about the liberties of citizens. In 1761 James Otis stirred up New England against writs of assistance (general search warrants); later, Patrick Henry proclaimed to a receptive Virginia, "Give me liberty, or give me death!" Authoritative statements on behalf of American prerogatives were also issued by the Continental Congress. Consider, for example, the 1774 Declaration and Resolves of the First Continental Congress (found in Appendix E-2 of this Commentary).

The complaints in the Declaration and Resolves do not speak of misconduct by the King (which was to be the thrust of the Declaration of Independence two years later) but rather of misconduct by Parliament. It was still assumed in 1774 that Americans would continue to be, and to enjoy the traditional privileges of, Englishmen. Their allegiance ran to the King rather than to a Parliament that did not rightfully govern them since it could not provide for their adequate representation.

Perhaps the most critical constitutional issue of that day, related to the claims of Parliament, may be seen therefore in the fourth resolution agreed to by the Continental Congress in this 1774 document:

> That the foundation of English liberty, and of all free government, is a right in the people to participate in their legislative council: and as the English colonists are not represented, and from their local and other circumstances, cannot properly be represented in the British parliament, they are entitled to a free and exclusive power of legislation in their several provincial legislatures, where their right of representation can alone be preserved, in all cases of taxation and internal polity, subject only to the negative of their sovereign, in such manner as has been heretofore used and accustomed: But, from the necessity of the case, and a regard to the mutual interest of both countries, we cheerfully consent to the operation of such acts of the British parliament, as are bona fide, restrained to the regulation of our external commerce, for the purpose of securing the commercial advantages of the whole empire to the mother country, and the commercial benefits of its respective members; excluding every idea of taxation internal or external, for raising a revenue on the subjects, in America, without their consent.

The two following 1774 resolutions remind us of what Americans had to build upon in their own constitutional development:

> That the respective colonies are entitled to the common law of England, and more especially to the great and inestimable privilege of being tried by their peers of the vicinage, according to the course of that law.

> That they are entitled to the benefit of such of the English statutes, as existed at the time of their colonization; and which they have, by

experience, respectively found to be applicable to their several local and other circumstances.

The emphasis throughout this 1774 document seems to be far more upon the political rights (if not powers) of a community or people than upon the personal rights of individuals.

Political rights, going back to the Glorious Revolution in England a century before, are reaffirmed in the third article of the Virginia Declaration of Rights (of June 12, 1776) (emphasis added):

> That government is, or ought to be instituted for the common bene-fit, protection, and security of *the people, nation, or community;* of all the various modes and forms of government, that is best which is capable of producing the greatest degree of happiness and safety, and is most effectually secured against the danger of maladministra-tion; and that, when any government shall be found inadequate or contrary to these purposes, a majority of the community hath an indubitable, unalienable, and indefeasible right to reform, alter, or abolish it, in such manner as shall be judged most conducive to the public weal.

The following month the Continental Congress issued the Declara-tion of Independence, invoking thereby that right "to reform, alter or abolish" government which is recognized in the Virginia Decla-ration of Rights.

VI

The Declaration of Independence, still another illustrious prede-cessor to the Bill of Rights of 1791, is to the American system what Magna Carta has been to the English system. Winston Churchill could even describe the Declaration of Independence as a restate-ment of the principles of the Whig Constitution developed in En-gland since Magna Carta.[48]

The Declaration of Independence restates general principles that found expression in particular rights that were, we have seen, so settled and known that they could be readily invoked in the long array of grievances collected in the Declaration. Guarantees with respect to various of these rights may be found both in the Consti-tution of 1787 and in the Bill of Rights of 1791. Those rights, it bears repeating, were not created by the Declaration of Independence, the Constitution, or the Bill of Rights.

If there is any major constitutional principle that is somewhat distinctive to the American development, it would probably be found in the radical implementation of the insistence in the Declaration of Independence "that all Men are created equal." Equality before the law is also important in English constitutional history, not least in the assurance in Chapter 39 of Magna Carta that no freeman should be acted against by government "excepting by the legal judgment of his peers, or by the law of the land." But it is liberty rather than equality that seems critical to the British constitutional development, a liberty that is grounded in the rule of law.

Implementation of the equality principle goes further in this Country than in Great Britain, and not only in that it nullifies the hereditary distinctions that remain important in the British constitutional system. The equality principle was vital to the American Civil War and to the three amendments (the Thirteenth, Fourteenth, and Fifteenth) that confirmed in the Constitution what had been done on the battlefields of that war. That principle may be seen as well in the provision in the Constitution for the exercise of ultimate authority by the people and in the provisions in various amendments (among others) for female suffrage, against poll taxes, and for the vote of eighteen year olds.

A particularly significant expression of the equality principle may be found in the concluding article of the Northwest Ordinance of 1787, which prohibits slavery in the Northwest Territory. This article, we have noticed, proved to be critical to the development of the United States and to the outcome of the Civil War.

That this article in the Northwest Ordinance also included a fugitive-slave provision should remind us of the necessity for community and hence mutual (however troublesome) accommodation on which an eventual full realization of a high principle can depend.

VII

The final item in our inventory of great predecessors to the Bill of Rights of 1791 is, as we have anticipated, the Constitution of 1787. This was preceded by the Articles of Confederation of 1776–1781. The American constitutional system evident from 1776 on is, in its pervasiveness, something like the common law in England.

We have seen that the Constitution of 1787 does recognize various rights in the body of the original instrument, such as the right of access to the writ of habeas corpus, the right of trial by jury, and the right of the people in every State to a republican form of government. We have also seen that restrictions are placed upon the control of the armed forces, the declaration of war, ex post facto laws, bills of attainder, and treason trials. Assurances are given about the revenue powers of the House of Representatives, about the suffrage of the people, about life tenure for judges, and about the ultimate subordination of both the President and the National Courts to the Congress. These assurances may be more important for the protection of civil liberties than most, if not all, of the rights collected in the Bill of Rights of 1791.

Perhaps most important for the origins of the Bill of Rights was the Constitution's reinforcement of the rule of law, with the supreme power in this Country recognized to reside in the people. The people ordain through their Constitution what government may do and how it may do it. The emphasis there is upon what is needed to make good governance most likely, with the protection of individual rights ultimately dependent upon the establishment and perpetuation of good government.

I have suggested the background against which the Bill of Rights should be read, the kind of background that unfortunately is not yet available to most peoples on this planet. (I return to this suggestion in Lecture No. 17 of this Commentary.) We have noticed that, however important a formal recognition of rights and liberties may be, they depend for their preservation and effective realization upon a well-ordered community.

A well-ordered community in turn depends upon a disciplined people. Such discipline is manifested in the craftsmanship with which the Constitution of 1787 was drafted, a discipline that is required in turn of every citizen who wants to understand and hence truly defend that remarkable document.

Only a disciplined people—a people that has been habituated to moderation somewhat in word as well as very much in deed—is apt to be able to make fruitful use, year in and year out, of the great guarantees enshrined in the Constitution of 1787 and its Bill of Rights.

4. The Purposes and Effects of the Bill of Rights of 1791

I

The Bill of Rights, which is the name by which we know the first ten amendments to the Constitution of 1787, was drafted in the first Congress that met pursuant to the Constitution. The role of James Madison of Virginia in the development of these amendments in the First Session of the First Congress is generally recognized. Madison is often called "The Father of the Constitution"; he could more justly be called "The Father of the Bill of Rights."

The records we have of Congressional deliberations and actions with respect to the drafting of the Bill of Rights are incomplete. We can get some idea of what happened in the House of Representatives, where Madison introduced his Bill of Rights resolution on June 8, 1789. (See Appendix J-1 of this Commentary.) But we have only the sketchiest notions of what happened in the Senate before the Bill of Rights resolution was returned to the House of Representatives for its acceptance of the changes made by the Senate. No records were made of the discussion, but only of the actions taken, in the Senate, which sat in executive session during most of the first decade of its existence.

We are reminded by the sketchiness of the records here of the limited records we also have of the framing of the Constitution at Philadelphia in 1787. In both cases, then, we are obliged to address the text itself—the Constitution, on the one hand, the Bill of Rights, on the other hand—in order to understand what was said and done. One advantage we have in reading the Constitution of 1787 is that it is a remarkably well-crafted text. Its craftsmanship permits, even invites, thinking about it. The Bill of Rights, however, appears more episodic and thus less obviously coherent in character. Even so it draws upon assertions of rights taken from that Anglo-American constitutional tradition which had been refined over the centuries by the English-speaking peoples in the light of natural-right doctrines. About the Bill of Rights, too, we are obliged to think, if we are to figure out what was intended and not intended, what was done and not done, and how it was ordered.

The amendments proposed by Congress were completed in September 1789 and sent to the States for ratification by their legislatures. All of the other amendments proposed by Congress during the past two centuries, except one (Amendment XXI), have also been sent to the State legislatures for ratification. Whatever the mode of ratification, the assent of three-fourths of the States is required.

Virginia completed ratification of the Bill of Rights on December 15, 1791.[49] Twelve amendments had been proposed by Congress in 1789. The first two of these failed to get the assents of enough State legislatures at that time to ratify them; one addressed the ratio of representation in the House of Representatives, the other the compensation of Members of Congress.[50]

Ratification of the Constitution of 1787 by the original States had taken less than two years (except for North Carolina, which ratified the Constitution in November 1789 after the Bill of Rights was proposed by Congress, and Rhode Island, which ratified in May 1790 after it became apparent that things could go on quite well without it). Ratification of the Bill of Rights took more than two years. The fact that it took longer to ratify these amendments than it did to ratify the Constitution suggests that there was less of a pressing need perceived for a bill of rights. In part this was, as we have seen, because it was generally recognized that American governments could be depended upon to continue to respect, as they had for some time, the rights and liberties of citizens.[51]

We shall see that what was done in providing for the Bill of Rights of 1791 was far less of a departure from established institutions, and hence far less controversial (as well as less urgent), than what had been done in providing for the Constitution of 1787. We shall also see that the generally accepted account of the way that the Bill of Rights came about is something of a myth, albeit (as in the case of Magna Carta) a somewhat salutary myth.

II

If the Bill of Rights was indeed less controversial than the Constitution, one might again wonder, why was there not a bill of rights provided by the Federal Convention with the original text of the Constitution that it produced in 1787? One obvious answer is that the Convention was too busy devising what almost all of the delegates believed was very much needed in fundamental constitutional reform (in implementing a natural constitutionalism) to take time to devise as well what was not perceived by many of them to be needed at all. Besides, as we have also seen, a bill of rights was regarded by many of the delegates to the Federal Convention as doing little more than reaffirming rights long secured and daily being exercised all over the Country.

Since what the form of the new national government should be and how powers should be allocated among the departments of that government had been controversial for some time before 1787, it is not surprising that the Federal Convention devoted most of its time to those issues. The effect of demands upon a conscientious assembly of other matters than the cause of civil liberty could later be seen as well in the First Congress, where Madison tried repeatedly to get the House of Representatives to set aside what it considered more pressing business (particularly provisions for taxes, for executive departments, and for the judiciary) in order to frame a Bill of Rights proposal.

This is not to deny that if the Framers of the Constitution had anticipated how much some opponents of the proposed Constitution would make of the lack of a designated bill of rights during the Ratification Campaign, they probably would have found time to draft a plausible declaration of rights. Even so, it seemed to many friends of the Constitution that much of the talk about such a lack came from critics who were far more troubled by the enhancement of national powers in the proposed Constitution than by the lack of a bill of rights. It must have been evident to many of those critics that attacks on the proposed form of government itself were not likely to be popular, especially considering such influential sponsors of it as George Washington and Benjamin Franklin. Accordingly there was a shift by those critics in the second half of the Ratification Campaign to the bill-of-rights theme as their major objection to the proposed constitution. On its merits alone, the proposed Constitution had been quickly ratified in one State after another in the early months of its being considered. The demand for a bill of rights was dramatized, perhaps deliberately if not cynically, as a way of avoiding further consideration of the document on its merits. This was countered by friends of the Constitution with promises that a bill of rights would be taken up during the First Congress. The sincere advocates of a bill of rights tended to be reassured by these promises, while the opponents of the Constitution recognized that this would leave them unsatisfied with respect to the one issue they were really troubled by, the considerable empowerment of a radically restructured national government under the new Constitution.

Half of the State Ratification Conventions in 1787–1788 proposed amendments to be considered by the First Congress. (See, for example, Appendixes I-1 and I-2 of this Commentary.) The preamble provided with the Bill of Rights proposal when it was sent by Congress to the States began by reporting that "[t]he Conventions of a number of the States [had] at the time of their adopting the Constitution, expressed a desire, in order to prevent misconstruction or abuse of its powers, that further declaratory and restrictive clauses should be added" to the new Constitution. It was then intimated that the amendments prepared by Congress were being submitted to the States because it was believed that "extending the ground of public confidence in the Government [would] best ensure the beneficent ends of its institution."[52] We shall see that, except perhaps for the Establishment Clause of the First Amendment, the only truly "restrictive clauses" (however minor) among the twelve amendments proposed by Congress in 1789 were in the two amendments not ratified by the States at that time.

III

Madison pressed for amendments in the First Congress in large part because he had promised his Virginia constituency that he would do so, a constituency in which there were (as elsewhere) sincere advocates of a bill of rights as well as some who were merely using this issue as a respectable way of resisting the empowerment of a new national government. In his First Inaugural

Address, President Washington had recognized a demand among the public at large for a bill of rights.[53]

A bill of rights was drafted in the First Congress in part to head off demands heard in some quarters during the Ratification Campaign for another Federal Convention, which would put the Country to the risk of wide-ranging changes to the body of the Constitution as well. We can be reminded of this concern when we notice the warnings today that any assembly called on demand by the States to consider, say, a balanced-budget amendment might turn into a "runaway" convention that would consider much more than that.[54]

Dozens of amendment suggestions had come out of the State Ratification Conventions, suggestions that were usually submitted in those conventions by the factions that had opposed ratification of the Constitution. Madison assured the First Congress that the amendments he was proposing would "make such alterations in the Constitution as will give satisfaction, without injuring or destroying any of its vital principles."[55] The rigorous sifting by Congress in 1789 of the proposed amendments showed that there was to be, at least by way of formal constitutional amendments, no fundamental change in the relations between the United States and the States or in the powers of the Government of the United States provided for in the Constitution of 1787.

We have also noticed the frustrations endured by those who tried to have the term *expressly* put into what is now the Tenth Amendment. It soon became apparent to opponents of the new Constitution in the First Congress that they were not going to get what they really wanted, so much so that they repeatedly had to be urged by Madison to take any interest at all in the development of the bill of rights they had once made so much of. The sort of changes that the opponents of the Constitution were truly interested in is suggested by one of the amendments proposed by Anti-Federalists in the First Congress:

> That the General Government of the United States ought never to impose direct taxes, but where the moneys arising from the duties of impost and excise are insufficient for the public exigencies, nor then, until Congress shall have made a requisition upon the States to assess, levy, and pay their respective portions of such requisitions; and in case any State shall neglect or refuse to pay its proportion, pursuant to such requisition, then Congress may assess and levy such State's proportion, together with interest thereon, at the rate of six

per cent, per annum, from the time of payment prescribed by such requisition.[56]

This proposal, representative of many that had been devised by opponents of the Constitution in the State Ratification Conventions (as may be seen in Appendixes I-1 and I-2 of this Commentary), was soundly rejected in the House of Representatives. No doubt, it smacked too much of the Articles of Confederation, which the Nationalists who controlled the First Congress had been determined to change radically in the Federal Convention.

A persistent desire of the opponents of the Constitution was that the States not be controlled very much, if at all, either by the Constitution of 1787 or by the General Government established by that Constitution. Those States' Rights advocates recognized, more than many judges and legal scholars since then have, the significant restraints placed upon the States by Section 10 of Article 1, by the Privileges and Immunities Clause and the Republican Form of Government Guarantee in Article IV, and by the Supremacy Clause in Article VI of the Constitution. These and other provisions are reinforced by the Necessary and Proper Clause in Section 8 of Article I.

Still, we have noticed, none of the amendments proposed by the First Congress and ratified by the States in 1791 cuts down any of the substantive powers of the Government of the United States provided by the Constitution of 1787. We should further notice that no amendment to the Constitution since the Bill of Rights has ever taken away from the Government of the United States any legislative power that the Framers intended it to have, except for the Twenty-seventh Amendment (which deals with a minor power that the Nationalists in the First Congress, as well as in the Federal Convention, were willing to see curbed). In fact, we may wonder whether any amendment has ever given to that Government any power that the Framers of 1787 did not want it to have. Some will argue that there has been an extra-constitutional, if not unconstitutional, growth of powers in the General Government as a result of legislative and judicial interpretations. But this argument may depend, in large part, upon a failure to see how broad the original powers are that were established by the Federal Convention for Congress under the Constitution. It may well be that what the Courts of the United States did in the twentieth century, partly in response to intense social and political pressure, was finally to recognize for Congress much of the power originally intended by the Framers of the Constitution.

Does not the absence, from the twenty-seven amendments we have had thus far to the Constitution, of any major curtailments in the powers of the General Government testify to the remarkable work done by the Federal Convention in 1787? It may also testify to the shaping of the American people and of their political life to conform to the Constitution, so much so that fundamental changes have become almost unthinkable.

IV

All kinds of arguments by proponents of the proposed Constitution had been used during the Ratification Campaign of 1787–1788 as to why no national bill of rights was needed. Some of these arguments were spurious (as were some arguments in favor of a bill of rights). I have suggested that a case was made against a bill of rights partly because advocates of the Constitution believed that they could not afford to risk serious delays by making concessions during the Ratification Campaign; they could only make promises for the First Congress to honor.

I have also suggested that if the Framers of the Constitution had anticipated the objections that would be made about the lack of a bill of rights, they probably would have tried to draft something appropriate in the Federal Convention. Or were the Framers so shrewd as to figure that it would be safer to have the more determined opponents of the Constitution complain about the lack of a bill of rights than to have them magnify other defects in the proposed Constitution? If those opponents could be busied with the bill-of-rights problem, they would be diverted from other alleged problems. Also, this "defect" could be easily remedied thereafter without damaging the Constitution that the Framers had fashioned.

Furthermore, as we have seen, friends of the Constitution might have sensed that critics who made much of the lack of a national bill of rights could not be taken too seriously by the people at large who knew that various of their rights were safe, whether or not the United States or the States had bills of rights. Friends of the Constitution could point out that its critics were not disturbed that half of

39

the States had no bill of rights in their State Constitutions, even though the domestic powers of those State governments had been considered virtually unlimited under the Articles of Confederation, while those of the new General Government could be said to be limited to what had been "enumerated."

We have also seen that the genuine popular demand for a bill of rights was lent support by the august place in British constitutional history of the 1689 Bill of Rights. We have seen as well that that constitutional document, one of several written parts of the British Constitution, had defined and limited the prerogatives of the Crown, had insisted upon the prerogatives of the Parliament, and had affirmed various other rights of the people. In this sense, it was pointed out by the friends of the Constitution, the entire Constitution of 1787 served the purpose of the 1689 Bill of Rights. But until there was something on paper that could be separately identified (however misleadingly) as a bill of rights, troublesome reservations would persist about the new Constitutional system, and this the friends of the Constitution undertook to provide in the First Congress under Madison's leadership.

Just as the name of a document could matter, so had the name mattered of the "party" advocating ratification of the Constitution in 1787–1788. That party took for itself the name of Federalists, even though the opponents of the Constitution (the "anti-Federalists") may have had the better claim to that evidently attractive name. The Federalists in the First Congress, we have seen, did not want the powers of the General Government reduced or hampered by any amendments (certainly none of a "federalizing" character) to the Constitution of 1787.

The more thoughtful of the Federalists might have been concerned as well about any shift in the Constitution from a primary concern with the powers and ends of government to a primary concern with the rights of individuals. The Constitution of 1787 looks in one direction; the Bill of Rights of 1791 seems to look in another direction. The shift that we have in part seen since 1787 is from a concern principally with political interests to a concern with individuality, a shift from the duties of the citizen to the privileges of the private person, even while the General Government has had its constitutional powers reinforced vis-à-vis the States.

Whatever the limitations in 1787–1789 of the case for a bill of rights, it is now salutary to consider the Bill of Rights of 1791 as the virtual completion of the constitutional framing that had begun in 1776.[57] The Bill of Rights could not now be eliminated or even abridged significantly without ominous political implications and without unhealthy effects upon citizen morale in this Country. Even tampering with it, as in response to such unfortunate provocations as the flag-burning cases, should be approached with the greatest caution.

Because of the powerful rhetorical presence and considerable political as well as judicial effects of the Bill of Rights, it is needed much more now than it was in 1789–1791. Or, put another way, one consequence of adding the first ten amendments to the Constitution, even though they may not have been needed, was to have made retention of the Bill of Rights absolutely necessary ever since.

V

I have suggested several times that the Bill of Rights of 1791 probably did not change anything essential. The Government of the United States could still concern itself after ratification of the Bill of Rights with the vital matters that had concerned it before that ratification, and could do so with all of its substantive powers unimpaired.

On the other hand, the Framers of the Constitution of 1787 did not establish the new government in order to abridge various long-recognized rights of the American people. In fact, they argued, only a national government with adequate powers could promote the prosperity and assure the safety necessary for a sustained flourishing of those rights.

Just as no recognized rights of the American people were subverted by the Constitution of 1787, no rights were created by the Bill of Rights of 1791, however much a few of them were adapted to republican circumstances and to the diversity among American States (as we shall see when we examine the First Amendment in my next lecture). Consider, as illustrative of the republican character of the American people well before Independence, what made the farmers fight in 1775. One of those farmers answered that question, years later, in this fashion: "We always had governed ourselves, and we always meant to. They [the British] didn't mean we should."[58] A more personal if not individualistic, or less political, way of expressing this position can be seen in the militiaman who went with his musket to confront the British, saying, "We'll see who's goin' t'own this farm!"[59]

It is not generally appreciated that the American Constitution, including its Bill of Rights, has worked as well as it has from the beginning in large part because so much of it was already being used, among the States if not nationally, when it was formally adopted in the late eighteenth century.[60] Nor is it generally appreciated that the Bill of Rights, in declaring and reaffirming those rights in 1791, does not itself suggest that any new remedy is available to secure such rights.

The notion that courts would be looked to in order to "enforce" the Bill of Rights (and all rights in the Constitution of 1787 also) did not take firm hold until well into the nineteenth century. This notion spilled over into the use of courts to police applications of various other provisions of the Constitution as well. In fact, the first act of Congress declared unconstitutional by the Supreme Court, in *Marbury* v. *Madison*,[61] did not run afoul of the Bill of Rights but rather of a technical jurisdiction-allocation provision in Article III of the Constitution. (In fact, what the Court did was done in such a way, in this case, as to deny a citizen an important right recognized by the Court to be due to him. William Marbury, after all, was not put in possession of the judicial office that the Court recognized as his due.)

It is far from clear that this kind of judicial supervision of Congress was intended by the Framers with respect to either the original Constitution or the Bill of Rights. This is not to deny, as we shall see in Lecture No. 7, that some of the guarantees in the Bill of Rights were meant to be binding upon (perhaps even binding primarily upon) the Courts.

VI

That few, if any, of the rights listed in the Bill of Rights of 1791 were new, however much some of them (such as the provisions in the First Amendment for freedom of speech and freedom of the press) became more significant in the United States than they had been before, is further testified to by the lack of difficulty in the First Congress in understanding what most of the proposed amendments meant.

We have noticed that how citizens generally conducted themselves did not seem to depend upon whether the State they were in had a bill of rights in its own State constitution. Americans tended to act the same wherever they were, so far as they were concerned about the responses of government to their conduct, just as today most Americans do not stop to notice what State they are in before they do what they do, for example, in their treatment of their children, in their business transactions, or in their sexual practices, however much the rules on the books with respect to these matters may vary from State to State.

An enterprising student of American constitutionalism could provide further illumination here by investigating whether the States that had no bill of rights in their State constitutions ever conducted themselves differently from the States that did: for example, in the Federal Convention, in the State Ratification Conventions, or in the First Congress when a bill of rights was being considered. The mobility of the American people from one State to another, a mobility taken for granted in the Federal Convention, made it unlikely that things would be done or thought of differently from one part of the Country to another, except perhaps when such a controversial institution as slavery intervened to color everything that was thought, said, and done.

It is useful to ask, in order to appreciate the likely sources of political liberty in the modern world, how various of the rights we deem important have been long recognized in Canada and Great Britain without the kind of bill of rights we have, regardless of what has recently been done in both countries to develop additional written guarantees. Have not many traditional rights been protected there for the same reasons that all of the American States were more or less respectful of the rights of citizens in 1789, whether or not they had a bill of rights in their State Constitutions?

The invocation of such rights in the Declaration of Independence testifies, I have argued, to how well established these rights were independent of a formal bill of rights. Even outside of the immediate influence of the English-speaking tradition, considerable respect for such rights has long been evident, as in France and the Scandinavian countries, and this despite different constitutional systems. On the other hand, there are all too many countries in the world today that have elaborate bills of rights (even copies of ours) that do not prevent tyranny.

Although the 1791 Bill of Rights might have done little to secure the long-established rights it enumerated, we have noticed that it may well have jeopardized the standing of other long-established rights that it did not enumerate, just as the rights subsequently listed in the Bill of Rights had been said by some in 1787–1788 to have been jeopardized by not having been among the rights mentioned (albeit for special reasons) in the Constitution of 1787. We shall see, in Lecture No. 8, how the Ninth Amendment was used to try to head off the unwelcome implications of such neglect.

There is, in Article IV of the Constitution of 1787, a Privileges and Immunities Clause, which could on its face be taken to assure, or at least to remind, citizens of the United States about long-established fundamental rights to which they are entitled, no matter where they happen to be in this Country. Did the listing of so many rights in the Bill of Rights tend to diminish the importance of the Privileges and Immunities Clause, especially with respect to the States, something that was attempted to be remedied in the Fourteenth Amendment?

Still another possible effect of enumerating so many rights in the Bill of Rights should be noticed: did enumeration of rights in this fashion induce some to make too much of enumeration as well of the powers of Congress in Section 8 of Article I? Just as only those rights that are expressly enumerated (except perhaps for "the right to privacy") have been made much of over the years by the courts and others, so only those powers that are expressly enumerated have been assigned to Congress without question. In both cases, the general spirit of the constitutional arrangement sometimes tends to be lost sight of. This too may contribute to a shift from politics and the common good to legalism and individualism as the prevailing mode of our life together.

VII

To emphasize legalism (and hence litigation?) is to encourage a positivistic approach both to law and to constitutional determinations. Law thus can come to be seen as the product of a sovereign, not as an emanation from some enduring standard of right and wrong. For example, a preference for authority (if not mere power) instead of reason may be seen in disparagements in some circles today of the significance of international law, which depends upon longstanding traditions and a body of reasoning about the proper relations between nations in a civilized world.

One consequence of positivistic developments in the United States is the steady depreciation of the status of the common law, which traditionally included an awareness of the spirit and ends of law for the English-speaking peoples. Thus, the common law could once be relied upon, emerging through the discoveries of judges under the guidance of their legislatures, to develop (in a sound and generally acceptable way) various relations and rights implicit in the prevailing political and social system. When the common-law discipline comes to be neglected, the interventions of judges become suspect, as may be seen in recent responses to the uses of the Ninth and Fourteenth Amendments in developing the right to privacy. The political repercussions here can be serious, especially if the development is seen to take on the appearance of judicial usurpation. Judicial usurpation is more likely whenever the natural differences between legislation and adjudication are obliterated.

It is not generally appreciated how much most of the guarantees in the Bill of Rights were embedded in the common law. This makes it difficult for us to understand fully the arguments of those in 1787–1789 who insisted that the most critical rights of Americans were already fully protected without a bill of rights, and this without any substantial experience of routine reliance theretofore upon courts to assess legislative acts for their constitutionality.

Most constitutional law scholars today do not seem even to be aware of the problems posed by what has been happening to the common law in this Country. Insofar as the Bill of Rights contributed to a more positivistic mode in the law, one can wonder whether the first ten amendments were in fact *amendments,* that is, improvements.[62]

To become more positivistic in our approach to law tends to diminish the status of natural right and a general reliance upon enduring standards. This in turn tends to encourage radical individuality, or "doing one's own thing," and various forms of hedonism. We can see positivistic assumptions in the arguments put forward from time to time by United States Supreme Court Justices and others to the effect that only enumerated fundamental rights, made explicitly applicable to the States, can be brought to bear by the National Government upon what is done by State Governments.

45

An emphasis upon law as that which is explicitly set forth undermines reliance upon, if not the majesty of, the common law. Does a seemingly comprehensive bill of rights tend to make the common-law process seem less important? Does it shift the attention of judges away from what is right to what is legal (or laid down)?

But however positivistic we become, and however much the demands of nature are disparaged, some standard beyond law and Constitution is implied in such provisions for amendments as those found in Article V. Some enduring standard is implied as well by the distinctively American assumption that a choice should be made by the people as to what constitution they want. A people cannot truly select or responsibly correct, to say nothing of being able to understand, their institutions without some awareness of nature and the truth about things. Intimations of the best possible regime, to which natural right looks, have to be drawn upon if the people are to be properly trained and sensibly guided.

Natural right means, among other things, that in the greatest emergencies even the most venerable constitutional arrangements can be temporarily suspended, as was sometimes done between 1774 and 1781 and between 1861 and 1865. A sensitivity to the demands of natural right also means, however, that far less threatening circumstances can be recognized and assessed for what they are, allowing our constitutional processes to work as intended. This understanding of natural right and constitutionalism leaves the people free to make prudent use of their prerogatives in governing themselves.

When all is said and done, therefore, the Bill of Rights we happen to have, along with the Constitution of 1787, can do for us what traditions, blood ties, and ancient institutions do for countries with longer and deeper histories than our own. That is, the Bill of Rights can suggest enduring standards of right and wrong and can encourage a healthy political restraint. Besides, people sometimes need to have available for veneration tangible manifestations of their most elevated aspirations. This is what the Constitution of 1787 and its Bill of Rights can provide for many. The Bill of Rights of 1791, properly understood and applied, promotes moderation (or civilization), liberty, and equal justice under law.

5. Amendment I

The amendments to the Constitution of 1787 that we know as the Bill of Rights were first proposed in the House of Representatives on June 8, 1789. At that time, and for two months thereafter, while the proposals were being debated and revised, the amendments we now have were designed for insertion at specified places in the original Constitution. If the ratified amendments had remained scattered in the body of the Constitution at the places originally designated for them, it would always have been obvious that all of the restrictions set forth in those amendments were directed against the Government of the United States, not against the States.

A few have argued, however, that the generality of the language of the restrictions in most of the Bill of Rights amendments, especially now that they stand alone in the collection of amendments appended to the Constitution, means that they should be considered applicable to all governments in the United States, not just to the General Government. But it is difficult to find evidence to support the proposition that the shift in placement of the proposed amendments was with a view to including the States within the sweep of those amendments, especially since there remained at one stage, even after the shift in placement, a proposed amendment that was clearly directed against State Governments. (See Appendix J-3 of this Commentary, as well as Section V of this lecture.) It is not likely that this separate proposed amendment, which was approved by the House of Representatives on August 24 but eliminated thereafter by the Senate, would have been resorted to if the other proposed amendments had been thought of as having a comprehensive application.

It can be argued that putting most of the amendments in general

47

terms, treating them as appendices to the Constitution, and eliminating the one amendment explicitly designed for the States had the (perhaps unintended) effect of making most of the Bill of Rights amendments comprehensive in their effects, restraining thereby the States as well as the General Government. But that would ignore the evident intentions and widely known understanding of the people involved in the shaping and ratification of those amendments. In such matters, common sense should be given its due.[63]

Very little is said in the available records as to why it was finally decided by the House of Representatives in 1789 not to insert its amendments into the body of the Constitution. The placement issue had been raised early in the amendment-preparation process that summer, with concern expressed about changing in any way the text of the document from what it had been when its distinguished Framers had put their names to it. No change was made, however, at that stage of the deliberations in the House of Representatives. Then, two months later, as the process was drawing to a close in that House, and before any draft was sent to the Senate for its initial consideration of amendments, the shift in placement was made without much recorded debate or explanation. (See Appendixes J-1, J-2, and J-3 of this Commentary.)

One effect of appending all amendments to the Constitution then and since has been to keep the 1787 document intact, preserving down to our day the integrity of its original appearance. This effect should have been welcomed by those who did not consider the Constitution to be amended in any critical respect by the Bill of Rights.

Another effect of the shift in position for the amendments drafted in 1789 was to make the Bill of Rights ratified in 1791 seem like a separate instrument, even like a kind of constitution itself. We are accustomed to seeing displayed the Congressional resolution, with its twelve proposed amendments, that was sent to the States for ratification, a document with its own preamble and signatures. (See Appendix J-5 of this Commentary.) This instrument has been invested with a mystique of its own as it stands somewhat in collaboration and somewhat in tension with the Constitution of 1787. I have observed that the Constitution reflects more what can be called natural sociability and the need for sound government; the Bill of Rights, with a perhaps different approach to the same ends or principles as the Constitution itself, reflects more the natural rights and civil liberties of a people.

The Bill of Rights of 1791 as a separate document invites study of its organization, just as the Constitution of 1787 does. It is evident in each case that care was taken in determining the arrangement settled upon. I have suggested in my Commentary on the Constitution of 1787 how that instrument is put together. I suggest, at the outset of my next lecture, how the Bill of Rights is put together. Such a study of the Bill of Rights should be useful as well for the light it can shed on the Constitution as a whole.

II

In a sense, virtually all of the Bill of Rights provisions represent restraints upon Congress. Of the twelve amendments proposed to the States by Congress in September 1789, most of them had been originally intended to be placed in Article I of the Constitution, with the others intended to be placed in Article III and VI. (See Appendixes J-1 and J-2 of this Commentary.)

Of the ten amendments originally designed for placement in Article I (the Legislative Article), the first two were to have been put where Congress is provided for (in Sections 2 and 6 of Article I), the other eight were to have been put where Congress is restrained in various ways (in Section 9 of Article I). The two amendments originally intended for Article III (the Judicial Article) were probably put there because they expanded provisions already in Article III with respect to jury trials.

It seems to have been routine for the Constitutionalists of 1789 to consider restraints upon Congress to be restraints as well upon the rest of the General Government. Most of what that Government does still depends on Congress. Congress must make the laws that the President executes and that the Courts interpret and apply. Also, Congress must create and finance the Executive Departments and the military and provide as well for the Courts and to some extent for their jurisdictions.

In short, Congress determines in large part who the Executive and the Courts are to be and much of what they are to do. President Washington had relatively little to do during his first nine months in office, and the Supreme Court did not convene for the first time until February 1790. Both Executive Officers and Courts had to wait until Congress provided for them and gave them something to do.

Thus to control Congress is largely to control all of the Government of the United States. This helps explain why most of the twelve amendments proposed in 1789 were originally intended for placement in the Legislative Article. Still, three of those amendments obviously deal more with Congress than do the others: the first is concerned with the composition of the House of Representatives; the second is concerned with the compensation of Members of Congress; and the third, which we now know as the First Amendment, begins, "Congress shall make no law . . ."

III

The first two of the twelve amendments proposed by Congress in September 1789 failed of ratification at that time by the State legislatures. They were, we have noticed, originally to have been placed in those parts of the Constitution (Sections 2 and 6, respectively, of Article I) that deal with the matters addressed in these two proposed amendments. (The ratification returns from the States are indicated in Appendix J-6 of this Commentary.)

The two proposed amendments that failed to be ratified in 1791 were these:

> After the first enumeration required by the first article of the Constitution, there shall be one Representative for every thirty thousand, until the number shall amount to one hundred, after which, the proportion shall be so regulated by Congress, that there shall be not less than one hundred Representatives, nor less than one Representative for every forty thousand persons, until the number of Representatives shall amount to two hundred; after which the proportion shall be so regulated by Congress, that there shall not be less than two hundred Representatives, nor more than one Representative for every fifty thousand persons.
>
> No law varying the compensation for the services of the Senators and Representatives shall take effect, until an election of Representatives shall have intervened.

Why did these proposed amendments fail to secure ratification? Was it sensed that these two provisions were not of the dignity of the others? Were they considered inappropriate for a bill of rights and hence better reserved for separate amendments or even for statutes?[64]

Still, it is significant what has happened to the two rejected amendments. The first was made obsolete by steady population growth in the United States. Concern had been expressed during the Ratification Campaign that the House of Representatives would not be large enough to be truly representative, with only sixty-five members of the House provided by the Constitution for the First Congress. It soon became evident, however, that there was no need to worry about having a large enough House of Representatives, but perhaps just the opposite.

The second failed amendment proposal, regulating the timing of changes in the compensation of Members of Congress, was long adhered to in practice. Congress routinely provided that increases in its own compensation would take effect only after an intervening Congressional election. Even so, it proved to be attractive (in 1992) for a few State legislatures to complete "ratification" of this amendment proposal, transforming what had been long ignored into what is now destined to be known as the Twenty-seventh Amendment. (We return to this amendment in Section VI of Lecture No. 16 of this Commentary.)

The American experience with these two initially rejected amendments, as well as with several others, reminds us that constitutional amendments in this Country are rarely controversial. That is, they usually deal with matters that either have been settled by events, such as the Civil War, or are already widely accepted. Even the Equal Rights Amendment proposed in 1972 has virtually been put into practice despite its having failed of formal ratification, a failure that may have been in part due to accidents in timing.

I have observed that none of the amendments to the Constitution during the past two centuries have cut down any significant power of Congress. The two Congressionally proposed amendments rejected in 1789–1791 by the States were designed to place minor restraints upon powers that Congress was given: the power to determine the composition of the House of Representatives and the power to determine the compensation of Congress. The Federal Convention had considered various ways of hedging both of these powers, including setting a permanent size for the House of Representatives and keying Congressional compensation to the price of

51

specified commodities. The Convention decided, however, that it had to rely, here as elsewhere, upon the integrity of the Members of Congress and upon the vigilance of the people who selected them, which is how matters still stand with respect to many like determinations.

IV

I have suggested that the first three of the twelve Congressionally proposed amendments of 1789 deal more with Congress than do the other nine. I have discussed, however briefly, the two proposals that failed to be ratified by the State legislatures in 1791. The last of these first three did secure ratification at that time, the proposal we now know as the First Amendment:

> Congress shall make no law respecting an establishment of religion, or prohibiting the free exercise thereof; or abridging the freedom of speech, or of the press; or the right of the people peaceably to assemble, and to petition the Government for a redress of grievances.

It is, because of the way the State legislatures happened to respond to the twelve amendments proposed in 1789, something of an accident that this should have become the *First* Amendment, a designation that people generally sense to be appropriate.[65]

The First Amendment is the only one of the first eight amendments that is somewhat innovative. All of the others, we have noticed, are copies of, or derivative from, respectable English prototypes. That is, Amendments II through VIII are reaffirmations of long-established rights of the English-speaking peoples, including those in North America.

There are two principal sets of concerns addressed in the First Amendment: concerns with religious freedom and religious establishments and concerns with freedom of speech and freedom of the press (and the related rights with respect to assembly and petition). A distinctively American response is given in each case, but perhaps necessarily in such a way as to leave questions for us to this day.

Freedom of the press has, even in this Country, some traditional features to it. English constitutional principles may be seen in the insistence among us that there can be no previous (or prior) restraint of the press (that is, no system of official censorship). These principles, described in William Blackstone's *Commentaries*, find their most dramatic advocacy in John Milton's *Areopagitica* of 1644.

Our freedom of speech provision, although in its scope more characteristic of the United States than of Great Britain, also draws upon English constitutional history. For centuries Members of Parliament had been assured immunity for whatever they said in the exercise of their duties. For example, the 1689 Bill of Rights (found in Appendix D of this Commentary) declared that "the Freedome of Speech and Debates or Proceedings in Parlyament ought not to be impeached or questioned in any Court or Place out of Parlyament." (We can see, in Appendix B of this Commentary, Thomas More's 1521 formulation of this immunity.) Similarly, the Constitution of 1787 provides, in Section 6 of Article I, that Senators and Representatives

> shall in all Cases, except Treason, Felony and Breach of the Peace, be privileged from Arrest during their Attendance at the Session of their respective Houses, and in going to and returning from the same; and for any Speech or Debate in either House, they shall not be questioned in any other Place.

The recognition in the First Amendment of the freedom of political discourse of the people at large, explicitly generalizing thereby the traditional immunity of what the 1689 Bill of Rights called "Freedome of Speech and Debates or Proceedings *In Parlyament*," testifies to what any truly self-governing body requires. The American people were already exercising this right by 1789, whether or not their States had bills of rights or guarantees in them of freedom of speech or of the press. These were rights that were confirmed, not created, by the speech, press, assembly, and petition provisions of the First Amendment.

The entire constitutional system in this Country depends upon a self-governing people that exercises popular control not only over what its governments do, but also over what the Constitution itself provides. The primary emphasis of the First Amendment here is upon free and open discussion of public affairs, as distinguished from what is now called *freedom of expression*. Freedom of speech and the press, unlike the much broader freedom of expression, may be necessary for effective self-government. An unregulated freedom of expression can, in some circumstances, undermine the character and education needed for sustained self-government. Freedom of expression, such as in artistic activity, is something that a people should want to see protected to a considerable extent, but there is not for it the absolute protection that is confirmed by the First Amendment for freedom of speech and of the press—that is, for completely unfettered (even "subversive," if not "treasonous") public discussion of the public business. Freedom of expression is protected more by our rights to property, liberty, and perhaps even privacy, interests that can be taken away or regulated by due process of law. The Constitutional provisions that protect property and liberty, such as the Fifth Amendment, are more individualistic and less civic-minded (or public-spirited) in their primary orientation than are the Speech and Press Clauses of the First Amendment.

A truly new way (compared to European practices) may be seen in the insistence in American constitutions (State as well as National) that the people are entitled, as the ultimate source of all governmental authority in this Country, to the right to discuss the public business as much as they wish, including in that public business not only the selecting and doings of officers of government but also the framing and amending of forms of government.[66] The American dedication to equality has come to have as a particularly dramatic manifestation that emphasis upon freedom of expression with which we have recently become familiar. This, too, is a new way, but one that may be more troublesome for the genuine Constitutionalist, even when it is recognized that this development may be partly in reaction to the imprudent and thus corrosive suppression of political discourse in the late 1940s and the 1950s.

V

We can be reminded of the federalist character of the American constitutional system by noticing that it is explicitly Congress (and, by implication, the General Government) that is restrained by the First Amendment from abridging the freedom of speech or of the press. The States are not addressed on this issue by the First Amendment.

But, we should also notice, Congress is not kept by the First Amendment from regulating State abridgments of freedom of speech or of the press. Such Congressional interventions on behalf of freedom of speech and of the press can be in the service of the General Government's Article IV obligation to guarantee each State in the Union a republican form of government, especially whenever State suppressions threaten the ability of the people to govern themselves.

We should immediately add, however, that self-government need not be subverted—indeed, it may even be enhanced—by prudent State efforts to control publications that threaten to undermine morality. The United States is more apt to try to regulate expression in the interest of national security (by acting against sedition, treason or, more loosely speaking, subversion), while the States are more apt to try to regulate expression in the interest of morality (by acting against corruption, licentiousness, and dissoluteness). But whatever government purports to do, and for whatever ends, freedom of speech and of the press protects those who want to examine what is being done by government or others and why it is being done.

Strictly speaking, then, it is not freedom of speech and of the press that the States are most apt to suppress but rather aspects of what we now call freedom of expression. Freedom of expression, I have suggested, is more of a property, liberty, or privacy interest that can be legitimately regulated by law for the sake of common morality and the general welfare than an absolutely privileged free-speech interest can be, however much it does resemble freedom of speech in some respects.

Is not freedom of expression critical to the appeal of religious freedom as well? Human beings, at least in the Western World, are now considered to be (in principle, at least) radically on their own with respect to spiritual matters, however much is made of religious communities. The appeal of freedom of expression, as well as a pervasive dedication to self-government, seems to provide a connection between the two kinds of freedom guaranteed by the First Amendment. There is a primacy to the kind of freedom guaranteed by the First Amendment, as may be seen in the one amendment proposal clearly applicable to the States that was developed in the House of Representatives: "No State shall infringe the right of trial by Jury in criminal cases, nor the rights of conscience, nor the freedom of speech, or of the press."[67] Thus, in addition to the traditional "right of trial by Jury in criminal cases," the only other great rights nominated by the House of Representatives for protection against State infringement in the Bill of Rights are those found in the First Amendment.

VI

The Religion Clauses of the First Amendment oblige Congress to stand clear of religious establishments, which means that Congress can neither provide for religious establishments of its own nor interfere with any State religious establishments then existing or later to be developed. The United States, in short, is to keep its hands off completely here. This means that all State establishments of religion are to be left alone by the General Government. State concerns here, as with the regulation of freedom of expression already referred to, reflect the police powers of the State, especially with respect to curbing licentiousness and corruption and promoting morality and education.

Although Congress cannot interfere at all with State religious establishments, it is evidently left free by the First Amendment to supervise State prohibitions of the free exercise of religion. Congress is kept from prohibiting the free exercise of religion, but it is not kept from correcting State interferences with the free exercise of religion. In this field, unlike that of religious establishments, the States need not be left alone by Congress to develop their local preferences in whatever way they choose.[68]

Even though I do not attempt in these lectures to recapitulate systematically how the Courts have interpreted the twenty-seven amendments we are reviewing, it can help us appreciate what the First Amendment does and does not provide by noticing how the Establishment Clause has been distorted by the Courts. That clause is now interpreted virtually to mean that governments cannot cooperate at all with religious institutions, for example, by providing some public funding of church-sponsored schools. This has long seemed to me a misreading of the First Amendment: the forbidden "establishment" does not refer to official cooperation with religion but rather to official preference for one or a few religious sects at the expense of all the others in the community.[69] Extensive, almost natural, collaboration between Church and State may be seen again and again in eighteenth-century America. Consider, for example, the concluding article of the Virginia Declaration of Rights (June 12,

1776), which declares that "all men are equally entitled to the free exercise of religion, according to the dictates of conscience." But that influential Declaration (found in Appendix F-1 of this Commentary) adds that "it is the mutual duty of all to practise Christian forbearance, love, and charity, towards each other."

Whatever problems there may be in interpreting the Religion Clauses, they are compounded when the Bill of Rights is said to have been made applicable, by means of the Fourteenth Amendment, against the States. For one thing, it is difficult to figure out how the Establishment Clause, with its obvious protection of the States from any Congressional interference with State religious establishments, can be made applicable against the States as well. Is there not something awkward about this particular transformation of the coverage of the First Amendment?

Now that the First Amendment is considered generally applicable to the States, it remains to be seen what the States, in collaboration with religious institutions, may continue to do against general corruption and in the service of common decency.

VII

We have already noticed that the First Amendment may be inherently the most controversial article in the Bill of Rights. All of the rights set forth in the other amendments from the Second through the Eighth are much more technical and long established, and hence less likely to be controversial, however troublesome particular applications of them may be from time to time.

That many rights seemed obvious enough to eighteenth-century Americans is evident from the way they were taken for granted in the Privileges and Immunities Clause in Article IV of the Constitution of 1787. Also, various rights seemed ascertainable enough to be capable of being referred to as they were in the Ninth Amendment. The First Amendment, on the other hand, seems less traditional in some of its implications.

We have also noticed that the Religion and Speech concerns of the First Amendment reinforce each other in critical respects. Both depend on, and encourage, that sense of personal responsibility and choice which we associate with effective self-government. The provisions of this amendment are, in the spirit that pervades them, distinctively American. The freedom of speech and of the press that the First Amendment affirms permits the American people to discuss fully and to assess deeply all of the other rights to which they are said to be entitled. That freedom also permits repeated examination of what rights the American people should have and how they should be exercised, with even the Constitution itself always subject to reconsideration and amendment. Thus, the Constitutional amendment that protects Americans in their devotion to the sacred also insures that no public policy will ever be regarded as so sacred in this Country that it cannot be subjected to the most searching inquiry.

6. Amendments II, III, and IV

I

We have observed that most of the restrictions of the Bill of Rights were directed in the first instance against Congress. This intention was indicated by the original plan of placing most of the proposed amendments in that part of the Constitution, Article I, Section 9, which collects many of the original restrictions upon Congress. The overall concern evident in the Constitution is that there be a rule of law, whatever may have to be done during extraordinary emergencies. This is reflected in the dominance of the legislature in the Constitutional system, which makes it even more important that Congress be held in check. Care is taken to make sure both how Congress is constituted and how legislation is enacted. The prohibitions of ex post facto laws and bills of attainder in Section 9 of Article I are designed to insure that Congress act only through properly developed legislation. The writ of habeas corpus, which is recognized in Section 9 of Article I, protects to some degree against the rule of law being cavalierly set aside.

The first three proposed amendments to the Constitution, two of which (as we have seen) were not ratified by the State legislatures in 1791, place direct limitations upon Congress. Limitations, in effect, upon the way Congress exercises its powers may be seen in most of the other amendments as well. But a few of them apply more than the others to the President, and these are our principal concern in this lecture.

The array of twelve proposed amendments prepared in the First Congress in 1789 is often regarded as rather haphazard in organization, a proposition that I have questioned. By noticing further the rationale of that arrangement, we might be better able to interpret those amendments. We cannot rely here simply upon what the Courts have said in interpreting these amendments, however much we may be obliged to conform to what the Courts do say from time to time. Judges, in adjusting to circumstances, do not always read a constitutional text with the care that it deserves, especially when they consider themselves obliged to build upon what their predecessors have ruled.

It can be said that the Bill of Rights amendments are organized according to their primary addressees. Of the twelve proposed amendments the first three (concluding with what we now know as Amendment I) address primarily Congress, the next three (Amendments II–IV) address primarily the President, the next four (Amendments V–VIII) address primarily the Courts, and the last two (Amendments IX–X) affirm general principles. The arrangement of the twelve proposed amendments of 1789 can be described in still another way: the sequence is determined by the order or stages of association between citizens and their government. We move from citizens shaping and directing the Congress to the citizen (or, more generally, the person) being subjected to a series of governmental actions.

The shaping and directing of Congress culminate in the First Amendment protection of the freedoms of speech, press, assembly, and petition required by citizens who are to inform, supply, and admonish Congress. (The Religion Clauses of the First Amendment contribute to the proper training of the citizens who control Congress.) The Second, Third, and Fourth Amendments deal with abuses apt to arise from the demands of government on citizens—for military services, for the quartering of soldiers, and for evidence. Government, particularly the Executive, can be seen as sometimes tempted to defend and otherwise serve the Country through the activities restrained in these three amendments. In Amendments V through VIII we can see a supervision of the stages of a trial, once evidence has been assembled pursuant to the restraints laid down in the Fourth Amendment.

We now consider, in turn, the three amendments by which the Executive, along with the Congress, is held in check, especially as the President tries to organize the defense of the Country. These are, again, Amendments II, III, and IV.

II

The Second Amendment provides, "A well regulated Militia, being necessary to the security of a free State, the right of the people to keep and bear Arms, shall not be infringed." The original intentions of this amendment may be, in some ways, the most difficult for us to agree upon, so divided and ingenious are advocates on both sides of the controversy about gun control in this Country today.

An early source of the Second Amendment may be found in the English Bill of Rights of 1689, where it is provided, "That the Subjects which are Protestants may have Arms for their Defense suitable to their Conditions and as allowed by Law." The vigorous case made by those who argue against extensive gun control is presented in the following account of the Second Amendment:

> However controversial the meaning of the Second Amendment is today, it was clear enough to the generation of 1789. The amendment assured to the people "their private arms," said an article which received James Madison's approval and was the only analysis available to Congress when it voted. Subsequent contemporaneous analysis is epitomized by the first American commentary on the writings of William Blackstone. Where Blackstone described arms for personal defense as among the "absolute rights of individuals" at common law, his eighteenth-century American editor commented that this right had been constitutionalized by the Second Amendment. Early constitutional commentators, including Joseph Story, William Rawle, and Thomas M. Cooley, described the amendment in terms of a republican philosophical tradition stemming from Aristotle's observation that basic to tyrants is a "mistrust of the people; hence they deprive them of arms." Political theorists from Cicero to John Locke and Jean-Jacques Rousseau also held arms possession to be symbolic of personal freedom and vital to the virtuous, self-reliant citizenry (defending itself from encroachment by outlaws, tyrants, and foreign invaders alike) that they deemed indispensable to popular government.[70]

Further on, this advocate argues:

> In contrast to the original interpretation of the amendment as a personal right to arms is the twentieth-century view that it protects

only the states' right to arm their own military forces, including their national guard units. . . .

> The states' rights interpretation simply cannot be squared with the amendment's words: "right of the people." It is impossible to believe that the First Congress used "right of the people" in the First Amendment to describe an individual right (freedom of assembly), but sixteen words later in the Second Amendment to describe a right vested exclusively in the states. Moreover, "right of the people" is used again to refer to personal rights in the Fourth Amendment and the Ninth Amendment, and the Tenth Amendment expressly distinguishes "the people" from "the states."[71]

I note, before suggesting a counterargument, that it is far from clear that "the Tenth Amendment expressly distinguishes 'the people' from 'the states.'" In fact, there have been scholars who have insisted that *people* is not distinguished from *States* in the Tenth Amendment, but rather is virtually its equivalent.[72] In any event, *people* there, and perhaps also when used with respect to the rights of assembly and petition in the First Amendment, seems to be an aggregate, not individuals, just as in the Declaration of Independence. And so also in the Second Amendment?

Some read the Second Amendment as protecting citizen-soldiers and the local militia against the depredations of the General Government, depredations that the State governments are obliged to resist. The militia is distinguished from the army, as may be seen in the Constitution of 1787.[73] Still, the militia too is subject to discipline, which is not something that most gun owners who make much of the Second Amendment today are personally eager for, especially if wartime service seems imminent.

The Second Amendment proposal, when initially brought before the First Congress in much the form we now have it, had a conscientious-objection exemption appended to it. Egbert Benson argued against this exemption in the House of Representatives:

> [He] moved to have the words "but no person religiously scrupulous shall be compelled to bear arms," struck out. He would always leave it to the benevolence of the Legislature, for, modify it as you please, it will be impossible to express it in such a manner as to clear it from ambiguity. No man can claim this indulgence of right. It may be a religious persuasion, but it is no natural right, and therefore ought to be left to the discretion of the Government. If this stands part of the

constitution, it will be a question before the Judiciary on every regulation of the militia, whether it comports with the declaration or not. It is extremely injudicious to intermix matters of doubt with fundamentals.

I have no reason to believe but the Legislature will always possess humanity enough to indulge this class of citizens in a manner they are so desirous of; but they ought to be left to their discretion.[74]

The way this issue was approached implies there was or could be a duty to bear arms, a duty that some might on occasion try to avoid by recourse, for example, to what we call a conscientious-objector status. Does not this approach tend to regard "the right of the people to keep and bear Arms" more as a prerogative of the local community (or the people) acting collectively than as a personal privilege of would-be gun owners? Did the proposal of a conscientious-objection exemption here reflect an understanding of the guarantee as recognizing a power in the States to conscript members of the militia? To emphasize a personal right in these circumstances, with little or no regard for the obligations and demands of the community in protecting itself, is something like putting the emphasis in the First Amendment upon the physical act of speaking without regard for the primary public-discourse aspect of the traditional right to freedom of speech.

It seems to have been understood from the beginning of Anglo-American constitutional history that whatever right to bear arms there was, it could properly be regulated by the community. The English Bill of Rights of 1689 referred, as we have just seen, to the possession of arms "as allowed by Law." The anti-gun-control advocate I have just quoted drew for support on William Blackstone and William Rawle. But those authors took for granted the regulation of all arms (which are not limited to firearms). Blackstone, in describing the arms one may have, speaks of "such as are allowed by law."[75] Rawle observed, in the early nineteenth century, "A disorderly militia is disgraceful to itself, and dangerous not to the enemy, but to its own country. The duty of the state government is to adopt such regulations as will tend to make good soldiers with the least interruptions of the ordinary and useful occupations of civil life."[76] Further on he added, "This right ought not, however, in any government, to be abused in the disturbance of the public peace."[77] Advocates of gun control today have considerable, and perhaps even steadily growing, "disturbance of the public peace" to point to as attributable to the remarkable proliferation of weapons among us. Even the anti-gun-control advocate from whom I have quoted at length concludes his article with major concessions to the power of government to regulate the ownership and use of weapons:

> Interpreting the Second Amendment as a guarantee of an individual right does not foreclose all gun controls. The ownership of firearms by minors, felons, and the mentally impaired—and the carrying of them outside the home by anyone—may be limited or banned. Moreover, the government may limit the types of arms that may be kept; there is no right, for example, to own artillery or automatic weapons, or the weapons of the footpad and gangster, such as sawed-off shotguns and blackjacks. Gun controls in the form of registration and licensing requirements are also permissible so long as the ordinary citizen's right to possess arms *for home protection* is respected.[78]

This advocate, who minimizes the militia orientation in the Second Amendment in his emphasis upon home protection, has enlisted Joseph Story in support of his reading of the original meaning of the Second Amendment. But the critical passage on the subject in Justice Story's *Commentary* is decidedly different in spirit from what this advocate has said:

> The importance of [the Second Amendment] will scarcely be doubted by any persons, who have duly reflected upon the subject. The militia is the natural defence of a free country against sudden foreign invasions, domestic insurrections, and domestic usurpations of power by rulers. It is against sound policy for a free people to keep up large military establishments and standing armies in time of peace, both from the enormous expenses, with which they are attended, and the facile means, which they afford to ambitious and unprincipled rulers, to subvert the government, or trample upon the rights of the people. The right of the citizens to keep and bear arms has justly been considered, as the palladium of the liberties of a republic; since it offers a strong moral check against the usurpation and arbitrary power of rulers; and will generally, even if these are successful in the first instance, enable the people to resist and triumph over them. And yet, though this truth would seem so clear, and the importance of a well regulated militia would seem so undeniable, it cannot be disguised, that among the American people there is a growing indifference to any system of militia discipline, and a strong disposition, from a sense of its burthens, to be rid of all regulations. *How it is practicable*

to keep the people armed without some organization, it is difficult to see. There is certainly no small danger, that indifference may lead to disgust, and disgust to contempt; and thus gradually undermine all the protection intended by this clause of our national bill of rights.[79]

It seems to me that the control of the private ownership of arms in this Country is a political, not a constitutional, issue. If the advocates of virtually unlimited access to firearms should be obliged to regard this as a political issue, they can be depended upon to continue to muster all their forces with the greatest possible effect without running the risk both of relying upon dubious constitutional support and of debasing constitutionalism itself.

III

The Third Amendment exhibits, as does the Second Amendment, the concern of eighteenth-century Americans about how the people are to be protected from the depredations of those whom they have to rely upon to protect them: "No Soldier shall, in time of peace be quartered in any house, without the consent of the Owner, nor in time of war, but in a manner to be prescribed by law."

This guarantee had found expression in the Petition of Right of 1628 (found in Appendix C of this Commentary):

> And whereas of late great Companies of Souldiers and Marriners have been dispersed into divers Counties of the Realme, and the inhabitants against their wills have been compelled to receive them into their houses, and there to suffer them to sojourne against the Lawes and Customes of this Realme and to the great grievance and vexacion of the people.

A century and a half later Americans expressed similar sentiments in the Declaration of Independence, with one of the grievances there turning around "quartering large bodies of armed troops among us." A decade earlier, Benjamin Franklin, while serving as one of the North American agents in London, had argued:

> All that the [American] agents contend for is, that *the same protection of property and domestic security which prevails in England, should be preserved in America.* Let [the British government] first try the effects of quartering soldiers on butchers, bakers, or other private houses here [in England], and then transport the measure to America.[80]

65

An attempt was made in the First Congress, when the Bill of Rights proposals were debated, to eliminate the "time of war" exception to the prohibition upon the quartering of soldiers in what is now the Third Amendment. The following proceedings in the House of Representatives on August 17, 1789, are illuminating:

> The fourth clause of the fourth proposition was taken up as follows: "No soldier shall, in time of peace, be quartered in any house, without the consent of the owner, nor in time of war, but in a manner to be prescribed by law."
>
> Mr. Sumter hoped soldiers would never be quartered on the inhabitants, either in time of peace or war, without the consent of the owner. It was a burthen, and very oppressive, even in cases where the owner gave his consent; but where this was wanting, it would be a hardship indeed! Their property would lie at the mercy of men irritated by a refusal, and well disposed to destroy the peace of the family.
>
> He moved to strike out all the words from the clause but "no soldier shall be quartered in any house without the consent of the owner."
>
> Mr. Sherman observed that it was absolutely necessary that marching troops should have quarters, whether in time of peace or war, and that it ought not to be put in the power of an individual to obstruct the public service; if quarters were not to be obtained in public barracks, they must be procured elsewhere. In England, where they paid considerable attention to private rights, they billeted the troops upon the keepers of public houses, and upon private houses also, with the consent of the magistracy.
>
> Mr. Sumter's motion being put, was lost by a majority of sixteen.[81]

It is salutary to be reminded, upon noticing Congress's refusal to remove the wartime exception in the Third Amendment, that there are community needs to be served in these matters. This protection of the public service against those individuals who would obstruct it is to be compared with the tendency of some today to deny the legitimate concerns of government with respect to the common defence, as may be seen in how the conscientious-objection cases have developed in this Country in recent decades.

I return to Justice Story for his discussion of the Third Amendment:

This provision speaks for itself. Its plain object is to secure the perfect enjoyment of that great right of the common law, that a man's house shall be his own castle, privileged against all civil and military intrusion. The billeting of soldiers in time of peace upon the people has been a common resort of arbitrary princes, and is full of inconvenience and peril. In the petition of right (3 Charles I.), it was declared by parliament to be a great grievance.[82]

The reference here to a man's home as his castle leads us naturally into the Search and Seizure provisions of the Fourth Amendment.

IV

Before we consider the Fourth Amendment, however, we should again notice the implications of the use of qualifications in some of the Amendments. For one thing, the presence of these qualifications points up their absence in other places, such as in the First Amendment, where Congress is forbidden to make any law respecting the establishment of religion, prohibiting the free exercise of religion, or abridging the freedom of speech, press, assembly, or petition. Thus, the First Amendment rights are unqualified, however much they depend on what such terms as *establishment of religion, free exercise [of religion],* and *freedom of speech, or of the press* mean.

In the Second, Third, and Fourth Amendments, unlike in the First Amendment, there are qualifications. In the Second Amendment, the right to bear arms is keyed to "the security of a free State" and is evidently related to the existence of a "well regulated Militia." According to the Third Amendment, the quartering of soldiers in houses without the consent of owners may be resorted to by the government only in wartime. And, as we shall see, not all searches and seizures are forbidden by the Fourth Amendment.

These qualifications, as is true with various qualifications in the Constitution of 1787, are with a view to the common good. The character and requirements of the community, especially a republican community, affect the purpose as well as the extent of various rights. These amendments assume not only personal interests and desires but also civic interests, keeping in view the contributions that only governments can make, as well as the threats that governments can pose, to the happiness of citizens.

The modern approach to these matters, we have seen, makes much more of "doing one's own thing." (We noticed in Lecture No. 5 how the absolute "freedom of speech [and] of the press" properly protected by the First Amendment is being improperly expanded to immunize practically all "freedom of expression" from regulation.) The muting of the original public-discourse aspect of the First Amendment is encouraged by the current eclipse of the assembly and petition elements in the First Amendment. This eclipse is in large part due to the scope and effectiveness of freedom of speech and of the press among us. An eloquent exercise of the right to petition may be seen, however, in the Declaration of Independence where a long list of grievances is recited, grievances that the Colonists had again and again called to the attention of their "British Brethren." Even as the development of a free press has made the right of petition (whether for public or private grievances) less significant, the primary purpose of a free press has sometimes been lost sight of.

The emphasis upon freedom of expression is not limited to readings of the First Amendment, with the consequent relaxation of restraints on pornography, libel, and advertising. This approach is seen in still another dramatic form today in the way that virtually unlimited access to handguns is insisted upon in some quarters, even though we now have every year firearm deaths that mount up to at least two-thirds of the total American battle-deaths of a decade of involvement in the Vietnam War.[83]

Related to, and perhaps reinforcing the insistence upon, a general freedom of expression is the appetite we are developing for more and more privacy, which is intended to be served to a limited extent by the "no religious Test" provision in Article VI of the Constitution, by such amendments as the Third, Fourth, Fifth and Eighth, and by the religion and the right-of-petition provisions in the First Amendment. The right to privacy about which we now hear so much seems to be the distinctively modern way of making a great deal of the ancient right of property. But property rights have always had built into them an awareness of the community that makes property possible. Privacy rights, on the other hand, tend to legitimize (and perhaps encourage) a radical separation from, if not even a repudiation of, the community, a repudiation in the name of what can be regarded as natural yearnings. All this leads to an intensification of individuality and hence a preoccupation with self-centeredness and of a corresponding depreciation, or at least a neglect, of citizenship and a commonly shared public sense of duty.

The movement toward more and more unfettered individuality and hence freedom of expression may be an inherent tendency of republics. There is something infectious about liberty, not least because of the considerable pleasure we usually get from saying and doing whatever we please. But an enduring liberty depends upon a stable community, which depends in turn upon a disciplined and enlightened people, a people equipped to remain truly self-governing. An appreciation of the care with which the Constitution of 1787 and its 1791 amendments were crafted should help us respect the requirements and blessings of public order.

V

The tension between a proper privacy and the needs of effective governance may be seen in the Fourth Amendment, which provides:

> The right of the people to be secure in their persons, houses, papers, and effects, against unreasonable searches and seizures, shall not be violated, and no Warrants shall issue, but upon probable cause, supported by Oath or affirmation, and particularly describing the place to be searched, and the persons or things to be seized.

Here, as elsewhere in the Bill of Rights, we see the affirmation of an old right that had been developed in England in response to even older abuses. One form these abuses took there, as well as in North America where they helped provoke the Revolution, was the use by the British government of general warrants (or writs of assistance), especially in tax matters. The right set forth in the Fourth Amendment is a right refined in the United States, going beyond what the English (whose government evidently still has access to general warrants) had insisted upon.

The development of the right not to be subjected to unreasonable searches and seizures was dramatized in England by the controversy about the publication there of an issue of the *North Briton* journal in 1763. Here is one scholar's account of the use of general warrants in that case and theretofore:

> The general warrant did not confine its reach to a particular person, place, or object but allowed its bearer to arrest, search, and seize as

his suspicions directed. In 1763, a typical warrant by the British secretaries of state commanded "diligent search" for the unidentified author, printer, and publisher of a satirical journal, *The North Briton, No. 45,* and the seizure of their papers. At least five houses were consequently searched, forty-nine (mostly innocent) persons arrested, and thousands of books and papers confiscated. Resentment against such invasions ultimately generated an antidote in the Fourth Amendment and is crucial to its understanding.

General warrants and general searches without warrant had a lengthy pedigree. In 1662, a statute codified writs of assistance that allowed searching all suspected places for goods concealed in violation of the customs laws. Such writs had been used since at least 1621 and themselves absorbed the language of royal commissions that had for centuries authorized general searches without warrant. Similarly promiscuous searches had existed for numerous applications: the pursuit of felons, suppression of political and religious deviance, regulation of printing, medieval craft guilds, naval and military impressment, counterfeiting, bankruptcy, excise and land taxes, vagrancy, game poaching, sumptuary behavior, and even the recovery of stolen personal items.[84]

In 1763 an English judge recorded his outrage upon reviewing the evidence in one such case:

> To enter a man's house by virtue of a nameless warrant, in order to procure evidence, is worse than the Spanish Inquisition; a law under which no Englishman would wish to live an hour; it was a most daring public attack made upon the liberty of the subject. I thought that the 29th chapter of Magna Charta, *Nullus liber homo capiatur vel imprisonetur, &c. nec super eum ibimus, &c. nisi per legale judicium parium suorum vel per legem terrae, &c.* which is pointed against arbitrary power, was violated.[85]

I return to the scholar I had quoted in order to notice the American responses to these issues:

> Although the right against unreasonable search and seizure has lengthy British roots, its cornerstone, the confinement of all searches, seizures, and arrests by warrant to the particular place, persons, and objects enumerated, derives from Massachusetts. A cluster of Massachusetts statutes and court decisions from 1756 to 1766, the third stage in a century-long process, uniformly restrained searches and arrests to the person or location designated in the warrant. Leg-

islation in the 1780s extended this specificity to the objects of seizure. The Fourth Amendment is thus the marriage of an ancient British right and a new, colonial interpretation that vastly extended its meaning.[86]

We are also told that eight States inserted guarantees against general warrants in their pre-1787 constitutions and that four State Ratification Conventions urged an amendment to the Constitution that would provide a corresponding restraint on searches by the new national government.

An elaborate predecessor to the Fourth Amendment may be found in the Massachusetts Constitution of 1780:

> Every subject has a right to be secure from all unreasonable searches, and seizures of his person, his house, his papers, and all his possessions. All warrants, therefore, are contrary to this right, if the cause or foundation of them be not previously supported by oath or affirmation, and if the order in the warrant to a civil officer, to make search in suspected places, or to arrest one or more suspected persons, or to seize their property, be not accompanied with a special designation of the persons or objects of search, arrest, or seizure: and no warrant ought to be issued but in cases, and with the formalities, prescribed by the laws.[87]

It is instructive to reflect upon the repeated use of the term *unreasonable* in a series of Search and Seizure declarations. Courts are told that they must use their judgment in issuing warrants. This reflects the power and duty of the Courts to assess these and like matters. The power left here with judges is evident in an account of pre-Revolutionary proceedings in Massachusetts:

> Writs of assistance came under attack in the American colonial courts. James Otis, a fiery young Massachusetts attorney, made a brilliant "higher law" assault on the writs in Paxton's Case (1761). Although Otis lost, most colonial courts refused to issue such writs when required to do so by the Townshend Act of 1767, and a series of pamphlets beginning with John Dickinson's *Farmer's Letters* joined in the assault.[88]

What are trial judges to do when prosecutors submit evidence that has been improperly seized by officers of government?[89] One way of dealing with this problem is what we now know as the Exclusionary Rule, which forbids governmental use in court of any such evidence. This rule is a possible but not a necessary implication of a guarantee that is designed, in large part, to keep the Executive in check. This Exclusionary Rule implication of the Fourth Amendment, developed by American judges, is rarely resorted to elsewhere. It is not, for example, the rule in other common-law jurisdictions such as Great Britain and Canada, where official disciplinary proceedings and (it is said) damage suits by aggrieved persons are relied upon to keep the police in line, with discretion left in the trial judge to exclude improperly seized evidence that seems unreliable.

What is the genesis of the American rule? It is considered unbecoming for governments to depend upon evidence that is tainted, even when the reliability of the evidence (say, a coerced confession) is not in question. Judges sometimes say that the honor of the community requires that only lawful means be used to secure convictions. Even more is made of the need to discipline not only the police but also the community at large. Various rules are defended as serving the development and maintenance of a moral sense in the community. This is a way of teaching that human relations are not to be merely the result of the random play of forces.

Many older lawyers and judges believe that the Exclusionary Rule and other such rules have had, despite occasional obvious injustices in their application, a generally salutary effect upon the police. The police, they remember, were all too often a law unto themselves before these judicial curbs were imposed upon them.

Even today some police are notorious for using supposed or minor traffic violations to stop, search, interrogate, and otherwise harass many drivers, especially members of minority groups, who are innocent of other offenses. Our automobiles have become so important to us that they are somewhat like the houses we have traditionally considered privileged places.

Law-enforcement authorities frequently testify that a well-disciplined police force is not likely to be adversely affected by the Exclusionary Rule, once the rule is properly publicized. Surprisingly few indictments, except perhaps in "the war against drugs" where the volume of offenses encourages even more official shortcuts than hard-pressed police routinely resort to, are dismissed because of the Exclusionary Rule. It is hard to determine, however, how many prosecutions are not initiated because of the Exclusionary Rule. Still, it should be noticed that criminal-law specialists generally believe that, contrary to a widespread public perception, the Exclusionary Rule has had relatively little adverse effect on the criminal-justice system and no discernible effect on the crime rate or on the ability of law-enforcement officers to control crime in this Country.

The Exclusionary Rule is a relatively minor offender among the various legal provisions that routinely deny prosecutors and judges access to the truth and otherwise protect guilty (as well as innocent) people. Far more important are such traditional immunities as the right against self-incrimination, the right of a defendant to remain silent when put on trial, the right one has not to testify against one's spouse in most situations, and the right of clients to speak in total confidence to their attorneys, all of which immunities are reinforced by the presumption of innocence. Even more pervasive in liberating our everyday life is the law of private property, which leaves a wide scope for unsupervised activity.

Do we want our lives organized in any other way with respect to such matters? After all, the police are sometimes rather confident about who the criminals are that are at large in the community. What do we want done to the people thus suspected, when there is no solid evidence available with which to prosecute them for any particular offense? Should torture (if not even summary executions) be routinely permitted when dealing with the more notorious suspects? Should there be more lie detector use with the typical suspect? And if we do not limit our efforts to suspects: Universal surveillance, including systematic eavesdropping on everyone's telephone conversations? Official monitoring of all financial transactions, of travel records, and even of social relations? Electronic implants that permit making an official record of everyone's whereabouts at all times?

Although we are reluctant to go this far, we still wonder what we can do to take proper care of ourselves.

VI

The education of our people, which includes a sound grounding in morality, is vital here. The provision of such grounding is one of the principal duties and opportunities of State Governments in our Constitutional system. How the States are to be guided and restrained by the Constitution in these and other matters may be even more controversial today than it has been from the beginning of the Republic.

We have noticed that the history of the drafting of the Bill of Rights, however comprehensive the language of most of these amendments may be, displays an intention to address only the General Government. The case of *Barron* v. *Baltimore*,[90] which elicited in 1833 a firm Opinion of the Court by Chief Justice John Marshall, is generally taken to dispose of attempts to make the Bill of Rights directly applicable to the States without benefit of any subsequent amendments.

There remains, however, the question of what Barron believed was available to him, because of the Bill of Rights, in his suit challenging State action. Perhaps he was trying (in a State with no Taking Clause in its constitution) to draw upon the implications of the fact that the Bill of Rights should be seen primarily as confirming rights that had always belonged to the American people, rights that had been developed in large part by common-law judges. We have noticed, for example, the repeated refusals of pre-Revolution Colonial judges in North America to issue the search warrants that British officers asked for.

That various critical rights of the American people did not depend upon the Constitution of the United States is evident in a State court case of 1814. Consider how a Connecticut appellate-court judge spoke on that occasion of a Search and Seizure issue on review before him:

> That this warrant was such as *no justice ought to have issued* will be admitted; for it is not only a warrant to search for stolen goods supposed to be concealed in a particular place, but it is a warrant to search all suspected places, stores, shops and barns in Wilton. Where those suspected places were in Wilton is not pointed out, or by whom suspected: so that all the dwelling-houses and out-houses within the town of Wilton were by this warrant made liable to search. The officer also was directed to search suspected persons, and arrest them. By whom they were suspected, whether by the justice, the officer, or complainant, is not mentioned; so that every citizen of the United States within the jurisdiction of the justice to try for theft, was liable to be arrested and carried before the justice for trial. The war-

74

rant was this: Search every house, store or barn within the town of Wilton, that is suspected of having certain bags concealed in it, said to be stolen, and all persons who are suspected of having stolen them. *This is a general search-warrant, which has always been determined to be illegal,* not only in cases of searching for stolen goods, but in all other cases.[91]

It is suggested by the materials I have been drawing upon that the laws and rights that guided all American governments before the Constitution was ratified should have continued to guide those governments after the Bill of Rights was ratified, except in those instances where the first eight amendments modified the previous arrangements. This means that the general legal system, with its Constitutional presuppositions about the privileges and immunities of Americans, should have continued to shape not only the Government of the United States but the State Governments as well. That general legal system has had a pervasive influence upon this Country, as have both the English heritage evident in our language and a market economy geared to vast territories available to be exploited by everyone.

VII

We have observed that most of the great rights recognized in the Bill of Rights of 1791 had been settled long before in the common law. The common law is taken for granted throughout our Constitutional system, particularly in the recognized capacity of judges to distinguish (with due regard for plausible expectations) between the reasonable and the unreasonable, between the just and the unjust, and hence between the acceptable and the unacceptable. To respect the common law is to take seriously both the constitutional heritage of a particular community and the enduring standards by which all communities should be guided.

Was not the United States Supreme Court, as the preeminent judicial body in this Country, assumed from the beginning to be at the apex of the common-law pyramid? Some such assumption may have been at the root of the decision by the plaintiff in *Barron* v. *Baltimore* to take his case to the United States Supreme Court.[92] May not the reliance by that plaintiff upon the Bill of Rights, which the Court ruled was obviously not applicable to the States, have

75

been little more than a convenient way of invoking traditional common-law guarantees that every government in the United States should respect?

The Courts of the United States are required to conduct their own proceedings in accordance with directives laid down in the Constitution and its amendments and in acts of Congress. These directives include provisions respecting jurisdiction and processes. How far may these National Courts go, in turn, in regulating the activities of other branches of the General Government?

Take, again, the directive to the National Courts by the Fourth Amendment that they not permit unreasonable searches and seizures. Perhaps they are entitled if not even obliged, in the spirit of this directive, not to admit any evidence that has been improperly gathered. Should grand juries also be kept from considering such evidence for any purpose? May the Courts go even further by expecting nonjudicial officers of the General Government not to make any use of material that is considered so tainted by the mode of its gathering that it should never be used in court? Is not this a variation upon the issue of judicial review that I discuss both in these lectures and in my Commentary on the Constitution of 1787? This issue, as well as the issue about the extent and effect of the Bill of Rights, should be further clarified by the investigation in my next lecture of those amendments (V–VIII) that are very much concerned with how judicial proceedings should be conducted, if not by all judges in this Country, at least by those who are both privileged and obliged in their routine judicial capacity to take their bearings primarily by the Constitution of 1787 and its amendments, as well as by whatever authoritative Constitutional interpretations that Congress may provide (something which was seen from the First Congress on).

7. Amendments V, VI, VII, and VIII

I

Of the three branches of the governments in the United States, the judiciary is the least affected by the Constitution of 1787, even though the General Government under the Articles of Confederation had no permanent judiciary of its own. The legislatures and executives of both the General and the State governments were much more affected by the new constitutional order after 1789 than were the judges in this Country. Once constituted, courts continued doing what they had been doing for centuries in English-speaking communities: interpreting statutes and constitutional provisions and developing and applying the common law.

Article III, the Judicial Article of the Constitution, permits Congress both to provide for the Supreme Court that is required by the Constitution and to establish a system of inferior courts. But the Constitution, unlike what it does in the Legislative and Executive Articles, assumes in the Judicial Article that the courts will continue operating much as they had long been operating in judicial proceedings, with the common law vital to the entire system of jurisprudence. It also assumes that legislatures will continue to provide guidance for the courts both with respect to the processes they employ and with respect to the substantive law they apply, supplementing what the Constitution itself supplies. It is important to notice here that courts cannot establish on their own the extent of their jurisdiction and powers. That must be left to the Constitution and to statutes made pursuant to the Constitution. In short, courts should not be expected to legislate.[93]

To say that the American judiciary was least affected by the Constitution of 1787 is to recognize that the principal activities of

English-speaking judges should not be much affected by political or perhaps even constitutional realignments. Where the judicial head of the community is to be found and what its jurisdiction includes may be political decisions, but how that court functions should not be. Similarly, the number of inferior courts and their scope may be political decisions, but how they operate should not be.

The system of government provided by the Constitution of 1787 could have operated indefinitely with no United States (Federal) courts inferior to the Supreme Court. State judges can be, and occasionally are, used to do what Federal judges do in recognizing and, if only rarely now, administering the laws of the United States. It is left to Congress to decide what inferior Federal courts the Country needs. The Constitutional system would not work properly, however, if State executives and State legislatures were depended upon to do much of what the President and the Congress do. That was attempted, with unsatisfactory consequences, under the Articles of Confederation.

All judges in this Country were expected, even before the Constitution, to apply the relevant National and State laws, including the common law, appropriate to the cases before them. There was no reason to believe that the common law would be different from what it had been before the Constitution was ratified. One reservation heard in the Federal Convention about reliance upon State judges was that many of them did not have life tenure, which kept them from being as independent of public opinion and of political considerations as the Framers believed that judges should be. The judges relied upon by the Constitution are expected to be fully, or truly, judges. They should therefore not be subject to routine correction by the people when they are believed to have gone astray. The cumbersome and rarely used impeachment remedy is the only means of holding judges personally responsible for what they do. This helps explain why the bulk of the provisions in the Bill of Rights (beginning with the Fifth, if not with the Fourth, Amendment and running through the Eighth Amendment) have as their principal concern the restraining of judges.

Congress, it seems, was considered to pose far less of a threat to the rights of the people. Not only was Congress subject to elections every two years, but it was also continuously exposed to the exercise by the people of their potent freedom of speech. The President, although subject to similar restraints, was considered a greater threat, especially because of his powers as Commander in Chief of the armed forces, military powers that are therefore placed under tight control by the Constitution. Congressional control of the purse is critical here, a restraint that was circumvented by the Iran arms–Contra aid shenanigans in the 1980s. Judicial tyranny, on the other hand, is harder to ward off in any particular case, especially if judges enjoy the considerable independence they require in order to be effective. The dangers posed by judges are evident in the elaborate precautions provided in the Judiciary Article with respect to the crime of treason, a crime that had been harshly dealt with and even extended by the English judges over the centuries.[94]

Reinforcing the perennial popular concern about how judges might conduct themselves is the mystery in which judges tend to be clothed. Because technicalities have to be important in the law, citizens are easily intimidated when they try to figure out what the law provides. This may be seen in difficulties one may have trying to explain to laymen today the nature of the common law or the intricacies of Article III of the Constitution.[95] Similar difficulties are encountered when one examines the provisions in the Bill of Rights that deal with the conduct of judicial proceedings, especially because those provisions obviously presuppose a well-developed (and once more familiar) system of law.[96]

A well-developed and indeed long-established system of law should again become apparent to us as we consider in turn the amendments (the Fifth through the Eighth) that are primarily concerned with potential abuses in the course of judicial proceedings. All officers of government are reminded here, as in the Second, Third, and Fourth Amendments, of privileges and immunities that had long been claimed as part of the heritage of the English-speaking peoples.

II

The Fourth Amendment, we have seen, was directed to both the Executive and the Judiciary. All of the first eight amendments, we have noticed, also have Legislative conduct in view. But the Fifth, Sixth, Seventh, and Eighth Amendments seem particularly concerned with the Courts, taking us as they do through the judicial process.

The Fifth and Sixth Amendments deal extensively with criminal proceedings, following upon the proper mode of securing evidence that is provided for in the Fourth Amendment. The text of the Fifth Amendment reads:

> No person shall be held to answer for a capital, or otherwise infamous crime, unless on a presentment or indictment of a Grand Jury, except in cases arising in the land or naval forces, or in the Militia, when in actual service in time of War or public danger; nor shall any person be subject for the same offence to be twice put in jeopardy of life or limb; nor shall be compelled in any criminal case to be a witness against himself, nor be deprived of life, liberty, or property, without due process of law; nor shall private property be taken for public use, without just compensation.

There are five elements set forth here. The first two specify who can be tried in a criminal proceeding. Action by a grand jury is a prerequisite (except for the trials of those in military service), but one can be tried only once for the same offence (that is, a second indictment will not be permitted or a retrial on the first indictment, once one is acquitted). Many technical questions have to be addressed, however, in any application of these two provisions.

For example, what is a grand jury, how does it work, and what form does its action have to take in order to provide the proper basis for a criminal trial? Both statutes and judicial determinations, stretching back to the days of Magna Carta and even before, have helped make the grand jury what it is. It is obvious that judges must be relied upon if we are to know what is called for on any particular occasion. The two dozen citizens assembled to determine whether any person should be subjected to a criminal trial can stand in the way of prosecutors and judges who might be inclined to oppress their fellow citizens. The grand jury can also serve to make officials of government more vigilant and vigorous in prosecuting and punishing criminals (including those who betray the public trust) than they might otherwise be.

Even more difficult technical questions are raised in the application of the double-jeopardy language of the Fifth Amendment. Double jeopardy, we have been told, "is the most ancient procedural guarantee provided by the American Bill of Rights."[97] Even so, many difficult questions remain to be resolved, usually by Courts, such as when precisely "jeopardy attaches." Thus, we are told, although the common law recognized the pleas of "former acquittal" and "former conviction," which would stand as bars to another trial on the same charge, the American law has taken a more expansive view of the right here: even a prior accusation without a verdict can sometimes result in a successful double-jeopardy plea. Complications extend to questions about whether the crime being charged is indeed the same as an earlier one that had been charged, especially when the same critical facts are the basis of the two charges, and about what the effects are of separate prosecutions for the same crime in State and Federal Courts.

Conscientious judges have to resolve these matters, and they must do so primarily on a case-by-case basis. Legislatures cannot do much more than provide general rules, especially if the spirit of the constitutional prohibitions of bills of attainder is to be respected. An independent judiciary is required if popular passions and zealous prosecutors are to be held in check. Moreover, judges need considerable instruction in how such matters have been dealt with by their predecessors. This instruction must promote an awareness of the considerations of fair play and social policy that generally guide judicial determinations.

Both the indictment and the double-jeopardy provisions presuppose the rule of law, including respect for the laws that govern how prosecutors and judges conduct themselves. However important technical requirements and learning may have to be, the Constitutionalist's understanding can help make it less likely that these privileges and immunities will be converted into delusions and snares.

III

The remaining three elements in the Fifth Amendment describe the limitations placed upon governmental efforts to take various things from a person: information he can provide about his activities; his life, liberty, or property; and private property desired for public use.

The first of these limitations is that no person "shall be compelled in any criminal case to be a witness against himself." No doubt, the defendant may often be the one person who knows most about what really happened on a particular occasion, but the government may still have to make its case against him without his cooperation. Here, by the way, is another of the places in our constitutional system where absolutes are relied upon.

There remain complicated questions to be resolved here also. What constitutes being "a witness against [oneself]"? Does it include having to provide blood and other bodily specimens? May incriminating testimony be compelled if comprehensive immunity from prosecution is provided? May one be compelled to testify against oneself in proceedings other than the criminal case in which one is a defendant? In addressing these and like questions, the traditional purposes of any privilege against self-incrimination have to be taken into account.

A considerable body of analysis takes account of the abuses that this and other privileges are intended to guard against and the respect for human dignity that they embody. We can be reminded here of something said about the Search and Seizure directives in the Fourth Amendment: "The law will not tempt a man to make a shipwreck of his conscience in order to disculpate himself."[98]

The second of the Fifth Amendment limitations upon deprivations is conditional: a person may be deprived of life, liberty or property with due process of law. This Due Process Clause is generally said to hearken back to the famous thirty-ninth chapter of Magna Carta, where the King's adherence to the law of the land was insisted upon. It has been reaffirmed many times since 1215, as in the third article of the Petition of Right of 1628 (found in Appendix C of of this Commentary):

> [B]y the Statute called The great Charter of the Liberties of England, It is declared and enacted, That no Freeman may be taken or imprisoned or be disseised of his Freehold or Liberties or his free Customes or be outlawed or exiled or in any manner destroyed, but by the lawfull Judgment of his Peeres or by the Law of the Land.

Three centuries earlier, in 1354, an act of Parliament, in reaffirming Magna Carta, had identified *law of the land* with *due process of law.*[99]

Due process became the preferred term in the United States once it was emphasized in the Fifth and Fourteenth Amendments. "Due process of law," it has been said, became "the most important and influential term in American constitutional law."[100] Part of that

82

influence has been dubious, taking the form as it did of a reading of the Due Process Clause that permitted courts to invalidate legislation even though that legislation did not disregard or violate the judicial processes that the clause was originally intended to require. The most notorious use of the Due Process Clause thus far has been in the *Dred Scott Case* of 1857, where it was held (in effect) that the Fifth Amendment kept Congress from trying to keep slavery out of the Territories of the United States, and this despite the significance of what had been done about slavery in the Northwest Ordinance both by the Confederation Congress and by the First Congress under the Constitution of 1787.

Although *Dred Scott* depended upon a misreading of the Fifth Amendment's Due Process Clause (which we shall consider at greater length when we discuss the Fourteenth Amendment and its Due Process Clause in Lecture No. 12), it should be conceded that some respect for due process may be seen even in a system that permits slavery. Slavery probably tends to be ameliorated when there is a general respect for the law of the land, which means that even the institutions of slavery have to be provided for by law. This is not to deny, however, that the underlying assumptions about the inestimable importance of a person's right to "life, liberty, [and] property" implicit in the Due Process Clause tend to call into question any system of slavery that is (in its fundamental lawlessness) based merely upon arbitrary racial differences.

Due process, or a respect for the law of the land in the ordering of judicial proceedings, is taken for granted throughout the Constitution of 1787, perhaps most dramatically in its recognition (in Section 9 of Article I) of the venerable privilege of the writ of habeas corpus. We are again reminded that what we see in our constitutional documents testifies to a much more extensive system of legal and political institutions than is made explicit on the surface of these documents. Even so, the Due Process Clause leaves open for determination what processes may be due on various occasions, something that the legislature may have to help to determine from time to time.

The third of the Fifth Amendment limitations on deprivations is also conditional: a person may have his "private property taken for public use" if "just compensation" is paid him. Here, too, it is evident upon examination of the controversies that courts routinely deal with that intricate questions have to be confronted. What is a taking? What is "public use"? How is "just compensation" to be determined? For example, if legislation or other governmental activity effectively prohibits the use by an owner of his property, is that to be considered a taking? A variety of circumstances have elicited a variety of responses by the courts. It is still generally believed in this Country that the property in question has to be physically taken over or deliberately destroyed by the community for it to be regarded as a taking requiring compensation. In nontaking instances, however, the community may sometimes want to pay something to owners whose continued use of property is made virtually impossible by something the community has done (perhaps unexpectedly) in its own interest—but that need not be a Taking Clause problem. There is a tendency in some quarters today to read the Taking Clause so broadly as to curtail sharply the activities of government, a reading for which there is little if any warrant in our Constitutional tradition.

By and large, the simpler, less sophisticated readings of the Bill of Rights provisions are better. We have noticed that these provisions were evidently so straightforward for the Congress which drafted the Bill of Rights that few of them required extended explanations. It is obvious from the available debates in Congress and in the Country at large that the drafters of the Bill of Rights in the First Congress knew that they were dealing with matters that had long been familiar to practitioners in common-law courts. Both the rights of the people and the powers of government could be expected to be developed, consistent with the spirit of the constitutional system, as circumstances changed.

IV

The Sixth Amendment was the only one of the first ten amendments that was intended, when first proposed, to replace a provision in the Constitution of 1787. One of the proposed amendments that was not ratified in 1791 by the States (changing the ratio of representation in the House of Representatives) was also intended to replace a provision in the Constitution. But that replacement represented a change in a constitutional provision, whereas the Sixth Amendment was advanced as an amplification of what was already there. Trial by jury in criminal cases is assured in the Constitution of 1787. The provision in Section 2 of Article III of the Constitution is primarily concerned, however, with the effect of division of the Country into States. Otherwise, the Article III Jury Trial Clause is a reminder of what was generally recognized as the right to trial by jury in criminal cases.

The original jury trial provision in Article III of the Constitution of 1787 reads:

> The Trial of all Crimes, except in Cases of Impeachment, shall be by Jury; and such Trial shall be held in the State where the said Crimes shall have been committed; but when not committed within any State, the Trial shall be at such Place or Places as the Congress may by Law have directed.

It is taken for granted that it is generally known what trial by jury is. The elements of a proper criminal trial are also considered to be known, but some of them were nevertheless spelled out in the Sixth Amendment where it is provided:

> In all criminal prosecutions, the accused shall enjoy the right to a speedy and public trial, by an impartial jury of the State and district wherein the crime shall have been committed, which district shall have been previously ascertained by law, and to be informed of the nature and cause of the accusation; to be confronted with the witnesses against him; to have compulsory process for obtaining witnesses in his favor, and to have the Assistance of Counsel for his defence.

The various elements of a trial were not only generally known, but long known. The elements collected here in the Sixth Amendment are still familiar today. What is now the status of the equally long-established elements not mentioned in the Sixth Amendment? Are some of them "saved" by the Due Process Clause of the Fifth Amendment? It is hardly likely that the drafters of the Bill of Rights intended to repudiate all elements of a proper trial other than those explicitly mentioned, especially since there is nothing to indicate that the elements collected there are of a different calibre from the ones not mentioned. All of these trial elements result from a long historical development, however much a few of them may be justified or cherished as somehow natural in their appeal. Certainly, it is natural that long-established rights, even if partly accidental in their origins or development, should be respected in a community.

It is almost certain, we have seen, that the elements of the criminal process set forth in the Fifth and Sixth Amendments would have been taken for granted by judges and lawyers in all American courts, even without the enactment of the Bill of Rights. Many of these elements, and others as well, have repeatedly been taken for granted, for two centuries now, in legislation pertaining to the courts of the United States. Even though the enumeration of some of the traditional elements may not have implicitly denied a constitutional status for other equally traditional elements that were not mentioned, that enumeration did tend to lead to the neglect of those not referred to explicitly. They have not always been regarded as worthy of the highest constitutional respect. What, for example, is the constitutional status of such traditional elements of trial by jury as the size of a jury, the right of challenge to prospective members of a jury, and the requirement of unanimity for a jury verdict?

The Sixth Amendment, amplifying as it does a provision in Article III, shows us what could have been done as well for many other provisions in the Constitution of 1787. What is the significance, if any, of amplification here but not elsewhere? Is the choice of what rights were to be thus spelled out in large part due to chance? We shall return to these questions in my next lecture when we consider the Ninth Amendment.

V

· We see in the Seventh Amendment, dealing with the right to trial by jury in civil cases, provision for a right that had been considered for inclusion in the Constitution by the Federal Convention and then rejected. As noted in Lecture No. 2 of this Commentary, the 1787 Convention found itself stymied in its efforts to settle upon what the traditional right to a civil-trial jury consisted of. A guarantee of this right was asked for on the last day of systematic review of the provisions of the constitution that was being prepared. But, it was argued in response, there was simply too much variation in practice from State to State to permit a statement of the right that would satisfy the Country at large. We have seen that one delegate put it thus, "The constitution of Juries is different in different States and the trial itself is *usual* in different cases in different States."[101]

Even so, the demand for a Constitutional guarantee was heard again in the First Congress—and so we have the Seventh Amendment, which reads:

In Suits at common law, where the value in controversy shall exceed twenty dollars, the right of trial by jury shall be preserved, and no fact tried by a jury, shall be otherwise re-examined in any Court of the United States, than according to the rules of the common law.

We can see here how the drafters of the Bill of Rights finessed the problem that had troubled the Federal Convention. It is simply said that "the right of trial by jury [in Suits at common law] shall be preserved," with nothing said about what that right consists of. The less said about that, it seems to have been thought, the better. This is in marked contrast to what is said in the Fifth and Sixth Amendments about the criminal process. Perhaps the judges were depended upon to help work out over the years a nationwide understanding about the proper conduct of civil cases. We must wonder whether this was also expected with respect to other rights that had begun to take somewhat different forms across the Country. The superintending role here of the United States Supreme Court, as well as of Congress, may have been depended upon as well.

The second half of the Seventh Amendment does spell out a feature of the right being preserved. The limitation there upon how a "fact tried by a jury" shall be dealt with on appeal was provided because of concerns that had been expressed about the implications of a provision in Section 2 of Article III of the Constitution of 1787:

In all Cases affecting Ambassadors, other public Ministers and Consuls, and those in which a State shall be a Party, the supreme Court shall have original Jurisdiction. In all the other Cases before mentioned, the supreme Court shall have appellate Jurisdiction, both as to Law and Fact, with such Exceptions, and under such Regulations as the Congress shall make.

Thus, the Seventh Amendment affirms the decisive role of the jury in American jurisprudence.

We should notice as well that the Seventh Amendment explicitly refers, for the first time either in the Constitution or in the Bill of Rights, to the common law (and this it does twice). The way it is referred to here again reminds us that the common law, which regulates many commercial and other relations between persons in this Country, was taken for granted throughout the Constitution without having had to be mentioned explicitly.

Whatever diversities had begun to develop in the procedural aspects of the common law from State to State, it is evident in the Constitution of 1787 and its Bill of Rights that the substantive aspects of the common law could be considered uniform or at least were considered capable of being made uniform under the guidance of Congress and the Supreme Court. Again and again, the Framers, whether of the Constitution or of the Bill of Rights, proceeded as if a general understanding of constitutional matters and legal practices could be developed and relied upon.

VI

Amendment VIII provides: "Excessive bail shall not be required, nor excessive fines imposed, nor cruel and unusual punishments inflicted." This guarantee goes back, in virtually the same language, to the English Bill of Rights of 1689. It was repeated many times, as in the Virginia Declaration of Rights in 1776, before the draft of the Eight Amendment was prepared by the First Congress in 1789. (The Virginia Declaration of Rights is found in Appendix F-1 of this Commentary.)

Legislators as well as judges are addressed by this amendment. We notice echoes here of the Fifth Amendment's Due Process Clause which attempts to protect "life, liberty, [and] property." The references to excessive bail, excessive fines, and cruel and unusual punishments deal, it seems, with liberty, property, and life in that order.

The opinions of one's day probably have to be drawn upon, in any particular case, to determine whether bail or fines are excessive and whether a punishment is cruel and unusual. Those opinions change from time to time. Moreover, bail, fines, and punishments should be tailored to the crime being charged. They may also have to be tailored to the circumstances of the person being charged. All this means that both the enduring standards of the community and the judgment and sense of humanity of lawyers, judges, and legislators must be drawn upon. The tough-mindedness of eighteenth-century statesmen is suggested by Samuel Livermore's comment in the First Congress on the "cruel and unusual punishments" clause:

> No cruel and unusual punishment is to be inflicted; it is sometimes necessary to hang a man, villains often deserve whipping, and perhaps having their ears cut off; but are we to be prevented from inflicting these punishments because they are cruel? If a more lenient mode of correcting vice and deterring others from the commission of it could be invented, it would be very prudent in the Legislature to adopt it; but until we have some security that this will be done, we ought not to be restrained from making necessary laws by any declaration of this kind.[102]

In recent decades considerable use has been made of the Eighth Amendment in efforts to have the death penalty declared unconstitutional by the courts. One obstacle for abolitionists here is that the Constitution and its Bill of Rights, like the common law before them, take it for granted that capital punishment may be properly resorted to. The Fifth Amendment, for example, refers to capital crimes and anticipates (as does the Fourteenth Amendment) that a person may be lawfully deprived of his life. It is also obvious that Congress, from the beginning, provided for the death penalty in its statutes as did probably all eighteenth-century State legislatures.[103]

Still, it is possible that radical changes in sensibilities, practices, or penology since 1791 have made capital punishment seem "cruel and unusual." Judges have to weigh contending arguments carefully if they are to adjudicate these matters in the spirit of the Eighth Amendment. Also relevant here is whether death sentences are distributed in such a way as to be either arbitrary or racially discriminatory, which would pose special problems under the Fifth and Fourteenth Amendments.

These are certainly considerations that officers of government, as well as the people at large, should be able to take into account in weighing the use of the death penalty. Here as elsewhere it may be better to rely upon legislatures to lay down overall policy, however important judges may have originally been in developing many of the rights enshrined in the Bill of Rights. It may be especially important to rely upon politically sensitive legislators in those instances where constitutional judgments should properly take account of changes in public opinion.

VII

One massive impression left by the Bill of Rights provisions we have been surveying in this lecture is that judges are relied upon to know well the constitutional heritage of the English-speaking peoples. Judges typically have the longest memories among the various officers of government in this Country. A judge keeps looking way back, while Congress and the President tend to be (and perhaps should be) much more responsive to the transient opinions of the Country at large, even as they attempt to interpret and apply the Constitution in an authoritative manner.

Judges should be learned and skilled. The primary concern we have is that judges be competent in the matters assigned to them, so much so that Judges (unlike Presidents and Members of Congress) need not be citizens of the United States. Judges are distinguished also by having life tenure and by not being liable to correction at the polls, however much the Courts of the United States may be subject under the Constitution to regulation by Congress.

We can see, when we consider the many restraints placed upon the Courts in the Bill of Rights and elsewhere, that adherence to the Constitution depends upon much more than judicial or any other official supervision. After all, what is it that makes judges, especially members of the Supreme Court, hew to the Constitutional line, since there is no nonjudicial body that routinely reviews what they do?

Perhaps the most important guide for officers of government is their, and ultimately the general, understanding of what the Constitution provides. How sensible that guidance is depends upon both how sound the Constitution itself is and how well it is understood. One question here, previously addressed in this Commentary, has to do with what was originally expected to be the significance of the Bill of Rights for the States. The presuppositions and tenor of the Bill of Rights suggest that it was generally understood that the restraints placed upon the judiciary in the Constitution continued to apply, even without the Bill of Rights, to the States, just as they applied to the Federal Judiciary prior to the Bill of Rights. For the most part, we have seen, the Bill of Rights recognized and refined rights that had been claimed and exercised by the American people well before Independence.

If judges were to continue to act as judges had long been acting, then State as well as Federal Judges could be expected to take their lead from the Bill of Rights, especially in how they conducted judicial proceedings. And if the reminders provided by Amendments Five through Eight were substantially those developed in the common law, a recognition of the United States Supreme Court as the paramount common-law court in the United States suggests that that Court was expected, even before the Fourteenth Amendment, to supervise to some degree how State courts conducted themselves. This is still another way of saying that the Constitution, from the beginning, anticipated that American courts (whether National or State) would continue acting as courts in the common-law tradition had "always" acted.

A sense of fairness, consistent with precedents, general expectations, and the political, social, economic, and religious opinions and institutions of the Country, is relied upon in how the law is to be developed and applied. The reference to "just compensation" in the Fifth Amendment is one of many reminders in our Constitutional documents of the moral standards taken for granted in all officers of government as well as in the people at large.

Fairness depends, as we have seen, upon an awareness of and an adaptation to circumstances as times change. We very much rely upon competent judges to develop, especially for judicial proceedings, long-established privileges and immunities. Not all of these rights are referred to in the Bill of Rights, but enough are collected there to provide judges guidance as to what is expected of them in the way they administer justice. Reasonableness should not be sacrificed in the administration of justice. Thus, for example, our ancient right to trial by jury does *not* mean that the more notorious someone's crime is, the more difficult it should be to convict and punish him. But then we do live in an era when two-thirds of each House of Congress are pressed to vote for a Constitutional amendment that would eventually require (at least on paper) a balanced national budget—and this effort is being made at a time and in circumstances when a mere one-half of each House can at once vote for a balanced budget if so minded. We can see here the kind of anomalies that the irrepressible Mark Twain exploited as a (sometimes unreasonable) critic of democratic institutions.

8. Amendments IX, X, XI, and XII

I

We have seen, in our survey of the Bill of Rights, that its orderliness reflects the orderliness of the Constitution of 1787. We have also seen that most, if not all, of the amendments proposed in 1789 seem to have been easily understood both by the Congress that prepared them and by the State legislatures that ratified them.

We have seen as well that the Bill of Rights reaffirmed rights that had long been claimed by the American people and that had been routinely respected by their governments. It is likely that little if anything changed in the conduct of the Government of the United States as a result of the ratification of the Bill of Rights in 1791. Since matters continued much as they had, there probably was little need to invoke the Bill of Rights before the Alien and Sedition Acts controversy in 1798.[104]

One effect that the Bill of Rights may eventually have had, I have suggested, was to obscure the traditional character of these rights. The more that came to be made of the Bill of Rights, the less evident it became that virtually all, if not all, of the rights found there had "always" been applicable against all governments in English-speaking North America.

The reaffirmation of rights found in the first eight amendments to the Constitution is carried further in the Ninth and Tenth Amendments, where the prerogatives of the people are recognized. These amendments do not add anything essential to what is evident in the Constitution and in the first eight amendments, or at least they do not add what some believe they add. The documents and other materials from which relevant information may be drawn about these matters have long been known to students of American constitutional developments. Also long known, but largely lost sight of these days, is how much is to be gathered from a sound assessment of the information that has been available since early in the nineteenth century about our Constitutional system.

We deal in turn now with the Ninth and Tenth Amendments and, thereafter, the two amendments that immediately supplement the Bill of Rights. We complete thereby our review of the amendments prepared by the founding generation in this Country.

II

The Ninth Amendment provides: "The enumeration in the Constitution, of certain rights, shall not be construed to deny or disparage others retained by the people." This amendment was designed to address one argument made repeatedly during the Ratification Campaign by proponents of the Constitution to justify the absence of a Bill of Rights: it is risky to list some already-recognized rights lest those not listed be implicitly negated. This argument was spoken to by James Madison when he first submitted to the House of Representatives his array of proposed amendments to the Constitution:

> It has been objected also against a bill of rights, that, by enumerating particular exceptions to the grant of power, it would disparage those rights which were not placed in that enumeration; and it might follow by implication, that those rights which were not singled out, were intended to be assigned into the hands of the General Government, and were consequently insecure. This is one of the most plausible arguments I have ever heard urged against the admission of a bill of rights into this system; but, I conceive, that it may be guarded against. I have attempted it, as gentlemen may see by turning to [what is now the Ninth Amendment].[105]

The implications of silence are thereby dealt with.

We are again reminded by the retention of rights insisted upon here of what had long been believed to be due to the English-speaking peoples independent of particular constitutional documents. A comprehensive constitutional system seems to have been assumed by both the Congress that prepared and the State legislatures that ratified the Bill of Rights. Consider, again, the implications of the Privileges and Immunities Clause of Article IV of the

93

Constitution, where it is provided, "The Citizens of each State shall be entitled to all Privileges and Immunities of Citizens in the several States." What was intended to be the effect of that clause? Is it something like the Equal Protection Clause of the Fourteenth Amendment, obliging each State to treat everyone in that State alike with respect to certain rights, whether they be citizens of that State or of another State? Or does it recognize certain rights that should be available to American citizens everywhere, rights that are consistent with, if not required from each State by, the Republican Form of Government Guarantee (also in Article IV)? In either case, the Privileges and Immunities Clause testifies to the opinion that there are rights (established, if not also incipient) that are not enumerated in the Constitution.

It is hard to say, however, what precisely was intended to be included among the rights referred to either in the Privileges and Immunities Clause or in the Ninth Amendment—or whether anything precise, or fixed, was intended. One problem here is how Courts should act in protecting such rights. Certainly, the judiciary should not try to conduct itself as a third branch of the legislature. The judiciary does not have the popular base or the political leadership and restraints needed for legislation, nor can it provide the comprehensive guidance that legislation is able to provide in dealing with any particular matter. And yet a kind of legislation seems to be resorted to when Courts exercise judicial review in developing substantive rights while policing the activities of legislatures.

Fewer difficulties are encountered when the Courts develop, as well as apply, procedural rights of the kind found in Amendments IV or V through VIII. Even so, we can again wonder, did the listing of rights in the Bill of Rights tend to "freeze" them in a way that they would not otherwise have been? Or has the United States Supreme Court been able to discover old, or develop new, procedural rights by elaborating those expressly laid down in the Bill of Rights? Some elaboration may be seen by the Congress as well, along with what has been done in providing for various "entitlements," which may be, in effect, new economic rights.

We wonder in this fashion about the other rights "retained by the people" that the Ninth Amendment contemplates. What, furthermore, is the status here of natural right? The Framers accepted and built upon the common law, which depends upon a grasp of natu-

ral right or, at least, upon the workings of and an awareness of natural right. But the lessons of history may be almost as important as
the guidance provided by nature, at least in what Courts are to do.[106]
It should matter to judges and others who try to apply the Ninth
Amendment what rights happened to emerge before 1791 in the
course of the centuries-old Anglo-American constitutional development.

Indications of those rights, and sometimes of the forms they have
taken, may be found in the extensive lists of rights recommended
by the State Ratification Conventions in 1787–1788.[107] We have seen
that the recommendations which called for cutting into the substantive powers of the new General Government were systematically
rejected by the First Congress. Were there left unenumerated by the
amendments proposed by Congress any State recommendations
with respect to rights similar to those that were acted upon by
Congress?

It can be argued that, but for the institution of slavery which had
to be accommodated in the late eighteenth century, an equal-protection principle might have found even more expression than it
did in the Constitution of 1787 and its Bill of Rights. Provision for,
as well as any pervasive reliance upon, the rule of law has equal-
protection implications. But the equal-protection principle, which
can be said to be implicit in Magna Carta, had to await the post–
Civil War amendments for its full (natural?) expression in this Country, most obviously with respect to slavery and its aftermath.

One major concern expressed again and again by advocates of a
bill of rights during the Ratification Campaign of 1787–1788 was
that there should be limitations placed upon standing armies in
time of peace.[108] But even so stout a civil libertarian as George Mason recognized "that an absolute prohibition of standing armies in
time of peace might be unsafe." He attempted instead to have precautions taken with respect to the establishment and use of the
militia.[109] A major precaution found in the Constitution that bears
upon these matters is the two-year limitation placed in Article I on
Congressional appropriations for the Army.

Perhaps it would be useful for us to study developments in Great
Britain the past two centuries to see what if any rights have been
further elaborated there by common-law judges, especially as attempts have been made to apply the common-law concerns with

natural justice and the common good to changing circumstances. In the United States, we have seen, the common law tends to be pushed aside, now that much more is made (by lawyers, judges, and legal scholars) of the will of the sovereign and much less of reasoning from first principles. It should be particularly instructive to consider what has been done with the right of privacy by British common-law judges, independent of legislative guidance. We have noticed that elements of a general respect for privacy may be found in various parts of the Constitution and the Bill of Rights, such as in the protection provided for both the right to liberty and the right to property. But it is difficult to recognize a general or comprehensive right to privacy without calling into question many of the seemingly legitimate powers of government. The right to privacy, if it is to be practicable, probably depends upon extensive legislative guidance, not only upon ad hoc judicial determinations. It is instructive to notice how much the prescriptions laid down by the Supreme Court in the 1973 *Abortion Cases*[110] resemble legislation. However dubious much of what the Court has said about abortion may be thus far, a woman's right to choose whether she will resort to an abortion is a claim that must be taken seriously, especially considering how deeply more and more women worldwide are evidently coming to feel about the subject (including many who would not themselves want an abortion). On the other hand, the limitations of deference to any extensive right to privacy (which is often coupled in our time with an innocent shamelessness) have been recognized across the millennia, as may be seen, for example, in Plato's *Laws:*

> For there are many little things, not visible to everyone, that take place in private and in the home, which, because of each person's pain, pleasure, and desire, go against the advice of the lawgiver, and would easily make the dispensations of the citizen diverse and dissimilar.[111]

This is related to the question of what the powers and duty of the community are with respect to the moral life of its citizens.

Whatever else the Ninth Amendment does, it recognizes and in effect ratifies a considerable constitutional history. A comprehensive constitutional system seems to be acknowledged, including (as we shall see in Section IV of this lecture) the perhaps most significant of the people's prerogatives "saved" by the Ninth Amendment: the right of revolution.

III

The Tenth Amendment provides: "The powers not delegated to the United States by the Constitution, nor prohibited by it to the States, are reserved to the States respectively, or to the people." This amendment says in effect, that the Constitution means what it seems to say. To suggest that the Tenth Amendment may be for the most part redundant is not a welcome message to those conventional States' Rights partisans who make so much of it.

Proposals were received by the First Congress from several States for some such affirmation as may be seen in the Tenth Amendment. What understanding of the Constitutional system is reflected in those proposals? The Ninth Amendment, we have just seen, addressed the implications of silence with respect to various rights of the people. The States' Rights proponents of something like what we now know as the Tenth Amendment also addressed the implications of silence. We have seen (in this Commentary and its companion volume) that those proponents attempted again and again to have the Government of the United States limited to the powers which were *expressly* delegated to it by the Constitution. This would have severely restricted, among other things, the scope of the Necessary and Proper Clause in Section 8 of Article I of the Constitution of 1787.

The attempts made in the First Congress to have what is now the Tenth Amendment begin, "The powers not *expressly* delegated to the United States," were, we have also seen, thwarted by the Federalists (that is, the Nationalists) who controlled the First Congress. They did not intend to dilute in any way the powers that had been developed for the General Government by the Federal Convention controlled by delegates of like mind. It is not surprising, that is, that Congress repeatedly refused to put in *expressly* or its equivalent, however much some interpreters of the Tenth Amendment (including all too many Justices of the United States Supreme Court) have since tried to do this. Instead, the Tenth Amendment recognizes that the Government of the United States does have the powers it has—that is, the powers provided for it in the Constitution of 1787. After it became evident to States' Rightists that they could not, either in the First Congress or thereafter, amend a Constitution that soon came to be generally venerated, they directed their efforts to curtailment of the powers of Congress by trying to shape the way that key provisions of the Constitution were read, particularly the vital Commerce Clause.

Perhaps the only powers that the Tenth Amendment denies to the General Government are those that may have been created, by implication, by various of the restrictions placed upon that government in the Bill of Rights. Some of those who tried to head off a Bill of Rights in 1787–1789 had argued for a very narrow reading of the grants of powers to Congress.[112] They had argued, we have seen, that there was no need for the declaration of many of the rights requested because the General Government did not have the power to do the things that those rights sought to prevent being done. The more successful the proponents of a bill of rights were in placing prohibitions upon the General Government, therefore, the more they seemed to expand the powers of that government by implication. The Tenth Amendment may provide some restraint here upon the powers implied by specific restraints. This amendment, like the Ninth Amendment, confirms an extensive and generally understood Constitutional system. These two amendments recognize that silence should not be taken as permitting a limitation either upon the rights of the American people or upon the powers of its General Government.[113]

Lest it be suspected that the unfashionable interpretation I have offered here is idiosyncratic, I call to the stand Justice Story for an extended passage (from his 1833 Commentary) on the Tenth Amendment, a passage which discusses the ill-fated *expressly* efforts that we have noticed:

> When this amendment was before congress, a proposition was moved, to insert the word "expressly" before "delegated," so as to read "the powers not *expressly* delegated to the United States by the constitution," &c. On that occasion it was remarked [replied], that it is impossible to confine a government to the exercise of express powers. There must necessarily be admitted powers by implication, unless the constitution descended to the most minute details. It is a general principle, that all corporate bodies possess all powers incident to a

corporate capacity, without being absolutely expressed. The motion was accordingly negatived. Indeed, one of the great defects of the [Articles of Confederation] was, (as we have already seen,) that it contained a clause, prohibiting the exercise of any power, jurisdiction, or right, not *expressly delegated*. The consequence was, that congress were crippled at every step of their progress; and were often compelled by the very necessities of the times to usurp powers, which they did not constitutionally possess; and thus, in effect, to break down all the great barriers against tyranny and oppression.

It is plain, therefore, that it could not have been the intention of the framers of [the Tenth Amendment] to give it effect, as an abridgment of any of the powers granted under the constitution, whether they are express or implied, direct or incidental. Its sole design is to exclude any interpretation, by which other powers should be assumed beyond those, which are granted. All that are granted in the original instrument, whether express or implied, whether direct or incidental, are left in their original state. All powers not delegated, (not all powers not *expressly* delegated,) and not prohibited, are reserved. The attempts, then, which have been made from time to time, to force upon this language an abridging, or restrictive influence, are utterly unfounded in any just rules of interpreting the words, or the sense of the instrument. Stripped of the ingenious disguises, in which they are clothed, they are neither more nor less, than attempts to foist into the text the word "expressly;" to qualify, what is general, and obscure, what is clear, and defined. They made the sense of the passage bend to the wishes and prejudices of the interpreter; and employ criticism to support a theory, and not to guide it. One should suppose, if the history of the human mind did not furnish abundant proof to the contrary, that no reasonable man would contend for an interpretation founded neither in the letter, nor in the spirit of an instrument. Where is controversy to end, if we desert both the letter and the spirit? What is to become of constitutions of government, if they are to rest, not upon the plain import of their words, but upon conjectural enlargements and restrictions, to suit the temporary passions and interests of the day? Let us never forget, that our constitutions of government are solemn instruments, addressed to the common sense of the people and designed to fix, and perpetuate their rights and their liberties. They are not to be frittered away to please the demagogues of the day. They are not to be violated to gratify the ambition of political leaders. They are to speak in the same voice now, and for ever. They are of no man's private interpretation. They are ordained by the will of the people; and can be changed only by the sovereign command of the people.[114]

IV

I have argued that the powers of the Government of the United States are kept in check by the Ninth Amendment, insofar as those powers are checked by the rights of the people acknowledged there. I have also argued that the powers of the Government of the United States are recognized for what they are in the Tenth Amendment. In both cases, the overall authority of the people is invoked.

One consequence of the Ninth and Tenth Amendments is the affirmation of the principle that it is We the People, not the States, who have made the Constitution. What these amendments did was, in this respect, not what some of their proponents wanted but perhaps just the opposite. The States are shown by the Tenth Amendment to be subordinated to the will of the same people that the United States is; the States, whatever their origins historically, are assumed not to exist independently either of the People or of their National Constitution. The Ninth Amendment, insofar as it explicitly recognizes rights that exist independently of the Constitution, may have subordinated the States even more to the general Constitutional system than the Constitution of 1787 had done.

The people, we see from the Ninth and Tenth Amendments, retain rights independent of all governments in the United States. We also see that the people have delegated the powers that governments possess, both nationally and locally, reserving to themselves what they have willed. Thus, the Ninth and Tenth Amendments gave the American people an opportunity to say about the constitutional dispensation found in the Constitution of 1787 and in its Bill of Rights, "We ourselves did it—and we really mean it!" It is startlingly evident from the Tenth Amendment that the People of the United States may determine the powers of and limitations upon the States, no matter what the people of any particular State may prefer.

The key right and power of such a self-governing people, implicitly recognized by the Ninth and Tenth Amendments, can be said to be what we cherish as the right of revolution, properly understood. Abraham Lincoln, in speeches made during his first few months as

President, conceded the right of revolution, the very right that was being invoked by some Southerners at the time in justifying their attempted secession from the Union. But he pointed out that this right, if it is to be properly invoked, requires a just cause. It is not merely a case either of desire or of might making right. Of course, both sides to a controversy may consider their respective causes just, even though both sides may also recognize that only one of them can be correct. The American Colonies had not allowed differences of opinion with Great Britain as to what was just to lead them to believe that they were not entitled to rebel. The importance of giving reasons in such circumstances should be evident. The Declaration of Independence, with its appeal to "a candid World," recognizes that there is an argument to be made. Arguments help all parties to do the right thing in such circumstances, however incapable one side or the other (or, sadly, both) may be, for the time being, in working out or accepting the best argument.

The Declaration of Independence suggests what has to be known and shown before recourse to the right of revolution is justified, at least in modern circumstances. Natural right, or a sense of what is by nature right, has to be used in assessing grievances and the particular situation, including the history and expectations of a people. An informed grasp of both principles and facts is vital to a proper determination of what is called for on any occasion.

The great right of revolution is not mentioned in the Bill of Rights. Certainly, it is not necessary to consider it a justiciable right. Nor does its validity depend upon any government's explicit recognition of it. The legal form that the right of revolution has taken from time to time in Anglo-American history is the repudiation of any requirement of nonresistance that governments have attempted to impose upon citizens. (This may be seen, for example, in Appendix I-1 of this Commentary, where Virginians are recorded as saying in 1788 "that the doctrine of non-resistance against arbitrary power and oppression is absurd, slavish, and destructive of the good and happiness of mankind.") Or, put in our terms today, an advocacy of the availability of the right of revolution is itself protected by the First Amendment. At the very least, the right of revolution acknowledges that there are standards, rooted both in nature and in the known political experience and constitutional history of a civilized people, that may be resorted to in assessing the claims and the deeds of governments. The authority of the people to make such assessments is recognized not only by the Ninth and Tenth Amendments, but also by the Preamble and Articles V and VII of the Constitution, and even by the First Amendment, which protects the right and power (if not even the duty) of the people to examine and discuss what their governments are saying and doing. A proper respect for the right of revolution can contribute to the perpetuity of any regime grounded in natural-right principles.

V

We have now reviewed the ten articles in the Bill of Rights of 1791. There were, we recall, originally twelve proposed articles in the Bill of Rights prepared by the First Congress in 1789. The first and second proposed articles, we also recall, were not ratified at that time by the States. (The ratification in 1992 of one of the amendment proposals rejected in 1791 has been noticed in Lecture No. 5 and will be discussed in Lecture No. 16 of this Commentary.)

In order to complete our survey of the amendments of the Constitutional Period, we now consider the Eleventh and Twelfth Amendments. These amendments, ratified in 1798 and 1804, respectively, can be said to have been in the spirit of the original Constitution, as were the amendments found in the Bill of Rights. That the period from 1776 to 1804 was a separate stage in our constitutional development is indicated by the fact that no further amendments were made to the Constitution for almost two-thirds of a century thereafter, the longest period in the history of the United States without the ratification of a constitutional amendment.

The Eleventh Amendment provides: "The Judicial power of the United States shall not be construed to extend to any suit in law or equity, commenced or prosecuted against one of the United States by Citizens of another State, or by Citizens or Subjects of any Foreign State." We see here, as in the Twelfth Amendment, the specificity that changes to the Constitution can have. There is here no statement of a principle or right, but merely a modification of an existing arrangement. The immediate cause of that modification was the decision that had been rendered in 1793 by the United States Supreme Court in *Chisholm v. Georgia.*[115] Whatever the original intentions of the Framers, Section 2 of Article III of the Constitution was interpreted by the Supreme Court in *Chisholm* to permit the kind of suits now forbidden by the Eleventh Amendment.[116]

If the conventional interpretation of Article III is correct, Congress could, by amending the Judiciary Act of 1789, have legislated the remedy provided by the Eleventh Amendment. Did the Third Congress want to make sure, by resorting to an amendment instead of to a statute, that no future Congress restored this jurisdiction to the Courts of the United States? Or did Congress believe that a Constitutionally granted judicial jurisdiction was beyond complete legislative removal? That is, did Congress then believe, contrary to the conventional interpretation of Article III today, that all of the jurisdiction of the Courts of the United States has to be recognized and provided for in one way or another by Congress? If so, the Eleventh Amendment may be one of the few amendments, if not the only amendment, that gave the States something that they had not had under the Constitution of 1787.

The Eleventh Amendment, like the *Chisholm* case that it responded to, implies that the Courts of the United States may use the common law in appropriate cases. Thus, the common law may have to be used to settle suits between citizens of different States as well as some of the suits involving States that are still within the jurisdiction of the United States Supreme Court. If the Courts of the United States are to use the common law in appropriate cases, must not Congress have available to it a power that common-law practitioners always recognized, the power of some legislature to supervise and, if need be, to correct or redirect what its courts do with the common law?

We find in *Hollingsworth* v. *Virginia* an early recognition of the effect of the Eleventh Amendment:

> The Court, on the day succeeding the argument, delivered an unanimous opinion, that the [Eleventh] amendment being constitutionally adopted, there could not be exercised any jurisdiction, in any case, past or future, in which a state was sued by the citizens of another state, or by citizens, or subjects, of any foreign state.[117]

Whether a State could be sued in its own courts by "the citizens of another state, or by citizens or subjects of any foreign state," depended upon what the constitution and laws of that State provided. That is how matters stood until the Fourteenth Amendment, which has of course made every State much more vulnerable to suits in Federal Courts by its own citizens as well as to suits by citizens of other States.

VI

The critical provision of the page-long Twelfth Amendment of 1804 reads: "The Electors shall meet in their respective states, and vote by ballot for President and Vice-President . . . ; they shall name in their ballots the person voted for as President, and in distinct ballots the person voted for as Vice-President . . ." This, like the Eleventh Amendment, is an early supplement to the Bill of Rights. The Twelfth Amendment responded to the Presidential electoral crisis of 1800–1801.

The problem of providing for the President is returned to again and again in Constitutional amendments. Americans have never been sure they have it quite right. Further changes are contemplated in some quarters today, such as the direct election of the President. But this (I have suggested, in Lecture No. 8 of my Commentary on the Constitution of 1787) could have unfortunate consequences, and not only because it would tend to make it even harder than it already is for Congress to exercise the control over the President (once popularly elected) that both the President and the Country need. In addition, the States would tend to be depreciated in their political influence as States by such a development. (Similar effects can be anticipated if many States should adopt the rules that Maine and Nebraska have for dividing the Presidential electors between candidates according to the proportions of votes they receive in those States.)

The obvious need for the Twelfth Amendment, or for Congressional legislation to the same effect, arose because of the emergence of nationwide, or at least multistate, political parties in the United States. This meant that two candidates could routinely end up with enough votes to be President because the Constitution of 1787 did not distinguish Presidential and Vice-Presidential choices in the original balloting on each occasion. The Twelfth Amendment not only removed this embarrassment but also made it virtually impossible to elect a President of one party and a Vice President of another party, which could be expected under the Constitution of

1787 and was indeed seen during the John Adams Administration, with Thomas Jefferson as Vice President.

One other effect of the Twelfth Amendment, or of the development of the political parties that helped lead to the amendment, was that recourse thereafter to the House of Representatives for the choice of a President would be rare.[118] The original constitutional expectation may have been that the House would have to settle most contests, with the original balloting in the States by the more or less independent electors usually serving only as a nominating stage.[119]

VII

The first twelve amendments are almost one-half of the amendments we now have. Although twenty-seven amendments have been considered ratified, two of them (the Eighteenth and the Twenty-first) virtually cancel each other out. The American people, once the first half (or I through XII) of the amendments we now have had been ratified, were still guided by the Constitution of 1787 in its essentials. The first twelve amendments adapted further the old constitutional system of the English-speaking peoples to republican conditions in North America.

By the time the Twelfth Amendment was ratified, the United States Supreme Court had asserted and exercised a power to review acts of Congress for their constitutionality. Although the Court was not to exercise that power again in so dramatic a way for half a century, it did mean that a fundamental change may have been in prospect for the Constitutional system, especially as the implications (both beneficent and threatening) of genuine self-government on a continental scale began to become apparent. One consequence of the judicial-review assertion by the Supreme Court has been to obscure the considerable part played by Congress in providing authoritative interpretations of the Constitution in the early decades of the Republic. Another significant threat to responsible self-government has been the tendency to insist upon unconstitutional "supermajorities" in conducting the Country's legislative affairs, a tendency that is evident in the Senate's tolerance for crippling filibusters. (I return to this problem in Lecture No. 13, Section VII, and in Lecture No. 17, Section I, of this Commentary.)

I have suggested that the first half of the amendments we have, through the Twelfth, left the original Constitutional arrangement essentially intact. The second half of our amendments, from the Thirteenth through the Twenty-seventh, shows the effects of profound social and political developments to which the emerging political parties contributed. These developments were generated in large part by the equality principle of the Declaration of Independence, a principle that is taken for granted (although it had to be compromised) in the Constitution of 1787. To say that the equality principle has found more and more vivid expression in our Constitutional development over the centuries is to recognize that modernity has had its effects, not least in the influence among us both of the Declaration of Independence and of life under the Constitution following upon that Declaration and its Revolution.

9. Education in the New Republic

I stand with this lecture at the midpoint of my Commentary on the Amendments to the Constitution of the United States. Once the Constitution of 1787 and its Bill of Rights were established (with unexpected technical questions about the Judiciary and Presidency disposed of in the Eleventh and Twelfth Amendments), the American people could settle down to governing themselves without worrying very much about forms of government. The education of that people and their leaders became critical in determining how competent American self-government would be. It is instructive for an assessment of this education to notice what early nineteenth-century Americans drew upon from antiquity, besides their considerable respect for the republican institutions (as well as some aspects of the Empire) of Rome. In a treatise on American constitutional law published two decades ago, I found myself looking for inspiration and guidance to both the *Apology* of Socrates as recorded by Plato and the Declaration of Independence of which Thomas Jefferson was the primary draftsman:

> The tension evident in this study may be inevitable for anyone who tries to "live with" both the *Apology* of Socrates and the Declaration of Independence—for anyone, that is, who finds himself drawn to two public declarations which are, despite their superficial compatibility, radically divergent in their presuppositions and implications. Thus, an attempt is made [in that 1971 study] to see American constitutional law and political thought from the perspective of our ancient teachers.[120]

How the ancients have come to be regarded by Americans was anticipated by what Jefferson and his contemporaries had to say

107

about Plato, perhaps the greatest of the philosophical writers of antiquity. Was not Jefferson's dismissal of that author (however special Jefferson's form of that dismissal) the typical American approach in the early nineteenth century? It seems that Plato and Aristotle were soon thereafter (if they were not already) reduced to insignificance in American political (if not also philosophical) thought. By the time of Abraham Lincoln, for example, Plato and Aristotle were rarely referred to by political men. This repudiation in public life of thinkers such as Plato and Aristotle seems to have come much later in Great Britain, where the great universities helped shape the principal politicians well into the twentieth century. (Winston Churchill, whose mother was an American and who did not himself have a university education, may appear to have been somewhat more in the Jeffersonian tradition with respect to classical philosophy. But Churchill, like Lincoln, was instructed in classical thought by Shakespeare. He tended to speak with more respect of both Athens and Jerusalem than Jefferson did.)

Jefferson's own high standing in American political thought is generally recognized:

> Thomas Jefferson is not the only spring of American political thought, but he is the primary one. All the principles of American political life, and all the tensions among those principles, show themselves in his works and words. He served in the Virginia House of Burgesses and House of Delegates and as governor of Virginia and was a delegate to the Continental Congress from 1775 to 1776 and again from 1783 to 1785.
>
> Appointed a member of a committee to which Congress assigned the task of drafting a statement declaring and justifying the separation of the American colonies from England, he was deferred to by his fellow committee members and thus emerged as the principal author of the Declaration of Independence. That Declaration, appealing before the opinions and judgment of all of mankind to principles of right embodied in nature, manifested the fundamentals upon which the United States rests and to which all modern liberal democracies look.[121]

My point of departure for this discussion is the proposition that two forms of excellence may be seen in the dialogues of Plato and in the political careers of Jefferson and his contemporaries. A review of the Jeffersonian response to Plato, however limited that review has to be in this context, should help us begin to investigate problems that many Americans have always had in sensing the amplitude and depth of the more thoughtful ancients. We may, after surveying that Jeffersonian response, be better able to understand the education of the men who not only developed the Constitution of 1787 and its first twelve amendments, but also (and perhaps more importantly) trained their successors. The reading of Plato that I rely upon in this lecture is, for the most part, the conventional reading.

II

My immediate texts for this discussion are Thomas Jefferson's letter from Virginia of July 5, 1814, to John Adams in Massachusetts, and Adams's reply of July 16, 1814.[122] These letters (set forth in Appendixes K-1 and K-2 of this Commentary) are part of the generous correspondence between the two former Presidents that was revived during the last decade and a half of their long lives. This intimate correspondence transcended the political differences they had had at the turn of the century, which culminated in Vice-President Jefferson's defeat of President Adams in the fateful Presidential contest of 1800–1801. It is difficult to imagine any prominent American politicians today being either inclined or equipped to carry on a private correspondence with the learning, grace, and seriousness evident in these letters. For one thing, both Jefferson and Adams exhibit a relaxed familiarity with the ancients and with what they called "classical reading," so much so that their opinions about the matters they range over still invite respectful attention.

In 1814 Jefferson was seventy-one years old; Adams was seventy-eight. Their correspondence, which had been renewed in 1812, continued into 1826. It was in that year that these last two surviving signers of the Declaration of Independence died on July 4th, fifty years to the day after their signing of that founding instrument. Adams, although he had long been somewhat more old-fashioned than Jefferson, found himself agreeing with much that Jefferson said, especially about the ancients. One can see in their 1814 exchange not only the Jeffersonian reading of the ancients but, one might say, a reading typical of many well-educated American public men, perhaps something of the modern democrat's reading.

Although old age was catching up with both men, who were by that time retired from active political life, they remained quite lively in their speculations. That old age was indeed catching up with them may be seen in what Jefferson could say, and Adams could agree to, about how their bodies were wearing out. They drew upon mechanical analogies in this July 1814 exchange and elsewhere as they spoke of their bodily machinery. This mechanistic materialism may be significant for any effort to understand why Jefferson and Adams think and talk as they do about the Platonic, and even the ancient, understanding of things.

I will work primarily from the Jefferson letter of July 5, 1814. My account is devoted to three related parts of this letter: the political, if not worldwide, circumstances of the day, particularly as seen in the career of Napoleon Bonaparte and in the activities of England; an extended critique of a Platonic dialogue; and the educational practices of the day, particularly with a view to reforms in the schooling of American youth.

III

Jefferson, after commenting on visitors and on matters of health, turns to the depredations abroad both of Napoleon Bonaparte and of England, who had been deadly opponents during the then-recent European wars. The Virginian characterizes the French leader as "the Attila of the age," adding, "Bonaparte was a lion in the field only. In civil life a cold-blooded, calculating unprincipled Usurper, without a virtue, no statesman, knowing nothing of commerce, political economy, or civil government, and supplying ignorance by bold presumption." Jefferson, after "rejoic[ing], for the good of mankind, in the deliverance of Europe from the havoc which would never have ceased while Bonaparte should have lived in power," wonders how the United States should respond to triumphant England: "I see with anxiety the tyrant of the ocean remaining in vigor, and even participating in the merit of crushing his brother tyrant." English impressment of American sailors (critical to the War of 1812) had offended Jefferson. He is now concerned about whether New England will stand up to English demands with respect to the fisheries that mean so much to Massachusetts. He hopes that Massachusetts will choose to fight for her rights—but he recognizes that New England, not Virginia or the South, should take the lead in the development of that policy.

Whatever the party and sectional differences in the United States concerning the War of 1812—it is partly for this reason that Jefferson proceeds with some delicacy here—Jefferson seems to find a sympathetic reader in Adams.[123] Adams has reservations, but he does not seem to be offended by, but rather endorses, what Jefferson says about both Napoleon Bonaparte and England. (Neither of them anticipated Napoleon's immediate resurgence, which culminated in his final defeat at Waterloo in 1815.)

We are reminded by Jefferson's remarks about foreign policy that much of Jefferson's thought has a political context. He, like Adams, is a vigorously practical-minded man. The whole world is their domain and universal respect for liberty under law is their end. This is both good and bad. It is important that political necessities, and hence common sense and natural right, be recognized. But may it not be impractical to make too much of the practical?

An undue emphasis upon the practical, or the utilitarian, may be seen in what has become of higher education in our own time. Consider, for example, the impressive ceremony I witnessed on October 3, 1991, on the campus of the University of Chicago, where a dozen honorary degrees were conferred in opening the university's year-long centennial celebration. Much was made, in these awards, of research, of creating new knowledge, and of the usefulness of such knowledge. Very little, if anything, was said about studying the ancients, including the founders of our highly productive scientific tradition. The spectacular, if not even wondrous, character of modern scientific research is epitomized in our time by that dramatic harnessing of nuclear energy which was demonstrated for the first time on the campus of the University of Chicago a half-century earlier on December 2, 1942. Too much talk is heard these days of creating knowledge, and not enough of discovering it. Is not rediscovery of what thoughtful human beings have always known one of the permanent tasks of any serious educational establishment? Few if any of the accomplishments celebrated these days will mean much, except perhaps as transitions, to thoughtful observers a quarter-century (to say nothing of a century) hence.

Another way of putting this is to say that the prudence and eloquence of the Founding Period in this Country drew upon intellectual and spiritual capital that was not adequately preserved by the education and training of the decades that followed. Lincoln and his colleagues had, by the middle of the nineteenth century, "used up" much of what remained of that intellectual capital, except as it continued to be incorporated in the plays of Shakespeare and in the Bible. A failure in sustaining our roots may be seen in what has become of both Biblical influences and classical education among us. Much of what is dull, shallow, and shortsighted (if not even shameless) in both our thought and our desires might be traced to that failure, however decent or, at times, self-sacrificing and even heroic we may be.

IV

The virtual abandonment of classical education in this Country (and elsewhere) was anticipated by such criticism as that found in the Jefferson-Adams correspondence that we are sampling. These two patriots' condemnation of Plato was prompted by Jefferson's unsuccessful attempt in 1814 to read the *Republic*, which most readers have always considered one of the more accessible of Plato's dialogues but which Jefferson found very difficult.

It was not for lack of trying on Jefferson's part. Much the same response to Plato is reported by Adams, who had once tried reading the dialogues in various translations, as well as by consulting the Greek texts. We notice the importance of leisure for such efforts, which is not unrelated to the aristocratic presuppositions of much of classical thought. Such presuppositions may put off the modern democrat somewhat, even when he is not fully aware of their implications.

Jefferson reports that his recent attempt to read the *Republic* seriously "was the heaviest task-work I ever went through." It was anything but "amusement." Rather he complains about having had to wade through "the whimsies, the puerilities, and unintelligible jargon of this work." The joy (as well as the profit) of reading Plato, to which many have testified across millennia, evidently eluded both Jefferson and Adams.[124]

What is it about Plato that so offended Jefferson and Adams? Not only his obscurity—for there are things about Plato that are so clear that they can be dismissed by Jefferson as "puerilities." One is reminded here of protests long ago by other democratic politicians: the Athenian Callicles, for example, is recorded in Plato's *Gorgias* as complaining vigorously about the puerilities of Socrates. This suggests that there is something in Plato's approach to serious matters that is likely to arouse the suspicion, and eventually the enmity, of practical-minded men, especially those with democratic inclinations—and this can be independent of the enlightened sophistication with which we have become familiar.

V

It is the republican in Jefferson who has a high opinion of certain Romans, especially Cicero. Here, as elsewhere, Jefferson expects Adams to agree with him for the most part. In fact, Adams says that Jefferson's opinion about Plato "perfectly harmonize[s]" with his own. Adams reports that one of the few things he ever learned from Plato was that sneezing was a reliable cure for hiccoughs.[125]

Jefferson can speak with respect elsewhere of the Roman Cato and of the Athenian Aristides.[126] These are virtuous men who are evidently considered republican in their sympathies. We are reminded again and again, upon reading Jefferson and his American contemporaries, that Rome was in their eyes the other great republic before the United States. Jefferson's republican sympathies are evident when he considers the great men of action of antiquity. We can see here how sensible the sturdy republican can be. That sturdiness can also be seen in the prudent letters of advice that Jefferson could write to young people.

Jefferson knows that Cicero thought highly of Plato. He does not try to figure out, however, what it was that the worthy Cicero could see in Plato. Perhaps he senses that there is in this a serious problem for him, but he does not dwell upon it. We seem to have here one more instance of the critical modern failing already alluded to: the ancient thinkers, including our most distinguished predecessors, need not be taken seriously. Predecessors are not apt to be given credit for intelligence, thoughtfulness, or sensitivity commensurate to our own. (One can wonder to what extent moderns have been influenced in this by David Hume and by the Enlightenment, if not by Niccolò Machiavelli and Thomas Hobbes.)

Democrats, both ancient and modern, tend to believe that they are equal to all others. This principle of equality applies to the past as well as to contemporaries. So why should we democrats defer to any authority of the past, especially since we are privileged (and not only because of modern science) to know more than our predecessors ever could? Besides, does not the desire for independence promote comprehensive liberation from the tyranny of the past?[127]

Even so, Jefferson has the intellectual integrity not to assume that it was only Plato's style that accounted for Cicero's high praise of Plato.

VI

Plato's style does dupe some readers, Jefferson believes. The "elegance of his diction" helps account for his reputation. A pleasing style can give the impression of wisdom. This may be seen, for example, in the much-acclaimed career of Oliver Wendell Holmes Jr. in this Country.

Elsewhere Jefferson refers to Greek as "the most beautiful of all languages."[128] Whatever reservations Jefferson has about Plato, he can, as a great stylist himself, recognize Plato as the master of a language.

Jefferson places emphasis, in explaining Plato's reputation, upon elements other than the Greek's thought: not only upon style, but also upon fashion and authority. Certainly, Plato's reputation has to be accounted for.

VII

The "dreams of Plato" are singled out by Jefferson for special condemnation. They are seen as fanciful, partaking, it seems, of Plato's questionable utopian projects.

Do not the dreams of Plato stand, somehow, in opposition to the American Dream? How are they to be distinguished? Is not much more made in the United States of the *pursuit* of happiness? Compare the classical emphasis upon happiness as something that is rooted in virtue. We are not likely to be comfortable in making much of a pursuit of virtue, especially if that pursuit should be guided by a moralistic community. Even Jefferson's advocacy of agrarian virtue can now be dismissed as obsolete, if not even as "judgmental" and as otherwise oppressive.

Jefferson, as perhaps the leading apostle among us of a dedication to the pursuit of happiness, is revealed in his letters to Adams as substantially modernist in his temperament. Elsewhere he endorses Epicureanism, which is not to be seen (he insists) as simple hedonism or as an invitation to indolence.[129] But is it not difficult to avoid a decline into mere hedonism if much is made of the pursuit of happiness?[130]

Certainly, hedonism is more apt to become dominant among a people if vulgar individualism is encouraged, something that is likely whenever happiness and its pursuit, rather than virtue, become of consuming interest.[131]

VIII

If Plato is tested by reason, Jefferson says to Adams, he is exposed as full of "sophisms, futilities, and incomprehensibilities." Although he is reputed to be "a great Philosopher," rigorous thinkers can now see that he is hardly competent in his arguments.

Jefferson does not have much doubt about this. His only difficulty here is that others do not see as well what is obvious enough to him—and what should have long been obvious to everyone who stopped to examine what Plato says. It remains a mystery to him that Plato can continue to be regarded by some as "a great Philosopher." In much of what Jefferson says here he seems to be backed up by Adams, who reports about his own study of "all [of Plato's] Work" some thirty years before, "My disappointment was very great, my Astonishment was greater and my disgust was shocking."

IX

Central to Jefferson's critique of Plato is the observation that he is "one of the race of genuine Sophists." Is this the peculiarly democratic response to serious philosophic thought? Or is it simply the modern response? Is all this what comes from being too practical (and hence truly impractical) in one's orientation? In any event, the modern intellectual knows that morality is not based upon reason; rather, it is based upon a moral sense (or conscience). The principal

115

English influences here seem to be Francis Bacon, David Hume, and Adam Smith, buttressed in critical respects by Jean-Jacques Rousseau.

For Athenian democrats, Socrates too was a sophist, whatever they thought of the more discreet Plato. That is, Socrates appeared to many Athenians to be much like the itinerant sophists. In Aristophanes' *Clouds,* for example, Socrates is portrayed as prepared to train a student to become a sophist—and, as such, to be able to avoid having to abide by the laws of the city. Consider also how Socrates has to defend himself in Plato's *Apology* and *Crito.* Jefferson spoke much more kindly of Socrates than he did of Plato—but he did not have to endure Socrates as a critic of his city and of American politicians and their democratic policies.[132]

What is there about sophistry that is particularly troublesome? Sophists are essentially outsiders, even when they are native born. They undermine the political integrity of the community, caring more for their own advancement than for the concerns of patriotic citizens. Since they care more for success and self-interest than for truth or the common good, they resort to arguments that are deeply flawed, however persuasive they may appear and however appealing they may be in some circumstances. In a sense, Jefferson reasons back to the sophistry of Plato by finding him guilty of using arguments that are far less conclusive than they are made out to be in the dialogue.

Jefferson does not seem to be sure whether Plato himself is aware of how flawed his arguments are. But perhaps that is the way sophists are: there must be some arguments that they depend upon, to guide them in their way of life, which they themselves do not appreciate the limitations of.

X

Jefferson, partly in order to account for the Platonic reputation, turns to a critique of the serious practical consequences of the general respect for Plato in the Western World. The allure of his style aside, Plato survives in large part (according to Jefferson) because "of the adoption and incorporation of his whimsies into the body of artificial Christianity." That is, it is suspicious for Jefferson that institutional Christianity finds Plato useful.[133] He does not say here how the Christians who used Plato really understood him.

This former President's suspicion of, if not hostility toward, institutionalized religion remained with him to the very end. (It may be found in abundance as well among intellectuals down to our day.) Thus Jefferson, in the last fortnight of his life, could still inveigh against "monkish ignorance and superstition,"[134] reflecting thereby the enduring influence upon him of the Enlightenment. He had long believed that a priest-ridden people could not maintain free government.[135] He did not tend to see organized religion as an aid to good government, challenging the supposition of some legal scholars of his day that "Christianity is part and parcel of the laws of England."[136] That Plato could be used the way he was by organized religion is, for Jefferson, both revealing and disturbing.

Adams does not fully share Jefferson's suspicion of organized religion, however much he too complains of the difficulty if not even the uselessness of the Platonic texts. Although he was prepared to grant the evils of the Roman Catholic Church that Jefferson referred to, he warns against the dangers of atheism.[137] Certainly, Adams is more respectful than Jefferson about the contribution that a proper Christianity can make to an effective political order.[138]

Has the modern intellectual's principled disavowal of religion, in the now-fashionable Jeffersonian mode, meant in effect that the more vital religious movements in this Country tend more and more to be dominated by passions that are not subject to the discipline of educated men and women who are incidentally adept in politics? The British situation still seems significantly different with respect to these matters.

XI

"The Christian priesthood," Jefferson argues, ". . . saw, in the mysticisms of Plato, materials with which they might build up an artificial system which might, from its indistinctness, admit everlasting controversy, give employment for their order, and introduce it to profit, power and pre-eminence." Thus, he believes, the obscurities of Plato could provide Churchmen personal advantages that the simple truths of Jesus could not. What makes Plato particularly attractive to Churchmen is that "nonsense can never be explained."[139] This means that there is no end to the mystery and speculation that self-serving religionists can exploit.

When Jefferson dealt with such matters he emphasized the motives of enterprising men in such a way as to rely primarily (if not exclusively) upon the low instead of the high. Whatever elevation that there may be in Plato's work cannot be seen by Jefferson and his disciples for what it is. Moderns have become accustomed, instead, to materialistic, or realistic, accounts of personalities and events. (See, on the proper relation between the high and the low, the observation by Leo Strauss that is included among the epigraphs for my Commentary on the Constitution of 1787.)

XII

Jefferson singles out, among what he considered the many dubious arguments of Plato, the case that is made in the dialogues for the immortality of the soul. He seems to be concerned about this in our 1814 letter not so much for what is said about immortality in the *Republic* (which is relatively little) but rather for the use made of this teaching (from other dialogues) by Christianity.[140]

We have noticed that Jefferson does not investigate what the intelligent and sober-minded Cicero saw in Plato. We move somewhat beyond the conventional reading of Plato by noticing that Jefferson does not consider what Plato himself believed in Socrates' arguments about such matters as the immortality of the individual soul. That is, Jefferson does not consider what it would mean if Plato (or, for that matter, Socrates) recognized (and indicated that he recognized) the limitations of (some, not all of) the critical arguments that are made in the dialogues. This bears upon whether moderns are really able to read the most serious writers of antiquity, even those writers who continue to be widely respected. This general disability comes down to our day, and not only among those interested primarily in politics.

Adams and Jefferson seem to be agreed that the thoughtful man should not be concerned about the immortality of his soul, certainly not if he has conducted himself justly. Nor, they are agreed, is total oblivion to be feared.[141] These calm, indeed noble, responses by them to the prospect of death find considerable support in the

Platonic dialogues, even as they have been traditionally understood, as well as in orthodox Christianity.

XIII

Jefferson was thankful that Plato's great influence on religion had not been matched by a like influence on social policy. He considered Plato's opinions about popular government to be politically harmful and believed it was fortunate that they did not catch on. Particularly to be guarded against is the provocative emphasis in the *Republic* upon the community of wives and children. (This is one of several outrageous features on the surface of the dialogue against which spirited politicians may naturally rebel.)

Adams is, here as elsewhere, somewhat more astute than Jefferson about the subtleties of ancient thought. Although he could be as critical as Jefferson of any seeming endorsement by Plato of a community of wives and children, he could also see this measure, however questionable, as a way of preventing the perpetuation of a system of crippling family privileges. (Jefferson, in his time, had worked to discredit primogeniture. His efforts no doubt seemed outrageous to some.) We, on the other hand, must wonder why neither Adams nor Jefferson took issue with Plato on the matters that modern democrats are usually troubled by, such as the reliance in the *Republic* upon a philosopher-king, the resort to various tyrannical-seeming institutions (including censorship), and the recourse to noble lies.[142]

Perhaps critical to the Adams-Jefferson dismissal of Plato and classical political philosophy is the accepted opinion of their own time that, as Adams put it, "Government has never been much studied by Mankind. But their Attention has been drawn to it, in the latter part of the last century and the beginning of this, more than at any former Period." This had led to "the vast Variety of experiments" in constitution-making that had been unprecedented and instructive. In these matters, it seems, the ancients had become obsolete, or so Americans could easily come to believe in the early nineteenth century once their new national constitution had taken hold. Americans were reinforced in these beliefs by the teachings of Hume, Smith, and others that ancient political life, continually torn by deadly faction and destructive wars, could not be relied upon to supply the conditions of security that make for enduring happiness. Thomas Jefferson's position with respect to these and related matters (including the vicious religious wars of then-recent centuries) was probably so American as to be compatible with that of such of his political rivals as Alexander Hamilton and Gouverneur Morris, as well as John Adams.

XIV

It may be vital to Jefferson's approach here that Plato be understood as having deceived his readers about Socrates. Socrates, Jefferson says, "had reason indeed to complain of the misrepresentations of Plato; for in truth his dialogues are libels on Socrates." Xenophon, for example, is regarded by Jefferson as a more reliable guide to the historical Socrates.[143]

Even so, the extensive distortions imposed with respect to Socrates by Plato were, according to Jefferson, exceeded by organized religion's distortions of the life and teachings of Jesus. This is a theme that Jefferson takes up again and again in his correspondence. He, as a rationalist, catalogues elsewhere what he considers the questionable doctrines engrafted upon the more reliable accounts discernible in the Bible of the historical Jesus.[144]

Jefferson is convinced that the discerning reader can detect beneath the surface of documents such as dialogues and gospels the simple, goodhearted men (Socrates and Jesus) who had inspired those documents. Does not this Jeffersonian conviction fail to appreciate how great and complex such men can be? This seems to go along with a failure to appreciate how difficult a serious reading of the most challenging works of the mind can be. The subtlety and playfulness, and hence the true seriousness, of a Plato or a Socrates (to say nothing of Jesus) are not apt to be noticed or given sufficient weight by the intellectual too impressed with his own enlightenment.

Is this a peculiarly modern tendency, reducing things as much as possible to a low, if not the lowest, common denominator? Or is this inherent to those of democratic inclinations, ancient as well as modern?

XV

Jefferson moves in his July 5, 1814, letter from a condemnation of Plato to a concern for the education of his day, especially because the young and others are being misled about Socrates, Jesus, and the like. Professional educators, he believes, have an interest in exaggerating the intricacies of Plato, and professional Churchmen have an interest in keeping people in thrall.

Furthermore, Jefferson complains, the attitudes and activities of too many young people of the time (1814) leave much to be desired. They are hardly serious about education. In fact, he reports, they are not much inclined toward formal education at all; they want to be completely self-sufficient; they resist being disciplined by any authority. (Are they attempting to imitate, albeit at a lower level, Jefferson's own approach to the ancient teachers in that they too intend to be independent?)

Observations of this kind about education later found full expression for Jefferson in the founding of the University of Virginia. The emphasis there also tends to be materialistic and utilitarian, albeit on a high level. For one thing, there seems to be little room in his curriculum for serious philosophy of the kind represented by Plato and Aristotle.

The arguments used by Jefferson to replace ancient book learning (except for history, logic, and rhetoric, and perhaps drama and poetry) with other, more modern, disciplines may have contributed to the already-developing American suspicion of book learning as such, something that Mark Twain could have great fun with a half-century later. One sees again and again down to our day that humane letters are squeezed out of curricula in this Country, and this by people of good intentions (teachers, benefactors, administrators, and students alike) who consider themselves quite practical.

All this may reflect the growing deference among us to excessive individualism and an increasing alienation from community, whether the community be the political community of one's own time or the community of learned men and women across the centuries. One consequence of this recourse to individualism is the widespread hostility among us toward any effort to legislate morality—that is, toward the effort by any community (religious as well as political) to insist upon the development and preservation of those opinions about right and wrong that routine law-abidingness and dedication to the common good usually presuppose.

The American Founders' critique of ancient political thought, even if for the sake of sound politics, may have contributed to a subversion among us of serious political thought and thereby of the political order itself.

XVI

Jefferson, Adams, and their fellows were political men. They seem, not unnaturally, to have been moved more by the spirited element in the soul than by the erotic. Perhaps this contributed to their inability to read Plato properly. Their misreading can help us to see Plato better—to see not only the importance for him of the erotic (however austere it should be), but also the secondary status (however significant) of the political and hence spiritedness even in such a civic-minded dialogue as the *Republic*. (Here, too, we may have moved somewhat beyond the conventional reading of Plato. I return, at the end of this Commentary, to questions about the proper place of the erotic in our life.)

Our concern in this lecture has not been so much with the opinions and education of Jefferson and Adams as with their influence and even more the influence of their generation upon the education and opinions of their successors. Jefferson's own openness to and personal reliance upon some of the classics is testified to by his repeated recourse to them in his old age, such as is reported in an 1819 letter: "My business is to beguile the wearisomeness of declining life, as I endeavor to do by the delights of classical reading and of mathematical truths, and by the consolations of a sound philosophy, equally indifferent to hope and fear."[145] Here, as elsewhere, the practice (including the state papers) of this great man was sounder than the preaching in some of his private correspondence.

We find in the American Founders competent, liberty-loving, political men who are distinguished by their dedication to the proposition that all men are created equal. This authoritative doctrine, which is at least in part attributable among us to Biblical influences, is grounded, to some extent, in nature. But does it not at the same time tend to ignore aspects of nature, and not only because of the widely heralded conquest of nature that is looked to as a means of making all mankind the beneficiaries of the resources available to be wrested from the sun and the earth?[146]

To the extent that nature seems, for Jefferson, more to be found in matter than in ideas, Plato should be suspected by him, especially since Plato's ideas are regarded by Jefferson as undisciplined and subject to abuse by conniving men. Perhaps no single topic is in as much need of serious examination today by thoughtful students of politics, as well as of philosophy, as is the topic of the nature of nature.

A proper place for Americans to begin such an inquiry is the Declaration of Independence. (See, for example, Section VII of Lecture No. 2 of my Commentary on the Constitution of 1787.) Not only should the Declaration's "created equal" language be examined, but also its teachings about inalienable rights. A consideration of what our venerable right of revolution implies about standards of right and wrong, of good and bad, should be vital to this inquiry. These standards do not depend upon what governments happen to demand from time to time. Nor do these standards look to chance personal preferences alone. Shakespeare continues to be instructive in these matters, bringing Biblical doctrines and classical thought together for us in an engaging and yet responsible manner.

XVII

Should one be drawn, as some of us are inclined to be, to both the *Apology* of Socrates and the Declaration of Independence? That question cannot be fully answered until one has examined both the Declaration and the *Apology* with the care that they invite, require, and deserve. Does not the Declaration itself reflect more of ancient yearnings than Jefferson himself recognized?

Jefferson recalled in 1825 that he had, upon drafting the Declaration, "intended [it] to be an expression of the American mind," drawing upon the books of Aristotle, Cicero, John Locke, and Algernon Sidney.[147] What, we may well wonder, did Jefferson get from Aristotle? And what, we may also wonder, did he consider the significance of the fact that Aristotle was one of Plato's greatest students (another was Cicero), a student who always spoke about Plato with great respect even when he seemed most to differ from him? (Some of Aristotle's criticisms of Plato are echoed in Jefferson— but a Jefferson who could not be, perhaps did not want to be, the philosopher that Aristotle was.)

Jefferson's draft of the Declaration, we should remember, was reviewed carefully and altered considerably by the Continental Congress. Even Jefferson's original version had been written with the American people in view, much more so than his private letters.[148] A deference to Anglo-American constitutional history is also evident in the Declaration. By and large, we have noticed, Jefferson was sounder in his public statements and public actions than in his private—and it was that public record (of Jefferson as dedicated citizen, not of Jefferson as speculative intellectual) that people such as Abraham Lincoln built upon and celebrated.

Thus, it can again be said, the Declaration of Independence reflects an awareness among the American people of that which is by nature right. Indeed, it can be argued that "the principal author of the Declaration of Independence" is not Jefferson but rather the American people. Old-fashioned notions about that which is by nature right, influenced it seems by a sense of morality reaffirmed and refined by long-established religious influences, helped shape the Declaration of Independence in ways that Plato and Aristotle can perhaps help us notice. Lincoln, for one, could see in the Declaration's insistence upon equality the basis for an eventual repudiation of slavery in the name of justice. Would mid-nineteenth-century Americans and their twentieth-century successors, better grounded in the ancient authors and less moved either by religious passion or by "anti-theological ire" (another form of religious passion?), have been able to deal more prudently than they did with the institutions and consequences both of chattel slavery and of radical individualism that have seriously threatened constitutional government in the United States?[149] This radical individualism (for which the self-centered "hero" of John Milton's *Paradise Lost* can be considered the patron saint) finds expression in the recourse among us to more and more privately held firearms and to less and less respect for community authority except, sometimes, for the making of war and the execution of murderers. Both serious education and the legislation of morality, as well as truly effective self-preservation, are thereby put at risk. An extreme form of this individualism found expression in the Southern insistence in 1860–1865 upon the sanctity of the right to continue to enjoy chattel slavery, to which we now turn.

10. The Confederate Constitution of 1861

I

The most drastic attempt thus far to "amend" the Constitution of 1787 was made by the leaders of the Southern Secessionist movement in 1860–1865.[150] Even so, the greatest tribute ever paid to the Constitution since the Founding Period may have been in 1861 by the framers of the Constitution of the Confederate States of America.

This 1861 tribute took two forms. First, there was the considerable reliance upon the 1787 Constitution in framing the Confederate Constitution. More than 90 percent of the 1861 Constitution repeats, with much the same ordering and even numbering of parts, what had been done in the Constitution of 1787 and in its Bill of Rights of 1791. The extensiveness of the 1861 imitation is illustrated by its provision for a seat of government:

> The Congress shall have power . . . To exercise exclusive legislation, in all cases whatsoever, over such district (not exceeding ten miles square) as may, by cession of one or more States [1787: "of particular States"] and the acceptance of Congress, become the seat of the government of the Confederate States [1787: "of the United States"] . . .[151]

I find it intriguing that such a provision, with its specification of "ten miles square," should be regarded as precisely what was still needed three-quarters of a century after the Constitution of 1787 was first drafted—and this despite the fact that part of the Federal District originally ceded to the United States (the part south of the Potomac) had been retroceded to Virginia.

The considerable, if not slavish, reliance in 1861 upon the 1787 Constitution is even more remarkable in light of the determination of the Confederate States to separate themselves from the government, if not from the way of life, called forth (whether or not properly) by the earlier Constitution. We come now to the second form that the 1861 tribute took: the pervasive effort by the Secessionists to frame the new Constitution so as to avoid the kind of central government against which they were rebelling. Was it not tacitly conceded by the 1861 changes made in the 1787 Constitution that without such modifications the new Confederate government might have been empowered to act, or at least might have been tempted on occasion to act, like the old government?

Light can be shed on our Constitutional processes by noticing some of the shifts made in 1861 by the Confederates when they undertook to rewrite a constitution, even as they justified their imitativeness by arguing that the South was the section trying to preserve the original Constitution. There can be illuminated thereby both the Constitution of 1787 and the amendments to it since the Civil War.

II

The Confederate Constitution implicitly concedes the plausibility of the interpretation of the 1787 Constitution that had been advanced by such Nationalists as George Washington, the young James Madison, Alexander Hamilton, John Marshall, Daniel Webster, Andrew Jackson, Henry Clay, Abraham Lincoln, and perhaps the young John Calhoun. The 1861 Confederate Constitution provides, in effect, a commentary upon the United States Constitution, as well as a challenge to its principles.

Several matters that had been controversial during the preceding half-century were disposed of in the 1861 Constitution. It was evidently understood that it would not be enough to count on new, and more congenial, interpretations of the constitutional provisions that had been so troublesome. That was too risky—and besides, there would always be some who would occasionally find it in their interest to advance the old interpretations. For example, the 1861 Constitution provides, "The principal officer in each of the executive departments, and all persons connected with the diplomatic service, may be removed from office at the pleasure of the President." Such a provision in the Constitution of 1787 might have

126

strengthened the position of President Andrew Johnson in 1868. Those determined to impeach him would have had to look for other offenses to allege. (The provision in Section 3 of Article II of the 1861 Constitution goes on to lay the groundwork for what we now know as the civil service.)

The Nationalists, once the Constitution of 1787 was ratified, had made much of those implied powers of Congress that some States' Rights people had sought to forestall in 1789 by trying to add *expressly* to the Tenth Amendment. It may seem somewhat surprising, therefore, that the Confederate framers did not say in their 1861 Constitution that their Congress would have only the powers *expressly* delegated to it. But it must have been recognized that to do so would have made it difficult for the new Confederate government to do effectively the things it was supposed to do. The 1861 framers seem to have believed that it was better to spell out restrictions upon their Confederate government instead of eliminating its implied powers altogether. It would have been too unsettling and crippling otherwise.

Some restrictions upon the Confederate government take the form of two-thirds-vote requirements for designated Congressional actions, especially with respect to certain revenue bills and certain appropriations, a dubious approach promoted by some today.

III

Various features in the 1861 Constitution reflect a radically different approach to the governance of a country from that found in the 1787 Constitution. This difference bears upon the controversy during the first half of the nineteenth century over whether tariffs should be used to promote domestic manufactures. Such promotion is forbidden by the 1861 Constitution, which provides (in Section 8 of Article I) that no "duties or taxes on importations from foreign nations [shall] be laid to promote or foster any branch of industry." Also forbidden is the allocation of federal funds for "any internal improvement intended to facilitate commerce." Even the Post Office had to become self-supporting within two years. These provisions indicate how far the Southern suspicion of commerce and the fear of subsidies for special or regional interests went.

The critical role of the States is emphasized in the 1861 Constitution. This shift in emphasis may be seen at the very beginning, with the Preamble announcing that this new Constitution is the deed of "We, the people of the Confederate States, each State acting in its sovereign and independent character . . ." It is a Constitution that aims not at the "more perfect Union" sought in the 1787 Preamble, but at a "permanent federal government." It is also a Constitution that is to be amended by the States, with the Congress having merely a ministerial part to play in that process. Another change from the old way is what is done with the Ninth Amendment of 1791: "the people" referred to there become (in Article VI of the 1861 Constitution) "the people of the several States." (A similar change is made when the 1791 Tenth Amendment is incorporated in Article VI of the 1861 Constitution.) We are given to understand, again and again, that there is to be no recognition this time around of the people of the country at large.

It is the States that matter, so much so that five (out of the by-then more than thirty American States) sufficed to form the new country in 1861—whereas nine (out of the original thirteen) had been required in 1787. (Only seven States had declared themselves seceded by the time the Confederate Constitution was drafted in March 1861.) These States, unlike under the 1787 Constitution, are permitted to interfere somewhat with movements between States; they can emit bills of credit; they can combine (without Congressional approval, it seems) to improve the navigation upon any river which "divides or flows through two or more States." Perhaps nothing indicates the enhanced status of the States under the 1861 Constitution more than the provision in Section 2 of its Article I that "any judicial or other Federal officer, resident and acting solely within the limits of any State, may be impeached by a vote of two-thirds of both branches of the Legislature [of that State]," which impeachment would then be tried by the Confederate Senate.

IV

Intimately related to the enhanced status of the States under the Confederate Constitution is its heightened and unembarrassed protection for slavery. If State sovereignty is attractive as a form of local government, a citizen's power over his slaves may bring effective local government a significant step closer to home. Such power may even be seen as a form of freedom of expression in the service of radical individualism.

The Confederate constitutional protection for slavery includes keeping the new Congress from interfering with the introduction of slavery into the territories of the Confederacy. The 1861 Constitution thus makes explicit provision for the position that had been taken four years earlier by the United States Supreme Court in the controversial *Dred Scott Case*.[152] Was it implicitly conceded, by the 1861 Constitution's doing this, that the ruling in *Dred Scott* was not required either by the Constitution of 1787 or by its Fifth Amendment?

On the other hand, the 1861 Constitution not only prohibits the international slave trade but even makes it a duty of Congress to suppress it. Is this done in such a way as to suggest that this power of suppression is not to be considered as an aspect of a broad commerce power in Congress, thereby protecting the domestic (including the "interstate") slave trade from any regulation by the new federal government?

The institution of slavery is recognized by the Confederate Constitution as vital to the new regime. So much is this so that the student of that constitution is obliged to ask whether the States in the Confederacy could on their own forbid slavery within their respective borders.[153] Whatever any State may do, it seems, the slave owner is entitled to move through and sojourn in every State in the Confederacy with his slaves.

V

Several differences between the system of 1787 and that of 1861 should be emphasized. The Confederacy depends far more upon the States, far less upon a national people (even in the South), than does the United States. Local government is made much more of, and so is property, especially property in slaves (which is, I have suggested, a peculiarly intensive form of home rule). At the same time, the Confederacy is less open to commerce than the 1787 regime. Certainly, the new federal government is severely restricted as to what it may do to encourage manufactures and trade. At the heart of these differences may be quite different notions about what human nature and a good life are like.

Government itself seems suspect in the 1861 Constitution; the further government is from local control, the more suspect it seems to be. This suspicion is accompanied by a determined sympathy for slavery as an institution. That kind of government is acceptable, despite its severity. All this means, in effect, that a general equality is sacrificed to the particular liberty of a privileged few, especially the major slaveholders in the South.

Two paths lay before the American people in 1860. One path led back to the Articles of Confederation and considerable State sovereignty, perhaps to more local sovereignty than had ever existed in North America before 1787. Progress for the Confederacy was a dubious prospect, especially if it should depend upon a concerted national effort. Abraham Lincoln (as we will see in Lecture No. 11 of this Commentary) could disparage the Confederate deference to the liberty of local self-determination as an invitation to anarchy.

The other path that lay before the American people in 1860 led (by way of the Civil War, if not by negotiations, and the Emancipation Proclamation) to the Thirteenth, Fourteenth, and Fifteenth Amendments with their abolition of slavery and their insistence upon a general equality, all at the expense of State sovereignty. The promise of the Declaration of Independence with respect to the elimination of tyranny was thereby reaffirmed.

This second path, in taking its bearings by the Declaration of Independence, assumes that the United States is older than the States. The Country is seen as having begun in 1776 (if not in 1774 or even earlier), not in 1787 or in 1789. For example, it is apparent that Lincoln's "Four score and seven years" at Gettysburg looks back to the issuance of the Declaration as the founding constitutional act for Americans.

To regard the Declaration of Independence as at the foundation of the American constitutional system is to ratify the grand opinion about human nature enshrined there. It is an opinion very much open to natural-right teachings, so much so that the Declaration of Independence can speak of "the Laws of Nature and of Nature's God." Somewhat more Biblical, and hence perhaps more conventionally pious, may be the Confederate Constitution, which adds to its Preamble not only an insistence upon "each State acting in its sovereign and independent character," but also an invocation of "the favor and guidance of Almighty God," something about which the Constitution of 1787 is silent.

Is it not true down to our day that an openness to State sovereignty and an openness to Biblical religion tend to go together? On the other hand, does not a reverence for the Country at large, as distinguished from a love of one's own, tend to replace piety as ordinarily understood? In this and other ways we may have much to learn from the Confederate Constitution of 1861.

VI

Among the things to consider in that 1861 Constitution, for what they may teach us about constitutional reforms in our day, are various experiments in government.

It is provided that "Congress may, by law, grant to the principal officer in each of the Executive Departments a seat upon the floor of either House, with the privilege of discussing any measures appertaining to his department." It is also provided that the President is to have a six-year term and that he is not eligible to succeed himself. It is provided as well that the President should be able to disapprove of particular items in any appropriations bill passed by Congress. Perhaps related to this is the insistence that every law should "relate to but one subject, and that shall be expressed in the title."[154]

Each of these experiments has its advocates today. Other changes of this character in the 1861 Constitution are less controversial, being merely efforts to clarify points in the 1787 Constitution. These include provisions with respect to recess appointments, the acquisition of new territories (the Louisiana Purchase problem?), and the shift from "cannot be convened" to "when . . . not in session."

Still other changes reflect changes in North America, as may be seen in raising the minimum electorate for a member of the House of Representatives from thirty thousand to fifty thousand. But it is odd that the twenty dollar figure is left undisturbed as the jurisdictional amount for a right to trial by jury in suits at common law.

VII

Any proposed reforms of the Constitution of 1787 should take into account both the purposes of existing provisions and the likely consequences of any changes. An understanding of the Constitution as a whole is obviously required if changes are to be prudent.

How well, we must wonder, did the Confederate framers of 1861 understand the Constitution of 1787? They made it explicit that the two-thirds required to expel a member of a House of Congress is "two-thirds of the whole number." But this is implicit in the original Constitution—and making this change here may have had the unintended effect of changing the meaning of other passages (retained unaltered) where the whole number of members had been similarly implied.

Another departure from the constitutional arrangement that the Confederate framers inherited may be seen in what they did with Amendments I through VIII of the Bill of Rights, which had been appended since 1791 to the United States Constitution. All of these amendments were placed in Article I, Section 9, of the Confederate Constitution, that section in which various restraints upon Congress are found. The Ninth and Tenth Amendments were placed in Article VI.

It is instructive that virtually no change is made in the wording of the first eight amendments upon their incorporation into the Confederate Constitution. Does this reflect the dependence of those and like rights upon historic associations and traditional formulations? This reminds us of the further question whether it had ever been necessary to spell out in 1787–1791 the rights now found in the Bill of Rights.

Both history and tradition ultimately depend for their authority upon the natural tendency of human beings to identify the old with the good. This in turn should remind us of the primacy of the natural—and of that which is by nature right. Is it not here that the Confederate Constitution, with its unfortunate deference to slavery, is most vulnerable? However much was made by Southern Secessionists of liberty, they did not want to see it extended to slaves exercising their natural right of revolution in order to secure the liberty of which they had been systematically deprived.

VIII

We have seen in these lectures what silences and implications may mean in a constitutional document. An instance of a revealing, indeed a most expressive, silence is the elimination from the 1861 Constitution of both of the references to the general welfare found in the 1787 Constitution (in its Preamble and in Article I, Section 8). Does not that elimination in 1861 concede that that phrase, as found in the 1787 Constitution, is quite potent? Should not this be taken into account by those today who make much of "original intent" in the mistaken expectation that this means a weaker national government?

Also revealing is the compatibility assumed between, on the one hand, the permanent system of slavery evidently envisioned by the Confederate Constitution and, on the other hand, the reaffirmation in that Constitution of the Bill of Rights, the Republican Form of Government Guarantee, and the invocation of the Blessings of Liberty. Is not the assumption of such compatibility indicative of fatal flaws in the Confederate Constitution? Does not all this remind us of the extent to which the accommodations to slavery in the Constitution of 1787 were meant to be temporary, a reluctant compromise that would permit the United States so to develop as to make slavery eventually impossible in North America? The Confederate attempt at Secession in 1860–1865 testifies to their opinion that the national endeavor to eliminate slavery pursuant to the Constitution of 1787 was dangerously far advanced.

IX

The significance of silences and implications in a Constitution reminds us also, if reminder we need, of the importance of words. The changes in terms used in the Confederate Constitution are revealing.

The framers of 1861 were careful to change all references in the 1787 Constitution that suggested the existence of a country prior to or superior in decisive respects to the States. Thus *Union* became *Confederation, United States* became *Confederate States,* and "a more perfect Union" became "a permanent federal government."[155]

The most revealing changes made by the 1861 framers had to do, of course, with slavery. We have noticed the protections extended to slavery, far more than had been available in the 1787 Constitution. But even more significant, perhaps, is the insistence in 1861 upon changing the 1787 usage ("all other Persons") to "all slaves." The Framers of 1787 had steadfastly refused to use in their Constitution the terms *slave* and *slavery*. This was explained, not only by Lincoln in the 1850s but also by various of the Framers in the 1780s, as a reflection of the confident hope that slavery would be eventually eliminated. The awkward circumlocutions when slavery was referred to in 1787 exposed the dubiousness of the institution being accommodated, something that was recognized in the 1780s as much by leading Southerners as by Northerners.

Southern statesmen could, in the late eighteenth century, routinely speak of slavery as a necessary evil, an institution that they could hope was in the course of ultimate extinction. It was much later (well into the nineteenth century) before their successors were moved, in their desperation, to speak routinely of slavery as a positive good. So desperate did they become that they felt obliged by 1861 to treat slavery as something they could not live without, when in fact it had become something that they as decent people could not really live with, especially since the humanity of the slaves had become all too evident once those Africans had adopted the English language and American ways (including Christianity).

Thus, to sum up this point, one particularly revealing difference between the Constitution of the United States and the Constitution of the Confederate States is that one constitution never used the terms *slave* and *slavery* until the time had come, at the end of the Civil War, to outlaw the institution for all time, while the other constitution freely (even defiantly and hence shamelessly) used these terms from its outset.[156]

What was done by Southerners in 1861 stands as a dramatic tribute to what was done by Southerners and Northerners alike in crafting not only the Constitution of 1787 but also the prophetic Northwest Ordinance (also of 1787) which laid down the terms upon which new States were to enter and to help redeem the Union.

11. The Emancipation Proclamation of 1862–1863[157]

I

I ventured to suggest in my last lecture that the greatest tribute ever paid to the Constitution of 1787 since the Founding Period may have been in 1861 by the framers of the Constitution of the Confederate States of America. Another great tribute—but one that was not perverse in some of its implications—was the measured response by Abraham Lincoln to the Great Rebellion. His Emancipation Proclamation was revealing of his constitutional understanding and political judgment, even as it opened the way to substantial political developments and constitutional amendments for more than a century thereafter.

There are, in responses to men singled out for our attention as Lincoln is, two tendencies among articulate citizens. One tendency is virtually to deify them as people somehow outside and above the Constitution. The other tendency is to denigrate them, even (as in the case of Lincoln) to dismiss them as "racists" and the like. Thus, one writer observed:

> However admirable the character of the American Constitution, it [is not] the most admirable expression of the regime. The Constitution is the highest American thing, only if one tries to understand the high in the light of the low. It is high because men are not angels, and because we do not have angels to govern us. Its strength lies in its ability to connect the interest of the man with the duty of the place. But the Constitution, in deference to man's nonangelic nature, made certain compromises with slavery. And partly because of those compromises, it dissolved in the presence of a great crisis. The man—or

the character of the man—who bore the nation through that crisis, seem[s] to me . . . the highest thing in the American regime.[158]

Thus, also, another writer (in the *Chicago Tribune,* taking issue with an editorial therein on President Lincoln) observed:

A close look at Lincoln, the Civil War, slavery, and the political, social, and economic movements and moral climate of that era convinces me that Lincoln should not be credited with freeing the slaves. Rather he was clearly forced by his critics and the urgencies of war to end chattel slavery or go down in defeat. No thinking person objects to Lincoln's adept use of the art of compromise. What I, as a black descendant of slaves, cannot escape is the fact that he also used that talent to delay as long as he could the recognition of a black human as something other than a piece of property.

This columnist added:

[Lincoln's] insistence that a slave was a property first and a person second resulted in the great Lincoln plan: the freeing of slaves thru (1) Southern state initiative (slavery forever); (2) government payment for slaves to be freed; (3) gradual emancipation (to be complete around the year 1900); (4) government aid to slave states suffering from loss of slaves (more sympathy for the criminal than for the victim); and (5) colonization of blacks out of the United States. To those unsung heroes who didn't permit Lincoln to "push thru his program," this one descendant of slaves belatedly thanks you.[159]

A defense of Lincoln (by the *Tribune* editorial, referred to in the column just quoted) had argued that Lincoln's attitudes and policies should not be judged by "today's standards."[160] Such a defense, however, misses the point. Does it not imply that we know better than Lincoln did what should have been done, that our consciences or our understanding or our feelings are somehow superior to his?

It is not only we who believe ourselves in a superior position. Many, perhaps most, of Lincoln's fellow citizens believed at one time or another that their judgments and consciences were also better than his. (At times, all they would give him credit for was a rough honesty, or sincerity.) Even his Secretary of State, William H. Seward, could observe in 1862 of Lincoln's Emancipation Proclamation policy: "[W]e show our sympathy with slavery by emancipating slaves where we cannot reach them, and holding them in bondage where we can set them free."[161]

But a more prudent assessment of that policy than may be found in most of the writings of either our contemporaries or Lincoln's is suggested by an oration delivered by Frederick Douglass on April 14, 1876, "on the occasion of the unveiling of the Freedmen's Monument [in Washington, D.C.] in memory of Abraham Lincoln." The distinguished former slave argued:

I have said that President Lincoln was a white man, and shared the prejudices common to his countrymen toward the colored race. Looking back to his times and to the condition of his country, we are compelled to admit that this unfriendly feeling on his part may be safely set down as one element of his wonderful success in organizing the loyal American people for the tremendous conflict before them, and bringing them safely through that conflict. His great mission was to accomplish two things: first, to save his country from dismemberment and ruin; and, second, to free his country from the great crime of slavery. To do one or the other, or both, he must have the earnest sympathy and the powerful co-operation of his loyal fellow-countrymen. Without this primary and essential condition to success his efforts must have been vain and utterly fruitless. *Had he put the abolition of slavery before the salvation of the Union, he would have inevitably driven from him a powerful class of the American people and rendered resistance to rebellion impossible.* Viewed from the genuine abolition ground, Mr. Lincoln seemed tardy, cold, dull, and indifferent; but measuring him by the sentiment of his country, a sentiment he was bound as a statesman to consult, he was swift, zealous, radical, and determined. Though Mr. Lincoln shared the prejudices of his white fellow-countrymen against the negro, it is hardly necessary to say that in his heart of hearts he loathed and hated slavery.[162]

Douglass quotes at this point Lincoln's letter of April 4, 1864, "I am naturally anti-slavery. If slavery is not wrong, nothing is wrong. I can not remember when I did not so think, and feel."[163] Whether Lincoln was, in fact, "prejudiced" would depend, first, on what one means by this term; second, on what all the causes were of African slavery; and, third, on what the effects were upon the slaves of their bondage.

Earlier in his 1876 oration, Douglass made an observation about his immediate response to the Emancipation Proclamation, an observation that can provide our point of departure both in considering that Presidential decree and in assessing Lincoln's political judgment:

Can any colored man, or any white man friendly to the freedom of all men, ever forget the night which followed the first day of January, 1863, when the world was to see if Abraham Lincoln would prove to be as good as his word [pledged the preceding September 22]? I shall never forget that memorable night, when in a distant city I waited and watched at a public meeting, with three thousand others not less anxious than myself, for the word of deliverance which we have heard read today. Nor shall I ever forget the outbursts of joy and thanksgiving that rent the air when the lightning [the telegraph] brought to us the emancipation proclamation. In that happy hour we forgot all delay, and forgot all tardiness, forgot that the President had bribed the rebels to lay down their arms by a promise to withhold the bolt which would smite the slave-system with destruction; and we were thenceforward willing to allow the President all the latitude of time, phraseology, *and every honorable device that statesmanship might require* for the achievement of a great and beneficent measure of liberty and progress.[164]

II

It is the statesmanship of Lincoln, as exhibited in the Emancipation Proclamation, with which we will be concerned in this lecture, thereby preparing the way for proper consideration in this Commentary of the Thirteenth, Fourteenth, and Fifteenth Amendments. In order to understand what happened in 1862–1863 and why, we must remind ourselves of the circumstances in which the Proclamation was issued. The first part, the Preliminary Proclamation, was issued September 22, 1862; the second part, the Final Proclamation, was issued January 1, 1863.

The general setting was, of course, the Civil War, the prosecution of which President Lincoln understood as primarily an effort, in accordance with his constitutional duty, to save the Union from unjustified dismemberment. Thus, he observed (in a statement of August 22, 1862, just one month before his issuance of the Preliminary Proclamation—a statement that continues to anger some of his antislavery critics down to our day):

I would save the Union. I would save it the shortest way under the Constitution. The sooner the national authority can be restored; the nearer the Union will be "the Union as it was." If there be those who would not save the Union, unless they could at the same time *save*

138

slavery, I do not agree with them. If there be those who would not save the Union unless they could at the same time *destroy* slavery, I do not agree with them. My paramount object in this struggle *is* to save the Union, and is *not* either to save or to destroy slavery. If I could save the Union without freeing *any* slave I would do it, and if I could save it by freeing *all* the slaves I would do it; and if I could save it by freeing some and leaving others alone I would also do that. What I do about slavery, and the colored race, I do because I believe it helps to save the Union; and what I forbear, I forbear because I do *not* believe it would help to save the Union. I shall do *less* whenever I shall believe what I am doing hurts the cause, and I shall do *more* whenever I shall believe doing more will help the cause.[165]

Lincoln concluded this statement—an open letter to Horace Greeley—with the assurance, "I intend no modification of my oft-expressed *personal* wish that all men every where could be free."[166] It should be noticed that Lincoln's flexibility, in his effort to save the Union, did not include a willingness to *enslave* anyone for that end. He observed on December 6, 1864:

I repeat the declaration made a year ago, that "while I remain in my present position I shall not attempt to retract or modify the emancipation proclamation, nor shall I return to slavery any person who is free by the terms of that proclamation, or by any of the Acts of Congress." If the people should, by whatever mode or means, make it an Executive duty to re-enslave such persons, another, and not I, must be their instrument to perform it.[167]

This suggests the limits of what Lincoln was willing to do or say in the service of "statesmanship."

That is, he was not willing to enslave or to re-enslave anyone, even though he was willing to live with slavery. But we should be clear what "living with slavery" meant for him. It meant that the Union would be preserved, a Union in which slavery would be permitted to continue in those Southern States where it happened to exist at the time Lincoln became President. He did not mean to touch it there but neither did he mean to let it expand into any new territory. Thus, he was a "Free-Soil Man," not an "Abolitionist." But, he also believed, if slavery could be contained, it would wither away—and in such a way as to leave both former slaves and former masters in the best possible condition for living with one another as free men. In the meantime, a South that continued to remain part of the Union could not help but be moderated by Northern opinion and Federal power in what it did to Africans, both at home and abroad.

The abolitionists insisted, "No union with slaveholders." It has been noticed that "[t]he extreme abolitionists, in the supposed purity of their principles, would have abandoned the four million slaves to their fate."[168] The alternative for them, of preserving the Union but destroying slavery, depended upon a successful war effort—and that, it was generally believed, depended upon a united effort on the part of the diverse factions loyal to the Union.

Among those factions were not only the abolitionists—Lincoln figured, no doubt, that they had nowhere else to go—but also Northerners who did not have strong opinions about slavery (but who did care about the Constitution and the Union) and Middle States men who retained both slaves and loyalty to the Constitution. These men of the Middle States were not, despite their slavery institutions, simply bad men; nor for that matter were the Southerners. Lincoln recognized that slavery was essentially a national affliction, that (for the most part) those who were burdened by it would have long since gotten rid of it if they could have seen a way to do so—a way both economically and socially feasible.

In this respect, Lincoln appreciated the long past of the Country and looked ahead to an even longer future. He recognized why one section of the Country was slave and why another was free. He had long hoped so to contain and thereby begin to ease out slavery as to make it possible for two races (both emancipated from the curse of slavery) to live thereafter, whether together or separated, in the best possible way. What was called for, he saw, was neither sentimental moralizing nor bitter recrimination. He was, we have seen, obliged so to conduct the war as not to lose the support of the many men in both the Northern and the Middle States who were, at best, indifferent about slavery. He believed that the goal for which the maximum support could be gathered was that of preserving the Union. Thus, "[f]ighting the war was always secondary to keeping alive the political coalition willing to fight the war."[169]

Once great sacrifices had been made, more could be ventured in explaining how matters truly stood. Once, that is, considerable Northern and Middle States blood had been shed on behalf of the Union, it was possible to direct the attention of the Country to slavery itself. "Slavery was what the rebel states were fighting for, and slavery enabled them to fight for slavery."[170] It had long been recognized by the laws of war that one could deprive an enemy of any property that helped keep him in the field. One could even appropriate such property for one's own use. The slaves were useful, perhaps even essential, property for the Southern war effort. It was on this basis, then, that Lincoln could mobilize Union men to move against Southern slavery, to ally themselves (in effect) with the freedom-seeking slaves held by the rebels.

The Emancipation Proclamation was thus a military fulfillment of the prophecy with which Lincoln had opened his famous "House Divided" speech of June 16, 1858:

> "A house divided against itself cannot stand." I believe this government cannot endure, permanently half *slave* and half *free*. I do not expect the Union to be *dissolved*—I do not expect the house to *fall*—but I *do* expect it will cease to be divided. It will become *all* one thing or *all* the other. Either the *opponents* of slavery, will arrest the further spread of it, and place it where the public mind shall rest in the belief that it is in course of ultimate extinction; or its *advocates* will push it forward, till it shall become alike lawful in *all* the States, *old* as well as *new—North* as well as *South*.[171]

III

Much of what I have said thus far should be generally familiar. Too much originality in such matters would be suspect. No doubt some may be inclined to question the assessment I have been tacitly making about Lincoln's judgment. That assessment is, to state it plainly, that Lincoln seems most impressive in his sure-footedness. He never seemed to err in the principles brought to bear upon the major moves he made in response to the South once he assumed the Presidency.

The mistakes he did make were due not to inadequate principles or to faulty judgment but to mistaken information, and in circumstances where he had to rely upon what was told him. Throughout the war, he was remarkably adept, knowing both what he should want and what he was doing. He was, in short, a model of prudential judgment, or at least as fine a practitioner of such judgment as we have had in government in this Country.

I can best illustrate what I mean—what prudence means in action, and especially in war circumstances (and a civil war, at that, where passions run particularly deep)—by examining in some detail the terms of the two documents which comprise the Emancipation Proclamation. By so doing, we can see as well what the Civil War meant and how it progressed, for the history of that war seems distilled in these documents. Perhaps even more important in the context of this Commentary, we can see how first-class practical reason works, the kind of reason evident in and nurtured by the Constitution of 1787 and its Bill of Rights.

The Emancipation Proclamation, unlike the Declaration of Independence and the Constitution, was in a sense the work of one man—and hence of one mind. It was carefully thought out by Lincoln, with only a few suggestions by his Cabinet added after he revealed to them what he proposed to do. It is, we will see, both bold in its conception and disciplined in its execution, the lawyer's art in its perfection. It is also, I suggest, more American than either the Declaration or the Constitution, in that its author had been fully shaped by the regime established after 1776.[172]

There are in our effort to grasp what Lincoln did both a challenge and an opportunity. There is the opportunity of fully asserting ourselves as citizens, in that we can, at least for the moment, walk with someone who thought as deeply as any American statesman has about the character, aspirations, and deficiencies of our regime. There is also a challenge, in that we are obliged to strive for a degree of seriousness to which we are no longer accustomed. We have become accustomed in our discussions of political things to the exposés and the superficialities of journalism and to the abnormalities and irrationalities of psychology—so much so that it is difficult to avoid either irrelevance or sensationalism. We have to make an effort, therefore, to understand the Emancipation Proclamation. But then, was not the Proclamation issued for the likes of us?

Lincoln challenges us to think; he challenges us to reconstruct the thinking he devoted to the problems he faced. We know that he devoted many hours to the text of the Emancipation Proclamation, especially the preliminary statement of September 22, 1862. If we should be able to work out what he took into account, and why, we can then be assured that we begin to understand the constitutional crisis of the Civil War as an eminently political man could and did.

To take seriously a statesman's carefully expressed thought is, after all, the best tribute we can pay to him. Such an attempt at the most noble imitation is worthy of our greatest efforts if we are to understand who we are, what we aspire to, and why.

IV

It is said that Lincoln issued no statement or argument to support the Emancipation Proclamation. "He let the paper go forth for whatever it might do."[173] But this is not to say that he never discussed it, for in a preparatory Cabinet meeting, he "proceeded to read his Emancipation Proclamation, making remarks on the several parts as he went on, and showing that he had fully considered the whole subject, in all the lights under which it has been presented to him." The discussion of the Proclamation on that occasion, we are told, included "the constitutional question, the war power, the expediency, and the effect of the movement."[174]

It is that discussion in Lincoln's Cabinet which we can, in effect, recreate if we are so minded. We turn first to an examination of the Preliminary Proclamation of September 22, 1862, the entire text of which (along with the entire text of the Final Proclamation of January 1, 1863) is set forth in italics in the course of this lecture.

i

I, Abraham Lincoln, President of the United States of America, and Commander-in-chief of the Army and Navy thereof, do hereby proclaim and declare that hereafter, as heretofore, the war will be prosecuted for the object of practically restoring the constitutional relation between the United States, and each of the states, and the people thereof, in which states that relation is, or may be suspended, or disturbed.

This is the first of Lincoln's proclamations as President that opens with his name and titles.[175] It is as if he intends to assert from the outset that this statement is especially his doing, that it emanates from his very being—and, insofar as he is a thinking being and this is well thought out, that is so.

This is only the second of his proclamations in which his title as Commander in Chief of the armed forces of the Country is invoked. Such invocation was not customary in Presidential proclamations.[176] We notice in passing the precision in his language: "proclaim and declare that hereafter, as heretofore." Such precision encourages us to expect that what he says throughout may profitably be read with care.

The insistence at the outset upon his status as Commander in Chief anticipates his insistence throughout upon this action as a legitimate war measure. No doubt he thought then what he was to say a year later (August 26, 1863) to a critic of the Proclamation:

> I think the constitution invests its commander-in-chief, with the law of war, in time of war. The most that can be said, if so much, is, that slaves are property. Is there—has there ever been—any question that by the law of war, property, both of enemies and friends, may be taken when needed? And is it not needed whenever taking it, helps us, or hurts the enemy? Armies, the world over, destroy enemies' property when they can not use it; and even destroy their own to keep it from the enemy. Civilized belligerents do all in their power to help themselves or hurt the enemy, except a few things regarded as barbarous or cruel. Among the exceptions are the massacre of vanquished foes, and non-combatants, male and female.[177]

We see in the opening paragraph of the Preliminary Proclamation an insistence as well upon the purpose of this war, that of restoring the constitutional relations among the States. An antislavery crusade would have been far more questionable than an effort to save the Union—and that was, in many quarters, questionable enough. We should remember that even today more citizens in this Country are in favor of "law and order" than are in favor of "racial justice" or "military justice" or "class justice."

For most citizens, justice is what the law prescribes. They cannot be depended on habitually to accept much more than that or even to want much more than that. Would "much more than that" be for them an unwelcome freedom? Does not Lincoln's approach recognize the limits of public opinion? Does it not recognize that respect for law is more "knowable" than respect for justice?

But, one is obliged to ask, are there not various kinds of constitutions (or master-laws)? Should this one have been established in the first place? That is, should the bargain ever have been made, that "constitutional relation" which permitted the States to retain jurisdiction over slaves? Was that bargain so immoral that it should never have been expected to hold? Still, what would have happened if the Southern States had been allowed to depart in peace, whether in 1787 or 1861? Had not the Union by 1861 served better the "Free

States," permitting them to grow to a stronger position in relation to the "Slave States" than they had been in the beginning?

Granted that the Union is to be preserved, upon what terms can it best be defended? Cannot people more readily be led to see that their interest is served by a constitutional regime (by orderly government, a continent-wide market, an absence of threatening neighbors) than it is served by a free regime (especially when the freedom yet to be sacrificed for is that of others, not obviously their own)? On the other hand, once the crusade for freedom is launched, it is much more difficult to control. Passions are much more likely to rage unchecked. Constitutionalism, however, has a sense of restraint built right into it.[178]

Besides, blatantly to attack slavery is to attack property rights and perhaps even the principle of property. Where is the stopping point once one starts down that path? Today, slaveholders; tomorrow, the wealthy? And the day after, anyone of talent or distinction? Is it not sensed by men and women of affairs that property depends on the arbitrary, on the accidental, on peculiarly local circumstances? Does it not also depend, at least in part, on the bargains that happen to be made from time to time?

Lincoln must insist upon the object of "restoring the constitutional relation" as critical, especially in light of what he is about to do. Cannot he effectively do what he is about to do partly because he has insisted heretofore on the proper constitutional relation, on constitutional technicalities and niceties?[179] Does one adhere scrupulously to a constitution and the law (as generally understood) in order to be able to rise above them at the propitious moment, thereby leading one's people to a higher or more solid constitutional plateau than they are accustomed to?

We notice the emphasis upon restoration. Things will go back to what they were—except for the opinion which some had held that secession was constitutionally proper. But full restoration will be impossible once that particular opinion is disavowed, for the status of slavery will never be the same again. Still, the closest the South can come to having the original Constitutional relation restored is by quickly acceding to the terms of the Preliminary Proclamation, thereby not "permitting" Lincoln to declare any slaves emancipated at this time.

We should notice as well that it is not only the South that threatens the Constitutional regime. Thaddeus Stevens, one of the radical abolitionist leaders in Congress, had proclaimed that there was no longer any Constitution and reported that he was weary of hearing the "never-ending gabble about the sacredness of the Constitution."[180]

Finally, we notice that the "constitutional relation" has not been destroyed; rather, it has been "suspended, or disturbed" in certain States—and it is there that immediate restoration is called for. Self-preservation calls for such restoration—that self-preservation which we shall later on see to be so critical a guide for human action.

Much more can be said about this first paragraph. But we must pass on to the subsequent paragraphs, about which far less than this must be said if we are to canvass the entire document on this occasion.

ii

That it is my purpose, upon the next meeting of Congress to again recommend the adoption of a practical measure tendering pecuniary aid to the free acceptance or rejection of all slave-states, so called, the people whereof may not then be in rebellion against the United States, and which states, may then have voluntarily adopted, or thereafter may voluntarily adopt, immediate, or gradual abolishment of slavery within their respective limits; and that the effort to colonize persons of African descent, with their consent, upon this continent, or elsewhere, with the previously obtained consent of the Governments existing there, will be continued.

Having laid in his opening paragraph the groundwork—that is, to paraphrase, "We are determined to restore the authoritative constitutional relation"—Lincoln can then indicate what would be an improvement consistent with such restored constitutional relation: compensated emancipation by nonrebellious slaveholders. This offer is extended, it seems, to all Slave States, "so called," those now in rebellion and those that had never been in rebellion against the United States. It was unlikely that the rebellious States would be won over, but what about the other Slave States, the loyal Middle States? They would not be directly affected by the impending proclamation, but was there not for them here, as there had been the preceding March, the suggestion that they would do better to "sell" their slaves now to the United States than to be deprived of them later upon the collapse of their ever more vulnerable systems of slavery?

Is not at least a useful appearance of fairness achieved by Lincoln's offer to pay for what he considered himself empowered, if not even obliged, to take? Does not this reinforce the Lincolnian position that it is not the slaveholder, but slavery, that is the critical problem here, that it is not punishment or political and social reform but rather a reaffirmed Union that he is after? If it is to be a Union in which the traditional role of the States is respected, it is up to the States "voluntarily" to adopt a program of abolishment of slavery.

Does he use "abolishment" rather than "abolition" in order to soften what he is asking for? That is, *abolition* may still have been seen as far too radical a term, even by many antislavery Northerners. Besides, Lincoln cannot abolish the institutions of slavery in any State; he can only emancipate certain people in certain places at a certain time. Abolition requires a more comprehensive change, of a permanent legislative character, than the President is constitutionally capable of making on his own authority.

The reference to "gradual abolishment" recognizes not only concerns among the public at large about the danger of precipitate action but those of Lincoln as well. What was to be done with the millions of people "of African descent" if they should be suddenly cut loose from their accustomed moorings in this Country? Would they thereafter be exploited even more than they had long been? Would they constitute a danger to the community? Could they be expected to know what to do with themselves? The difficulties seen then in any program of wholesale emancipation remain to a considerable extent in American race relations down to this day. Was time needed, then as now, to effect a proper transition? Or, failing that, should the removal of most (if not all) Africans from this Country be planned, for their own good as well as that of the Caucasians? Did Lincoln have to explore alternatives in this way, if only to indicate that he understood what many of his countrymen, North and South, were concerned about? By so indicating, did he not make it more likely that the public would eventually accept whatever he decided upon and offered as the least objectionable way of achieving the desired end? If he had failed to appreciate alternative positions, he probably would not have been trusted the way that he came to be.

But to appreciate is not necessarily to agree; it is rather to grasp why another should make the mistakes he is making. Slavery was, to say the least, a mistake, not only a moral mistake but (perhaps even more important for the future of the regime) a constitutional mistake. Was not American constitutionalism, with its rule of law and its dependence upon substantial equality, bound eventually to undermine slavery or to be undermined by it? Was not slavery somehow hostile to the principles of the American regime? The Slave States depended on the law-abidingness of the Free States— on the respect of Free States for such Constitutional arrangements as the Fugitive Slave Clause—in order to be protected in an institution that was, in a sense, lawless.

Finally, we notice the double emphasis upon the necessity for consent: the consent of those to be colonized, the consent of those governments that would receive the colonists. This, along with the deference to voluntariness on the part of the Slave States, points up once again the vulnerability of slavery in any regime where consent of the governed is made as much of as it has always been in ours.[181]

iii

That on the first day of January in the year of our Lord, one thousand eight hundred and sixty-three, all persons held as slaves within any state, or designated part of a state, the people whereof shall then be in rebellion against the United States shall be then, thenceforward, and forever free; and the executive government of the United States, including the military and naval authority thereof, will recognize and maintain the freedom of such persons, and will do no act or acts to repress such persons, or any of them, in any efforts they may make for their actual freedom.

One offer has just been made, that of compensated emancipation. Now comes another offer to this effect: "You can keep your slaves, if you wish, so long as you return to your allegiance." This once again emphasizes that it is the Union which Lincoln seeks to preserve, not Slavery which he seeks to destroy. One hundred days are provided rebellious slaveholders in which to take advantage of this offer. Some of the North still needed to be assured that Southern property and the American Constitution were being dealt with fairly.

"[A]ll persons held as slaves": does not this formulation permit the inference that they are not truly slaves? One who is called a

148

slave may be no more than someone held as a slave, perhaps as a prisoner of war. May he merely be regarded as a slave? Is not slavery as practiced in North America at that time only conventional slavery, with its convention arbitrarily guided by color differences and its enslavements based primarily upon force? Yet, even if slavery originated in injustice, it may have compounded the original injustice to have tried to free all slaves at once or to have freed them one way rather than another.

Notice that Lincoln can command only the response of the "executive government of the United States." The Courts and Congress act independently. We can see in the second paragraph of the Preliminary Proclamation that it is Congress, not the Executive, which can provide the "pecuniary aid" Lincoln speaks of there.

Notice also that freedom comes in two stages, so to speak: recognized freedom and actual freedom. Recognized freedom is what comes to someone from the sayings and doings of others; actual freedom depends more upon one's own efforts. It should go without saying that not everyone who is recognized to be free is actually free. Men who have lived for generations in slavery may need generations of purgation and training before they become actually free—as the Israelites' forty years in the desert suggest.

iv

That the executive will, on the first day of January aforesaid, by proclamation, designate the States, and parts of states, if any, in which the people thereof respectively, shall then be in rebellion against the United States; and the fact that any state, or the people thereof shall, on that day be, in good faith represented in the Congress of the United States, by members chosen thereto, at elections wherein a majority of the qualified voters of such state shall have participated, shall, in the absence of strong countervailing testimony, be deemed conclusive evidence that such state and the people thereof, are not then in rebellion against the United States.

A promise is made as to what Lincoln will do on January 1: designate the States, or parts of States, if any, in which the people thereof shall then be in rebellion. Is not that to be the principal purpose of that January 1 proclamation? What follows from such designation will have already been indicated in this September 22 proclamation. Little more needs to be added on January 1: the emancipation then will even have the effect of a promise fulfilled. That revolutionary step will be living up to a bargain already struck. There is about this sequence a psychological master-stroke.

By thus pointing ahead Lincoln succeeded in shifting attention to an occasion that was expected and even demanded by a kind of contract. (The designation required for that day was, for the most part, perfunctory. Most of the States designated could have been designated by anyone; as we shall see, they in effect designated themselves.) Lincoln succeeded so well in shifting attention to the expected measure (on January 1) from the extraordinary measure (of September 22) that the January 1 statement (which is, except for its concluding language, more pedestrian) has become the one which is remembered and reproduced in anthologies, not the earlier one that had truly been decisive.

Notice Lincoln's precise use of "if any"—"the States, and parts of states, *if any*." After all, an offer has been made; it must not be assumed in advance that it will be rejected by anyone. To do so would be virtually to admit that it is a mere form (as was seen later, for example, in the world-shaking July 1914 ultimatum delivered by Austria-Hungary to Serbia). It would, besides, deny the rationality and hence the humanity of those in rebellion. They must be considered as, in principle, open to argument. They, too, are American citizens.

Notice, also, that the decisive indication that a State is not in rebellion is its good-faith representation in the Congress. Lincoln says, in effect, "If you wish to avoid the harsh effects of this necessary military measure, exercise your rights as free men; send representatives of your choice to Congress; return to your seats in the national legislature and resume the duty and power you have always had there to help run the country." Does not this approach acknowledge the fundamentally republican character of the Country, a character to which the military power is ultimately subservient? We need not concern ourselves here with whether Congress would have immediately accepted such representatives from the States that had been in rebellion. It suffices to notice that republican standards were apparently relied upon even in those trying times.

Notice, finally, that Lincoln in effect cedes to rebellious States the power to decide for themselves whether they are again to be in good standing. "[I]n the absence of strong countervailing testimony," their recourse to Congressional elections will "be deemed conclusive evidence" that they "are not then in rebellion against the United States." Is there not something generous about this also? Indeed, does not generosity pervade the Proclamation, the generosity of a truly magnanimous man who can be at the same time shrewd and knowing about the usefulness (as well as the limitations) of generosity?

V

That attention is hereby called to an act of Congress entitled "An act to make an additional Article of War" approved March 13, 1862, and which act is in the words and figure following:

Be it enacted by the Senate and House of Representatives of the United States of America in Congress assembled, That hereafter the following shall be promulgated as an additional article of war for the government of the army of the United States, and shall be obeyed and observed as such:

Article—. All officers or persons in the military or naval service of the United States are prohibited from employing any of the forces under their respective commands for the purpose of returning fugitives from service or labor, who may have escaped from any persons to whom such service or labor is claimed to be due, and any officer who shall be found guilty by a court-martial of violating this article shall be dismissed from the service.

Sec. 2. And be it further enacted, That this act shall take effect from and after its passage.

Also [attention is hereby called] to the ninth and tenth sections of an act entitled "An Act to suppress Insurrection, to punish Treason and Rebellion, to seize and confiscate property of rebels, and for other purposes," approved July 17, 1862, and which sections are in the words and figures following:

Sec. 9. And be it further enacted, That all slaves of persons who shall hereafter be engaged in rebellion against the government of the United States, or who shall in any way give aid or comfort thereto, escaping from such persons and taking refuge within the lines of the army; and all slaves captured from such persons or deserted by them and coming under the control of the government of the United States; and all slaves of such persons found on [or] being within any place occupied by rebel forces and afterwards occupied by the forces of the United States, shall be deemed captives of war, and shall be forever free of their servitude and not again held as slaves.

Sec. 10. And be it further enacted, That no slave escaping into any State, Territory, or the District of Columbia, from any other State, shall

151

be delivered up, or in any way impeded or hindered of his liberty, ex-
cept for crime, or some offence against the laws, unless the person claim-
ing said fugitive shall first make oath that the person to whom the labor
or service of such fugitive is alleged to be due is his lawful owner, and
has not borne arms against the United States in the present rebellion,
nor in any way given aid and comfort thereto; and no person engaged
in the military or naval service of the United States shall, under any
pretence whatever, assume to decide on the validity of the claim of
any person to the service or labor of any other person, or surrender up
any such person to the claimant, on pain of being dismissed from the
service.

And I do hereby enjoin upon and order all persons engaged in the
military and naval service of the United States to observe, obey, and enforce,
within their respective spheres of service, the act, and sections above re-
cited.[182]

This passage draws attention to two acts of Congress: one prohibits military officers from returning certain fugitive slaves, and
the other (in the sections quoted from it) declares certain fugitive
slaves free and places restrictions upon the return of certain other
fugitive slaves to their masters. The passage thereafter orders "all
persons engaged in the military and naval service of the United
States to observe, obey, and enforce, within their respective spheres
of service, the act, and sections above recited."

What is all this doing in here? Perhaps it is partly to suggest that
what Lincoln is now doing is not without Congressional precedent.
This passage may address itself to the more conservative Unionists.
They are assured that all this is not simply executive usurpation on
the President's part, that there may even be some Congressional
guidance for what the President is doing. Perhaps, also, it is partly
to counter the hostility of abolitionists who would not like an emancipation decree framed in so qualified and so partial a manner as
this one is. Such single-minded critics are reminded that at least the
notorious Fugitive Slave Clause has been in effect suspended, permitting "captives of war" to become "forever free."

In addition, there are other hints. The first Act that Lincoln calls
attention to is reproduced in its entirety, including the superfluous
enacting clause (the title of the Act, also given, would have sufficed) and the immediate-effect clause. But only two sections of the
second Act are called to our attention, in marked (and intended?)

contrast to what was done with the first Act. Does Lincoln thereby tacitly repudiate the other sections of the second Act?

We cannot, on this occasion, explore this question; it suffices to notice that several of the sections of the second Act which Lincoln does not mention here are quite harsh, authorizing death sentences and comprehensive confiscation of all property. That harsh spirit is against what Lincoln is interested in establishing in the Proclamation. Property in slaves is to be confiscated, so to speak; but, after all, free men will thereby come into being.

The emphasis here is upon fugitive slaves. Does not this suggest who may be able to take advantage at once of the Proclamation—those who flee from rebel territory? Is not an implicit invitation issued? This anticipates and to some extent deals with the complaint that the Proclamation emancipates only where the Union army is not.

Finally, we cannot help but notice that the language of Congress is less precise, less carefully thought out, than that of Lincoln. Is this intended to show the reader that Lincoln is truly more worthy of being taken seriously? In any event, the Proclamation will free all slaves within the designated areas, regardless of whether their masters are able or willing to "make Oath" about their constant loyalty to the United States—and no matter what compensation they may happen either to be entitled to or to be in a position to collect.

vi

And the executive will in due time recommend that all citizens of the United States who shall have remained loyal thereto throughout the rebellion, shall (upon the restoration of the constitutional relation between the United States, and their respective states, and people, if that relation shall have been suspended or disturbed) be compensated for all losses by acts of the United States, including the loss of slaves.

Once again, we see that the demands of war are not to be permitted to obscure permanently either the desire or the duty to see justice done. Certainly, loyalty must be noticed and, if possible, rewarded. And, it has to be said, the United States should recognize that there has existed up to now an acknowledged property interest in slaves that must still be taken into account. Does this remark (the closing one among the substantive paragraphs of the Preliminary Proclamation) appeal to the apprehensive Middle States Unionists, just as the preceding passage incorporating the Acts of Congress appealed in large part to impatient Abolitionists? Do we once again see that Lincoln must keep quite divergent, but vitally necessary, horses yoked together if the war chariot is to advance? (See, on the limits of "compensat[ion] for . . . the loss of slaves," Section X of Lecture No. 12 of this Commentary.)

vii

In witness whereof, I have hereunto set my hand, and caused the seal of the United States to be affixed.

This is the standard testamentary statement for such proclamations. We will return to it at the end of the Final Proclamation.

viii

Done at the City of Washington, this twenty second day of September, in the year of our Lord, one thousand eight hundred and sixty two, and of the Independence of the United States, the eighty seventh.

The eighty-seventh year hearkens back to 1776 and the Declaration of Independence. It is that "eighty seventh" which Lincoln will transform into "four score and seven" when he speaks in November of 1863 at Gettysburg.

Why September 22? Lincoln had planned to issue this Preliminary Proclamation some weeks earlier (in fact, in July). But he had been dissuaded by Secretary Seward's argument that he should at least wait until the Union forces won another victory rather than make the proclamation seem an act of desperation—for it had been a time of one defeat after another. Then there came the "victory" of Antietam, in the middle of September 1862, and a few days later, the Emancipation Proclamation.[183]

Did Lincoln choose an interval of one hundred days so that the final proclamation would fall on New Year's Day, a day of rebirth and rededication?

ix

There is, in the handwritten original of the Preliminary Proclamation of September 22, 1862, the repetition of "sixty two," in this fashion, "in the year of our Lord, one thousand, eight hundred and sixty two, and sixty two, and of the Independence of the United States the eighty seventh." This passage is in the handwriting of a clerk.[184]

Here, for the only time in this commentary upon the Emancipation Proclamation, I move from what Lincoln thought and intended, to what may have been "unconscious" (and hence "inspired"?). This inadvertent repetition by a clerk of "sixty two" suggests that he, at least, made much of the date—as if to emphasize, "It is late 1862, not early 1861. We loyalists have tried for a year and a half to put down this dreadful rebellion with conventional measures. We can now proceed in good faith to a measure that we have had to be cautious in using, not only because it challenges longstanding constitutional arrangements (after all, it is a constitution we are defending) but also because it conforms to and gratifies the deepest desires of those of us who have always hated slavery. It is 1862!"

I must leave further poetic probings of the unconscious (or of the providential?) to others. Still, one can wonder whether Lincoln himself ever noticed this slip of the pen and, if so, what he (a master psychologist) thought of it.

We turn now to the Final Proclamation (of January 1, 1863). Much of what might be said about the parts of this proclamation has already been said in my review of the Preliminary Proclamation. We can therefore be brief.

X

Whereas, on the twentysecond day of September, in the year of our Lord one thousand eight hundred and sixty two, a proclamation was issued by the President of the United States, containing, among other things, the following, towit:

"That on the first day of January, in the year of our Lord one thousand eight hundred and sixty-three, all persons held as slaves within any State or designated part of a State, the people whereof shall then be in rebellion against the United States, shall be then, thenceforward, and forever free; and the Executive Government of the United States, including the military and naval authority thereof, will recognize and maintain the freedom of such persons, and will do no act or acts to repress such persons, or any of them, in any efforts they may make for their actual freedom.

"That the Executive will, on the first day of January aforesaid, by proclamation, designate the States and parts of States, if any, in which

the people thereof, respectively, shall then be in rebellion against the United States; and the fact that any State, or the people thereof, shall on that day be, in good faith, represented in the Congress of the United States by members chosen thereto at elections wherein a majority of the qualified voters of such State shall have participated, shall, in the absence of strong countervailing testimony, be deemed conclusive evidence that such State, and the people thereof, are not then in rebellion against the United States."

A solemn version of the date of the Preliminary Proclamation is given, that version used in the final paragraph of that proclamation. We recall that when the dates were given for Acts of Congress in that first proclamation, simpler versions of their dates were given (that is, "March 13, 1862," "July 17, 1862"). Is a proclamation somehow of greater dignity than an Act of Congress? Does the Presidency, properly employed, tend to have a greater dignity than the Congress? Is this one reason why a Presidential proclamation about Southern slaves means more, and has a greater effect, than Congressional enactments? Is the Commander in Chief of the armed forces in time of war somehow the decisive ruler of a country, especially when the war is a civil war—for that makes war comprehensive?

These questions lead us to notice that there is nothing said about Congress in the Final Proclamation. Lincoln quoted at length from Congress in the Preliminary Proclamation; here he quotes only from himself. Both Congress and the States take second place in the constitutional drama now being enacted. They have served their purpose; they have had their chance—and now the President must get on with conducting the war to save the Union.

We also notice that nothing is said about compensation for voluntary emancipation; nor is anything said about compensation for loss of slaves by loyal slaveowners. Both of these had been proposed, as promised, to Congress. But nothing substantial had come from the proposals. (Later on, the Fourteenth Amendment would forbid such compensation by any government in the United States.) The emphasis is now upon this emancipation and its consequences.

A new stage has been reached in the war—but a stage which, it can be argued, developed constitutionally from the preceding stage. This proclamation gets right down to business. There are no "frills" or offers or alternatives, but rather a judgment set forth in prosaic yet somehow solemn terms.

xi

Now, therefore I, Abraham Lincoln, President of the United States, by virtue of the power in me vested as Commander-in-Chief, of the Army and Navy of the United States in time of actual armed rebellion against authority and government of the United States, and as a fit and necessary war measure for suppressing said rebellion, do, on this first day of January, in the year of our Lord one thousand eight hundred and sixty three, and in accordance with my purpose so to do publicly proclaimed for the full period of one hundred days, from the day first above mentioned, order and designate as the States and parts of States wherein the people thereof respectively, are this day in rebellion against the United States, the following, towit:

Arkansas, Texas, Louisiana, (except the Parishes of St. Bernard, Plaquemines, Jefferson, St. Johns, St. Charles, St. James, Ascension, Assumption, Terrebonne, Lafourche, St. Mary, St. Martin, and Orleans, including the city of New Orleans) Mississippi, Alabama, Florida, Georgia, South-Carolina, North-Carolina, and Virginia, (except the fortyeight counties designated as West Virginia, and also the counties of Berkley, Accomac, Northampton, Elizabeth-City, York, Princess Ann, and Norfolk, including the cities of Norfolk & Portsmouth); and which excepted parts are, for the present, left precisely as if this proclamation were not issued.

Lincoln's status of Commander in Chief is again emphasized, and reinforced further by the references to "time of actual armed rebellion" and "fit and necessary war measure." A solemn version of the date is again relied on as he draws in this decree upon the full majesty of the language as well as upon the full force of the war power.

But the war power is properly to be employed for a certain purpose. It must be used discriminatingly, if constitutional government is truly to be defended. This is recognized by the exceptions Lincoln insisted upon making, in the application of his proclamation, for those parishes in Louisiana and those counties in Virginia where Union forces were already in control. Might not Lincoln also have thought that such exceptions made his policy seem discriminating and hence contributed to its effectiveness?

Secretary of the Treasury Salmon P. Chase argued against such exceptions and kept after the President thereafter to extend the Emancipation Proclamation to all of Virginia and Louisiana. Lincoln replied on September 2, 1863:

> Knowing your great anxiety that the emancipation proclamation shall now be applied to certain parts of Virginia and Louisiana which were exempted from it last January, I state briefly what appear to me to be difficulties in the way of such a step. The original proclamation has no constitutional or legal justification, except as a military measure. The exemptions were made because the military necessity did not apply to the exempted localities. Nor does that necessity apply to them now any more than it did then. If I take the step must I not do so, without the argument of military necessity, and so, without any argument, except the one that I think the measure politically expedient, and morally right? Would I not thus give up all footing upon constitution or law? Would I not thus be in the boundless field of absolutism? Could this pass unnoticed, or unresisted? Could it fail to be perceived that without any further stretch, I might do the same in Delaware, Maryland, Kentucky, Tennessee, and Missouri; and even change any law in any State?[185]

Notice the words, "Could this pass unnoticed . . . ?", "Could it fail to be perceived . . . ?" It is important for constitutional government what the people of the Country understand their officers to be doing and on what authority. It is also important that the people be trained to expect the basis of governmental authority to be evident, even when extraordinary measures have to be resorted to.

Yet, we might ask, in what sense are the "excepted parts" "left precisely as if this proclamation were not issued"? Should it not have been evident to all—was it not evident to (and perhaps even intended by) Lincoln—that if the proclamation was effective with respect to the States and parts of States listed, then the system of slavery would collapse not only in the rebellious States but also in the loyal Middle States and in the "excepted" counties and parishes of Virginia and Louisiana?

The emancipation of so massive a body of slaves made slavery itself quite vulnerable in the Country at large. Such slavery as then existed in North America could find enough intelligent defenders in this Country only if virtually all members of the slaves' race were subjected to slavery. If a significant number were free, and could develop themselves as free and responsible residents here, the supposed natural basis for slavery would no longer be tenable. Slavery could not survive, in a regime such as ours, if it clearly rested as much as it would have had to rest (after the Emancipation Proclamation) upon obvious accidents of geography and history. The moral basis of slavery would have been undermined insofar as everyday morality rests in large part upon the customary and the uniform.

Consider finally, in this passage, how the States are listed. They are not alphabetical, nor in the order of admission to the Union, nor in order of secession. Rather, Lincoln begins with the only landlocked state among them (Arkansas), and then moves along the coast, starting with the State farthest away from him (Texas) and coming closer and closer to Washington (ending with Virginia). It is as if he sweeps them all in to himself. (States are listed differently in other proclamations.) Lincoln displays here a methodical and yet imaginative turn of mind, a combination familiar to us in poets.

In this way, too, we should be reassured to notice, he avoids "the boundless field of absolutism"—and this means that we can safely think about what he is doing, for then we are thinking about thinking rather than trying to think about that which is irrational or accidental and hence not truly knowable.

xii

And by virtue of the power, and for the purpose aforesaid, I do order and declare that all persons held as slaves within said designated States, and parts of States, are, and henceforward shall be free; and that the Executive government of the United States, including the military and naval authorities thereof, will recognize and maintain the freedom of said persons.

We see here brought to completion what had been promised on September 22. We again see that Lincoln's formal control is limited to "the Executive government of the United States." Most of what one might say about this paragraph has already been anticipated in this lecture.

But what about "order and declare"? Perhaps he realizes that he can order only some things, that he can merely express a strong preference or hope with respect to other things. Consider other pairs of terms in this paragraph: "are, and henceforward shall be free"; "recognize and maintain the freedom of said persons." Does he *order* such persons to be free *now*? Does he *order* such freedom to be recognized *now*? He can do that, perhaps. But he cannot order that such freedom exist "henceforward" or that it be maintained. Will not that depend on future governments and future circumstances, perhaps ultimately on the judgment and will of the American people, including the freed slaves and their descendants?

I note in passing that "maintain" had been put into the Preliminary Proclamation at the suggestion of a cabinet member; but Lincoln had misgivings about it. He was reluctant, he indicated, to promise something he did not know he could perform. He retained "maintain" here but perhaps not without hinting at his reservations.

xiii

And I hereby enjoin upon the people so declared to be free to abstain from all violence, unless in necessary self-defence; and I recommend to them that, in all cases when allowed, they labor faithfully for reasonable wages.

We see here one great problem of the future, a problem that continues to this day. In dealing with the freed people, Lincoln recognizes what he can and cannot say. He can, as President, *enjoin* them to "abstain from all violence." That is what the law ordains. But he cannot *enjoin* them to work. If they are truly free men, they must decide that on their own. Here he can only recommend. They can be urged to work faithfully; their prospective employers are implicitly instructed to pay them reasonable wages. Emancipation is one thing; preparation for self-government is quite another—for that takes time and such willingness as Lincoln himself had to face up to facts and to restrain himself. What can be proclaimed, therefore, is neither virtue nor genuine freedom but, at best, the removal of chains and a provision of opportunities. Education and training, as well as experience, must thereafter do their part.

Are not the serious problems with immediate comprehensive abolition reflected in the virtually complete silence about what is to become of the emancipated slaves? Is it sensible to expect them to manage on their own like other free men? Is not this why Lincoln had argued again and again for gradual, compensated emancipation, a mode of emancipation that could both motivate and empower masters to provide a proper transition for their slaves into a free life? Such a mode would have had the minimum of bitterness and of general poverty (due to the passions and ravages of war) to contend with.

Violence on the part of freed slaves is forbidden. Lincoln is speaking here to long-standing fears among slaveowners of bloody slave rebellions, fears which Middle States Unionists as well as Northern humanitarians shared. If such violence had broken out on a large scale, the Union cause might have been discredited. The old concerns of slaveholders and the repressive measures in the South might have then appeared justified. Still, violence is understood to be permitted to the freed slaves for "necessary self-defense." Is this a law of nature? Would it be self-defense to use force against the master who wants to retain his emancipated slave?

We see in this "necessary self-defense" an echo of the "necessary war measure" Lincoln had declared himself obliged to resort to in defense of the Union. Indeed, self-defense had promoted and permitted the original compromises with slavery in 1776 and 1787—that is, the defense of the several States, threatened by European powers and by continual war among themselves.

xiv

And I further declare and make known, that such persons of suitable condition, will be received into the armed service of the United States to garrison forts, positions, stations, and other places, and to man vessels of all sorts in said service.

This sentence is quietly stated; the use of "declare and make known" almost suggests he is reporting something rather than ordering something—reporting something that is happening, that is bound to happen. The military uses to which freed slaves may be put are not immediately, or obviously, combative. Lincoln still has to think of Southern fears and Northern prejudices, both of which can lead to actions harmful either to the slaves or to Lincoln's government. There would be something shocking, perhaps even unnatural, many must have felt, in former slaves fighting against their former masters. This was a development that took some time getting used to, but it eventually came about on a significant scale.

Southerners themselves were finally reduced to freeing slaves who would serve in their army. This too testified to Lincoln's policy as a genuine war measure, a war measure that made chattel slavery thereafter untenable among Americans.

XV

And upon this act, sincerely believed to be an act of justice, warranted by the Constitution, upon military necessity, I invoke the considerate judgment of mankind, and the gracious favor of Almighty God.

This is perhaps the most complicated sentence in the two stages of the Proclamation. We must settle on this occasion for a few preliminary observations about it. Interpretation is made even more difficult when one understands it to have been supplied (in large part?) by a member of the Cabinet, not by Lincoln himself. If that should be so, what appears to be complexity may only be confusion.

Still, a few questions may be in order: "this act" is considered to be "warranted by the Constitution, upon military necessity." Is it done because it is warranted? Or it is done for some other reason, and the power to do so is provided by "military necessity"? An "act of justice" is pointed to as somehow involved here. Is this the true purpose? Or is it understood that a respect for justice is itself good military strategy? Notice that it is regarded as certainly a "military necessity" but that it is only "sincerely believed" to be "an act of justice." Is the truth about justice far harder to arrive at than truth about military strategy? The President had delayed a long time in doing this. He had had to decide what the right thing to do was, and that depended not only on military strategy, natural right, and political circumstances, but also on his Constitutional powers, duties, and limitations.

The "considerate judgment of mankind" reminds us of the Declaration of Independence's "Opinions of Mankind" and "a candid World." Mankind has "judgment"; Almighty God has "gracious favor." It is not for human beings to assess what moves God or, indeed, to determine whether God moves at all. They, it seems, must do what they think right, and then hope or pray for the best. The references to both mankind and God serve to remind the citizen that immediate, personal concerns should not be permitted to usurp in us the proper, one might even say the constitutional, role of the truly human, the justly divine.

xvi

In witness whereof, I have hereunto set my hand and caused the seal of the United States to be affixed.

It is said that the issuance of the Emancipation Proclamation was delayed on January 1 because when it came to be signed in the morning, another formal testamentary paragraph, one appropriate for another kind of proclamation, had been inadvertently used in the place of this one in the official copy. It had to be sent back to the State Department to be redone. (It is this, along with a reception Lincoln had to attend for much of the day, that contributed to the delay indicated in one of the passages I have quoted from Frederick Douglass. Compare the earlier inadvertent use of "sixty-two.")

We can see even here, in constitutional matters as in worship, the importance of forms, of appearances, and perhaps of chance.

xvii

Done at the City of Washington, this first day of January, in the year of our Lord one thousand eight hundred and sixty three, and of the Independence of the United States of America the eighty-seventh.

Nothing more (in addition to what has been said about the conclusion of the Preliminary Proclamation) needs to be said about this concluding sentence, except perhaps to notice that it is in the City of Washington that the decisive declaration against slavery was issued, that system of servitude which even the slaveholders of Washington's generation, including Washington himself, can be said to have looked forward to ending in a responsible manner as the Republic matured.

A responsible examination of the Emancipation Proclamation suggests that if Lincoln, as Washington's legitimate successor, could have constitutionally "save[d] the Union" either by "sav[ing] slavery" or by "destroy[ing] slavery," he would have preferred to do so by taking advantage of this opportunity to destroy slavery. Indeed, to preserve the Union on Lincoln's terms was, even without the Emancipation Proclamation, to destroy slavery.

V

Three topics remain to be discussed—but not at length in this lecture. I will suggest the sorts of things that need to be considered.

There is needed, first, a consideration of the effects of the Emancipation Proclamation. One should note first and foremost that it did work—in that it promoted the flight of slaves from the South, in that it undermined the economy and the moral standing of the South both at home and in Europe, and in that it contributed a significant military force of freed slaves to the North. We can see that, in order for such a policy to work, timing was critical. Also critical was that the President should have had a clear notion of standards and goals. This means that his ultimate considerations drew upon prudence and justice more than upon either liberty or equality (as these are generally understood).

As the Union army moved South, thereafter, it "naturally" left freed slaves in its wake. This had, it seems, a great moral effect upon what the North was doing and what it was seen to be doing. For example, the Proclamation began to emancipate Lincoln himself and people like him, as well as the Constitution itself and the very idea of republican government, from the burden of slavery.

We can see as well that ideas do matter in political life. One might even say that only ideas matter for long. That which we now call "symbolic" can be very important. One should, in considering such matters, begin with the fact that the Proclamation was at once regarded as important. Only the Thirteenth Amendment, abolishing all slavery in the United States (adopted by Congress early in 1865 for ratification by the States), produced as enthusiastic a response from the antislavery people as the Proclamation had done. To be regarded as important is, in political matters, to be at least somewhat important.

It should be evident to us, upon thinking about the Proclamation and its effect, how critical the opinion of the public is for law and, in turn, how critical law is for morality and for civilization. Above all, it should be evident to us how critical it is to know what one is doing.

It should also be evident to us that the Proclamation and the war effort it served have had bad effects as well. The ascendancy of Executive power in the United States was made eminently respectable because of the Civil War; the separation of powers was undermined as were the States; the war power was magnified; and the notion of "total war" was made respectable.

Should not a political man of Lincoln's understanding and temperament now devote himself to redefining, for our changed circumstances, what is now appropriate in our constitutional relations? Would not Lincoln himself insist today that practical (but not necessarily constitutional) reforms, some of a far-reaching character, should be made if we are to address ourselves sensibly and safely to the new challenges that confront us?

VI

That is one topic which should be developed. I have already touched upon my second remaining topic in this lecture—that which addresses itself to what we can learn, of a more general nature, from our study of the Emancipation Proclamation.

We see, of course, what prudence can mean in a particular situation—and hence what prudence itself means. One must adjust to one's materials, including the prejudices and limitations of one's community. Such adjustment often includes settling for less than the best. But the most useful adjustment is not possible unless one knows what the very best would be. We can also sense, upon the study of the doings of prudent men and women, how important chance is in human affairs—and hence how limited we often are in what we can do, even when we know what should be done.

We should notice as well, and guard against, that fashionable opinion which dismisses what is reasonable and deliberate as cold-blooded and calculating. It is important, however, if one is to be most effective as a reasonable, deliberate, and deliberating human being, to seem other than cold-blooded and calculating—that is, it is important to be a good politician. Once again we are reminded of the importance in political things of appearances, of a healthy respect for the opinions (and hence the errors as well as the sound intuition) of mankind.

Certainly, self-righteousness should always be held in check, but not always a show of indignation. Still, indignation even in a good cause should be carefully watched. Consider, for example, the famous abolitionist William Lloyd Garrison's 1831 promise:

> I *will* be as harsh as truth, and as uncompromising as justice. On this subject I do not wish to think, or to speak, or write, with moderation. No! No! Tell a man whose house is on fire to give a moderate alarm; tell him to moderately rescue his wife from the hand of the ravisher; tell the mother to gradually extricate her babe from the fire into which it has fallen;—but urge me not to use moderation in a cause

like the present. I am in earnest—I will not equivocate—I will not excuse—I will not retreat a single inch—AND I WILL BE HEARD.[186]

Such passion may be useful, even necessary, if great evils are to be corrected, but only if a Lincoln should become available to supervise what finally happens and to deal prudently with others (zealous friends and sincere enemies alike) with a remarkable, even godlike, magnanimity.

VII

Now, to my final topic for the future, which I preface with three quotations that can serve to illuminate as well the commentary in this lecture on the Emancipation Proclamation.

The first quotation is from the New Testament. "Behold, I send you forth as sheep in the midst of wolves: be ye therefore wise as serpents, and harmless as doves."[187]

The second is from Stephen A. Douglas, who said of Lincoln in the course of their celebrated Illinois debates in 1858 that Lincoln "has a fertile genius in devising language to conceal his thoughts."[188]

The third is from Lincoln himself who once observed, "I am very little inclined on any occasion to say anything unless I hope to produce some good by it."[189]

Artemus Ward was evidently Lincoln's favorite humorist during the Civil War:

> The President's reading of the humorist's story, "High-Handed Outrage at Utica" to his cabinet before presenting them with the Emancipation Proclamation [on September 22, 1862] is well known. "With the fearful strain that is upon me night and day," said Lincoln, "if I did not laugh I should die, and you need this medicine as much as I do."[190]

There may be even more to this famous episode than has heretofore been recognized, except perhaps by Lincoln himself. Why was that particular story selected by him for this occasion? The story Lincoln read to his cabinet is amusing. But notice, also, that it is about a great traitor, perhaps indeed the greatest traitor who has ever lived. This traitor is dealt with soundly, if irrationally, in the story.[191]

Consider the title: "High-Handed Outrage at Utica." Utica was the famous African city that allied itself to republican Rome in the mighty struggle against Carthage. Did not Lincoln intend to gather to the cause of the American Republic an African power (the "persons of African descent" dealt with in the Emancipation Proclamation) against the threatening Carthage represented by the South?

But perhaps he recognized that there was in his own action something questionable, something dubious, even high-handed and outrageous—at least there would be in appearance, especially if he did not handle it properly. Thus, he saw himself as others saw him, or as others might see him, and laughed at himself.

This would be, of course, most subtle and far higher humor than anything Artemus Ward was ever capable of. But if Lincoln was so subtle, so detached, should not that really make us take notice? It points up the deliberateness, the self-conscious artistry, the coolness of Lincoln. This is, indeed, startling self-criticism, which he would share with his most perceptive observers. Or should what I am now drawing upon be dismissed as mere chance and hence unsound speculation? So be it—for those who would have it so.

In any event, we are obliged to emphasize, even more than we have already, that Lincoln must have known what he was doing, including what impression he needed to make. This citizen is truly a remarkable child (indeed, a prodigy) of the American constitutional regime. He is, in this sense at least, subordinate to the constitutional regime. Should not these observations induce us to return to the Emancipation Proclamation and to take it, as well as the Constitution that it both draws upon and serves, even more seriously than we have? We have examined merely the Proclamation's surface—but in doing so, we have been reminded that the surface, the appearances of things, can be critical for responsible political action, however inconclusive appearances may ultimately be.

The words one uses—and the words one keeps to oneself—contribute to the appearances of things and hence to one's effects. In this sense, a word fitly spoken is like apples of gold in settings of silver.[192]

12. Amendments XIII, XIV, and XV

I

The three Civil War amendments to the Constitution of 1787 continued the deep wartime division in this Country by pitting one section against another, at least until the passions of war had subsided enough to permit everyone to see that the new order was truly preferable in key respects to that with which the Framers of the Constitution had been saddled in 1787. No respectable defenders of slavery are heard among us today. Even the segregation of a half-century ago has come to be generally recognized as no longer defensible, however useful it may have once seemed to many during a period of transition following the Civil War and Reconstruction. The merits of the new order are so widely appreciated that little is heard these days either about the way in which ratifications were gotten out of State legislatures for one or more of the Civil War amendments or about the way the United States Supreme Court explained itself in dealing the mortal blow to official segregation that it did in 1954.

We have noticed the orderliness of the arrangement of the first ten amendments and, to a lesser extent, of the next two amendments as well. But, we have also noticed, there is far less of a pattern to the amendments after the Twelfth, except as responses to historical developments and unpredictable events around the world or within the United States. The amendments since the Bill of Rights, as well as the Articles of Confederation of 1776–1781 and the Confederate Constitution of 1861, testify to what happens when constitution-making is done primarily in response to events or circumstances.

The Constitution of 1787, on the other hand, rose above circumstances to a remarkable degree, however much it was prompted by the problems of that day. Even so, the need for amendments was anticipated by the Constitution's Framers, especially by those who recognized that there had to be compromises that would keep the Constitution from conforming even more than it did to that natural constitutionalism which it is salutary to recognize as guiding the strivings of Americans from the beginning.

Amendments to the Constitution, I have suggested, have tended thus far to refine, if not merely to confirm, what has already happened. Even the three Civil War amendments, which are regarded as the most far-reaching of the twenty-seven amendments there have been thus far to the Constitution of 1787, reflect what had already happened in this Country. The war was over, and now the Union victory had to be "ratified." One way or another, this was going to be done, even though it has taken more than a century to work out much (not yet all) of what was intended by the three amendments. Even without formal amendments, most of what has happened in adjusting constitutional arrangements to the outcome of the Civil War would probably have come about anyway, especially as Americans responded and conformed to worldwide developments in race relations and with respect to human rights. Still, the Civil War amendments have long helped shape, or at least illuminate and define, developments in this Country.

II

Foremost among the developments to be "ratified" by the Civil War amendments was the abolition of slavery—not only the raw institution itself but much that permitted if not required it and virtually everything questionable that flowed from it. One way or another, the practices, principles, and legacies of slavery were to be eliminated.

Slavery had been a worrisome problem in the Federal Convention of 1787 and thereafter in the Constitution itself. It was widely recognized in 1787 that slavery was a serious defect in the American system; but it was also widely recognized that it simply had to be put up with, that it could not be immediately abolished in the Country as a whole. That those citizens in the South who were so unfortunate in 1787 as to be personally dependent upon slavery were aware of the general detestation of slavery in the United States is revealed by the precautions they took in insisting upon provisions in the Constitution that would protect aspects of the slavery system from immediate suppression.

All human beings resident in the United States are, according to the Civil War amendments, to have access to the principal legal prerogatives of everyone else who lives here. The deep-rooted equality principle finally came to terms with slavery. In the United States this vital principle is nourished by venerable doctrines and is reinforced, if not even taught, by considerable experience. One significant influence upon American opinion has been the fact that virtually anyone with productive capacities could move West, set up an establishment, and hence be independent. Everyone, therefore, could readily consider themselves to be as good as anyone else. Hereditary privilege, monopolistic advantages, and sometimes even family attachments, fell before an openness to self-development. This openness remains, if not on some Western frontier, at least in the realm of the economic opportunities and social advancement to which Americans have long been accustomed, fueled as they now are by scientific discoveries and technological innovations.

The equality principle has been drawn upon in several Constitutional amendments for more than a century now. But the Civil War amendments were particularly important here, with the Fourteenth Amendment providing, in effect, a second Bill of Rights in that it guaranteed critical rights as against the States and in that it sought to bring everyone living in this Country under its coverage. Just as the Constitution of 1787 permitted the General Government to reach citizens directly without depending upon the States (for example, in taxing and conscripting them), so the Fourteenth Amendment permitted citizens to look to the General Government for protection against State infringements of traditional (if not even natural) rights.

The principles of the Fourteenth Amendment could not be taken with full seriousness, however, until slavery had been truly abolished throughout the United States. This was the objective to which the Thirteenth Amendment had been dedicated and to which the Fifteenth Amendment returned.

III

Section 1 of the Thirteenth Amendment provides: "Neither slavery nor involuntary servitude, except as a punishment for crime whereof the party shall have been duly convicted, shall exist within the United States, or any place subject to their jurisdiction."

This absolute prohibition of chattel slavery in this Country implicitly relied upon the "created equal" statement in the Declaration of Independence, a statement that Lincoln for one had emphasized in developing his political principles in the 1850s. Just as Americans had had to put up with the Articles of Confederation arrangement in order to get on with the Revolutionary War in 1776, so too they had had to put up with slavery in order to get on with the development and ratification of the Constitution in 1787. But in both cases these accommodations were generally recognized to be temporary expedients.

We recall that the natural inclination of Americans who had subscribed to the principles of the Declaration of Independence may be seen in the Northwest Ordinance, which had been enacted by the Confederation Congress in New York City during the same summer that the Constitution was drafted in Philadelphia. The last major provision in the Ordinance of '87 reads,

> There shall be neither slavery nor involuntary servitude in the said territory, otherwise than in punishment of crimes whereof the party shall have been duly convicted: Provided always, that any person escaping into the same, from whom labor or service is lawfully claimed in any one of the original states, such fugitive may be lawfully reclaimed and conveyed to the person claiming his or her labor or service as aforesaid.

It can be seen where the decisive language of the Thirteenth Amendment was probably taken from sixty years later.[193] Even so, the prohibition of slavery in the Northwest Territory did depend upon an accommodation to slavery interests in "the original states." A fugitive-slave assurance had to be added lest the institution of slavery in those States be steadily undermined by flights of slaves to the northwest.[194]

The Thirteenth Amendment was anticipated by executive actions taken during the Civil War, culminating (as we have seen) in

171

the Emancipation Proclamation of President Lincoln on January 1, 1863. We have observed that this kind of executive action, reflecting considerable expansion of Presidential power, is to be expected in wartime. Even so, the Thirteenth Amendment goes further: the Emancipation Proclamation had freed slaves held in the areas still in rebellion; the Amendment provides that slavery simply "shall [not] exist within the United States." All slavery, future as well as present, is thereby forbidden and invalidated, no matter under whose auspices slaves are held in this Country.[195]

The abolition of slavery by the Thirteenth Amendment in 1865 is in dramatic contrast to the amendment that had been proposed by a desperate Congress in 1861 in an effort to reassure the South and thereby to head off the drive to secession:

> No amendment shall be made to the Constitution which will authorize or give to Congress the power to abolish or interfere, within any State, with the domestic institutions thereof, including that of persons held to labor or service by the laws of said State.[196]

The Thirteenth Amendment is to be contrasted as well, we saw in Lecture No. 10 of this Commentary, to the Constitution of the Confederate States of America. We noticed in Lecture No. 1 that no later State government ever again aspired to the power in the Union that the States in the Confederation exercised between 1860 and 1865. The successful Union effort to suppress those State pretensions led among us to that magnification of the national powers which has been virtually impossible ever since to reverse, and not only during periods of crisis.

The Thirteenth Amendment of 1865 was followed three years later by the Fourteenth and two years after that by the Fifteenth. The Thirteenth Amendment "merely" abolished slavery and empowered Congress to make certain that the abolition would be as thorough as the Country wanted it to be. Had it been evident from the outset that the emancipated slaves would not be permanently discriminated against—if it had been evident, say, that they would be treated like the newly arrived and hence somewhat handicapped immigrants who are usually permitted to do as well as their talents and initiative permit—then the Fourteenth and Fifteenth Amendments might not have been resorted to by Congress. Without those two amendments, the powers and immunities of the States might have remained, at least for a while, pretty much what they had been under the Constitution of 1787.

We will never know what would have happened if the abolition of slavery by the Thirteenth Amendment had been immediately accepted in good faith in the South, just as we will never know what would have happened if another ordinance in the 1780s had, like the Northwest Ordinance in its terms, forbidden as well the spread of slavery to what was then the Southwest Territory.

IV

Whereas the Thirteenth Amendment is fairly simple and straight-forward, the Fourteenth Amendment is much more complicated. Even more complicated is what has been done with the Fourteenth Amendment by courts, scholars, and others, so much so that nothing I could say here is apt to provide more than the barest guidance to anyone familiar with the amendment, its interpretations, and its implementations.

Still, I offer enough of an account of the Fourteenth Amendment to permit it and its interpretations to be fitted into a comprehensive scheme. It is critical, in approaching the amendment, to remember that once the Union forces had prevailed against a radical "State Sovereignty" position in the Civil War, the States would eventually be obliged to recognize the fundamental rights of Americans, at least those great rights that had been celebrated, even before the Bill of Rights, as part of the inheritance of the English-speaking peoples.

There are, in the first section of the Fourteenth Amendment, four elements. I shall consider each of these elements in turn before going on tó the other four sections in the amendment. The amendment begins: "All persons born or naturalized in the United States, and subject to the jurisdiction thereof, are citizens of the United States and of the State wherein they reside."

This sentence reverses, in effect, the ruling by the United States Supreme Court a decade before in the explosive *Dred Scott Case.* On that occasion the Court had seemed to many to rule in effect, despite the precedent of the Northwest Ordinance (which had been reenacted with appropriate modifications by the First Congress in 1789), that the Due Process Clause of the Fifth Amendment kept Congress from prohibiting the introduction of slavery into any territory of the United States. Opposition to that ruling, which deeply divided the Country, had been vital to the platform of the Republican Party which nominated Abraham Lincoln for the Presidency in 1860.

Among the things said by the Supreme Court in *Dred Scott* was that no one of African descent could, for Constitutional purposes, ever be considered a citizen of the United States, whatever individual States might say or do. It was even argued on that occasion, in support of this ruling, that the authors of the Declaration of Independence had not meant to include anyone of African descent within the scope of the challenging pronouncement that "all Men are created equal." The most elaborate contemporaneous discussion of this issue may be found in the celebrated Lincoln-Douglas debates conducted in Illinois in 1858.[197]

Thus, this part of the Fourteenth Amendment, like the Eleventh Amendment before it and the Sixteenth Amendment and to some extent the Twenty-sixth Amendment after it, came in response to a Supreme Court ruling. A different kind of response to questionable Court rulings is the effort to change the composition of the Court, a response that is easier to make than an amendment but that may not be as reassuring because of the long-term unpredictability of the Justices who may be appointed. Our general deference to the law makes it likely that even a wrongheaded decision by the United States Supreme Court will be so respected, once established, that only a constitutional amendment may be considered adequate to reverse it.

Although the Thirteenth Amendment abolished slavery in 1865, the influence of a Supreme Court ruling is such that it was still believed by many that something had to be done to rid the Country of the pernicious effect of the 1857 *Dred Scott* ruling with respect to the nature of American citizenship. One consequence of the opening sentence of the Fourteenth Amendment was to require the States to surrender much if not all of the considerable power that they had had theretofore with respect to definitions of State citizenship.

V

The drafters of the Fourteenth Amendment, once they had addressed the citizenship issue, could go on to provide for some of the prerogatives of citizenship: "No State shall make or enforce any law which shall abridge the privileges or immunities of citizens of the United States."

It seems to be generally agreed that the Fourteenth Amendment was intended to apply to the States various of the Constitutional restraints that had been applied theretofore only to the General Government. Reliance upon the Privileges or Immunities Clause of the amendment seems the most obvious way to carry out such an intention.

There has been, for more than a half-century now, considerable argument as to which restraints on government are to be made applicable against the States. Some say that all of the Bill of Rights should be extended to the States; others say that most of the Bill of Rights should be extended; a few attempt to add to the Bill of Rights still other restraints for the States to be bound by.

It seems to me that "the privileges or immunities of citizens of the United States" binding upon the States should include at least those rights not of a peculiarly federal character that may be recognized in the Constitution of 1787 and in its Bill of Rights. It is obvious that privileges and immunities were believed to be identifiable prior to the drafting of the Bill of Rights in 1789 because there is a Privileges and Immunities Clause in Article IV of the Constitution of 1787 as well. The Bill of Rights, we should always remember, did not create the rights set forth therein but, for the most part, reaffirmed and refined long-established rights. The Ninth Amendment also reminds us that rights exist for the American people independently of their enumeration in the Bill of Rights. State constitutions can be looked to, therefore, as well as other constitutional documents (including the Constitution of 1787 and its Bill of Rights), to determine what rights (and what kind of rights) are taken seriously by the American people.[198]

This problem is complicated, however, by the modern tendency to rely primarily upon courts to protect the rights we have, a tendency which, curiously enough, goes along with the refusal to take the common law (with the rights it recognized) as seriously as it was once taken. The emphasis in the Fourteenth Amendment is upon the making or enforcing of any law, which provides a guide to State legislatures and executives as well as to State courts. If there are privileges and immunities of citizens of the United States that the States are bound to respect, does not that mean that the General

Government should (independent of explicit provisions either in the Bill of Rights or in the Fourteenth Amendment) also be bound to respect them?

I have suggested that the straightforward way of extending against the States the rights otherwise recognized by the Constitution is through the Privileges or Immunities Clause of the Fourteenth Amendment.[199] But an 1873 ruling by the Supreme Court[200] slaughtered the Privileges or Immunities Clause of the Fourteenth Amendment and effectively removed it (for more than a century thereafter) from serious consideration as the means for assuring restraints upon the States. This has led to one distortion after another as, once again, the American people, in their pursuit of the aspirations evident in the Declaration of Independence and the Constitution of the United States, have been obliged to work their way around what the Supreme Court and others have wrought.[201]

VI

Section 1 of the Fourteenth Amendment continues: "nor shall any State deprive any person of life, liberty, or property, without due process of law." This draws upon a provision found in the Fifth Amendment. There is no reason to believe that this 1868 provision should be read differently from the 1791 provision, which, as we have seen, reminds judges in the Courts of the United States of due-process obligations of long standing in Anglo-American jurisprudence. Indicative of what due process means are such references to it as that found in the Thirteenth Amendment: "crime whereof the party shall have been duly convicted."

Notice that the two Due Process Clauses cover all persons, not only citizens of the United States. Everyone is entitled to a fair trial when he is about to be deprived in this Country of his "life, liberty, or property."[202] It can be argued that the right to a fair trial, in both criminal and civil cases, is one of the privileges and immunities of citizens of the United States—and, if so, the Due Process Clause in the Fourteenth Amendment is superfluous. But the Privileges or Immunities Clause seems to be primarily concerned with the making or enforcing of statutes that may be questionable, while the Due Process Clause looks primarily to the conduct of judicial proceedings, including common-law cases, aside from what may be done through the use of statutes. Thus, the sequence in Section 1 of the Fourteenth Amendment ("mak[ing]," "enforc[ing]," and "process") follows more or less the sequence of the first three articles of the Constitution (Legislative, Executive, and Judicial).

Even though the Due Process Clause of the Fifth Amendment continues to be read as primarily a guide for judges (in the National Courts), the Due Process Clause in the Fourteenth Amendment has been used as the means for bringing to bear upon State governments (not just upon State judges) an array of rights due to people living in the United States. That is, the Due Process Clause has been relied upon to do what the Privileges or Immunities Clause in the Fourteenth Amendment was originally believed to do. The Supreme Court could effectively get rid of the Privileges or Immunities Clause in 1873, but it eventually felt obliged (considering certain inherent tendencies in the American regime) to find some other way to subject the States to the principles and restraints that Americans had long believed should be respected by all governments. These principles and restraints are invoked, we have seen, in such documents as the Declaration of Independence.

However defensible this use of the Fourteenth Amendment's Due Process Clause may have been in the circumstances, it has not promoted care in reading of the Constitution. When virtually identical provisions, as those in the Fifth and Fourteenth Amendments, can be read so differently, people come to suspect that the Constitution is no more than what the judges happen to say it is. If the Due Process Clause of the Fourteenth Amendment can be expanded the way it has been, there seem to be no limits upon what may be done with it. Perhaps even more significant, if the extension of rights against the States is accomplished by means of the Due Process Clause, the primary guardian of those rights is more likely to be taken to be the courts, since due process has traditionally been associated with judicial proceedings. But it is evident, as we shall see when we come to Section 5 of the Fourteenth Amendment, that Congress was looked to for leadership in protecting the rights of the American people, just as Parliament has always been looked to in England. *Dred Scott* taught thoughtful citizens that the United States Supreme Court could not be left to its own devices here.

VII

Section 1 of the Fourteenth Amendment concludes: "nor [shall any State] deny to any person within its jurisdiction the equal protection of the laws." The principle of equality fundamental to the American regime, which goes back, in some form, at least to Magna Carta and which was proclaimed in the Declaration of Independence, is for the first time made explicit in the Constitution.

It is likely that the recently emancipated slaves were the primary concern of the framers of the Fourteenth Amendment. They are to have the rights that others have. But that means, in effect, that all others have those rights also, and perhaps have them now more firmly than ever before, whatever individual States may want to do.

The sequence of the provisions in Section 1 of the Fourteenth Amendment suggests that they do not cover the same things. First, citizens are identified: that is the constitutional bedrock, or the people, upon which everything else is built. It is then provided that State governments may not abridge the privileges or immunities of citizens. But, it seems to be recognized, due process may be denied in particular cases even though the privileges and immunities of citizens may be generally respected by the laws that are made and enforced—and so the Due Process Clause is added. But, it then seems to be recognized, although privileges and immunities may be respected and due process may be routinely available, some persons may be mistreated by being subjected to laws that do not apply in the same way to others—and so the Equal Protection Clause is added. Or, as it has recently been put, this Clause "requires every State to govern impartially."[203]

The Equal Protection Clause is implied, it can again be said, by Magna Carta and its Rule of Law. Perhaps, indeed, it is implied in the American constitutional system from the beginning, however much it was compromised by the institution of slavery. One way or another, it has come to be argued, Equal Protection criteria should be applied against the General Government as well.[204]

We have seen that the equality principle has been so powerful in the United States that one Constitutional provision after another is developed by those who want to see that all governments in the United States respect, for all persons, the rights that Americans have long believed are due not only to them but to all human beings in appropriate circumstances. Critical here may be that natural right—that sense of what is by nature right—to which I have several times referred.[205]

Section 1 of the Fourteenth Amendment, with its disciplining of the States by bringing to bear against them the rights traditionally recognized by the American people, ushered in a significantly revised constitutional arrangement in the United States. The Gettysburg Address, which serves as preamble to this new Constitution, argues in effect that this redefined American regime was implicit from the very beginning.

VIII

Section 2 of the Fourteenth Amendment provides that "Representatives shall be apportioned among the several States according to their respective numbers, counting the whole number of persons in each State, excluding Indians not taxed." One immediate consequence of this was to increase the voting power of the Southern States in the national councils, since the emancipated slaves were now to be given full weight (not the three-fifths that had originally been provided for slaves).

Thus, equality immediately proved threatening for Northerners who could see themselves substantially weakened in Congress by their victory in the Civil War. The first sentence of Section 2 may not have been needed, since the counting for apportionment purposes would routinely include the citizens identified in Section 1. This sentence seems to be there as an introduction to what follows: the limitation placed upon those States that deny the right to vote "to any of the male inhabitants of such State, being twenty-one years of age, and citizens of the United States."

This provision does not assure voting rights to those improperly denied them, but rather penalizes States that do deny them. Perhaps the Equal Protection Clause invalidates such denials, but it does not suggest an immediate remedy. And so Congress is empowered by Section 2 of the Fourteenth Amendment to reduce in the House of Representatives "the basis of representation" for offending States.

The Northerners who controlled the Congress that wrote the Fourteenth Amendment were willing to have the emancipated slaves counted if they could vote. Presumably they could, as voters, affect who was chosen to go to Congress and to fill various posts in State governments. (The exclusion with respect to Indians reminds us of the vital relation between taxation and representation in the American regime. In 1924 Congress passed the Indian Citizenship Act, which provided "That all non-citizen Indians born within the territorial limits of the United States be, and they are hereby, declared to be citizens of the United States . . .")

IX

Section 3 of the Fourteenth Amendment represents another attempt by the Congress to hold Southerners in check, at least for a generation. Public office, National as well as State, was denied to certain persons "who, having previously taken an oath . . . to support the Constitution of the United States, [had] engaged in insurrection or rebellion against the same."

We are reminded by this provision that the equality principle can be suspended, in its application, by one's circumstances or conduct. Criminals, for example, are routinely denied various civil rights. Just as slavery had kept people of African descent from full access to the privileges and immunities of Americans, so could rebellion affect the full access of others. (Congress was given the power, by a two-thirds vote of each House, to remove this disability for rebellion.)

One implication of Section 3, and of Section 4 as well, seems to be to declare secession itself to be unconstitutional, for the disability here seems to refer not only to previous but also to future rebellions.

X

Section 3 of the Fourteenth Amendment provided for penalizing rebels in their public capacities. Section 4 provides for penalizing rebels in their private capacities: "neither the United States nor any State shall assume or pay any debt or obligation incurred in aid of insurrection or rebellion against the United States, or any claim for the loss or emancipation of any slave."

Among the purposes of this provision, it would seem, was to head off any claims against the United States for the loss or emancipation of slaves, perhaps by recourse to such provisions as the Taking Clause of the Fifth Amendment. Such claims would have had little chance of success insofar as emancipation came by way of the Thirteenth Amendment. But what about earlier losses and emancipation that had come by way of military action and executive decrees? The Fourteenth Amendment says, in effect, that people who have lost slaves at any time or in any way may not be compensated by any public funds, National or State, no matter what was anticipated by the Emancipation Proclamation, by Acts of Congress, or by State legislation.

XI

The drafters of Constitutional amendments, beginning with the Thirteenth, have taken to adding a provision empowering Congress to enforce the amendment. Such provisions may be found in more than half of the amendments since the Twelfth Amendment.

Section 5 of the Fourteenth Amendment reads, "The Congress shall have power to enforce, by appropriate legislation, the provisions of this article." Much is left for Congress to do in working out implications of the Fourteenth Amendment. This provision recognizes the supervisory role of Congress in these matters.

Does such a provision add anything to what the Necessary and Proper Clause does in empowering Congress? In fact, does the use of such a provision in some amendments implicitly, however inadvertently, limit the powers of Congress with respect to the matters covered in those amendments that do not happen to have such a provision?[206]

What constitutes "appropriate legislation" by Congress in "enforc[ing] the provisions" of the Fourteenth Amendment? Is Congress limited simply to making sure that the various provisions in the amendment are carried out? For example, Congress may act to ensure that no person is deprived of equal protection of the laws. But may Congress also act to serve the purposes for which equal protection is evidently desired? It is here that one case for the authority to use affirmative-action programs may be made. This would be authority for the majority to do on behalf of a minority at the immediate expense of the majority what could not be done on behalf of the majority at the expense of the minority. Such action would be designed to serve the interest of the entire community as well as of the minority.

It can be argued that the ultimate concern of Section 5 of the Fourteenth Amendment is not to ensure State compliance with specified formal standards but rather to permit the United States to advance racial justice. It may not be enough, considering the lingering effects of centuries of oppression for African-Americans in this Country and elsewhere, merely to forbid formal State actions of a certain character hereafter. Certainly the early Congresses under the Fourteenth Amendment, including the Congress that drafted it, considered it within their power to provide special programs on behalf of the recently emancipated slaves.

XII

The Fourteenth Amendment recognized the integrity of the Union that had been sealed in blood by the Civil War. That war had made many feel that they now had a Country—the Nation they had fought for and across. The war may even have provided ordinary Americans a depth and dignity they had not had before, with sacrifices made in 1861–1865 that (some have argued) should have been made from 1787 on to dispose of slavery at the outset in an authoritative and permanent fashion, however long the process of disposition might have taken at that time.

Once the integrity of the Union had been affirmed by a great war, especially through a struggle that began for the National Government as an effort to keep the Union together and ended as a crusade against slavery, the Fifteenth Amendment followed naturally enough upon the Thirteenth and Fourteenth Amendments: "The right of citizens of the United States to vote shall not be denied or abridged by the United States or by any State on account of race, color, or previous condition of servitude."

The primary concern of both the Thirteenth and the Fifteenth Amendments is with the condition and treatment of the former slaves. This makes it likely that the Fourteenth Amendment is also very much concerned with those people, however much others may benefit as well because of the reaffirmation and application in that amendment of various general principles.

Perhaps it was originally believed by the framers of the Fourteenth Amendment that it would guarantee voting rights for the former slaves. Those rights are taken for granted in Section 2 of that amendment. But it seems to have become evident fairly soon that more direct or explicit provisions about something so fundamental as voting were needed. Even the Fifteenth Amendment required almost a century to take hold.

The insistence in the second half of the twentieth century upon voting rights proved decisive, especially when underwritten and directed by Congressional mandates. Invocations of the equality principle made it easier to insist upon such rights.

XIII

All branches of the General Government have contributed to accomplishing the aims of the Civil War Amendments. This is something that is much easier for the General Government than for the State Governments to try to do, even though the Southern States have been substantially (not yet completely) liberated by the War and its amendments from crippling institutions.

Congress started the implementation of these amendments with legislation in the 1860s and 1870s and has continued down to our day, culminating in the recent Civil Rights and Voting Rights legislation. African-Americans have not been the only beneficiaries of some of this legislation. Even when they have been intended as the principal immediate beneficiaries, the entire Country has been strengthened by the empowerment, reassurance, and development of a significant minority within it.

The Executive, too, started implementation of these amendments in the 1860s and 1870s: this was anticipated by the Emancipation Proclamation and was furthered by directives issued to, and promulgated by, armies of occupation in the South. Since the Second World War, executive orders have been critical in the curtailment of racial discrimination in the armed forces and Executive departments of the United States, so much so that an African-American four-star general was widely respected as the Chairman of the Joint Chiefs of Staff in charge of the overall military conduct of the 1990–1991 crisis in the Persian Gulf region.

The record of the Judiciary regarding civil-rights matters seems to have been spottier than that of the Congress and the Executive.

Rulings by the Supreme Court in the decades following the Civil War seriously hampered what Congress had tried to do.[207] The rulings with respect to State actions in *Plessy* v. *Ferguson*[208] did not help either. The Court's most dramatic manifestation of a more enlightened position may be seen in the 1954 school-desegregation case, *Brown* v. *Board of Education*[209]—but *Brown* and like cases might not have been needed to the extent or in the way that they were if the Court had been more sensible in its readings of the Fourteenth Amendment in the last quarter of the nineteenth century.

I have suggested that the affirmative-action issue has yet to be sensibly settled by the Courts. Another issue in need of sensible resolution is the status of "State action" under the Fourteenth Amendment. It is often said by the Courts that Congress, in enforcing the provisions of this amendment, can only direct its attention to actions taken by the State governments that deny equal protection of the laws. Private actions, it is argued, are beyond the scope of Congress under the Fourteenth Amendment, whatever Congress may do pursuant to other powers it may have (such as the Commerce Power).

But it is evident in the sequence of Civil War amendments and related legislation that Congress attempted to deal with one subterfuge after another whereby efforts might be made to deny various rights to the former slaves. If communities, by custom and other means which can have the force of law, do informally what they obviously cannot do formally (that is, by explicit statutory provisions or other governmental action), may nothing be done by the General Government to check them? Suppose, for example, that two neighboring American communities practice obvious racial segregation with respect to the same activities, with one of the communities achieving this result through the use of a statute and the other achieving it through the use of a determined and authoritative public opinion. Why should not Congress, pursuant to Section 5 of the Fourteenth Amendment, be able to deal the same way with both? However that may be, Congress in the 1860s believed it was authorized to supervise private activities bearing upon race relations, but the Supreme Court in the following decades thought otherwise. (Compare the 1772 *Somerset* opinion found in Appendix L-1 of this Commentary: Lord Mansfield was confident that the habeas corpus remedy extended to private acts of confinement.

Somerset also suggests, by the way, that the Courts of the United States should have been able, even before the Fourteenth Amendment, to provide habeas corpus remedies with respect to some instances of confinement by the States, especially in circumstances where the Privileges and Immunities Clause of Article IV of the Constitution was applicable. In some circumstances, American slavery itself might have been vulnerable to such a challenge.)

Again one must consider whether the evident purposes of the Fourteenth Amendment suggest what Congress might do to deal with any actions and conditions that thwart a just and humane national purpose. In these and related matters it is sounder for Congress to take the lead; it usually can decide better than can judges how much of the private activity in and of a community is to be regulated and in what way. After all, is it not really the community that is often expressing itself through these private activities, even to the extent of trying in effect to amend the Constitution? And if so, is it not better to counter that form of public effort with another form of public effort of a more official character, something that the Congress (as the branch of government most sensitively representative of the people) is usually better equipped to develop than either the President or the Courts? The people are thereby confronted by themselves, but in a more elevated form. The people, in their most elevated form, have their political sentiments nourished by the Biblical as well as by the Classical tradition. This may be seen most dramatically in the Gettysburg Address and the Second Inaugural Address of Abraham Lincoln. Celebration of victory over slavery may be heard in the 1878 Sacred Harp song, *Babylon Is Fallen*, with its joyous proclamation, "Babylon is fallen, is fallen, is fallen, Babylon is fallen to rise no more." (This kind of sentiment is anticipated in William Shakespeare's bittersweet examination of republican virtue, *Julius Caesar*. Plutarch's biography of Timoleon, as well as of Julius Caesar, is also instructive here.) Another stirring Sacred Harp song, the *Easter Anthem* of 1787, could well have served as the hymn of the American Revolution (just as the 1862 *Battle Hymn of the Republic* was to do during the Civil War), its most stirring lines about ushering in a New World being, "Then first humanity triumphant passed the crystal ports of light, and seized eternal youth." The Civil War amendments may be seen as apt instruments for a prudent rejuvenation of the American Republic, or a new birth of freedom.

185

13. Amendments XVI, XVII, and XIX

I

The Sixteenth, Seventeenth, and Nineteenth Amendments, along with the Eighteenth Amendment (which we will consider in our next lecture along with the amendment that repealed it, the Twenty-first), all reflect populist developments in the United States during the first quarter of the twentieth century.

More than forty years passed between the Civil War amendments (1865, 1868, and 1870) and these three amendments of 1913 and 1920. It took more than half a century to spell out the populist implications grounded in the equality principle that began to be drawn upon in the 1860s with the radically democratic response to the oligarchic features of the attempt at secession. (The complexity of American sectional relations, however, is suggested upon noticing the democratic impulse in the Southern invocation of home-rule and liberty and the oligarchic impulse in the Northern financial and industrial development.)

The three Civil War amendments obscure a significant fact of American constitutional history: more than a century passed (from 1804 to 1913) before any amendments were fashioned primarily for changing the way the General Government worked in this Country. The Civil War amendments, as we have seen, were mostly directed to curbing the States, and powers were given to the General Government to serve that end.

I have attempted to develop, both in my Commentary on the Constitution of 1787 and thus far in this Commentary on the Amendments, the order in which things are arranged, an order keyed to the matters dealt with both in the Constitution and in those amendments. We have noticed that when one goes beyond the Twelfth

Amendment, or for that matter when one goes beyond the Tenth Amendment, the order of the Amendments is determined by history. This means that chance is likely to play a greater part, making the overall American constitutional movement more difficult to subject to rational analysis.[210]

II

A change in the way that the General Government worked may be seen in the Sixteenth Amendment: "The Congress shall have power to lay and collect taxes on incomes, from whatever source derived, without apportionment among the several States, and without regard to any census or enumeration."

This change, unlike the changes curtailing the States in the Civil War amendments and elsewhere, was primarily in order to expand the power of the General Government. In fact, we have noticed, there has never been a constitutional amendment that has curbed any of the major legislative powers originally desired by the Framers of the Constitution of 1787 for the Government of the United States.[211]

The Sixteenth Amendment might never have been needed if the Supreme Court had not cast doubt in 1895 upon the power of Congress to tax incomes,[212] something Congress had done during the Civil War and thereafter. The difficulty perceived here had come from the provision in Section 9 of Article I of the Constitution: "No Capitation, or other direct, Tax shall be laid, unless in Proportion to the Census or Enumeration herein before directed to be taken." It is difficult to see, however, that an income tax violated the obvious purposes of the limitation upon "Capitation, or other direct, Tax," a limitation that aimed at uniform treatment of taxpayers throughout the several States.

The Sixteenth Amendment is still another indication that citizens can be dealt with directly by the General Government, without any mediation by the States in any way. This has been seen recently in what can evidently be done by the General Government with the National Guard of a State.

187

III

The Seventeenth Amendment provides for direct popular election of Senators, taking that power of selection away from the State legislatures:

> The Senate of the United States shall be composed of two Senators from each State, elected by the people thereof, for six years; and each Senator shall have one vote. The electors in each State shall have the qualifications requisite for electors of the most numerous branch of the State legislatures.

This shift can be said to have been anticipated by, among other things, the highly publicized contest between Abraham Lincoln and Stephen A. Douglas in Illinois in 1858. Although that election still depended on the State legislature, the debates between Lincoln and Douglas were intended to influence the choice by the people of the members of the State legislature that would in turn choose a Senator that year.

The national movement that led to direct election of Senators has been described in this fashion:

> Selection of United States senators by state legislatures had been an object of criticism for many years. Direct election of senators was first proposed in 1826; and after 1893 a constitutional amendment to establish direct election was proposed in Congress every year. Even without a constitutional amendment, popular choice of senators was becoming the rule. By 1912, twenty-nine of the forty-eight states had provided either for nomination by party primaries, with the individual legislators bound to vote for their party's nominee, or for a statewide general election, the result of which was binding on the legislature.
>
> The objectives of direct election included reducing corruption in selection of senators, elimination of national-party domination of state legislatures, and immediate representation of the people in the Senate.[213]

The stipulation in the Seventeenth Amendment that "each Senator shall have one vote" simply repeats a provision in Section 3 of Article I of the Constitution: it had been prudent to make that point there, lest it be argued that the two Senators chosen by a State legislature should have no votes on their own but rather should act as their State legislature directed.[214]

The provision in the Seventeenth Amendment about the electors of Senators is taken from Section 2 of Article I where the qualifications of the electors of Representatives are described. We can see here, as elsewhere in the amendments, signs of the steady democratization (keyed to the equality principle) that it is salutary to regard as having been implicit in the American constitutional system from its beginning. Perhaps this is evident as well in the second paragraph of the Seventeenth Amendment, where it is clear that a State's temporary replacement of a Senator, pending an election, is ultimately under the control of the legislature, not of the governor.

Students of the Constitution have wondered whether the popular election of Senators has been a good thing for the Country. It is sometimes said that popular election of Senators has opened the way to more demagoguery in Senators, as well as to more costly elections, than we might otherwise have had. Or, as some have put it, all or practically all of the good Senators we have had since 1913 could have been chosen by their State legislatures as well, but most if not all of our bad Senators would not have been chosen (or at least not kept for a second term) by State legislatures. This assessment presupposes, it seems, that the worst Senators we have had would not have been chosen by people who really knew them—and State legislators are much more apt to know Senatorial candidates intimately than is the man in the street. Of course, it can be answered, the man in the street is more likely to be moral, if not moralistic, in his political judgment than the professional politician. The question is left whether it is better in such matters to lean more toward morality or more toward competence, as each of these is ordinarily understood.

The difficulty in any recourse to a completely popular election of the President may be seen in the problem any one of us has in trying to figure out what appeal a questionable Senator from another State could possibly have in the State from which he is elected. We can still rely somewhat upon party and State organizations to screen our Presidential candidates for us, a screening that direct popular election would tend to discourage, just as popular election of Senators and much more reliance upon Presidential primaries have tended to do.

IV

We find in the Seventeenth Amendment, just as in the Sixteenth Amendment, that the role of the States is cut down in our Constitutional system. As a result of the Sixteenth Amendment, we have seen, citizens can be dealt with directly by the United States as tax collector, without any reference at all to the States. As a result of the Seventeenth Amendment, we have also seen, citizens can directly choose their own Senators. The State legislatures are not to filter out and weigh popular opinions and desires in making a choice.

The qualifications of electors of Senators in a State are keyed in the Seventeenth Amendment to the broadest base possible among the standards employed by the State in identifying electors for its legislature. Subsequent amendments, beginning with the Nineteenth, whittle away at even this degree of control of the electorate by State governments. This development may have been encouraged, if not somewhat required, by the Republican Form of Government Guarantee in the Constitution of 1787; it may also have been contemplated by the Fourteenth and Fifteenth Amendments. We can see, that is, that there may be something inevitable, or at least highly likely, about all this: once massive change begins accelerating, as the result of something as cataclysmic as the Civil War, it is hard to reverse the movement. In much of the Country States' Rights had come to mean Slavery and Rebellion—and so the States have found their powers steadily curtailed, both by formal constitutional amendments and by everyday political rearrangements.

Still, it is instructive to notice that the changes made thus far by Constitutional amendments do not emphasize the duties that government might have. Except for the Preamble and the Republican Form of Government Guarantee, none of the provisions for the rights of individuals in the Constitution and its amendments require the Government of the United States to do anything on behalf of citizens; rather, the Government is kept, by the declaration of these rights, from doing certain things. Economic and social rights, as in the United Nations declarations of human rights, require governments to provide various things. But it is evident that judicial attempts to enforce such rights can be frustrating. The American approach, on the other hand, still tends to proceed on the assumption that the Constitution of the United States should do no more than empower and restrain government, leaving it up to the people to decide both what to do with their personal resources and what political measures they want their governments to fashion for them with the powers made available to government. I return to these matters in Lecture No. 17 of this Commentary.

V

The Nineteenth Amendment provides: "The right of citizens of the United States to vote shall not be denied or abridged by the United States or by any State on account of sex." The "denied or abridged" form had been used before, as in the Fifteenth Amendment; it is intended to make sure that neither outright deprivation nor a cutting down will be tolerated here.

The background to the emergence of the Nineteenth Amendment has been described in this fashion:

> Political agitation for enfranchisement [of women] began in 1848, at the first women's rights convention in Seneca Falls, New York. In its Declaration of Sentiments, the convention included suffrage as one of the "inalienable rights" to which women were entitled. As the century progressed, the vote assumed increasing importance, both as a symbolic affirmation of women's equality and as a means to address a vast array of sex-based discrimination in employment, education, domestic law, and related areas. Once the Supreme Court ruled [in 1875] that suffrage was not one of the Privileges and Immunities guaranteed by the Fourteenth Amendment to women as citizens, the necessity for a state or federal constitutional amendment became apparent.
>
> The struggle for women's rights was a response to various forces. Urbanization, industrialization, declining birth rates, and expanding educational and employment opportunities tended to diminish women's role in the private domestic sphere while encouraging their participation in the public sphere. So too, women's involvement, first with abolitionism and later with other progressive causes, generated political commitments and experiences that fueled demands for equal rights.[215]

The enfranchisement of women did not begin in the United States with the Nineteenth Amendment. Some States had already begun to allow women to vote well before the Nineteenth Amendment. It should be noticed that the Constitution of 1787 never kept the States from allowing women to vote (even though the Fourteenth Amendment presupposed male voters). The States are not left free to implement the Nineteenth Amendment as they wish; we again see that Congress is given power "to enforce this article by appropriate legislation."

The suffrage guarantee in the Nineteenth Amendment is, it seems to me, far more important than the Equal Rights Amendment proposed by Congress in 1972. The 1972 proposal, which barely failed of ratification by the States, provides, "Equality of rights under the law shall not be denied or abridged by the United States or by any State on account of sex." Women, who need not be a minority in the United States, are equipped, by the use of the votes they do have, to get by means of legislation everything that they should want to get from an Equal Rights Amendment. Congressional and State legislation, backed up by judicial interpretations, have already accomplished much of what the Equal Rights Amendment would have, and perhaps in a healthier way—that is, without the kind of recrimination that has come from reliance upon judicial rather than political development of, say, abortion rights.[216]

VI

There have been, since the Civil War, three principal constitutional developments by way of amendments (the first two of which we have already had illustrations of): the equality principle is implemented further; the States are played down; and Presidential arrangements are tinkered with. These three developments may be related to one another. Thus, the extension of suffrage by means of the Fifteenth and Nineteenth Amendments has meant that the States have lost some of the control of elections that they originally had. The States, however important they are bound to remain, have been partly but decisively eclipsed in their institutionalized or collective capacity.

It is well to notice again that the Constitutional amendments we have had are, by and large, consistent with the original Constitution. Many of them, I have suggested, can be said to have been called for, or at least encouraged, by the spirit of the Constitution of 1787. This may even be said of the Civil War amendments. After all, an explanation was needed, from the beginning, to justify the accommodations to slavery in the Constitution of 1787; but no explanation was needed to justify the abolition of slavery in 1865, especially since this had already happened in most of the Western World. In these matters, the United States often leads but also sometimes follows what is happening elsewhere.

VII

I return to the significance of steadily playing down the States in our Constitutional system. This can also mean playing down the Congress, with a related ascendancy of the Presidency. Consider, again, how the Congressional prerogative with respect to the declaration of war was virtually foreclosed by the Presidential decision, announced on November 8, 1990, to transform the emergency-oriented American forces in Saudi Arabia from a defensive to an offensive stance. Such unilateral action by the President, effectively limiting what Congress could do thereafter, would have once been generally condemned as being unconstitutional in spirit. That the determination to take this action was concealed from view by the President during the 1990 Congressional elections was also disquieting. (One can be reminded by all this of Congressman Abraham Lincoln's reservations about how the United States got into the Mexican War. One can be reminded as well of the remarkably destructive maneuvers by Germany and Austria-Hungary toward Serbia in July 1914.)

The States and the Congress go together more than do the President and the States. However Senators are chosen, they are selected State by State; the same is true of members of the House of Representatives. But the current tendency is more and more to turn the election of the President into a national event, even without going all the way to a direct popular election.

It has always been in Congress that the States have been most effective. For Congress reflects, much more than any President can, the States as States. It is easy, sometimes perhaps even necessary, to identify the Nation with the Executive Officer, especially during a crisis. This is probably reinforced by technological developments that make it easy, as well as more interesting, to play up the drama of individual leaders acting. Our Presidents, however, are by and large much more like chief executives in countries around the world than our Congress is like most parliamentary bodies (which are typically controlled by their executives). Deliberative bodies tend to be far less exciting than chief executives. But is it not in Congress that We the People do our most distinctive as well as our most effective "peopling" most of the time? This makes ever more troublesome, if not eventually dangerous, the current unconstitutional tendency to permit both interests-driven referenda in the States and the "supermajority" rules (including routine filibusters) in legislative bodies to subvert the deliberate workings of the will of the people's duly elected representatives. (I return to this problem in Lecture No. 17, Section I, of this Commentary.)

14. Amendments XVIII and XXI

I

The Eighteenth Amendment, ratified just after the First World War, provided in its first section:

> After one year from the ratification of this article the manufacture, sale, or transportation of intoxicating liquors within, the importation thereof into, or the exportation thereof from the United States and all territory subject to the jurisdiction thereof for beverage purposes is hereby prohibited.

One author has observed about the post–First World War era:

> That was a time of great hopes and high endeavors, with the Progressive movement making successful efforts to revive income taxation, to provide for the popular election of Senators and for women's suffrage, to institute the direct primary, initiative and referendum, and ballot reform, to regulate business, and to improve the lot of the underprivileged.[217]

The United States had just fought a war that was defined, in this Country at least, as aiming to make the world safe for democracy. Now, it was widely believed in the United States, a general abstention from intoxicating liquors would help make democracy safer for the world by moderating the passions and strengthening the moral fibre of the American people. The Eighteenth Amendment, combining as it did high-minded aspirations and dismal consequences, became the Vietnam War of our Constitutional amendments.

One of the concerns that prohibitionists had as they agitated against intoxicating beverages in this Country was that prohibition not be identified with the sumptuary laws familiar to the eighteenth century. Those laws, directed at excessive consumption and display, were often condemned by Americans as infringements of liberty. The desire of prohibitionists not to have their efforts resisted as sumptuary laws helps account for the exclusion from the Eighteenth Amendment of any restriction upon the *consumption* of intoxicating beverages. Rather, it was argued, prohibition addressed the misconduct of the merchants of alcohol, not the morals or the personal liberty of the American people.[218]

II

The Eighteenth Amendment was an unnecessary amendment in that it followed upon misreadings of parts of the Constitution. Much if not all of what the amendment was intended to accomplish could have been done by the use of Congressional powers. This would have been more obvious than it was, in the first decades of the twentieth century, if the Commerce Clause had always been recognized in its amplitude by the United States Supreme Court.

Alcohol could be regulated, even to the extent of prohibition, by Congressional statute, without the need of any constitutional amendment, just as many narcotics (including tobacco), various weapons, and the products of child labor are dealt with today.[219] The suppression of child labor is particularly instructive in that it was first attempted by Congressional statute, then by constitutional amendment when the statute was said by the Supreme Court to be unconstitutional, and then again by statute with the Supreme Court reversing itself as to the constitutionality of child labor regulations, making it unnecessary to press further for the ratification of the proposed amendment. Since the physical and social effects of alcohol in this Country have probably always been far worse than those of narcotics, it would seem that if the sale of narcotics can be regulated as it is by Congressional statutes, so can the sale of alcohol.

It is not only the Commerce Clause that can be said to provide Congress the basis for the regulation of the manufacture and sale of intoxicating liquors. The revenue powers of Congress were looked to in the first session of the First Congress for this purpose; a tariff on the importation of molasses was justified, in part, for what it would do to help curb the manufacture and consumption of rum in this Country.[220]

Prohibition did not begin in this Country with the Eighteenth Amendment. It had been anticipated in more than half of the States by statewide measures and in the Country at large during the First World War by the Wartime Prohibition Act. The States were understood to be exercising their traditional powers to safeguard the health and morals of their people; Congress was understood to be exercising its defense powers in curtailing the making of products that used grains needed for the war effort and that undermined the efficiency of the work force. Thus, the Country was largely dry, by acts of Congress and of the States, before the Eighteenth Amendment took effect.[221]

If the prohibitionists (who were evidently strengthened significantly by the newly established female suffrage) had restricted themselves to State efforts and to Congressional statutes, they might have been more successful in the long run than they have been, in that they could have been more discriminating and otherwise accommodating in the measures they relied upon. Did recourse to a constitutional amendment make it much more likely that there would be an all-or-nothing approach, with the dire consequences for the cause of prohibition that we have seen? We are reminded here that care must be taken lest the Constitution and constitutional interpretations be used as repositories for a variety of social and economic reforms that are better left to statutes that can be much more easily adjusted as circumstances change.

III

I have suggested that a constitutional amendment in this Country usually is seen following upon, rather than leading to, a general development. For example, the reliance upon either preferential primaries or statewide general elections for the popular choice of Senators preceded the Seventeenth Amendment in one-half of the States.[222] We have seen that the Lincoln-Douglas Debates contributed to developments here. We have also seen that the 1913 Women's Suffrage Amendment, too, was anticipated by innovations in the States.[223]

We have noticed as well that legal prohibition of intoxicating beverages was widely provided for before the Eighteenth Amendment was ratified. Much of the impetus for prohibition at the turn of the twentieth century came from a campaign against the evils of saloons. This campaign helped put the emphasis, as did the Eighteenth Amendment later on, not upon the immorality of drinkers but rather upon the greed and misconduct of producers and suppliers.[224]

It can seem implausible to us today that two-thirds of the Congress and three-fourths of the States could agree, evidently with considerable enthusiasm, that the manufacture and sale of intoxicating beverages should be generally suppressed in this Country. This was in large part due, it seems, to a widespread and perhaps justified public opinion, developed in the nineteenth century, about the devastating effects of alcohol consumption. We can get some notion of what that devastation must have looked like by noticing today the problems that the Russians have with alcohol and that we have with drugs.

We will see, further on, how shifts in public opinion contributed to the repeal of the Eighteenth Amendment.

IV

The terms of the Eighteenth Amendment do not pose much of a problem in figuring out what was intended. It was recognized, however, that Congress would have to be relied upon to determine what should be considered "intoxicating liquors." This Congress did in the Volstead Act of 1919,[225] which also provided means for enforcing the prohibitions of the Eighteenth Amendment.

Some have argued that the amendment, instead of using the term *intoxicating liquors,* should have referred to and thus forbidden various forms of alcohol, such as beer, rum, whiskey, and wine. One may wonder, as well, whether intoxicating pills and powders should have been considered within the scope of the term, *for beverage purposes.*[226] But these do not seem to have been the difficult problems in enforcing this amendment.

In critical respects, moreover, the Eighteenth Amendment was self-executing, once its year of grace had run.[227] The restriction in the amendment upon exportation seems to have served at least two purposes. First, it would be easier to control the domestic sales of alcohol if none could be made for export either, since the potential diversion to the domestic market of alcohol said to be manufactured for export would always have been a problem. Second, some of the prohibitionists saw the American development as the forerunner of a salutary worldwide movement. They did not want to permit a foisting upon the rest of the world of what was now recognized to be harmful in the United States. (Consider here the concerns among us today about our irresponsible exportation of tobacco products, medicines, and environmental pollutants that are restricted in the United States.)

Questions were raised, as the Volstead Act was prepared and enforced, about whether the absolutist character of the Eighteenth Amendment overrode other Constitutional provisions, including those that recognized the effects of treaties and that enshrined (as in the Bill of Rights) traditional guarantees. Certainly, Constitutional interpretations and relations, as well as the general political system in this Country, were substantially shaken by attempted implementations of the Eighteenth Amendment.

Symbolic perhaps of the distortions following upon this amendment are the directions laid down in the third section of the Eighteenth Amendment:

> This article shall be inoperative unless it shall have been ratified as an amendment to the Constitution by the legislatures of the several States, as provided in the Constitution, within seven years from the date of the submission hereof to the States by the Congress.

This kind of provision also came to be used in Amendments XX, XXI, and XXII. There was thereby some thirty years of burdening the Constitution with decidedly unconstitutional language, language that could have been adequately provided for (as it is now) in the Congressional resolutions submitting proposed amendments to the States for their ratification.

Thus, it can be said, the purpose of Section 3 of the Eighteenth Amendment could have been accomplished without adding that section to the amendment just as the principal purpose of the Eighteenth Amendment itself could have been accomplished (and, indeed, perhaps better accomplished) without adding that amendment to the Constitution.

V

This, then, was what came to be known as The Noble Experiment—first, sincerely, by its proponents; later, sardonically, by its critics. This became, in some ways, *the* American Issue. The alcohol prohibition movement was largely rooted in several of the Protestant churches in this Country.[228] Some may be tempted, therefore, to regard it to have been in spirit, even if not in terms, a partial modification of the Religion Clauses of the First Amendment.

Certainly religious enthusiasm stimulated and sustained the alcohol-prohibition movement, just as it had done a half-century before with the slavery-abolition movement. Prohibitionists, in their determination to stamp out the evils of the intoxicating-liquors industry, were themselves intoxicated by what they believed could be accomplished by law. They tried to eliminate the slavery of addiction to alcohol by the Eighteenth Amendment, just as had been done for the slavery of the African race by the Thirteenth Amendment. In both cases, the War Powers of the Government of the United States were used to anticipate what Constitutional amendments later aimed at. One would not be allowed to become a slave voluntarily, it seems to have been argued, so why should one be allowed to become enslaved by alcohol, even if voluntarily? And, it could also have been argued, it is the *blessings*, not the *curses*, of liberty that the Constitution is designed to secure.

Opponents to national prohibition questioned it on several accounts:

> As in the debates over state prohibition, the opponents of the amendment argued that drinking was a deeply rooted custom and that many people, especially wage earners and persons of foreign stock, would regard prohibition as a violation of their personal liberty and refuse to obey it. The result, they warned, would be to discredit the law.[229]

Senator Henry Cabot Lodge, of Massachusetts (one of the States that refused to ratify the Eighteenth Amendment), predicted:

> As a measure of prohibition the practical difficulties . . . will cause it to fail, and my own belief is that in a very short time we shall settle down to a condition like that presented by the Amendments which attempted to confer full political rights upon the negroes of the United States, where the constitutional provision is entirely disregarded.[230]

Consider, also, Lincoln's pre–Civil War position with respect to both alcohol and slavery. Although both a nondrinker and an anti-slavery man, he had reservations about the imprudent, and hence impolitic, measures sometimes advocated by both the prohibition-ists and the abolitionists of his day.[231]

Others even argued that since the proposed amendment would control personal conduct and destroy a species of private property, it was somehow inappropriate for the Constitution. This led in turn to questions about how the amendment should be ratified, with some insisting that only the people themselves could approve such an innovation.[232] All this reminds us of an old question: Are there any amendments that would be improper, if not impossible, to add to the Constitution? We shall return, however briefly, to this ques-tion in the final lecture of this Commentary.

The United States can be said to have "turned eighteen" in more ways than one with this amendment. It did "grow up" somewhat with this experiment, for it led to a traumatic loss of innocence. The quixotic effort made here, with the nobility that it represented, may have been unprecedented in the Western world, at least in modern times.

VI

Loss of innocence may be seen in the social and political turmoil that contributed to the prompt repudiation of the Eighteenth Amend-ment. *Repeal* became as generally known a term as *prohibition* had been, enlisting enthusiasts of its own.

The movement for repeal probably had at its roots the appetite that many have always had for alcohol, an appetite that is consid-ered so natural by some people that the United States could look ridiculous abroad (except perhaps in some, not all, of the Muslim countries) for what it was trying to do. It may well be, however, that national prohibition worked much better in the 1920s than it is now recognized to have done, reducing significantly the waste and dam-age associated with alcohol consumption, waste and damage that we can still see among us in large measure. We also have consider-able experience with and testimony from people who have bene-fited immeasurably by personally turning away from alcohol. Such people do not consider their liberty infringed, but rather enhanced, by having given up intoxicating liquors.

Even so, a critical perceived consequence of prohibition was the breakdown of law and order in this Country, including the corruption of public officials connected with crime, something we are quite familiar with because of what has been happening with respect to drugs in recent decades.[233] The morale, tastes, and dedication to law-abidingness of citizens were undermined by the struggle over enforcement of prohibition statutes. And, it is said, the Mob was permanently established in American life. Thus, several serious consequences of the Eighteenth Amendment outlasted the amendment itself.

VII

A shift in American sentiment doomed, first, national prohibition and, then, most long-standing State restrictions on the sale of alcohol. This shift was due, in part, to the general disillusionment that evidently set in after the Great War and, in part, to the Great Depression, which left many people thirsting for legitimate diversion that promised to cheer them up in gloomy times. This shift in sentiment reflected a shift in power from a middle-class, largely rural and small-town America to a nation in which the poor, the foreign-born, and the city dweller became much more important. The region strongest for prohibition remained the South of the Old Confederacy.[234]

One account of the coming of prohibition ends with observations that sum up the development I have been describing:

> Out of an earnest desire to revitalize and preserve American democracy, middle-class Americans had turned to prohibition as one means of achieving their goal. And having secured prohibition, they now believed that they were passing into a new era of humanity, a new era of struggle, progress, and achievement. It remained to be seen, however, whether in adopting such a perfectionist measure they had overreached themselves; whether in trying to impose a rigid standard of sobriety on the entire nation by law they had undertaken something that the working classes would not accept and that they themselves would often not obey. If so, they would either have to try to enforce the law through measures that smacked of tyranny, or they would have to acquiesce in a defiance of the law that would only create worse evils than the law was designed to cure. In either case the result would be reaction, not progress.[235]

The advocates of Repeal presented themselves as enemies of tyranny, making much of free choice and individuality. Arguments similar to theirs may be heard today from Pro-Choice advocates with respect to both abortions and drugs.

The Twenty-first Amendment, which repeals the Eighteenth, has been the only amendment ratified by State conventions rather than by State legislatures. Congress, which designates the mode of amendment ratification, selected the convention mode "because proponents of repeal feared that anti-liquor sentiment was dominant in many State legislatures because of the relative overrepresentation [at that time] of rural areas."[236]

Congress can provide for the use of State conventions in such a way as to turn the selections of delegates for those conventions into a popular referendum on the matter being considered. The only other time this was done nationwide in American history, also in order to permit the people rather than the State legislatures to decide the issue at hand, was when the Constitution itself was up for ratification in 1787–1788. If the proponents of the Equal Rights Amendment had anticipated in 1972 the organized resistance they eventually encountered, they would have been well-advised to have chosen the State-conventions mode of ratification. This would have permitted, in effect, a national referendum on an issue that women, as voters, probably could have controlled instead of having to rely upon largely male State legislatures elected in other circumstances and on other issues.

The Twenty-first Amendment was proposed by Congress in February 1933, after Franklin Roosevelt had been elected President but before he took office. It was ratified by December 1933. Repeal was seen by many as a new beginning, mandated by the people directly, just as the Constitution of 1787 had seemed to be one hundred and fifty years before. The despotism of prohibition was no doubt more benevolent in intention than that of George III and his Ministers, but it came to be widely resented as despotism nevertheless.

VIII

The first section of the Twenty-first Amendment comes right to the point: "The eighteenth article of amendment to the Constitution of the United States is hereby repealed." The second section of this

203

amendment reinforces whatever power that the States may have always had to regulate the alcohol industry within their borders: "The transportation or importation into any State, Territory, or possession of the United States for delivery or use therein of intoxicating liquors, in violation of the laws thereof, is hereby prohibited."

The second section of the Eighteenth Amendment had provided: "The Congress and the several States shall have concurrent power to enforce this article by appropriate legislation." Both amendments, then, took care not to interfere with efforts by the States to develop their own prohibition measures. Those readings of the Commerce Clause that had limited what the States could do to burden "interstate commerce" were in effect set aside insofar as they bore upon State regulation of the trade in alcohol.[237] This confirmed what Congress had done by statute, before the Eighteenth Amendment, to empower the States to deal on their own with "interstate commerce" in alcohol.

The Twenty-first Amendment refers to the Eighteenth Amendment by number, thereby implicitly numbering all of the amendments, something that had been anticipated by Congress's numbering of the Thirteenth, Fourteenth, Fifteenth, and Sixteenth Amendments. The series of amendments may thus be seen as a whole, perhaps as a separate constitutional effort ranging across two centuries. But if the series is a whole, it is largely as a collection of fragments, responding to one challenge after another rather than incorporating the coherent constitutional message that the Constitution of 1787 (and perhaps also its Bill of Rights) did. Even so, as we have seen, the amendments illuminate many features of the Constitution of 1787. (The designation, *this Constitution,* is used in the body of the Constitution but not in any of the amendments, where *the Constitution* is again and again referred to as if it should still be regarded as something that stands apart.)

IX

Students of the Prohibition Era are often dubious about any effort today to use the law for "allegedly moral ends."[238] It seems that the prohibition experience reinforced in this Country a widespread questioning of the propriety of attempting to legislate morality among us. The questioners here tend to forget that morality has always been critical to the law both as a condition of law-abidingness and as an end of many laws.[239] It has not been only the Prohibitionists among us, therefore, who have assumed that the community is entitled, and perhaps even obliged, to care for the people's moral condition, especially if that people is to be able truly to govern itself.

One may see throughout the Constitution and its amendments repeated indications of moral concerns and standards. Various moral and physical failings or vices are ruled out, or at least deplored, in those documents, such as high crimes and misdemeanors, felonies, and treason. Morality for us includes respect for liberty (or excellence) and for equality (or justice), however muted these concerns have sometimes been with respect to the status and treatment both of imported slaves and of the indigenous peoples of this continent. Some of the rights we claim, such as to freedom of speech and of the press, imply duties that accompany the privileges protected. The religious freedom we insist upon is also intimately related to morality.

The common law, which is (as we have seen) very much taken for granted by the Constitution of 1787 and its Bill of Rights, is along with religion a significant carrier of morality in this Country. The common law attempts, through the arguments of lawyers, the opinions of judges, and the reflections of scholars, to apply enduring natural-right teachings to the ever changing circumstances of the day.[240]

Considerable power still remains in the Government of the United States, despite the repeal of the Eighteenth Amendment, to control the production and sale of alcohol in this Country. For example, this power permits Congress to address the abuses of alcohol advertising, just as it has done for tobacco advertising, in an effort to protect the young and the weak from exploitation. We have yet to appreciate the extent to which beer advertising on radio and television has corrupted not only professional but also college athletics in this Country.

But then, we have yet to appreciate the extent of corruption visited upon us by television itself.[241] Our ineptness with respect to such matters reflects the fact that all too many of us tend to believe that moral training and the moral tone of the community are beyond both the legitimate purview and the effective control of the community itself. Both self-confidence and self-restraint are needed if morality is to continue to be usefully legislated, however harmful the ill-fated American experience with Prohibition is believed to have been and however beneficial the invocation of cultural pluralism may often be. Some questionable aspects of the old-time prohibitionists may be seen in the unfelicitous language of the Balanced Budget Amendment approved for permanent enshrinement in the Constitution by the House of Representatives on January 26, 1995:

> Section 1. Total outlays for any fiscal year shall not exceed total receipts for that fiscal year, unless three-fifths of the whole number of each House of Congress shall provide by law for a specific excess of outlays over receipts by a rollcall vote. . . .

> Section 4. No bill to increase revenue shall become law unless approved by a majority of the whole number of each House by a rollcall vote.

> Section 5. The Congress may waive the provisions of this article for any fiscal year in which a declaration of war is in effect. The provisions of this article may be waived for any fiscal year in which the United States is engaged in military conflict which causes an imminent and serious military threat to national security and is so declared by a joint resolution, adopted by a majority of the whole number of each House, which becomes law. . . .

> Section 7. Total receipts shall include all receipts of the United States Government except those derived from borrowing. Total outlays shall include all outlays of the United States Government except for those for repayment of debt principal. . . .

(I return to this, our most recent exercise in Constitutional frivolity, in Lecture No. 17, Section II, of this Commentary.)

206

15. Amendments XX, XXII, XXIII, and XXV

I

We return, with these four amendments, to the place of the President in the American Constitutional system. A large part of the space devoted to Amendments since 1787 deals with the President. Some of that is done indirectly, as in Amendments II, III, IV, and XIV. Even more is done directly, beginning with Amendment XII. None of the Constitutional amendments that bear upon the President are offered as empowerments of the Executive Branch. The considerable, perhaps even sometimes improper, changes made since 1787 in the influence and hence powers of the President do not rely upon constitutional amendments.

We have seen that the Civil War was significant in this expansion of Presidential influence. The President became most critical during that war in that the continued existence of the Country in what seemed its divinely ordained integrity depended upon extensive military activities that naturally made much more of the "Commander in Chief of the Army and Navy of the United States."

A Presidency enhanced in this way, however, may still have relatively little effective control over serious domestic developments in this Country, except perhaps in an economic crisis that is so severe as to be warlike.

II

The Twentieth Amendment designates when the terms of office both of the President and of Members of Congress should end (and when the terms of their successors should begin) and when Congress should assemble. The amendment provides as well for what is to happen if the President-elect should die before his term begins and for related matters.

Some of the matters addressed in this amendment, it is further provided, can be dealt with otherwise, or can be supplemented, by Congress. All of the matters addressed by the Twentieth Amendment had been left by the Federal Convention for Congress to handle as it chose from time to time. To a considerable extent, then, this amendment was unnecessary.

In fact, surprisingly little of Amendment XX is immune from Congressional rearrangement; it is again and again said that Congress may "by law" alter the dispositions made there. It does seem to be unalterable, however, that the terms of the President and Vice President "shall end at noon on the 20th day of January." Congress cannot "appoint a different day" in the way that it can for its January 3 date of assembly.

Congress, it seems, is to be kept from fiddling with the President's term of office. So long as Congress "assemble[s] at least once in every year," it does not seem to matter as much when Congress does assemble, perhaps partly because Congress can usually be expected to be largely the same from one term to another.

Also unalterable by Congress is this provision: "If at the time fixed for the beginning of the term of the President, the President elect shall have died, the Vice President elect shall become President." It is an odd feature of this amendment that the emphasis is upon when the terms referred to end, not when they should begin. This seems to be due primarily to the need to have existing terms cut down when the amendment goes into effect.

One might question the prudence of removing from Congress the power to consider who should be President if the President elect dies before taking office. The Vice President elect in these circumstances, who can be rather unimpressive, often has not had the seasoning that service as Vice President can provide.

III

The Twenty-second Amendment reflects the determination by the Republican Party to repudiate the invincible Franklin Roosevelt by establishing as the permanent law of the land the two-term limit that George Washington, Thomas Jefferson, James Madison, James Monroe, and Andrew Jackson had established as custom. The amendment was prepared by the only Congress controlled in both Houses by Republicans between the Herbert Hoover Administration and 1995. It is, strictly speaking, not a two-term limit but rather a two-and-a-half term limit, permitting the President ten years altogether (provided that the President finishes the last two years of his predecessor's term).

This limitation is not likely to mean much in practice. A decade of running for, and serving as, President is probably more than enough for anyone; a person is likely by then to have done all that one can do for the Country.[242] Nevertheless, it is true that there can be a crisis which makes it appear that only the incumbent can serve effectively as President, but such an appearance is almost always an illusion (especially since the soon-to-be ineligible incumbent could serve as the most intimate advisor of his successor). The serious crisis we could really have some day because of this amendment would involve the argument that the description here, "acted as President," includes service as the "Acting President" provided for in the Twenty-fifth Amendment. Although it should not be read thus, the argument could still be made, not without some plausibility, especially by the ambitious.

An exemption from the two-term limitation is made for the incumbent either at the time that the amendment was proposed to the States or at the time that it was ratified (for the remainder of the incumbent's term). The latter provision avoids an upheaval in midterm; the former provision, as well as perhaps the latter provision, keeps personalities out of the decision by Congress and the States in considering the amendment. Besides, it was Franklin Roosevelt, not Harry Truman (the incumbent when the amendment was proposed to the States by Congress), that the Republican Party was finally defeating.

The Republican Party, it seems, is also largely responsible for the recent agitation for term limitations for Members of Congress as well as for State legislators.[243] It hardly makes sense, however, to exclude permanently from the legislative councils of the Country our more experienced elders. The January 1991 debates in Congress about the prospects of a Persian Gulf war illustrated the usefulness of having some Members with recollections of similar circumstances they had confronted as Members of Congress a generation before, something that the currently proposed twelve-year limitation would deprive us of. What other major enterprise in this Country or what other government elsewhere around the world thus forbids itself the services of seasoned personnel?

The agitation for term limitations reflects the spirit both of equality and of mobility (or liberty) among us. It is to be hoped that Congress, if only out of self-interest, will resist those who would, with perhaps the best of intentions, subvert the institutional memory of Congress.[244]

IV

The Twenty-third Amendment, to which I return in my next lecture, provides that "[t]he District constituting the seat of Government of the United States," the place we call the District of Columbia,

> shall appoint . . . [a] number of electors of President and Vice President equal to the whole number of Senators and Representatives in Congress to which the District would be entitled if it were a State, but in no event more than the least populous State . . .

The vote of the people of this District, so far as this amendment is concerned, applies only to the election of the President and Vice President, not to the choice of members of the Senate or of the House of Representatives. It was evidently believed by the framers of this amendment that these people, who have long had a say in their local government, should be able to participate as well in national elections. But the only national election that now counts, it sometimes seems to be believed, is the Presidential election.[245]

In some ways, however, the Twenty-third Amendment is little more than a token recognition of the political rights of the residents of the District of Columbia. The few electoral votes for President and Vice President to which they are now entitled will rarely have a significant effect on the outcome of a Presidential election. Residents of the District would obviously have a much more effective say about those who could look out for their interests in the General Government if they chose instead voting members of Congress, especially as those members acquired seniority in their respective Houses.

Even with respect to Presidential elections, the residents of the District are not to be fully like citizens in the States, for they can have no more votes than the least populous State. This means, in practice, three votes. A constitutional amendment was proposed by Congress in 1978 to have the District of Columbia treated as a State for national-elections purposes, but that failed of ratification. The power rests in Congress to admit the District to the Union as a regular State. This is something that Congress is able to do without either Presidential approval or the approval of the States (except perhaps the States which originally ceded the territory used for the District).[246]

Whatever the effect of the Congressional-empowerment section added to several amendments since the Thirteenth, it does seem superfluous here. The opening sentence of the amendment provides that the District's selection of its Presidential and Vice Presidential electors shall be done "in such manner as the Congress may direct." That alone should assure Congress all of the power that it needs to enforce provisions of this amendment.

V

The Twenty-fifth Amendment is devoted to Presidential succession, Presidential disability, and Vice Presidential replacement. The dominant concern here is that the Country be able to identify who properly exercises, at any particular moment, the powers of the President. This is especially important when much is made of the President as Commander in Chief of the armed forces.

This concern does not account, however, for the provision in this amendment for a Vice President whenever that office is vacant. Before the Twenty-fifth Amendment was added to the Constitution, succession to the Presidency in such circumstances was prescribed by acts of Congress. This usually meant that the Speaker of the House was next in line, which could be "certain" enough.

But this order of succession could mean a midterm shift of the Presidency from one political party to another, something that is now considered somewhat dubious. It could also mean that the new President might be too much under the influence of the Congress that had in effect selected him. This possibility seems to offend modern sensibilities nurtured by more and more reliance upon the Presidency.

211

The Framers, on the other hand, drafted a Constitution that leaves Congress in charge of the Country, at least so far as the branches of the General Government are concerned. It is likely, we have noticed in our discussion of the Twelfth Amendment, that it was originally expected that the President would often be chosen by the House of Representatives after an inconclusive casting of ballots by the Presidential electors in the several States. We have also noticed that the rise and discipline of political parties changed that expectation.

VI

However much Congress has been eclipsed by the President in the twentieth century, it is still difficult to avoid ultimate reliance upon Congress to determine who should at any particular moment be, or at least act as, President. This reliance upon Congress is evident in the extended provision in the Twenty-fifth Amendment for Presidential disability.

The provision for filling the vacated office of Vice President may be justified primarily as a condition for the most efficient response to Presidential disability. It is much easier to have the Vice President rather than, say, the Speaker of the House of Representatives temporarily take over the office of a disabled President. This concern with disability is related to the provision in the Twenty-fifth Amendment for the creation of the position of Acting President.[247]

The addition of a disability provision was spurred by recollections of the protracted, debilitating illness of Woodrow Wilson, the concealed physical decline in office of Franklin Roosevelt, and the illnesses of Dwight Eisenhower. The amendment was ratified four years after John Kennedy's assassination.

Any disability provision, if it is to anticipate instances in which the President may not only be unaware of his disability but may even contest the opinions of others that he is disabled, is bound to be complicated. Amendment XXV provides in part:

> [Whenever] the President transmits to the President pro tempore of the Senate and the Speaker of the House of Representatives his written declaration that no inability exists [for him to serve as President], he shall resume the powers and duties of his office unless the Vice President and a majority of either the principal officers of the execu-

tive department or of such other body as Congress may by law provide, transmit within four days to the President pro tempore of the Senate and the Speaker of the House of Representatives their written declaration that the President is unable to discharge the powers and duties of his office. Thereupon Congress shall decide the issue, assembling within forty-eight hours for that purpose if not in session. If the Congress, within twenty-one days after receipt of the latter written declaration, or, if Congress is not in session, within twenty-one days after Congress is required to assemble, determines by two-thirds vote of both Houses that the President is unable to discharge the powers and duties of his office, the Vice President shall continue to discharge the same as Acting President; otherwise, the President shall resume the powers and duties of his office.

We can see here another reason for having a Vice President on hand, rather than relying upon either the Speaker of the House of Representatives or the President pro tempore of the Senate to be next in line: if Congress is obliged to settle any disability dispute between the President and the person next in line (in association with, say, "the principal officers of the executive department"), it would hardly do to have the one next in line be stationed in the Congress. The complications in the disability provision invite speculations regarding the assumptions about human nature implicit in this amendment.

The two-thirds vote of both houses of Congress required if the Vice President is to prevail over the President here is the same proportion needed for the Senate to remove a President from office after impeachment by the House of Representatives. Therefore, the Twenty-fifth Amendment cannot be used to remove an unwilling President (by declaring him disabled) when those who would remove him do not have at least the Senate votes needed to convict him upon an impeachment.

VII

The provision in the Twenty-fifth Amendment for replacement of the Vice President can again remind us of the mode originally intended for the selection of both the President and the Vice President by the Electoral College.[248] That is, it was expected that selections would be made not directly by the people at large but rather after thoughtful deliberation by electors chosen, one way or another, by the people.

I have suggested (as in a letter to the editor published by the *New York Times* on September 20, 1992) that, considering how running mates have come to be chosen by Presidential candidates since the Second World War (if not well before), it would make more sense to have the newly elected President nominate a Vice President in the manner prescribed in the Twenty-fifth Amendment when there is a vacancy in the office of Vice President. I suspect that we would usually get better Vice Presidents that way, or at least Vice Presidents who would seem to be somewhat less the products of chance than all too many have been. Of course, a candidate for the Presidency could announce in advance of the election his likely nominee for Vice President.

Whatever may be done about reforming the Vice Presidential selection process, it is hardly likely that any approach to Presidential selection that depends upon the judgment of any deliberative body would be generally accepted today. Rather, it may be that all that thoughtful citizens can do these days is to keep the United States from resorting to direct popular elections of Presidents, an innovation that we do hear agitated from time to time. (I discuss this in my Commentary on the Constitution of 1787.) It remains difficult to determine what the consequences of such a change would be. Would it not be likely to confirm, if not even to reinforce, certain questionable tendencies implicit in the Presidency, at least since the First World War? Particularly troublesome here would be any further strengthening of the President in his relations with Congress.

VIII

One formidable obstacle to any effort to return the Presidency to constitutional size is that modern Presidential politics "play" much better on television than do Congressional politics. Television dotes on the Presidency; it does not matter whether the incumbent is personally liked or disliked by the mass media. The President is easy to dramatize; the Congress tends to be boring. All that the Congress does is talk (or deliberate); the President acts (with little or no show of deliberation required). That which can be readily presented by television in an "interesting" way affects what we are now apt to consider government to be.

Whether what television usually offers is truly interesting is another question. But it can still come to dominate what people take to be significant, and this public perception can affect what political men and women do and how they present themselves. It can also affect our education as well as theirs, going along with, and promoting, shallower politics, if not a shallower people. Consider, for example, the finding "in 1986 that 66 percent of the public claimed that television was their main source of news about what was going on in the world, while 36 percent named newspapers and 14 percent, radio."[249]

The modern ascendancy of the Presidency is related also to the movement toward universal suffrage, something that will be examined in my next lecture. Who the President is, or how inclusive the electorate is, may matter less if it should be recognized that a somewhat representative and seriously deliberative body is really in charge of the Country.

IX

The key question now may not be who precisely is President or when a particular President's term begins or who can vote for that office. Rather, it must be asked, what is the President to be able to do?

The presumptuousness of Presidents, especially during much of the twentieth century, has been disturbing. This stance should be contrasted with the deference toward Congressional authority displayed repeatedly by George Washington and Dwight Eisenhower. Presidential presumptuousness was dramatically exposed during the Iran arms–Contra aid scandal in 1987. The prerogatives of Congress were usurped by the Reagan-Bush Administration in selling arms and "appropriating" money in a clandestine fashion. A decade earlier there had been the Watergate scandal, which had seen clumsy attempts made by another administration to usurp the prerogatives of the electorate during a Presidential election campaign.[250]

Despite the chastening effects of those two dubious episodes, the Presidency has since then exhibited again and again a spirit foreign to that expected by the Framers of the Constitution. Particularly disquieting for the Constitutionalist, as we have noticed, is how the

1990–1991 Gulf War was conducted by the United States. The people at large may never appreciate the enormity and implications of the damage (political as well as physical) done by us in that war. We were far too captivated, both by the brilliance of our technical efforts and by the evils of our principal adversary on that occasion, to see things clearly.[251]

It should be evident from these developments both what the 1787 Framers were fearful of at the hands of anyone who wields the powers of the Commander in Chief of the armed forces and how profound transformations (including an incipient Caesarism) can come about in a constitutional regime without any authorization by formal amendment of the Constitution.

16. Amendments XXIII, XXIV, XXVI, and XXVII

I

The Declaration and Resolves by the First Continental Congress, of October 14, 1774, included the following passages:

> That the inhabitants of the English colonies in North-America, by the immutable laws of nature, the principles of the English constitution, and the several charters or compacts, have the following RIGHTS: . . .

> That the foundation of English liberty, and of all free government, is a right in the people to participate in their legislative council: and as the English colonists are not represented, and from their local and other circumstances, cannot properly be represented in the British parliament, they are entitled to a free and exclusive power of legislation in their several provincial legislatures, where their right of representation can alone be preserved, in all cases of taxation and internal polity, subject only to the negative of their sovereign, in such manner as has been heretofore used and accustomed . . .

It is this ancient "right of the people to participate in their legislative council" which underlies that movement in the United States toward universal suffrage evident in the Twenty-third, Twenty-fourth, and Twenty-sixth Amendments. I suggested in my last lecture that the modern ascendancy of the Presidency is related to this movement. The right of the people "to participate in their legislative council" may be implied as well in the 1992 ratification of the Twenty-seventh Amendment.

A movement toward universal suffrage can be seen also in several of the other amendments I have discussed, including those

217

assuring the vote for emancipated slaves and their descendants and for women. The growing recourse to universal suffrage is manifested in several ways.

It is most obvious in making the vote available to ever more groups in the United States, including those that were once excluded on the basis of race, gender, or age. It is also obvious in the making of more public posts subject to direct selection by the electorate, while at the same time keeping qualifications for such posts to a minimum. We now have popular elections of Senators; there is, we have noticed, the agitation from time to time, for popular election of the President.

Following upon and reinforcing this movement toward universal suffrage is the growing reliance upon increasingly sophisticated public opinion polls. As more and more depends upon divining what the public believes and perhaps wants, the fewer moderating factors are there likely to be in the development of public policies.

II

We return now to the Twenty-third Amendment, which we have already considered for what it tells us about the role and influence of the President today. Presidential selection is the primary concern in that amendment on behalf of the residents of the Federal District.

It is taken for granted in the amendments dealing with voting rights that for the most part voters will be designated, and the conduct of elections will be provided for, by local governments. Local election laws are devised in the District of Columbia by Congress or by whatever local government may be authorized by Congress for the District.

The local control exercised in the implementation of election laws is a significant check upon national tyranny. This can call to mind the "natural" powers of the barons responsible for Magna Carta. The wide dispersal of the wealth of the community in the form of private property can have a like effect.

Local election laws and their application are subject to review, by the Congress and Courts of the United States, in the light of constitutional standards, whether the standards are of a general character or are primarily concerned with elections. In addition, Congress has always had, under the Constitution, power (seldom exercised) to modify considerably the election laws of the States, even when such laws are constitutional.

Congress attempted to go even further than the Twenty-third Amendment on behalf of the residents of the District of Columbia by proposing in 1978 a Constitutional amendment to this effect:

> For purposes of representation in the Congress, election of the President and Vice President, and article V of this Constitution, the District constituting the seat of government of the United States shall be treated as though it were a State.

Congress would have provided for the exercise of the electoral rights of the people of the District pursuant to this amendment.

This proposed amendment of 1978, which was not ratified, would have repealed the Twenty-third Amendment. It remains to be seen whether Congress will ever, in furtherance of the principal purpose of this proposed amendment, exercise the power it may have to admit the District of Columbia to the Union as a State. (It was evidently easier to muster a two-thirds vote in each House of Congress to submit this amendment proposal to the States for possible ratification by three-fourths of them than it now is to get a majority of each House to transform the District of Columbia into a State. Did Congress rely upon the State legislatures to prevent a controversial development that its Members did not find it expedient to reject?)

We are reminded by these considerations of the role of the legislature (whether National or State and Local) in directing all kinds of activities, including electoral, executive, judicial, and Constitution-amending activities.

III

We have seen in Lecture No. 15 of this Commentary that the voting referred to in the Twenty-third Amendment applies only to the election of the President and Vice President. The officers dealt with in the Twenty-fourth Amendment are expanded:

> The right of citizens of the United States to vote in any primary or other election for President or Vice President, for electors for President or Vice President, or for Senator or Representative in Congress, shall not be denied or abridged by the United States or any State by reason of failure to pay any poll tax or other tax.

Even so, such expansion leaves this amendment with less coverage than others such as the Fifteenth, the Nineteenth and, later, the Twenty-sixth Amendments, which apply to all elections in the United States, State as well as National.

The Twenty-fourth Amendment is the only constitutional provision thus far that explicitly recognizes the role of political parties in the American political system. This it does by governing "primary or other election[s]." The primary elections referred to are those in which the candidates of political parties are chosen. This precaution was evidently believed necessary here because of the efforts once made in some States to circumvent prohibitions of racial discrimination by having the critical election choices made by privileged voters in party primaries, not in general elections governed by those prohibitions.

It does not seem that the poll tax was a significant restriction upon voting by the time the Twenty-fourth Amendment was ratified in 1964. That tax can stir up ancestral memories of repression, however, which have been evident (as we have seen) in the sometimes violent controversy during the 1980s in Great Britain about a levy called a poll tax by its opponents.

IV

The Twenty-fourth Amendment, with its elimination of the "failure to pay any poll tax or other tax" as a factor in a voter's eligibility (at least in National elections), testifies to the now-prevalent opinion that financial considerations or economic interests should not bear upon one's eligibility or power to vote.

Why did not this amendment cover State elections as well? The taxes dealt with were State revenues, sometimes fairly substantial revenues, with control of access to the ballot as an important aspect of the efforts to collect the needed money. May Congress (pursuant to, say, the Republican Form of Government Guarantee) regulate State power to control access to the ballot in State election? If it can, it would want to consider the legitimate uses of this power by the States, which can include property and other qualifications for local elections. In any event, the States today would usually find it difficult, if not politically impossible, to provide for separate rolls of voters for State and National elections. I comment further on this kind of problem in my discussion of Amendment XXVI in the next section of this lecture.

We must wonder whether the deep-rooted drive for equality in this Country is likely to undermine, if not a respect for discriminating choices, at least any conditions designed to make sensible choices more likely.[252] Thus we have seen educational requirements come under suspicion as a basis for determining voters' eligibility, in part because they have obviously been used on occasion to exclude some people arbitrarily and unfairly. (Compare the discussion, in the central lecture of this Commentary, of the Jefferson-Adams concern that citizens be adequately prepared for self-government.)

Corrective measures here have come from both Congress and the courts. It is now generally accepted that whatever advantages the wealthy and the educated may have in practice, there should be no special provision for them in the law. But we have gone further than this, in effect, perhaps without recognizing what is happening. This may be seen in the elimination, both by amendments and by changes in practice, of institutional arrangements that had been intended to encourage, as well as to permit, formal deliberation, especially in choices of officers of government such as Senators and Presidents.

Whatever restrictions there had once been upon voters' qualifications, including education and character restrictions, they were imposed from the beginning of the Republic by the States. By and large, the Constitution of 1787 relied upon republican States to designate and qualify voters. The efforts of the Nation for two centuries now, whether by amendments or by statute, have tended both to expand the electorate and to moderate State restrictions. Less and less provision is made, or is permitted to be made, by law for the calibre of voters as such. Thus, we must take our general educational system more seriously, if only to help people learn to whom, if not to what, they should defer in making the important political decisions they do.

V

The Twenty-sixth Amendment, which was ratified in 1971, provides:

The right of citizens of the United States, who are eighteen years of age or older, to vote shall not be denied or abridged by the United States or by any State on account of age.

With this provision we have probably taken assurances for the rights of people as voters about as far as we can go.

We are not apt to set the voting age much lower than eighteen. Although students in high schools and grade schools do participate in instructive school elections and student councils, the lowering of the general voting age to eighteen had been prompted, in large part, by the eligibility of eighteen-year-olds for military conscription. If the draft age should ever be lowered, Congress on its own can lower the general voting age as well, arguing that this is an exercise by Congress of a power necessary and proper to carry into execution its war powers.[253]

It is only when youngsters go off to war, or live apart from their parents, that they are apt to exhibit much concern about a right to vote. To give unemancipated children the vote simply adds, in the typical situation, to the votes that their parents control. Even so, the young have considerable influence among us because of their tastes (as in music) and because of their considerable spending power.

The Twenty-sixth Amendment applies to State as well as to National elections. The principal spur to the speedy formulation and ratification of this amendment was the prospect of an impending general election that would have had, because of Congressional and Judicial developments, different constituencies for the National and State officers on the ballots of some States, an awkward situation indeed. This amendment testifies once again to the American impulse to include as many as possible, as soon as possible, in the national political body.

Restrictions upon voting remain to this day, including requirements with respect to registration and residency. Related questions have to do with the extent and significance of political constituencies within a State and, for that matter, with whether or how the States themselves should count in Presidential elections.

Also, what should the status of resident aliens be in American elections? Is it not sensible that they should be able to have a say in those local elections in which such an element as property ownership or having children in the school system is the key to the interest or eligibility of voters?

It has long been evident to the American people that other rights and various conditions and privileges are related to the adjustable right of suffrage. No matter what one's condition (for example, mental incompetency), one is entitled to, say, due process of law when one is about to be deprived by some government of life, liberty, or property in this Country. But the right to the vote has always depended somewhat on legislative determinations, probably necessarily so, especially with repect to the competency of voters.

We have seen again and again that once any group gains effective access to the ballot in this Country, other privileges and immunities are apt to follow. We have noticed, for example, how women have been able, because of their obvious voting strength, to secure by legislation many of the rights and privileges that had been sought through the Equal Rights Amendment. Whatever Congress and the State legislatures do not provide, enterprising Courts (which are aware both of election returns and the direction of public opinion) are likely to supply, drawing upon the Fourteenth and Fifteenth Amendments. One consequence of the empowerment of Congress in the Fifteenth, Nineteenth, Twenty-fourth and Twenty-sixth Amendments is that it establishes, if it does not recognize, a considerable supervisory authority in the General Government with respect to the conduct of elections in the States.

VI

The Twenty-seventh Amendment happens to be far less important for its substance than for what it teaches us not only about the amendment process itself but also about the ratification and authority of constitutional documents in general. Amendment XXVII provides: "No law varying the compensation for the services of the Senators and Representatives shall take effect, until an election of Representatives shall have intervened." The 1992 ratification of this amendment, initially prepared by the First Congress along with what we now know as the Bill of Rights, confirmed the practice usually adhered to by Congress with respect to the timing of changes in its compensation. I have, in Section III of Lecture No. 5 of this Commentary, anticipated my discussion here of the Twenty-seventh Amendment.

The ratification of this amendment, stretched out as it has been over two centuries, was highly irregular. Completion of that ratification in 1992 was something of a fluke, if not even a exercise in constitutional frivolity, reflecting as it did public exasperation at

223

that time with Congress, if not with government itself. Not much should be read, however, into the substance of this amendment as a reflection of American opinion in the late twentieth century; after all, this provision is something that Congress drafted in 1789 for submission to the States—and that the States have been "ratifying" ever since. (I have discussed, in Section IV of Lecture No. 14 of this Commentary, Congress's sensible practice since 1919 of limiting the viability [usually, seven years] of amendment proposals. It would probably be prudent for Congress to withdraw all of its pre-1919 amendment proposals that have not been ratified.)

Although Amendment XXVII did little more than confirm a long-established practice with respect to Congressional compensation, it can prove mischievous because of the questions it leaves, some of which may be litigated from time to time. What is to be considered compensation? Do cost-of-living adjustments (automatic or other-wise) constitute "compensation for services" that must be delayed? What about changes in the perquisites of office (such as franking privileges), reimbursement for expenses, and other payments to Members of Congress and their staffs? Still, it should be noticed that underlying the appeal of the Twenty-seventh Amendment was the suspicion of special governmental privileges that found expression among eighteenth-century Americans in repeated suggestions that monopolies and other such governmental grants be prohibited. The two prohibitions of titles of nobility in the Constitution of 1787 display one form of this state of mind.

We are reminded by the way the Twenty-seventh Amendment was ratified that what is a constitutional fact is ultimately a political decision. This means, among other things, that (as Aristotle pointed out long ago and as may be seen in the Leo Strauss quotation among the epigraphs for this Commentary) rules cannot be made to cover all contingencies. Consider, as examples, the irregulari-ties that had to be resorted to by Americans in the issuance of the Declaration of Independence in 1776, in the call of the Federal Con-vention in 1787, in the standards laid down in Article VII of the Constitution of 1787 for ratification of that document, in the acqui-sition of vast territories by the United States from the Indians, the French, the Mexicans, and others, in the powers exercised by Presi-dent Lincoln during the Civil War, in the separation of West Vir-ginia from an unwilling State of Virginia, and in the ratification of the Thirteenth, Fourteenth, and Fifteenth Amendments. Presidential power has sometimes had to be assumed and expanded, extra-constitutionally; in other extreme circumstances, Congressional power may have to be similarly resorted to.

Whether a country has a constitution of authority may itself be as much subject to indefinable, or at least undefined, criteria as what constitutes a community and whether *it* exists in a variety of circumstances and in what form. These considerations are related to the question of when the right of revolution should be resorted to and what the effects of its invocation should be. The ultimate considerations here are apt to be moral and political, or prudential—not legal and technical—and these considerations may be somewhat dependent upon chance. Indeed, there may be something arbitrary about any founding or self-constituting act by a community. Even so, such apparent arbitrariness may reflect something natural. Do not communities somehow sense their existence or integrity? When we notice the role of chance in these matters, we can better appreciate the limits of politics. We can better appreciate also that there are things more important than politics, things that communities, constitutions, and laws prepare the way for and permit. Although there are private activities higher than politics—activities colored by erotic yearnings and addressed by philosophy and by theology—they should be distinguished from both individualism for its own sake and from that hedonism and shamelessness into which uninhibited individualism can deteriorate. A concern with law, justice, and the common good is certainly superior to personal self-expression. A proper inquiry into the great ends of public life can help us understand better the eternal and the truly knowable, which may well be what the community instinctively strives for.

VII

Who "We the People" happen to be in our circumstances, including what follows from this identification, has been spelled out for two centuries now. The challenge of self-knowledge continues to face the people of the United States. Consider, for example, the 1991 report that New York City, perhaps the greatest metropolis in the Western World, now has a majority of minorities. It is said to be "the most ethnically and racially diverse city in the world."[254] Having expanded our electorate in the existing States to virtually its natural limit, we have seen that this extension includes enlarging significantly the scope of the matters that the electorate decides directly. (Experiments in California and elsewhere with referenda suggest the limits of this development.) Related developments have been the restriction upon the powers of States as separate entities (a development that goes back to the Civil War Amendments) and the sanctification (somewhat defensive in character) of the Right to Privacy.

We have done all this, one can suspect, without adequate provisions either for the character and education or for the civic attachments of the electorate. Should we not want the thoughtfulness, rather than the number, of the people voting to be our principal concern? How would we regard these matters if there were here, as in some other countries in the Western World, penalties or inducements designed to promote a higher rate of participation by the people in elections? Is a citizen who has to be encouraged (if not forced) to vote not likely to care enough to inform himself properly about the issues under consideration?

We have seen in the twentieth century that making our system ever more democratic (but not by going as far as was done in ancient Athens, where key officials could be routinely chosen by lot) does not automatically help us to solve our most pressing problems. Radical democratization may even intensify those problems, if not bring on some of its own.

The growing democratization of the election process during the past century is now being matched, at least in this Country, by an increasing number of efforts to limit the activities of government. Now that almost all of the adults legally in this Country are eventually able to vote and to choose more officers directly (including, however inadequately, judges in many States), some advocates are considering, as solutions to our deepening problems, greater shackling of the governments that the people can choose. A symptom of this tendency, however trivial, is the way that the Twenty-seventh Amendment was ratified in response to an aroused public opinion. Another symptom, but far less trivial, may be seen in the movements in support of a balanced-budget amendment and in support of term limitations for members of legislatures. The people are encouraged to try to do more and more of the legislating themselves, which is what much of the constitution amending that is currently advocated amounts to.

These developments, reinforced by growing reliance upon public opinion polls and referenda, suggest that we may be moving from a republican regime grounded in representative legislatures to a plebiscitary democracy in which much is made of Presidents and other executive officers who cannot fail to disappoint the expectations of those who depend upon them, both at home and abroad. This trend was evident in the calamities visited in the closing decade of a much-troubled century upon people in Iraq, especially upon those (such as the Kurds) who discovered that one should not put much trust in princes, even when one of them happens to be a President of the United States.

17. The Constitution in the Twenty-first Century

I

There have not been, for two decades now, any amendments to the Constitution, except for the 1992 ratification by State legislatures of the long-neglected 1789 Congressional pay proposal. Two of the amendments proposed during this period—the Equal Rights and the District of Columbia proposals—failed to be ratified.

Informal constitutional adjustments continue to be made, of course, and some of these may eventually have the effect of formal amendments. We have seen, for example, what has become of the original reliance upon State electors for the selection of Presidents. The emergence of political parties and party discipline is reflected in how Presidents are in fact selected, with the discretionary voting by State electors having long been little more than a formality that should be eliminated, if only to remove an occasion for mischief. A disturbing use of party discipline is a minority's repeated recourse to filibustering in the United States Senate, thereby obstructing the intended power of the majority to rule. (The proposals for amendments submitted to the First Congress in 1789 included many suggestions that what we call a "supermajority" be required on one issue after another. The First Congress refused to change what the Framers had done in limiting severely—that is, to a half-dozen instances—the matters for which more than a majority is needed.) The current Senate rule that keeps a bare majority from ending debate, after a reasonable time for discussion of the relevant issues, is probably unconstitutional. A resourceful Senate majority, with the cooperation of the presiding officer, should be able, by the use of points of order, to revise both the Senate filibuster rule requiring a three-fifths vote to end debate and the Senate rule requiring a two-thirds vote to change the rules of that body. (The threat of such a move may suffice to discourage routine recourse to filibusters.) Less dramatic, but still important, have been some of the technical changes limiting the jurisdiction but expanding the activities (for example, with respect to judicial review) of the Courts of the United States. Some of these rules, too, are probably unconstitutional.

We should be aware, in any event, of how limited in effect formal amendments can be. Some amendments have been precise enough to be easily enforced by a people determined to use them, such as the ban on slavery in the Thirteenth Amendment, the provision for female suffrage in the Nineteenth Amendment, and the electoral empowerment of eighteen-year-olds in the Twenty-sixth Amendment.

But many of the most illustrious amendments, those that make up the Bill of Rights, had little if any immediate effect after their ratification. This was true not only of the Tenth Amendment, which has long been recognized by many as mostly a truism (to the effect that the government of the United States indeed has the powers it has), but it was true as well of most of the first eight amendments, confirming and refining as they did many rights that the American people of 1789 had always believed they were entitled to and were already exercising.

Again we see that the Constitution and its amendments presuppose an established constitutional and legal system. The amendments ratified from time to time have either acknowledged rights already recognized or adjusted arrangements in a way consistent with the overall system. American experience with the Eighteenth Amendment illustrates what is likely to happen if an amendment (whatever its initial appeal may happen to be) does not truly fit in with what is already there.

II

It is instructive to notice the kind of amendment proposals that might be considered during the opening quarter of the twenty-first century. Various such proposals have been glanced at throughout this Commentary.

Some proposals are likely to be impulsive responses, all too often exploited by the cynical, to passing provocations, such as the amendment advocated as a response to occasional desecrations of the Flag. The immediate stimulus in these cases can be a judicial interpretation of the Constitution. Judicial interpretations that have affected the implementations of treaties, public-school prayers, admission of lawyers to State bars, State legislative apportionment, and access to abortions have in turn led to controversial amendment proposals.

We do have considerable talk these days of a balanced-budget amendment and of a legislative term-limitations amendment. Both would probably be troublesome if ratified: the first (another exercise in constitutional frivolity) because it is not likely to work, thereby disillusioning and perhaps demoralizing people; the second because it *is* likely to work, thereby crippling the Government of the United States.

Those who recognize how a balanced-budget amendment could readily be circumvented by both legislatures and executives suggest other ways of accomplishing such an amendment's purposes. One response is that a limitation be placed upon the amount of taxation that is permitted annually. But circumvention is likely here also, as may be seen in how State governments have had to work their way around such limitations. In fact, no mechanical rule or formula can take the place in such matters of political judgment on the part of both the people and their government, if there is to be sound guidance of the economy in varying circumstances. Such guidance depends upon sensible assessments not only of the causes and consequences of deficits but also of the costs, consequences, and desirability of balancing the national budget at any particular time.[255] Here, as elsewhere, myths and misinformation have to be reckoned with. Many of these questions about economic and fiscal policies are better addressed directly, and preferably by legislatures, as circumstances change.

Those who recognize that term limitations for legislators can truly be crippling look to other remedies to deal with what they conceive to be the underlying problem. One set of remedies has to do with changes that could reduce the advantages of incumbency, including severe limitations upon political contributions and campaign expenditures. (A reconsideration by the United States Supreme Court of its unfortunate First Amendment rulings with respect to these matters should be encouraged.) Most of these remedies, too, are more appropriate for legislation than for constitutional amendments, especially since experiments and revisions are apt to be needed.

It is often said that those who hold legislative offices today are virtually impossible to defeat. But this is not, as many seem to believe, because incumbents are immune from public scrutiny and control. On the contrary, incumbents these days tend to be very sensitive, perhaps unduly so, to the opinions of their constituents. Indicative of what has long been happening is the fact that incumbents do say quite different things on the issues of the day, depending on precisely where they are from and what electorate they rely upon. Public opinion polling makes it easier for each incumbent to tailor his words and deeds to the opinions and immediate desires of his constituents. It should be instructive, moreover, to consider what changes there have been and why, in recent decades, in the average length of service of Members of Congress.[256]

It is likely, or so it seems to me, that most if not all of the constitutional-amendment matters being agitated these days (including the line-item veto) would be much better dealt with through legislation that can be readily adjusted and, if need be, repealed as circumstances change.

III

I do not mean to suggest by my reservations about the proposed amendments of our day that the Constitution is now perfect, but only that most proposals we hear for its amendment either would not get far, or would not be likely to have the effects intended by their proponents, or would do better as legislative proposals.

I myself continue to believe, for example, that much is now to be said for routinely choosing all Vice Presidents the way that the office of Vice President is filled when it falls vacant between elections. The mode provided in the Twenty-fifth Amendment, which induces the President to nominate someone that the Congress is likely to approve, would make it far more likely that greater care would be used in selecting Vice Presidents than we have witnessed during the hurly-burly of our quadrennial political conventions in recent decades. The mode I propose here hearkens back, in spirit, to the original Electoral College mode of selecting Presidents.

Also to be encouraged are serious proposals that would restore effective local government. Much is likely to be different when the Country is made up of a quarter of a billion people, instead of the three to four million of 1787. Can the American Union now be effectively broken up for certain purposes? (The South will rise again? It is prudent to notice, however, that Southern passions, which can sometimes be attractive, are also displayed in the steady drumbeat of executions to which we have become accustomed from that part of this fair land.) Or do we need, instead, to consider further integrating both Canada and Mexico into our economic, if not even our political, Union? Can only an effective world government permit the responsible elimination of national armed forces that would make executive power less needed and local autonomy more feasible?

Neither a humane world government (in which countries would likely be represented by their chief executives) nor an effective local autonomy seems to be immediately available. But neither would have to be looked to as much as they are if there could be greater reliance among us upon personal (but not apolitical) self-sufficiency and integrity. This is something that all of us should be able to do something about wherever we happen to be.

IV

Most of the concerns we encounter these days for constitutional amendments take the form of curbing either the Congress or the Courts. How deep these concerns really run may be questioned, especially if the American people should, by and large, be fairly well satisfied with their way of life.

Far less is heard these days about the need to place curbs upon the Presidency.[257] Rather, some of the changes suggested (such as the line-item veto, term limitations for Congress, and the direct election of the President) would tend to strengthen the Presidency even more than it has naturally been strengthened in an era of perpetual crisis.

Transformation of our General Government into a parliamentary system, dominated in effect by the President, is sometimes advocated as a means of avoiding institutional gridlock. This transformation (with or without proportional representation) would require radical changes, with unpredictable consequences, in our deep-rooted bicameral legislative arrangements (which contribute to a salutary separation of powers) as well as in our way of choosing the President. Furthermore, a parliamentary system probably depends for political stability on public opinion less volatile than ours can sometimes be. Experiments along these lines, if risked at all, might better be made first in a few of our States. (Also contributing to our separation of powers, but not always in a salutary way, is the modern insistence upon the distinction between "state" and "society." This includes the subordination of the political to psychological, economic, and sociological considerations. One result of this is an emphasis upon the Right to Privacy, with the related suspicion of any Legislation of Morality.)

Should the Presidency, in the system we now have, be confined? Or should it be recognized for what it has become and perhaps has to be? What is the status, for example, of the 1973 War Powers Resolution?[258] Should not more reliance be placed than has been the case in recent decades upon the exclusive Congressional power to declare war? Congress already has the power to curb adventurous Presidents, beginning with what it can do to military and other appropriations. What is needed here, then, are not constitutional amendments but rather the willingness of an alert Congress, guided by an informed people, to exercise properly the power with which Congress has always been entrusted by the Constitution.

The Constitutional lessons of the 1990–1991 Gulf War are yet to be drawn. The more we see of the disastrous consequences of that war, some of which (already apparent) were predicted and others of which will take years to appreciate, the sounder the much more cautious prewar Congressional judgment appears to have been on that occasion. Much of the high-minded talk about a new world order we once heard from hard liners is already being shown up as hollow moral posturing—and innocent people in the Middle East (or, at least, people probably as innocent as we have been in recent decades) have suffered grievously by the hundreds of thousands in part because of what we have and have not done.

The moral sensibilities of our leaders need to be rigorously questioned in such situations. We have noticed again and again that fundamental to our capacity to govern ourselves, and fundamental also to our power to provide our leaders the curbs and guidance they need, are our right and ability to judge the governments upon which we have to rely. Critical to our ability to judge properly are our character and our education as one people.

V

I have touched upon some of the institutional reforms that have been suggested in this Country from time to time. This survey has not been offered as exhaustive but rather as illustrative of the issues. I attempt thereby to suggest how such Constitutional amendment proposals should be assessed.

Other amendment proposals look more to the assertion of the personal rights of citizens. What, for example, remains to be mined out of the Ninth Amendment? Can the Courts be relied upon to develop properly the Right to Privacy? Or is that better left to the legislatures of this Country (State as well as National) to deal with? Certainly, much has been done and continues to be done by statute. A reliable assessment of what the Courts should do here could well begin with a careful study of the political as well as the legal and constitutional consequences of the massive judicial intervention in the abortion controversy in recent decades.

Whether anything should be done now by explicit constitutional amendment to curb the Courts can be doubted. Perhaps argument remains the best way to induce the Courts to become ever more cautious in exercising the power of judicial review of acts of Congress. That power has been appropriated by judges in the name of principles that need to be continually reexamined. Argument, not a recourse to frivolous constitutional amendments, is also called for when the Courts come up, as they do from time to time, with wrongheaded constitutional interpretations.

One vital right implicitly recognized by the Ninth Amendment should be reaffirmed (reaffirmed, but not exercised) from time to time. That is the great right of revolution dramatically exercised in the establishment of Magna Carta. Sober reaffirmations of this right and duty, as in the Declaration of Independence, serve to remind us that there are standards—enduring moral and political standards grounded in "the Laws of Nature and of Nature's God"—that can and should be looked to in judging what our governments do. A proper respect for the right of revolution calls into question the contemporary tendency to sacrifice the common good to the right of privacy. Care must be taken lest the assertion of this foundational right of revolution take the form of mindless rebelliousness against a proper civic-mindedness.

VI

Still another kind of constitutional amendment is likely to be proposed more and more in the coming decades: amendments providing for various social, economic, and environmental (including child and animal) rights. Models are available in numerous constitutions and declarations around the world. These include rights to a living wage, to education, to medical treatment, to family assistance, and to a sound habitat. We even hear talk of "a right to die" and a right to the benefits of euthanasia: such rights are intriguing (some would say, perverse) derivations from our ancient rights to "Life, Liberty, and the Pursuit of Happiness."

In some respects contemporary declarations of rights presuppose a political system that is not itself examined. Are not the constitutional amendments that might be relied upon here likely to be either unduly confining or simply ineffectual? Most people in this Country still tend to believe that the objectives sought to be served by such declarations are better dealt with through the constantly changing political process and by the maintenance of an economy that permits a steady rise in the general standard of living, a standard of living that in turn permits both governments and private parties to address the dislocations and misery perhaps inevitable in any large-scale institutional arrangements. Whether part of that misery, of rich and poor alike, can be traced back to a generally accepted article of faith—that we should become more and more comfortable as well as more and more secure—is a question that it would be prudent for us to consider seriously in the coming decades.

One consequence of the virtually universal adult suffrage we now have in this Country for citizens is that underprivileged groups can better make themselves felt in the political process, if only they can be organized to do so. The powers of the Government of the United States are now recognized to be so extensive that that government can do whatever we believe needs to be done to serve the social and economic needs of the American people.

It remains to be seen, however, whether artificial constitutional difficulties will be imagined that will interfere with what may need to be done with affirmative action, population control, moral training, cultural enrichment, and other such programs. Both the General and State Governments have much to do here, however skeptical we should all remain about what any government can do. With respect to education, our underlying need as a community is (and perhaps always has been) to look to the best that is available. This concern was evident in the remarkable Jefferson-Adams correspondence drawn upon in Lecture No. 9 of this Commentary.

Critical at this time may be a reassessment of two prevailing but questionable opinions: that there is a Constitutional right to establish nonpublic schools in this Country and that there is a Constitutional barrier to providing public funds to sectarian and other "private" schools. By and large, we must insist, the Constitution should not be understood to keep us from doing what is good and sensible, whether by curtailing or by supporting (in a doctrinally nonsectarian manner) all nonpublic schools.

VII

What, then, are the amendments we truly need? They would genuinely be *amend*ments in the sense of *making things better.*

The moral judgment, including the sense of civility, of our people should be for us a constant concern. Such judgment depends upon that reaffirmation of natural right to which I have several times referred in the course of this Commentary. Unlike two centuries ago, virtue is more likely to be seen these days primarily in terms of private rather than of public conduct. Much more needs to be made among us of civic virtue, hearkening back to the time when the best people in this Country, who could be generally recognized to be such, devoted themselves mostly to politics, to the military, and to the ministry (a different form, perhaps, of politics).

A mature people, morally and politically, is less likely to be imposed upon for long by its leaders. Consider, for example, how we have been deliberately manipulated in recent years by images of such despicable characters as Willie Horton (1988) and Saddam Hussein (1990–1992). Irresponsible sloganeering has usurped the place of serious discussion.

Vital to the proper training of our people, generation after generation, is that the community recognize that it is entitled and obliged to do much here, both directly and indirectly. In such training the emphasis should be placed more upon *duties* than upon *rights*. Even so, a proper regard for rights can promote a sense of dignity and a respect for nature—and that in turn can contribute to taking one's duties seriously.

Charles de Gaulle, in dealing with the French, once asked, "How can you be expected to govern a country which has 246 kinds of cheese?"[259] Similarly, we can ask, how is it possible to train our people properly when the dramatic arts (including sports) and public discourse are as much fragmented and polluted by selling as ours have become? That we put up with so much relentless, if not brutal, exploitation of our legitimate interests and attention is remarkable.

What is not remarkable is that our experience in and ability for serious public deliberation should be deteriorating, especially as we become more and more accustomed to being entertained and less and less resentful of being cheated and brutalized. Instead we are much more likely to resent, if not even to penalize, those who presume to question our tastes, our illusions, and our transformation into mere consumers. Both our ever-growing appetites as consumers and our heightened sensitivity to various rights are among the social, intellectual, and political implications of the Industrial Revolution that have to be reckoned with.

A properly disciplined and self-confident community depends in the modern world upon a constitution that a people recognizes can and should be read with care, a constitution that is, because of its scope and flexibility, useful in a variety of circumstances. It is remarkable that extended discussions of the Declaration of Independence, of the Constitution of 1787, and of its Bill of Rights have had respectable audiences during one Bicentennial Celebration after another in this Country since 1976. The American language and experience still permit, and may even encourage, our politics to be sensible.

I have heard that love sentiments are easier to convey in Italian or modern Greek or Spanish than in English. Has this, if true, helped to keep Americans from becoming either too skilled in or unduly preoccupied with matters of love? Have we, as perhaps the preeminent self-governing community on a grand scale in modern times, been fortunate in being "naturally" better at politics than at something so promising but yet so absorbing and distracting as love? To what extent is our escalating appetite for personal self-expression (both in public and in private) an ill-conceived attempt to make up for (as well as contributing to) growing deficiencies among us with respect to both politics and love? Particularly to be amended by a self-governing people is any deficiency in knowing what in human beings and in citizens is truly to be cherished.[260]

APPENDIXES AND SOURCES

The documents reproduced in these appendixes are taken immediately from the sources indicated below. The ultimate sources of the major documents are also indicated. There are some departures here, from the sources drawn upon, in the use of headings, indentations, line placements, capitalization of entire words, and italics. Paragraphing, punctuation, spelling, and other such details can vary from one source to another. All of the documents reprinted here are complete unless otherwise indicated.

A. Magna Carta (1215)

This is based upon an early nineteenth-century translation of the Latin original. See Richard Thomson, *An Historical Essay on the Magna Carta of King John* (London: John Major and Robert Jennings, 1829). This version may represent the nearest date in time available today, for an English translation, to the Founding Period in the United States. (In Chapter 39, "or exiled" is inserted and "the laws of the land" has been changed to the more familiar "law of the land." Compare Chapters 45 and 55.) The bracketed additions in the text are in the 1829 edition, except for the Latin text provided for Chapter 39 and the data provided in Chapter 62 and in the Conclusion. The chapter numbers, although not in the Latin original, are traditional. The numberings of chapters were changed in the many reissues of Magna Carta as parts were dropped or added. See, for the complete Latin text, as well as another English translation of the 1215 document signed by King John, J. C. Holt, *Magna Carta* (2d ed.; Cambridge: Cambridge University Press, 1992), 448f. See, for still another translation of Magna Carta, "The Making of the Bill of Rights," *Great Ideas Today*, 329 (1991).

B. Thomas More's Petition to Henry VIII on Parliamentary Freedom of Speech (1521)

This is based upon William Roper, *The Lyfe of Sir Thomas Moore, Knighte,* Elsie Vaughan Hitchcok, ed. (London: Oxford University Press, 1935), 12–16. The author is identified on the title page as "William Roper, Esquire, whiche married Margreat, daughter of the sayed Thomas Moore." This document displays sixteenth-century spelling. See, for another version of this document, George Anastaplo, *The Constitutionalist: Notes on the First Amendment* (Dallas: Southern Methodist University Press, 1971), 538–39.

C. The Petition of Right (1628)

This is based upon *The Statutes of the Realm, Printed by Command of His Majesty King George III, in Pursuance of an Address of the House of Commons of Great Britain* (1819), 5: 23–24. The bracketed numbers are taken from the margins of the 1819 copy.

D. The English Bill of Rights (1689)

This is based upon *The Statutes of the Realm* (see Item C, above), 6: 142–45.

E. Declarations by American Congresses (1765–1776)
E-1. Declarations of Rights & Grievances by the Stamp Act Congress (1765)

This is based upon the copy in C. A. Weslager, *The Stamp Act Congress, With an Exact Copy of the Complete Journal* (Newark, Delaware: University of Delaware Press, 1976), 200–3.

E-2. Declaration and Resolves by the First Continental Congress (1774)

This is based upon *Journals of Congress Containing Their Proceedings from September 5, 1774, to January 1, 1776* (Philadelphia: Folwell's Press, 1800), 1: 26–30.

E-3. The Declaration of Independence (1776)

This is based upon the copy in *The Declaration of Independence and the Constitution of the United States,* 96th Congress, 1st Session, House Document No. 96–143 (Washington, D.C.: Government Printing Office, 1979), 1–5. That version of the Declaration of Independence was reprinted in accord with the text and typographical style of the original printed by John Dunlap at Philadelphia for the Continental Congress.

F. Declarations of Rights (1776–1780)

These Virginia and Massachusetts bills of rights are based upon the copies in *The Federal and State Constitutions, Colonial Charters and Other Organic Laws of the States, Territories, and Colonies Now or Heretofore Forming the United States of America,* Francis Newton Thorpe, ed. (Washington, D.C.: Government Printing Office, 1909), 3: 1888–93, 1914–15, 7: 3812–14. Harry V. Jaffa has observed, "The two most celebrated American statements of why men enter civil society—next to the Declaration of Independence itself—are the bills of rights of Virginia (1776) and of Massachusetts (1780)." See, for another Virginia-Massachusetts collaboration, Appendix K, below.

G. Virginia Statute of Religious Liberty (1785)

This is based upon *Statutes at Large of Virginia,* William Waller Hening, ed. (Richmond, Virginia, 1823), 12: 84–86. In the spirit of this statute is President George Washington's 1790 letter to the Hebrew Congregation of Newport, Rhode Island, which may be found in note 69 of this Commentary.

H. The Principal Bill of Rights Discussions in James Madison's *Notes of Debates in The Federal Convention* (1787)

These excerpts are taken from the copy of James Madison's *Notes* reprinted in *The Records of the Federal Convention of 1787,* Max Farrand, ed. (New Haven: Yale University Press, 1937), 2: 340–42, 587–88, 628, 631–33. The August 20, 1787, entry is taken in the Farrand collection from the *Journal* of the Convention of that date. Madison's entry for that day may be found in Section II of Lecture No. 2 of this Commentary.

I. Amendment Proposals by the Last States to Ratify the Constitution before Its Initial Implementation (1788)

These sets of amendment proposals (one set from a leading Southern State, the other set from a leading Northern State) are based upon the copies in *Documents Illustrative of the Formation of the Union of the American States,* 69th Congress, 1st Session, House Document No. 398 (Washington, D.C.: Government Printing Office, 1927), 1027–44. The Virginia proposals were taken from *Documentary History of the Constitution* (1894), 2: 145, 146, 160, 377–855; the New York proposals were taken from *Documentary History of the Constitution* (1894), 2: 190–203. The Ratification Campaign arguments in *Federalist* No. 84 (1788), against the need for a bill of rights, may be found in note 14 of this Commentary.

J. Stages of the Bill of Rights in the First Congress and in the State Legislatures (1789–1791)

These materials are based upon the *Annals of Congress,* 1: 433–37 (1789); Edward Dumbauld, *The Bill of Rights and What It Means Today* (Norman: University of Oklahoma Press, 1957), 210–22; Helen E. Veit, Kenneth R. Bowling, & Charlene Bangs Bickford, eds., *Creating the Bill of Rights: The Documentary Record from the First Federal Congress* (Baltimore: Johns Hopkins University Press, 1991), 3–5, 29–33, 37–41, 47, 48; and (for ratification returns from the States) Jonathan Elliot, ed., *The Debates in the Several State Conventions on the Adoption of the Federal Convention* (2d ed.; Philadelphia: J. B. Lippincott Company, 1901), 1: 339–40. The French Declaration of the Rights of Man and the Citizen (1789) may be found in note 60 of this Commentary.

K. Letters Exchanged by Thomas Jefferson and John Adams (1814)

These are copied from *The Adams-Jefferson Letters: The Complete Correspondence between Thomas Jefferson and Abigail and John Adams,* Lester J. Cappon, ed. (New York: Clarion Books, Simon and Schuster, 1959), 430–39. The page numbers in the Cappon edition are indicated by the numbers in brackets. The original spelling and punctuation are left unchanged, except where indicated in brackets. Brackets are also used to enclose translations and other explanatory material.

L. Anglo-American Responses to Slavery (1771–1863)

L-1. Somerset's Case (1771–1772)

This is based upon *Reports of Case Adjudged in the Court of King's Bench* (from Easter Term, 12 George III to Michaelmas, 14 George III),

Capal Lofft, ed. (Dublin, 1790), 1, 17–19. Minor changes in the Lofft version have been made upon consulting another edition (in *English Reports* [Edinburgh, 1909]), 98: 489, 509–10).

L-2. THE CONSTITUTION OF THE CONFEDERATE STATES OF AMERICA (1861)

This is based upon the copy in Senate Document No. 234, 58th Congress, 2d Session (Washington, D.C.: Government Printing Office, 1904), 909–23. That version came from *Journal of the Congress of the Confederate States of America* (1861–1865). The Constitution of the Provisional Government of the Confederate States of America is also reprinted in Senate Document No. 234 (1904), 899–909.

L-3. THE EMANCIPATION PROCLAMATION (1862–1863)

The entire text of the two stages of the Emancipation Proclamation is set forth *in italics* in the course of Lecture No. 11 of this Commentary. That text is taken from *The Collected Works of Abraham Lincoln*, Roy P. Basler, ed. (New Brunswick, New Jersey: Rutgers University Press, 1953), 5: 433–36, 6: 28–31, where elaborate notes are provided with respect to the ultimate sources of the text.

M. THE CONSTITUTION OF 1787 WITH AMENDMENTS (1787–1992)

The text of the Constitution of 1787 is based upon the copy in *Documents Illustrative of the Formation of the Union of the American States* (see Item I, above), 989–1002. That version was taken from the engrossed Constitution, in four sheets, as signed by the delegates to the Federal Convention. A few minor changes have been made in light of the version of the Constitution reprinted in William W. Crosskey, *Politics and the Constitution in the History of the United States* (Chicago: University of Chicago Press, 1953), 2: 1225–33.

The text of the Amendments to the Constitution is based upon the copy of the Amendments in *The Declaration of Independence and the Constitution of the United States* (see Item E-3, above), 31–40, 43. My mode of numbering each Amendment here is adapted from the mode used by the Twenty-first Amendment in referring to the Eighteenth Amendment. The year is given in which each of the Amendments was ratified.

A. Magna Carta (1215)

MAGNA CARTA

John, by the Grace of God, King of England, Lord of Ireland, Duke of Normandy and Aquitaine, and Earl of Anjou, to his Archbishops, Bishops, Abbots, Earls, Barons, Justiciaries, Foresters, Sheriffs, Governors, Officers, and to all Bailiffs, and his faithful subjects,—Greeting.

Know ye, that We, in the presence of God, and for the salvation of our own soul, and of the souls of all our ancestors, and of our heirs, to the honour of God, and the exaltation of the Holy Church and amendment of our Kingdom, by the counsel of our venerable fathers, Stephen Archbishop of Canterbury, Primate of all England, and Cardinal of the Holy Roman Church, Henry Archbishop of Dublin, William of London, Peter of Winchester, Joceline of Bath and Glastonbury, Hugh of Lincoln, Walter of Worcester, William of Coventry, and Benedict of Rochester, Bishops; Master Pandulph our Lord the Pope's Subdeacon and familiar, Brother Almeric, Master of the Knights-Templars in England, and of these noble persons, William Mareschal Earl of Pembroke, William Earl of Salisbury, William Earl of Warren, William Earl of Arundel, Alan de Galloway Constable of Scotland, Warin Fitz-Gerald, Hubert de Burgh Seneschal of Poictou, Peter Fitz-Herbert, Hugh de Nevil, Matthew Fitz-Herbert, Thomas Basset, Alan Basset, Philip de Albiniac, Robert de Roppel, John Mareschal, John Fitz-Hugh, and others our liegemen:

[1] [We] have in the First place granted to God, and by this our present Charter, have confirmed, for us and our heirs for ever: That the English Church shall be free, and shall have her whole rights and her liberties inviolable; and we will this to be observed in such a manner, that it may appear from thence, that the freedom of

elections, which was reputed most requisite to the English Church, which we granted, and by our Charter confirmed, and obtained the Confirmation of the same, from our Lord Pope Innocent the Third, before the rupture between us and our Barons, was of our own free will: which Charter we shall observe, and we will it to be observed with good faith, by our heirs for ever.

We have also granted to all the Freemen of our Kingdom, for us and our heirs for ever, all the underwritten Liberties, to be enjoyed and held by them and by their heirs, from us and from our heirs.

[2] If any of our Earls or Barons, or others who hold of us in chief by military service, shall die, and at his death his heir shall be of full age, and shall owe a relief, he shall have his inheritance by the ancient relief; that is to say, the heir or heirs of an Earl, a whole Earl's Barony for one hundred pounds: the heir or heirs of a Baron for a whole Barony, by one hundred pounds; the heir or heirs of a Knight, for a whole Knight's Fee, by one hundred shillings at most: and he who owes less, shall give less, according to the ancient custom of fees.

[3] But if the heir of any such be under age, and in wardship, when he comes to age he shall have his inheritance without relief and without fine.

[4] The warden of the land of such heir who shall be under age, shall not take from the lands of the heir any but reasonable issues, and reasonable customs, and reasonable services, and that without destruction and waste of the men or goods, and if we commit the custody of any such lands to a Sheriff, or any other person who is bound to us for the issues of them, and he shall make destruction or waste upon the ward-lands we will recover damages from him, and the lands shall be committed to two lawful and discreet men of that fee, who shall answer for the issues to us, or to him to whom we have assigned them. And if we shall give or sell to any one the custody of any such lands, and he shall make destruction or waste upon them, he shall lose the custody; and it shall be committed to two lawful and discreet men of that fee, who shall answer to us in like manner as it is said before.

[5] But the warden, as long as he hath the custody of the lands, shall keep up and maintain the houses, parks, warrens, ponds, mills, and other things belonging to them, out of their issues; and shall restore to the heir when he comes of full age, his whole estate,

provided with ploughs and other implements of husbandry, according as the time of Wainage shall require, and the issues of the lands can reasonably afford.

[6] Heirs shall be married without disparagement, so that before the marriage be contracted, it shall be notified to the relations of the heir by consanguinity.

[7] A widow, after the death of her husband, shall immediately, and without difficulty have her marriage and her inheritance; nor shall she give any thing for her dower, or for her marriage, or for her inheritance, which her husband and she held at the day of his death: and she may remain in her husband's house forty days after his death, within which time her dower shall be assigned.

[8] No widow shall be distrained to marry herself, while she is willing to live without a husband; but yet she shall give security that she will not marry herself without our consent, if she hold of us, or without the consent of the lord of whom she does hold, if she hold of another.

[9] Neither we nor our Bailiffs, will seize any land or rent for any debt, while the chattels of the debtor are sufficient for the payment of the debt; nor shall the sureties of the debtor be distrained, while the principal debtor is able to pay the debt; and if the principal debtor fail in payment of the debt, not having wherewith to discharge it, the sureties shall answer for the debt; and if they be willing, they shall have the lands and rents of the debtor, until satisfaction be made to them for the debt which they had before paid for him, unless the principal debtor can shew himself acquitted thereof against the said sureties.

[10] If any one hath borrowed any thing from the Jews, more or less, and die before that debt be paid, the debt shall pay no interest so long as the heir shall be under age, of whomsoever he may hold; and if that debt shall fall into our hands, we will not take any thing except the chattel contained in the bond.

[11] And if any one shall die indebted to the Jews, his wife shall have her dower and shall pay nothing of that debt; and if children of the deceased shall remain who are under age, necessaries shall be provided for them, according to the tenement which belonged to the deceased: and out of the residue the debt shall be paid, saving the rights of the lords [of whom the lands are held]. In like manner let it be with debts owing to others than Jews.

[12] No scutage nor aid shall be imposed in our kingdom, unless by the common council of our kingdom; excepting to redeem our person, to make our eldest son a knight, and once to marry our eldest daughter, and not for these, unless a reasonable aid shall be demanded.

[13] In like manner let it be concerning the aids of the City of London. And the City of London should have all it's ancient liberties, and it's free customs, as well by land as by water. Furthermore, we will and grant that all other Cities, and Burghs, and Towns, and Ports, should have all their liberties and free customs.

[14] And also to have the common council of the kingdom, to assess and aid, otherwise than in the three cases aforesaid: and for the assessing of scutages, we will cause to be summoned the Archbishops, Bishops, Abbots, Earls, and great Barons, individually, by our letters. And besides, we will cause to be summoned in general by our Sheriffs and Bailiffs, all those who hold of us in chief, at a certain day, that is to say at the distance of forty days [before their meeting], at the least, and to a certain place; and in all the letters of summons, we will express the cause of the summons: and the summons being thus made, the business shall proceed on the day appointed, according to the counsel of those who shall be present, although all who had been summoned have not come.

[15] We will not give leave to any one, for the future, to take an aid of his own free-men, except for redeeming his own body, and for making his eldest son a knight, and for marrying once his eldest daughter; and not that unless it be a reasonable aid.

[16] None shall be distrained to do more service for a Knight's-Fee, nor for any other free tenement, than what is due from thence.

[17] Common Pleas shall not follow our court, but shall be held in any certain place.

[18] Trials upon the Writs of *Novel Disseisin*, of *Mort d'Ancestre* [Death of the Ancestor], and *Darrien Presentment* [Last Presentation], shall not be taken but in their proper counties, and in this manner: We, or our Chief Justiciary, if we are out of the kingdom, will send two Justiciaries into each county, four times in the year, who, with four knights of each county, chosen by the county, shall hold the aforesaid assizes, within the county on the day, and at the place appointed.

[19] And if the aforesaid assizes cannot be taken on the day of the

county-court, let as many knights and freeholders, of those who were present at the county-court remain behind, as shall be sufficient to do justice, according to the great or less importance of the business.

[20] A free-man shall not be amerced for a small offence, but only according to the degree of the offence; and for a great delinquency, according to the magnitude of the delinquency, saving his contenement: a Merchant shall be amerced in the same manner, saving his merchandise, and a villain shall be amerced after the same manner, saving to him his Wainage, if he shall fall into our mercy; and none of the aforesaid amerciaments shall be assessed, but by the oath of honest men of the vicinage.

[21] Earls and Barons shall not be amerced but by their Peers, and that only according to the degree of their delinquency.

[22] No Clerk shall be amerced for his lay-tenement, but according to the manner of the others as aforesaid, and not according to the quantity of his ecclesiastical benefice.

[23] Neither a town nor any person shall be distrained to build bridges or embankments, excepting those which anciently, and of right, are bound to do it.

[24] No Sheriff, Constable, Coroners, nor other of our Bailiffs, shall hold pleas of our crown.

[25] All Counties, and Hundreds, Trethings, and Wapontakes, shall be at the ancient rent, without any increase, excepting in our Demesne-manors.

[26] If any one holding of us a lay-fee dies, and the Sheriff or our Bailiff, shall shew our letters-patent of summons concerning the debt which the defunct owed to us, it shall be lawful for the Sheriff or our Bailiff to attach and register the chattels of the defunct found on that lay-fee, to the amount of that debt, by the view of lawful men, so that nothing shall be removed from thence until our debt be paid to us; and the rest shall be left to the executors to fulfil the will of the defunct; and if nothing be owing to us by him, all the chattels shall fall to the defunct, saving to his wife and children their reasonable shares.

[27] If any free-man shall die intestate, his chattels shall be distributed by the hands of his nearest relations and friends, by the view of the Church, saving to every one the debts which the defunct owed.

[28] No Constable nor other Bailiff of ours shall take the corn or other goods of any one, without instantly paying money for them, unless he can obtain respite from the free will of the seller.

[29] No Constable [Governor of a Castle] shall distrain any Knight to give money for castle-guard, if he be willing to perform it in his own person, or by another able man, if he cannot perform it himself, for a reasonable cause: and if we have carried or sent him into the army, he shall be excused from castle-guard, according to the time that he shall be in the army by our command.

[30] No Sheriff nor Bailiff of ours, nor any other person shall take the horses or carts of any free-man, for the purpose of carriage, without the consent of the said free-man.

[31] Neither we, nor our Bailiffs, will take another man's wood, for our castle or other uses, unless by the consent of him to whom the wood belongs.

[32] We will not retain the lands of those who have been convicted of felony, excepting for one year and one day, and then they shall be given up to the lord of the fee.

[33] All kydells [fish-weirs] for the future shall be quite removed out of the Thames, and the Medway, and through all England, excepting upon the sea-coast.

[34] The writ which is called *Præcipe*, for the future shall not be granted to any one of any tenement, by which a free-man may lose his court.

[35] There shall be one measure of wine throughout all our kingdom, and one measure of ale, and one measure of corn, namely the quarter of London; and one breadth of dyed cloth, and of russets, and of halberjects, namely, two ells within the lists. Also it shall be the same with weights as with measures.

[36] Nothing shall be given or taken for the future for the Writ of Inquisition of life or limb; but it shall be given without charge, and not denied.

[37] If any hold of us by Fee-Farm, or Socage, or Burgage, and hold land of another by Military Service, we will not have the custody of the heir, nor of his lands, which are of the fee of another, on account of that Fee-Farm, or Socage, or Burgage; nor will we have the custody of the Fee-Farm, Socage, or Burgage, unless the Fee-Farm owe Military Service. We will not have the custody of the

heir, nor of the lands of any one, which he holds of another by Military Service, on account of any Petty-Sergeantry which he holds of us by the service of giving us daggers, or arrows, or the like.

[38] No Bailiff, for the future, shall put any man to his law, upon his own simple affirmation, without credible witnesses produced for that purpose.

[39] No freeman shall be seized, or imprisoned, or dispossessed, or outlawed, or exiled, or in any way destroyed; nor will we condemn him, nor will we commit him to prison, excepting by the legal judgment of his peers, or by the law of the land. [In the Latin original: *Nullus liber homo capiatur, vel imprisonetur, aut disseisiatur, aut utlagetur, aut exuletur, aut aliquo modo destruatur, nec super eum ibimus, nec super eum mittemus, nisi per legale judicium parium suorum vel per legem terre.*]

[40] To none will we sell, to none will we deny, to none will we delay right or justice.

[41] All Merchants shall have safety and security in coming into England, and going out of England, and in staying and in travelling through England, as well by land as by water, to buy and sell, without any unjust exactions, according to ancient and right customs, excepting in the time of war, and if they be of a country at war against us: and if such are found in our land at the beginning of a war, they shall be apprehended without injury of their bodies and goods, until it be known to us, or to our Chief Justiciary, how the Merchants of our country are treated who are found in the country at war against us; and if ours be in safety there, the others shall be in safety in our land.

[42] It shall be lawful to any person, for the future, to go out of our kingdom, and to return, safely and securely, by land or by water, saving his allegiance to us, unless it be in time of war, for some short space, for the common good of the kingdom: excepting prisoners and outlaws, according to the laws of the land, and of the people of the nation at war against us, and Merchants who shall be treated as it is said above.

[43] If any hold of any escheat, as of the Honour of Wallingford, Nottingham, Boulogne, Lancaster, or of other escheats which are in our hand, and are Baronies, and shall die, his heir shall not give any other relief, nor do any other service to us, than he should have done to the Baron, if that Barony had been in the hands of the Baron; and we will hold it in the same manner that the Baron held it.

[44] Men who dwell without the Forest, shall not come, for the future, before our Justiciaries of the Forest on a common summons; unless they be parties in a plea, or sureties for some person or persons who are attached for the Forest.

[45] We will not make Justiciaries, Constables, Sheriffs, or Bailiffs, excepting of such as know the laws of the land, and are well disposed to observe them.

[46] All Barons who have founded Abbies, which they hold by charters from the Kings of England, or by ancient tenure, shall have the custody of them when they become vacant, as they ought to have.

[47] All Forests which have been made in our time, shall be immediately disforested; and it shall be so done with Water-banks, which have been taken or fenced in by us during our reign.

[48] All evil customs of Forests and Warrens, and of Foresters and Warreners, Sheriffs and their officers, Water-banks and their keepers, shall immediately be inquired into by twelve Knights of the same county, upon oath, who shall be elected by good men of the same county; and within forty days after the inquisition is made, they shall be altogether destroyed by them never to be restored; provided that this be notified to us before it be done, or to our Justiciary, if we be not in England.

[49] We will immediately restore all hostages and charters, which have been delivered to us by the English, in security of the peace and of their faithful service.

[50] We will remove from their bailiwicks the relations of Gerard de Athyes, so that, for the future, they shall have no bailiwick in England; Engelard de Cygony, Andrew, Peter, and Gyone de Chancell, Gyone de Cygony, Geoffrey de Martin, and his brothers, Philip Mark, and his brothers, and Geoffrey his nephew, and all their followers.

[51] And immediately after the conclusion of the peace, we will remove out of the kingdom all foreign knights, cross-bow-men, and stipendiary soldiers, who have come with horses and arms to the molestation of the kingdom.

[52] If any have been disseised or dispossessed by us, without a legal verdict of their peers, of their lands, castles, liberties, or rights, we will immediately restore these things to them; and if any dispute shall arise on this head, then it shall be determined by the

verdict of the twenty-five Barons, of whom mention is made below, for the security of the peace. Concerning all those things of which any one hath been disseised or dispossessed, without the legal verdict of his peers by King Henry our father, or King Richard our brother, which we have in our hand, or others hold with our warrants, we shall have respite, until the common term of the Croisaders, excepting those concerning which a plea had been moved, or an inquisition taken, by our precept, before our taking the Cross; but as soon as we shall return from our expedition, or if, by chance, we should not go upon our expedition, we will immediately do complete justice therein.

[53] The same respite will we have, and the same justice shall be done, concerning the disforestation of the forests, or the forests which remain to be disforested, which Henry our father, or Richard our brother, have afforested; and the same concerning the wardship of lands which are in another's fee, but the wardship of which we have hitherto had, occasioned by any of our fees held by Military Service; and for Abbies founded in any other fee than our own, in which the Lord of the fee hath claimed a right; and when we shall have returned, or if we shall stay from our expedition, we shall immediately do complete justice in all these pleas.

[54] No man shall be apprehended or imprisoned on the appeal of a woman, for the death of any other man than her husband.

[55] All fines that have been made by us unjustly, or contrary to the laws of the land; and all amerciaments that have been imposed unjustly, or contrary to the laws of the land, shall be wholly remitted, or ordered by the verdict of the twenty-five Barons, of whom mention is made below, for the security of the peace, or by the verdict of the greater part of them, together with the aforesaid Stephen, Archbishop of Canterbury, if he can be present, and others whom he may think fit to bring with him: and if he cannot be present, the business shall proceed, notwithstanding, without him; but so, that if any one or more of the aforesaid twenty-five Barons have a similar plea, let them be removed from that particular trial, and others elected and sworn by the residue of the same twenty-five, be substituted in their room, only for that trial.

[56] If we have disseised or dispossessed any Welshmen of their lands, or liberties, or other things, without a legal verdict of their peers, in England or in Wales, they shall be immediately restored to

them; and if any dispute shall arise upon this head, then let it be determined in the Marches by the verdict of their peers: for a tenement of England, according to the law of England; for a tenement of Wales, according to the law of Wales; for a tenement of the Marches, according to the law of the Marches. The Welsh shall do the same to us and to our subjects.

[57] Also concerning those things of which any Welshman hath been disseised or dispossessed without the legal verdict of his peers, by King Henry our father, or King Richard our brother, which we have in our hand, or others hold with our warrant, we shall have respite, until the common term of the Croisaders, excepting for those concerning which a plea had been moved, or an inquisition made, by our precept, before our taking the Cross. But as soon as we shall return from our expedition, or if, by chance, we should not go upon our expedition, we shall immediately do complete justice therein, according to the laws of Wales, and the parts aforesaid.

[58] We will immediately deliver up the son of Llewelin, and all the hostages of Wales, and release them from their engagements which were made with us, for the security of the peace.

[59] We shall do to Alexander King of Scotland, concerning the restoration of his sisters and hostages, and his liberties and rights, according to the form in which we act to our other Barons of England, unless it ought to be otherwise by the charters which we have from his father William, the late King of Scotland; and this shall be by the verdict of his peers in our court.

[60] Also all these customs and liberties aforesaid, which we have granted to be held in our kingdom, for so much of it as belongs to us, all our subjects, as well clergy as laity, shall observe towards their tenants as far as concerns them.

[61] But since we have granted all these things aforesaid, for GOD, and for the amendment of our kingdom, and for the better extinguishing the discord which has arisen between us and our Barons, we being desirous that these things should possess entire and unshaken stability for ever, give and grant to them the security underwritten; namely, that the Barons may elect twenty-five Barons of the kingdom, whom they please, who shall with their whole power, observe, keep, and cause to be observed, the peace and liberties which we have granted to them, and have confirmed by this our present charter, in this manner: that is to say, if we, or our

Justiciary, or our bailiffs, or any of our officers, shall have injured any one in any thing, or shall have violated any article of the peace or security, and the injury shall have been shown to four of the aforesaid twenty-five Barons, the said four Barons shall come to us, or to our Justiciary if we be out of the kingdom, and making known to us the excess committed, petition that we cause that excess to be redressed without delay. And if we shall not have redressed the excess, or, if we have been out of the kingdom, our Justiciary shall not have redressed it within the term of forty days, computing from the time when it shall have been made known to us, or to our Justiciary if we have been out of the kingdom, the aforesaid four Barons, shall lay that cause before the residue of the twenty-five Barons; and they, the twenty-five Barons, with the community of the whole land, shall distress and harass us by all the ways in which they are able; that is to say, by the taking of our castles, lands, and possessions, and by any other means in their power, until the excess shall have been redressed, according to their verdict; saving harmless our person, and the persons of our Queen and children; and when it hath been redressed, they shall behave to us as they have done before. And whoever of our land pleaseth, may swear, that he will obey the commands of the aforesaid twenty-five Barons, in accomplishing all the things aforesaid, and that with them he will harass us to the utmost of his power: and we publicly and freely give leave to every one to swear who is willing to swear; and we will never forbid any to swear. But all those of our land, who, of themselves, and of their own accord, are unwilling to swear to the twenty-five Barons, to distress and harass us together with them, we will compel them by our command, to swear as aforesaid. And if any one of the twenty-five Barons shall die, or remove out of the land, or in any other way shall be prevented from executing the things above said, they who remain of the twenty-five Barons shall elect another in his place, according to their own pleasure, who shall be sworn in the same manner as the rest. In all those things which are appointed to be done by these twenty-five Barons, if it happen that all the twenty-five Barons have been present, and have differed in their opinions about any thing, or if some of them who had been summoned, would not, or could not be present, that which the greater part of those who were present shall have provided and decreed, shall be held as firm and as valid, as if all the twenty-five had agreed in it: and the aforesaid twenty-five shall swear, that they will faithfully observe, and, with all their power, cause to be observed, all the things mentioned above. And we will obtain nothing from any one, by ourselves, nor by another, by which any of these concessions and liberties may be revoked or diminished. And if any such thing shall have been obtained, let it be void and null: and we will never use it, neither by ourselves nor by another.

[62] And we have fully remitted and pardoned to all men, all the ill-will, rancour, and resentments, which have arisen between us and our subjects, both clergy and laity, from the commencement of the discord. Moreover, we have fully remitted to all the clergy and laity, and as far as belongs to us, have fully pardoned all transgressions committed by occasion of the said discord, for Easter, in the sixteenth year of our reign [i.e. 1215] until the conclusion of the peace. And, moreover, we have caused to be made to them testimonial letters-patent of the Lord Stephen, Archbishop of Canterbury, the Lord Henry, Archbishop of Dublin, and of the aforesaid Bishops, and of Master Pandulph concerning this security, and the aforesaid concessions.

[63] Wherefore, our will is, and we firmly command that the Church of England be free, and that the men in our kingdom have and hold the aforesaid liberties, rights, and concessions, well and in peace, freely and quietly, fully and entirely, to them and their heirs, of us and our heirs, in all things and places, for ever as is aforesaid. It is also sworn, both on our part, and on that of the Barons, that all the aforesaid shall be observed in good faith, and without any evil intention.

Witnessed by the above, and many others. Given by our hand in the Meadow which is called Runningmead, between Windsor and Staines, this 15th day of June, in the 17th year of our reign [i.e., 1215: the new regal year began on 28 May].

B. Thomas More's Petition to Henry VIII on Parliamentary Freedom of Speech (1521)

Sythe I perceive, most redoubted soveraigne, that it standethe not with your highe pleasure to reforme this election [of Thomas More as Speaker of the House of Commons] and cause it to be changed, but have by the mouth of the most reverend father in god, the legate, your highnes Chauncellor [i.e., Cardinal Wolsey], therunto geven your most royal assent, and have of your benignity determyned, farre above that I may beare, to enhable me and for this office to repute me meete, rather then ye should seeme to impute unto your comons [i.e., the House of Commons] that they had unmeetely chosen, I am therefore, and alway shalbe, ready obediently to conforme my self to thaccomplishment of your highe commandement, In my most humble wise beseeching your most noble maiestie that I may with your graces favour, before I farther enter therunto, make mine humble intercession unto your highnes for two lowly petitions: The one privately concerning my self, the other the whole assembly of your comon house.

For my self, gratious Soveraigne, that if it misshapp me in anye thinge hereafter that is on the behalf of your comons in your highe presence to be declared, to mistake my message, and in the lack of good utteraunce, by my misrehersall, to perverte or impaire their prudent instuctions, It may then like your most noble maiestie, of your aboundant grace, with the eye of your accostomed pitye, to pardon my simplenes, geving me leave to repaire againe to the comen house, and there to conferre with them, and to take their substancial advise what thing and in what wise I shall on their behalf utter and speak before your noble grace, To thentente their prudent devises and affaires be not by my simplenes and Folly

256

hindered or impaired: which thing, if it should so mishappe, as it were well likely to mishappe in me, if your gratious benignity releaved not my oversight, It could not faile to be during my life a perpetuall grudge and hevines to my harte, The helpe and remedy whereof, in manner aforesaid remembred, is, most gracious soveraigne, my first lowly suit and humble petition unto your most noble grace.

Mine other humble request, moste excellent Prince, is this: Forasmuche as there be of your comons, heare by your highe commandment assembled for your parliament, a greate number which are, after thaccustomed manner, appointed in the comen house to treate and advise of the comon affaires among themselfes aparte; And albeit, most deere leige Lord, that according to your prudent advise, by your honorable writes every wheare declared, there hath bine as due diligens used in sending upp to your highnes courte of parliament the most discreete persons out of every quarter that men could esteeme meete thereunto, Wherby it is not to be doubted but that there is a very substanciall assembly of right wise and politicke persons; yeat, most victorious Prince, sith among so many wise men neyther is every man wise alike, nor among so many men, like well witted, every man like well spoken, And it often happeneth that, likewise as much folly is uttered with painted polished speache, so many, boystyous and rude in language, see deepe indeed, and give right substanciall councell; And sithe also in matters of great importaunce, the mynd is often so occupied in the matter that a man rather studieth what to say then howe, By reson whereof the wisest man and the best spoken in a whole country fortuneth among, while his mynd is fervent in the matter, somewhat to speake in such wise as he wold afterward wishe to have bine uttered otherwise, and yeat no wors will had when he spake it, then he hath when he wold so gladly chaunge it; Therefore, most gracious soveraigne, considering that in your highe court of parliament is nothing intreated but matter of weight and importance concerning your realme and your owne roiall estate, It could not faile to let and put to silence from the geving of their advice and councell many of your discreete comons, to the greate hinderaunce of the comon affaires, excepte that every of your comons were utterly discharged of all doubte and feare howe any thing that it should happen them to speake, should happen of your highnes to be taken. And in this point, though your well knowen and proved benignity puttethe every man in ryght good hope, yeat such is the waight of the matter, such is the reverend dread that the tymorous hartes of your naturall subiectes conceave toward your highe maiestie, our most redoubted king and undoubted soveraigne, that they cannot in this point finde themselfes satisfied, except your gracious bounty therin declared put away the scruple of their timorous myndes, and animate and incourage them, and put them out of doubte. It may therefore like your moste aboundant grace, our most benigne and godly kinge, to give to all your comons heare assembled your most gracious licens and pardon, freely, without doubte of your dreadfull displeasure, every man to dischárge his consciens, and boldlye in every thinge incident among us to declare his advise; and whatsoever happen any man to say, that it may like your noble maiestye, of your inestimable goodnes, to take all in good parte, interpreting every mans wordes, howe unconingly soever they be couched, to proceed yeat of good zeale towardes the profit of your realme and honor of your royall person, the prosperous estate and preservation whereof, most excellent soveraigne, is the thinge which we all, your most humble loving subiectes, according to the most bounden duty of our naturall alleageans, moste highlye desire and pray for.

C. The Petition of Right (1628)

The Peticion Exhibited to His Majestie [Charles I] by the Lords Spirituall and Temporall and Commons in this present Parliament assembled concerning divers Rights and Liberties of the Subjects: with the Kings Majesties Royall Aunswera thereunto in full Parliament.

To the King's most Excellent Majestie.

Humbly shew unto our Soveraigne Lord the King the Lords Spirituall and Temporall and Commons in Parliament assembled, That whereas it is declared and enacted by a Statute made in the tyme of the Raigne of King Edward the first commonly called Statutum de Tallagio non concedendo, That no Tallage or Ayde should be layd or levyed by the King or his Heires in this Realme without the good will and assent of the Archbishopps Bishopps Earles Barons Knights Burgesses and other the Freemen of the Commonaltie of this Realme, And by Authoritie of Parliament holden in the five and twentith yeare of the raigne of King Edward the third, it is declared and enacted, That from thenceforth no person should be compelled to make any Loanes to the King against his will because such Loanes were against reason and the franchise of the Land, And by other Lawes of this Realme it is provided, that none should be charged by any charge or Imposicion called a Benevolence nor by such like Charge by which the Statutes before mencioned and other the good Lawes and Statutes of this Realme your Subjects have inherited this Freedome That they should not be compelled to contribute to any Taxe Tallage Ayde or other like Charge not sett by common consent in Parliament.

[II] Yet neverthelesse of late divers Commissions directed to sundry Commissioners in severall Counties with Instruccions have issued, by means whereof your people have been in divers places assembled and required to lend certain sommes of mony unto your Majestie, and many of them uppon their refusall soe to doe have had an Oath administred unto them not warrantable by the Lawes or Statutes of this Realme and have been constrayned to become bound to make apparance and give attendance before your Privie Councell and in other places; and others of them have been therefore imprisoned confined and sondry other waies molested and disquieted And divers other charges have been laid and levied upon your people in severall Counties by Lord Lieutenants Deputie Lieutenants Commissioners for Musters Justices of Peace and others by Commaund or Direccion from your Majestie or your Privie Councell against the Lawes and free Customes of the Realme.

[III] And where alsoe by the Statute called The great Charter of the Liberties of England [Magna Carta], It is declared and enacted [in Chapter 39], That no Freeman may be taken or imprisoned or be disseised of his Freehold or Liberties or his free Customes or be outlawed or exiled or in any manner destroyed, but by the lawfull Judgment of his Peeres or by the Law of the Land.

[IV] And in the eight and twentith yeere of the raigne of King Edward the third it was declared and enacted by authoritie of Parliament, that no man of what estate or condicion that he be, should be put out of his Land or Tenements nor taken nor imprisoned nor disherited nor put to death without being brought to aunswere by due processe of Lawe.

[V] Neverthelesse against the tenor of the said Statutes and other the good Lawes and Statutes of your Realme to that end provided, divers of your Subjects have of late been imprisoned without any cause shewed: And when for their deliverance they were brought before your Justices by your Majesties Writts of Habeas corpus there to undergoe and receive as the Court should order, and their Keepers commaunded to certifie the causes of their detayner, no cause was certified, but that they were deteined by your Majesties speciall commaund signified by the Lords of your Privie Councill, and yet were returned backe to severall prisons without being charged with any thing to which they might make aunswere according to the Lawe.

[VI] And whereas of late great Companies of Souldiers and Marriners have been dispersed into divers Counties of the Realme, and the inhabitants against their wills have been compelled to receive them into their houses, and there to suffer them to sojourne against the Lawes and Customes of this Realme and to the great greivance and vexacion of the people.

[VII] And whereas alsoe by authoritie of Parliament in the five and twentith yeare of the Raigne of King Edward the third it is declared and enacted that no man should be forejudged of life or limbe against the forme of the Great Charter and the Lawe of the Land, And by the said Great Charter, and other the Lawes and Statutes of this your Realme no man ought to be adjudged to death but by the Lawes established in this your Realme either by the customes of the same Realme or by Acts of Parliament. And whereas no offender of what kinde soever is exempted from the proceedings to be used and punishments to be inflicted by the Lawes and Statutes of this your Realme, Nevertheless of late tyme divers Commissions under your Majesties great Seale have issued forth, by which certaine persons have been assigned and appointed Commissioners with power and authoritie to proceed within the land according to the Justice of Martiall Lawe against such Souldiers or Marriners or other dissolute persons joyning with them as should committ any murther robbery felony mutiny or other outrage or misdemeanor whatsoever, and by such summary course and order as is agreeable to Martiall Lawe and as is used in Armies in tyme of warr, to proceed to the tryall and condemnacion of such offenders, and them to cause to be executed and put to death according to the Lawe Martiall.

By pretext whereof some of your Majesties Subjects have been by some of the said Commissioners put to death, when and where, if by the Lawes and Statutes of the land they had deserved death, by the same Lawes and Statutes alsoe they might and by no other ought to have byn judged and executed.

And alsoe sundrie greivous offendors by colour thereof clayming an exempcion have escaped the punishments due to them by the Lawes and Statutes of this your Realme, by reason that divers of your Officers and ministers of Justice have unjustlie refused or forborne to proceed against such Offendors according to the same Lawes and Statutes upon pretence that the said offendors were punishable onlie by Martiall law and by authoritie of such Commissions as aforesaid. Which Commissions and all other of like

261

nature are wholly and directlie contrary to the said Lawes and Statutes of this your Realme.

[VIII] They doe therefore humblie pray your most Excellent Majestie, that no man hereafter be compelled to make or yeild any Guift Loane Benevolence Taxe or such like Charge without common consent by Act of Parliament, And that none be called to make aunswere or take such Oath or to give attendance or be confined or otherwise molested or disquieted concerning the same or for refusall thereof. And that no freeman in any such manner as is before mencioned be imprisoned or deteined. And that your Majestie would be pleased to remove the said Souldiers and Mariners and that your people may not be soe burthened in tyme to come. And that the aforesaid Commissions for proceeding by Martiall Lawe may be revoked and annulled. And that hereafter no Commissions of like nature may issue forth to any person or persons whatsoever to be executed as aforesaid, lest by colour of them any of your Majesties Subjects be destroyed or put to death contrary to the Lawes and Franchise of the Land.

All which they most humblie pray of your most Excellent Majestie as their Rights and Liberties according to the Lawes and Statutes of this Realme, And that your Majestie would alsoe vouchsafe to declare that the Awards doings and proceedings to the prejudice of your people in any of the premisses shall not be drawne hereafter into consequence or example. And that your Majestie would be also graciouslie pleased for the further comfort and safetie of your people to declare your Royall will and pleasure, That in the things aforesaid all your Officers and Ministers shall serve you according to the Lawes and Statutes of this Realme as they tender the Honor of your Majestie and the prosperitie of this Kingdome.

Qua quidem Peticione lecta et plenius interllecta per dictum Dominum Regem taliter est responsum in pleno Parliamento, viz. Soit droit fait come est desire. [Which Petition having been read and fully understood, the answer by word of the Lord King in full Parliament was, "Let it be made law as is desired."]

D. The English Bill of Rights (1689)

An Act declareing the Rights and Liberties of the Subject and Setleing the Succession of the Crowne.

Whereas the Lords Spirituall and Temporall and Commons assembled at Westminster lawfully fully and freely representing all the Estates of the People of this Realme did upon the thirteenth day of February in the yeare of our Lord one thousand six hundred eighty eight present unto their Majesties then called and known by the Names and Stile of William and Mary Prince and Princesse of Orange being present in their proper Persons a certaine Declaration in writeing made by the said Lords and Commons in the words following viz

Whereas the late King James the Second by the Assistance of diverse evill Councellors Judges and Ministers imployed by him did endeavour to subvert and extirpate the Protestant Religion and the Lawes and Liberties of this Kingdome

[1] By Assumeing and Exerciseing a Power of Dispensing with and Suspending of Lawes and the Execution of Lawes without Consent of Parlyament.

[2] By Committing and Prosecuting diverse Worthy Prelates for humbly Petitioning to be excused from Concurring to the said Assumed Power.

[3] By issueing and causeing to be executed a Commission under the Great Seale for Erecting a Court called The Court of Commissioners for Ecclesiasticall Causes.

[4] By Levying Money for and to the Use of the Crowne by pretence of Prerogative for other time and in other manner then the same was granted by Parlyament.

[5] By raising and keeping a Standing Army within this King-

dome in time of Peace without Consent of Parlyament and Quartering Soldiers contrary to Law.

[6] By causing severall good Subjects being Protestants to be disarmed at the same time when Papists were both Armed and Imployed contrary to Law.

[7] By Violating the Freedome of Election of Members to serve in Parlyament.

[8] By Prosecutions in the Court of Kings Bench for Matters and Causes cognizable onely in Parlyament and by diverse other Arbitrary and Illegall Courses.

[9] And whereas of late yeares Partiall Corrupt and Unqualifyed Persons have been returned and served on Juryes in Tryals and particularly divers Jurors in Tryalls for High Treason which were not Freeholders.

[10] And excessive Baile hath beene required of Persons committed in Criminall Cases to elude the Benefit of the Lawes made for the Liberty of the Subjects.

[11] And excessive Fines have beene imposed.

[12] And illegall and cruell Punishments inflicted.

[13] And several Grants and Promises made of Fines and Forfeitures before any Conviction or Judgment against the Persons upon whome the same were to be levyed.

All which are utterly and directly contrary to the knowne Lawes and Statutes and Freedome of this Realme.

And whereas the said late King James the Second haveing Abdicated the Government and the Throne being thereby Vacant His Highnesse the Prince of Orange (whome it hath pleased Almighty God to make the glorious Instrument of Delivering this Kingdome from Popery and Arbitrary Power) did (by the Advice of the Lords Spirituall and Temporall and diverse principall Persons of the Commons) cause Letters to be written to the Lords Spirituall and Temporall being Protestants and other Letters to the severall Countyes Cityes Universities Burroughs and Cinque Ports for the Choosing of such Persons to represent them as were of right to be sent to Parlyament to meete and sitt at Westminster upon the two and twentyeth day of January in this Yeare one thousand six hundred eighty and eight in order to such an Establishment as that their Religion Lawes and Liberties might not againe be in danger of being Subverted, Upon which Letters Elections haveing been accordingly made.

And thereupon the said Lords Spirituall and Temporall and Commons pursuant to their respective Letters and Elections being now assembled in a full and free Representative of this Nation takeing into their most serious Consideration the best meanes for attaining the Ends aforesaid Doe in the first place (as their Auncestors in like case have usually done) for the Vindicating and Asserting their auntient Rights and Liberties, Declare

[1] That the pretended Power of Suspending of Laws or the Execution of Laws by Regall Authority without Consent of Parlyament is illegall.

[2] That the pretended Power of Dispensing with Laws or the Execution of Laws by Regall Authority as it hath beene assumed and exercised of late is illegall.

[3] That the Commission for erecting the late Court of Commissioners for Ecclesiastical Causes and all other Commissions and Courts of like nature are Illegal and Pernicious.

[4] That levying Money for or to the Use of the Crowne by pretence of Prerogative without Grant of Parlyament for longer time or in other manner than the same is or shall be granted is Illegall.

[5] That it is the Right of the Subjects to petition the King and all Committments and Prosecutions for such Petitioning are Illegall.

[6] That the raising or keeping a standing Army within the Kingdome in time of Peace unlesse it be with Consent of Parlyament is against Law.

[7] That the Subjects which are Protestants may have Arms for their Defence suitable to their Conditions and as allowed by Law.

[8] That Election of Members of Parlyament ought to be free.

[9] That the Freedome of Speech and Debates or Proceedings in Parlyament ought not to be impeached or questioned in any Court or Place out of Parlyament.

[10] That excessive Baile ought not to be required nor excessive Fines imposed nor cruell and unusuall Punishments inflicted.

[11] That Jurors ought to be duely impannelled and returned and Jurors which passe upon Men in Trialls for High Treason ought to be Freeholders.

[12] That all Grants and Promises of Fines and Forfeitures of particular persons before Conviction are illegall and void.

[13] And that for Redress of all Grievances and for the amending strengthening and preserveing of the Lawes Parlyaments ought to be held frequently.

And they doe Claime Demand and Insist upon all and singular the Premises as their undoubted Rights and Liberties and that noe Declarations Judgements Doeings or Proceedings to the Prejudice of the People in any of the said Premisses ought in any wise to be drawn hereafter into Consequence or Example. To which Demand of their Rights they are particularly encouraged by the Declaration of his Highnesse the Prince of Orange as being the onely meanes for obtaining a full Redresse and Remedy therein. Haveing therefore an intire Confidence That his said Highnesse the Prince of Orange will perfect the Deliverance soe farr advanced by him and will still preserve them from the Violation of their Rights which they have here asserted and from all other Attempts upon their Religion Rights and Liberties. The said Lords Spirituall and Temporall and Commons assembled at Westminster doe Resolve That William and Mary Prince and Princess of Orange be and be declared King and Queene of England France and Ireland and the Dominions thereunto belonging to hold the Crowne and Royall Dignity of the said Kingdomes and Dominions to them the said Prince and Princesse dureing their Lives and the Life of the Survivour of them And that the sole and full Exercise of the Regall Power be onely in and executed by the said Prince of Orange in the Names of the said Prince and Princesse dureing their joynt Lives And after their Deceases the said Crowne and Royall Dignitie of the said Kingdoms and Dominions to be to the Heires of the Body of the said Princess. And for default of such Issue to the Princesse Anne of Denmarke and the Heires of her Body And for default of such Issue to the Heires of the Body of the said Prince of Orange. And the Lords Spirituall and Temporall and Commons doe pray the said Prince and Princesse to accept the same accordingly. And that the Oathes hereafter mentioned be taken by all Persons of whome the Oathes of Allegiance and Supremacy might be required by Law instead of them And that the said Oathes of Allegiance and Supremacy be abrogated.

I A B doe sincerely promise, and sweare That I will be faithfull and beare true Allegiance to their Majestyes King William and Queene Mary

Soe helpe me God.

I A B doe sweare That I doe from my Heart Abhorr, Detest and Abjure as Impious and Hereticall this damnable Doctrine and Position That Princes Excommunicated or Deprived by the Pope or any Authority of the See of Rome may be deposed or murdered by their Subjects or any other whatsoever. And I doe declare That noe Forreigne Prince Person Prelate, State or Potentate hath or ought to have any Jurisdiction Power Superiority Preeminence or Authoritie Ecclesiasticall or Spirituall within this Realme

Soe help me God.

Upon which their said Majestyes did accept the Crowne and Royall Dignitie of the Kingdoms of England France and Ireland and the Dominions thereunto belonging according to the Resolution and Desire of the said Lords and Commons contained in the said Declaration. And thereupon their Majestyes were pleased That the said Lords Spirituall and Temporall and Commons being the two Houses of Parlyament should continue to sitt and with their Majesties Royall Concurrence make effectuall Provision for the Setlement of the Religion Lawes and Liberties of this Kingdome soe that the same for the future might not be in danger againe of being subverted, To which the said Lords Spirituall and Temporall and Commons did agree and proceede to act accordingly. Now in pursuance of the Premisses the said Lords Spirituall and Temporall and Commons in Parlyament assembled for the ratifying confirming and establishing the said Declaration and the Articles Clauses Matters and Things therein contained by the Force of a Law made in due Forme by Authority of Parlyament doe pray that it may be declared and enacted That all and singular the Rights and Liberties asserted and claimed in the said Declaration are the true auntient and indubitable Rights and Liberties of the People of this Kingdome and soe shall be esteemed allowed adjudged deemed and taken to be and that all and every the particulars aforesaid shall be firmly and strictly holden and observed as they are expressed in the said Declaration And all Officers and Ministers whatsoever shall serve their Majestyes and their Successors according to the same in all times to come. . . . All which Their Majestyes are contented and pleased shall be declared enacted and established by authoritie of this present Parliament and shall stand remaine and be the Law of this Realme for ever And the same are by their said Majesties by and with the advice and consent of the Lords Spirituall and Temporall and Commons in Parlyament assembled and by the authoritie of the same declared enacted and established accordingly . . .

E. Declarations by American Congresses (1765–1776)

E-1. DECLARATIONS OF RIGHTS & GRIEVANCES BY THE STAMP ACT CONGRESS (1765)

Saterday, October 19th 1765 AM

The Congress met according to Adjournment and Resumed &c as Yesterday—And upon Mature Deliberation agreed to the following Declarations of the Rights & Grievances of the Colonists, in America which were ordered to be inserted

The Members of this Congress sincerely devoted with the warmest Sentiments, of Affection and Duty to his Majestys [George III's] Person & Government, inv[io]lably attached to the present happy Establishment of the Protestant Succession, and with Minds deeply impressed by a Sense of the present, and impending Misfortunes of the British Colonies on this Continent, haveing Considered as Maturely as time will permit, the Circumstances of the said Colonies esteem it our indispensable Duty to make the following Declarations of Our Humble Opinion respecting the most essential Rights, and Liberties of the Colonists, and of the Grievances, under which they labour, by Reason of Several late Acts of Parliament.

1st That his Majesty's Subjects in these Colonies Owe the same Allegiance to the Crown of Great Britain, that is Owing from his Subjects born within the Realm, and all due Subordination to that August Body the Parliament of Great Britain.

2d That his Majestys liege Subjects in these Colonies are intituld to all the Inherent Rights and liberties of his Natural Bornd Subjects, within the Kingdom of Great Britain.

3d That it is inseparably essential to the Freedom of a People, and the Undoubted Right of Englishmen, that no Taxes be imposed on them, but with their own Consent, given personally or by their Representatives.

4th That the People of these Colonies are not and from their local Circumstances cannot be Represented in the House of Commons in Great Britain.

5th That the only Representatives of the People of these Colonies are persons chosen therein, by themselves & that no Taxes ever have been or can be consititutionally imposed on them but by their respective Legislatures.

6th That all Supplies to the Crown, being free Gifts of the People, it is unreasonable, and inconsistent with the principles and Spirit of the British Constitution, for the People of Great Britain, to Grant to his Majesty, the property of the Colonists.

7th That Trial by Jury is the inherent and invaluable Right of every British Subject, in these Colonies.

8th That the late Act of Parliament, intituled, "An Act for Granting and applying certain Stamp Duties, and other Duties in the British Colonies and Plantations in America &c," by imposing Taxes on the Inhabitants of these Colonies, and the said Act, and several other acts, by extending the Jurisdiction of the Courts of Admiralty, beyond its Ancient limits, have a Manifest tendency to Subvert the Rights, and liberties of the Colonists.

9th That the Duties imposed by several late Acts of Parliament from the peculiar Circumstances of these Colonies, will be extremely Burthensome & Grevious; and from the Scarcity of Specie, the Payment of them absolutely impracticable.

10th That as the profits of the Trade of these Colonies ultimately center in Great Britain, to pay for the Manufactures which they are Obliged to take from thence, they eventually contribute very largely to all Supplies Granted there to the Crown.

11th That the Restrictions imposed by several late Acts of Parliament on the Trade of these Colonies, will render them unable to purchase the Manufactures of Great Britain.

12th That the Encrease Prosperity and hapiness of these Colonies, depend on the full and free Enjoyment of their Rights and Liberties, and an Intercourse with Great Britain mutually Affectionate and Advantageous.

13th That it is the Right of the British Subjects in these Colonies to Petition the King, or either House of Parliament.

Lastly That it is the indispensable duty of these Colonies to the best of Soverigns, to the Mother Country, and to themselves, to endeavour by a loyal and dutifull Address to his Majesty, and humble Applications to both Houses of Parliament, to procure the Repeal of the Act for Granting and applying certain Stamp Duties, of all Clauses of any other Acts of Parliament, whereby the Jurisdiction of the Admiralty is extended as aforesaid, and of the other late Acts for the Restriction of American Commerce.

Upon Motion Voted, That Robert R. Livingston, Wm Samuel Johnson, and William Murdock Esqrs be a Committee to prepare an address to his Majesty and lay the same before the Congress, on Monday next.

Voted allso that John Rutledge, Edward Tilghman and Philip Livingston Esqrs be a Committee to prepare a Memorial and Petition to the Lords in Parliament, and lay the same before the Congress on Monday Next.

Voted also, that Thomas Lynch, James Otis and Thomas McKean Esqrs be a Committee to prepare a Peticion to the House of Commons of Great Britain, and lay the same before the Congress on Monday next. Then the Congress Adjourned to Monday next at 12 OClock

E-2. DECLARATION AND RESOLVES BY THE FIRST CONTINENTAL CONGRESS (1774)

Friday, October 14, 1774

The Congress met according to adjournment, and resuming the consideration of the subject under debate—made the following *declarations* and *resolves:*

Whereas, since the close of the last war, the British parliament, claiming a power, of right, to bind the people of America by statutes in all cases whatsoever, hath, in some acts, expressly imposed taxes on them, and in others, under various pretences, but in fact for the purpose of raising a revenue, hath imposed rates and duties payable in these colonies, established a board of commissioners, with unconstitutional powers, and extended the jurisdiction of courts of admiralty, not only for collecting the said duties, but for the trial of causes merely arising within the body of a county.

And whereas, in consequence of other statutes, judges, who before held only estates at will in their offices, have been made dependant on the crown alone for their salaries, and standing armies kept in times of peace: And whereas it has lately been resolved in parliament, that by force of a statute, made in the thirty-fifth year of the reign of king Henry the eighth, colonists may be transported to England, and tried there upon accusations for treasons and misprisions, or concealments of treasons committed in the colonies, and by a late statute, such trials have been directed in cases therein mentioned:

And whereas, in the last session of parliament, three statutes were made; one entitled, "An act to discontinue, in such manner and for such time as are therein mentioned, the landing and discharging, lading, or shipping of goods, wares and merchandize, at the town, and within the harbour of Boston, in the province of Massachusetts-Bay in North-America;" another entitled, "An act for the better regulating the government of the province of Massachusetts-Bay in New England;" and another entitled, "An act for the impartial administration of justice, in the cases of persons questioned for any act done by them in the execution of the law, or for the suppression of riots and tumults, in the province of the Massachusetts-Bay in New England;" and another statute was then made, "for making more effectual provision for the government of the province of Quebec, &c." All which statutes are impolitic, unjust, and cruel, as well as unconstitutional, and most dangerous and destructive of American rights:

And whereas, assemblies have been frequently dissolved, contrary to the rights of the people, when they attempted to deliberate on grievances; and their dutiful, humble, loyal, and reasonable petitions to the crown for redress, have been repeatedly treated with contempt, by his majesty's ministers of state:

The good people of the several colonies of New-Hampshire, Massachusetts-Bay, Rhode-Island and Providence Plantations, Connecticut, New-York, New-Jersey, Pennsylvania, Newcastle, Kent, and Sussex on Delaware, Maryland, Virginia, North-Carolina, and South-Carolina, justly alarmed at these arbitrary proceedings of parliament and administration, have severally elected, constituted, and appointed deputies to meet, and sit in general Congress, in the city of Philadelphia, in order to obtain such establishment, as that their religion, laws, and liberties, may not be subverted: Whereupon the deputies so appointed being now assembled, in a full and free representation of these colonies, taking into their most serious consideration, the best means of attaining the ends aforesaid, do, in the first place, as Englishmen, their ancestors in like cases have usually done, for asserting and vindicating their rights and liberties, DECLARE,

That the inhabitants of the English colonies in North-America, by the immutable laws of nature, the principles of the English constitution, and the several charters or compacts, have the following RIGHTS:

Resolved, N. C. D. [No one dissenting] 1. That they are entitled to life, liberty and property: and they have never ceded to any sovereign power whatever, a right to dispose of either without their consent.

Resolved, N. C. D. 2. That our ancestors, who first settled these colonies, were at the time of their emigration from the mother country, entitled to all the rights, liberties, and immunities of free and natural-born subjects, within the realm of England.

Resolved, N. C. D. 3. That by such emigration they by no means forfeited, surrendered, or lost any of those rights, but that they were, and their descendants now are, entitled to the exercise and enjoyment of all such of them, as their local and other circumstances enable them to exercise and enjoy.

Resolved, 4. That the foundation of English liberty, and of all free government, is a right in the people to participate in their legislative council: and as the English colonists are not represented, and from their local and other circumstances, cannot properly be represented in the British parliament, they are entitled to a free and exclusive power of legislation in their several provincial legislatures, where their right of representation can alone be preserved, in all cases of taxation and internal polity, subject only to the negative of their sovereign, in such manner as has been heretofore used and accustomed: But, from the necessity of the case, and a regard to the mutual interest of both countries, we cheerfully consent to the operation of such acts of the British parliament, as are bona fide, restrained to the regulation of our external commerce, for the purpose of securing the commercial advantages of the whole empire to the mother country, and the commercial benefits of its respective members; excluding every idea of taxation internal or external, for raising a revenue on the subjects, in America, without their consent.

Resolved, N. C. D. 5. That the respective colonies are entitled to the common law of England, and more especially to the great and inestimable privilege of being tried by their peers of the vicinage, according to the course of that law.

Resolved, 6. That they are entitled to the benefit of such of the English statutes, as existed at the time of their colonization; and which they have, by experience, respectively found to be applicable to their several local and other circumstances.

Resolved, N. C. D. 7. That these, his majesty's colonies, are likewise entitled to all the immunities and privileges granted and confirmed to them by royal charters, or secured by their several codes of provincial laws.

Resolved, N. C. D. 8. That they have a right peaceably to assemble, consider of their grievances, and petition the king; and that all prosecutions, prohibitory proclamations, and commitments for the same, are illegal.

Resolved, N. C. D. 9. That the keeping a standing army in these colonies, in times of peace, without the consent of the legislature of that colony, in which such army is kept, is against law.

Resolved, N. C. D. 10. It is indispensably necessary to good government, and rendered essential by the English constitution, that the constituent branches of the legislature be independent of each other; that, therefore, the exercise of legislative power in several colonies, by a council appointed, during pleasure, by the crown, is unconstitutional, dangerous and destructive to the freedom of American legislation.

All and each of which the aforesaid deputies, in behalf of themselves, and their constituents, do claim, demand, and insist on, as their indubitable rights and liberties; which cannot be legally taken from them, altered or abridged by any power whatever, without their own consent, by their representatives in their several provincial legislatures.

In the course of our inquiry, we find many infringements and violations of the foregoing rights, which, from an ardent desire, that harmony and mutual intercourse of affection and interest may be restored, we pass over for the present, and proceed to state such acts and measures as have been adopted since the last war, which demonstrate a system formed to enslave America.

Resolved, N. C. D. That the following acts of parliament are infringements and violations of the rights of the colonists; and that the repeal of them is essentially necessary, in order to restore harmony between Great-Britain and the American colonies, viz.

The several acts of 4 Geo. III. ch. 15. and ch. 34.—5 Geo. III. ch. 25.— 6 Geo. III. ch. 52.—7 Geo. III. ch. 41. and ch. 46.—8 Geo. III. ch. 22. which impose duties for the purpose of raising a revenue in America, extend the power of the admiralty courts beyond their ancient limits, deprive the American subject of trial by jury, authorise the judges certificate to indemnify the prosecutor from damages, that he might otherwise be liable to, requiring oppressive security from a claimant of ships and goods seized, before he shall be allowed to defend his property, and are subversive of American rights.

Also 12 Geo. III. ch. 24. intituled, "An act for the better securing his majesty's dock-yards, magazines, ships, ammunition, and stores," which declares a new offence in America, and deprives the American subject of a constitutional trial by jury of the vicinage, by authorising the trial of any person, charged with the committing any offence described in the said act, out of the realm, to be indicted and tried for the same in any shire or county within the realm.

Also the three acts passed in the last session of parliament, for stopping the port and blocking up the harbour of Boston, for altering the charter and government of Massachusetts-Bay, and that which is entitled, "An act for the better administration of justice, &c."

Also the act passed in the same session for establishing the Roman Catholic religion, in the province of Quebec, abolishing the equitable system of English laws, and erecting a tyranny there, to the great danger, (from so total a dissimilarity of religion, law and government) of the neighbouring British colonies, by the assistance of whose blood and treasure the said country was conquered from France.

Also the act passed in the same session, for the better providing suitable quarters for officers and soldiers in his majesty's service, in North-America.

Also, that the keeping a standing army in several of these colonies, in time of peace, without the consent of the legislature of that colony, in which such army is kept, is against law.

To these grievous acts and measures, Americans cannot submit, but in hopes their fellow subjects in Great-Britain will, on a revision of them, restore us to that state, in which both countries found happiness and prosperity, we have for the present, only resolved to pursue the following peaceable measures: 1. To enter into a non-importation, non-consumption, and non-exportation agreement or association. 2. To prepare an address to the people of Great-Britain, and a memorial to the inhabitants of British America: and 3. To prepare a loyal address to his majesty, agreeable to resolutions already entered into.

A letter being received from several gentlemen in Georgia, was read.

E-3. THE DECLARATION OF INDEPENDENCE (1776)

In CONGRESS, July 4, 1776.
A DECLARATION
By the REPRESENTATIVES of the
UNITED STATES OF AMERICA,
In GENERAL CONGRESS ASSEMBLED.

When in the Course of human Events, it becomes necessary for one People to dissolve the Political Bands which have connected them with another, and to assume among the Powers of the Earth, the separate and equal Station to which the Laws of Nature and of Nature's God entitle them, a decent Respect to the Opinions of Mankind requires that they should declare the causes which impel them to the Separation.

We hold these Truths to be self-evident, that all Men are created equal, that they are endowed by their Creator with certain unalienable Rights, that among these are Life, Liberty, and the Pursuit of Happiness—That to secure these Rights, Governments are instituted among Men, deriving their just Powers from the Consent of the Governed, that whenever any Form of Government becomes destructive of these Ends, it is the Right of the People to alter or to abolish it, and to institute new Government, laying its Foundation on such Principles, and organizing its Powers in such Form, as to them shall seem most likely to effect their Safety and Happiness. Prudence, indeed, will dictate that Governments long established should not be changed for light and transient Causes; and accordingly all Experience hath shewn, that Mankind are more disposed to suffer, while Evils are sufferable, than to right themselves by abolishing the Forms to which they are accustomed. But when a long Train of Abuses and Usurpations, pursuing invariably the same Object, evinces a Design to reduce them under absolute Despotism, it is their Right, it is their Duty, to throw off such Government, and to provide new Guards for their future Security. Such has been the patient Sufferance of these Colonies; and such is now the Necessity which constrains them to alter their former Systems of Government. The History of the present King of Great-Britain is a History of repeated Injuries and Usurpations, all having in direct Object the Establishment of an absolute Tyranny over these States. To prove this, let Facts be submitted to a candid World.

He has refused his Assent to Laws, the most wholesome and necessary for the public Good.

He has forbidden his Governors to pass Laws of immediate and pressing Importance, unless suspended in their Operation till his Assent should be obtained; and when so suspended, he has utterly neglected to attend to them.

He has refused to pass other Laws for the Accommodation of large Districts of People, unless those People would relinquish the Right of Representation in the Legislature, a Right inestimable to them, and formidable to Tyrants only.

He has called together Legislative Bodies at Places unusual, uncomfortable, and distant from the Depository of their public Records, for the sole Purpose of fatiguing them into Compliance with his Measures.

He has dissolved Representative Houses repeatedly, for opposing with manly Firmness his Invasions on the Rights of the People.

He has refused for a long Time, after such Dissolutions, to cause others to be elected; whereby the Legislative Powers, incapable of Annihilation, have returned to the People at large for their exercise; the State remaining in the mean time exposed to all the Dangers of Invasion from without, and Convulsions within.

He has endeavoured to prevent the Population of these States; for that Purpose obstructing the Laws for Naturalization of Foreigners;

277

refusing to pass others to encourage their Migrations hither, and raising the Conditions of new Appropriations of Lands.

He has obstructed the Administration of Justice, by refusing his Assent to Laws for establishing Judiciary Powers.

He has made Judges dependent on his Will alone, for the Tenure of their Offices, and the Amount and Payment of their Salaries.

He has erected a Multitude of new Offices, and sent hither Swarms of Officers to harass our People, and eat out their Substance.

He has kept among us, in Times of Peace, Standing Armies, without the consent of our Legislatures.

He has affected to render the Military independent of and superior to the Civil Power.

He has combined with others to subject us to a Jurisdiction foreign to our Constitution, and unacknowledged by our Laws; giving his Assent to their Acts of pretended Legislation:

For quartering large Bodies of Armed Troops among us:

For protecting them, by a mock Trial, from Punishment for any Murders which they should commit on the Inhabitants of these States:

For cutting off our Trade with all Parts of the World:

For imposing Taxes on us without our Consent:

For depriving us, in many Cases, of the Benefits of Trial by Jury:

For transporting us beyond Seas to be tried for pretended Offences:

For abolishing the free System of English Laws in a neighbouring Province, establishing therein an arbitrary Government, and enlarging its Boundaries, so as to render it at once an Example and fit Instrument for introducing the same absolute Rule into these Colonies:

For taking away our Charters, abolishing our most valuable Laws, and altering fundamentally the Forms of our Governments:

For suspending our own Legislatures, and declaring themselves invested with Power to legislate for us in all Cases whatsoever.

He has abdicated Government here, by declaring us out of his Protection and waging War against us.

He has plundered our Seas, ravaged our Coasts, burnt our Towns, and destroyed the Lives of our People.

He is, at this Time, transporting large Armies of foreign Mercenaries to compleat the Works of Death, Desolation, and Tyranny, already begun with circumstances of Cruelty and Perfidy, scarcely paralleled in the most barbarous Ages, and totally unworthy the Head of a civilized Nation.

He has constrained our fellow Citizens taken Captive on the high Seas to bear Arms against their Country, to become the Executioners of their Friends and Brethren, or to fall themselves by their Hands.

He has excited domestic Insurrections amongst us, and has endeavoured to bring on the Inhabitants of our Frontiers, the merciless Indian Savages, whose known Rule of Warfare, is an undistinguished Destruction, of all Ages, Sexes and Conditions.

In every stage of these Oppressions we have Petitioned for Redress in the most humble Terms: Our repeated Petitions have been answered only by repeated Injury. A Prince, whose Character is thus marked by every act which may define a Tyrant, is unfit to be the Ruler of a free People.

Nor have we been wanting in Attentions to our British Brethren. We have warned them from Time to Time of Attempts by their Legislature to extend an unwarrantable Jurisdiction over us. We have reminded them of the Circumstances of our Emigration and Settlement here. We have appealed to their native Justice and Magnanimity, and we have conjured them by the Ties of our common Kindred to disavow these Usurpations, which, would inevitably interrupt our Connections and Correspondence. They too have been deaf to the Voice of Justice and of Consanguinity. We must, therefore, acquiesce in the Necessity, which denounces our Separation, and hold them, as we hold the rest of Mankind, Enemies in War, in Peace, Friends.

We, therefore, the Representatives of the UNITED STATES OF AMERICA, in General Congress, Assembled, appealing to the Supreme Judge of the World for the Rectitude of our Intentions, do, in the Name, and by Authority of the good People of these Colonies, solemnly Publish and Declare, That these United Colonies are, and of Right ought to be, Free and Independent States; that they are absolved from all Allegiance to the British Crown, and that all political Connection between them and the State of Great-Britain, is and ought to be totally dissolved; and that as Free and Independent States, they have full Power to levy War, conclude Peace, contract Alliances, establish Commerce, and to do all other Acts and Things which Independent States may of right do. And for the support of this Declaration, with a firm Reliance on the Protection of divine Providence, we mutually pledge to each other our Lives, our Fortunes, and our sacred Honor.

Signed by Order and in Behalf of the Congress . . . [The names of the signers are collected by States, following upon the signature of John Hancock as President of the Continental Congress: *New Hampshire:* Josiah Bartlett, Wm. Whipple, Matthew Thornton; *Massachusetts-Bay:* Saml. Adams, John Adams, Robt. Treat Paine, Elbridge Gerry; *Rhode-Island and Providence, &c.:* Step. Hopkins, William Ellery; *Connecticut:* Roger Sherman, Saml. Huntington, Wm. Williams, Oliver Wolcott; *New-York:* Wm. Floyd, Phil. Livingston, Frans. Lewis, Lewis Morris; *New Jersey:* Richd. Stockton, Jno. Witherspoon, Fras. Hopkinson, John Hart, Abra. Clark; *Pennsylvania:* Robt. Morris, Benjamin Rush, Benja. Franklin, John Morton, Geo. Clymer, Jas. Smith, Geo. Taylor, James Wilson, Geo. Ross; *Delaware:* Caesar Rodney, Geo. Read, (Tho M:Kean); *Maryland:* Samuel Chase, Wm. Paca, Thos. Stone, Charles Carroll, of Carrollton; *Virginia:* George Wythe, Richard Henry Lee, Ths. Jefferson, Benja. Harrison, Thos. Nelson, jr., Francis Lightfoot Lee, Carter Braxton; *North-Carolina:* Wm. Hooper, Joseph Hewes, John Penn; *South-Carolina:* Edward Rutledge, Thos. Heyward, junr, Thomas Lynch, junr., Arthur Middleton; and *Georgia:* Button Gwinnett, Lyman Hall, Geo. Walton.]

F. Declarations of Rights (1776–1780)

F-1. VIRGINIA DECLARATION OF RIGHTS (1776)

A declaration of rights made by the representatives of the good people of Virginia, assembled in full and free convention; which rights do pertain to them, and their posterity, as the basis and foundation of government.

SECTION 1. That all men are by nature equally free and independent, and have certain inherent rights, of which, when they enter into a state of society, they cannot, by any compact, deprive or divest their posterity; namely, the enjoyment of life and liberty, with the means of acquiring and possessing property, and pursuing and obtaining happiness and safety.

SEC. 2. That all power is vested in, and consequently derived from, the people; that magistrates are their trustees and servants, and at all times amenable to them.

SEC. 3. That government is, or ought to be instituted for the common benefit, protection, and security of the people, nation, or community; of all the various modes and forms of government, that is best which is capable of producing the greatest degree of happiness and safety, and is most effectually secured against the danger of maladministration; and that, when any government shall be found inadequate or contrary to these purposes, a majority of the community hath an indubitable, unalienable, and indefeasible right to reform, alter, or abolish it, in such manner as shall be judged most conducive to the public weal.

SEC. 4. That no man, or set of men, are entitled to exclusive or separate emoluments or privileges from the community, but in consideration of public services; which, not being descendible, neither ought the offices of magistrate, legislator, or judge to be hereditary.

SEC. 5. That the legislative and executive powers of the State should be separate and distinct from the judiciary; and that the members of the two first may be restrained from oppression, by feeling and participating the burdens of the people, they should, at fixed periods, be reduced to a private station, return into that body from which they were originally taken, and the vacancies be supplied by frequent, certain, and regular elections, in which all, or any part of the former members, to be again eligible, or ineligible, as the laws shall direct.

SEC. 6. That elections of members to serve as representatives of the people, in assembly, ought to be free; and that all men, having sufficient evidence of permanent common interest with, and attachment to, the community, have the right of suffrage. and cannot be taxed or deprived of their property for public uses, without their own consent, or that of their representatives so elected, nor bound by any law to which they have not, in like manner, [assented] for the public good.

SEC. 7. That all power of suspending laws, or the execution of laws, by any authority, without consent of the representatives of the people, is injurious to their rights, and ought not to be exercised.

SEC. 8. That in all capital or criminal prosecutions a man hath a right to demand the cause and nature of his accusation, to be confronted with the accusers and witnesses, to call for evidence in his favor, and to a speedy trial by an impartial jury of twelve men of his vicinage, without whose unanimous consent he cannot be found guilty; nor can he be compelled to give evidence against himself; that no man be deprived of his liberty, except by the law of the land or the judgment of his peers.

SEC. 9. That excessive bail ought not to be required, nor excessive fines imposed, nor cruel and unusual punishments inflicted.

SEC. 10. That general warrants, whereby any officer or messenger may be commanded to search suspected places without evidence of a fact committed, or to seize any person or persons not named, or whose offence is not particularly described and supported by evidence, are grievous and oppressive, and ought not to be granted.

SEC. 11. That in controversies respecting property, and in suits between man and man, the ancient trial by jury is preferable to any other, and ought to be held sacred.

SEC. 12. That the freedom of the press is one of the great bulwarks of liberty, and can never be restrained but by despotic governments.

SEC. 13. That a well-regulated militia, composed of the body of the people, trained to arms, is the proper, natural, and safe defence of a free State; that standing armies, in time of peace, should be avoided, as dangerous to liberty; and that in all cases the military should be under strict subordination to, and governed by, the civil power.

SEC. 14. That the people have a right to uniform government; and, therefore, that no government separate from, or independent of the government of Virginia, ought to be erected or established within the limits thereof.

SEC. 15. That no free government, or the blessings of liberty, can be preserved to any people, but by a firm adherence to justice, moderation, temperance, frugality, and virtue, and by frequent recurrence to fundamental principles.

SEC. 16. That religion, or the duty which we owe to our Creator, and the manner of discharging it, can be directed only by reason and conviction, not by force or violence; and therefore all men are equally entitled to the free excercise of religion, according to the dictates of conscience; and that it is the mutual duty of all to practise Christian forbearance, love, and charity towards each other.

[This "Declaration of Rights" is followed by "The Constitution or Form of Government &c."]

F-2. MASSACHUSETTS DECLARATION OF RIGHTS (1780)

Preamble

The end of the institution, maintenance, and administration of government, is to secure the existence of the body politic, to protect it, and to funish the individuals who compose it with the power of enjoying in safety and tranquillity their natural rights, and the blessings of life: and whenever these great objects are not obtained, the people have a right to alter the government, and to take measures necessary for their safety, prosperity, and happiness.

The body politic is formed by a voluntary association of individuals: it is a social compact, by which the whole people covenants with each citizen, and each citizen with the whole people, that all shall be governed by certain laws for the common good. It is the duty of the people, therefore, in framing a constitution of government, to provide for an equitable mode of making laws, as well as for an impartial interpretation and a faithful execution of them; that every man may, at all times, find his security in them.

We, therefore, the people of Massachusetts, acknowledging, with grateful hearts, the goodness of the great Legislator of the universe, in affording us, in the course of His providence, an opportunity, deliberately and peaceably, without fraud, violence, or surprise, of entering into an original, explicit, and solemn compact with each other; and of forming a new constitution of civil government, for ourselves and posterity; and devoutly imploring His direction in so interesting a design, do agree upon, ordain, and establish, the following *Declaration of Rights, and Frame of Government*, as the CONSTITUTION OF THE COMMONWEALTH OF MASSACHUSETTS.

PART THE FIRST
A DECLARATION OF THE RIGHTS OF THE INHABITANTS
OF THE COMMONWEALTH OF MASSACHUSETTS

ARTICLE I. All men are born free and equal, and have certain natural, essential, and unalienable rights; among which may be reckoned the right of enjoying and defending their lives and liberties; that of acquiring, possessing, and protecting property; in fine, that of seeking and obtaining their safety and happiness.

II. It is the right as well as the duty of all men in society, publicly, and at stated seasons, to worship the SUPREME BEING, the great Creator and Preserver of the universe. And no subject shall be hurt, molested, or restrained, in his person, liberty, or estate, for worshipping GOD in the manner and season most agreeable to the dictates of his own conscience; or for his religious profession of sentiments; provided he doth not disturb the public peace, or obstruct others in their religious worship.

III. As the happiness of a people, and the good order and preservation of civil government, essentially depend upon piety, religion, and morality; and as these cannot be generally diffused through a community but by the institution of the public worship of GOD, and of public instructions in piety, religion, morality: Therefore, to

284

promote their happiness, and to secure the good order and preservation of their government, the people of this commonwealth have a right to invest their legislature with power to authorize and require, and the legislature shall, from time to time, authorize and require, the several towns, parishes, precincts, and other bodies politic, or religious societies, to make suitable provision, at their own expense, for the institution of the public worship of GOD, and for the support and maintenance of public Protestant teachers of piety, religion, and morality, in all cases where such provision shall not be made voluntarily.

And the people of this commonwealth have also a right to, and do, invest their legislature with authority to enjoin upon all the subjects an attendance upon the instructions of the public teachers aforesaid, at stated times and seasons, if there be any on whose instructions they can conscientiously and conveniently attend.

Provided, notwithstanding, that the several towns, parishes, precincts, and other bodies politic, or religious societies, shall, at all times, have the exclusive right of electing their public teachers, and of contracting with them for their support and maintenance.

And all moneys paid by the subject to the support of public worship, and of the public teachers aforesaid, shall, if he require it, be uniformly applied to the support of the public teacher or teachers of his own religious sect or denomination, provided there be any on whose instructions he attends; otherwise it may be paid towards the support of the teacher or teacheres of the parish or precinct in which the said moneys are raised.

And every denomination of Christians, demeaning themselves peaceably, and as good subjects of the commonwealth, shall be equally under the protection of the law: and no subordination of any one sect or denomination to another shall ever be established by law.

[In 1833, Section III was amended to read, "As the public worship of GOD and instructions in piety, religion, and morality, promote the happiness and prosperity of a people, and the security of a republican government; therefore, the several religious societies of this commonwealth, whether corporate or unincorporate, at any meeting legally warned and holden for that purpose, shall ever have the right to elect their pastors or religious teachers, to contract with them for their support, to raise money for erecting and repair-

285

ing houses for public worship, for the maintenance of religious instruction, and for the payment of necessary expenses; and all persons belonging to any religous society shall be taken and held to be members, until they shall file with the clerk of such society a written notice, declaring the dissolution of their membership, and thenceforth shall not be liable for any grant or contract which may be thereafter made, or entered into by such society; and all religious sects and denominations, demeaning themselves peaceably, and as good citizens of the commonwealth, shall be equally under the protection of the law; and no subordination of any one sect or denomination to another shall ever be established by law."]

IV. The people of this commonwealth have the sole and exclusive right of governing themselves, as a free, sovereign, and independent state; and do, and forever hereafter shall, exercise and enjoy every power, jurisdiction, and right, which is not, or may not hereafter be, by them expressly delegated to the United States of America, in Congress assembled.

V. All power residing originally in the people, and being derived from them, the several magistrates and officers of government, vested with authority, whether legislative, executive, or judicial, are their substitutes and agents, and are at all times accountable to them.

VI. No man, nor corporation, or association of men, have any other title to obtain advantages, or particular and exclusive privileges, distinct from those of the community, than what arises from the consideration of services rendered to the public; and this title being in nature neither hereditary, nor transmissible to children, or descendants, or relations by blood, the idea of a man born a magistrate, lawgiver, or judge, is absurd and unnatural.

VII. Government is instituted for the common good; for the protection, safety, prosperity, and happiness of the people; and not for the profit, honor, or private interest of any one man, family, or class of men: Therefore the people alone have an incontestible unalienable, and indefeasible right to institute government; and to reform, alter, or totally change the same, when their protection, safety, prosperity, and happiness require it.

VIII. In order to prevent those who are vested with authority from becoming oppressors, the people have a right, at such periods and in such manner as they shall establish by their frame of government, to cause their public officers to return to private life; and to fill up vacant places by certain and regular elections and appointments.

IX. All elections ought to be free; and all the inhabitants of this commonwealth, having such qualifications as they shall establish by their frame of government, have an equal right to elect officers, and to be elected, for public employments.

X. Each individual of the society has a right to be protected by it in the enjoyment of his life, liberty, and property, according to standing laws. He is obliged, consequently, to contribute his share to the expense of this protection; to give his personal service, or an equivalent, when necessary: but no part of the property of any individual can, with justice, be taken from him, or applied to public uses, without his own consent, or that of the representative body of the people. In fine, the people of this commonwealth are not controllable by any other laws than those to which their constitutional representative body have given their consent. And whenever the public exigencies require that the property of any individual should be appropriated to public uses, he shall receive a reasonable compensation therefor.

XI. Every subject of the commonwealth ought to find a certain remedy, by having recourse to the laws, for all injuries or wrongs which he may receive in his person, property, or character. He ought to obtain right and justice freely, and without being obliged to purchase it; completely, and without any denial; promptly, and without delay; conformably to the laws.

XII. No subject shall be held to answer for any crimes or offence, until the same is fully and plainly, substantially, and formally, described to him; or be compelled to accuse, or furnish evidence against himself. And every subject shall have a right to produce all proofs that may be favorable to him; to meet the witnesses against him face to face, and to be fully heard in his defence by himself, or his counsel, at his election. And no subject shall be arrested, imprisoned, despoiled, or deprived of his property, immunities, or privileges, put out of the protection of the law, exiled, or deprived of his life, liberty, or estate, but by the judgment of his peers, or the law of the land.

And the legislature shall not make any law that shall subject any person to a capital or infamous punishment, excepting for the government of the army and navy, without trial by jury.

XIII. In criminal prosecutions, the verification of facts, in the vicinity where they happen, is one of the greatest securities of the life, liberty, and property of the citizen.

XIV. Every subject has a right to be secure from all unreasonable searches, and seizures, of his person, his houses, his papers, and all his possessions. All warrants, therefore, are contrary to this right, if the cause or foundation of them be not previously supported by oath or affirmation, and if the order in the warrant to a civil officer, to make search in suspected places, or to arrest one or more suspected persons, or to seize their property, be not accompanied with a special designation of the persons or objects of search, arrest, or seizure; and no warrant ought to be issued but in cases, and with the formalities prescribed by the laws.

XV. In all controversies concerning property, and in all suits between two or more persons, except in cases in which it has heretofore been otherways used and practised, the parties have a right to a trial by jury; and this method of procedure shall be held sacred, unless, in causes arising on the high seas, and such as relate to mariners' wages, the legislature shall hereafter find it necessary to alter it.

XVI. The liberty of the press is essential to the security of freedom in a state it ought not, therefore, to be restricted in this commonwealth.

XVII. The people have a right to keep and to bear arms for the common defence. And as, in time of peace, armies are dangerous to liberty, they ought not to be maintained without the consent of the legislature; and the military power shall always be held in an exact subordination to the civil authority, and be governed by it.

XVIII. A frequent recurrence to the fundamental principles of the constitution, and a constant adherence to those of piety, justice, moderation, temperance, industry, and frugality, are absolutely necessary to preserve the advantages of liberty, and to maintain a free government. The people ought, consequently, to have a particular attention to all those principles, in the choice of their officers and representatives: and they have a right to require of their lawgivers and magistrates an exact and constant observance of them, in the formation and execution of the laws necessary for the good administration of the commonwealth.

XIX. The people have a right, in an orderly and peaceable manner, to assemble to consult upon the common good; give instructions to their representatives, and to request of the legislative body, by the way of addresses, petitions, or remonstrances, redress of the wrongs done them, and of the grievances they suffer.

XX. The power of suspending the laws, or the execution of the laws, ought never to be exercised but by the legislature, or by authority derived from it, to be exercised in such particular cases only as the legislature shall expressly provide for.

XXI. The freedom of deliberation, speech, and debate, in either house of the legislature, is so essential to the rights of the people, that it cannot be the foundation of any accusation or prosecution, action or complaint, in any other court or place whatsoever.

XXII. The legislature ought frequently to assemble for the redress of grievances, for correcting, strengthening, and confirming the laws, and for making new laws, as the common good may require.

XXIII. No subsidy, charge, tax, impost, or duties ought to be established, fixed, laid, or levied, under any pretext whatsoever, without the consent of the people or their representatives in the legislature.

XXIV. Laws made to punish for actions done before the existence of such laws, and which have not been declared crimes by preceding laws, are unjust, oppressive, and inconsistent with the fundamental principles of a free government.

XXV. No subject ought, in any case, or in any time, to be declared guilty of treason or felony by the legislature.

XXVI. No magistrate or court of law shall demand excessive bail or sureties, impose excessive fines, or inflict cruel or unusual punishments.

XXVII. In time of peace, no soldier ought to be quartered in any house without the consent of the owner; and in time of war, such quarters ought not to be made but by the civil magistrate, in a manner ordained by the legislature.

XXVIII. No person can in any case be subject to law-martial, or to any penalties or pains, by virtue of that law, except those employed in the army or navy, and except the militia in actual service, but by authority of the legislature.

XXIX. It is essential to the preservation of the rights of every individual, his life, liberty, property, and character, that there be an impartial interpretation of the laws, and administration of justice. It is the right of every citizen to be tried by judges as free, impartial, and independent as the lot of humanity will admit. It is, therefore, not only the best policy, but for the security of the rights of the people, and of every citizen, that the judges of the supreme judicial court should hold their offices as long as they behave themselves well; and that they should have honorable salaries ascertained and established by standing laws.

XXX. In the government of this commonwealth, the legislative department shall never exercise the executive and judicial powers, or either of them: the executive shall never exercise the legislative and judicial powers, or either of them; the judicial shall never exercise the legislative and executive powers, or either of them: to the end it may be a government of laws and not of men.

[This "Declaration of Rights" is followed by "Part the Second: The Frame of Government."]

G. Virginia Statute of Religious Liberty (1785)

AN ACT FOR ESTABLISHING RELIGIOUS FREEDOM.

I. Whereas Almighty God hath created the mind free; that all attempts to influence it by temporal punishments or burthens, or by civil incapacitations, tend only to beget habits of hypocrisy and meanness, and are a departure from the plan of the Holy author of our religion, who being Lord both of body and mind, yet chose not to propagate it by coercions on either, as was in his Almighty power to do; that the impious presumption of legislators and rulers, civil as well as ecclesiastical, who being themselves but fallible and uninspired men, have assumed dominion over the faith of others, setting up their own opinions and modes of thinking as the only true and infallible, and as such endeavouring to impose them on others, hath established and maintained false religions over the greatest part of the world, and through all time; that to compel a man to furnish contributions of money for the propagation of opinions which he disbelieves, is sinful and tyrannical; that even the forcing him to support this or that teacher of his own religious persuasion, is depriving him of the comfortable liberty of giving his contributions to the particular pastor, whose morals he would make his pattern, and whose powers he feels most persuasive to righteousness, and is withdrawing from the ministry those temporary rewards, which proceeding from an approbation of their personal conduct, are an additional incitement to earnest and unremitting labours for the instruction of mankind; that our civil rights have no dependence on our religious opinions, any more than our opinions in physics or geometry; that therefore the proscribing any citizen as unworthy the public confidence by laying upon him an incapacity of being called to offices of trust and emolument, unless he profess or renounce this or that religious opinion, is depriving him injuriously of those privileges and advantages to which in common with his fellow-citizens he has a natural right; that it tends only to corrupt the principles of that religion it is meant to encourage, by bribing with a monopoly of worldly honours and emoluments, those who will externally profess and conform to it; that though indeed these are criminal who do not withstand such temptation, yet neither are those innocent who lay the bait in their way; that to suffer the civil magistrate to intrude his powers into the field of opinion, and to restrain the profession or propagation of principles on supposition of their ill tendency, is a dangerous fallacy, which at once destroys all religious liberty, because he being of course judge of that tendency will make his opinions the rule of judgment, and approve or condemn the sentiments of others only as they shall square with or differ from his own; that it is time enough for the rightful purposes of civil government, for its officers to interfere when principles break out into overt acts against peace and good order; and finally, that truth is great and will prevail if left to herself, that she is the proper and sufficient antagonist to error, and has nothing to fear from the conflict, unless by human interposition disarmed of her natural weapons, free argument and debate, errors ceasing to be dangerous when it is permitted freely to contradict them:

II. *Be it enacted by the General Assembly*, That no man shall be compelled to frequent or support any religious worship, place, or ministry whatsoever, nor shall be enforced, restrained, molested, or burthened in his body or goods, nor shall otherwise suffer on account of his religious opinions or belief; but that all men shall be free to profess, and by argument to maintain, their opinion in matters of religion, and that the same shall in no wise diminish, enlarge, or affect their civil capacities.

III. And though we well know that this assembly, elected by the people for the ordinary purposes of legislation only, have no power to restrain the acts of succeeding assemblies, constituted with powers equal to our own, and that therefore to declare this act to be irrevocable would be of no effect in law; yet we are free to declare, and do declare, that the rights hereby asserted are of the natural rights of mankind, and that if any act shall be hereafter passed to repeal the present, or to narrow its operation, such act will be an infringement of natural right.

H. The Principal Bill of Rights Discussions in James Madison's *Notes of Debates in the Federal Convention* (1787)

H-1. MONDAY, AUGUST 20, 1787

Mr. [Charles] Pinkney submitted to the House, in order to be referred to the Committee of detail, the following propositions— "Each House shall be the Judge of its own privileges, and shall have authority to punish by imprisonment every person violating the same; or who, in the place where the Legislature may be sitting and during the time of its Session, shall threaten any of its members for any thing said or done on the House, or who shall assault any of them therefor—or who shall assault or arrest any witness or other person ordered to attend either of the Houses in his way going or returning; or who shall rescue any person arrested by their order."

"Each branch of the Legislature, as well as the Supreme Executive shall have authority to require the opinions of the supreme Judicial Court upon important questions of law, and upon solemn occasions"

"The privileges and benefit of the Writ of Habeas corpus shall be enjoyed in this Government in the most expeditious and ample manner; and shall not be suspended by the Legislature except upon the most urgent and pressing occasions, and for a limited time not exceeding   months."

"The liberty of the Press shall be inviolably preserved"

"No troops shall be kept up in time of peace, but by consent of the Legislature"

"The military shall always be subordinate to the Civil power, and

293

no grants of money shall be made by the Legislature for supporting military Land forces, for more than one year at a time"

"No soldier shall be quartered in any House in time of peace without consent of the owner."

"No person holding the office of President of the U.S., a Judge of their Supreme Court, Secretary for the department of Foreign Affairs, of Finance, of Marine, of War, or of   , shall be capable of holding at the same time any other office of Trust or Emolument under the U.S. or an individual State"

"No religious test or qualification shall ever be annexed to any oath of office under the authority of the U.S."

"The U.S. shall be for ever considered as one Body corporate and politic in law, and entitled to all the rights privileges, and immunities, which to Bodies corporate do or ought to appertain"

"The Legislature of the U.S. shall have the power of making the great Seal which shall be kept by the President of the U.S. or in his absence by the President of the Senate, to be used by them as the occasion may require.—It shall be called the great Seal of the U.S. and shall be affixed to all laws."

"All Commissions and writs shall run in the name of the U.S."

"The Jurisdiction of the supreme Court shall be extended to all controversies between the U.S. and an individual State, or the U.S. and the Citizens of an individual State"

These propositions were referred to the Committee of detail without debate or consideration of them, by the House. . . .

H-2. WEDNESDAY, SEPTEMBER 12, 1787

. . . Mr. [Hugh] Williamson, observed to the House that no provision was yet made for juries in Civil cases and suggested the necessity of it.

Mr. [Nathaniel] Gorham. It is not possible to discriminate equity cases from those in which juries are proper. The Representatives of the people may be safely trusted in this matter.

Mr. [Elbridge] Gerry urged the necessity of Juries to guard against corrupt Judges. He proposed that the Committee last appointed should be directed to provide a clause for securing the trial by Juries.

Col. [George] Mason perceived the difficulty mentioned by Mr.

Gorham. The jury cases can not be specified. A general principle laid down on this and some other points would be sufficient. He wished the plan [the Constitution] had been prefaced with a Bill of Rights, & would second a Motion if made for the purpose—It would give great quiet to the people; and with the aid of the State declarations, a bill might be prepared in a few hours.

Mr Gerry concurred in the idea & moved for a Committee to prepare a Bill of Rights. Col: Mason 2ded the motion.

Mr. [Roger] Sherman. was for securing the rights of the people where requisite. The State Declarations of Rights are not repealed by this Constitution; and being in force are sufficient—There are many cases where juries are proper which cannot be discriminated. The Legislature may be safely trusted.

Col. [George] Mason. The Laws of the U.S. are to be paramount to State Bills of Rights. On the question for a Com[mittee] to prepare a Bill of Rights

N.H. no. Mas. abst. Ct no. N— J— no. Pa. no. Del— no. Md no. Va no. N— C. no. S— C— no. Geo no. [Ayes—0; noes—10; absent—1.] . . .

H-3. SATURDAY, SEPTEMBER 15, 1787

. . . Art. III. sect. 2. parag: 3. Mr. Pinkney & Mr. Gerry moved to annex to the end. "And a trial by jury shall be preserved as usual in civil cases."

Mr. Gorham. The constitution of Juries is different in different States and the trial itself is *usual* in different cases in different States,

Mr. [Rufus] King urged the same objections

Genl. [Charles Cotesworth] Pinkney also. He thought such a clause in the Constitution would be pregnant with embarrassments

The motion was disagreed to nem: con: [no one contradicting].

Art. IV. sect. 2. parag: 3. the term "legally" was struck out, and "under the laws thereof" inserted [after the word "State,"] in compliance with the wish of some who thought the term ["legal"] equivocal, and favoring the idea that slavery was legal in a moral view . . .

Mr. [Edmund] Randolph animadverting on the indefinite and dangerous power given by the Constitution to Congress, expressing the pain he felt at differing from the body of the Convention, on the close of the great & awful subject of their labours, and anxiously wishing for some accommodating expedient which would relieve him from his embarrassments, made a motion importing "that amend ments to the plan might be offered by the State Conventions, which should be submitted to and finally decided on by another general Convention." Should this proposition be disregarded, it would he said be impossible for him to put his name to the instrument. Whether he should oppose it afterwards he would not then decide but he would not deprive himself of the freedom to do so in his own State, if that course should be prescribed by his final judgment—

Col: Mason 2ded. & followed Mr. Randolph in animadversions on the dangerous power and structure of the Government, concluding that it would end either in monarchy, or a tyrannical aristocracy; which, he was in doubt, but one or other, he was sure. This Constitution had been formed without the knowledge or idea of the people. A second Convention will know more of the sense of the people, and be able to provide a system more consonant to it. It was improper to say to the people, take this or nothing. As the Constitution now stands, he could neither give it his support or vote in Virginia; and he could not sign here what he could not support there. With the expedient of another Convention as proposed, he could sign.

Mr. Pinkney. These declarations from members so respectable at the close of this important scene, give a peculiar solemnity to the present moment. He descanted on the consequences of calling forth the deliberations & amendments of the different States on the subject of Government at large. Nothing but confusion & contrariety could spring from the experiment. The States will never agree in their plans—And the Deputies to a second Convention coming together under the discordant impressions of their Constituents, will never agree. Conventions are serious things, and ought not to be repeated—He was not without objections as well as others to the plan [the Constitution]. He objected to the contemptible weakness & dependence of the Executive. He objected to the power of a majority only of Cong[res]s over Commerce. But apprehending the danger of a general confusion, and an ultimate decision by the Sword, he should give the plan his support.

Mr. Gerry, stated the objections which determined him to withhold his name from the Constitution. 1. the duration and re-eligibility of the Senate. 2. the power of the House of Representatives to conceal their journals. 3—the power of Congress over the places of election. 4. the unlimited power of Congress over their own compensations. 5. Massachusetts has not a due share of Representatives allotted to her. 6. 3/5 of the Blacks are to be represented as if they were freemen. 7. *Under* the power over commerce, monopolies may be established. 8. The vice president being made head of the Senate. He could however he said get over all these, if the rights of the Citizens were not rendered insecure 1. by the general power of the Legislature to make what laws they may please to call necessary and proper. 2. raise armies and money without limit. 3. to establish a tribunal without juries, which will be a Star-chamber as to Civil cases. Under such a view of the Constitution, the best that could be done he conceived was to provide for a second general Convention.

On the question on the proposition of Mr Randolph. All the States answered—no

On the question to agree to the Constitution, as amended. All the States ay.

The Constitution was then ordered to be engrossed.

And the House adjourned [until its final

session on Monday, September 17, 1787.]

I. Amendment Proposals by the Last States to Ratify the Constitution before Its Initial Implementation (1788)

I-1. VIRGINIA RATIFICATION CONVENTION (JUNE 26–27, 1788)

We the Delegates of the People of Virginia duly elected in pursuance of a recommendation from the General Assembly and now met in Convention having fully and freely investigated and discussed the proceedings of the Federal Convention and being prepared as well as the most mature deliberation hath enabled us to decide thereon Do in the name and in behalf of the People of Virginia declare and make known that the powers granted under the Constitution being derived from the People of the United States may be resumed by them whensoever the same shall be perverted to their injury or oppression and that every power not granted thereby remains with them and at their will: that therefore no right of any denomination can be cancelled abridged restrained or modified by the Congress by the Senate or House of Representatives acting in any Capacity by the President or any Department or Officer of the United States except in those instances in which power is given by the Constitution for those purposes: & that among other essential rights the liberty of Conscience and of the Press cannot be cancelled abridged restrained or modified by any authority of the United States. With these impressions with a solemn appeal to the Searcher of hearts for the purity of our intentions and under the conviction that whatsoever imperfections may exist in the Constitution ought rather to be examined in the mode prescribed therein than to bring the Union into danger by a delay with a hope of obtaining Amendments previous to the Ratification, We the said Delegates in the name and in behalf of the People of Virginia do by these presents assent to and ratify the Constitution recommended on the seventeenth day of September one thousand seven hundred and eighty seven by the Federal Convention for the Government of the United States hereby announcing to all those whom it may concern that the said Constitution is binding upon the said People according to an authentic Copy hereto annexed in the Words following . . . [The Constitution of 1787 is set forth here.]

Subsequent Amendments agreed to in [the Virginia] Convention as necessary to the proposed Constitution of Government for the United States, recommended to the consideration of the Congress which shall first assemble under the said Constitution to be acted upon according to the mode prescribed in the fifth article thereof: . . .

That there be a Declaration or Bill of Rights asserting and securing from encroachment the essential and unalienable Rights of the People in some such manner as the folowings:

[Proposed Declaration or Bill of Rights]

[1] That there are certain natural rights of which men, when they form a social compact cannot deprive or divest their posterity, among which are the enjoyment of life and liberty, with the means of acquiring, possessing and protecting property, and pursuing and obtaining happiness and safety.

[2] That all power is naturally vested in and consequently derived from the people; that Magistrates, therefore, are their trustees and agents and at all times amenable to them.

[3] That government ought to be instituted for the common benefit, protection and security of the People; and that the doctrine of non-resistance against arbitrary power and oppression is absurd slavish, and destructive of the good and happiness of mankind.

[4] That no man or set of Men are entitled to exclusive or separate public emoluments or privileges from the community, but in Consideration of public services; which not being descendible, neither ought the offices of Magistrate, Legislator or Judge, or any other public office to be hereditary.

[5] That the legislative, executive, and judiciary powers of Government should be seperate and distinct, and that the members of

the two first may be restrained from oppression by feeling and participating the public burthens, they should, at fixt periods be reduced to a private station, return into the mass of the people; and the vacancies be supplied by certain and regular elections; in which all or any part of the former members to be eligible or ineligible, as the rules of the Constitution of Government, and the laws shall direct.

[6] That elections of representatives in the legislature ought to be free and frequent, and all men having sufficient evidence of permanent common interest with and attachment to the Community ought to have the right of suffrage: and no aid, charge, tax or fee can be set, rated, or levied upon the people without their own consent, or that of their representatives so elected, nor can they be bound by any law to which they have not in like manner assented for the public good.

[7] That all power of suspending laws or the execution of laws by any authority, without the consent of the representatives of the people in the legislature is injurious to their rights, and ought not to be exercised.

[8] That in all capital and criminal prosecutions, a man hath a right to demand the cause and nature of his accusation, to be confronted with the accusers and witnesses, to call for evidence and be allowed counsel in his favor, and to a fair and speedy trial by an impartial Jury of his vicinage, without whose unanimous consent he cannot be found guilty, (except in the government of the land and naval forces) nor can he be compelled to give evidence against himself.

[9] That no freeman ought to be taken, imprisoned, or disseised of his freehold, liberties, privileges or franchises, or outlawed or exiled, or in any manner destroyed or deprived of his life, liberty, or property but by the law of the land.

[10] That every freeman restrained of his liberty is entitled to a remedy to enquire into the lawfulness thereof, and to remove the same, if unlawful, and that such remedy ought not to be denied nor delayed.

[11] That in controversies respecting property, and in suits between man and man, the ancient trial by Jury is one of the greatest Securities to the rights of the people, and ought to remain sacred and inviolable.

[12] That every freeman ought to find a certain remedy by re-course to the laws for all injuries and wrongs he may receive in his person, property or character. He ought to obtain right and justice freely without sale, compleatly and without denial, promptly and without delay, and that all establishments or regulations contraven-ing these rights, are oppressive and unjust.

[13] That excessive Bail ought not to be required, nor excessive fines imposed, nor cruel and unusual punishments inflicted.

[14] That every freeman has a right to be secure from all unrea-sonable searches and seizures of his person, his papers and his property; all warrants, therefore, to search suspected places, or seize any freeman, his papers or property, without information upon Oath (or affirmation of a person religiously scrupulous of taking an oath) of legal and sufficient cause, are grievous and oppressive; and all general Warrants to search suspected places, or to apprehend any suspected person, without specially naming or describing the place or person, are dangerous, and ought not to be granted.

[15] That the people have a right peaceably to assemble together to consult for the common good, or to instruct their Representa-tives; and that every freeman has a right to petition or apply to the legislature for redress of grievances.

[16] That the people have a right to freedom of speech, and of writing and publishing their Sentiments; but the freedom of the press is one of the greatest bulwarks of liberty, and ought not to be violated.

[17] That the people have a right to keep and bear arms; that a well regulated Militia composed of the body of the people trained to arms is the proper, natural and safe defence of a free State. That standing armies in time of peace are dangerous to liberty, and therefore ought to be avoided, as far as the circumstances and protection of the Community will admit; and that in all cases the military should be under strict subordination to and governed by the Civil power.

[18] That no Soldier in time of peace ought to be quartered in any house without the consent of the owner, and in time of war in such manner only as the laws direct.

[19] That any person religiously scrupulous of bearing arms ought to be exempted upon payment of an equivalent to employ another to bear arms in his stead.

[20] That religion or the duty which we owe to our Creator, and the manner of discharging it can be directed only by reason and conviction, not by force or violence, and therefore all men have an equal, natural and unalienable right to the free exercise of religion according to the dictates of conscience, and that no particular religious sect or society ought to be favored or established by Law in preference to others.

[Proposed] Amendments to the Body of the Constitution

[1] That each State in the Union shall respectively retain every power, jurisdiction and right which is not by this Constitution delegated to the Congress of the United States or to the departments of the Federal Government.

[2] That there shall be one representative for every thirty thousand, according to the Enumeration or Census mentioned in the Constitution, until the whole number of representatives amounts to two hundred; after which that number shall be continued or encreased as the Congress shall direct, upon the principles fixed by the Constitution by apportioning the Representatives of each State to some greater number of people from time to time as population encreases.

[3] When Congress shall lay direct taxes or excises, they shall immediately inform the Executive power of each State of the quota of such state according to the Census herein directed, which is proposed to be thereby raised; And if the Legislature of any State shall pass a law which shall be effectual for raising such quota at the time required by Congress, the taxes and excises laid by Congress shall not be collected, in such State.

[4] That the members of the Senate and House of Representatives shall be ineligible to, and incapable of holding, any civil office under the authority of the United States, during the time for which they shall respectively be elected.

[5] That the Journals of the proceedings of the Senate and House of Representatives shall be published at least once in every year, except such parts thereof relating to treaties, alliances or military operations, as in their judgment require secrecy.

[6] That a regular statement and account of the receipts and ex-

penditures of all public money shall be published at least once in every year.

[7] That no commercial treaty shall be ratified without the concurrence of two thirds of the whole number of the members of the Senate; and no Treaty ceding, contracting, restraining or suspending the territorial rights or claims of the United States, or any of them or their, or any of their rights or claims to fishing in the American seas, or navigating the American rivers shall be [made] but in cases of the most urgent and extreme necessity, nor shall any such treaty be ratified without the concurrence of three fourths of the whole number of the members of both houses respectively.

[8] That no navigation law, or law regulating Commerce shall be passed without the consent of two thirds of the Members present in both houses.

[9] That no standing army or regular troops shall be raised or kept up in time of peace, without the consent of two thirds of the members present in both houses.

[10] That no soldier shall be inlisted for any longer term than four years, except in time of war, and then for no longer term than the continuance of the war.

[11] That each State respectively shall have the power to provide for organizing, arming and disciplining it's own Militia, whensoever Congress shall omit or neglect to provide for the same. That the Militia shall not be subject to Martial law, except when in actual service in time of war, invasion, or rebellion; and when not in the actual service of the United States, shall be subject only to such fines, penalties and punishments as shall be directed or inflicted by the laws of its own State.

[12] That the exclusive power of legislation given to Congress over the Federal Town and its adjacent District and other places purchased or to be purchased by Congress [from] any of the States shall extend only to such regulations as respect the police and good government thereof.

[13] That no person shall be capable of being President of the United States for more than eight years in any term of sixteen years.

[14] That the judicial power of the United States shall be vested in one supreme Court, and in such courts of Admiralty as Congress may from time to time ordain and establish in any of the different States: The Judicial power shall extend to all cases in Law and

Equity arising under treaties made, or which shall be made under the authority of the United States; to all cases affecting ambassadors other foreign ministers and consuls; to all cases of Admiralty and maritime jurisdiction; to controversies to which the United States shall be a party; to controversies between two or more States, and between parties claiming lands under the grants of different States. In all cases affecting ambassadors, other foreign ministers and Consuls, and those in which a State shall be a party, the supreme court shall have original jurisdiction; in all other cases before mentioned the supreme Court shall have appellate jurisdiction as to matters of law only: except in cases of equity, and of admiralty and maritime jurisdiction, in which the Supreme Court shall have appellate jurisdiction both as to law and fact, with such exceptions and under such regulations as the Congress shall make. But the judicial power of the United States shall extend to no case where the cause of action shall have originated before the ratification of this Constitution; except in disputes between States about their Territory, disputes between persons claiming lands under the grants of different States, and suits for debts due to the United States.

[15] That in criminal prosecutions no man shall be restrained in the exercise of the usual and accustomed right of challenging or excepting to the Jury.

[16] That Congress shall not alter, modify or interfere in the times, places, or manner of holding elections for Senators and Representatives or either of them, except when the legislature of any State shall neglect, refuse or be disabled by invasion or rebellion to prescribe the same.

[17] That those clauses which declare that Congress shall not exercise certain powers be not interpreted in any manner whatsoever to extend the powers of Congress. But that they may be construed either as making exceptions to the specified powers where this shall be the case, or otherwise as inserted merely for greater caution.

[18] That the laws ascertaining the compensation of Senators and Representatives for their services be postponed in their operation, until after the election of Representatives immediately succeeding the passing thereof; that excepted, which shall first be passed on the Subject.

[19] That some Tribunal other than the Senate be provided for trying impeachments of Senators.

[20] That the Salary of a Judge shall not be encreased or diminished during his continuance in Office, otherwise than by general regulations of Salary which may take place on a revision of the subject at stated periods of not less than seven years to commence from the time such Salaries shall be first ascertained by Congress.

And the Convention [of the Delegates of the People of Virginia] do, in the name and behalf of the People of this Commonwealth enjoin it upon their Representatives in Congress to exert all their influence and use all reasonable and legal methods to obtain a Ratification of the foregoing alterations and provisions in the manner provided by the fifth article of the said Constitution; and in all Congressional laws to be passed in the mean time, to conform to the spirit of those Amendments as far as the said Constitution will admit. [The formal conclusion is omitted.]

I-2. NEW YORK RATIFICATION CONVENTION (JULY 26, 1788)

We the Delegates of the People of the State of New York, duly elected and Met in Convention, having maturely considered the Constitution for the United States of America, agreed to on the seventeenth day of September, in the year One thousand Seven hundred and Eighty seven, by the Convention then assembled at Philadelphia in the Commonwealth of Pennsylvania (a Copy whereof precedes these presents) and having also seriously and deliberately considered the present situation of the United States, Do declare and make known:

[Declaration or Bill of Rights]

[1] That all Power is originally vested in and consequently derived from the People, and that Government is instituted by them for their common Interest Protection and Security.

[2] That the enjoyment of Life, Liberty and the pursuit of Happiness are essential rights which every Government ought to respect and preserve.

[3] That the Powers of Government may be reassumed by the People, whensoever it shall become necessary to their Happiness; that every Power, Jurisdiction and right, which is not by the said

Constitution clearly delegated to the Congress of the United States, or the departments of the Government thereof, remains to the People of the several States, or to their respective State Governments to whom they may have granted the same; And that those Clauses in the said Constitution, which declare, that Congress shall not have or exercise certain Powers, do not imply that Congress is entitled to any Powers not given by the said Constitution; but such Clauses are to be construed either as exceptions to certain specified Powers, or as inserted merely for greater Caution.

[4] That the People have an equal, natural and unalienable right, freely and peaceably to Exercise their Religion according to the dictates of Conscience, and that no Religious Sect or Society ought to be favoured or established by Law in preference of others.

[5] That the People have a right to keep and bear Arms; that a well regulated Militia, including the body of the People *capable of bearing Arms,* is the proper, natural and safe defence of a free State;

[6] That the Militia should not be subject to Martial Law except in time of War, Rebellion or Insurrection.

[7] That standing Armies in time of Peace are dangerous to Liberty, and ought not to be kept up, except in Cases of necessity; and that at all times, the Military should be under strict Subordination to the civil Power.

[8] That in time of Peace no Soldier ought to be quartered in any House without the consent of the Owner, and in time of War only by the Civil Magistrate in such manner as the Laws may direct.

[9] That no Person ought to be taken imprisoned or disseised of his freehold, or be exiled or deprived of his Privileges, Franchises, Life, Liberty or Property but by due process of Law.

[10] That no Person ought to be put twice in Jeopardy of Life or Limb for one and the same Offence, nor, unless in case of impeachment, be punished more than once for the same Offence.

[11] That every Person restrained of his Liberty is entitled to an enquiry into the lawfulness of such restraint, and to a removal thereof if unlawful, and that such enquiry and removal ought not to be denied or delayed, except when on account of Public Danger the Congress shall suspend the privilege of the Writ of Habeas Corpus.

[12] That excessive Bail ought not to be required; nor excessive Fines imposed; nor Cruel or unusual Punishments inflicted.

[13] That (except in the Government of the Land and Naval

Forces, and of the Militia when in actual Service, and in cases of Impeachment) a Presentment or Indictment by a Grand Jury ought to be observed as a necessary preliminary to the trial of all Crimes cognizable by the Judiciary of the United States, and such Trial should be speedy, public, and by an impartial Jury of the County where the Crime was committed; and that no person can be found Guilty without the unanimous consent of such Jury. But in cases of Crimes not committed within any County of any of the United States, and in Cases of Crimes committed within any County in which a general Insurrection may prevail, or which may be in the possession of a foreign Enemy, the enquiry and trial may be in such County as the Congress shall by Law direct; which County in the two Cases last mentioned should be as near as conveniently may be to that County in which the Crime may have been committed. And that in all Criminal Prosecutions, the Accused ought to be informed of the cause and nature of his Accusation, to be confronted with his accusers and the Witnesses against him, to have the means of producing his Witnesses, and the assistance of Council for his defense, and should not be compelled to give Evidence against himself.

[14] That the trial by Jury in the extent that it obtains by the Common Law of England is one of the greatest securities to the rights of a free People, and ought to remain inviolate.

[15] That every Freeman has a right to be secure from all unreasonable searches and selzures of hls person his papers or hls property, and therefore, that all Warrants to search suspected places or seize any Freeman his papers or property, without information upon Oath or Affirmation of sufficient cause, are grievous and oppressive; and that all general Warrants (or such in which the place or person suspected are not particularly designated) are dangerous and ought not to be granted.

[16] That the People have a right peaceably to assemble together to consult for their common good, or to instruct their Representatives; and that every person has a right to Petition or apply to the Legislature for redress of Grievances.   That the Freedom of the Press ought not to be violated or restrained.

[17] That there should be once in four years an Election of the President and Vice President, so that no Officer who may be appointed by the Congress to act as President in case of the removal, death, resignation or inability of the President and Vice President

307

can in any case continue to act beyond the termination of the period for which the last President and Vice President were elected.

[18] That nothing contained in the said Constitution is to be construed to prevent the Legislature of any State from passing Laws at its discretion from time to time to divide such State into convenient Districts, and to apportion its Representatives to and amongst such Districts.

[19] That the Prohibition contained in the said Constitution against *ex post facto* Laws, extends only to Laws concerning Crimes.

[20] That all Appeals in Causes determinable according to the course of the common Law, ought to be by Writ of Error and not otherwise.

[21] That the Judicial Power of the United States in cases in which a State may be a party, does not extend to criminal Prosecutions, or to authorize any Suit by any Person against a State.

[22] That the Judicial Power of the United States as to Controversies between Citizens of the same State claiming Lands under Grants [by] different States is not to be construed to extend to any other Controversies between them except those which relate to such Lands, so claimed under Grants [by] different States.

[23] That the Jurisdiction of the Supreme Court of the United States, or of any other Court to be instituted by the Congress, is not in any case to be encreased enlarged or extended by any Fiction Collusion or mere suggestion;—And That no Treaty is to be construed so to operate as to alter the Constitution of any State.

Under these impressions and declaring that the rights aforesaid cannot be abridged or violated, and that the Explanations aforesaid are consistent with the said Constitution, And in confidence that the Amendments which shall have been proposed to the said Constitution will receive an early and mature Consideration: We the said Delegates, in the Name and in the behalf of the People of the State of New York Do, by these presents Assent to and Ratify the said Constitution. In full Confidence nevertheless that until a Convention shall be called and convened for proposing Amendments to the said Constitution, the Militia of this State will not be continued in Service out of this State for a longer term than six weeks without the Consent of the Legislature thereof;—that the Congress will not make or alter any Regulation in this State respecting the times places and manner of holding Elections for Senators or Representatives unless the Legislature of this State shall neglect or refuse to make Laws or regulations for the purpose, or from any circumstance be incapable of making the same, and that in those cases such power will only be exercised until the Legislature of this State shall make provision in the Premises;—that no Excise will be imposed on any Article of the Growth production or Manufacture of the United States, or any of them within this State, Ardent Spirits excepted; And that the Congress will not lay direct Taxes within this State, but when the Monies arising from the Impost and Excise shall be insufficient for the public Exigencies, nor then, until Congress shall first have made a Requisition upon this State to assess levy and pay the Amount of such Requisition made agreably to the Census fixed in the said Constitution in such way and manner as the Legislature of this State shall judge best, but that in such case, if the State shall neglect or refuse to pay its proportion pursuant to such Requisition, then the Congress may assess and levy this States proportion together with Interest at the Rate of six per Centum per Annum from the time at which the same was required to be paid. . . .

And the Convention do in the Name and Behalf of the People of the State of New York enjoin it upon their Representatives in the Congress, to Exert all their Influence and use all reasonable means to Obtain a Ratification of the following Amendments to the said Constitution in the manner prescribed therein; and in all Laws to be passed by the Congress in the meantime to conform to the spirit of the said Amendments as far as the Constitution will admit.

[*Proposed Amendments to the Constitution*]

[1] That there shall be one Representative for every thirty thousand Inhabitants, according to the enumeration or Census mentioned in the Constitution, until the whole number of Representatives amounts to two hundred; after which that number shall be continued or encreased but not diminished, as Congress shall direct, and according to such ratio as the Congress shall fix, in conformity to the rule prescribed for the Apportionment of Representatives and direct Taxes.

[2] That the Congress do not impose any Excise on any Article (except Ardent Spirits) of the Growth Production or Manufacture of the United States, or any of them.

[3] That Congress do not lay direct Taxes but when the Monies arising from the Impost and Excise shall be insufficient for the Public Exigencies, nor then until Congress shall first have made a Requisition upon the States to assess levy and pay their respective proportions of such Requisition, agreably to the Census fixed in the said Constitution, in such way and manner as the Legislatures of the respective States shall judge best; and in such Case, if any State shall neglect or refuse to pay its proportion pursuant to such Requisition, then Congress may assess and levy such States proportion, together with Interest at the rate of six per Centum per Annum, from the time of Payment prescribed in such Requisition.

[4] That the Congress shall not make or alter any Regulation in any State respecting the times places and manner of holding Elections for Senators or Representatives, unless the Legislature of such State shall neglect or refuse to make Laws or Regulations for the purpose, or from any circumstance be incapable of making the same; and then only until the Legislature of such State shall make provision in the premises; provided that Congress may prescribe the time for the Election of Representatives.

[5] That no Persons except natural born Citizens, or such as were Citizens on or before the fourth day of July one thousand seven hundred and seventy six, or such as held Commissions under the United States during the War, and have at any time since the fourth day of July one thousand seven hundred and seventy six become Citizens of one or other of the United States, and who shall be Freeholders, shall be eligible to the places of President, Vice President, or Members of either House of the Congress of the United States.

[6] That the Congress do not grant Monopolies or erect any Company with exclusive Advantages of Commerce.

[7] That no standing Army or regular Troops shall be raised or kept up in time of peace, without the consent of two-thirds of the Senators and Representatives present, in each House.

[8] That no Money be borrowed on the Credit of the United States without the Assent of two-thirds of the Senators and Representatives present in each House.

[9] That the Congress shall not declare War without the concurrence of two-thirds of the Senators and Representatives present in each House.

[10] That the Privilege of the *Habeas Corpus* shall not by any Law be suspended for a longer term than six Months, or until twenty days after the Meeting of the Congress next following the passing the Act for such suspension.

[11] That the Right of the Congress to exercise exclusive Legislation over such District, not exceeding ten Miles square, as may by cession of a particular State, and the acceptance of Congress, become the Seat of the Government of the United States, shall not be so exercised, as to exempt the Inhabitants of such District from paying the like Taxes Imposts Duties and Excises, as shall be imposed on the other Inhabitants of the State in which such District may be; and that no person shall be privileged within the said District from Arrest for Crimes committed, or Debts contracted out of the said District.

[12] That the Right of exclusive Legislation with respect to such places as may be purchased for Forts, Magazines, Arsenals, Dockyards and other needful Buildings, shall not authorize the Congress to make any Law to prevent the Laws of the States respectively in which they may be, from extending to such places in all civil and Criminal Matters except as to such Persons as shall be in the Service of the United States; nor to them with respect to Crimes committed without such Places.

[13] That the Compensation for the Senators and Representatives be ascertained by standing Laws; and that no alteration of the existing rate of Compensation shall operate for the Benefit of the Representatives, until after a subsequent Election shall have been had.

[14] That the Journals of the Congress shall be published at least once a year, with the exception of such parts relating to Treaties or Military operations, as in the Judgement of either House shall require Secrecy; and that both Houses of Congress shall always keep their Doors open during their Sessions, unless the Business may in their Opinion require Secrecy. That the yeas & nays shall be entered on the Journals whenever two Members in either House may require it.

[15] That no Capitation Tax shall ever be laid by Congress.

[16] That no Person be eligible as a Senator for more than six years in any term of twelve years; and that the Legislatures of the respective States may recal their Senators or either of them, and elect others in their stead, to serve the remainder of the time for which the Senators so recalled were appointed.

[17] That no Senator or Representative shall during the time for which he was elected be appointed to any Office under the Authority of the United States.

[18] That the Authority given to the Executives of the States to fill the vacancies of Senators be abolished, and that such vacancies be filled by the respective Legislatures.

[19] That the Power of Congress to pass uniform Laws concerning Bankruptcy shall only extend to Merchants and other Traders; and that the States respectively may pass Laws for the relief of other Insolvent Debtors.

[20] That no Person shall be eligible to the Office of President of the United States a third time.

[21] That the Executive shall not grant Pardons for Treason, unless with the Consent of the Congress; but may at his discretion grant Reprieves to persons convicted of Treason, until their Cases, can be laid before the Congress.

[22] That the President or person exercising his Powers for the time being, shall not command an Army in the Field in person, without the previous desire of the Congress.

[23] That all Letters Patent, Commissions, Pardons, Writs and Process of the United States, shall run in the Name of *the People of the United States*, and be tested in the name of the President of the United State, or the person exercising his powers for the time being, or the first Judge of the Court out of which the same shall issue, as the case may be.

[24] That the Congress shall not constitute ordain or establish any Tribunals of Inferior Courts, with any other than Appellate Jurisdiction, except such as may be necessary for the Tryal of caues of Admiralty and Maritime Jurisdiction, and for the Trial of Piracies and Felonies committed on the High Seas; and in all other Cases to which the Judicial Power of the United States extends, and in which the Supreme Court of the United States has not original Jurisdiction, the Causes shall be heard tried, and determined in some one of the State Courts, with the right of Appeal to the Supreme Court of the United States, or other proper Tribunal to be established for that purpose by the Congress, with such exceptions, and under such regulations as the Congress shall make.

[25] That the Court for the Trial of Impeachments shall consist of the Senate, the Judges of the Supreme Court of the United States,

and the first or Senior Judge for the time being, of the highest Court of general and ordinary common Law Jurisdiction in each State;— that the Congress shall by standing Laws designate the Courts in the respective States answering this Description, and in States having no Courts exactly answering this Description, shall designate some other Court, preferring such if any there be, whose Judge or Judges may hold their places during good Behavior—Provided that no more than one Judge, other than Judges of the Supreme Court of the United States, shall come from one State—That the Congress be authorized to pass Laws for compensating the said Judges for such Services and for compelling their Attendance—and that a Majority at least of the said Judges shall be requisite to constitute the said Court—that no person impeached shall sit as a Member thereof. That each Member shall previous to the entering upon any Trial take an Oath or Affirmation, honestly and impartially to hear and determine the Cause—and that a Majority of the Members present shall be necessary to a Conviction.

[26] That persons aggrieved by any Judgment, Sentence or Decree of the Supreme Court of the United States, in any Cause in which that Court has original Jurisdiction, with such exceptions and under such Regulations as the Congress shall make concerning the same, shall upon application, have a Commission to be issued by the President of the United States, to such Men learned in the Law as he shall nominate, and by and with the Advice and consent of the Senate appoint, not less than seven, authorizing such Commissioners, or any seven or more of them, to correct the Errors in such Judgment or to review such Sentence and Decree, as the case may be, and to do Justice to the parties in the Premises.

[27] That no Judge of the Supreme Court of the United States shall hold any other Office under the United States, or any of them.

[28] That the Judicial Power of the United States shall extend to no Controversies respecting Land, unless it relate to Claims of Territory or Jurisdiction between States, or to Claims of Land between Individuals, or betweem States and Individuals under the Grants of different States.

[29] That the Militia of any State shall not be compelled to serve without the limits of the State for a longer term than six weeks, without the Consent of the Legislature thereof.

[30] That the words *without the Consent of the Congress* in the

seventh Clause of the ninth Section of the first Article of the Constitution, be expunged.

[31] That the Senators and Representatives and all Executive and Judicial Officers of the United States shall be bound by Oath or Affirmation not to infringe or violate the Constitutions or rights of the respective States.

[32] That the Legislatures of the respective States may make provision by Law, that the Electors of the Election Districts to be by them appointed shall chuse a Citizen of the United States who shall have been an Inhabitant of such District for the Term of one year immediately preceding the time of his Election, for one of the Representatives of such State. [The formal conclusion is omitted.]

J. Stages of the Bill of Rights in the First Congress and in the State Legislatures (1789–1791)

J-1. JAMES MADISON'S PROPOSALS IN THE HOUSE OF REPRESENTATIVES (JUNE 8, 1789)

... I believe that the great mass of the people who opposed it [the Constitution in 1787–1788], disliked it because it did not contain effectual provisions against the encroachments on particular rights, and those safeguards which they have been long accustomed to have interposed between them and the magistrate who exercises the sovereign power; nor ought we to consider them safe, while a great number of our fellow-citizens think these securities necessary.

It is a fortunate thing that the objection to the Government has been made on the ground I stated; because it will be practicable, on that ground, to obviate the objection, so far as to satisfy the pub-mind that their liberties will be perpetual, and this without endangering any part of the Constitution, which is considered as essential to the existence of the Government by those who promoted its adoption.

The amendments which have occurred to me, proper to be recommended by Congress to the State Legislatures, are these:

First. That there be prefixed to the Constitution a declaration, that all power is originally vested in, and consequently derived from, the people.

That Government is instituted and ought to be exercised for the benefit of the people; which consists in the enjoyment of life and libery, with the right of acquiring and using property, and generally of pursuing and obtaining happiness and safety.

That the people have an indubitable, unalienable, and indefeasible right to reform or change their Government, whenever it be found adverse or inadequate to the purposes of its institution.

Secondly. That in article 1st, section 2, clause 3, these words be struck out, to wit: "The number of Representatives shall not exceed one for every thirty thousand, but each State shall have at least one Representative, and until such enumeration shall be made;" and that in place thereof be inserted these words, to wit: "After the first actual enumeration, there shall be one Representative for every thirty thousand, until the number amounts to   , after which the proportion shall be so regulated by Congress, that the number shall never be less than   , nor more than   , but each State shall, after the first enumeration, have at least two Representatives; and prior thereto."

Thirdly. That in article 1st, section 6, clause 1, there be added to the end of the first sentence, these words, to wit: "But no law varying the compensation last ascertained shall operate before the next ensuing election of Representatives."

Fourthly. That in article 1st, section 9, between clauses 3 and 4, be inserted these clauses, to wit: The civil rights of none shall be abridged on account of religious belief or worship, nor shall any national religion be established, nor shall the full and equal rights of conscience be in any manner, or on any pretext, infringed.

The people shall not be deprived or abridged of their right to speak, to write, or to publish their sentiments; and the freedom of the press, as one of the great bulwarks of liberty, shall be inviolable.

The people shall not be restrained from peaceably assembling and consulting for their common good; nor from applying to the Legislature by petitions, or remonstrances, for redress of their grievances.

The right of the people to keep and bear arms shall not be infringed; a well armed and well regulated militia being the best security of a free country: but no person religiously scrupulous of bearing arms shall be compelled to render military service in person.

No soldier shall in time of peace be quartered in any house without the consent of the owner; nor at any time, but in a manner warranted by law.

No person shall be subject, except in cases of impeachment, to more than one punishment or one trial for the same offence; nor shall be compelled to be a witness against himself; nor be deprived of life, liberty, or property, without due process of law; nor be obliged to relinquish his property, where it may be necessary for public use, without a just compensation.

Excessive bail shall not be required, nor excessive fines imposed, nor cruel and unusual punishments inflicted.

The rights of the people to be secured in their persons; their houses, their papers, and their other property, from all unreasonable searches and seizures, shall not be violated by warrants issued without probable cause, supported by oath or affirmation, or not particularly describing the places to be searched, or the persons or things to be seized.

In all criminal prosecutions, the accused shall enjoy the right to a speedy and public trial, to be informed of the cause and nature of the accusation, to be confronted with his accusers, and the witnesses against him; to have a compulsory process for obtaining witnesses in his favor; and to have the assistance of counsel for his defence.

The exceptions here or elsewhere in the Constitution, made in favor of particular rights, shall not be so construed as to diminish the just importance of other rights retained by the people, or as to enlarge the powers delegated by the Constitution; but either as actual limitations of such powers, or as inserted merely for greater caution.

Fifthly. That in article 1st, section 10, between clauses 1 and 2, be inserted this clause, to wit:

No State shall violate the equal rights of conscience, or the freedom of the press, or the trial by jury in criminal cases.

Sixthly. That, in article 3d, section 2, be annexed to the end of clause 2d, these words, to wit:

But no appeal to such court shall be allowed where the value in controversy shall not amount to   dollars: nor shall any fact triable by jury, according to the course of common law, be otherwise re-examinable than may consist with the principles of common law.

Seventhly. That in article 3d, section 2, the third clause be struck out, and in its place be inserted the clauses following, to wit:

The trial of all crimes (except in cases of impeachments, and cases arising in the land or naval forces, or the militia when on actual service, in time of war or public danger) shall be by an impartial jury of freeholders of the vicinage, with the requisite of unanimity for conviction, of the right of challenge, and other accustomed requisites; and in all crimes punishable with loss of life or member, presentment or indictment by a grand jury shall be an essential preliminary, provided that in cases of crimes committed within any county which may be in possession of an enemy, or in which a general insurrection may prevail, the trial may by law be authorized in some other county of the same State, as near as may be to the seat of the offence.

In cases of crimes committed not within any county, the trial may by law be in such county as the laws shall have prescribed. In suits at common law, between man and man, the trial by jury, as one of the best securities to the rights of the people, ought to remain inviolate.

Eighthly. That immediately after article 6th, be inserted, as article 7th, the clauses following, to wit:

The powers delegated by this Constitution are appropriated to the departments to which they are respectively distributed: so that the Legislative Department shall never exercise the powers vested in the Executive or Judicial, nor the Executive exercise the powers vested in the Legislative or Judicial, nor the Judicial exercise the powers vested in the Legislative or Executive Departments.

The powers not delegated by this Constitution, nor prohibited by it to the States, are reserved to the States respectively.

Ninthly. That article 7th be numbered as article 8th.

The first of these amendments relates to what may be called a bill of rights. I will own that I never considered this provision so essential to the Federal Constitution as to make it improper to ratify it, until such an amendment was added; at the same time, I always conceived, that in a certain form, and to a certain extent, such a provision was neither improper nor altogether useless. I am aware that a great number of the most respectable friends to the Government, and champions for republican liberty, have thought such a provision not only unnecessary, but even improper; nay, I believe some have gone so far as to think it even dangerous. Some policy has been made use of, perhaps, by gentlemen on both sides of the question: I acknowledge the ingenuity of those arguments which were drawn against the Constitution, by a comparison with the policy of Great Britain, in establishing a declaration of rights; but there is too great a difference in the case to warrant the comparison: therefore, the arguments drawn from that source were in a great measure inapplicable. In the declaration of rights which that country has established, the truth is, they have gone no farther than to raise a barrier against the power of the Crown; the power of the Legislature is left altogether indefinite. Although I know whenever the great rights, the trial by jury, freedom of the press, or liberty of conscience, come in question in that body, the invasion of them is resisted by able advocates, yet their Magna Charta does not contain any one provision for the security of those rights, respecting which the people of America are most alarmed. The freedom of the press and rights of conscience, those choicest privileges of the people, are unguarded in the British Constitution.

But although the case may be widely different, and it may not be thought necessary to provide limits for the legislative power in that country, yet a different opinion prevails in the United States. The people of many States have thought it necessary to raise barriers against power in all forms and departments of Government, and I am inclined to believe, if once bill of rights are established in all the States as well as the Federal Constitution, we shall find that although some of them are rather unimportant, yet, upon the whole, they will have a salutary tendency. It may be said, in some instances, they do no more than state the perfect equality of mankind. This, to be sure, is an absolute truth, yet it is not absolutely necessary to be inserted at the head of a Constitution.

In some instances they assert those rights which are exercised by the people in forming and establishing a plan of Government. In other instances, they specify those rights which are retained when particular powers are given up to be exercised by the Legislature. In other instances, they specify positive rights, which may seem to result from the nature of the compact. Trial by jury cannot be considered as a natural right, but a right resulting from a social compact, which regulates the action of the community, but is as essential to secure the liberty of the people as any one of the pre-existent rights of nature. In other instances, they lay down dogmatic maxims with respect to the construction of the Government; declaring that the Legislative, Executive, and Judicial branches shall be kept separate and distinct. Perhaps the best way of securing this in practice is, to provide such checks as will prevent the encroachment of the one upon the other.

But whatever may be the form which the several States have adopted in making declarations in favor of particular rights, the great object in view is to limit and qualify the powers of Government, by excepting out of the grant of power those cases in which the Government ought not to act, or to act only in a particular mode. They point these exceptions sometimes against the abuse of the Executive power, sometimes against the Legislative, and, in some cases, against the community itself; or, in other words, against the majority in favor of the minority.

In our Government it is, perhaps, less necessary to guard against the abuse in the Executive Department than any other; because it is not the stronger branch of the system, but the weaker. It therefore must be levelled against the Legislative, for it is the most powerful, and most likely to be abused, because it is under the least control. Hence, so far as a declaration of rights can tend to prevent the exercise of undue power, it cannot be doubted but such declaration is proper. But I confess that I do conceive, that in a Government modified like this of the United States, the great danger lies rather in the abuse of the community than in the Legislative body. The prescription in favor of liberty ought to be levelled against that quarter where the greatest danger lies, namely, that which possesses the highest prerogative of power. But this is not found in either the Executive or Legislative Departments of Government, but in the body of the people, operating by the majority against the minority.

It may be thought that all paper barriers against the power of the community are too weak to be worthy of attention. I am sensible they are not so strong as to satisfy gentlemen of every description who have seen and examined thoroughly the texture of such a defence; yet, as they have a tendency to impress some degree of respect for them, to establish the public opinion in their favor, and rouse the attention of the whole community, it may be one means to control the majority from those acts to which they might be otherwise inclined. . . .

J-2. AMENDMENTS REPORTED BY A HOUSE OF REPRESENTATIVES COMMITTEE (JULY 28, 1789)

[1] In the introductory paragraph before the words, "*We the people*," add, "Government being intended for the benefit of the peo-

ple, and the rightful establishment thereof being derived from their authority alone."

[2] ART. 1, SEC. 2, PAR. 3—Strike out all between the words, *"direct"* and *"and until such,"* and instead thereof insert, "After the first enumeration there shall be one representative for every thirty thousand until the number shall amount to one hundred; after which the proportion shall be so regulated by Congress that the number of Representatives shall never be less than one hundred, nor more than one hundred and seventy-five, but each State shall always have at least one Representative."

[3] ART. 1, SEC. 6—Between the words *"United States,"* and *"shall in all cases,"* strike out *"they,"* and insert, "But no law varying the compensation shall take effect until an election of Representatives shall have intervened. The members."

[4] ART. 1, SEC. 9—Between PAR. 2 and 3 insert, "No religion shall be established by law, nor shall the equal rights of conscience be infringed."

[5] "The freedom of speech, and of the press, and the right of the people peaceably to assemble and consult for their common good, and to apply to the government for redress of grievances, shall not be infringed."

[6] "A well regulated militia, composed of the body of the people, being the best security of a free State, the right of the people to keep and bear arms shall not be infringed, but no person religiously scrupulous shall be compelled to bear arms."

[7] "No soldier shall in time of peace be quartered in any house without the consent of the owner, nor in time of war but in a manner to be prescribed by law."

[8] "No person shall be subject, except in case of impeachment, to more than one trial or one punishment for the same offence, nor shall be compelled to be a witness against himself, nor be deprived of life, liberty, or property without due process of law; nor shall private property be taken for public use without just compensation."

[9] "Excessive bail shall not be required, nor excessive fines imposed, nor cruel and unusual punishments inflicted."

[10] "The right of the people to be secure in their person, houses, papers and effects, shall not be violated by warrants issuing, without probable cause supported by oath or affirmation, and not par-

ticularly describing the places to be searched, and the persons or things to be seized."

[11] "The enumeration in this Constitution of certain rights shall not be construed to deny or disparage others retained by the people."

[12] ART. 1, SEC. 10, between the 1st and 2d PAR. insert, "No State shall infringe the equal rights of conscience, nor the freedom of speech, or of the press, nor of the right of trial by jury in criminal cases."

[13] ART. 3, SEC. 2, add to the 2d PAR. "But no appeal to such court shall be allowed, where the value in controversy shall not amount to one thousand dollars; nor shall any fact, triable by a Jury according to the course of the common law, be otherwise re-examinable than according to the rules of common law."

[14] ART. 3, SEC. 2—Strike out the whole of the 3d paragraph, and insert—"In all criminal prosecutions the accused shall enjoy the right to a speedy and public trial, to be informed of the nature and cause of the accusation, to be confronted with the witnesses against him, to have compulsory process for obtaining witnesses in his favor, and to have the assistance of counsel for his defence."

[15] "The trial of all crimes (except in cases of impeachment, and in cases arising in the land or naval forces, or in the militia, when in actual service in time of war or public danger) shall be by an impartial jury of freeholders of the vicinage, with the requisite of unanimity for conviction, the right of challenge and other accustomed requisites; and no person shall be held to answer for a capital, or otherwise infamous crime, unless on a presentment or indictment by a Grand Jury; but if a crime be committed in a place in the possession of an enemy, or in which an insurrection may prevail, the indictment and trial may by law be authorized in some other place within the same State; and if it be committed in a place not within a State, the indictment and trial may be at such place or places as the law may have directed."

[16] "In suits at common law the right of trial by jury shall be preserved."

[17] Immediately after ART. 6, the following to be inserted as ART. 7.

"The powers delegated by this Constitution to the government of the United States, shall be exercised as therein appropriated, so that the Legislative shall never exercise the powers vested in the

322

Executive or the Judicial; nor the Executive the powers vested in the Legislative or Judicial; nor the Judicial the powers vested in the Legislative or Executive."

[18] "The powers not delegated by this Constitution, nor prohibited by it to the States, are reserved to the States respectively."

[19] ART. 7 to be made ART 8.

J-3. AMENDMENTS PASSED BY THE HOUSE OF REPRESENTATIVES (AUGUST 24, 1789)

... [1] After the first enumeration, required by the first Article of the Constitution, there shall be one Representative for every thirty thousand, until the number shall amount to one hundred, after which the proportion shall be so regulated by Congress, that there shall be not less than one hundred Representatives, nor less than one Representative for every forty thousand persons, until the number of Representatives shall amount to two hundred, after which the proportion shall be so regulated by Congress, that there shall not be less than two hundred Representatives, nor less than one Representative for every fifty thousand persons.

[2] No law varying the compensation to the members of Congress, shall take effect, until an election of Representatives shall have intervened.

[3] Congress shall make no law establishing religion or prohibiting the free exercise thereof, nor shall the rights of Conscience be infringed.

[4] The Freedom of Speech, and of the Press, and the right of the People peaceably to assemble, and consult for their common good, and to apply to the Government for a redress of grievances, shall not be infringed.

[5] A well regulated militia, composed of the body of the People, being the best security of a free State, the right of the People to keep and bear arms, shall not be infringed, but no one religiously scrupulous of bearing arms, shall be compelled to render military service in person.

[6] No soldier shall, in time of peace, be quartered in any house without the consent of the owner, nor in time of war, but in a manner to be prescribed by law.

[7] The right of the People to be secure in their persons, houses,

papers and effects, against unreasonable searches and seizures, shall not be violated, and no warrants shall issue, but upon probable cause supported by oath or affirmation, and particularly describing the place to be searched, and the persons or things to be seized.

[8] No person shall be subject, except in case of impeachment, to more than one trial, or one punishment for the same offense, nor shall be compelled in any criminal case, to be a witness against himself, nor be deprived of life, liberty or property, without due process of law; nor shall private property be taken for public use without just compensation.

[9] In all criminal prosecutions, the accused shall enjoy the right to a speedy and public trial, to be informed of the nature and cause of the accusation, to be confronted with the witnesses against him, to have compulsory process for obtaining witnesses in his favor, and to have the assistance of counsel for his defence.

[10] The trial of all crimes (except in cases of impeachment, and in cases arising in the land or naval forces, or in the militia when in actual service in time of War or public danger) shall be by an impartial Jury of the Vicinage, with the requisite of unanimity for conviction, the right of challenge, and other accostomed requisites; and no person shall be held to answer for a capital, or otherways infamous crime, unless on a presentment or indictment by a Grand Jury; but if a crime be committed in a place in the possession of an enemy, or in which an insurrection may prevail, the indictment and trial may by law be authorized in some other place within the same State.

[11] No appeal to the Supreme Court of the United States, shall be allowed, where the value in controversy shall not amount to one thousand dollars, nor shall any fact, triable by a Jury according to the course of the common law, be otherwise re-examinable, than according to the rules of common law.

[12] In suits at common law, the right of trial by Jury shall be preserved.

[13] Excessive bail shall not be required, nor excessive fines imposed, nor cruel and unusual punishments inflicted.

[14] No State shall infringe the right of trial by Jury in criminal cases, nor the rights of conscience, nor the freedom of speech, or of the press.

[15] The enumeration in the Constitution of certain rights, shall not be construed to deny or disparage others retained by the people.

[16] The powers delegated by the Constitution to the government of the United States, shall be exercised as therein appropriated, so that the Legislative shall never exercise the powers vested in the Executive or Judicial; nor the Executive the powers vested in the Legislative or Judicial; nor the Judicial the powers vested in the Legislative or Executive.

[17] The powers not delegated by the Constitution, nor prohibited by it, to the States, are reserved to the States respectively.

J-4. AMENDMENTS PASSED BY THE SENATE (SEPTEMBER 9, 1789)

... [1] After the first enumeration, required by the first article of the Constitution, there shall be one Representative for every thirty thousand, until the number shall amount to one hundred; to which number one Representative shall be added for every subsequent increase of forty thousand, until the Representatives shall amount to two hundred, to which number one Representative shall be added for every subsequent increase of sixty thousand persons.

[2] No law, varying the compensation for the services of the Senators and Representatives, shall take effect, until an election of Representatives shall have intervened.

[3] Congress shall make no law establishing articles of faith, or a mode of worship, or prohibiting the free exercise of religion, or abridging the freedom of speech, or of the press, or the right of the people peaceably to assemble, and to petition to the government for a redress of grievances.

[4] A well regulated militia, being necessary to the security of a free State, the right of the people to keep and bear arms, shall not be infringed.

[5] No soldier shall, in time of peace, be quartered in any house, without the consent of the owner, nor in time of war, but in a manner to be prescribed by law.

[6] The right of the people to be secure in their persons, houses, papers, and effects, against unreasonable searches and seizures, shall not be violated, and no warrants shall issue, but upon probable cause, supported by oath or affirmation, and particularly describing the place to be searched, and the persons or things to be seized.

[7] No person shall be held to answer for a capital, or otherwise

infamous crime, unless on a presentment or indictment of a Grand Jury, except in cases arising in the land or naval forces, or in the militia, when in actual service in time of war or public danger; nor shall any person be subject for the same offence to be twice put in jeopardy of life or limb; nor shall be compelled in any criminal case, to be a witness against himself, nor be deprived of life, liberty or property, without due process of law; nor shall private property be taken for public use without just compensation.

[8] In all criminal prosecutions, the accused shall enjoy the right to a speedy and public trial, to be informed of the nature and cause of the accusation, to be confronted with the witnesses against him, to have compulsory process for obtaining witnesses in his favour, and to have the assistance of counsel for his defence.

[9] In suits at common law, where the value in controversy shall exceed twenty dollars, the right of trial by Jury shall be preserved, and no fact, tried by a Jury, shall be otherwise re-examined in any court of the United States, than according to the rules of the common law.

[10] Excessive bail shall not be required, nor excessive fines imposed, nor cruel and unusual punishments inflicted.

[11] The enumeration in the Constitution of certain rights, shall not be construed to deny or disparage others retained by the people.

[12] The powers not delegated to the United States by the Constitution, nor prohibited by it to the States, are reserved to the States respectively, or to the people.

J-5. AMENDMENTS PROPOSED BY CONGRESS FOR RATIFICATION BY THE STATES (SEPTEMBER 25, 1789)

*Congress of the United States
Begun and held at the City of New York, on
Wednesday, the 4th of March, 1789.*

The Conventions of a number of the States, having at the time of their adopting the Constitution, expressed a desire, in order to prevent misconstruction or abuse of its powers, that further declaratory and restrictive clauses should be added: And as extending the ground of public confidence in the Government, will best ensure the beneficent ends of its institution

RESOLVED by the Senate and House of Representatives of the United States of America, in Congress assembled, two thirds of both Houses concurring, that the following Articles be proposed to the Legislatures of the several States, as amendments to the Constitution of the United States, all or any of which Articles, when ratified by three fourths of the said Legislatures, to be valid to all intents and purposes, as part of the said Constitution; vizt.

ARTICLES in addition to, and amendment of the Constitution of the United States of America, proposed by Congress, and ratified by the Legislatures of the several States, pursuant to the fifth Article of the original Constitution.

ARTICLE THE FIRST. After the first enumeration required by the first Article of the Constitution, there shall be one Representative for every thirty thousand, until the number shall amount to one hundred, after which, the proportion shall be so regulated by Congress, that there shall not be less than one hundred Representatives, nor less than one Representative for every forty thousand persons, until the number of Representatives shall amount to two hundred, after which the proportion shall be so regulated by Congress, that there shall not be less than two hundred Representatives, nor more than one Representative for every fifty thousand persons.

ARTICLE THE SECOND. No law varying the compensation for the services of the Senators and Representatives shall take effect until an election of Representatives shall have intervened.

ARTICLE THE THIRD. Congress shall make no law respecting an establishment of religion, or prohibiting the free exercise thereof; or abridging the freedom of speech, or of the press, or the right of the people peaceably to assemble, and to petition the Government for a redress of grievances.

ARTICLE THE FOURTH. A well regulated Militia, being necessary to the security of a free State, the right of the people to keep and bear Arms, shall not be infringed.

ARTICLE THE FIFTH. No Soldier shall, in time of peace be quartered in any house, without the consent of the Owner, nor in time of war, but in a manner to be prescribed by law.

ARTICLE THE SIXTH. The right of the people to be secure in their persons, houses, papers, and effects, against unreasonable searches and seizures, shall not be violated, and no Warrants shall issue, but upon probable cause, supported by Oath or affirmation, and particularly describing the place to be searched, and the persons or things to be seized.

ARTICLE THE SEVENTH. No person shall be held to answer for a capital, or otherwise infamous crime, unless on a presentment or indictment of a Grand Jury, except in cases arising in the land or naval forces, or in the Militia, when in actual service in time of War or public danger; nor shall any person be subject for the same offence to be twice put in jeopardy of life or limb, nor shall be compelled in any criminal case to be a witness against himself, nor be deprived of life, liberty, or property, without due process of law; nor shall private property be taken for public use without just compensation.

ARTICLE THE EIGHTH. In all criminal prosecutions, the accused shall enjoy the right to a speedy and public trial, by an impartial jury of the State and district wherein the crime shall have been committed, which district shall have been previously ascertained by law, and to be informed of the nature and cause of the accusation; to be confronted with the witnesses against him; to have compulsory process for obtaining witnesses in his favor, and to have the Assistance of Counsel for his defence.

ARTICLE THE NINTH. In Suits at common law, where the value in controversy shall exceed twenty dollars, the right of trial by jury shall be preserved, and no fact tried by a jury shall be otherwise re-examined in any Court of the United States, than according to the rules of the common law.

ARTICLE THE TENTH. Excessive bail shall not be required, nor excessive fines imposed, nor cruel and unusual punishments inflicted.

ARTICLE THE ELEVENTH. The enumeration in the Constitution, of certain rights, shall not be construed to deny or disparage others retained by the people.

ARTICLE THE TWELFTH. The powers not delegated to the United States by the Constitution, nor prohibited by it to the States, are reserved to the States respectively, or to the people.

> Frederick Augustus Muhlenberg
> Speaker of the House of Representative
> John Adams
> Vice-President of the United States,
> and President of the Senate

Attest,
John Beckley, Clerk of the House of Representative.
Samuel A. Otis, *Secretary of the Senate* [September 25, 1789].

J-6. RATIFICATION RETURNS FROM THE STATES (NOVEMBER 20, 1789–DECEMBER 15, 1791)

[The twelve aproposed articles of amendment,] being transmitted to the several state legislatures, were decided upon by them, according to the following returns:—

By the State of New Hampshire. [November 20, 1787].—Agreed to the whole of the said amendments, except the 2d article.

By the State of New York.—Agreed to the whole of the said amendments, except the 2d article.

By the State of Pennsylvania.—Agreed to the 3d, 4th, 5th, 6th, 7th, 8th, 9th, 10th, 11th, and 12th articles of the said amendments.

By the State of Delaware.—Agreed to the whole of the said amendments, except the 1st article.

By the State of Maryland.—Agreed to the whole of the said twelve amendments.

By the State of South Carolina.—Agreed to the whole [of the] said twelve amendments.

By the State of North Carolina.—Agreed to the whole of the said twelve amendments.

By the State of Rhode Island and Providence Plantations.—Agreed to the whole of the said twelve articles.

By the State of New Jersey.—Agreed to the whole of the said amendments, except the second article.

By the State of Virginia [December 15, 1791].—Agreed to the whole of the said twelve articles.

No returns were made by the states of Massachusetts, Connecticut, Georgia, and Kentucky.

The amendments thus proposed became a part of the Constitution, the first and second of them excepted, which were not ratified by a sufficient number of the state legislatures. [Thus, of the ten State ratifications required, the first proposal received eight; the second (now the Twenty-seventh Amendment), six.]

K. Letters Exchanged by Thomas Jefferson and John Adams (1814)

─────────────

K-1. LETTER FROM THOMAS JEFFERSON TO JOHN ADAMS

Monticello July 5. [18]14.

DEAR SIR

Since mine of Jan. 24. yours of Mar. 14. was recieved. It was not acknoleged in the short one [from Jefferson] of May 18. [delivered] by Mr. Rives, the only object of that having been to enable one of our most promising young men to have the advantage of making his bow to you. I learned with great regret the serious illness mentioned in your letter: and I hope Mr. Rives will be able to tell me you are entirely restored. But our machines have now been running for 70. or 80. years, and we must expect that, worn as they are, here a pivot, there a wheel, now a pinion, next a spring, will be giving way: and however we may tinker them up for awhile, all will at length surcease motion. Our watches, with works of brass and steel, wear out within that period. Shall you and I last to see the course the seven-fold wonders of the times will take? The Attila of the age [Napoleon Bonaparte] dethroned, the ruthless destroyer of 10. millions of the human race, whose thirst for blood appeared unquenchable, the great oppressor of the rights and liberties of the world, shut up within the circuit of a little island of the Mediterranean [Elba], and dwindled to the condition of an humble and degraded pensioner on the bounty of those he had most injured. How miserably, how meanly, has he closed his inflated career! What a sample of the Bathos will his history present! [He was, after his defeat at Waterloo on June 18, 1815, banished for the rest of his life to the island of St. Helena, in the South Atlantic.] He should have perished on the swords of his enemies, under the walls of Paris.

'Leon piagato a morte	['The lion stricken to death
Sente mancar la vita,	realizes that he is dying,
Guarda la sua ferita,	and looks at his wounds from which
Ne s'avilisce ancor.	he grows ever weaker and weaker.
Cosi fra l'ire estrema	[Then with his final wrath
rugge, minaccia, e freme,	he roars, threatens, and screams,
Che fa tremar morendo	which makes the hunter
Tal volta il cacciator.'	tremble at him dying.']
Metast[asio,] *Adriano*	
[*in Siria*, II, 11]	

But Bonaparte was a lion in the field only. In civil life a cold-blooded, calculating unprincipled Ursurper, without a virtue, no statesman, knowing nothing of commerce, political economy, or civil government, and supplying ignorance by bold presumption. I had supposed him a great man until his entrance into the Assembly des cinq cens, 18. Brumaire (an 8.) [November 9, 1799]. From that date however I set him down as a great scoundrel only. To the wonders of his rise and fall, we may add that of a Czar of Muscovy [Alexander I] dictating, *in Paris* [in 1814], laws and limits to all the successors of the Caesars, and holding even the balance in which the fortunes of this new world are suspended. I own that, while I rejoice, for the good of mankind, in the deliverance of Europe from the havoc which would have never ceased while Bonaparte should have lived in power, I see with anxiety the tyrant of the ocean [England] remaining in vigor, and even participating in the merit of crushing his brother tyrant. While the world is thus turned up side down, on which side of it are we? All the strong reasons indeed place us on the side of peace; the interests of the continent, their friendly dispositions, and even the interests of England. Her passions alone are opposed to it. Peace would seem now to be an easy work, the causes of the war being removed. Her orders of council will no doubt be taken care of by the allied powers, and, war ceasing, her impressment of our seamen ceases of course. But I fear there is foundation for the design intimated in the public papers, of demanding a cession of our right in the fisheries [off the northern coast of North America]. What will Massachusets say to this? I mean her majority, which must be considered as speaking, thro' the organs it has appointed itself, as the Index of it's will. She chose to sacrifice the liberty of our seafaring citizens, in which we were all interested, and with them her obligations to the Co-states; rather than war with England. Will she now sacrifice the fisheries to the same partialities? This question is interesting to her alone: for to the middle, the Southern and Western States they are of no direct concern; of no more than the culture of tobacco, rice and cotton to Massachusets. I am really at a loss to conjecture what our refractory sister will say on this occasion. I know what, as a citizen of the Union, I would say to her. 'Take this question ad referendum. It concerns you alone. If you would rather give up the fisheries than war with England, we give them up. If you had rather fight for them, we will defend your interests to the last drop of our blood, chusing rather to set a good example than follow a bad one.' And I hope she will determine to fight for them. With this however you and I shall have nothing to do; ours being truly the case wherein 'non tali auxilio, nec defensoribus istis Tempus eget.' ['We do not, at this time, want such aid as that, nor such defenders.' Virgil, *Aeneid*, II, 521.] Quitting this subject therefore I will turn over another leaf.

I am just returned from one of my long absences, having been at my other home for five weeks past. Having more leisure there than here for reading, I amused myself with reading seriously Plato's republic. I am wrong however in calling it amusement, for it was the heaviest task-work I ever went through. I had occasionally before taken up some of his other works, but scarcely ever had patience to go through a whole dialogue. While wading thro' the whimsies, the puerilities, and unintelligible jargon of this work, I laid it down often to ask myself how it could have been that the world should have so long consented to give reputation to such nonsense as this? How the soi-disant Christian world indeed should have done it, is a piece of historical curiosity. But how could the Roman good sense do it? And particularly how could Cicero bestow such eulogies on Plato? Altho' Cicero did not wield the dense logic of Demosthenes, yet he was able, learned, laborious, practised in the business of the world, and honest. He could not be the dupe of mere style, of which he was himself the first master in the world. With the Moderns, I think, it is rather a matter of fashion and authority. Education is chiefly in the hands of persons who, from their profession, have an interest in the reputation and the dreams of Plato. They give the tone while at school, and few, in their after-years, have occasion to revise their college opinions. But fashion and authority apart, and bringing Plato to the test of reason, take from him his sophisms, futilities, and incomprehensibilities, and what remains? In truth, he is one of the race of genuine Sophists, who has escaped the oblivion of his brethren, first by the elegance of his diction, but chiefly by the adoption and incorporation of his whimsies into the body of artificial Christianity. His foggy mind, is forever presenting the semblances of objects which, half seen thro' a mist, can be defined neither in form or dimension. Yet this which should have consigned him to early oblivion really procured him immortality of fame and reverence. The Christian priesthood, finding the doctrines of Christ levelled to every understanding, and too plain to need explanation, saw, in the mysticisms of Plato, materials with which they might build up an artificial system which might, from it's indistinctness, admit everlasting controversy, give employment for their order, and introduce it to profit, power and pre-eminence. The doctrines which flowed from the lips of Jesus himself are within the comprehension of a child; but thousands of volumes have not yet explained the Platonisms engrafted on them: and for this obvious reason that nonsense can never be explained. Their purposes however are answered. Plato is canonized; and it is now deemed as impious to question his merits as those of an Apostle of Jesus. He is peculiarly appealed to as an advocate of the immortality of the soul; and yet I will venture to say that were there no better arguments than his in proof of it, not a man in the world would believe it. It is fortunate for us that Platonic republicanism has not obtained the same favor as Platonic Christianity; or we should now have been all living, men, women and children, pell mell together, like beasts of the field or forest. Yet 'Plato is a great Philosopher,' said La Fontaine. But says Fontenelle 'do you find his ideas very clear?' 'Oh no! he is of an obscurity impenetrable.' 'Do you not find him full of contradictions?' 'Certainly,' replied La Fontaine, "he is but a Sophist." Yet immediately after, he exclaims again, 'Oh Plato was a great Philosopher.' Socrates had reason indeed to complain of the misrepresentations of Plato; for in truth his dialogues are libels on Socrates.

But why am I dosing you with these Ante-diluvian topics? Because I am glad to have some one to whom they are familiar, and who will not recieve them as if dropped from the moon. Our post-revolutionary youth are born under happier stars than you and I were. They acquire all learning in their mothers' womb, and bring it into the world ready-made. The information of books is no longer necessary; and all knolege which is not innate, is in contempt, or neglect at least. Every folly must run it's round; and so, I suppose, must that of self-learning, and self sufficiency; of rejecting the knolege acquired in past ages, and starting on the new ground of intuition. When sobered by experience I hope our successors will turn their attention to the advantages of education. I mean of education on the broad scale, and not that of the petty *academies*, as they call themselves, which are starting up in every neighborhood, and where one or two men, possessing Latin, and sometimes Greek, a knolege of the globes, and the first six books of Euclid, imagine and communicate this as the sum of science. They commit their pupils to the theatre of the world with just taste enough of learning to be alienated from industrious pursuits, and not enough to do service in the ranks of science. We have some exceptions indeed. I presented one to you lately, and we have some others. But the terms I use are general truths. I hope the necessity will at length be seen of establishing institutions, here as in Europe, where every branch of science, useful at this day, may be taught in it's highest degrees. Have you ever turned your thoughts to the plan of such an institution? I mean to a specification of the particular sciences of real use in human affairs, and how they might be so grouped as to require so many professors only as might bring them within the views of a just but enlightened economy? I should be happy in a communication of your ideas on this problem, either loose or digested. But to avoid my being run away with by another subject, and adding to the length and ennui of the present letter, I will here present to Mrs. Adams and yourself the assurance of my constant and sincere friendship and respect.

TH: JEFFERSON

K-2. LETTER FROM JOHN ADAMS TO THOMAS JEFFERSON

Quincy July 16. 1814

DEAR SIR

I recd. this morning your favour of the 5th. and as I can never let a Sheet of your's rest I sit down immediately to acknowledge it.

Whenever Mr. Rives, of whom I have heard nothing, shall arrive he shall receive all the cordial Civilities in my power.

I am sometimes afraid that my "Machine" will not "surcease motion" soon enough; for I dread nothing so much as "dying at top" and expiring like Dean Swift "a driveller and a Show" or like Sam. Adams, a Grief and distress to his Family, a weeping helpless Object of Compassion for Years.

I am bold to say that neither you nor I, will live to see the Course which "the Wonders of the Times" will take. Many Years, and perhaps Centuries must pass, before the current will acquire a settled direction. If the Christian Religion as I understand it, or as you understand it, should maintain its Ground as I believe it will; Yet Platonick Pythagoric, Hindoo, and cabballistical Christianity which is Catholic Christianity, and which has prevailed for 1500 Years, has recd. a mortal Wound of which the Monster must finally die; Yet so strong is his constitution that he may endure for Centuries before he expires. Government has never been much studied by Mankind. But their Attention has been drawn to it, in the latter part of the last Century and the begining of this, more than at any former Period: and the vast Variety of experiments that have been made of Constitutions, in America in France, in Holland, in Geneva in Switzerland, and even in Spain and South America, can never be forgotten. They will be studied, and their immediate and remote Effects, and final Catastrophys noted. The result in time will be Improvements. And I have no doubt that the horrors We have experienced for the last forty Years, will ultimately, terminate in the Advancement of civil and religious Liberty, and Ameliorations, in the condition of Mankind. For I am a Believer, in the probable improvability and Improvement, the Ameliorabi[li]ty and Amelioration in human Affairs: though I never could understand the Doctrine of the Perfectability of the human Mind. This has always appeared to me, like the Phylosophy or Theology of the Gentoos, viz. "that a Brachman by certain Studies for a certain time pursued, and by certain Ceremonies a certain number of times repeated, becomes Omniscient and Almighty."

Our hopes however of sudden tranquility ought not to be too sanguine. Fanaticism and Superstition will still be selfish, subtle, intriguing, and at times furious. Despotism will still struggle for domination; Monarchy will still study to rival nobility in popularity; Aristocracy will continue to envy all above it, and despize and oppress all below it; Democracy will envy all, contend with all, endeavour to pull down all; and when by chance it happens to get the Upper hand for a short time, it will be revengefull bloody and cruel. These and other Elements of Fanaticism and Anarchy will yet for a long time continue a Fermentation, which will excite alarms and require Vigilance.

Napoleon is a Military Fanatic like Achilles, Alexander, Caesar, Mahomet, Zingis Kouli, Charles 12th. etc. The Maxim and Principle of all of them was the same "Jura negat sibi cata [i.e., nata], nihil non arrogat Armis." ["He denies that laws were made for him; he arrogates everything to himself by force of arms." Horace, *Ars Poetica*, 122.]

But is it strict, to call him An Usurper? Was not his Elevation to the Empire of France as legitimate and authentic a national Act as that of William 3d. or the House of Hanover to the throne of the 3 Kingdoms or as the Election of Washington to the command of our Army or to the Chair of the States.

Human Nature, in no form of it, ever could bear Prosperity. That peculiar tribe of Men, called Conquerors, more remarkably than any other have been swelled with Vanity by any Series of Victories. Napoleon won so many mighty Battles in such quick succession and for so long a time, that it was no Wonder his brain became compleatly intoxicated and his enterprises, rash, extravagant and mad.

Though France is humbled, Britain is not. Though Bona is banished a greater Tyrant and wider Usurper still domineers. John Bull is quite as unfeeling, as unprincipled, more powerful, has shed more blood, than Bona. John by his money his Intrigues and Arms, by exciting Coalition after coalition against him made him what he was, and at last, what he is. How shall the Tyrant of Tyrants, be brought low? Aye! there's the rub. I still think Bona great, at least as any of the Conquerors. "The Wonders of his rise and fall," may be seen in the Life of King Theodore, or Pascall Paoli or Rienzi, or Dyonisius or Mazzionelli, or Jack Cade or Wat Tyler. The only difference is that between miniatures and full length pictures. The Schoolmaster at Corinth, was a greater Man, than the Tyrant of Syracuse; upon the Principle, that he who conquers himself is greater than he who takes a City. Tho' the ferocious Roar of the wounded Lion, may terrify the Hunter with the possibility of another dangerous leap; Bona was shot dead at once, by France. He could no longer roar or struggle growl or paw, he could only gasp the grin of death. I wish that France may not still regret him. But these are Speculations in the Clouds. I agree with you that the Milk of human kindness in the Bourbons is safer for Mankind than the fierce Ambition of Napoleon.

The Autocrator [of Russia] appears in an imposing Light. Fifty Years ago English Writers, held up terrible Consequences from "thawing out the monstrous northern Snake." If Cossacks and Tartars, and Goths and Vandalls and Hunns and Ripuarians, should get a taste of European Sweets, what may happen? Could Wellingtons or Bonapartes, resist them? The greatest trait of Sagacity, that [Czar] Alexander [of Russia] has yet exhibited to the World is his Courtship of the United States. But whether this is a mature well digested Policy or only a transient gleam of thought, still remains to be explained and proved by time.

The "refractory Sister" [Massachusetts] will not give up the Fisheries. Not a Man here dares to hint at so base a thought.

I am very glad you have seriously read Plato: and still more rejoiced to find that your reflections upon him so perfectly harmonize with mine. Some thirty Years ago I took upon me the severe task of going through all his Works. With the help of two Latin Translations, and one English and one French Translation and comparing some of the most remarkable passages with the Greek, I laboured through the tedious toil. My disappointment was very great, my Astonishment was greater and my disgust was shocking. Two Things only did I learn from him. 1. that Franklins Ideas of exempting Husbandmen and Mariners etc. from the depredations of War were borrowed from him. 2. that Sneezing is a cure for the Hickups. Accordingly I have cured myself and all my Friends of that provoking disorder, for thirty Years with a Pinch of Snuff.

Some Parts of some of his Dialogues are entertaining, like the Writings of Rousseau: but his Laws and his Republick from which I expected most, disappointed me most. I could scarcely exclude the suspicion that he intended the latter as a bitter Satyre upon all Republican Government, as Xenophon undoubtedly designed by his Essay on Democracy, to ridicule that Species of Republick. In a late letter to the learned and ingenious Mr. Taylor of Hazelwood, I suggested to him the Project of writing a Novel, in which The Hero should be sent upon his travels through Plato's Republick, and all his Adventures, with his Observations on the principles and Opinions, the Arts and Sciences, the manners Customs and habits of the Citizens should be recorded. Nothing can be conceived more destructive of human happiness; more infallibly contrived to transform Men and Women into Brutes, Yahoos, or Daemons than a Community of Wives and Property. Yet, in what, are the Writings of Rousseau and Helvetius wiser than those of Plato? "The Man who first fenced a Tobacco Yard, and said this is mine ought instantly to have been put to death" says Rousseau. "The Man who first pronounced the barbarous Word "Dieu," ought to have been immediately destroyed," says Diderot. In short Philosophers antient and modern appear to me as Mad as Hindoos, Mahomitans, and Christians. No doubt they would all think me mad; and for any thing I know this globe may be, the bedlam, Le Bicatre [i.e., Bicêtre] of the Universe.

After all; as long as Property exists, it will accumulate in Individuals and Families. As long as Marriage exists, Knowledge, Property and Influence will accumulate in Families. Your and our equal Partition of intestate Estates, instead of preventing will in time augment the Evil, if it is one.

The French Revolutionists saw this, and were so far consistent. When they burned Pedigrees and genealogical Trees, they anni[hi]-lated, as far as they could, Marriages, knowing that Marriage, among a thousand other things was an infallible Source of Aristocracy. I repeat it, so sure as the Idea and the existence of PROPERTY is admitted and established in Society, Accumulations of it will be made, the Snow ball will grow as it rolls.

Cicero was educated in the Groves of Academus where the Name and Memory of Plato, were idolized to such a degree, that if he had wholly renounced the Prejudices of his Education his Reputation would have been lessened, if not injured and ruined. In his two Volumes of Discourses of Government We may presume, that he fully examined Plato's Laws and Republick as well as Aristotles Writings on Government. But these have been carefully destroyed; not improbably, with the general Consent of Philosophers, Politicians and Priests. The Loss is as much to be regretted as that of any Production of Antiquity.

Nothing seizes the Attention, of the stareing Animal, so surely, as Paradox, Riddle, Mystery, Invention, discovery, Mystery, Wonder, Temerity.

Plato and his Disciples, from the fourth Century Christians, to Rousseau and Tom Paine, have been fully sensible of this Weakness in Mankind, and have too successfully grounded upon it their Pretensions to Fame. I might indeed, have mentioned Bolingbroke, Hume, Gibbon Voltaire Turgot Helvetius Diderot, Condorcet, Buffon De La Lande and fifty others; all a little cracked! Be to their faults a little blind; to their Virtues ever kind.

Education! Oh Education! The greatest Grief of my heart, and the greatest Affliction of my Life! To my mortification I must confess, that I have never closely thought, or very deliberately reflected upon the Subject, which never occurs to me now, without producing a deep Sigh, an heavy groan and sometimes Tears. My cruel Destiny seperated me from my Children, allmost continually from their Birth to their Manhood. I was compelled to leave them to the ordinary routine of reading writing and Latin School, Accademy and Colledge. John alone was much with me, and he, but occasionally. If I venture to give you any thoughts at all, they must be very crude. I have turned over Locke, Milton, Condilac Rousseau and even Miss. Edgeworth as a bird flies through the Air. The Praecepter [by Robert Dodsley], I have thought a good Book. Grammar, Rhetorick, Logic, Ethicks mathematicks, cannot be neglected; Classicks, in spight of our Friend Rush, I must think indispensable. [Benjamin Rush advocated dropping Greek and Latin from the school curriculum, except for the few students who would go to college.] Natural History, Mechanicks, and experimental Philosophy, Chymistry etc att least their Rudiments, can not be forgotten. Geography Ast[ron]omy, and even History and Chronology, tho' I am myself afflicted with a kind of Pyrrhonism in the two latter, I presume cannot be omitted. Theology I would leave to Ray, Derham, Nicuenteyt and Payley, rather than to Luther Zinzindorph, Sweedenborg Westley, or Whitefield, or Thomas Aquinas or Wollebius [i.e., to the naturalists rather than to the revealed religionists]. Metaphysics I would leave in the Clouds with the Materialists and Spirtualists, with Leibnits, Berkley Priestley and Edwards, and I might add Hume and Reed, or if permitted to be read, it should be with Romances and Novels. What shall I say of Musick, drawing, fencing, dancing and Gymnastic Exercises? What of Languages Oriental or Occidental? of French Italian German or Russian? of Sanscrit or Chinese?

The Task you have prescribed to me of Grouping these Sciences, or Arts, under Professors, within the Views of an inlightened Economy, is far beyond my forces. Loose indeed and indigested must be all the hints, I can note. Might Gramar, Rhetoric, Logick and Ethicks be under One Professor? Might Mathematicks, Mechanicks, Natural Phylosophy, be under another? Geography and Astro[no]my under a third. Laws and Goverment, History and Chronology under a fourth. Classicks might require a fifth.

Condelacs course of Study has excellent Parts. Among many Systems of Mathematicks English, French and American, there is none preferable to Besouts Course La Harps Course of Litterature is very valuable.

But I am ashamed to add any thing more to the broken innuendos except Assurances of the continued Friendship of
JOHN ADAMS

340

L. Anglo-American Responses to Slavery (1771–1863)

L-1. SOMERSET'S CASE (1771–1772)

Somerset against *Stewart.*
Easter Term, May 14, 1772

On return to [a writ of] *habeas corpus*, requiring Captain [*John*] *Knowles* to shew cause for the seizure and detainure of the complainant [*James*] *Somerset*, a negro—The case appeared to be this—

That the negro had been a slave to Mr. [*Charles*] *Stewart*, in *Virginia*, had been purchased from the *African* coast, in the course of the slave-trade, as tolerated in the [North American] plantations; that he had been brought over to *England* by his master, who intending to return, by force sent him on board of Captain *Knowles's* vessel, lying in the river; and was there, by the order of his master, in the custody of Captain *Knowles*, detained against his consent; until returned in obedience to the writ [in December 1771]. And under this order, and the facts stated, Captain *Knowles* relied in his justification. [Extensive arguments by counsel follow.]

Lord *Mansfield*: The question is, if the owner had a right to detain the slave, for the sending of him over to be sold in *Jamaica*. In five or six cases of this nature, I have known it to be accommodated by agreement between the parties: On its first coming before me [in December 1771], I strongly recommended it here. But if the parties will have it decided, we must give our opinion. Compassion will not, on the one hand, nor inconvenience on the other, be to decide; but the law: In which the difficulty will be principally from the inconvenience on both sides. Contract for sale of a slave is good here; the sale is a matter to which the law properly and readily attaches, and will maintain the price according to the agreement. But here the person of the slave himself is immediately the object of enquiry; which makes a very material difference. The now question is, whether any dominion, authority or coercion can be exercised in this country, on a slave according to the *American* laws? The difficulty of adopting the relation, without adopting it in all its consequences, is indeed extreme; and yet, many of those consequences are absolutely contrary to the municipal law of *England*. We have no authority to regulate the conditions in which law shall operate. On the other hand, should we think the coercive power cannot be exercised: 'Tis now about fifty years since the opinion given by two of the greatest men of their own or any times, (since which no contract has been brought to trial, between the masters and slaves;) the service performed by the slaves without wages, is a clear indication they did not think themselves free by coming hither. The setting 14,000 or 15,000 men at once free loose by a solemn opinion, is much disagreeable in the effects it threatens. There is a case in *Hobart*, (*Coventry* and *Woodfall*,) where a man had contracted to go as a mariner: But the now case will not come within that decision. Mr. *Stewart* advances no claim on contract; he rests his whole demand on a right to the negro as slave, and mentions the purpose of detainure to be the sending of him over to be sold in *Jamaica*. If the parties will have judgment, *fiat justitia, ruat coelum*, let justice be done whatever be the consequence. 50 [pounds] a head may not be a high price; then a loss follows to the proprietors of above 700,000 [pounds] sterling. How would the law stand with respect to their settlement; their wages? How many actions for any slight coercion by the master? We cannot in any of these points direct the law; the law must rule us. In these particulars, it may be matter of weighty consideration, what provisions are made or set by law. Mr. *Stewart* may end the question, by discharging or giving freedom to the negro. I did think at first to put the matter to a more solemn way of argument: But if my brothers agree, there seems no occasion. I do not imagine, after the point has been discussed on both sides so extremely well, any new light could be thrown on the subject. If the parties chuse to refer it to the Common Pleas, they can give them-[selves] that satisfaction whenever they think fit. An application to parliament, if the merchants think the question of great commercial concern, is the best, and perhaps the only method of settling the point for the future. The court is greatly obliged to the gentlemen of the bar who have spoke on the subject; and by whose care and abilities so much has been effected, that the rule of decision will be reduced to a very easy compass. I cannot omit to express particular happiness in seeing young men, just called to the bar, have been able so much to profit by their reading. I think it right the matter should stand over; and if we are called on for a decision, proper notice shall be given.

Trinity Term, June 22, 1772.

Lord *Mansfield*: On the part of *Somerset*, the case which we gave notice should be decided this day, the court now proceeds to give its opinion. I shall recite the return to the writ of *habeas corpus*, as the ground of our determination; omitting only words of form. The captain of the ship on board of which the negro was taken, makes his return to the writ in terms signifying that there have been, and still are, slaves to a great number in *Africa*; and that the trade in them is authorized by the laws and opinions of *Virginia* and *Jamaica*; that they are goods and chattels; and, as such, saleable and sold. That *James Somerset*, is a negro of *Africa*, and long before the return of the king's writ was brought to be sold, and was sold to *Charles Stewart*, Esq. then in *Jamaica*, and has not been manumitted since; that Mr. *Stewart*, having occasion to transact business, came over hither, with an intention to return; and brought *Somerset*, to attend and abide with him, and to carry him back as soon as the business should be transacted. That such intention has been, and still continues; and that the negro did remain till the time of his departure, in the service of his master Mr. *Stewart*, and quitted it without his consent; and thereupon, before the return of the king's writ, the said *Charles Stewart* did commit the slave on board the *Ann* and *Mary*, to save custody, to be kept till he should set sail, and then to be taken with him to *Jamaica*, and there sold as a slave. And this is the cause why he, Captain *Knowles*, who was then and now is, commander of the above vessel, then and now lying in the river of *Thames*, did the said negro, committed to his custody, detain; and on which he now renders him to the orders of the court. We pay all due attention to the opinion of Sir *Philip Yorke*, and Lord Chief Justice *Talbot*, whereby they pledged themselves to the *British* planters, for all the legal consequences of slaves coming over to this kingdom or being baptized, recognized by Lord *Hardwicke*, sitting as Chancellor on the 19th of *October* 1749, that *trover* would lie: That a notion had prevailed, if a negro came over, or became a christian, he was emancipated, but no ground in law; that he and Lord *Talbot*, when Attorney and Solicitor-General, were of opinion, that no such claim for freedom was valid; that tho' the Statute of Tenures had abolished villains regardant to a manor, yet he did not conceive but that a man might still become a villain in gross, by confessing himself such in open court. We are so well agreed, that we think there is no occasion of having it argued (as I intimated an intention at first,) before all the judges, as is usual, for obvious reasons, on a return to a *habeas corpus*; the only question before us is, whether the cause on the return is sufficient? If it is, the negro must be remanded; if it is not, he must be discharged. Accordingly, the return states, that the slave departed and refused to serve; whereupon he was kept, to be sold abroad. So high an act of dominion must be recognized by the law of the country where it is used. The power of a master over his slave has been extremely different, in different countries. The state of slavery is of such a nature, that it is incapable of being introduced on any reasons, moral or political; but only [by] positive law, which preserves its force long after the reasons, occasion, and time itself from whence it was created, is erased from memory: It's so odious, that nothing can be suffered to support it, but positive law. Whatever inconveniences, therefore, may follow from a decision, I cannot say this case is allowed or approved by the law of *England*; and therefore the black must be discharged.

L-2. THE CONSTITUTION OF THE CONFEDERATE STATES OF AMERICA (1861)

Constitution Of The Confederate States Of America

We, the people of the Confederate States, each State acting in its sovereign and independent character, in order to form a permanent federal government, establish justice, insure domestic tranquility, and secure the blessings of liberty to ourselves and our posterity—

344

invoking the favor and guidance of Almighty God—do ordain and establish this Constitution for the Confederate States of America.

Article 1.
Section 1.

All legislative powers herein delegated shall be vested in a Congress of the Confederate States, which shall consist of a Senate and a House of Representatives.

Section 2.

1. The House of Representatives shall be composed of members chosen every second year by the people of the several States; and the electors in each State shall be citizens of the Confederate States, and have the qualifications requisite for electors of the most numerous branch of the State Legislature; but no person of foreign birth, not a citizen of the Confederate States, shall be allowed to vote for any officer, civil or political, State or Federal.

2. No person shall be a Representative who shall not have attained the age of twenty-five years, and be a citizen of the Confederate States, and who shall not, when elected, be an inhabitant of that State in which he shall be chosen.

3. Representatives and direct taxes shall be apportioned among the several States, which may be included within this Confederacy, according to their respective numbers, which shall be determined, by adding to the whole number of free persons, including those bound to service for a term of years, and excluding Indians not taxed, three-fifths of all slaves. The actual enumeration shall be made within three years after the first meeting of the Congress of the Confederate States, and within every subsequent term of ten years, in such manner as they shall by law direct. The number of Representatives shall not exceed one for every fifty thousand, but each State shall have at least one Representative; and until such enumeration shall be made, the State of South Carolina shall be entitled to choose six; the State of Georgia ten; the State of Alabama nine; the State of Florida two; the State of Mississippi seven; the State of Louisiana six; and the State of Texas six.

4. When vacancies happen in the representation from any State,

the Executive authority thereof shall issue writs of election to fill such vacancies.

5. The House of Representatives shall choose their Speaker and other officers; and shall have the sole power of impeachment; except that any judicial or other Federal officer, resident and acting solely within the limits of any State, may be impeached by a vote of two-thirds of both branches of the Legislature thereof.

Section 3.

1. The Senate of the Confederate States shall be composed of two Senators from each State, chosen for six years by the Legislature thereof, at the regular session next immediately preceding the commencement of the term of service; and each Senator shall have one vote.

2. Immediately after they shall be assembled, in consequence of the first election, they shall be divided as equally as may be into three classes. The seats of the Senators of the first class shall be vacated at the expiration of the second year; of the second class at the expiration of the fourth year; and of the third class at the expiration of the sixth year; so that one-third may be chosen every second year; and if vacancies happen by resignation, or otherwise, during the recess of the Legislature of any State, the Executive thereof may make temporary appointments until the next meeting of the Legislature which shall then fill such vacancies.

3. No person shall be a Senator who shall not have attained the age of thirty years, and be a citizen of the Confederate States; and who shall not, when elected, be an inhabitant of the State for which he shall be chosen.

4. The Vice President of the Confederate States shall be President of the Senate, but shall have no vote unless they be equally divided.

5. The Senate shall choose their other officers; and also a President *pro tempore* in the absence of the Vice President, or when he shall exercise the office of President of the Confederate States.

6. The Senate shall have the sole power to try all impeachments. When sitting for that purpose, they shall be on oath or affirmation. When the President of the Confederate States is tried, the Chief Justice shall preside; and no person shall be convicted without the concurrence of two-thirds of the members present.

7. Judgment in cases of impeachment shall not extend further than to removal from office, and disqualification to hold and enjoy any office of honor, trust or profit, under the Confederate States; but the party convicted shall, nevertheless, be liable and subject to indictment, trial, judgment and punishment according to law.

Section 4.

1. The times, places and manner of holding elections for Senators and Representatives, shall be prescribed in each State by the Legislature thereof, subject to the provisions of this Constitution; but the Congress may, at any time, by law, make or alter such regulations, except as to the times and places of choosing Senators.

2. The Congress shall assemble at least once in every year; and such meeting shall be on the first Monday in December, unless they shall, by law, appoint a different day.

Section 5.

1. Each House shall be the judge of the elections, returns, and qualifications of its own members, and a majority of each shall constitute a quorum to do business; but a smaller number may adjourn from day to day, and may be authorized to compel the attendance of absent members, in such manner and under such penalties as each House may provide.

2. Each House may determine the rules of its proceedings, punish its members for disorderly behavior, and with the concurrence of two-thirds of the whole number expel a member.

3. Each House shall keep a journal of its proceedings, and from time to time publish the same, excepting such parts as may in their judgment require secrecy; and the yeas and nays of the members of either House, on any question, shall, at the desire of one-fifth of those present, be entered on the journal.

4. Neither House, during the session of Congress, shall without the consent of the other, adjourn for more than three days, nor to may other place than that in which the two Houses shall be sitting.

Section 6.

1. The Senators and Representatives shall receive a compensation for their services, to be ascertained by law, and paid out of the treasury of the Confederate States. They shall, in all cases, except treason, felony, and breach of the peace, be privileged from arrest during their attendance at the session of their respective Houses, and in going to and returning from the same; and for any speech or debate in either House, they shall not be questioned in any other place.

2. No Senator or Representative shall, during the time for which he was elected, be appointed to any civil office under the authority of the Confederate States, which shall have been created, or the emoluments whereof shall have been increased during such time; and no person holding any office under the Confederate States shall be a member of either House during his continuance in office. But Congress may, by law, grant to the principal officer in each of the Executive Departments a seat upon the floor of either House, with the privilege of discussing any measures appertaining to his department.

Section 7.

1. All bills for raising revenue shall originate in the House of Representatives; but the Senate may propose or concur with amendments, as on other bills.

2. Every bill which shall have passed both Houses, shall, before it becomes a law, be presented to the President of the Confederate States; if he approve, he shall sign it; but if not, he shall return it, with his objections, to that House in which it shall have originated, who shall enter the objections at large on their journal, and proceed to reconsider it. If, after such reconsideration, two-thirds of that House shall agree to pass the bill, it shall be sent, together with the objections, to the other House, by which it shall likewise be reconsidered, and if approved by two-thirds of that House, it shall become a law. But in all such cases, the votes of both Houses shall be determined by yeas and nays, and the names of the persons voting for and against the bill shall be entered on the journal of each House respectively. If any bill shall not be returned by the President within ten days (Sundays excepted) after it shall have been pre-

sented to him, the same shall be a law, in like manner as if he had signed it, unless the Congress, by their adjournment, prevent its return; in which case it shall not be a law. The President may approve any appropriation and disapprove any other appropriation in the same bill. In such case he shall, in signing the bill, designate the appropriations disapproved; and shall return a copy of such appropriations, with his objections, to the House in which the bill shall have originated; and the same proceedings shall then be had as in case of other bills disapproved by the President.

3. Every order, resolution or vote, to which the concurrence of both Houses may be necessary, (except on a question of adjournment,) shall be presented to the President of the Confederate States; and before the same shall take effect, shall be approved by him; or being disapproved by him, shall be re-passed by two-thirds of both Houses, according to the rules and limitations prescribed in case of a bill.

Section 8.

The Congress shall have power—

1. To lay and collect taxes, duties, imposts, and excises, for revenue necessary to pay the debts, provide for the common defence, and carry on the government of the Confederate States; but no bounties shall be granted from the treasury; nor shall any duties or taxes on importations from foreign nations be laid to promote or foster any branch of industry; and all duties, imposts, and excises shall be uniform throughout the Confederate States:

2. To borrow money on the credit of the Confederate States:

3. To regulate commerce with foreign nations, and among the several States, and with the Indian tribes; but neither this, nor any other clause contained in the constitution, shall ever be construed to delegate the power to Congress to appropriate money for any internal improvement intended to facilitate commerce; except for the purpose of furnishing lights, beacons, and buoys, and other aids to navigation upon the coasts, and the improvement of harbors and the removing of obstructions in river navigation, in all which cases, such duties shall be laid on the navigation facilitated thereby, as may be necessary to pay the costs and expenses thereof:

4. To establish uniform laws of naturalization, and uniform laws

on the subject of bankruptcies, throughout the Confederate States; but no law of Congress shall discharge any debt contracted before the passage of the same:

5. To coin money, regulate the value thereof and of foreign coin, and fix the standard of weights and measures:

6. To provide for the punishment of counterfeiting the securities and current coin of the Confederate States:

7. To establish post-offices and post-routes; but the expenses of the Post-office Department, after the first day of March, in the year of our Lord eighteen hundred and sixty-three, shall be paid out of its own revenues:

8. To promote the progress of science and useful arts, by securing for limited times to authors and inventors the exclusive right to their respective writings and discoveries:

9. To constitute tribunals inferior to the Supreme Court:

10. To define and punish piracies and felonies committed on the high seas, and offences against the law of nations:

11. To declare war, grant letters of marque and reprisal, and make rules concerning captures on land and water:

12. To raise and support armies; but no appropriation of money to that use shall be for a longer term than two years:

13. To provide and maintain a navy:

14. To make rules for the government and regulation of the land and naval forces:

15. To provide for calling forth the militia to execute the laws of the Confederate States, suppress insurrections, and repel invasions:

16. To provide for organizing, arming, and disciplining the militia, and for governing such part of them as may be employed in the service of the Confederate States; reserving to the States, respectively, the appointment of the officers, and the authority of training the militia according to the discipline prescribed by Congress:

17. To exercise exclusive legislation, in all cases whatsoever, over such district (not exceeding ten miles square) as may, by cession of one or more States and the acceptance of Congress, become the seat of the government of the Confederate States; and to exercise like authority over all places purchased by the consent of the legislature of the State in which the same shall be, for the erection of forts, magazines, arsenals, dockyards, and other needful buildings: and

18. To make all laws which shall be necessary and proper for

carrying into execution the foregoing powers, and all other powers vested by this Constitution in the government of the Confederate States, or in any department or officer thereof.

Section 9.

1. The importation of negroes of the African race, from any foreign country, other than the slaveholding States or Territories of the United States of America, is hereby forbidden; and Congress is required to pass such laws as shall effectually prevent the same.

2. Congress shall also have power to prohibit the introduction of slaves from any State not a member of, or Territory not belonging to, this Confederacy.

3. The privilege of the writ of *habeas corpus* shall not be suspended, unless when in cases of rebellion or invasion the public safety may require it.

4. No bill of attainder, *ex post facto* law, or law denying or impairing the right of property in negro slaves shall be passed.

5. No capitation or other direct tax shall be laid, unless in proportion to the census or enumeration hereinbefore directed to be taken.

6. No tax or duty shall be laid on articles exported from any State, except by a vote of two-thirds of both Houses.

7. No preference shall be given by any regulation of commerce or revenue to the ports of one State over those of another.

8. No money shall be drawn from the treasury, but in consequence of appropriations made by law; and a regular statement and account of the receipts and expenditures of all public money shall be published from time to time.

9. Congress shall appropriate no money from the treasury except by a vote of two-thirds of both Houses, taken by yeas and nays, unless it be asked and estimated for by some one of the heads of departments, and submitted to Congress by the President; or for the purpose of paying its own expenses and contingencies; or for the payment of claims against the Confederate States, the justice of which shall have been judicially declared by a tribunal for the investigation of claims against the government, which it is hereby made the duty of Congress to establish.

10. All bills appropriating money shall specify in federal cur-

rency, the exact amount of each appropriation and the purposes for which it is made; and Congress shall grant no extra compensation to any public contractor, officer, agent or servant, after such contract shall have been made or such service rendered.

11. No title of nobility shall be granted by the Confederate States; and no person holding any office of profit or trust under them, shall, without the consent of the Congress, accept of any present, emolument, office or title of any kind whatever, from any king, prince, or foreign state.

12. Congress shall make no law respecting an establishment of religion, or prohibiting the free exercise thereof; or abridging the freedom of speech, or of the press; or the right of the people peaceably to assemble and petition the government for a redress of grievances.

13. A well-regulated militia, being necessary to the security of a free state, the right of the people to keep and bear arms shall not be infringed.

14. No soldier shall, in time of peace, be quartered in any house, without the consent of the owner; nor in time of war, but in a manner to be prescribed by law.

15. The right of the people to be secure in their persons, houses, papers, and effects, against unreasonable searches and seizures, shall not be violated; and no warrants shall issue but upon probable cause, supported by oath or affirmation, and particularly describing the place to be searched, and the persons or things to be seized.

16. No person shall be held to answer for a capital or otherwise infamous crime, unless on a presentment or indictment of a grand jury, except in cases arising in the land or naval forces, or in the militia, when in actual service in time of war or public danger; nor shall any person be subject for the same offence to be twice put in jeopardy of life or limb; nor be compelled, in any criminal case, to be a witness against himself; nor be deprived of life, liberty, or property, without due process of law; nor shall private property be taken for public use, without just compensation.

17. In all criminal prosecutions, the accused shall enjoy the right to a speedy and public trial, by an impartial jury of the State and district wherein the crime shall have been committed, which district shall have been previously ascertained by law, and to be informed of the nature and cause of the accusation; to be confronted with the witnesses against him; to have compulsory process for

obtaining witnesses in his favor; and to have the assistance of counsel for his defence.

18. In suits at common law, where the value in controversy shall exceed twenty dollars, the right of trial by jury shall be preserved; and no fact so tried by a jury shall be otherwise re-examined in any court of the Confederacy, than according to the rules of common law.

19. Excessive bail shall not be required, nor excessive fines imposed, nor cruel and unusual punishments inflicted.

20. Every law, or resolution having the force of law, shall relate to but one subject, and that shall be expressed in the title.

Section 10.

1. No State shall enter into any treaty, alliance, or confederation; grant letters of marque and reprisal; coin money; make any thing but gold and silver coin a tender in payment of debts; pass any bill of attainder, or *ex post facto* law, or law impairing the obligation of contracts; or grant any title of nobility.

2. No State shall, without the consent of the Congress, lay any imposts or duties on imports or exports, except what may be absolutely necessary for executing its inspection laws; and the net produce of all duties and imposts, laid by any State on imports or exports, shall be for the use of the Treasury of the Confederate States; and all such laws shall be subject to the revision and control of Congress.

3. No State shall, without the consent of Congress, lay any duty on tonnage, except on sea-going vessels, for the improvement of its rivers and harbors navigated by the said vessels; but such duties shall not conflict with any treaties of the Confederate States with foreign nations; and any surplus revenue, thus derived, shall, after making such improvement, be paid into the common treasury. Nor shall any State keep troops or ships-of-war in time of peace, enter into any agreement or compact with another State, or with a foreign power, or engage in war, unless actually invaded, or in such imminent danger as will not admit of delay. But when any river divides or flows through two or more States, they may enter into compacts with each other to improve the navigation thereof.

353

Article II.
Section 1.

1. The executive power shall be vested in a President of the Confederate States of America. He and the Vice President shall hold their offices for the term of six years; but the President shall not be re-eligible. The President and Vice President shall be elected as follows:

2. Each State shall appoint, in such manner as the legislature thereof may direct, a number of electors equal to the whole number of Senators and Representatives to which the State may be entitled in the Congress; but no Senator or Representative or person holding an office of trust or profit under the Confederate States, shall be appointed an elector.

3. The electors shall meet in their respective States and vote by ballot for President and Vice President, one of whom, at least, shall not be an inhabitant of the same State with themselves; they shall name in their ballots the person voted for as President, and in distinct ballots the person voted for as Vice President, and they shall make distinct lists of all persons voted for as President, and of all persons voted for as Vice President, and of the number of votes for each, which lists they shall sign and certify, and transmit, sealed, to the seat of the government of the Confederate States, directed to the President of the Senate; the President of the Senate shall, in the presence of the Senate and House of Representatives, open all the certificates, and the votes shall then be counted; the person having the greatest number of votes for President shall be the President, if such number be a majority of the whole number of electors appointed; and if no person have such majority, then, from the persons having the highest numbers, not exceeding three, on the list of those voted for as President, the House of Representatives shall choose immediately, by ballot, the President. But in choosing the President, the votes shall be taken by States—the representation from each State having one vote; a quorum for this purpose shall consist of a member or members from two-thirds of the States, and a majority of all the States shall be necessary to a choice. And if the House of Representatives shall not choose a President, whenever the right of choice shall devolve upon them, before the fourth day of March next following,

then the Vice-President shall act as President, as in case of the death, or other constitutional disability of the President.

4. The person having the greatest number of votes as Vice President, shall be the Vice President, if such number be a majority of the whole number of electors appointed; and if no person have a majority, then, from the two highest numbers on the list, the Senate shall choose the Vice President; a quorum for the purpose shall consist of two-thirds of the whole number of Senators, and a majority of the whole number shall be necessary to a choice.

5. But no person constitutionally ineligible to the office of President shall be eligible to that of Vice President of the Confederate States.

6. The Congress may determine the time of choosing the electors, and the day on which they shall give their votes; which day shall be the same throughout the Confederate States.

7. No person except a natural born citizen of the Confederate States, or a citizen thereof at the time of the adoption of this Constitution, or a citizen thereof born in the United States prior to the 20th of December, 1860, shall be eligible to the office of President; neither shall any person be eligible to that office who shall not have attained the age of thirty-five years, and been fourteen years a resident within the limits of the Confederate States, as they may exist at the time of his election.

8. In case of the removal of the President from office, or of his death, resignation, or inability to discharge the powers and duties of said office, the same shall devolve on the Vice President; and the Congress may, by law, provide for the case of removal, death, resignation, or inability, both of the President and Vice President, declaring what officer shall then act as President; and such officer shall act accordingly, until the disability be removed or a President shall be elected.

9. The President shall, at stated times, receive for his services a compensation, which shall neither be increased nor diminished during the period for which he shall have been elected; and he shall not receive within that period any other emolument from the Confederate States, or any of them.

10. Before he enters on the execution of his office, he shall take the following oath or affirmation:

"I do solemnly swear (or affirm) that I will faithfully execute the office of President of the Confederate States, and will, to the best of my ability, preserve, protect, and defend the Constitution thereof."

Section 2.

1. The President shall be commander-in-chief of the army and navy of the Confederate States, and of the militia of the several States, when called into the actual service of the Confederate States; he may require the opinion, in writing, of the principal officer in each of the executive departments, upon any subject relating to the duties of their respective offices; and he shall have power to grant reprieves and pardons for offences against the Confederate States, except in cases of impeachment.

2. He shall have power, by and with the advice and consent of the Senate, to make treaties; provided two-thirds of the Senators present concur; and he shall nominate, and by and with the advice and consent of the Senate, shall appoint ambassadors, other public ministers and consuls, judges of the Supreme Court, and all other officers of the Confederate States whose appointments are not herein otherwise provided for, and which shall be established by law; but the Congress may, by law, vest the appointment of such inferior officers, as they think proper, in the President alone, in the courts of law, or in the heads of departments.

3. The principal officer in each of the executive departments, and all persons connected with the diplomatic service, may be removed from office at the pleasure of the President. All other civil officers of the executive departments may be removed at any time by the President, or other appointing power, when their services are unnecessary, or for dishonesty, incapacity, inefficiency, misconduct, or neglect of duty; and when so removed, the removal shall be reported to the Senate, together with the reasons therefor.

4. The President shall have power to fill all vacancies that may happen during the recess of the Senate, by granting commissions which shall expire at the end of their next session; but no person rejected by the Senate shall be re-appointed to the same office during their ensuring recess.

Section 3.

1. The President shall, from time to time, give to the Congress information of the state of the Confederacy, and recommend to their consideration such measures as he shall judge necessary and expedient; he may, on extraordinary occasions, convene both Houses, or either of them; and in case of disagreement between them, with respect to the time of adjournment, he may adjourn them to such time as he shall think proper; he shall receive ambassadors and other public ministers; he shall take care that the laws be faithfully executed, and shall commission all the officers of the Confederate States.

Section 4.

1. The President, Vice President, and all civil officers of the Confederate States, shall be removed from office on impeachment for, and conviction of, treason, bribery, or other high crimes and misdemeanors.

Article III.
Section 1.

1. The judicial power of the Confederate States shall be vested in one Supreme Court, and in such inferior courts as the Congress may, from time to time, ordain and establish. The judges, both of the Supreme and inferior courts, shall hold their offices during good behavior, and shall, at stated times, receive for their services a compensation which shall not be diminished during their continuance in office.

Section 2.

1. The judicial power shall extend to all cases arising under this Constitution, the laws of the Confederate States; and treaties made, or which shall be made, under their authority; to all cases affecting ambassadors, other public ministers and consuls; to all cases of admiralty and maritime jurisdiction; to controversies to which the Confederate States shall be a party; to controversies between two or more States; between a State and citizens of another State, where

the State is plaintiff; between citizens claiming lands under grants of different States; and between a State or the citizens thereof, and foreign states, citizens or subjects; but no State shall be sued by a citizen or subject of any foreign state.

2. In all cases affecting ambassadors, other public ministers and consuls, and those in which a State shall be a party, the Supreme Court shall have original jurisdiction. In all the other cases before mentioned, the Supreme Court shall have appellate jurisdiction both as to law and fact, with such exceptions and under such regulations as the Congress shall make.

3. The trial of all crimes, except in cases of impeachment, shall be by jury, and such trial shall be held in the State where the said crimes shall have been committed; but when not committed within any State, the trial shall be at such place or places as the Congress may by law have directed.

Section 3.

1. Treason against the Confederate States shall consist only in levying war against them, or in adhering to their enemies, giving them aid and comfort. No person shall be convicted of treason unless on the testimony of two witnesses to the same overt act, or on confession in open court.

2. The Congress shall have power to declare the punishment of treason; but no attainder of treason shall work corruption of blood, or forfeiture, except during the life of the person attainted.

Article IV.
Section 1.

1. Full faith and credit shall be given in each State to the public acts, records, and judicial proceedings of every other State. And the Congress may, by general laws, prescribe the manner in which such acts, records, and proceedings shall be proved, and the effect thereof.

Section 2.

1. The citizens of each State shall be entitled to all the privileges and immunities of citizens in the several States; and shall have the

right of transit and sojourn in any State of this Confederacy, with their slaves and other property; and the right of property in said slaves shall not be thereby impaired.

2. A person charged in any State with treason, felony, or other crime against the laws of such State, who shall flee from justice, and be found in another State, shall, on demand of the executive authority of the State from which he fled, be delivered up, to be removed to the State having jurisdiction of the crime.

3. No slave or other person held to service or labor in any State or Territory of the Confederate States, under the laws thereof, escaping or lawfully carried into another, shall, in consequence of any law or regulation therein, be discharged from such service or labor: but shall be delivered up on claim of the party to whom such slave belongs, or to whom such service or labor may be due.

Section 3.

1. Other States may be admitted into this Confederacy by a vote of two-thirds of the whole House of Representatives and two-thirds of the Senate, the Senate voting by States; but no new State shall be formed or erected within the jurisdiction of any other State; nor any State be formed by the junction of two or more States, or parts of States, without the consent of the legislatures of the States concerned, as well as of the Congress.

2. The Congress shall have power to dispose of and make all needful rules and regulations concerning the property of the Confederate States, including the lands thereof.

3. The Confederate States may acquire new territory; and Congress shall have power to legislate and provide governments for the inhabitants of all territory belonging to the Confederate States, lying without the limits of the several States; and may permit them, at such times, and in such manner as it may by law provide, to form States to be admitted into the Confederacy. In all such territory, the institution of negro slavery, as it now exists in the Confederate States, shall be recognized and protected by Congress and by the territorial government: and the inhabitants of the several Confederate States and Territories shall have the right to take to such territory any slaves lawfully held by them in any of the States or Territories of the Confederate States.

4. The Confederate States shall guarantee to every State that now is, or hereafter may become, a member of this Confederacy, a republican form of government; and shall protect each of them against invasion; and on application of the legislature, (or of the executive, when the legislature is not in session,) against domestic violence.

Article V.
Section 1.

1. Upon the demand of any three States, legally assembled in their several conventions, the Congress shall summon a convention of all the States, to take into consideration such amendments to the Constitution as the said States shall concur in suggesting at the time when the said demand is made; and should any of the proposed amendments to the Constitution be agreed on by the said convention—voting by States—and the same be ratified by the legislatures of two-thirds of the several States, or by conventions in two-thirds thereof—as the one or the other mode of ratification may be proposed by the general convention—they shall thenceforward form a part of this Constitution. But no State shall, without its consent, be deprived of its equal representation in the Senate.

Article VI.

1. The Government established by this Constitution is successor of the Provisional Government of the Confederate States of America, and all the laws passed by the latter shall continue in force until the same shall be repealed or modified; and all the officers appointed by the same shall remain in office until their successors are appointed and qualified, or the offices abolished.

2. All debts contracted and engagements entered into before the adoption of this Constitution shall be as valid against the Confederate States under this Constitution, as under the Provisional Government.

3. This Constitution, and the laws of the Confederate States, made in pursuance thereof, and all treaties made, or which shall be made, under the authority of the Confederate States, shall be the supreme law of the land; and the judges in every State shall be

bound thereby, anything in the Constitution or laws of any State to the contrary notwithstanding.

4. The Senators and Representatives before mentioned, and the members of the several State Legislatures, and all executive and judicial officers, both of the Confederate States and of the several States, shall be bound by oath or affirmation to support this Constitution; but no religious test shall ever be required as a qualification to any office or public trust under the Confederate States.

5. The enumeration, in the Constitution, of certain rights, shall not be construed to deny or disparage others retained by the people of the several States.

6. The powers not delegated to the Confederate States by the Constitution, nor prohibited by it to the States, are reserved to the States, respectively, or to the people thereof.

Article VII.

1. The ratification of the conventions of five States shall be sufficient for the establishment of this Constitution between the States so ratifying the same.

2. When five States shall have ratified this Constitution, in the manner before specified, the Congress under the Provisional Constitution shall prescribe the time for holding the election of President and Vice President; and for the meeting of the Electoral College; and for counting the votes, and inaugurating the President. They shall also prescribe the time for holding the first election of members of Congress under this Constitution, and the time for assembling the same. Until the assembling of such Congress, the Congress under the Provisional Constitution shall continue to exercise the legislative powers granted them; not extending beyond the time limited by the Constitution of the Provisional Government.

Adopted unanimously by the Congress of the Confederate States of South Carolina, Georgia, Florida, Alabama, Mississippi, Louisiana and Texas, sitting in Convention at the capitol, in the city of Montgomery, Alabama, on the Eleventh day of March, in the Year Eighteen Hundred and Sixty-One. . . .

L-3. THE EMANCIPATION PROCLAMATION
(1862–1863)

[The entire text of the two parts of the Emancipation Proclamation (September 22, 1862 and January 1, 1863) is set forth *in italics* in the course of the Eleventh Lecture in this Commentary. The Emancipation Proclamation was confirmed and extended by the Thirteenth Amendment (1865), where it is provided, "Neither slavery nor involuntary servitude, except as a punishment for crime whereof the party shall have been duly convicted, shall exist within the United States, or any place subject to their jurisdiction." This provision had been anticipated by the Northwest Ordinance (1787), where it is provided (in Article VI), "There shall be neither slavery nor involuntary servitude in the said territory [the Northwest Territory], otherwise than in punishment of crimes whereof the party shall have been duly convicted . . ."]

M. The Constitution of 1787 with Amendments (1787–1992)

M-1. THE CONSTITUTION OF 1787 (1787)

The Constitution of the United States

We the People of the United States, in Order to form a more perfect Union, establish Justice, insure domestic Tranquility, provide for the common defence, promote the general Welfare, and secure the Blessings of Liberty to ourselves and our Posterity, do ordain and establish this Constitution for the United States of America.

Article. I.

Section. 1. All legislative Powers herein granted shall be vested in a Congress of the United States, which shall consist of a Senate and a House of Representatives.

Section. 2. The House of Representatives shall be composed of Members chosen every second Year by the People of the several States, and the Electors in each State shall have the Qualifications requisite for Electors of the most numerous Branch of the State Legislature.

No person shall be a Representative who shall not have attained to the Age of twenty five Years, and been seven Years a Citizen of the United States, and who shall not, when elected, be an Inhabitant of that State in which he shall be chosen.

Representatives and direct Taxes shall be apportioned among the several States which may be included within this Union, according to their respective Numbers, which shall be determined by adding to the whole Number of free Persons, including those bound to

Service for a Term of Years, and excluding Indians not taxed, three fifths of all other Persons. The actual Enumeration shall be made within three Years after the first Meeting of the Congress of the United States, and within every subsequent Term of ten Years, in such Manner as they shall by Law direct. The Number of Representatives shall not exceed one for every thirty Thousand, but each State shall have at Least one Representative; and until such enumeration shall be made, the State of New Hampshire shall be entitled to chuse three, Massachusetts eight, Rhode-Island and Providence Plantations one, Connecticut five, New-York six, New Jersey four, Pennsylvania eight, Delaware one, Maryland six, Virginia ten, North Carolina five, South Carolina five, and Georgia three.

When vacancies happen in the Representation from any State, the Executive Authority thereof shall issue Writs of Election to fill such Vacancies.

The House of Representatives shall chuse their Speaker and other Officers; and shall have the sole Power of Impeachment.

Section. 3. The Senate of the United States shall be composed of two Senators from each State, chosen by the Legislature thereof, for six Years; and each Senator shall have one Vote.

Immediately after they shall be assembled in Consequence of the first Election, they shall be divided as equally as may be into three Classes. The Seats of the Senators of the first Class shall be vacated at the Expiration of the second Year, of the second Class at the Expiration of the fourth Year, and of the third Class at the Expiration of the sixth Year, so that one third may be chosen every second Year; and if Vacancies happen by Resignation, or otherwise, during the Recess of the Legislature of any State, the Executive thereof may make temporary Appointments until the next Meeting of the Legislature, which shall then fill such Vacancies.

No Person shall be a Senator who shall not have attained to the Age of thirty Years, and been nine Years a Citizen of the United States, and who shall not, when elected, be an Inhabitant of that State for which he shall be chosen.

The Vice President of the United States shall be President of the Senate, but shall have no Vote, unless they be equally divided.

The Senate shall chuse their other Officers, and also a President pro tempore, in the Absence of the Vice President, or when he shall exercise the Office of President of the United States.

The Senate shall have the sole Power to try all Impeachments. When sitting for that Purpose, they shall be on Oath or Affirmation. When the President of the United States is tried, the Chief Justice shall preside: And no Person shall be convicted without the Concurrence of two thirds of the Members present.

Judgment in Cases of Impeachment shall not extend further than to removal from Office, and disqualification to hold and enjoy any Office of honor, Trust or Profit under the United States: but the Party convicted shall nevertheless be liable and subject to Indictment, Trial, Judgment and Punishment, according to Law.

Section. 4. The Times, Places and Manner of holding Elections for Senators and Representatives, shall be prescribed in each State by the Legislature thereof; but the Congress may at any time by Law make or alter such Regulations, except as to the Places of chusing Senators.

The Congress shall assemble at least once in every Year, and such Meeting shall be on the first Monday in December, unless they shall by Law appoint a different Day.

Section. 5. Each House shall be the Judge of the Elections, Returns and Qualifications of its own Members, and a Majority of each shall constitute a Quorum to do Business; but a smaller Number may adjourn from day to day, and may be authorized to compel the Attendance of absent Members, in such Manner, and under such Penalties as each House may provide.

Each House may determine the Rules of its Proceedings, punish its Members for disorderly Behaviour, and, with the Concurrence of two thirds, expel a Member.

Each House shall keep a Journal of its Proceedings, and from time to time publish the same, excepting such Parts as may in their Judgment require Secrecy; and the Yeas and Nays of the Members of either House on any question shall, at the Desire of one fifth of those Present, be entered on the Journal.

Neither House, during the Session of Congress, shall, without the Consent of the other, adjourn for more than three days, nor to any other Place than that in which the two Houses shall be sitting.

Section. 6. The Senators and Representatives shall receive a Compensation for their Services, to be ascertained by Law, and paid out of the Treasury of the United States. They shall in all Cases, except Treason, Felony and Breach of the Peace, be privileged from Arrest during their Attendance at the Session of their respective Houses, and in going to and returning from the same; and for any Speech or Debate in either House, they shall not be questioned in any other Place.

No Senator or Representative shall, during the Time for which he was elected, be appointed to any civil Office under the Authority of the United States, which shall have been created, or the Emoluments whereof shall have been encreased during such time; and no Person holding any Office under the United States, shall be a Member of either House during his Continuance in Office.

Section. 7. All Bills for raising Revenue shall originate in the House of Representatives; but the Senate may propose or concur with Amendments as on other Bills.

Every Bill which shall have passed the House of Representatives and the Senate, shall, before it become a Law, be presented to the President of the United States; If he approve he shall sign it, but if not he shall return it, with his Objections to that House in which it shall have originated, who shall enter the Objections at large on their Journal, and proceed to reconsider it. If after such Reconsideration two thirds of that House shall agree to pass the Bill, it shall be sent, together with the Objections, to the other House, by which it shall likewise be reconsidered, and if approved by two thirds of that House, it shall become a Law. But in all such Cases the Votes of both Houses shall be determined by yeas and Nays, and the Names of the Persons voting for and against the Bill shall be entered on the Journal of each House respectively. If any Bill shall not be returned by the President within ten days (Sundays excepted) after it shall have been presented to him, the Same shall be a Law, in like Manner as if he had signed it, unless the Congress by their Adjournment prevent its Return in which Case it shall not be a Law.

Every Order, Resolution, or Vote to which the Concurrence of the Senate and House of Representatives may be necessary (except on a question of Adjournment) shall be presented to the President of the United States; and before the Same shall take Effect, shall be approved by him, or being disapproved by him, shall be repassed by two thirds of the Senate and House of Representatives, according to the Rules and Limitations prescribed in the Case of a Bill.

Section. 8. The Congress shall have Power

To lay and collect Taxes, Duties, Imposts and Excises, to pay the

Debts and provide for the common Defence and general Welfare of the United States; but all Duties, Imposts and Excises shall be uniform throughout the United States;

To borrow Money on the credit of the United States;

To regulate Commerce with foreign Nations, and among the several States, and with the Indian Tribes;

To establish an uniform Rule of Naturalization, and uniform Laws on the subject of Bankruptcies throughout the United States;

To coin Money, regulate the Value thereof, and of foreign Coin, and fix the Standard of Weights and Measures;

To provide for the Punishment of counterfeiting the Securities and current Coin of the United States;

To establish Post Offices and post Roads;

To promote the Progress of Science and useful Arts, by securing for limited Times to Authors and Inventors the exclusive Right to their respective Writings and Discoveries;

To constitute Tribunals inferior to the supreme Court;

To define and punish Piracies and Felonies committed on the high Seas, and Offences against the Law of Nations;

To declare War, grant Letters of Marque and Reprisal, and make Rules concerning Captures on Land and Water;

To raise and support Armies, but no Appropriation of Money to that Use shall be for a longer Term than two Years;

To provide and maintain a Navy;

To make Rules for the Government and Regulation of the land and naval Forces;

To provide for calling forth the Militia to execute the Laws of the Union, suppress Insurrections and repel Invasions;

To provide for organizing, arming, and disciplining, the Militia, and for governing such Part of them as may be employed in the Service of the United States, reserving to the States respectively, the Appointment of the Officers, and the Authority of training the Militia according to the discipline prescribed by Congress;

To exercise exclusive Legislation in all Cases whatsoever, over such District (not exceeding ten Miles square) as may, by Cession of particular States, and the Acceptance of Congress, become the Seat of the Government of the Unites States, and to exercise like Authority over all Places purchased by the Consent of the Legislature of the State in which the Same shall be, for the Erection of Forts,

Magazines, Arsenals, dock-Yards, and other needful Buildings; —And

To make all Laws which shall be necessary and proper for carrying into Execution the foregoing Powers, and all other Powers vested by this Constitution in the Government of the United States, or in any Department or Officer thereof.

Section. 9. The Migration or Importation of such Persons as any of the States now existing shall think proper to admit, shall not be prohibited by the Congress prior to the Year one thousand eight hundred and eight, but a Tax or duty may be imposed on such Importation, not exceeding ten dollars for each Person.

The Privilege of the Writ of Habeas Corpus shall not be suspended, unless when in Cases of Rebellion or Invasion the public Safety may require it.

No Bill of Attainder or ex post facto Law shall be passed.

No Capitation, or other direct, Tax shall be laid, unless in Proportion to the Census or Enumeration herein before directed to be taken.

No Tax or Duty shall be laid on Articles exported from any State.

No Preference shall be given by any Regulation of Commerce or Revenue to the Ports of one State over those of another: nor shall Vessels bound to, or from, one State, be obliged to enter, clear, or pay Duties in another.

No Money shall be drawn from the Treasury, but in Consequence of Appropriations made by Law; and a regular Statement and Account of the Receipts and Expenditures of all public Money shall be published from time to time.

No Title of Nobility shall be granted by the United States: And no Person holding any Office of Profit or Trust under them, shall, without the Consent of the Congress, accept of any present, Emolument, Office, or Title, of any kind whatever, from any King, Prince, or foreign State.

Section. 10. No State shall enter into any Treaty, Alliance, or Confederation; grant Letters of Marque and Reprisal; coin Money; emit Bills of Credit; make any Thing but gold and silver Coin a Tender in Payment of Debts; pass any Bill of Attainder, ex post facto Law, or Law impairing the Obligation of Contracts, or grant any Title of Nobility.

No State shall, without the Consent of the Congress, lay any

Imposts or Duties on Imports or Exports, except what may be absolutely necessary for executing it's inspection Laws: and the net Produce of all Duties and Imposts, laid by any State on Imports or Exports, shall be for the Use of the Treasury of the United States; and all such Laws shall be subject to the Revision and Controul of the Congress.

No State shall, without the Consent of Congress, lay any Duty of Tonnage, keep Troops, or Ships of War in time of Peace, enter into any Agreement or Compact with another State, or with a foreign Power, or engage in War, unless actually invaded, or in such imminent Danger as will not admit of delay.

Article. II.

Section. 1. The executive Power shall be vested in a President of the United States of America. He shall hold his Office during the Term of four Years, and, together with the Vice President, chosen for the same Term, be elected, as follows

Each State shall appoint, in such Manner as the Legislature thereof may direct, a Number of Electors, equal to the whole Number of Senators and Representatives to which the State may be entitled in the Congress: but no Senator or Representative, or Person holding an Office of Trust or Profit under the United States, shall be appointed an Elector.

The Electors shall meet in their respective States, and vote by Ballot for two Persons, of whom one at least shall not be an Inhabitant of the same State with themselves. And they shall make a List of all the Persons voted for, and of the Number of Votes for each; which List they shall sign and certify, and transmit sealed to the Seat of the Government of the United States, directed to the President of the Senate. The President of the Senate shall, in the Presence of the Senate and House of Representatives, open all the Certificates, and the Votes shall then be counted. The Person having the greatest Number of Votes shall be the President, if such Number be a Majority of the whole Number of Electors appointed; and if there be more than one who have such Majority, and have an equal Number of Votes, then the House of Representatives shall immediately chuse by Ballot one of them for President; and if no Person have a Majority, then from the five highest on the List the said

House shall in like Manner chuse the President. But in chusing the President, the Votes shall be taken by States, the Representation from each State having one Vote; A quorum for this Purpose shall consist of a Member or Members from two thirds of the States, and a Majority of all the States shall be necessary to a Choice. In every Case, after the Choice of the President, the Person having the greatest Number of Votes of the Electors shall be the Vice President. But if there should remain two or more who have equal Votes, the Senate shall chuse from them by Ballot the Vice President.

The Congress may determine the Time of chusing the Electors, and the Day on which they shall give their Votes; which Day shall be the same throughout the United States.

No Person except a natural born Citizen, or a Citizen of the United States, at the time of the Adoption of this Constitution, shall be eligible to the Office of President; neither shall any Person be eligible to that Office who shall not have attained to the Age of thirty five Years, and been fourteen Years a Resident within the United States.

In Case of the Removal of the President from Office, or of his Death, Resignation, or Inability to discharge the Powers and Duties of the said Office, the Same shall devolve on the Vice President, and the Congress may by Law provide for the Case of Removal, Death, Resignation or Inability, both of the President and Vice President, declaring what Officer shall then act as President, and such Officer shall act accordingly, until the Disability be removed, or a President shall be elected.

The President shall, at stated Times, receive for his Services, a Compensation, which shall neither be encreased nor diminished during the Period for which he shall have been elected, and he shall not receive within that Period any other Emolument from the United States, or any of them.

Before he enter on the Execution of his Office, he shall take the following Oath or Affirmation:—"I do solemnly swear (or affirm) that I will faithfully execute the Office of President of the United States, and will to the best of my Ability, preserve, protect and defend the Constitution of the United States."

Section. 2. The President shall be Commander in Chief of the Army and Navy of the United States, and of the Militia of the several States, when called into the actual Service of the United

States; he may require the Opinion, in writing, of the principal Officer in each of the executive Departments, upon any Subject relating to the Duties of their respective Offices, and he shall have Power to grant Reprieves and Pardons for Offences against the United States, except in Cases of Impeachment.

He shall have Power, by and with the Advice and Consent of the Senate, to make Treaties, provided two thirds of the Senators present concur; and he shall nominate, and by and with the Advice and Consent of the Senate, shall appoint Ambassadors, other public Ministers and Consuls, Judges of the supreme Court, and all other Officers of the United States, whose Appointments are not herein otherwise provided for, and which shall be established by Law: but the Congress may by Law vest the Appointment of such inferior Officers, as they think proper, in the President alone, in the Courts of Law, or in the Heads of Departments.

The President shall have Power to fill up all Vacancies that may happen during the Recess of the Senate, by granting Commissions which shall expire at the End of their next Session.

Section. 3. He shall from time to time give to the Congress Information of the State of the Union, and recommend to their Consideration such Measures as he shall judge necessary and expedient; he may, on extraordinary Occasions, convene both Houses, or either of them, and in Case of Disagreement between them, with Respect to the Time of Adjournment, he may adjourn them to such Time as he shall think proper; he shall receive Ambassadors and other public Ministers; he shall take Care that the Laws be faithfully executed, and shall Commission all the Officers of the United States.

Section. 4. The President, Vice President and all civil Officers of the United States, shall be removed from Office on Impeachment for, and Conviction of, Treason, Bribery, or other high Crimes and Misdemeanors.

Article. III.

Section. 1. The judicial Power of the United States, shall be vested in one supreme Court, and in such inferior Courts as the Congress may from time to time ordain and establish. The Judges, both of the supreme and inferior Courts, shall hold their Offices during good Behaviour, and shall, at stated Times, receive for their Services, a

Compensation, which shall not be diminished during their Continuance in Office.

Section. 2. The judicial Power shall extend to all Cases, in Law and Equity, arising under this Constitution, the Laws of the United States, and Treaties made, or which shall be made, under their Authority;—to all Cases affecting Ambassadors, other public Ministers and Consuls;—to all Cases of admiralty and maritime Jurisdiction;—to Controversies to which the United States shall be a Party;—to Controversies between two or more States;—between a State and Citizens of another State;—between Citizens of different States,—between Citizens of the same State claiming Lands under Grants of different States, and between a State, or the Citizens thereof, and foreign States, Citizens or Subjects.

In all Cases affecting Ambassadors, other public Ministers and Consuls, and those in which a State shall be a Party, the supreme Court shall have original Jurisdiction. In all the other Cases before mentioned, the supreme Court shall have appellate Jurisdiction, both as to Law and Fact, with such Exceptions, and under such Regulations as the Congress shall make.

The Trial of all Crimes, except in Cases of Impeachment, shall be by Jury; and such Trial shall be held in the State where the said Crimes shall have been committed; but when not committed within any State, the Trial shall be at such Place or Places as the Congress may by Law have directed.

Section. 3. Treason against the United States, shall consist only in levying War against them, or in adhering to their Enemies, giving them Aid and Comfort. No Person shall be convicted of Treason unless on the Testimony of two Witnesses to the same overt Act, or on Confession in open Court.

The Congress shall have Power to declare the Punishment of Treason, but no Attainder of Treason shall work Corruption of Blood, or Forfeiture except during the Life of the Person attainted.

Article. IV.

Section. 1. Full Faith and Credit shall be given in each State to the public Acts, Records, and judicial Proceedings of every other State. And the Congress may by general Laws prescribe the Manner in which such Acts, Records and Proceedings shall be proved, and the Effect thereof.

Section. 2. The Citizens of each State shall be entitled to all Privileges and Immunities of Citizens in the several States.

A Person charged in any State with Treason, Felony, or other Crime, who shall flee from Justice, and be found in another State, shall on Demand of the executive Authority of the State from which he fled, be delivered up, to be removed to the State having Jurisdiction of the Crime.

No Person held to Service or Labour in one State, under the Laws thereof, escaping into another, shall, in Consequence of any Law or Regulation therein, be discharged from such Service or Labour, but shall be delivered up on Claim of the Party to whom such Service or Labour may be due.

Section. 3. New States may be admitted by the Congress into this Union; but no new State shall be formed or erected within the Jurisdiction of any other State; nor any State be formed by the Junction of two or more States, or Parts of States, without the Consent of the Legislatures of the States concerned as well as of the Congress.

The Congress shall have Power to dispose of and make all needful Rules and Regulations respecting the Territory or other Property belonging to the United States; and nothing in this Constitution shall be so construed as to Prejudice any Claims of the United States, or of any particular State.

Section. 4. The United States shall guarantee to every State in this Union a Republican Form of Government, and shall protect each of them against Invasion; and on Application of the Legislature, or of the Executive (when the Legislature cannot be convened) against domestic Violence.

Article. V.

The Congress, whenever two thirds of both Houses shall deem it necessary, shall propose Amendments to this Constitution, or, on the Application of the Legislatures of two thirds of the several States, shall call a Convention for proposing Amendments, which, in either Case, shall be valid to all Intents and Purposes, as Part of this Constitution, when ratified by the Legislatures of three fourths of the several States, or by Conventions in three fourths thereof, as the one or the other Mode of Ratification may be proposed by the Congress; Provided that no Amendment which may be made prior to the Year One thousand eight hundred and eight shall in any Manner affect the first and fourth Clauses in the Ninth Section of the first Article; and that no State, without its Consent, shall be deprived of it's equal Suffrage in the Senate.

Article. VI.

All Debts contracted and Engagements entered into, before the Adoption of this Constitution, shall be as valid against the United States under this Constitution, as under the Confederation.

This Constitution, and the Laws of the United States which shall be made in Pursuance thereof; and all Treaties made, or which shall be made, under the Authority of the United States, shall be the supreme Law of the Land; and the Judges in every State shall be bound thereby, any Thing in the Constitution or Laws of any State to the Contrary notwithstanding.

The Senators and Representatives before mentioned, and the Members of the several State Legislatures, and all executive and judicial Officers, both of the United States and of the several States, shall be bound by Oath or Affirmation, to support this Constitution; but no religious Test shall ever be required as a Qualification to any Office or public Trust under the United States.

Article. VII.

The Ratification of the Conventions of nine States, shall be sufficient for the Establishment of this Constitution between the States so ratifying the Same.

done in Convention by the Unanimous Consent of the States present the Seventeenth Day of September in the Year of our Lord one thousand seven hundred and Eighty seven and of the Independence of the United States of America the Twelfth In Witness whereof We have hereunto subscribed our Names, . . . [The names of the witnesses are collected by States, following upon the signature of George Washington as President of the Federal Convention: *New Hampshire*: John Langdon, Nicholas Gilman; *Massachusetts*: Nathaniel Gorham, Rufus King; *Connecticut*: Wm Saml Johnson, Roger Sherman; *New York*: Alexander Hamilton; *New Jersey*: Wil: Livingston, David Brearley, Wm Paterson, Jona: Dayton; *Pennsylvania*: B. Franklin, Thomas Mifflin, Robt Morris, Geo. Clymer, Thos Fitz-Simons, Jared Ingersoll, James Wilson, Gouv Morris; *Delaware*: Geo: Read, Gunning Bedford jun, John Dickinson, Richard Bassett, Jaco: Broom; *Maryland*: James McHenry, Dan of St Thos Jenifer, Danl Carroll; *Virginia*: John Blair, James Madison Jr.; *North Carolina*: Wm Blount, Richd Dobbs Spaight, Hu Williamson; *South Carolina*: J. Rutledge, Charles Cotesworth Pinckney, Charles Pinckney, Pierce Butler; *Georgia*: William Few, Abr Baldwin.]

M-2. AMENDMENTS TO THE CONSTITUTION OF 1787 (1791–1992)

Amendments to the Constitution

First Article of Amendment [1791]

Congress shall make no law respecting an establishment of religion, or prohibiting the free exercise thereof; or abridging the freedom of speech, or of the press, or the right of the people peaceably to assemble, and to petition the Government for a redress of grievances.

Second Article of Amendment [1791]

A well regulated Militia, being necessary to the security of a free State, the right of the people to keep and bear Arms, shall not be infringed.

Third Article of Amendment [1791]

No Soldier shall, in time of peace be quartered in any house, without the consent of the Owner, nor in time of war, but in a manner to be prescribed by law.

Fourth Article of Amendment [1791]

The right of the people to be secure in their persons, houses, papers, and effects, against unreasonable searches and seizures, shall not be violated, and no Warrants shall issue, but upon probable cause, supported by Oath or affirmation, and particularly describing the place to be searched, and the persons or things to be seized.

Fifth Article of Amendment [1791]

No person shall be held to answer for a capital, or otherwise infamous crime, unless on a presentment or indictment of a Grand Jury, except in cases arising in the land or naval forces, or in the Militia, when in actual service in time of War or public danger; nor shall any person be subject for the same offence to be twice put in jeopardy of life or limb, nor shall be compelled in any criminal case to be a witness against himself, nor be deprived of life, liberty, or property, without due process of law; nor shall private property be taken for public use without just compensation.

Sixth Article of Amendment [1791]

In all criminal prosecutions, the accused shall enjoy the right to a speedy and public trial, by an impartial jury of the State and district wherein the crime shall have been committed, which district shall have been previously ascertained by law, and to be informed of the nature and cause of the accusation; to be confronted with the witnesses against him; to have compulsory process for obtaining witnesses in his favor, and to have the Assistance of Counsel for his defence.

Seventh Article of Amendment [1791]

In Suits at common law, where the value in controversy shall exceed twenty dollars, the right of trial by jury shall be preserved, and no fact tried by a jury shall be otherwise re-examined in any Court of the United States, than according to the rules of the common law.

Eighth Article of Amendment [1791]

Excessive bail shall not be required, nor excessive fines imposed, nor cruel and unusual punishments inflicted.

Ninth Article of Amendment [1791]

The enumeration in the Constitution, of certain rights, shall not be construed to deny or disparage others retained by the people.

Tenth Article of Amendment [1791]

The powers not delegated to the United States by the Constitution, nor prohibited by it to the States, are reserved to the States respectively, or to the people.

Eleventh Article of Amendment [1798]

The Judicial power of the United States shall not be construed to extend to any suit in law or equity, commenced or prosecuted against one of the United States by Citizens of another State, or by Citizens or Subjects of any Foreign State.

Twelfth Article of Amendment [1804]

The Electors shall meet in their respective states, and vote by ballot for President and Vice-President, one of whom, at least, shall not be an inhabitant of the same state with themselves; they shall name in their ballots the person voted for as President, and in distinct ballots the person voted for as Vice-President, and they shall make distinct lists of all persons voted for as President, and of all persons voted for as Vice-President, and of the number of votes for each, which lists they shall sign and certify, and transmit sealed to the seat of the government of the United States, directed to the President of the Senate;—The President of the Senate shall, in the presence of the Senate and House of Representatives, open all the certificates and the votes shall then be counted;—The person having the greatest number of votes for President, shall be the President, if such number be a majority of the whole number of Electors appointed; and if no person have such majority, then from the persons having the highest numbers not exceeding three on the list of those voted for as President, the House of Representatives shall choose immediately, by ballot, the President. But in choosing the President, the votes shall be taken by states, the representation from each state having one vote; a quorum for this purpose shall consist of a member or members from two-thirds of the states, and a majority of all the states shall be necessary to a choice. And if the House of Representatives shall not choose a President whenever the right of choice shall devolve upon them, before the fourth day of March next following, then the Vice-President shall act as President, as in the case of the death or other constitutional disability of the President.—

377

The person having the greatest number of votes as Vice-President, shall be the Vice-President, if such number be a majority of the whole number of Electors appointed, and if no person have a majority, then from the two highest numbers on the list, the Senate shall choose the Vice-President; a quorum for the purpose shall consist of two-thirds of the whole number of Senators, and a majority of the whole number shall be necessary to a choice. But no person constitutionally ineligible to the office of President shall be eligible to that of Vice-President of the United States.

Thirteenth Article of Amendment [1865]

Section 1. Neither slavery nor involuntary servitude, except as a punishment for crime whereof the party shall have been duly convicted, shall exist within the United States, or any place subject to their jurisdiction.

Section 2. Congress shall have power to enforce this article by appropriate legislation.

Fourteenth Article of Amendment [1868]

Section 1. All persons born or naturalized in the United States, and subject to the jurisdiction thereof, are citizens of the United States and of the State wherein they reside. No State shall make or enforce any law which shall abridge the privileges or immunities of citizens of the United States; nor shall any State deprive any person of life, liberty, or property, without due process of law; nor deny to any person within its jurisdiction the equal protection of the laws.

Section 2. Representatives shall be apportioned among the several States according to their respective numbers, counting the whole number of persons in each State, excluding Indians not taxed. But when the right to vote at any election for the choice of electors for President and Vice President of the United States, Representatives in Congress, the Executive and Judicial officers of a State, or the members of the Legislature thereof, is denied to any of the male inhabitants of such State, being twenty-one years of age, and citizens of the United States, or in any way abridged, except for participation in rebellion, or other crime, the basis of representation therein shall be reduced in the proportion which the number of such male citizens shall bear to the whole number of male citizens twenty-one years of age in such State.

Section 3. No person shall be a Senator or Representative in Congress, or elector of President and Vice President, or hold any office, civil or military, under the United States, or under any State, who, having previously taken an oath, as a member of Congress, or as an officer of the United States, or as a member of any State legislature, or as an executive or judicial officer of any State, to support the Constitution of the United States, shall have engaged in insurrection or rebellion against the same, or given aid or comfort to the enemies thereof. But Congress may be a vote of two-thirds of each House, remove such disability.

Section 4. The validity of the public debt of the United States, authorized by law, including debts incurred for payment of pensions and bounties for services in suppressing insurrection or rebellion, shall not be questioned. But neither the United States nor any State shall assume or pay any debt or obligation incurred in aid of insurrection or rebellion against the United States, or any claim for the loss or emancipation of any slave; but all such debts, obligations and claims shall be held illegal and void.

Section 5. The Congress shall have power to enforce, by appropriate legislation, the provisions of this article.

Fifteenth Article of Amendment [1870]

Section 1. The right of citizens of the United States to vote shall not be denied or abridged by the United States or by any State on account of race, color, or previous condition of servitude.

Section 2. The Congress shall have power to enforce this article by appropriate legislation.

Sixteenth Article of Amendment [1913]

The Congress shall have power to lay and collect taxes on incomes, from whatever source derived, without apportionment among the several States, and without regard to any census or enumeration.

Seventeenth Article of Amendment [1913]

The Senate of the United States shall be composed of two Senators from each State, elected by the people thereof, for six years; and each Senator shall have one vote. The electors in each State shall have the qualifications requisite for electors of the most numerous branch of the State legislatures.

When vacancies happen in the representation of any State in the Senate, the executive authority of such State shall issue writs of election to fill such vacancies: *Provided,* That the legislature of any State may empower the executive thereof to make temporary appointments until the people fill the vacancies by election as the legislature may direct.

This amendment shall not be so construed as to affect the election or term of any Senator chosen before it becomes valid as part of the Constitution.

Eighteenth Article of Amendment [1919]

Section 1. After one year from the ratification of this article the manufacture, sale, or transportation of intoxicating liquors within, the importation thereof into, or the exportation thereof from the United States and all territory subject to the jurisdiction thereof for beverage purposes is hereby prohibited.

Sec. 2. The Congress and the several States shall have concurrent power to enforce this article by appropriate legislation.

Sec. 3. This article shall be inoperative unless it shall have been ratified as an amendment to the Constitution by the legislatures of the several States, as provided in the Constitution, within seven years from the date of the submission hereof to the States by the Congress.

Nineteenth Article of Amendment [1920]

The right of citizens of the United States to vote shall not be denied or abridged by the United States or by any State on account of sex.

Congress shall have power to enforce this article by appropriate legislation.

Twentieth Article of Amendment [1933]

Section 1. The terms of the President and Vice President shall end at noon on the 20th day of January, and the terms of Senators and

Representatives at noon on the 3d day of January, of the years in which such terms would have ended if this article had not been ratified; and the terms of their successors shall then begin.

Sec. 2. The Congress shall assemble at least once in every year, and such meeting shall begin at noon on the 3d day of January, unless they shall by law appoint a different day.

Sec. 3. If, at the time fixed for the beginning of the term of the President, the President elect shall have died, the Vice President elect shall become President. If a President shall not have been chosen before the time fixed for the beginning of his term, or if the President elect shall have failed to qualify, then the Vice President elect shall act as President until a President shall have qualified; and the Congress may by law provide for the case wherein neither a President elect nor a Vice President elect shall have qualified, declaring who shall then act as President, or the manner in which one who is to act shall be selected, and such person shall act accordingly until a President or Vice President shall have qualified.

Sec. 4. The Congress may by law provide for the case of the death of any of the persons from whom the House of Representatives may choose a President whenever the right of choice shall have devolved upon them, and for the case of the death of any of the persons from whom the Senate may choose a Vice President whenever the right of choice shall have devolved upon them.

Sec. 5. Sections 1 and 2 shall take effect on the 15th day of October following the ratification of this article.

Sec. 6. This article shall be inoperative unless it shall have been ratified as an amendment to the Constitution by the legislatures of three-fourths of the several States within seven years from the date of its submission.

Twenty-first Article of Amendment [1933]

Section 1. The eighteenth article of amendment to the Constitution of the United States is hereby repealed.

Sec. 2. The transportation or importation into any State, Territory, or possession of the United States for delivery or use therein of intoxicating liquors, in violation of the laws thereof, is hereby prohibited.

Sec. 3. This article shall be inoperative unless it shall have been ratified as an amendment to the Constitution by conventions in the several States, as provided in the Constitution, within seven years from the date of the submission hereof to the States by the Congress.

Twenty-second Article of Amendment [1951]

Section 1. No person shall be elected to the office of the President more than twice, and no person who has held the office of President, or acted as President, for more than two years of a term to which some other person was elected President shall be elected to the office of the President more than once. But this Article shall not apply to any person holding the office of President when this Article was proposed by the Congress, and shall not prevent any person who may be holding the office of President, or acting as President, during the term within which this Article becomes operative from holding the office of President or acting as President during the remainder of such term.

Sec. 2. This article shall be inoperative unless it shall have been ratified as an amendment to the Constitution by the legislatures of three-fourths of the several States within seven years from the date of its submission to the States by the Congress.

Twenty-third Article of Amendment [1961]

Section 1. The District constituting the seat of Government of the United States shall appoint in such manner as the Congress may direct:

A number of electors of President and Vice President equal to the whole number of Senators and Representatives in Congress to which the District would be entitled if it were a State, but in no event more than the least populous State; they shall be in addition to those appointed by the States, but they shall be considered, for the purposes of the election of President and Vice President, to be electors appointed by a State; and they shall meet in the District and perform such duties as provided by the twelfth article of amendment.

Section 2. The Congress shall have power to enforce this article by appropriate legislation.

Twenty-fourth Article of Amendment [1964]

Section 1. The right of citizens of the United States to vote in any primary or other election for President or Vice President, for electors for President or Vice President, or for Senator or Representative in Congress, shall not be denied or abridged by the United States or any State by reason of failure to pay any poll tax or other tax.

Section 2. The Congress shall have power to enforce this article by appropriate legislation.

Twenty-fifth Article of Amendment [1967]

Section 1. In case of the removal of the President from office or of his death or resignation, the Vice President shall become President.

Sec. 2. Whenever there is a vacancy in the office of the Vice President, the President shall nominate a Vice President who shall take office upon confirmation by a majority vote of both Houses of Congress.

Sec. 3. Whenever the President transmits to the President pro tempore of the Senate and the Speaker of the House of Representatives his written declaration that he is unable to discharge the powers and duties of his office, and until he transmits to them a written declaration to the contrary, such powers and duties shall be discharged by the Vice President as Acting President.

Sec. 4. Whenever the Vice President and a majority of either the principal officers of the executive departments or of such other body as Congress may by law provide, transmit to the President pro tempore of the Senate and the Speaker of the House of Representatives their written declaration that the President is unable to discharge the powers and duties of his office, the Vice President shall immediately assume the powers and duties of the office as Acting President.

Thereafter, when the President transmits to the President pro tempore of the Senate and the Speaker of the House of Representatives his written declaration that no inability exists, he shall resume the powers and duties of his office unless the Vice President and a majority of either the principal officers of the executive department or of such other body as Congress may by law provide, transmit within four days to the President pro tempore of the Senate and the Speaker of the House of Representatives their written declaration that the President is unable to discharge the powers and duties of his office. Thereupon Congress shall decide the issue, assembling within forty-eight hours for that purpose if not in session. If the

383

Congress, within twenty-one days after receipt of the latter written declaration, or, if Congress is not in session, within twenty-one days after Congress is required to assemble, determines by two-thirds vote of both Houses that the President is unable to discharge the powers and duties of his office, the Vice President shall continue to discharge the same as Acting President; otherwise, the President shall resume the powers and duties of his office.

Twenty-sixth Article of Amendment [1971]

Sec. 1. The right of citizens of the United States, who are eighteen years of age or older, to vote shall not be denied or abridged by the United States or by any State on account of age.

Sec. 2. The Congress shall have power to enforce this article by appropriate legislation.

Twenty-seventh Article of Amendment [1992]

No law varying the compensation for the services of the Senators and Representative shall take effect until an election of Representatives shall have intervened.

[Excerpts from the version of a Balanced Budget Amendment approved by the House of Representatives on January 26, 1995, may be found in Lecture No. 14, Section IX, of this Commentary. This proposed amendment, if it should happen to be approved by the Senate and by three-fourths of the States, would be the twenty-eighth Amendment.]

Notes

1. The American Revolutionary War struggle, ending with the Treaty of Paris (1783–1784), can be said to have begun in 1774 with the first meeting of the Continental Congress. See Lecture No. 1, Section II, of this Commentary. "That [George III] failed in the central problems of his reign may, in the long run of events, have been fortunate for the ultimate liberty of England. Out of the disasters that ensued, rose the Parliamentary system of government as we now know it." Winston Churchill, *A History of the English-Speaking Peoples* (New York: Bantam Books, 1963), 136.

The American Civil War struggle, ending with the disintegration of the Confederacy in 1865 after the surrender of his army by General Robert E. Lee, can be said to have begun in 1857 with the remarkably divisive action by the United States Supreme Court in *Dred Scott* v. *Sanford*, 60 U.S. (19 How.) 393 (1857), if not with the Kansas-Nebraska Act of 1854. See Lecture No. 7, Section III, of this Commentary. The Civil War may have done for the American Republic what the killing by Junius Brutus of his sons did for the Roman Republic. See Niccolò Machiavelli, *Discourses on the First Decade of Titus Livy*, III, 3; Anastaplo, "The Constitution at Two Hundred: Explorations," *Texas Tech Law Review*, 22: 968, 978 (1991); notes 146, 195, and 260, below; Lecture No. 12, Section XII, of this Commentary. (For a helpful translation of the *Discourses*, see the English-language version to be published in 1995 by Leo Paul S. de Alvarez, who provided us as well the first reliable translation into English of Machiavelli's *The Prince*.)

Two other great struggles on this Continent, which have had some of the features of civil wars, were the relentless campaigns against the indigenous tribes (to which the Mexican War is related) and the complicated efforts to deal properly with enslaved Africans and their partially emancipated descendants. See the texts at notes 166 and 177 of this Commentary. See, on the fate of indigenous tribes in this Country, Anastaplo, "An Introduction to North American Indian Thought," *Great Ideas Today*, 1993: 252 (1993). See also note 177, below. See as well the end of Section VIII of Lecture No. 12 of this Commentary.

The hopes and related challenges of the American enterprise are suggested in note 134, below. Its risks and related challenges are indicated in notes 130 and 131, below. See, for further discussions by me of American constitutionalism and related matters, "George Anastaplo: An Autobiographical Bibliography (1947–1992)," in *Law and Philosophy: The Practice of Theory,* John A. Murley, Robert L. Stone & William T. Braithwaite, eds. (Athens, Ohio: Ohio University Press, 1992), 2: 1073–1146. (Cited hereafter as *Law and Philosophy.*) See, for reviews over the years of my books, *Law and Philosophy,* 1: 539–600. See also notes 12 and 106, below. (My bibliography is brought up to date by entries in the general bibliography in political philosophy prepared by Professor Murley of the Rochester Institute of Technology.)

The sources of the nine epigraphs for this Commentary are the following:

1. Plato: *Euthydemus* 296A–B.
2. Acts of the Apostles: Acts 22: 25–26, 29. See also George Anastaplo, "Rome, Piety, and Law: Explorations," *Loyola of New Orleans Law Review,* 39: 1, 32, 39 (1993). (Cited hereafter as "Rome, Piety, and Law.")
3. Thomas Jefferson: *Autobiography* (1821), in S. K. Padover, ed., *The Complete Jefferson* (New York: Duell, Sloan & Pearce, 1943), 1191. See also William Blackstone, *Commentaries on the Laws of England* (1765–1769, 1: 304f. (Cited hereafter as Blackstone. I use here the four Blackstone volumes republished recently by the University of Chicago Press.) See as well note 33, below.
4. Winston S. Churchill: Howard La Fay, "'Be Ye Men of Valor,'" *National Geographic,* August 1965, 150, 151.
5. Leo Strauss: *Socrates and Aristophanes* (New York: Basic Books, 1966), 184.
6. Edmund Burke: *Reflections on the Revolution in France* (Indianapolis: Library of Liberal Arts, Bobbs-Merrill Co., 1965), 24.
7. Harry V. Jaffa: *Original Intent and the Framers of the Constitution* (Washington, D.C.: Regnery Gateway, 1994), 386 n. 12. (Cited hereafter as *Original Intent.*) Even so, Abraham Lincoln addressed in his First Inaugural Address and thereafter the question of the proper exercise of the right of revolution. See note 232, below. See also note 11, below.
8. Ulysses S. Grant: *Personal Memoirs* (New York: Charles L. Webster and Co., 1894), 629–30, 665. See also note 156, below.
9. Hugo L. Black: *The Bar Admission Cases,* 366 U.S. 82, 116 (1961) (dissenting opinion). See also Studs Terkel, "We Must Not Be Afraid To Be Free: Interviews With George Anastaplo," in *Law and Philosophy,* 1: 504; Harry Kalven, Jr., "Wondrous Complexity," The Bar Admission Cases," ibid., 1: 413; Laurence Berns, "Two Old Conservatives," ibid., 1: 496; Irving Dilliard, "Mr. Justice Black," ibid., 1: 478; Andrew Patner, "The Quest of George Anastaplo," ibid., 1: 582; Maurice F. X. Donohue, "Making a Living, Making a Life," ibid., 1: 597; Anastaplo, "What Is Still Wrong With George Anastaplo?," *DePaul Law Review,* 35: 559 n. 38, 575 (1986), "Freedom of Speech and the First Amendment: Explorations," *Texas Tech Law Review,* 21: 2041–51, 2065–84 (Parts VII and IX) (1990); Jaffa, *Original Intent,* 232–34 n. 33, 375f, 385 n. 10; note 66, below. ("Freedom of Speech and the First Amendment" has been reprinted in James L. Swanson, ed., *First Amendment Law Handbook, 1993–1994* [New York:

Clark Boardman Callaghan, 1993], 61–184. See as well Roger K. Newman, *Hugo Black: A Biography* (New York: Pantheon Books, 1994), 502–7; the Conley-Kaminsky citation, note 260, below.

2. The Declaration of Independence and the Gettysburg Address are among the items collected in the Appendixes of George Anastaplo, *The Constitution of 1787: A Commentary* (Baltimore: Johns Hopkins University Press, 1989), 235–302. (Cited hereafter as *The Constitution of 1787.*) If any American or English constitutional document is quoted in the text of this Commentary without citation, it is likely to be found either in the Appendixes of *The Constitution of 1787* or in the Appendixes of this Commentary, *The Amendments to the Constitution.* All italics in the quotations in this Commentary are in the sources quoted, unless otherwise indicated.

The Appendixes of *The Constitution of 1787* include the following items: The Declaration of Independence (1776); The Articles of Confederation and Perpetual Union (1776–1781); Congressional Resolution Calling the Federal Convention (1787); The Northwest Ordinance (1787) (with the Act of the First Congress reenacting the Northwest Ordinance); The United States Constitution (1787); Resolutions of the Federal Convention Providing for Transmittal of the Proposed Constitution to the Confederation Congress (1787); Letter Transmitting the Proposed Constitution from the Federal Convention to the Confederation Congress (1787); Congressional Resolution Transmitting the Proposed Constitution to the States (1787); Congressional Act for Putting the Constitution into Operation (1788) (with a listing of the States' ratifications of the Constitution); Amendments to the Constitution of the United States (1791–1971); Proposed Amendments to the Constitution Not Ratified by the States (1789–1978); The Gettysburg Address (1863); and the Second Inaugural Address of Abraham Lincoln (1865). That Commentary, as indicated in its Index, includes discussions of various amendments to the Constitution. See, for a survey of the Constitution of the United States, Anastaplo, "The Constitution at Two Hundred," 1024. See also note 41, below.

3. Magna Carta, the Petition of Right, and the English Bill of Rights may be found in Appendixes A, C, and D of this Commentary. See Lecture No. 3, Sections II–IV, of this Commentary. See also note 48, below.

4. Leonard W. Levy, "The Continental Congress," in Leonard W. Levy, Kenneth L. Karst, and Dennis J. Mahoney, eds., *Encyclopedia of the American Constitution* (New York: Macmillan Co, 1986), 2: 493. (Cited hereafter as *Ency. Am. Const.*) The 1774 Declarations and Resolves by the First Continental Congress may be found in Appendix E-2 of this Commentary. An earlier stage of this controversy, illustrated by the 1765 Stamp Act Congress's Declarations of Rights & Grievances, may be found in Appendix E-1. See, for a lively account of these troubles, Churchill, *A History of the English-Speaking Peoples*, 3: 141f.

5. Dennis J. Mahoney, "The Association," in *Ency. Am. Const.*, 1: 79. See note 257, below.

6. Ibid.

7. Ibid.

8. Levy, "The Continental Congress," in *Ency. Am. Const.*, 2: 493.

9. Ibid.

10. Thus, the 1991 Bicentennial of the December 15, 1791, ratification of the Bill of Rights occurred in the 216th year "of the Independence of the United States of America." The four "organic laws of the United States" are the Declaration of Independence, the Articles of Confederation, the Northwest Ordinance, and the Constitution (including its amendments).

11. See Anastaplo, "American Constitutionalism and the Virtue of Prudence: Philadelphia, Paris, Washington, Gettysburg," in *Abraham Lincoln, The Gettysburg Address and American Constitutionalism*, Leo Paul S. de Alvarez, ed. (Irving, Texas: University of Dallas Press, 1976), 165–68 (originally published, in a shorter version, in *Loyola of Los Angeles Law Review*, 8: 77 [1976]). (Cited hereafter as "American Constitutionalism.") See also the two sets of exchanges between Harry V. Jaffa and me, in Jaffa, *Original Intent*; notes 131 and 168, below. See, on Professor Jaffa, Laurence Berns, "Aristotle and the Moderns on Freedom and Equality," in Kenneth L. Deutsch and Walter Soffer, eds., *The Crisis of Liberal Democracy: A Straussian Perspective* (Albany: State University of New York Press, 1987), 156; Anastaplo, *Human Being and Citizen: Essays on Virtue, Freedom and the Common Good* (Chicago: Swallow Press/Ohio University Press, 1975), 61–73. (Cited hereafter as *Human Being and Citizen*.) See also notes 158, 168, and 255, below. An unfortunate review by Robert H. Bork of Mr. Jaffa's *Original Intent* (*National Review*, Feb. 7, 1994, 61) permitted Mr. Jaffa to enjoy himself hugely in his instructive responses. See, on Judge Bork, Anastaplo, Book Review, *Northwestern University Law Review*, 84: 1142 (1990). Critical to the Bork position is his failure to appreciate the fact that the Declaration of Independence has been considered from the beginning one of the "organic laws of the United States." See note 10, above.

12. See, on prudence, George Anastaplo, *The American Moralist: On Law, Ethics, and Government* (Athens, Ohio: Ohio University Press, 1992), xvi, 618. (Cited hereafter as *The American Moralist*.) See also Harrison J. Sheppard, "American Principles, Prudence, and Practice," *Review of Politics*, 55: 719 (1993); John A. Murley, Book Review, *Journal of Church and State*, 35: 407 (1993); Jonathan K. Van Patten, Book Review, *Constitutional Commentary*, 11:—(1995); note 11, above, notes 63 and 68, below; Lecture No. 11 of this Commentary. See as well my two reviews of Allan Bloom's work in Robert L. Stone, ed., *Essays on the Closing of the American Mind* (Chicago: Chicago Review Press, 1989), 225–34, 267–84. Compare Sara Prince Anastaplo, "Allan Bloom at 26," in *Law and Philosophy*, 2: 1034.

13. This quotation is taken from the following passage in a review of *The Constitution of 1787* by a respected constitutional scholar who is a United States Senior District Court Judge in Pennsylvania:

> [George Anastaplo's] comments [in his *Commentary*] are based primarily on analysis of the original text of the Constitution itself and reflections

about it, with scant regard for "judicial and other official interpretations and applications of the Constitution." He proclaims at the outset (and often thereafter) his nationalistic orientation and recognition of the supremacy of the legislative branch, and he acknowledges the influence of his teachers William Winslow Crosskey and Leo Strauss. Another characteristic of his treatment is his frequently expressed appreciation of the skill and craftsmanship with which the Constitution is drafted. The author discusses the various parts of the Constitution in the sequence established by the document itself. He strives to discern a systematic scheme or pattern in which the parts coherently come together and to speculate about why a particular portion is placed where it is.

Edward Dumbauld, *Journal of American History*, 77: 290 (1990) (reprinted in *Law and Philosophy*, 1: 573). Additional reviews of or comments upon *The Constitution of 1787* are the following: J. Jackson Barlow, *Interpretation*, 18: 475 (1991); Laurence Berns, "Foreword," in *Law and Philosophy*, 1, xvi (1992); John Braeman, *Choice*, 27: 203 (1989); Milton Cantor, *Library Journal*, 114: 86 (1989); Thomas Engeman, *Review of Politics*, 51: 612 (1989); Timothy Fuller, *Interpretation*, 18: 467 (1991); Ben Gelman, *Southern Illinoisan*, Carbondale, Ill., Sept. 10, 1989, p. 42 (reprinted in *Greek Star*, Chicago, Ill., Oct. 5, 1989, p. 5); Robert A. Licht, *Legal Studies Forum*, 15: 75 (1991) (reprinted in *Law and Philosophy*, 1: 575); *Loyola World*, Aug. 17, 1989, p. 13; Robert C. Power, *Northwestern University Law Review*, 84: 711 (1990); Glen E. Thurow, *Publius*, 20: 15, 19 n. 8 (1990); Jonathan K. Van Patten, *South Dakota Law Review*, 34: 440 (1989).

My comments on the work of William W. Crosskey and of Leo Strauss include the following: "Mr. Crosskey, the American Constitution, and the Natures of Things," *Loyola University of Chicago Law Journal*, 15: 181 (1984); *The Artist as Thinker: From Shakespeare to Joyce* (Athens, Ohio: Ohio University Press, 1983), 249. (Cited hereafter as *The Artist as Thinker.*) See notes 49, 52, 61, 66, and 120, below. See, on the Crosskey "blockbuster," C. Herman Pritchett, Book Review, in *Law and Philosophy*, 1: 539.

14. See, e.g., *The Federalist*, No. 84, in which Publius made the following arguments (in New York City, on May 28, 1788):

. . . The most considerable of [the] remaining objections [to the proposed constitution] is, that the plan of the [Federal Convention] contains no bill of rights. Among other answers given to this, it has been upon different occasions remarked, that the constitutions of several of the states are in a similar predicament. I add, that New-York is of this number. And yet the opposers of the new system in this state, who profess an unlimited admiration for [New-York's] constitution, are among the most intemperate partizans of a bill of rights. To justify their zeal in this matter, they alledge two things; one is, that though the constitution of New-York has no bill of rights prefixed to it, yet it contains in the body of it various provisions in favour of particular privileges and rights, which in substance amount to the same thing; the other is, that the constitution [of New-York] adopts in their full extent the common and statute law of Great Britain, by which many other rights not expressed in it are equally secured.

To the first I answer, that the constitution proposed by the [Federal Convention] contains, as well as the constitution of this state [of New-York], a number of such provisions.

Independent of those, which relate to the structure of the government, we find the following: Article I, section 3, clause 7. "Judgment in cases of impeachment shall not extend further than to removal from office, and disqualification to hold and enjoy any office of honour, trust or profit under the United States; but the party convicted shall nevertheless be liable and subject to indictment, trial, judgment and punishment according to law." Section 9 of the same article, clause 2. "The privilege of the writ of *habeas corpus* shall not be suspended, unless when in cases of rebellion or invasion the public safety may require it." Clause 3. "No bill of attainder or *ex post facto* law shall be passed." Clause 7. "No title of nobility shall be granted by the United States: And no person holding any office of profit or trust under them, shall, without the consent of congress, accept of any present, emolument, office or title, of any kind whatever, from any king, prince or foreign state." Article III, section 2, clause 3. "The trial of all crimes, except in cases of impeachment, shall be by jury; and such trial shall be held in the state where the said crimes shall have been committed; but when not committed within any state, the trial shall be at such place or places as the congress may by law have directed." Section 3, of the same article. "Treason against the United States shall consist only in levying war against them, or in adhering to their enemies, giving them aid and comfort. No person shall be convicted of treason unless on the testimony of two witnesses to the same overt act, or on confession in open court." And clause 3, of the same section. "The congress shall have power to declare the punishment of treason, but no attainder of treason shall work corruption of blood, or forfeiture, except during the life of the person attainted."

It may well be a question whether these are not upon the whole, of equal importance with any which are to be found in the constitution of this state [of New-York]. The establishment of the writ of *habeas corpus,* the prohibition of *ex post facto* laws, and of TITLES OF NOBILITY, *to which we have no corresponding provision in our [state] constitution,* are perhaps greater securities to liberty and republicanism than any [our state constitution] contains. The creation of crimes after the commission of the fact, or in other words, the subjecting of men to punishment for things which, when they were done, were breaches of no law, and the practice of arbitrary imprisonments have been in all ages the favourite and most formidable instruments of tyranny. The observations of the judicious Blackstone [*Commentaries*, 1: 136] in reference to the latter, are well worthy of recital: "To bereave a man of life (says he) or by violence to confiscate his estate, without accusation or trial, would be so gross and notorious an act of despotism, as must at once convey the alarm of tyranny throughout the whole nation; but confinement of the person by secretly hurrying him to

[jail], where his sufferings are unknown or forgotten, is a less public, a less striking, and therefore *a more dangerous engine* of arbitrary government." And as a remedy for this fatal evil, he is every where peculiarly emphatical in his encomiums on the *habeas corpus* act, which in one place he calls "the BULWARK of the British constitution."

Nothing need be said to illustrate the importance of the prohibition of titles of nobility. This may truly be denominated the corner stone of republican government; for so long as they are excluded, there can never be serious danger that the government will be any other than that of the people.

To the second, that is, to the pretended establishment of the common and statute law by the constitution [of New-York], I answer, that they are expressly made subject "to such alterations and provisions as the legislature shall from time to time make concerning the same." They are therefore at any moment liable to repeal by the ordinary legislative power, and of course have no constitutional sanction. The only use of the declaration was to recognize the ancient law, and to remove doubts which might have been occasioned by the revolution. This consequently can be considered as no part of a declaration of rights, which under our constitutions must be intended as limitations of the power of the government itself.

It has been several times truly remarked, that bills of rights are in their origin, stipulations between kings and their subjects, abridgments of prerogative in favor of privilege, reservations of rights not surrendered to the prince. Such was MAGNA CHARTA, obtained by the Barons, sword in hand, from king John. [See Appendix A of this Commentary.] Such were the subsequent confirmations of that charter by subsequent princes. Such was the *petition of right* assented to by Charles the First, in the beginning of his reign. [See Appendix C of this Commentary.] Such also was the declaration of right presented by the lords and commons to the prince or Orange in 1688, and afterwards thrown into the form of an act of parliament, called the bill of rights. [See Appendix D of this Commentary.] It is evident, therefore, that according to their primitive signification, they have no application to constitutions professedly founded upon the power of the people, and executed by their immediate representatives and servants. Here, in strictness, the people surrender nothing, and as they retain every thing, they have no need of particular reservations. "WE THE PEOPLE of the United States, to secure the blessings of liberty to ourselves and our posterity, do *ordain* and *establish* this constitution for the United States of America." Here is a better recognition of popular rights than volumes of those aphorisms which make the principal figure in several of our state bills of rights, and which would sound much better in a treatise of ethics than in a constitution of government.

But a minute detail of particular rights is certainly far less applicable to a constitution like that under consideration, which is merely intended to regulate the general political interests of the nation, than to a constitution [such as in New-York] which has the regulation of every species of personal and private concerns. If therefore the loud clamours against the plan of the convention on this score, are well founded, no epithets of reprobation will be too strong for the constitution of this state [of New-York]. But the truth is, that both [constitutions] contain all, which in relation to their objects, is reasonably to be desired.

I go further, and affirm that bills of rights, in the sense and in the extent in which they are contended for, are not only unnecessary in the proposed constitution, but would even be dangerous. They would contain various exceptions to powers which are not granted; and on this very account, would afford a colourable pretext to claim more [powers] than were granted. For why declare that things shall not be done which there is no power to do? Why for instance, should it be said, that the liberty of the press shall not be restrained, when no power is given by which restrictions may be imposed? I will not contend that such a provision would confer a regulating power; but it is evident that it would furnish, to men disposed to usurp, a plausible pretence for claiming that power. They might urge with a semblance of reason, that the constitution ought not to be charged with the absurdity of providing against the abuse of an authority, which was not given, and that the provision against restraining the liberty of the press afforded a clear implication, that a power to prescribe proper regulations concerning it, was intended to be vested in the national government. This may serve as a specimen of the numerous handles which would be given to the doctrine of constructive powers, by the indulgence of an injudicious zeal for bills of rights.

On the subject of the liberty of the press, as much has been said, I cannot forbear adding a remark or two: In the first place, I observe that there is not a syllable concerning it in the constitution of this state [of New-York], and in the next, I contend that whatever has been said about it in [the constitution] of any other state, amounts to nothing. What signifies a declaration that "the liberty of the press shall be inviolably preserved?" What is the liberty of the press? Who can give it any definition which would not leave the utmost latitude for evasion? I hold it to be impracticable; and from this, I infer, that its security, whatever fine declarations may be inserted in any constitution respecting it, must altogether depend on public opinion, and on the general spirit of the people and of the government. [*Publius' note:* To show that there is a power in the constitution by which the liberty of the press may be affected, recourse has been had to the power of taxation. It is said that duties may be laid upon publications so high as to amount to a prohibition. I know not by what logic it could be maintained that the declarations, in the state constitutions, in favour of the freedom of the press, would be a constitutional impediment to the imposition of duties upon publications by the state legislatures. It cannot certainly be pretended that any degree of duties, however low, would be an abridgement of the liberty of the press. We know that newspapers are taxed in Great-Britain, and yet it is notorious that the press no where enjoys greater liberty than in that country. And if duties of any kind may be laid without a violation of that liberty, it is evident that the extent must depend on legislative discretion, regulated by public opinion; so that after all, general declarations respecting the liberty of the press will give it no greater security than it will have without them. The same invasions of it may be effected under the state constitutions which contain those declarations through the means of taxation, as under the proposed constitution which has nothing of the kind. It would be quite as significant to declare that government ought to be free, that taxes ought not to be excessive, &c., as that the liberty of the press ought not to be restrained.] And here, after all, as intimated upon another occasion, must we seek for the only solid basis of all our rights.

There remains but one other view of this matter to conclude the point. The truth is, after all the declamation we have heard, that the [proposed] constitution is itself in every rational sense, and to every useful purpose, A BILL OF RIGHTS. The several bills of rights, in Great-Britain, form its constitution, and conversely the constitution of each state is its bill of rights. And the proposed constitution, if adopted, will be the bill of rights of the union. Is it one object of a bill of rights to declare and specify the political privileges of the citizens in the structure and administration of the government? This is done in the most ample and precise manner in the plan of the [Federal Convention], comprehending various precautions for the public security, which are not to be found in any of the state constitutions. Is another object of a bill of rights to define certain immunities and modes of proceeding, which are relative to personal and private concerns? This we have seen has also been attended to, in a variety of cases, in the same plan. Adverting therefore to the substantial meaning of a bill of rights, it is absurd to allege that it is not to be found in the work of the [Federal Convention]. It may be said that it does not go far enough, though it will not be easy to make this appear; but it can with no propriety be contended that there is no such thing. It certainly must be immaterial what mode is observed as to the order of declaring the rights of the citizens, if they are to be found in any part of the instrument which establishes the government. And hence it must be apparent that much of what has been said on this subject rests merely on verbal and nominal distinctions, which are entirely foreign from the substance of the thing. . . .

Selected Writings and Speeches of Alexander Hamilton, Morton J. Frisch, ed. (Washington, D.C.: American Enterprise Institute, 1985), 186–91. See also Appendix J-1 of this Commentary. It is instructive to notice here how bills of rights could be regarded. It should also be noticed that nothing is said, including in Publius' long note about threats to liberty of the press, about judicial review of Acts of Congress as a way of applying constitutional safeguards. Consider also the implications of the concluding lines of the Virginia Statute of Religious Liberty (found in Appendix G of this Commentary). Compare Sotirios A. Barber, "Judicial Review and *The Federalist,*" *University of Chicago Law Review,* 55: 836 (1988); notes 61, 68, 74, and 134, below. See, for reservations with respect to the *Federalist,* the work of William W. Crosskey (note 13, above, note 52, below). See as well Anastaplo, *The Constitution of 1787*, 334; Book Review, *Ethics*, 99: 655 (1989); "The Constitution at Two Hundred," 1042; note 209, below. See also Anastaplo, *The Constitutionalist: Notes on the First Amendment* (Dallas: Southern Methodist University Press, 1971), 819 (on Publius). (Cited hereafter as *The Constitutionalist.*) See as well note 66, below.

15. The Federal Convention, we recall, began on May 25 and ended on September 17, 1787. See note 216, below.

16. Max Farrand, ed., *The Records of the Federal Convention of 1787* (New Haven: Yale University Press, 1937), 2: 341–42. (Cited hereafter as Farrand.) James Madison's *Notes of Debates in the Federal Convention of 1787*, found in the first two Farrand volumes, is available in paperback from the Ohio University Press. See, for a fuller account of the bill-of-rights proposals suggested by Charles Pinckney on August 20 and found in Appendix H-1 of this Commentary, Farrand, 2: 341–42. (The Pinckney cited to in note 112, below, is an older relative of this more volatile Pinckney.)

17. Ibid., 2: 340 n. 4.

18. Ibid., 2: 341 n. 4.

19. Ibid., 3: 122.

20. Ibid.

21. Ibid., 2: 587–88. George Mason had been the author of the Virginia Declaration of Rights in 1776. That Declaration of Rights is found in Appendix F-1 of this Commentary.

22. The New York delegation in the Federal Convention no longer had a quorum available, two of its three members having gone home (evidently because they did not like the course that the Convention was following). The third New York member, Alexander Hamilton, could continue to speak in Convention debates but could not cast his State's vote. See *Selected Writings and Speeches of Alexander Hamilton*, 124; Farrand, 3: 367, 448, 474, 521, 529–31, 537. Rhode Island never sent a delegation to the Federal Convention, nor did it ratify the Constitution until May 29, 1790. See, for all of the original States' ratification dates, Anastaplo, *The Constitution of 1787*, 286–87.

23. Letter from George Washington to La Fayette (Apr. 28, 1788), reprinted in Farrand, 3: 298.

24. Farrand, 2: 638.

25. Ibid., 2: 588. See, for a salutary reminder of what can (perhaps even should) be done with State constitutional law today, Ronald K. L. Collins, "Reliance on State Constitutions: Some Random Thoughts," *Mississippi Law Journal*, 54: 371 (1984). See also the text at note 198 of this Commentary.

26. Farrand, 2: 628.

27. Ibid., 2: 630. Madison's warning anticipated the concern of the Federalists throughout the Ratification Campaign about reopening matters already settled by the Federal Convention.

28. Ibid., 2: 632–33. See note 257, below. See also Anastaplo, "The Constitution at Two Hundred," 1013.

29. Farrand, 2: 628. This action occurred immediately after the civil-jury

proposal was dealt with. The tenor of the remark recorded here, by Madison a Virginian, indicates how slavery could then be talked about, even among Southerners. See notes 186 and 259, below. See also note 152, below.

30. Plutarch, *Lives,* John Dryden and Arthur Hugh Clough, trans. (Modern Library edition), 1110 (*Antony, IX*). Consider the advice give by Gouverneur Morris (from Paris) to President elect Washington:

> Will you excuse me, my dear Sir, . . . for making one Remark on the subject of Economy and Example taken into joint Consideration. I think it of very great Importance to fix the Taste of our Country properly, and I think your Example will go very far in that Respect. It is therefore my Wish that every Thing about you should be substantially good and majestically plain; made to endure.

Anastaplo, "American Constitutionalism," 149 n. 37. See note 62, below. See, on sumptuary laws, note 218, below, and the text at note 32 of this Commentary. Consider also the advice of Cyrus to the Persians with which Herodotus concludes his *History* (David Grene translation; 9: 122): "From soft countries come soft men. It is not possible that from the same land stems a growth of wondrous fruit and men who are good soldiers." Consider as well the counsel to Xerxes recorded in the Preface to this Commentary. Ibid., 7: 16. Compare our unseemly, if not even corrupting, addiction to State-run lotteries in recent decades. See, e.g., Peter Applebume, "Casino Boom along Gulf Coast Brings Fears of Glut and High Cost," *New York Times,* Jan. 10, 1994, p. A1. Machiavelli, *Discourses,* II, 19 ("[A]cquisitions, in republics which are not well-ordered and which do not proceed according to Roman virtue, are to their ruin and not to their exaltation."); notes 60 and 130, below. See also notes 68, 135, 240, and 260 below.

31. Farrand, 2: 344. See notes 99 and 251, below.

32. Ibid., 2: 606–7. See Lawrence Zelic Freedman, "Greed: Law, Morality, and Pathology," in *Law and Philosophy,* 1: 379. See also note 218, below.

33. Farrand, 2: 342. See, on the recent British "poll tax," Bagehot, "The Cursed Tax," *Economist,* March 9, 1991, p. 60; Craig R. Whitney, "Britain Will Abandon Its Fiercely Disputed 'Poll Tax'," *New York Times,* March 22, 1991, p. A3. See also the Jefferson quotation among the epigraphs for this Commentary.

34. See, e.g., Farrand, 2: 617.

35. Ibid., 2: 342. See note 16, above. See, for the epitaphic tribute to the Charleston lawyer James Louis Petigru, a Unionist who opposed Secession and a Constitutionalist who opposed Nullification, Anastaplo, "We the People: The Rulers and the Ruled," *Great Ideas Today,* 1987: 72 (1987). Compare note 259, below.

36. See, e.g., Anastaplo, *The Constitution of 1787,* 124–48. See also Blackstone, 1: 17f, 70f; William T. Braithwaite, "The Common Law and the Judicial Power: An Introduction to *Swift-Erie,*" in *Law and Philosophy,* 774; notes 62 and 240, below. Consider, as testimony to the existence of a general common law, the reliance in Amendment VII upon "the rules of the common law."

37. Theodore F. T. Plucknett, *A Concise History of the Common Law* (5th ed.; Boston: Little, Brown and Co., 1956), 17. (Cited hereafter as Plucknett.) Consider, on the implications of the struggle between Henry II and Thomas Becket, Anastaplo, "Rome, Piety, and Law," 138–46.

38. Plucknett, 22–23.

39. Ibid., 23. See note 85, below.

40. Ibid., 25. Magna Carta is found in Appendix A of this Commentary. See, on Magna Carta, Blackstone, 1: 123–24, 129–36, 2: 52, 4: 416–17, 420; Anastaplo, "On Freedom: Explorations," *Oklahoma City University Law Review,* 17: 465, 481 (1992). (Cited hereafter as "On Freedom.")

41. The much-quoted original Latin version of this provision, Chapter 39 of Magna Carta, accompanies its English translation in Appendix A of this Commentary. See Blackstone, 4: 417: "And, lastly, (which alone would have merited the title that it bears, of the *great* charter) it protected every individual of the nation in the free enjoyment of his life, his liberty, and his property, unless declared to be forfeited by the judgment of his peers or the law of the land." See also ibid., 134, 389; note 85, below. It is important to notice that government is taken seriously by the people of Magna Carta. Consider, for example, what (according, for example, to Chapter 39) may be done to someone pursuant to "the law of the land." Consider also the teachings of John Stuart Mill about the differences between civilization and barbarism and how government should respond to each. See Anastaplo, "On Freedom," 509–17; notes 60 and 68, below. It is also evident in Magna Carta that any incipient individualism is curbed by the complex system of allegiances upon which claims to property depend. See note 133, below. Compare, on the status of authority in the Western World, note 100, below.

42. Habeas Corpus Act, 1679. See also Star Chamber Act, 1641. The Habeas Corpus Act has been acclaimed as "that second *Magna carta,* and stable bulwark of our liberties." Blackstone, 1: 133. "*Magna carta* only, in general terms, declared, that no man shall be imprisoned contrary to law: the *habeas corpus* act points him out effectual means, as well to release himself, though committed even by the king in council, as to punish all those who shall thus unconstitutionally misuse him" Ibid., 4: 432. See, on the writ of habeas corpus, Anastaplo, *The Constitutionalist,* 814.

43. See Blackstone, 1: 129–38. See also Plucknett, 57–58.

44. Plucknett, 53–55. See Lecture No. 1, Section I, of this Commentary.

45. Ibid., 59 (emphasis added). The English Bill of Rights (1689) is found in Appendix D of this Commentary. The care with which President Lincoln developed his policy of emancipation testifies to his awareness of the fact that it does not suffice to promote a policy that is "intrinsically an advance" if the way has not been prepared for it. See Lecture No. 11 of this Commentary.

46. See Blackstone, 1: 204–8, 323, 356.

47. Plucknett, 60. See Harvey C. Mansfield, Jr., "Party Government and the Settlement of 1688," *American Political Science Review,* 58: 933 (1964).

48. See Churchill, *A History of the English-Speaking Peoples,* 3: 156: "The Declaration [of Independence] was in the main a restatement of the principles which had animated the Whig struggle against the later Stuarts and the English Revolution of 1688, and it now became the symbol and rallying centre of the Patriot cause." It could be said by a learned English judge in 1765 that "our constitution [has] arrived at it's full perfection." Blackstone, 1: 257. See also note 134, below.

49. That Virginia's vote happened to be the final one required for ratification of the Bill of Rights was fitting in light of the key role played by Madison in the Congressional drafting of the amendments. (Three-quarters of a century later, Lincoln considered it worthy of notice that his State, Illinois, had been the first to ratify the proposed Thirteenth Amendment. See note 193, below.) Instructive (and usefully complementary) descriptions of Madison's Bill of Rights efforts in the First Congress may be found in Paul Finkelman, "James Madison and the Bill of Rights: A Reluctant Paternity," *Supreme Court Review,* 1990: 301 (1990); Robert A. Goldwin, "Congressman Madison Proposes Amendments to the Constitution," *Public Interest Law Review,* 1: 47 (1991). See, on the drafting and intended scope of the Bill of Rights, William W. Crosskey, *Politics and the Constitution in the History of the United States* (Chicago: University of Chicago Press, 1953), 2: 1056–82. (Cited hereafter as Crosskey.)

50. See, for these two proposed amendments, the text at note 64 of this Commentary. See, on the 1992 "ratification" of the 1789 Congressional-pay amendment, Lecture No. 5, Section III, and Lecture No. 16, Sections VI and VII, of this Commentary.

51. The rate of ratification of the Bill of Rights depend upon when State legislatures would be meeting. But that had been true also when the proposed Constitution was ratified. On that occasion, not only had State legislatures had to meet in 1787–1788, but also, thereafter, the State Ratification Conventions had had to be provided for by the State legislatures. This makes the speed with which the Constitution was ratified, as compared to the Bill of Rights, quite striking, especially considering how extended the discussions of the Constitution of 1787 were in some of the State Ratification Conventions. Compare note 64, below.

52. See, on the importance of preambles, Crosskey, 1: 370–79, 391, 394, 399, 400; 2: 1065. See also Anastaplo, *The Constitution of 1787,* 13–25; note 13, above, note 66, below. The preamble provided with the proposed Bill of Rights sent by Congress to the States is included in Appendix J-5 of this Commentary. The Declaration of Independence can be considered the preamble for our constitutional efforts, beginning with the Articles of Confederation and the Constitution of 1787. (Mr. Crosskey, by the way, was an unrelenting critic of Thomas Jefferson and James Madison, much preferring instead the constitutional contributions of George Washington, Alexander Hamilton, John Marshall, James Wilson, and Gouverneur Morris.)

53. See, e.g., Samuel E. Morison, *The Oxford History of the American People* (New York: Oxford University Press, 1972), 319. (Cited hereafter as Morison.)

54. See Anastaplo, *The Constitution of 1787,* 183.

55. *The Roots of The Bill of Rights,* Bernard Schwartz, ed. (New York: Chelsea House Publishers, 1980), 5: 1065 (Madison's statement of August 13, 1787). See also Anastaplo, *The Constitution of 1787,* 52, 60, 67, 229.

56. See Bennett B. Patterson, *The Forgotten Ninth Amendment* (Indianapolis: Bobbs-Merrill Co., 1955), 215.

57. See Anastaplo, *The Constitution of 1787,* 24. We shall see that the Eleventh and Twelfth Amendments can also be considered part of that post-Convention effort at completion represented by the first ten amendments. See Lecture No. 8 of this Commentary.

58. Morison, 213.

59. Ibid., 227–28. These farmers' recollections bear upon the gun-control issues discussed in Lecture No. 6 of this Commentary. See also notes 134 and 176, below.

60. See, on the quite different prospects in Eastern Europe today, Anastaplo, *The American Moralist,* 555–69. See also Anastaplo, "On Freedom," 630; note 41, above.

European politics for two centuries now have been profoundly influenced by late eighteenth-century developments in France similar to, but yet significantly different from, what has happened in the United States since 1774. A month before the First Congress completed its work on the American Bill of Rights, the French National Constituent Assembly (on August 26, 1789) promulgated (well in advance of a French constitution) their celebrated Declaration of the Rights of Man and the Citizen:

> The representatives of the French people, constituted as a National Assembly, considering that ignorance, disregard or contempt of the rights of man are the sole causes of public misfortunes and governmental corruption, have resolved to set forth a solemn declaration of the natural, inalienable and sacred rights of man: in order that this declaration, by being constantly present to all members of the social body, may keep them at all times aware of their rights and duties; that the acts of both the legislative and executive powers, by being liable at every moment to comparison with the aim of all political institutions, may be the more fully respected; and that demands of the citizens, by being founded henceforward on simple and incontestable principles, may always redound to the maintenance of the constitution and the general welfare.
>
> The Assembly consequently recognizes and declares, in the presence and under the auspices of the Supreme Being, the following rights of man and the citizen:
>
> I. Men are born and remain free and equal in rights. Social distinctions may be based only on common utility.
>
> II. The aim of all political association is to preserve the natural and imprescriptible rights of man. These rights are liberty, property, security and resistance to oppression.

III. The principle of all sovereignty rests essentially in the nation. No body and no individual may exercise authority which does not emanate from the nation expressly.

IV. Liberty consists in the ability to do whatever does not harm another; hence the exercise of the natural rights of each man has no limits except those which assure to other members of society the enjoyment of the same rights. These limits can only be determined by law.

V. Law may rightfully prohibit only those actions which are injurious to society. No hindrance should be put in the way of anything not prohibited by law, nor may any man be forced to do what the law does not require.

VI. Law is the expression of the general will. All citizens have the right to take part, in person or by their representatives, in its formation. It must be the same for all whether it protects or penalizes. All citizens being equal in its eyes are equally admissible to all public dignities, offices and employments, according to their capacity, and with no other distinction than that of their virtues and talents.

VII. No man may be indicted, arrested or detained except in cases determined by law and according to the forms which it has prescribed. Those who instigate, expedite, execute or cause to be executed arbitrary orders should be punished; but any citizen summoned or seized by virtue of the law should obey instantly, and renders himself guilty by resistance.

VIII. Only strictly necessary punishments may be established by law, and no one may be punished except by virtue of a law established and promulgated before the time of the offense, and legally put into force.

IX. Every man being presumed innocent until judged guilty, if it is deemed indispensable to keep him under arrest, all rigor not necessary to secure his person should be severely repressed by law.

X. No one may be disturbed for his opinions, even in religion, provided that their manifestation does not trouble public order as established by law.

XI. Free communication of thought and opinion is one of the most precious of the rights of man. Every citizen may therefore speak, write and print freely, on his own responsibility for abuse of this liberty in cases determined by law.

XII. Preservation of the rights of man and the citizen requires the existence of public forces. These forces are therefore instituted for the advantage of all, not for the private benefit of those to whom they are entrusted.

XIII. For maintenance of public forces and for expenses of administration common taxation is necessary. It should be apportioned equally among all citizens according to their capacity to pay.

XIV. All citizens have the right, by themselves or through their representatives, to have demonstrated to them the necessity of public taxes, to consent to them freely, to follow the use made of the proceeds and to determine the shares to be paid, the means of assessment and collection and the duration.

XV. Society has the right to hold accountable every public agent of administration.

XVI. Any society in which the guarantee of rights is not assured or the separation of powers not determined has no constitution.

XVII. Property being an inviolable and sacred right, no one may be deprived of it except for an obvious requirement of public necessity, certified by law, and then on condition of a just compensation in advance.

George Lefebvre, *The Coming of the French Revolution* (R. R. Palmer, trans.; Princeton: Princeton University Press, 1967), 221–23. "It is a commonplace of counterrevolutionary polemics to find fault with the Declaration [of the Rights of Man and the Citizen] for being too philosophical and abstract. . . . As the historian [Alphonse] Aulard put it, the Declaration is essentially the *death certificate of the Old Regime.*" Ibid., 173–74. See note 198, below.

Important as "the natural, inalienable and sacred rights of man" are in this Declaration, there is also considerable emphasis upon public order and the authority of that law which is "the expression of the general will." See, for English parallels, Blackstone, 1: 6, 121–23; Anastaplo, "Freedom of Speech and the Silence of the Law," *Texas Law Review,* 64: 443 (1985); notes 99 and 134, below. A distinguished French historian concluded his study (originally prepared in 1939) of the Declaration of the Rights of Man and the Citizen with these observations:

> We come here to the deeper meaning of the Declaration. It is a direction of intention; it therefore requires of the citizens an integrity of purpose, which is to say a critical spirit, patriotism in the proper sense of the word, respect for the rights of others, reasoned devotion to the national community, "virtue" in the language of Montesquieu, Rousseau and Robespierre. "The soul of the Republic," wrote Robespierre in 1792, "is virtue, love of country, the generous devotion that fuses all interests into the general interest." The Declaration in proclaiming the rights of man appeals at the same time to discipline freely consented to, to sacrifice if need be, to cultivation of character *and to the mind.* Liberty is by no means an invitation to indifference or to irresponsible power; nor is it the promise of unlimited well-being without a counterpart of toil and effort. It supposes application, perpetual effort, strict government of self, sacrifice in contingencies, civic and private virtues. It is therefore more difficult to live as a free man than to live as a slave, and that is why men so often renounce their freedom; for freedom is in its way an invitation to a life of courage, and sometimes of heroism, as the freedom of the Christian is an invitation to a life of sainthood.

Lefebvre, *The Coming of the French Revolution,* 219–20. See also note 149, below.

See, for critical differences (and not only as to the meaning of *virtue*) between the American and French revolutions, Anastaplo, "American Constitutionalism," 94–106 (as observed by Gouverneur Morris while serving as the American Minister to France). See also note 30, above, notes 130 and 146, below. See, on the Bonapartism that (naturally?) followed the French Revolution, Lecture No. 9 of this Commentary. See, for the perennial tension between the general and the particular among the French (and, no doubt, among others also), the text at note 259 of this Commentary. See also note 259, below.

61. 5 U.S. (1 Cranch) 137 (1803). See, for the most challenging study of this much-discussed case, Crosskey, 2: 978, 1035–46, 1327. See, on judicial review *of Acts of Congress*, Anastaplo, *The Constitution of 1787*, 124–48; note 14, above, notes 74 and 134, below. See also Blackstone, 1: 8, 91. (Such judicial review— of the kind vigorously condemned by both Judge Blackstone (1: 91) and Professor Crosskey (2: 943)—should be distinguished from the obviously authorized review of State legislative, executive, and judicial activity by the General Government of the United States. It should also be distinguished from the power that the United States Supreme Court may have to protect its prerogatives.) See, for other questionable uses of judicial power, *Powell* v. *McCormack*, 395 U.S. 486 (1969), and *United States* v. *Nixon*, 418 U.S. 683 (1974). (See, on the *Powell* problem, Blackstone, 1: 159. See, on President Nixon and Watergate, Stephen E. Ambrose, *Nixon* (New York: Simon & Schuster, 1991), 3: 381f, 581f; Anastaplo, *Human Being and Citizen*, 160, *The American Moralist*, 431.) Reservations about judicial review are indicated in the course of the discussion in the Senate, on January 31, 1803, of a petition submitted by William Marbury and others. See *Annals of Congress*, 12: 34–50 (1803). (The years given by me in this Commentary for the *Annals of Congress* refer to the dates of the Congressional debates cited, not to the dates of the publication of the *Annals* volumes.)

The traditional reluctance of Anglo-American courts to invalidate acts of the supreme legislature is reflected in an observation by Chief Justice Marshall in *United States* v. *Fisher*, 6 U.S. (2 Cranch) 358, at 390 (1804): "Where rights are infringed, where fundamental principles are overthrown, where the general system of the laws is departed from, the legislative intention must be expressed with irresistible clearness to induce a court of justice to suppose a design to effect such objects." Congress, for example, must be willing to insist upon what it is doing if it proposes to act improperly. See, on the independence of the judiciary, Ronald K. L. Collins, "The Principles of Power," in *Law and Philosophy*, 2: 671; Kenneth M. Holland, "Implications of the Canadian Charter of Rights and Freedoms for Judicial Service on Royal Commissions of Inquiry," ibid., 2: 852.

62. The decline of the common law may be seen in the resort to comprehensive codification, which perhaps was stimulated by what was happening to the common law in the United States. (Did not Justinian try to do the same, also with mixed results? See, e.g., Anastaplo, "Rome, Piety, and Law," 98.) On the merits of the common-law approach rather than codification, see John Winthrop's *Journal* (Sept. 1639) (reprinted in *Original Narratives of Early*

American History, James K. Hosmer, ed. [New York: C. Seribner's Sons, 1908], Winthrop (Boston: Little, Brown, 1958), 167–68. See also note 36, above. Is there not something positivistic, or at least the beginning of a turn away from a grander form of expression, in the partial shift in the Bill of Rights from the extensive mode of capitalization (with its implicit respect for substantives) employed in the Declaration of Independence and in the Constitution of 1787? This, at least, was a "constitutional" innovation in the Bill of Rights. (See, for an example of the routine use of capitalization by Gouverneur Morris [the principal draftsman of the Constitution], note 30, above.)

63. Both the common-law system and the natural-right tradition (by which the common-law system is nourished) respect common sense. See, e.g., Blackstone, 1: 70; note 12, above, note 106, below. There is something commonsensical (and hence Aristotelian) about a common refrain in the ancient Buddhist text, *Questions of Milinda:* "That man might say whatever he would, but all the same . . . ," as in "That man might say whatever he would, but all the same, that grown woman came straight from that young girl." See Anastaplo, "An Introduction to Buddhist Thought," *Great Ideas Today,* 1992: 244 n. 45 (1992).

64. We have no records of extended debates in State legislatures on this issue, where the first of these provisions failed by two States and the second by four States. (Ten States were required at that time for ratification.) See Appendix J-6 of this Commentary. See, on the actions by State legislatures "ratifying" the proposed Congressional-pay amendment of 1789, *Federal Register,* 57: 21187–88 (May 18, 1992) (the Archivist of the United States); Richard B. Bernstein, "The Sleeper Wakes: The History and Legacy of the Twenty-seventh Amendment," *Fordham Law Review,* 61: 497 (1992); William Van Alstyne, "What Do You Think About the Twenty-seventh Amendment?," *Constitutional Commentary,* 10: 9 (1993). See also Lecture No. 16, Section VI, of this Commentary. I find it puzzling that the Archivist of the United States (rather than, say, Congress) should have been relied upon to play the decisive role he evidently did in the authoritative determination of whether the Twenty-seventh Amendment had been ratified.

The Founders' Constitution, Philip B. Kurland and Ralph Lerner, eds. (Chicago: University of Chicago Press, 1987), is very useful for students of the Constitution and of the Bill of Rights, as is the *Encyclopedia of the American Constitution* (note 4, above). See also note 108, below. See, for the relevant documentary record from the First Congress with respect to the Bill of Rights, Helen E. Veit, Kenneth R. Bowling, and Carlene Bangs Bickford, eds., *Creating the Bill of Rights* (Baltimore: Johns Hopkins University Press, 1991). See also note 55, above.

65. One of the two amendments rejected in 1791 did not fail by much. See note 64, above. It should also be noticed that for some time after 1791 the articles of the Bill of Rights were sometimes referred to by their original numbers, evidently by people who had only the original Congressional resolution to draw upon and who did not realize that not all of the pro-

posed amendments in that resolution had been ratified. See, e.g., *Annals of Congress*, 8: 1955 (1798). What does this suggest about the immediate significance of the Bill of Rights upon its ratification? Consider as well the significance of the "accident" of names touched upon in Lecture No. 4, Section IV, of this Commentary.

66. See Anastaplo, "Censorship," *Encyclopedia Britannica* (15th edition, beginning with the 1986 printing). That article serves as a summary of several critical First Amendment arguments made in Anastaplo, *The Constitutionalist*. See, on the First Amendment, Anastaplo, *The Constitution of 1787*, 334; *The American Moralist*, 223–316; note 1 (end), above; notes 99 and 125, below. The intermittent campaigns we have had to endure, at the hands of the fearful and the self-righteous, against our invaluable freedom of political discourse in this Country deliver "tremenjis blow[s] to the hed" of our ability to govern ourselves sensibly. See note 191, below. See also note 11, above (on the Jaffa-Anastaplo exchanges), notes 134 and 254, below.

Ulysses S. Grant was moved, after the Civil War, to compare the press North and South during the war: "The press of the South, like the people who remained at home, were loyal to the Southern cause. . . . In the North the press was free up to the point of open treason." *Memoirs*, 637. But did not Northern freedom, troublesome as it could be, contribute significantly to the moral superiority and hence the success of the North in the Civil War? See notes 258 and 259, below. See, on the Joseph McCarthy Period and its victims, Anastaplo, "On Freedom," 518, 540.

A distinctive school of First Amendment free-speech doctrine (complementing William W. Crosskey's constitutional studies [see notes 13 and 52, above]) flourished at the University of Chicago for more than two decades after the Second World War. It was there, during my first year in the College (while I was enrolled in a philosophy course taught by his son Donald), that Alexander Meiklejohn gave a series of lectures on freedom of speech which captivated Malcolm P. Sharp and Harry Kalven Jr. of the Law School faculty. See Meiklejohn, *Political Freedom: The Constitutional Powers of the People* (New York: Harper, 1960; first edition, 1948); Sharp, "Crosskey, Anastaplo and Meiklejohn on the United States Constitution," *University of Chicago Law School Record*, Spring 1973, 3; Kalven, *A Worthy Tradition: Freedom of Speech in America* (New York: Harper & Row, 1988); Anastaplo, "Mr. Crosskey, The American Constitution, and the Natures of Things," 193–96, 198, 225–26 n. 50, 233 n. 95, 259–60 n. 220. The Meiklejohn influence thereafter upon Justice Black became significant. All of these relations are explored in Newman, *Hugo Black*. See also, on the Black epigraph for this Commentary, note 1, above.

The spirit of those troubled times is reflected in this tribute to Harry Kalven that Malcolm Sharp (then in his late seventies and long an anti–Cold Warrior), prepared at my request not long after Mr. Kalven died in 1974:

Harry Kalven is particularly associated, for me, with the comfort and support he gave during the 1950's and the consequences of the 1950's, which continue, in changed form, until the present day. Many other personal ties were strained. In isolation, one tended to doubt one's judgment. Harry was always friendly and reassuring and cooperative. We did not always agree, but disagreement was for him, as for me, an occasion for friendly argument, and for defining and often reducing the scope of disagreement. Our personal ties with him and his family always were strong; and they completed a relationship which is a treasure in a long life.

See, on Mr. Meiklejohn, Mr. Sharp, Mr. Kalven, and Justice Black, respectively, Anastaplo, (1) "American Constitutionalism," 144–45, (2) "Malcolm P. Sharp and the Spirit of '76," *University of Chicago Law Alumni Journal*, Summer 1976, 18, "On Trial: Explorations," *Loyola University of Chicago Law Journal*, 22: 765, 994–1009 (1991) (cited hereafter as "On Trial"), (3) "A Little Touch of Harry," *University of Chicago Law Review* 43: 13 (1975) (in which the Sharp recollection of Harry Kalven should have been included), and (4) "Justice Black, His Generous Common Sense, and the Bar Admission Cases," *Southwestern University Law Review*, 9: 977 (1977). See also C. Herman Pritchett, Book Review, in *Law and Philosophy*, 1: 539; Malcolm P. Sharp, Book Review, ibid., 1: 551; Sharp, *Was Justice Done? The Rosenberg-Sobell Case* (New York: Monthly Review Press, 1956); Anastaplo, *The American Moralist*, 588, 621 (on Malcolm Sharp), "Freedom of Speech and the First Amendment," 2016 (Part VII).

See, on the stages of the First Amendment in the First Congress, Anastaplo, *The Constitutionalist*, 287–93. See, on the right of petition, note 134, below. The appropriate "self-expression," as distinguished from the "political-discourse," aspects of the right of petition are suggested by this counsel (of some four thousand years ago) from a ruler to his son:

> If you are a man who leads, listen calmly to the speech of one who pleads; don't stop him from purging his body of that which he planned to tell. A man in distress wants to pour out his heart more than that his case be won. About him who stops a plea one says: "Why does he reject it?" Not all one pleads for can be granted, but a good hearing soothes the heart.

"The Instruction of Ptahhotep," in Miriam Lichtheim, ed., *Ancient Egyptian Literature* (Berkeley: University of California Press, 1973), 1: 68. A critical argument for free political discourse was made to Xerxes when he was reminded that "when no opposing opinions are presented, it is impossible to choose the better, but one must accept what is proposed." Herodotus, *History*, 7: 10. I have examined in some detail, in *The Constitutionalist*, what is and (almost as important) what is not absolutely protected by the First Amendment.

See, for how academic pedants can try to defend their "turf" by dismissing as "top-of-the-head self-expressiveness" the efforts of interpreters who presume to take important texts seriously without displaying all of the conventional scholarship that they may be aware of, Book Notice, *Journal of Modern Literature*, 11: 374 (1984). Compare John Alvis, Book Review, in *Law and Philosophy*, 1: 561: "One realizes that much has been lost to academic professionalism that can yet be recovered by mere lovers of good writing who are willing, as Socrates was willing, to ask of poets what they knew about living a good life." Compare also Frederick Vaughan, "On First Looking into Popper's Plato," ibid., 1: 128; Christina von Nolcken Kazazis, "Meaning and Generic Interplay in the Plays of Aristophanes," ibid., 2: 886.

67. See Appendix J-3 of this Commentary. It is a prophetic curiosity of American history that this States-limiting proposition (of August 24, 1789), which was rejected by the Senate (Appendix J-4), was the *fourteenth* in the list prepared by the House of Representatives. See, on the Fourteenth Amendment, Lecture No. 12 of this Commentary.

68. Congress did not seem to be concerned, in framing the First Amendment, about the standards that the United States (or the people generally) might use in policing State prohibitions of the free exercise of religion. The applicable standards, subject to development and adaptation, seem to have been generally understood. See, on religious freedom, Robert E. Rodes, Jr., "On the Fiftieth Anniversary of St. Thomas More's Canonization," in *Law and Philosophy*, 1: 272; Anastaplo, "On Trial," 950; Anastaplo, "Church and State: Explorations," *Loyola University of Chicago Law Journal*, 19: 61 (1987). (Cited hereafter as "Church and State.") See also note 135, below; Appendix G of this Commentary. See, on how "the Separation of Church and State" was *not* regarded in the Founding Period, Anastaplo, *The Constitution of 1787*, Lecture No. 15, Section IX.

See, for salutary instruction in how to tailor to one's audience whatever one has to say publicly about sensitive subjects, the following account:

A sixth species of offences against God and religion, of which our ancient books are full, is a crime of which one knows not well what account to give. I mean the offence of *witchcraft, conjuration, inchantment,* or *sorcery.* To deny the possibility, nay, actual existence, of witchcraft and sorcery, is at once flatly to contradict the revealed word or God, in various passage both of the old and new testament: and the thing itself is a truth to which every nation in the world hath in it's turn borne testimony, by either examples seemingly well attested, or prohibitory laws, which at least suppose the possibility of a commerce with evil spirits. The civil law punishes with death not only the sorcerers themselves, but also those who consult them; imitating in the former the express law of God, "thou shalt not suffer a witch to live" [citing Exodus, 22: 18]. And our own laws, both before and since the conquest, have been equally penal; ranking this crime in the same class with heresy, and condemning both to the flames [citing Edward Coke, *Institutes*, 3: 44]. The president Montesquieu [citing *The Spirit of the Laws*, bk. 12, chap. 5] ranks them also both together, but with a very different view: laying it down as an important maxim, that we ought to be very circumspect in the prosecution of magic and heresy; because the most unexceptionable conduct, the purest morals, and the constant practice of every duty in life, are not a sufficient security against the suspicion of crimes like these. And indeed the ridiculous stories that are generally told, and the many impostures and delusions that have been discovered in all ages, are enough to demolish all faith in such a dubious crime; if the contrary evidence were not also extremely strong. Wherefore it seems to be the most eligible way to conclude, with an ingenious writer of our own [citing Joseph Addison, *The Spectator,* no. 117], that in general there has been such a thing as witchcraft; though one cannot give credit to any particular modern instance of it.

Blackstone, 4: 60. See, on the trials of witches, Anastaplo, "Church and State," 65. See also notes 255 and 260, below. See, on due process, note 99, below. (The cautions expressed here by Blackstone with respect to witch-craft should be extended to such other serious charges that are difficult to handle properly as subversion in the 1950s and child abuse in the 1990s.) See, on discretion in speaking, notes 142, 187, and 188, below.

Compare the unfortunate case of *Church of the Lukumi Babalu Aye* v. *City of Hialeah,* 113 S. Ct. 2217 (1993). A community may regard certain activities (such as communal animal sacrifices) as likely to be corrupting, whether done under the auspices of a religious sect or under the auspices of a secular association (such as a sports team). What is particularly disturbing about the *Hialeah* case in the United States Supreme Court is that there seems to be, neither in the opinions of the Justices nor in the related briefs and commentary that I have seen, any awareness of the moral stance that can properly be taken, in modern circumstances, against such practices as communal animal sacrifices.

The First Amendment should not keep us from recognizing that all too many people believe and do things in the name of religion that are highly questionable. Does not a community have at least as much of a duty to be concerned about pollution of human souls as it has to be concerned about pollution of the environment? (Among the activities that the community may regulate are abortion and sexual conduct. See, e.g., Anastaplo, *The American Moralist,* 389, 399; notes 110, 255 and 259, below.) Critical to the decline that we are witnessing is the abandonment by the community of both moral self-confidence and a reliance upon prudence. See note 12, above. See also 30 and 41, above.

What will be the long-run effects of the Religious Freedom Restoration Act of 1993? Although this statute attempts to revive questionable Su-preme Court readings of the Religion Clauses, it does have the merit of being subject to *statutory* correction if its effects should be dubious. See note 259, below. It is salutary, in any event, that Congress too should be seen as one of the guardians of the rights and liberties of the people. See notes 205 and 209, below.

69. The Virginia Ratification Convention included, in the last article of its proposed bill of rights in June 1788: "[N]o particular religious sect or society ought to be favored or established by Law in preference to others." The New York Ratification Convention, in July 1788, suggested the same

amendment (except for "particular"). See Appendixes I-1 and I-2 of this Commentary. See also notes 135 and 259, below.

Consider, on the intentions of the Religion Clauses of the First Amendment, President George Washington's 1790 letter to the Hebrew Congregation in Newport, Rhode Island:

> While I receive, with much satisfaction, your Address replete with expressions of affection and esteem, I rejoice in the opportunity of assuring you, that I shall always retain a grateful remembrance of the cordial welcome I experienced in my visit to Newport [on August 17, 1790], from all classes of Citizens.
>
> The reflection on the days of difficulty and danger which are past is rendered the more sweet from a consciousness that they are succeeded by days of uncommon prosperity and security. If we have wisdom to make the best use of the advantages with which we are now favored, we cannot fail, under the just administration of a good Government, to become a great and a happy people.
>
> The Citizens of the United States of America have a right to applaud themselves for having given to Mankind examples of an enlarged and liberal policy: a policy worthy of imitation. All possess alike liberty of conscience and immunities of citizenship. It is now no more that toleration is spoken of as if it was by the indulgence of one class of people, that another enjoyed the exercise of their inherent natural rights. For happily the Government of the United States, which gives to bigotry no sanction, to persecution no assistance, requires only that they who live under its protection, should demean themselves as good citizens, in giving it on all occasions their effectual support.
>
> It would be inconsistent with the frankness of my character not to avow that I am pleased with your favorable opinion of my Administration, and fervent wishes for my felicity. May the Children of the Stock of Abraham, who dwell in this land, continue to merit and enjoy the good will of the other Inhabitants; while every one shall sit in safety under his own vine and figtree, and there shall be none to make him afraid. May the father of all mercies scatter light and not darkness in our paths, and make us all in our several vocations useful here, and in his own due time and way everlastingly happy.

See *Papers of George Washington,* Library of Congress, CCCXXXV, 19–20; Morris A. Gutstein, ed., *To Bigotry No Sanction* (New York: Block Publishing Co., 1958), 87–92; Morris U. Schappes, ed., *A Documentary History of the Jews in the United States, 1654–1875* (New York: Citadel Press, 1950), 79–81; Paul F. Boller, Jr., *George Washington and Religion* (Dallas: Southern Methodist University Press, 1963), 185–87. This "immortal document" has been "rank[ed] with the Gettysburg Address as a testament of the human spirit." Harry V. Jaffa, "Were the Founding Fathers Christian?" *This World,* Spring/ Summer 1984, 4. See also Appendix G of this Commentary. Compare Appendix A, chapters 10 and 11, of this Commentary. See as well Henry Wadsworth Longfellow's poem, "The Jewish Cemetery at Newport" (1852).

70. Don B. Kates, Jr., "Second Amendment," in *Ency. Am. Const.*, 4: 1639.

71. Ibid., 4: 1639–40.

72. See, e.g., Crosskey, 1: 705.

73. See Letter from Joseph Hawley to Elbridge Gerry (Feb. 18, 1776), in *The Founders' Constitution*, 5: 216.

74. *Annals of Congress*, 1: 752 (1789). See also *The Founders' Constitution*, 5: 211. The possibility of judicial review is suggested in this Benson quotation. See, on the constitutional right (if any) to conscientious objection to military service, Anastaplo, "Church and State," 127–45, "On Freedom," 566.

75. Blackstone, 1: 139. See also ibid., 1: 140; note 134, below.

76. William Rawle, *A View of the Constitution of the United States* (2d. ed., 1829), 125–26, in *The Founders' Constitution*, 5: 213.

77. Rawle, in *The Founders' Constitution*, 5: 214.

78. Kates, "Second Amendment," 4: 1640 (emphasis added). If the argument is put this way, do not the kind and the degree of gun control become (as they should be) political, not constitutional, questions? See "Handguns Kill More Than They Protect," *Chicago Tribune* (editorial), Sept. 14, 1992, sec. 1, p. 16; "Of Guns and 2nd Amendment Myths," *Chicago Tribune* (editorial), Dec. 2, 1993, sec. 1, p. 22. Compare Robert J. Cottrol and Raymond T. Diamond, "The Second Amendment: Toward an Afro-Americanist Reconsideration," *Georgetown Law Journal*, 80: 309 (1991).

79. Joseph Story, *Commentaries on the Constitution of the United States* (1833), 3: 1890 (emphasis added), in *The Founders' Constitution*, 5: 214. One can see something of the old-fashioned American militia in Israel and in Switzerland today. On more than one occasion during the Summer of 1989, I felt quite safe (as a motorist traveling in Israel with my wife and two of our grandchildren) in picking up hitchhiking men and women in uniform who were carrying submachine guns and other weapons. However, stones thrown at our rented car on two occasions by "the Intifada" (in Bethlehem and in Hebron) were quite another matter.

Consider this suggestion, which provoked some angry letters to the editor: "Congress has the constitutional power to enact a Militia Act of 1992, to require every person who owns a gun or aspires to own one to 'enroll' in the militia. In plain 1990s English, if you want to own a gun, sign up with the National Guard." Robert A. Goldwin, "Gun Control Is Constitutional," *Wall Street Journal*, Dec. 12, 1991, p. A15. See also Letters to the Editor, *Wall Street Journal*, Jan. 14, 1992, p. A15, Dec. 13, 1993, p. A15; Anastaplo, *The American Moralist*, 367–74. See as well note 176, below, and the texts at notes 59 and 109 of this Commentary.

80. Benjamin Franklin, *The Gazetter and New Daily Advertiser*, May 2, 1765, in *The Founders' Constitution*, 5: 215 (emphasis added). See also Dennis J. Mahoney, "Third Amendment," in *Ency. Am. Const.*, 4: 1890.

81. *Annals of Congress*, 1: 752 (1789), in *The Founders' Constitution*, 5: 217–18.

82. Story, 3: 1893, in *The Founders' Constitution*, 5: 218.

83. See *World Almanac* (1992), 702, 940, 954; Erik Eckhom, "A Basic Issue: Whose Hands Should Guns Be Kept Out Of?," *New York Times,* April 3, 1992, p. A1. ("[F]irearms deaths . . . totalled 35,000 in 1989, including 18,000 suicides, 15,000 homicides, 1,500 accidents and others unspecified.") We may still have each year in most States more fatalities on the highways than from firearms, but many more people and resources are devoted to highway travel than to the use of guns. (Besides, the utilitarian can point out, the advantages of our massive motor traffic, despite its human costs, are generally recognized. Are not many more lives made possible, as well as saved, because of our highway traffic than are lost there?) See William Recktenwald, "Guns Lead a Deadly Race: More Illinoisans Die from Bullets Than from Car Crashes," *Chicago Tribune,* Nov. 1, 1983, sec. 1, p. 1. "Degrees of Terror," *Economist,* July 10, 1993, 24: "By comparison with anywhere else in the developed world, America is an astonishingly violent place. Belfast, let us suppose, is a 'terrorist' city; Washington, D.C. is not. Yet in the year up to the end of June, there had been just 11 deaths by violence in Belfast; in the year up to July 6th there had been 230 homicides in Washington."

We need not assume that Americans are significantly more violent in their passions than most other peoples—but Americans do insist upon having more lethal means readily available with which to "express" their passions. Thus we are told that "nine out of ten murders in industrialized nations occur in the United States." Colman McCarthy, Column, *National Catholic Reporter,* Oct. 15, 1993, p. 23. We are also told, "Handguns are virtually banned in Great Britain, Japan and Canada, with not-too-surprising results. In 1990, handguns killed only 22 people in Great Britain, 87 in Japan and 68 in Canada, compared to 10,567 in the USA." Barbara Reynolds, Column, *USA Today,* Jan. 7, 1994, p. 11A. Akira Kurosawa's 1949 film, *Stray Dog,* dramatizes, even more than do these handgun-killings statistics, profound divergences between ways of life. This movie depicts efforts by a police detective to recover the Colt pistol stolen from him. We see here the differences that one illicitly held gun may make in a community. But we see in this film even more a way of life, with oppressive as well as attractive features, that can make the strictest gun control feasible. (In Chicago, we are told, a couple of hundred illegal guns are seized by the police on a typical weekend. See William Recktenwald, "Best News of '94: Record Gun Seizure," *Chicago Tribune,* Jan. 4, 1994, sec. 1, p. 1.) See, on Japan and the United States, note 255, below. See, as additional reminders of how different another way of life can be, Kurosawa's classic films *Rashomon* and *The Seven Samurai.*

The widespread ownership of guns in the United States may be peculiarly fitting for a people who make as much as we do of both liberty and equality. One need not depend upon the law or champions (including *samurai*): that is, one is free (no matter how weak one happens to be physically) literally to take measures into one's own hands (either in self-defense or for revenge, to say nothing of increasing one's assets). On the other hand, the fear that many have of being gunned down on our streets in hardly liberating.

Two reports, published in the press on the same day, reflect the distinctive failings of two quite different ways of life:

Nearly 50,000 children and teenagers were killed by guns from 1970 through 1991 [in the United States], a total roughly equal to the number of [American] battle casualties in the Vietnam War, the Children's Defense Fund said Thursday. . . . Guns are regulated less [in the United States] than teddy bears or toasters, the group asserted. . . .

The report said juveniles now account for both a high and rapidly growing share of homicide offenders as well as victims. Of the nearly 50,000 children and teenagers killed by firearms from 1979 through 1991, there were 24,552 homicides, 16,614 suicides with a firearm, and 7,257 gun accidents. The figures come from the National Center for Health Statistics.

Associated Press, "Guns Killed 50,000 Kids in 13 Years," *Chicago Tribune,* Jan. 21, 1994, sec. 1, p. 15.

A huge store of gold, accumulated by Ferdinand E. Marcos during his 21-year rule of the Philippines, is lying in an airport warehouse in Switzerland, according to the British television program "Dispatches." The report said about 1,240 tons of gold, worth about $15.5 billion, was stored in a bonded warehouse at Zurich's Kloten airport. If the figure is correct, the hoard of gold would be equivalent to about 15 percent of the gold the U.S. government holds in Fort Knox.

"Marcos Fortune," *Chicago Sun-Times,* Jan. 21, 1994, p. 10. See, for periodic combinations of widespread domestic violence and official financial corruption, "A Survey of Nigeria," *Economist,* Aug. 21, 1993.

84. William J. Cuddihy, "Fourth Amendment (Historical Origins)," in *Ency. Am. Const.,* 2: 761.

85. *Huckle* v. *Money,* 95 Eng. Rep. 768 (C.P. 1763), in *The Founders' Constitution,* 5: 230. This was Chapter 39 of Magna Carta when it was originally issued in 1215. Chapters in Magna Carta were modified, added, or dropped in its various reissues. See note 41, above.

86. Cuddihy, 2: 763.

87. Massachusetts Constitution of 1780, Part One, Art. XIV. See Appendix F-2 of this Commentary.

88. Cuddihy, 2: 762.

89. The discussion that follows is adapted from my "Constitutional Comment" for Gera-Lind Kolarik and Wayne Klatt, *Freed to Kill: The True Story of Serial Murderer Larry Eyler* (New York: Avon Books, 1992), 418–21.

90. 32 U.S. (7 Pet.) 243 (1833). See note 92, below.

91. *Grumon* v. *Raymond,* 1 Conn. 40 (1814) (Reeve, C.J.), in *The Founders' Constitution,* 5: 240 (emphasis added). Whether judges are now as vigilant as they should be in supervising prosecutorial intrusions has been questioned:

The courts are often seen as a safeguard against encroachments on our fundamental liberties. But, from the numbers in a recent federal report on eavesdropping, it doesn't appear that judges nationwide put much value on any right we might have to converse privately.

In 1992 federal and state judges approved all 919 requests filed by prosecutors seeking permission for wiretaps or other electronic surveillance, according to the annual report on wiretaps by the Administrative Office of the U.S. Courts. It was the fourth consecutive year that judges had approved all requests for electronic surveillance. In fact, in the last decade the courts have approved 8,393 such wiretap requests and turned down only 7. . . .

But a former federal prosecutor with experience in wiretap cases says the statistics should be no cause for alarm. Federal prosecutors need approval from Department of Justice higher-ups before requesting permission from the courts, he said and there is careful review of such requests.

Still, one wonders whether the courts are a check in wiretap cases or a rubber stamp.

"On the Law," *Chicago Tribune,* May 18, 1993, sec. 3, p. 3.

92. See, for a challenging discussion of *Barron* v. *Baltimore* (as well as of the drafting and scope of the Bill of Rights), Crosskey, 2: 1056–82, 1090–1, 1101, 1124, 1134. See also note 206, below.

93. See Anastaplo, *The Constitution of 1787,* 133–34, 139. See also Anastaplo, "The Supreme Court Is Indeed a Court," in Rubert A. Licht, ed., *Is the Supreme Court the Guardian of the Constitution?* (Washington, D.C.: The AEI Press, 1993), 22; Ronald K. L. Collins, "The Principles of Power," in *Law and Philosophy,* 2: 671. See, on the proper guardians of the Constitution, Blackstone, 1: 7–9; Crosskey, 2: 1082. See also Ralph A. Rossum, "Civic Virtue and Republican Government: The Practice of James Wilson's Constitutional Theory," in *Law and Philosophy,* 2: 684.

94. See Blackstone, 4: 74–93; Farrand, 2: 345–50; Crosskey, 1: 444, 470–77; Anastaplo, *The Constitution of 1787,* 146–47. See also Jonathan K. Van Patten, "Magic, Prophecy, and the Law of Treason in Reformation England," *American Journal of Legal History,* 27: 1 (1983). Consider as well how Blackstone (4: 92–93) describes the punishments inflicted upon conviction of treason:

The punishment of high treason in general is very solemn and terrible. 1. That the offender be drawn to the gallows, and not be carried or walk; though usually a sledge or hurdle is allowed, to preserve the offender from the extreme torment of being dragged on the gound or pavement. 2. That he be hanged by the neck, and then cut down alive. 3. That his entrails be taken out, and burned, while he is yet alive. 4. That his head be cut off. 5. That his body be divided into four parts. 6. That his head and quarters be at the king's disposal. (Blackstone's note: This punishment for treason sir Edward Coke tells us, is warranted by divers examples in scripture; for Joab was drawn, Bithan was hanged, Judas was embowelled, and so of the rest. [3 Inst. 211])

The king may, and often doth discharge all the punishment, except beheading, especially where any of noble blood are attainted. . . .

In the case of coining, which is a treason of a different complexion from the rest, the punishment is milder for male offenders; being only to be drawn, and hanged by the neck till dead. But in treasons of every kind the punishment of women is the same, and different from that of men. For, as the natural modesty of the sex forbids the exposing and publicly mangling their bodies, their sentence (which is to the full as terrible to sense as the other) is to be drawn to the gallows, and there to be burned alive.

See, for perhaps related differences between male and female and how women may further "benefit" from the natural solicitude of men for their welfare, note 216, below.

95. See Anastaplo, *The Constitution of 1787*, 124–25.

96. One can see again and again in Plato's *Laws*, even when a new city is being founded in words by the participants in that dialogue, that many complicated ways of doing things among the Greeks must be taken into account. I have twice used, with considerable success, the *Laws* (in the excellent translation by Thomas L. Pangle) as the sole text in law-school jurisprudence courses. My Loyola colleague, Professor William T. Braithwaite, has had similar experiences. Compare note 124, below.

97. Jay A. Sigler, "Double Jeopardy," in *Ency. Am. Const.*, 2: 576. See also Blackstone, 4: 256.

98. *The King* v. *Dr. Purnell*, 96 Eng. Rep. 20 (K.B. 1748), in *The Founders' Constitution*, 5: 219.

99. Leonard W. Levy, "Due Process of Law," in *Ency. Am. Const.*, 5: 589. These phrases may not have been regarded as synonymous. This is aside from the highly questionable recourse there has been in the United States to that peculiar hybrid called "substantive due process." See, e.g., note 204, below. See, on due process, *Speiser* v. *Randall*, 357 U.S. 513 (1958); Anastaplo, "Due Process and the Freedom of Speech: A Celebration of *Speiser* v. *Randall*," *John Marshall Law Review*, 20: 7 (1986); note 106, below. But Blackstone counsels us (4: 226), "[T]he law [should] not suffer itself to be trifled with by [certain] evasions, especially under the cloke of legal process." See also notes 66 and 68, above.

Has the law been "trifled with" in the Felix Bloch matter? See David Wise, "The Felix Bloch Affair," *New York Times Magazine*, May 13, 1990, 29. "Felix Bloch's case is extraordinary. Never before has a high-ranking official of the [United States] Government been publicly branded as a suspected spy for the Soviet Union, followed around for months by the F.B.I., the television networks, and the press, yet not formally accused, indicted, or brought to trial." Ibid., 31. See also Anna Quindlen, "A Woman Scorned," *New York Times*, Jan. 29, 1994, p. 15. Four years later the Director of the Central Intelligence Agency condemned an exposed spy within the Agency as "a malignant betrayer of his country who killed a number of people who helped the United States and the West win the cold war." He also said that these agents "died because this warped, murdering traitor wanted a bigger house and a Jaguar." Tim Weiner, "Agency Chief Pledges to Overhaul 'Fraternity' Atmosphere at C.I.A.," *New York Times,* July 19, 1994, p. A10. See notes 258 and 260, below. See, on the Alger Hiss case, Anastaplo, *The American Moralist,* 201–4.

100. Levy, "Due Process of Law," 589, 591. Our reservations in the Western World about the exercise of authority may be colored by the fact that the two great trials at the foundations of the philosophic and Christian traditions are generally believed to have been unjustly decided. See, on the trials of Socrates and of Jesus, Anastaplo, *Human Being and Citizen,* 8, 203, "On Trial," 882, 900. See also note 41, above, note 120, below.

101. Farrand, 2: 628 (Sept. 15, 1787) (Nathanial Gorham of Massachusetts). See Lecture No. 2, Section V, of this Commentary. See, on how various elements of trial by jury may be discussed, John A. Murley, "Numbers, Justice, and Trial by Jury," in *Law and Philosophy,* 2: 819.

102. *Annals of Congress,* 1: 754 (1789), in *The Founders' Constitution,* 5: 377.

103. Compare James Wilson, "A Charge Delivered to the Grand Jury" (1791) (advocating use of the death penalty) with Benjamin Rush, "On Punishing Murder by Death" (1792) (questioning the effectiveness of harsh punishments). See *The Founders' Constitution,* 5: 378–79. See, on capital punishment, Blackstone, 4: 18–19; Anastaplo, *The American Moralist,* 605. See also note 134, below. Reliance on more and more prisons and executions to reduce crime among us is like reliance on price controls to promote market fairness. Matters are probably made worse, at least in our circumstances, by recourse to such measures. See, e.g., "Dear Mr. President . . . ," *Wall Street Journal,* Jan. 14, 1994, p. A10 (signed by 562 economists): "Price controls produce shortages, black markets and reduced quality. This has been the universal experience in the 4,000 years that governments have tried to artificially hold prices down using regulations." This is not to deny that communities are naturally inclined to experiment both with price controls and with capital punishment and prisons, no matter what competent economists and competent criminologists may happen to say from time to time. See the columns by Mike Royko and Stephen Chapman, *Chicago Tribune,* Jan. 27, 1994, sec. 1, pp. 3, 23. See also note 233, below.

104. See Merrill D. Peterson, "Alien and Sedition Acts," in *Ency. Am. Const.,* 5: 43–44. See also Anastaplo, *The Constitutionalist,* 810.

105. *Annals of Congress,* 1: 439 (1789), in *The Founders' Constitution,* 5: 399. See also note 14, above.

Consider how Blackstone's description of the privileges of Parliament, and why they should never be completely enumerated, applies to the rights of the people of the United States:

The *privileges* of parliament are likewise very large and indefinite; which has occasioned an observation, that the principal privilege of parliament consisted in this, that it's privileges were not generally known to any but the parliament itself. . . . Privilege of parliament was principally established, in order to protect it's members not only from being molested by their fellow-subjects, but also more especially from being oppressed by the power of the crown. If therefore all the privileges of parliament were once to be set down and ascertained, and no privilege to be allowed but what was so defined and determined, it were easy for the executive power to devise some new case, not within the line of privilege, and under pretence thereof to harass any refractory member and violate the freedom of parliament. The dignity and independence of the two houses are therefore in great measure preserved by keeping their privileges indefinite. Some however of the more notorious privileges of the members of either house are, privilege of speech, of person, of their domestics, and of their lands and goods. As to the first, privilege of speech, it is declared by the statute 1 W. & M. st. 2. c. 2. as one of the liberties of the people, "that the freedom of speech, and debates, and proceedings in parliament, ought not to be impeached or questioned in any court or place out of parliament." And this freedom of speech is particularly demanded of the king in person, by the speaker of the house of commons, at the opening of every new parliament.

Blackstone, 1: 159–60. Notice that a parliamentary privilege is referred to as "one of the liberties *of the people*" (emphasis added). See, on Thomas More and the freedom of speech "demanded of the king in person," Appendix B of this Commentary. (See, on the kind of monarch Thomas More had to deal with in Henry VIII, Blackstone, 4: 25, 424. That monarch was partly responsible for the transformation, if not the virtual nullification, of the opening chapter of Magna Carta.) Underlying the prudence of keeping the privileges, or rights, of the people "indefinite" may be a recognition of the ultimate right of revolution. See, on that great right, Blackstone, 1: 157, 4: 82; Appendix E-3 of this Commentary. See, on "the slavish and exploded doctrine of non-resistance," Blackstone, 1: 326, 356.

106. For example, although natural right may dictate that no one (except in the most extraordinary circumstances) should be condemned without a fair trial, this does not by itself either make trial by jury necessary or identify the indispensable elements of a proper trial by jury in a criminal case. Does the American emphasis upon a written constitution tend to undermine that reliance upon an unwritten constitution which might be more sensitive to natural right? See, on natural right, Blackstone, 1: 27, 32, 54, 4: 66f; Leo Strauss, "Natural Law," in *International Encyclopedia of the Social Sciences* (1964); Yves R. Simon, *The Tradition of Natural Law: A Philosopher's Reflection* (New York: Fordham University Press, 1992); Anastaplo, *Human Being and Citizen*, 46, 74, "Justice Brennan, Natural Right, and Constitutional Interpretation," *Cardozo Law Review*, 10: 201 (1988), "Natural Law or Natural Right? An Appreciation of James V. Schall, S.J.," *Loyola of New Orleans Law Review*, 38: 915 (1993); notes 63 and 99, above, notes 120, 130, 198, and 216, below. (Unfortunately, a last-minute printer's error turned "Natural Right" into "Natural Rights" in the title of this *Loyola of New*

Orleans article.) Consider Stephen Vanderslice, "A Natural Right Perspective on Contemporary Moral Questions," in *Law and Philosophy*, 1: 130; James Lehrberger, "Crime without Punishment: Thomistic Natural Law and the Problem of Sanctions," ibid., 1: 237; John A. Gueguen, "Beyond Legal Positivism and Legal Naturalism," ibid., 1: 258; Pamela Werrbach Proietti, "Natural Right(s) and Natural Law: John Locke and the Scholastic Tradition," ibid., 1: 280. See, for assessments of a series of ancient and modern trials, Anastaplo, "On Trial." A review of this 1991 *Loyola University of Chicago Law Journal* collection (22: 765–1118), along with a review of *The American Moralist*, has been prepared by Christopher A. Colmo for the *Political Science Reviewer*. Additional reviews of my work, including constitutional studies, have been prepared by others for the same journal and for a 1995 American Political Science Association meeting panel.

See, for an explanation of the "natural meaning" of a maxim, Story, 3: 1898, in *The Founders' Constitution*, 5: 400.

107. See Jonathan Elliot, ed., *The Debates in the Several State Conventions on the Adoption of the Federal Constitution* (2d ed.; Philadelphia: J. B. Lippincott Co., 1876). See also Anastaplo, *The Constitution of 1787*, 308 n. 19; Appendixes I-1 and I-2 of this Commentary.

108. See, for discussions during the Ratification Campaign of standing-armies limitations, *The Complete Anti-Federalist*, Herbert J. Storing and Murray Dry, eds. (Chicago: University of Chicago Press, 1981) (another quite useful collection); Blackstone (St. George Tucker, ed.), 1: 300–01, in *The Founders' Constitution*, 5: 218. See also note 176, below.

109. Farrand, 2: 616–17 (Sept. 14, 1787). See note 176, below, and Lecture No. 6, Section II, of this Commentary.

110. *Roe* v. *Wade*, 410 U.S. 113 (1973); *Doe* v. *Bolton*, 410 U.S. 179 (1973). Much the same can be said about the Executive Order invalidated in *The Steel Seizure Case* (*Youngstown Sheet & Tube Company* v. *Sawyer*, 343 U.S. 579 [1952]). See Anastaplo, *The Constitution of 1787*, 114, 316 n. 77. See, on the abortion issue and the limits of abortion regulation today, Anastaplo, *The American Moralist*, 399, 603; note 68, above.

111. Plato, *Laws* 788A-B. See note 96, above.

112. See, e.g., Charles Cotesworth Pinckney, Speech in the South Carolina House of Representatives (Jan. 18, 1788), in Farrand, 3: 256–57; note 14, above.

113. See, on the Tenth Amendment, Crosskey, 1: 675–708; Anastaplo, *The Constitution of 1787*, 338. See also, in Appendix J-5 of this Commentary, the preamble for the Bill of Rights proposals sent by Congress to the States.

114. Story, 3: 1900–1, in *The Founders' Constitution*, 5: 406–7.

115. 2 U.S. (2 Dall.) 419 (1793).

116. Ibid. Notice the use of *construed* in the Eleventh Amendment. Congress may have been suggesting that it was interpreting, perhaps even properly interpreting, the Constitution, rather than amending it. Much the same can be said about the use of *construed* in the Ninth Amendment. Compare the Seventeenth Amendment.

117. 3 U.S. (3 Dall.) 378, 382 (1798).

118. Since 1801, when Thomas Jefferson was elected President by the House of Representatives, John Quincy Adams has been the only President to have been truly elected in the same manner. That was in 1825. The Hayes-Tilden contest in 1877, a much more complicated affair, was only formally resolved by the House of Representatives. See C. Vann Woodward, "Compromise of 1877," in *Ency. Am. Const.*, 1: 338–39.

119. The emergence of political parties has also led to the virtual elimination of the Presidential electors in the States. (It is probably time to get rid of them altogether.) A related change is the designation in the Twelfth Amendment of three, rather than five, as the number of candidates to be considered by the House of Representatives in the event that no candidate has a majority of Presidential electors. Party discipline makes it far less likely, than the Framers originally anticipated, that there would be more than two or three serious Presidential candidates for the House to have to consider on any particular occasion.

120. Anastaplo, *The Constitutionalist*, 420. See notes 146 and 149, below. See also notes 132 and 147, below.

See, for another effort to bring together the teachings of the Declaration of Independence and of ancient philosphers (or modern constitutional democracy and classic natural right), Leo Strauss, *Natural Right and History* (Chicago: University of Chicago Press, 1952), e.g., 3, 7–8. Compare ibid., 324. Consider Hilail Gildin, "Leo Strauss and the Crisis of Liberal Democracy," in Deutsch and Soffer, eds., *The Crisis of Liberal Democracy*, 92–93:

> The extent to which [Leo] Strauss's work reflects his concern with the contemporary crisis of philosphy—a crisis that, in his opinion, is at the bottom of the theoretical crisis of modern liberalism—seems to support the belief that his political preferences derive from his concern for the future of philosophy. Yet it would be a mistake to conclude that Strauss cared about the fate of constitutional democracy only to the extent to which it was linked to the fate of philosophy. Like Socrates, he was just in more than one sense. His support of liberal democracy can be compared to his support of political Zionism. No one who knew Strauss ever doubted the depth and genuineness of his concern for Israel. Nor could anyone who knew him think that this concern was based on the belief that the fate of philosophy in some mysterious way depended on the survival of Israel. He thought no such thing. His support of political Zionism was unhesitating even though his approval of it was not unqualified.

Compare Victor Gourevitch, "A Reply to Gildin," ibid., 112–13, and Gildin, "A Response to Gourevitch," ibid., 118f; Harry Neumann, "Leo Strauss or Nihilism? The Case against Politics," in *Law and Philosophy*, 1: 391. See also Jaffa, *Original Intent*, 225–26, n. 11; note 260, below.

Consider as well Leo Strauss, *The City and Man* (Chicago: Rand McNally and Company, 1964), 122:

> By answering the question of how the good city is possible, Socrates introduces philosophy as a theme of the *Republic* [473C-D]. This means

416

that in the *Republic* philosophy is not introduced as the end of man but as a means for realizing justice and therefore the just city, the city as armed camp which is characterized by absolute communism and equality of the sexes in the upper class, the class of warriors. Since the rule of philosophers is not introduced as an ingredient of the just city but only as a means for its realization, Aristotle legitimately disregards that institution in his critical analysis of the *Republic*.

See notes 135, 147, and 260, below. See also note 100, above.

Both the ancient philosophers and the Declaration of Independence had to take account of citizen piety. See, for the Declaration's uses of the Divine, note 135, below. See, on natural theology, Kenneth Hart Green, *Jew and Philosopher: The Return to Maimonides in the Jewish Thought of Leo Strauss* (Albany: State University of New York Press, 1993), 238; Plato, *Laws*, bk 10. See also ibid., 232–33. See as well notes 138, 144, and 149, below.

121. *The Political Thought of American Statesmen*, Morton J. Frisch and Richard G. Stevens, eds. (Itasca, Ill.: F. E. Peacock, 1973), 6.

122. Unless otherwise indicated, all quotations in the text of Lecture No. 9 of this Commentary from the Jefferson-Adams correspondence are taken from their letters of July 5 and July 16, 1814. These two letters, which are set forth in Appendixes K-1 and K-2 of this Commentary, are taken from *The Adams-Jefferson Letters*, Lester J. Cappon, ed. (New York: Simon and Schuster, 1971), 430–49. (Cited hereafter as *Adams-Jefferson Letters*.) I use modern spellings whenever I quote from these letters in the text of Lecture No. 9.

Thomas Jefferson is associated with the Declaration of Independence (found in Appendix E-3) and the Virginia Statute of Religious Liberty (found in Appendix G). John Adams is associated with the Massachusetts Declaration of Rights (found in Appendix F-2). Adams and Jefferson were the first Presidential leaders of their respective political parties.

123. See, e.g., Letter from Jefferson to Don Valentin de Foronda Coruna (Dec. 14, 1813), *The Writings of Thomas Jefferson*, Andrew A. Lipscomb, ed. (Washington, D.C.: Thomas Jefferson Memorial Association, 1905), 14: 32. (Cited hereafter as *Writings of Jefferson*.) See Letter from Adams to Jefferson (Mar. 2, 1816), ibid., 14: 441; also *Adams-Jefferson Letters*, 464.

124. Similar criticisms are made by them elsewhere. See, e.g., Letter from Jefferson to John Short (Oct. 31, 1819), *Writings of Jefferson*, 15: 219.

A kinder dismissal of Plato for Americans may be seen in the course of an 1845 comment by Edgar Allan Poe on Plato's *Laws* (see note 96, above):

> No one can doubt the purity and nobility of the Platonian soul, or the ingenuity of the Platonian intellect. But if the question be put to-day, what is the value of the Platonian philosophy, the proper answer is, "exactly nothing at all." We do not believe that any good purpose is answered by popularizing his dreams; on the contrary we do believe that they have a strong tendency of ill—intellectually of course.

James A. Harrison, ed., *The Complete Works of Edgar Allan Poe* (New York: Thomas Y. Crowell & Co., 1902), 12: 164–65. (See, on the dreams of Plato,

Section VIII of this lecture, No. 9. See also note 146, below.) "We know from various accounts that Plato was considered by the founding fathers as a poor guide in practical affairs. He was considered a radical, a constructor of imaginary utopias—an idealist in the most pejorative sense." Aryeh L. Motzkin, Book Review, *Review of Metaphysics*, June 1993, 864. Compare how Plato could be regarded in Italy during the High Renaissance:

> [The Platonic Academy in Florence] was dedicated to study of Plato and of the Neoplatonists. The presumed birthday of the philosopher was celebrated every year on November 7 with amiable discussions of one or more of the dialogues. Plato's philosophy was taken to be universally applicable, and [Marsilio] Ficino liked to say that one could be neither a good citizen nor a good Christian without being a Platonist as well

Bonner Mitchell, *Rome in the High Renaissance: The Age of Leo X* (Norman: University of Oklahoma Press, 1973), 15.

125. See Plato, *Symposium* 185D–E. See also Strauss, *Socrates and Aristophanes*; note 132, below. It can be startling to notice how much the self-deprecating Socrates displays himself as in fact knowing. See Anastaplo, "Freedom of Speech and the First Amendment," 1945–58 (Part I). See note 1 (end), above. See also Anastaplo, "On Freedom," 666.

126. See Letter from Jefferson to William Canby (Sept. 18, 1813), *Writings of Jefferson*, 13: 377. See also note 60, above.

127. See Anastaplo, *The American Moralist*, 350.

128. Letter from Jefferson to Nathaniel F. Moore (Sept. 22, 1818), *Writings of Jefferson*, 15: 218.

129. See Letter from Jefferson to William Short (Oct. 31, 1819), ibid., 15: 219, 222–24.

130. See, on the Declaration of Independence and the pursuit of happiness, Anastaplo, "The Constitution at Two Hundred," 987. Consider also Laurence Berns's remarks at a St. John's College memorial service in 1979 for Simon Kaplan:

> [H]e was concerned for the land of his refuge. What troubled him has been called many things: pseudo-sophistication, permissiveness, moral decline. His own way of putting it was much simpler: barbarism and, most dangerous of all for America, hedonism. What seemed to bother him was the fact that when people cease to observe and impose limits on themselves, it becomes natural to think more about having limits imposed by others from above.

Anastaplo, *The American Moralist*, 294. And not only "from above," as Nazi Germany showed us? Consider as well *Haggai* 1: 2–4:

> Thus says the Lord of hosts: "This people say the time has not yet come to rebuild the house of the Lord." Then the word of the Lord came to Haggai the prophet, "Is it time for you yourselves to dwell in your paneled houses, while this house [of the Lord] lies in ruin?"

Compare 1 *Chronicles* 17:1. See, on the Nazis, natural right, and the 1945–1946 Nuremberg Trial, Anastaplo, "On Trial," 977. See also notes 30 and 60, above, note 252, below.

Central to the purpose of this Commentary and its companion Commentary, at least for lawyers and judges, is this advice from Blackstone in response to the suggestion that the training of lawyers "drop all liberal education, as of no use to lawyers; and to place [would-be lawyers], in it's stead, at the desk of some skilful attorney; in order to initiate them early in all the depths of practice, and render them more dextrous in the mechanical part of the business" (1: 32):

> Making therefore due allowance for one or two shining exceptions, experience may teach us to foretell that a lawyer thus educated to the bar, in subservience to attorneys and solicitors, will find that he has begun at the wrong end. If practice be the whole he is taught, practice must also be the whole he will ever know: if he be uninstructed in the elements and first principles upon which the rule of practice is founded, the least variation from established precedents will totally distract and bewilder him: *ita lex scripta est* is the utmost his knowledge will arrive at; he must never aspire to form, and seldom expect to comprehend any arguments drawn *a priori*, from the spirit of the laws and the natural foundations of justice.

See also Eugene Miller, "Washington's Patronage of Education," in *Law and Philosophy*, 2: 700; Anastaplo, "The Constitution at Two Hundred," 1060.

The "liberal education" that Blackstone recommends for lawyers must take less for granted in our time than in his with respect to the preparation of youngsters before they come to the study of law. This is reflected in suggestions I have made for law-school curriculum reform:

> Curriculum reform . . . should include the provision for a mandatory year-long course (preferably in the first year of law school, but no later than the second year) in the two great texts of the English-speaking world: half of the year in this course should be devoted to the Bible (preferably in the King James translation because of the wonders and influence of its language); the other half of that year should be devoted to Shakespeare, I have tried to make the case, in my Commentary on the Constitution, for the influence of Shakespeare as a condition for sustained republican government on a large scale in the modern world. In addition, Shakespeare brings together for us, in an inspired way, the teachings both of the Bible and of the Greek and Roman classics.

> A sound acquaintance with the Biblical and Shakespearean texts (and thus, indirectly, with the classics) has always been important for the accomplished American lawyer, promoting as it does a seriousness of thought as well as a better grasp of the language and the great heritage of the Western World. One's ability both to read and to write is likely to be significantly enhanced. A common exposure to such texts also provides a sound basis for meaningful discourse about the matters that we should be (and indeed are) interested in. True, these are texts that students *should* be quite

familiar with by the time they come to law school but, alas, that is not the case. . . . Serious attention to the greatest texts of the Western World does help us respect the tried-and-true and to discourage novelty. All this serves as well to counter the effects of our productive and invaluable market economy, an economy that does tend to encourage constant change, if not even ruthlessness.

A not unrelated law-curriculum proposal is less utopian. I refer to the suggestion that Constitutional Law courses in our law schools should work in large part from a careful reading of the Constitution, which requires as preparation a few weeks of studying such constitutional documents as the Declaration of Independence, the Articles of Confederation, and the Northwest Ordinance before turning first to the Constitution itself and then to the cases that purport to interpret and apply that instrument. My impression has long been that such a study of the Constitution best equips the student of law to grasp what the United States Supreme Court and other courts happen to say from time to time.

Anastaplo, "Rome, Piety, and Law," 108–10. See also Anastaplo, "On Freedom," 724–26. See, on the limitations of (perhaps *especially* of) the best law schools, *Law and Philosophy*, 2: 771 (headnote). See, for useful introductions to various of Shakespeare's works, John Alvis and Thomas West, eds., *Shakespeare as Political Thinker* (Durham: Carolina Academic Press, 1981); Alvis, *Shakespeare's Understanding of Honor* (Durham: Carolina Academic Press, 1990); Allan Bloom with Harry V. Jaffa, *Shakespeare's Politics* (New York: Basic Books, 1964); Michael Platt, *Rome and Romans According to Shakespeare* (Salzburg: Institut für Englische Sprache und Literatur, 1976). See also David Grene, "*Measure for Measure:* Mythological History, Reality, and the Stage," in *Law and Philosophy*, 2: 871; Michael Platt, "To Emulate or To Be (Aeneas and Hamlet)," ibid., 2: 917; Leo Paul S. de Alvarez, "Biblical Allusions in *The Comedy of Errors*," ibid., 2: 981; note 188, below. See as well Elmer Gertz, Book Review, ibid., 1: 562; Wendy Ann Braithwaite, "Shaw and Shakespeare," ibid., 2: 1052; Gisela N. Berns, "Schiller's Drama: Fulfillment of History and Philosophy in Poetry," ibid., 2: 989.

A distinguished member of the United States Department of Justice has written to me upon reading my curriculum-reform proposals, "I strongly agree with your 'utopian' proposal about the potential value in the legal curriculum of a Bible/Shakespeare course. Both as a law teacher and as a practicing lawyer I have become acutely aware of the impoverished cultural background many of the best-educated law students and young lawyers bring to the understanding of the law." He added that he is "pessimistic about the survival of our legal tradition when it is so cut off from its roots." See notes 149 and 250, below. Consider also this assessment of George III: "His mind was Hanoverian, with an infinite capacity for mastering detail, and limited success in dealing with large issues and main principles." Churchill, *A History of the English-Speaking Peoples*, 3: 143. Compare the observation of an effusive character in Jane Austen, *Mansfield Park* (chap. 34): "But Shakespeare one gets acquainted with without knowing how. It is a part of an Englishman's constitution. His thoughts and beauties are so spread abroad that one touches them every where, one is intimate with him by instinct."

131. See, for Adams's assessment of the thinkers of his own time, Letter from Adams to Jefferson (Dec. 25, 1813), *Writings of Jefferson*, 15: 33–34; also *Adams-Jefferson Letters*, 409. Consider the following instructive account of the American heritage:

> The political thought guiding the Founding, and hence the subsequent constitutional order, emerges out of and in some sense rebels against three complex, diverse, and competing traditions of Western political and republican theorizing. These traditions are: (1) the theocratic tradition rooted in the Bible, (2) the classical republican tradition rooted in classical political philosophy, and (3) the liberal tradition which originated out of a vast rebellion against the first two in a radically new rationalism and politics spearheaded by Machiavelli, Bacon, and Descartes. I would characterize the political thought of the American Founding as occupying, if you will, a tension-ridden field of spiritual and intellectual energy emanating from these three poles of radiation. The attaining of a clear view of the distinctive and even warring forces emanating from these three poles is fundamental to any accurate conceptualization of the Founders' enterprise. Only by such a careful delineation can we begin to understand what truly defines, and in some degree distinguishes, the thought of the various American Founders. That definition consists partly in the Founders' firm agreement with one pole—that of rebellious modern rationalism—over and against the two older poles, but also partly in various Founders' sometimes elegant, but oftentimes awkward, attempts to create new syntheses of ancient and modern rationalist and religious political thinking.

Thomas L. Pangle, "The Classical Challenge to the American Constitution," *Chicago-Kent Law Review*, 66: 145, 148 (1990). (Cited hereafter as Pangle.) See as well Anastaplo, *The American Moralist*, xiv–xvi. All this is not to deny that "the pursuit of happiness" may be approached in a more wholesome manner; a healthy hedonism and a sturdy individualism (disciplined by the right kind of art) can be rooted in the pursuit by the virtuous of happiness, properly understood. See, on music and the Constitution, the text at note 260 of this Commentary. See also Plato, *Republic* 424B-D. See, on "how Americans combat individualism by the doctrine of interest well understood," Ken Masugi, ed., *Interpreting Tocqueville's "Democracy in America"* (Savage, Md.: Rowman and Littlefield, 1991), 425. Compare Mera Flaumenhaft, "Housebound or Floating Free: The American Home in *Huckleberry Finn*," in *Law and Philosophy*, 2: 1011.

Central to the presuppositions of this Commentary is this proposition:

> The implications of a principle can go far beyond what the immediate framers of that principle were either able to recognize or willing to put up with. This can be said not only about [John Milton's] *Areopagitica*, but also

about such other great statements of principle in the Anglo-American heritage as Magna Carta, the Declaration of Independence, and the Fourteenth Amendment.

Anastaplo, "On Freedom," 560–61. See Lecture No. 3, Section II, of this Commentary. See also note 69, above.

132. Particularly helpful translations of Plato's *Apology* and *Crito* and of Aristophanes' *Clouds*, by Thomas G. West and Grace Starry West, have been published by the Cornell University Press. See also Willmoore Kendall, *Contra Mundum* (New Rochelle, N.Y.: Arlington House, 1971), 149; Patrick Coby, *Socrates and the Sophistic Enlightenment: A Commentary on Plato's "Protagoras"* (Lewisburg: Bucknell University Press, 1987); Coby, "The Philosopher Outside the City: The Apolitical Socrates of the *Crito*," in *Law and Philosophy*, 1: 84; Walter Nicgorski, "Assessment of 'The Socratic Turn'," ibid., 1: 213; David L. Schaefer, "Was Socrates a Corrupter?," ibid., 1: 73, Anastaplo, *Human Being and Citizen*, 8, 84, 203 (on the *Apology*, *Meno*, and *Crito* of Plato); note 125, above. See, on Jean-Jacques Rousseau, Hilail Gildin, "A Note on Leo Strauss's Interpretation of Rousseau," in *Law and Philosophy*, 1: 311; Leonard R. Sorenson, "The 'Good Man' and the 'Virtuous Citizen' in Rousseau's Republic," ibid., 1: 318; Mary P. Nichols, "Rousseau's Influence on Current Theories of Education," ibid., 1: 329. Perhaps Jefferson was exposed to Rousseau's influence more than any other American statesman of note.

133. Jefferson repeats this in an 1819 letter. Letter from Jefferson to William Short (Oct. 31, 1819), *Writings of Jefferson*, 15: 219–20. He anticipates here the critique of Platonized Christianity by Friedrich Nietzsche. See, on Nietzsche upon Christianity as Platonism for the people, Leo Strauss, "Philosophy as Rigorous Science and Political Philosophy," *Interpretation*, 2: 5 (1971). See, on the relation between egalitarian individualism and Nietzsche's "last man," ibid., 2: 4; notes 144, 149, and 172, below. See, on Nietzsche, Anastaplo, *The American Moralist*, 125.

134. Letter from Jefferson to Roger C. Weightman (June 24, 1826), ibid., 16: 182. Jefferson also observed in this letter, as he anticipated the celebration of the fiftieth anniversary of the greatest Fourth of July:

> All eyes are opened, or opening, to the rights of man. The general spread of the light of science has already laid open to every view the palpable truth, that the mass of mankind has not been born with saddles on their backs, nor a favored few booted and spurred, ready to ride them legitimately, by the grace of God. These are grounds of hope for others.

Compare, on the Jeffersonian recognition of the aristocratic imperatives of a democratic age, Anastaplo, *The American Moralist*, 103–7. Even so, even the most aristocratically minded American is not apt to speak in the following terms about class differences:

> Death is ordered to be punished with death; not because one is equivalent to the other, for that would be expiation, and not punishment. Nor is

death always an equivalent for death: the execution of a needy decrepit assassin is a poor satisfaction for the murder of a nobleman in the bloom of his youth, and full enjoyment of his friends, his honours, and his fortune. But the reason upon which this sentence is grounded seems to be, that this is the highest penalty that man can inflict, and tends most to the security of the world, by removing one murderer from the earth, and setting a dreadful example to deter others: so that even this grand instance proceeds upon other principles than those of retaliation.

Blackstone, 4: 14. See note 103, above. See also Gary D. Glenn, "Cyrus' Corruption of Aristocracy," in *Law and Philosophy*, 1: 147.

Is it not the aristocratic inclination of the British constitution that encourages an emphasis upon excellence and hence liberty more than an emphasis upon justice and hence equality? Thus Blackstone could observe (1: 140–41):

To preserve these [rights] from violation, it is necessary that the constitution of parliaments be supported in it's full vigor; and limits certainly known, be set to the royal prerogative. And, lastly, to vindicate these rights, when actually violated or attacked, the subjects of England are entitled, in the first place, to the regular administration and free course of justice in the courts of law; next to the right of petitioning the king and parliament for redress of grievances; and lastly to the right of having and using arms for self-preservation and defence. And all these rights and liberties it is our birthright to enjoy entire; unless where the laws of our country have laid them under necessary restraints. Restraints in themselves so gentle and moderate, as will appear upon farther enquiry, that no man of sense or probity would wish to see them slackened. For all of us have it in our choice to do every thing that a good man would desire to do; and are restrained from nothing, but what would be pernicious either to ourselves or to our fellow citizens. So that this review of our situation may fully justify the observation of a learned French author, who indeed generally both thought and wrote in the spirit of a genuine freedom [citing Montesquieu, *The Spirit of the Laws*, bk. 11, chap. 5]; and who hath not scrupled to profess, even in the very bosom of his native country, that the English is the only nation in the world, where political or civil liberty is the direct end of it's constitution.

See also Blackstone, 1: 6; notes 48 and 60, above. Consider the relation of liberty to equality that is discussed throughout this book, anticipated as it is in the eleventh paragraph of the Preface of this Commentary.

The importance of the character of the people for the proper combination of liberty and equality is anticipated in the final paragraph of the Preface of this Commentary. Unity has always been regarded as vital to the effectiveness of a people, as may be seen in an 1843 circular prepared by Abraham Lincoln and two political allies:

That "union is strength" is a truth that has been known, illustrated and declared, in various ways and forms in all ages of the world. That great fabulist and philosopher, Aesop, illustrated it by his fable of the bundle of sticks, and he whose wisdom surpasses that of all philosophers, has declared that "a house divided against itself cannot stand."

Collected Works of Lincoln, 315. A general familiarity not only with the Bible but also with Aesop seems to be assumed here. The equality principle, so critical to American self-respect and hopes, is challenged by the awareness, throughout the Aesop stories, of a hierarchy rooted in nature and enhanced by virtue. Illustrative of Aesop's understanding of the dictates of nature are two of his shortest fables, one of them set in what could be called the state of nature, the other set in a political context. The first story tells us:

A vixen sneered at a lioness because she never bore more than one cub. "Only one," she replied, "but a lion."

Fables of Aesop, S. A. Handford (London: Penguin Books, 1964), 19. See also ibid., 73. The other story tells us:

When the hares addressed a public meeting and claimed that all should have fair shares, the lions answered: "A good speech, Hairy-Feet, but it lacks claws and teeth such as we have."

Ibid., 27. See also ibid., 15, 23, 46, 48. Compare ibid., 41 (about the lion unexpectedly saved by the mouse he had spared), 72. One can see in Lincoln's thought, however guarded his public statements had to be, a recognition of the facts of political life taught by Aesop. See notes 211 and 225, below.

135. See, e.g., Letter from Jefferson to Alexander von Humboldt (Dec. 6, 1813), ibid., 14: 21. Jefferson routinely included the Protestant clergy among the "priests" to be countered by the enlightened. See Anastaplo, *The Constitution of 1787,* 213.

Enlightened Americans of Jefferson's day regarded the bloody European history since the Reformation as a vivid warning against the dangers of combining church and state. Even Blackstone, who preferred to be respectful of the past, could speak (4: 45) of "those days of blind zeal and pious cruelty." The advantages here of commerce, as well as of the disestablishment of religion, were apparent to early Americans, however troublesome the legitimation of acquisitiveness could be. See, e.g., *Federalist* No. 10; note 30, above, notes 240 and 259, below.

Both our free-enterprise system of commerce and our (related) disestablishment of religion contribute to the separation of powers critical to our Constitutional system. See also, on the State/Society distinction, Lecture No. 17, Section IV, of this Commentary. See as well Strauss, *The City and Man,* 30–34; note 260, below. Only the truly or fully wise (and hence good) can be trusted to combine properly the prudently separated powers of government. Such a combination may be expected (only?) of the Divine, which is displayed in the Declaration of Independence as exercising legislative, judicial, and executive powers. See Anastaplo, *The Constitution of 1787*, 21–22, 308 n. 16, *The American Moralist*, 107. See also Blackstone, 1:38–42. Compare Plato, *Republic* 473C–D; Strauss, *The City and Man*, 121f; notes 68, 69, and 120, above.

136. See, e.g., Letter from Jefferson to Adams (Jan. 24, 1814), ibid., 14: 74; also *Adams-Jefferson Letters*, 421. See as well Blackstone, 4: 59.

137. See Letter from Adams to Jefferson (Mar. 2, 1816), *Writings of Jefferson*, 14: 439; also *Adams-Jefferson Letters*, 464.

138. See Letter from Thomas Jefferson to Henry Dearborn (June 14, 1809), *Writings of Jefferson*, 14: 292. Thus, Adams probably endorsed most if not all of Edward Gibbon's famous remark about the multiplicity of religions in the ancient Roman world: "The various modes of worship were all conceived by the people as equally true; by the philosophers, as equally false; and by the magistrates, as equally useful." *The Decline and Fall of the Roman Empire*, chap. 15. See note 120, above, note 144, below.

139. Letter from Jefferson to Wilson C. Nicholas (Apr. 2, 1816), ibid., 14: 449. Nietzsche again comes to mind. See note 133, above. "What philosophers find prolematic is itself a problem." A. W. H. Adkins, "Ignorance, Socialization, and Culpability in Robert Owen and Aristotle," in *Law and Philosophy*, 1: 164.

140. One of Lincoln's few written references to Plato is with respect to the immortality of the soul. See *The Collected Works of Abraham Lincoln*, Roy P. Basler, ed. (New Brunswick, N.J.: Rutgers University Press, 1953), 3: 357. (Cited hereafter as *Collected Works of Lincoln*.) Did Lincoln pick this up, indirectly if not directly, from Jefferson? See note 149, below.

141. See Letter from Adams to Jefferson (Dec. 25, 1813), *Writings of Jefferson*, 14: 123; also *Adams-Jefferson Letters*, 409. See as well Letter from Adams to Jefferson (Sept. 14, 1813), *Writings of Jefferson*, 13: 372–73 (on whether the universe is infinite and eternal); Letter from Adams to Jefferson (Mar. 2, 1816), ibid., 14: 440 ("Why then should We abhor the Word God, and fall in Love with the Word Fate? We know there exist Energy and Intellect enough to produce such a World as this, which is a sublime and beautiful one, and a very benevolent one."); also *Adams-Jefferson Letters*, 372, 465. See, on Aristotle and the sweetness of existence, Anastaplo, *The American Moralist*, 600.

142. Jefferson acknowledged that he occasionally tailored what he had to say to his audience. Letter from Jefferson to William Canby (Sept. 18, 1813), *Writings of Jefferson*, 13: 376. See Leo Strauss, *Persecution and the Art of Writing* (Glencoe, Illinois: The Free Press, 1952); Anastaplo, *The American Moralist*, 27 (on the Kantian alternative). See also note 68, above, notes 159 and 188, below, and the texts at notes 148 and 187 of this Commentary. See, on the marginality of the philosopher-king in Plato's *Republic*, note 120, above.

143. See, e.g., Letter from Jefferson to William Short (Oct. 31, 1814), *Writings of Jefferson*, 15: 220. See also Pangle, 147: "Xenophon was probably the most widely read and cited classical political theorist at the time of the [American] Founding." See, for influential teachings about ancient political life, David Hume, "The Populousness of Ancient and Modern Nations";

Adam Smith, *Theory of Moral Sentiments,* e.g., VII, ii, I, 28 ([Indianapolis: Liberty Classics, 1982], 281–82). "The most popular work of ancient literature (always excepting the Bible) in America for about 250 years was Plutarch's *Lives.*" Reinhold Meyer, *Classica Americana: The Greek and Roman Heritage in the United States* (Detroit: Wayne State University Press, 1984), 250. See note 149, below.

144. The questionable Christian doctrines for Jefferson are "[t]he immaculate conception of Jesus, His deification, the creation of the world by Him, His miraculous powers, His resurrection and visible ascension, His corporeal presence in the Eucharist, the Trinity, original sin, atonement, regeneration, election, orders of Hierarchy, etc." Letter from Jefferson to William Short (Oct. 31, 1819), *Writings of Jefferson,* 15: 221 n. 1. See also ibid., 15: 220–21; Letter from Jefferson to Timothy Pickering (Feb. 27, 1821), ibid., 15: 323–34. Various Enlightenment thinkers anticipated Jefferson with respect to both Jesus and Plato. See, e.g., Voltaire, *Philosophical Dictionary* (Paris: E. R. DuMont, 1901), 8: 18–19, 210–11. See as well notes 120 and 138, above. Still, is it not likely that the individualism (as well as the equality) advanced by the Enlightenment was nourished by orthodox Christianity? If each human being can be trusted to choose his religion and how to practice it, at the risk of eternal damnation, why should he not be trusted to choose many other things as well for himself? See Paul Eidelberg, "The Rise of Secularism: From Socrates to Machiavelli," in *Law and Philosophy,* 1: 55; Richard G. Stevens, "The People, the Great, and the Wise," ibid., 1:359. See also note 133, above.

145. Letter from Jefferson to William Short (Oct. 31, 1819), *Writings of Jefferson,* 15: 221. There is something Lucretian in this stance.

146. Jefferson's admiration of Bacon and Newton is instructive here. See, e.g., Letter from Jefferson to William Clark (Jan. 27, 1814), ibid., 14: 79. Jefferson, in his comments on Plato, seems to echo Isaac Newton: "We are certainly not to relinquish the evidence of experiments for the sake of dreams and vain fictions of our own devising." *Principia,* Book III, Rule III (1685). See, on the dreams of Plato, note 124, above. See, for eighteenth-century reservations about Aristotle's natural science, Blackstone, 4: 410–11. See, on the self-regulating integrity of the modern scientific enterprise, Hellmut Fritzsche, "Of Things That Are Not," in *Law and Philosophy,* 1: 3. See, on Jefferson's thought, Eva T. H. Brann, *Paradoxes of Education in a Republic* (Chicago: University of Chicago Press, 1979), 170; Larry Arnhart, *Political Questions: Political Philosophy from Plato to Rawls* (New York: Macmillan, 1987), 378. See also the sources cited in notes 121 and 131, above. See as well Brann, "Was Jefferson a Philosopher?," in *Law and Philosophy,* 2: 654. The concluding paragraphs of Professor Brann's article reflect the splendors of a truly noteworthy man (ibid., 2: 669–70 [emphasis added]):

Hegel regards the Enlightenment as the layman's movement in philosophy. We may say that Jefferson was the layman of the layman's movement, its deliberate dilettante. Much of what appears thoughtlessly shallow, obtusely idiosyncratic, willfully unreflective in his writings is directly attributable to his resistance to making professions, to being a professional philosopher. Hence the unity and wholeness of his views remains implicit, appearing only as reflected in the unmistakable stamp of his style. His thought is fragmented, incomplete, curtailed.

In part, this curtailment is the consequnce of the often lamented lack of leisure resulting from public service. The Founding Fathers frequently express a Mosaic sense of preparing a world in which they cannot share. Thus Adams: "I must study politics and war, that my sons may have liberty to study mathematics and philosophy." But, in part, at least in Jefferson's case, this curtailment aided the success of his political work, for it guaranteed the absence of that intellectual fanaticism of a thoroughgoing, book-bred reason that marks the French Revolution.

The answer, then, to the title question is, No, Jefferson is not a philosopher in the full sense. But in his wide delectation for inquiry he makes plain the way for philosophy. *It seems to me unjust to blame on Jefferson any supposed prejudice against philosophical depth in American life. On the contrary, Madison's appreciation of Jefferson is exact and just: the Genius of Philosophy ever walked hand in hand with him.*

See Strauss, *The City and Man*, 37–38, 49; note 60, above. The more successful the Founders were, the less likely it would be that talented Americans thereafter would devote themselves primarily to politics, except during times of great crises. See, e.g., *Collected Works of Lincoln*, 1: 113–14 ("On the Perpetuation of Our Political Institutions"). Compare Harry Neumann, *Liberalism* (Durham: Carolina Academic Press, 1991), 292: "Nations, like individuals, reach their peak and then die spiritually, if not physically. Prussia and France reached their peak at Verdun (just as the United States probably reached its peak during the Civil War)." But see Anastaplo, *The Constitutionalist*, 784–85: "Churchill lamented in 1956 that Great Britain had 'answered all the tests' confronting her in the twentieth century, but that 'it was useless.' . . . But had she not failed the first great test of the century, and in such a way as to make all later tests merely valiant rearguard actions, by not stopping the First World War before it wrecked Europe spiritually as well as physically?" We had, instead, a Thirty Years War and thereafter the follies of the Cold War, if not even an Eighty Years War altogether. See, e.g., the Geiss citation in note 251, below.

147. Letter from Jefferson to Henry Lee (May 8, 1825), *Writings of Jefferson*, 16: 118–19. See Anastaplo, "The Declaration of Independence," *St. Louis University Law Review*, 9: 390 (1965). See, for Aristotle's grasp of Plato's *Republic*, note 120, above, note 260, below. Cicero's understanding of the *Republic* is suggested in these observations by Leo Strauss (*The City and Man*, 138):

[Plato's] *Republic* then indeed makes clear what justice is. As Cicero has observed [citing Cicero, *De republica*, II, 52], the *Republic* does not bring to light the best possible regime but rather the nature of political things—the nature of the city. Socrates makes clear in the *Republic* of what character the city would have to be in order to satisfy the highest need of man. By letting us see that the city constructed in accordance with this requirement is not possible, he lets us see the essential limits, the nature, of the city.

Did Jefferson, as a preeminently political man, sense the fundamental challenge posed by Plato's *Republic* to his way of life? See the text at note 260 of this Commentary. See, on Cicero, John R. MacCormack, "Morality and Politics in Cicero's Defense of the Roman Republic," in *Law and Philosophy*, 1: 195. See also John Alvis, "Virgil's Rome: An Empire by Nature?," ibid., 2: 905.

148. See Letter from Jefferson to Timothy Pickering (Feb. 27, 1821), *Writings of Jefferson*, 15: 324; note 142, above.

149. Abraham Lincoln did not have ready access to the classics, except for Euclid, Aesop, and perhaps Plutarch. See, e.g., *Collected Works of Lincoln*, 1: 315, 4: 62; note 134, below. See also note 143, above. However, Lincoln did know the Bible, as well as Shakespeare. We have observed that it was in part through Shakespeare that lessons from the classical world have had a profound effect on the English-speaking peoples. See Anastaplo, "American Constitutionalism," 113–25, *The Constitution of 1787*, 338, *The Artist as Thinker*, 15; note 130, above.

The phrase, "anti-theological ire," comes from Leo Strauss's study of Machiavelli. See also Anastaplo, "Rome, Piety, and Law," 11–12. Recognition of the contributions of both classical thought and Biblical religion to the political thought of the West may be seen in this 1939 recapitulation by a French historian:

> Through the course of centuries our Western world, formed by Christianity yet inheriting ancient thought, has directed its effort through a thousand vicissitudes toward the liberation of the human person. The Church upheld the freedom of the individual so that he might work in peace for his salvation and entrance into heaven. From the sixteenth to the eighteenth centuries philosophers proposed that man also throw off the fetters that held down his rise on earth; they urged him to become the master of nature and make his kind the true ruler of creation. Different though such doctrine seemed from that of the Church, the two were at one in recognizing the eminent dignity of the human person and commanding respect for it, in attributing to man certain natural and imprescriptible rights and in assigning to the authority of the state no other purpose than to protect these rights and to help the individual make himself worthy of them.
>
> The West, inspired by the same masters, continued also to acknowledge the unity of mankind. The Church promised salvation to all without distinction of race, language or nation. To this universalism the new thinkers remained faithful. They secularized the idea of the Christian community, but they kept it alive.

Lefebvre, *The Coming of the French Revolution*, 215. See also notes 60 and 133, above, and the text at note 120 of this Commentary. The excesses of would-be Christians have their historians also. See, e.g., Yitzhak F. Baer, *Galut* (New York: Schocken Books, 1947), 22–26.

150. There were eventually thirteen States that were said *by some* in those States to have seceded from the Union during the Civil War. See "Confederate States of America," in *Encyclopedia Britannica* (14th ed., 1972), 6: 285. (Most scholars, however, seem to count eleven States in the Confederacy. The Confederate States of America was formed on February 8, 1861, by South Carolina, Georgia, Florida, Alabama, Louisiana, and Mississippi and was joined by Texas on March 2, 1861 [overriding the opposition of Governor Sam Houston]. Virginia, North Carolina, Tennessee, and Arkansas joined the Confederate States after the capture of Fort Sumter, in April 1861.) The seven States that had seceded by the time that the Confederate Constitution was drafted in March 1861 were operating pursuant to a Provisional Constitution. See, for the Constitution of the Provisional Government of the Confederate States, Senate Document No. 234, 58th Congress, 2d Session (Washington, D.C.: Government Printing Office, 1904), 899–909.

151. Confederate Constitution of February 8, 1861, art. I, sec. 8, cl. 17. All the quotations in the text of Lecture No. 10 of this Commentary are, unless otherwise indicated, to the Confederate Constitution of March 11, 1861, as set forth in Appendix L-2 of this Commentary. (A slightly different version of that constitution is appended to the edition of this Commentary published in *Loyola University of Chicago Law Journal*, 23: 631, 849–65 [1992]).

152. *Dred Scott v. Sandford*, 60 U.S. (19 How.) 393 (1857). See Anastaplo, "Slavery and the Constitution," 732, *The Constitution of 1787*, 333; note 1, above. Thus, slavery was guaranteed from the outset in the territories of the Confederacy, rather than allowing residents in the territories to choose, as most Southerners had advocated in the 1850s for the territories of the United States. See, for an 1860 argument that the Constitution was fundamentally antislavery, *The Frederick Douglass Papers*, John W. Blassingame, ed. (New Haven: Yale University Press, 1985), 3: 340. Critical to the Douglass position was the recognition that once the Government of the United States became determined to abolish slavery, it would be able to find adequate provisions in the Constitution that would permit it to do so. Southerners too could see this and could see as well (by 1860) that all branches of the National Government were likely to grow aggressively hostile to slavery. See also the text at notes 162–164 of this Commentary. See as well note 45, above, note 186, below, and Lecture No. 13, Section XIII (end), of this Commentary.

153. See, e.g., Confederate Constitution of 1861, art. IV, sec. 2, cl. 1. This was consistent with Lincoln's warnings in 1858 that the *Dred Scott* Court and its "co-conspirators" in the Executive and Congress were aiming to make it difficult, if not virtually impossible, for any State to forbid slavery within its borders. See, e.g., *Collected Works of Lincoln*, 2: 466–69.

154. Confederate Constitution of 1861, art. I, sec. 9, cl. 20. All this bears upon what we call a "line-item veto." See Lecture No. 17, Section IV, of this Commentary.

155. In addition, notice the uses of the term *federal* in the Confederate Constitution (as in the Preamble, and in Article I, Sections 2 and 9 (clause 10), a term never used in the Constitution of 1787. Consider as well the following report:

> The United States went to war in 1861 to preserve the *Union;* it emerged from war in 1865 having created a *nation.* Before 1861 the two words "United States" were generally used as a plural noun: "the United States are a republic." After 1865 the United States became a singular noun. The loose union of states became a nation. Lincoln's wartime speeches marked this transition. In his first inaugural address he mentioned the "Union" twenty times but the nation not once. In his first message to Congress, on July 4, 1861, Lincoln used the word "Union" thirty-two times and "nation" only three times. But in his Gettysburg Address two and one-half years later, the president did not mention the Union at all but spoke of the "nation" five times to invoke a new birth of freedom and nationhood. And in his second inaugural address on March 4, 1865, Lincoln spoke of the South seeking to dissolve the Union in 1861 and the North accepting the challenge to preserve the nation.

James M. McPherson, *Abraham Lincoln and the Second American Revolution* (New York: Oxford University Press, 1990), viii. See also Lecture No. 11 of this Commentary. See, on the term *Electoral College*, note 248, below.

156. Confederate Constitution of 1861, art. I, sec. 2, cl. 3; sec. 9, cls. 1, 2, 4; art. IV, sec. 2, cls. 1, 3; sec. 3, cl. 3. See, for a twentieth-century defense of the Confederacy, note 259, below. Does such a defense recognize the significance of the extent to which the range of national power that had been developed pursuant to the Constitution of 1787 was retained in the Confederate Constitution of 1861? See Don E. Fehrenbacher, *Constitutions and Constitutionalism in the Slaveholding South* (Athens: University of Georgia Press, 1989), 61–67.

Constitutional considerations aside, Southern secession should not have been permitted insofar as it consolidated, if it did not even advance, the cause of slavery, that slavery to which all of the United States had contributed one way or another. "Technicalities" aside, justice (as well as an enduring domestic tranquillity) called for stopping the South (and hence slaveholding) in its immoral endeavor. (Compare how we respond at this time to the possible breakup of the Canadian union, unfortunate as that would be. Moral issues, as ordinarily understood, are clearly secondary there. See, e.g., Anastaplo, *Human Being and Citizen,* 139; Storer H. Rowley, "Quebec Already Separate, Canadian Parliament Told," *Chicago Tribune,* Jan. 20, 1994, sec. 1, p. 8. Consider also the concluding remarks of a study of the "Hitler Youth" army division during the Second World War:

> An entire nation, unlike a deranged potentate in a Shakespearean play, cannot decide to turn evil; on the contrary, what is most disturbing about the Nazi period is how adroitly the National Socialist leadership was able

to harness the considerable moral and physical energies of a decent and capable people to the pursuit of largely criminal objectives. To reach their nefarious goals, the Nazis did not hesitate to exploit the trust and idealism of Germany's younger generation. Steeped in traditions of public service and self-sacrifice, the boys of the 12th SS Panzer Division "Hitler Youth" were plunged into the abyss of blood and darkness that is modern total war. Too young to fear death, yet old enough to face it and die, they were "worthy of a better cause than that which the man whose name they once bore had to offer."

Craig W. H. Luther, *Blood and Honor: The History of the 12th SS Panzer Division "Hitler Youth," 1943–1945* (San Jose, California: R. James Bender Publishing, 1987), 244–45. The Ulysses S. Grant quotation, among the epigraphs for this Commentary, again comes to mind.)

We can see in *Robert's Rules of Order,* where the American political sense is systematized for everyday affairs, how genuine emergencies may require temporarily setting aside the rules by which an association is routinely governed. See, on emergencies, *Robert's Rules of Order, Newly Revised* (New York: Scott Foresman, 1990), 675. See also Blackstone, 1: 147–48, 188–89, 2: 345. Compare the misleading "clear and present danger" test imposed upon this Country by Justice Holmes. See *Schenck* v. *United States,* 249 U.S. 47 (1919); Anastaplo, *The Constitutionalist,* 812.

157. Lecture No. 11 of this Commentary originated as a talk given on April 14, 1974, at the K.A.M.–Isaiah Israel Congregation, in Chicago, Illinois. It also served, in printed form, as the basis for a Center Dialogue on June 19, 1974, at the Center for the Study of Democratic Institutions, in Santa Barbara, California. See Anastaplo, *The Artist as Thinker,* 279–83. The original 1974 lecture was further developed for publication in *Constitutional Government in America,* Ronald K. L. Collins, ed. (Durham: Carolina Academic Press, 1980), 421–46. See David Fellman, Book Review, *American Political Science Review,* 75: 192–94 (1981). My earlier discussions of the Emancipation Proclamation are adapted for use here, with much of the instructive material available in the notes of the useful Collins volume omitted on this occasion. See note 192, below.

The texts of the Preliminary Proclamation (of September 22, 1862) and of the Final Proclamation (of January 1, 1863), which together constitute the Emancipation Proclamation and which are set forth in Lecture No. 11, are taken from *Collected Works of Lincoln,* 5: 433–36, 6: 28–30. See note 175, below.

158. Harry V. Jaffa, *The Conditions of Freedom: Essays in Political Philosophy* (Baltimore: Johns Hopkins University Press, 1975), 8. See Anastaplo, "American Constitutionalism," 165–68 n. 64, Anastaplo, *The Artist as Thinker,* 476 n. 285. See also note 11, above, notes 168 and 259, below.

159. Vernon Jarrett, "Why We Must Re-evaluate Heroes of the Past," *Chicago Tribune,* Feb. 20, 1974, sec. 1, p. 14. It should be remembered that Lincoln always had to contend with the anti-Negro prejudices of Unionists

in the North and Middle States. See, for Lincoln's periodic, deliberate recourse to talk about "colonization of blacks" as his way of lulling the racial fears of white Unionists, Stephen B. Oates, *With Malice Toward None: The Life of Abraham Lincoln* (New York: Harper and Row, 1977), 268, 297–99, 307, 312–13, 322, 325–26, 330–31, 339–42. (Cited hereafter as *With Malice Toward None.*) See also note 45, above, note 259, below. See as well note 142, above, note 188, below.

160. Editorial, *Chicago Tribune*, Feb. 15, 1974, sec. 1, p. 12.

161. Carl Sandburg, *Abraham Lincoln: The War Years* (New York: Harcourt, Brace and Co. 1939), 2: 21–22. Secretary of State Seward had just said, "I mean that the Emancipation Proclamation was uttered in the first gun fired at Fort Sumter, and we have been the last to hear it." Ibid., 2: 21.

162. *What Country Have I? Political Writings of Black Americans*, Herbert J. Storing, ed. (New York: St. Martin's Press, 1970), 52–53 (emphasis added). (Cited hereafter as *What Country Have I?*)

163. Letter from Lincoln to Albert G. Hodges, Apr. 4, 1864, *Collected Works of Lincoln*, 7: 281. See note 259, below.

164. *What Country Have I?*, 51–52 (emphasis added). See also notes 45 and 152 above.

165. *Collected Works of Lincoln*, 5: 388–89.

166. Ibid., 5: 389.

167. Ibid., 8: 152 (Annual Message to Congress, Dec. 6, 1864).

168. Harry V. Jaffa, *Equality and Liberty: Theory and Practice in American Politics* (New York: Oxford University Press, 1965), 157. (Cited hereafter as *Equality and Liberty.*) Today, students of Lincoln and the Civil War are fortunate to have available to them the pioneering work of Mr. Jaffa, particularly his *Crisis of the House Divided: An Interpretation of the Issues in the Lincoln-Douglas Debates* (Garden City, N.Y.: Doubleday & Co., 1959). My own considerable debt to Mr. Jaffa is particularly evident in Lecture No. 11, Sections I and II, of this Commentary. See also notes 11 and 158, above. (It is appropriate to notice, considering how much I draw upon the classics in my work, that comparable to the contributions in recent decades of Harry Jaffa to the study of American political thought have been the contributions of Seth Benardete to classical scholarship. Both of these remarkably [if not even enviably] gifted and radically imaginative men studied with Leo Strauss. See Anastaplo, *The American Moralist*, 587–89.)

See, for further discussion of Lincoln and the Civil War, Anastaplo, "Slavery and the Constitution: Explorations," *Texas Tech Law Review*, 19: 677 (1989), *The American Moralist*, 537, *Human Being and Citizen*, 61, 203. See also Laurence Berns, "Xenophon's Alcibiades and Pericles on the Question of Law, with Applications to the Polity of the United States," in *Law and Philosophy*, 1: 464; Michael P. Zuckert, "Lincoln and the Problem of Civil Religion," ibid., 2: 720.

169. Jaffa, *Equality and Liberty*, 158.

170. Ibid., 163. See, on how the South was able to mobilize its slaves for its war efforts, Grant, *Memoirs*, 636.

171. *Collected Works of Lincoln*, 2: 461–62.

172. Similarly, it can be said that Christian thought (as we have come to know it) may be better seen in someone such as St. Augustine than in Jesus, if only because Jesus (insofar as he was human) was raised as a Jew with relatively little exposure to the philosophical tradition of the Greeks that has been incorporated in Christianity. See, on St. Augustine, Anastaplo, "Rome, Piety, and Law," 83. See, on St. Paul (who was born a Roman citizen), ibid., 32, 39. See also note 133, above, note 260, below.

173. Sandburg, *Abraham Lincoln: The War Years*, 2: 20. Among the things that Lincoln's "paper" did, when he let it "go forth," was to provoke these responses:

> Southern reaction to the proclamation was predictably negative, damning it as an invitation to slaves to murder their masters. The reaction in the north was mixed, with the legislature of Lincoln's own state, Illinois, declaring the proclamation "a gigantic usurpation . . . violent liberation of 3,000,000 Negro slaves . . ."

Family Encyclopedia of American History (Pleasantville, N.Y.: Reader's Digest Association, 1975), 383. Three million, we recall, was roughly the number of free men and women in the United States in 1776.

174. John G. Nicolay and John Hay, *Abraham Lincoln: A History* (New York: Century Co., 1914), 6: 161–62. (Cited hereafter as Nicolay and Hay.)

175. *Collected Works of Lincoln*, 5: 433. There are collected in the Appendix to the United States Statutes thirteen of Lincoln's proclamations prior to this one. Both the Preliminary Proclamation and the Final Proclamation bear the superscription, "By the President of the United States: A Proclamation" (and their respective dates); both bear the signature, "By the President: Abraham Lincoln/William H. Seward, Secretary of State." The complete texts of the two documents are set forth, in order, in Lecture No. 11 of this Commentary. The passages of these documents are the only quotations set off *in italics* in the text of Lecture No. 11. See note 157, above.

176. See James G. Randall, *Lincoln, the President* (New York: Dodd, Mead, 1945), 4: 162. Too much is made these days of the President as *"our* Commander in Chief." He is, according to the Constitution, merely "Commander in Chief of the Army and Navy of the United States, and of the Militia of the several States, when called into the actual Service of the United States." Consider here the concurring opinion by Justice Jackson in *Youngstown Sheet & Tube Company* v. *Sawyer*, 343 U.S. 579, 643–44 (1952):

> There are indications that the Constitution did not contemplate that the title Commander-in-Chief *of the Army and Navy* will constitute him also Commander-in-Chief of the country, its industries and its inhabitants. He has no monopoly of "war powers," whatever they are. While Congress cannot deprive the President of the command of the army and navy, only Congress can provide him an army or navy to command. It is also empowered to make rules for the "Government and Regulation of land and naval forces," by which it may to some unknown extent impinge upon

even command functions. That military powers were not to supersede representative government of internal affairs seems obvious from the Constitution and from elementary American history.

It is salutary to keep in mind here what have been described as massive antitheses, grinding one another in gigantic contention, that go back to the earliest decades of this Republic:

The Antifederalists complained [in 1787–1789] of the absence of a bill of rights, but, more than that, of the presence (or the likely presence) of a standing army. That army would be used to enforce the laws because, they said, in a territory so extensive, comprising people with interests, habits and customs so diverse, [the laws] could not be enforced in any other way.

But the Federalists saw the necessity of a strong executive, making him commander in chief of the Army (which, on a few occasions—Little Rock, Ark., in 1957 and Oxford, Miss., in 1962—has indeed been used to enforce the laws). The Constitution "has an awful squinting," Patrick Henry said; "it squints toward monarchy," and for the Antifederalists monarchy meant the possibility of tyranny. . . .

The Antifederalists lost the debate on the Constitution, and probably ought to have lost it, but their arguments were not without merit and deserve careful consideration even (and perhaps especially) today.

Walter Berns, Book Review, *Washington Times,* July 4, 1993, pp. B7–B8. See, on standing armies, the text at notes 108–9 of this Commentary. Should there not be added to the "few occasions [when the army] has indeed been used to enforce the laws," the massive response by President Lincoln to Southern secessionist efforts? See note 216, below. See also the text at note 59 of this Commentary.

177. *Collected Works of Lincoln,* 6: 407–8. There are echoes here of one of the grievances in the Declaration of Independence: "He has . . . endeavoured to bring on the Inhabitants of our Frontiers, the merciless Indian Savages, whose known Rule of Warfare, is an undistinguished Destruction, of all Ages, Sexes and Conditions." See Blackstone, 4: 312. See also note 1, above.

178. One need read only the youthful Lincoln's Temperance Speech in Springfield, Illinois, on February 22, 1842, to sense his lifelong concern about moral passion. See *Collected Works of Lincoln,* 1: 271. See also Jaffa, *Crisis of the House Divided,* 233; the text at notes 228 and 231 of this Commentary; note 259, below.

179. We should remember that Lincoln had even repudiated unauthorized decrees or acts of emancipation by various of his generals in the field. See, e.g., Lord Charnwood, *Abraham Lincoln* (Garden City, N.Y.: Garden City Publishing Co., 1917), 268–70, 313–37. Ultimate political control of the military was evidently taken for granted throughout the Civil War, in both the North and the South, however much civilians were abused by armies on both sides.

180. John T. Morse, Jr., *Abraham Lincoln* (Boston: Houghton, Mifflin, 1893), 2: 109.

181. The two "consent" qualifications are said to have been inserted in the Preliminary Proclamation at the suggestion of Secretary of State Seward. See *Collected Works of Lincoln*, 5: 434 n. 4.

182. The Emancipation Proclamation refers to all slaves in a rebellious State or part of a State, whereas in Section 9 of this Act Congress had referred primarily to "all slaves of persons who shall hereafter be engaged in rebellion, or who in any way give aid or comfort thereto." See note 185, below.

183. See Randall, *Lincoln, the President*, 156–57; Oates, *With Malice Toward None*, 311, 317–20.

184. The clerk had written in everything at the end of what is otherwise Lincoln's handwritten original of the Preliminary Proclamation (beginning at "In witness whereof"). See *Collected Works of Lincoln*, 5: 56.

185. Letter from Lincoln to Salmon P. Chase, Sept. 2, 1863, *Collected Works of Lincoln*, 6: 428–29. See Morse, *Abraham Lincoln*, 2: 3, 99–100; Nicolay and Hay, 6: 405. Lincoln's letter to Chase (whom he later appointed to the Supreme Court) continues: "Would not many of our friends shrink away appalled? Would it not lose us the elections, and with them, the very cause we seek to advance?" *Collected Works of Lincoln*, 6: 429. See note 45, above. We have noticed that a respect for the Constitution may be seen in Lincoln's provision that the decisive indication that a State is not in rebellion is that it is properly represented in Congress. The republican form of government is thereby deferred to. See note 182, above, note 259, below.

186. William Lloyd Garrison, *The Liberator*, No. 1, Jan. 1, 1831, in John L. Thomas, *The Liberator: William Lloyd Garrison, A Biography* (Boston: Little, Brown, 1963), 128. See, for Garrison's "extremist" position, *Documents of Upheaval: Selections from William Lloyd Garrison's "The Liberator," 1831–1865*, Truman Nelson, ed. (New York: Hill and Wang, 1966), xiii. Another "extremist," but far less obviously so, is the Lord Mansfield of *Somerset's Case* (1772). See Appendix L-1 of this Commentary; Blackstone, 1: 412–13, 4: 29. See also William M. Wiecek, "*Somerset*: Lord Mansfield and the Legitimacy of Slavery in the Anglo-American World," *University of Chicago Law Review*, 42: 86 (1974); Anastaplo, "On Freedom," 715. See also note 152, above.

187. Matthew 10: 16.

188. *Collected Works of Lincoln*, 3: 261. Compare ibid., 3: 249–50, 277, 279–81. See, on salutary concealments, Plato, *Republic* 414E; Thucydides, *Peloponnesian War*, II, 65; Blackstone, 1: 238, 2: 117, 4: 33; Gibbon, *The Decline and Fall of the Roman Empire*, chap. 15 (opening and closing paragraphs). See also Jules Gleicher, "Deception and Ennoblement in *Henry V*," in *Law and Philosophy*, 2: 959; Stanley D. McKenzie, "The Prudence and Kinship of Prince Hal and John of Lancaster in *2 Henry IV*," ibid., 2: 937; notes 68, 142 and 148, above, note 251, below. Compare, on the perhaps misguided campaign to change "an arcane House [of Representatives] procedural rule that allows members to block legislation in secret while supporting it

in public," Clifford Krauss, "Conservatives Push to End Secrecy in House Rules," *New York Times*, Sept. 14, 1993, p. A15; "Outflanked by Talk Shows, House Drops Secrecy Rule," *Chicago Tribune*, Sept. 29, 1993, sec. 1, p. 6. See also Adam Clymer, "Broad Change Proposed in How Congress Works," *New York Times*, Nov. 23, 1993, p. A14.

189. *Collected Works of Lincoln*, 5: 358.

190. James C. Austin, *Artemus Ward* (New York: Twayne Publishers, 1964), 107–8. See Oates, *With Malice Toward None*, 318–19; Sandburg, *Abraham Lincoln: The War Years*, 1: 583.

191. I take the full text of "High-Handed Outrage at Utica" from Charles Farrar Browne, *The Complete Works of Artemus Ward*, (New York: G. W. Dillingham Co., 1898), 36–37:

> In the Faul of 1856, I showed my show in Utiky, a trooly grate sitty in the State of New York.
>
> The people gave me a cordyal recepshun. The press was loud in her prases.
>
> 1 day as I was givin a descripshun of my Beests and Snaiks in my usual flowry stile what was my skorn disgust to see a big burly feller walk up to the cage containin my wax figgers of the Lord's Last Supper, and cease Judas Iscarrot by the feet and drag him out on the ground. He then commenced fur to pound him as hard as he cood.
>
> "What under the son are you abowt?" cried I.
>
> Sez he, "What did you bring this pussylanermus cuss here fur?" and he hit the wax figger another tremenjis blow on the hed.
>
> Sez I, "You egrejus ass, that air's a wax figger—a representashun of the false 'Postle."
>
> Sez he, "That's all very well for you to say, but I tell you, old man, that Judas Iscarrot can't show hisself in Utiky with impunerty by a darn site!" with which observashun he kaved in Judassis hed. The young man belonged to 1 of the first famerlies in Utiky. I sood him, and the Joory brawt in a verdick of Arson in the 3d degree.

See, for an anticipation of the "big burly feller," Gibbon, *The Decline and Fall of the Roman Empire* (Modern Library edition), II, 390–91 (the "indiscreet fury" of Clovis). See also note 66, above. The Artemus Ward volume includes a number of instructive pieces on slavery, Lincoln, and the Civil War. See, for the crippling consequences of not taking Lincoln seriously enough, note 259, below.

192. See Proverbs 25: 11: "A word fitly spoken is like apples of gold in pictures of silver." (This verse served as the epigraph upon the publication by me, in 1974 and in 1980, of earlier forms of Lecture No. 11 of this Commentary. See note 157, above.)

Lincoln, aware that the Emancipation Proclamation was necessarily limited in scope and not without problems as to its authority, encouraged in due time the constitutional amendment prohibiting slavery for which his Proclamation and then the Gettysburg Address can be said to have prepared the way. He announced on June 9, 1864, that he approved his party's "declaration of so amending the Constitution as to prohibit slavery throughout the nation":

> When the people in revolt, with a hundred days of explicit notice, that they could, within those days, resume their allegiance, without the over-throw of their institution [of slavery], and that they could not so resume it afterwards, elected to stand out, such an amendment of the Constitution as is now proposed, became a fitting, and necessary conclusion to the final success of the Union cause. Such [an amendment] alone can meet and cover all cavils. *Now, the unconditional Union men, North and South, perceive its importance, and embrace it.* In the joint names of Liberty and Union, let us labor to give it legal form, and practical effect.

Collected Works of Lincoln, 7: 380 (emphasis added). See, for the party plat-form on which Lincoln was commenting, ibid., 7: 381–82, 411. See also note 259, below. See, for the salutary Aesopian lessons taught to Lincoln's gen-eration about the limits of the equality principle, note 134, above.

193. The principal draftsman in 1865 of the Thirteenth Amendment was Senator Lyman Trumbull of Illinois, a State carved out of the Northwest Territory. See, for Lincoln's celebration of Illinois's taking the lead in ratify-ing this amendment, ibid., 8: 254–55. See also note 49, above.

194. Northwest Ordinance, art. VI (note 2, above). See Appendix L-3 of this Commentary. See also note 240, below, and the text at note 29 of this Commentary. See, on the Northwest Ordinance, Anastaplo, "The Northwest Ordinance of 1787: Illinois' First Constitution," *Illinois Bar Journal*, 75: 123 (1986); *The Constitution of 1787*, 304, 336. See also notes 2, 10, and 152, above.

195. An exception is made for persons "duly convicted" of crimes. Our sentiments about slavery are now such that we can be troubled by the use of the term *slave* to designate the convicted criminal serving his sentence. (Are we not, in our understandable squeamishness about certain terms, and especially *slavery*, somewhat like the Roman Republic was about any use in Italy of the term *king*? See, for example, the second scene in Shake-speare's *Julius Caesar*. See also note 1, above.) The Thirteenth Amendment exception indicates not only that forced labor is still possible for convicted criminals but also that slavery should not be disguised as a system of forced labor for nominal criminals.

196. Anastaplo, *The Constitution of 1787*, 299. Three States ratified this exercise in desperation before Secession had to be dealt with. Compare Lincoln's own proposed amendment, in his Annual Message to Congress of December 1, 1862, which provided for compensated emancipation of the slaves. *Collected Works of Lincoln*, 5: 530.

197. See, for the texts of these seven debates (which began at Ottawa, Illinois, on August 21, 1858, and which ended at Alton, Illinois, on Octo-

ber 15, 1858), ibid., 3: 1–76, 102–44, 207–44, 283–325. See also Jaffa, *Crisis of the House Divided;* Anastaplo, "Slavery and the Constitution," 732.

198. See note 25, above. See, on "the privileges or immunities of citizens of the United States," Crosskey, 2: 1083–89, 1119–34. See, for a review of recent literature as to what rights should be taken seriously hereafter, Daniel N. Hoffman, "What Makes a Right Fundamental?," *Review of Politics,* 49: 515 (1987); Mortimer J. Adler, "Six Amendments to the Constitution," in *Law and Philosophy,* 2: 747. See, for the French Declaration of the Rights of Man and the Citizen, note 60, above. See, for its twentieth-century counterpart in the 1948 Universal Declaration of Human Rights, Anastaplo, "How to Read the Constitution of the United States," *Loyola University of Chicago Law Journal,* 17: 1, 55–64 (1985); Anastaplo, "On the Use, Neglect, and Abuse of Veils: The Parliaments of the World's Religions," *Great Ideas Today,* 1994: 30 (1994). Still other twentieth-century counterparts are the 1966 International Covenants on Human Rights (on Economic, Social and Cultural Rights, on Civil and Political Rights). See also Bernard Weisberg, Ellen Flaum, Frank Kruesi, and others, *Final Report of the Governor's Commission on Individual Liberty and Personal Privacy,* State of Illinois, Jan. 28, 1976 (reprinted, in part, in *Focus/Midwest,* 11: 16 [1976]); Anastaplo, "The Public Interest in Privacy: On Becoming and Being Human," *De Paul Law Review,* 26: 767 (1977). See as well note 216, below.

199. This way was also available, to a limited extent, through the Republican Form of Government Guarantee in Article IV of the Constitution.

200. *The Slaughter-House Cases,* 83 U.S. (16 Wall.) 36 (1873).

201. The lamentable end to the baseball career of Dizzy Dean again comes to mind. See Anastaplo, *The Constitution of 1787,* xvii. See also Machiavelli, *Discourses,* II, 20: "[T]he ambition of man is so great that to satisfy a present wish, he does not think of the evil that in a short time results from it."

202. The emphasis does seem to be upon human beings, whatever consideration may be given by plausible extension to business corporations and other organizations.

203. *Craig v. Boren,* 429 U.S. 190, 211 (1976) (Justice Stevens, concurring). See Anastaplo, *The Constitutionalist,* 710–11 n. 83.

204. This has been done, in such cases as *Bolling v. Sharpe,* 347 U.S. 497 (1954), not by making use either of the Privileges and Immunities Clause of Article IV (which is, however, directed to the States) or of the Ninth Amendment, but rather by expanding the meaning of the Due Process Clause of the Fifth Amendment. Nor does it seem to be appreciated that it may be prudent, as was evidently intended by the drafters of the Fourteenth Amendment, to leave in some government in the United States immunity from the full equal-protection restraints. Blackstone, for example, speaks (1: 156) of "that absolute despotic power, which must in all governments reside somewhere." See note 232, below. See also note 99, above, note 211, below.

205. One problem with the use of the Equal Protection Clause to accomplish what could be better done otherwise may be seen in *The Reappor-*

tionment Cases (*Baker* v. *Carr,* 369 U.S. 186 [1962], and *Reynolds* v. *Sims,* 377 U.S. 533 [1964]). Is a more mechanical approach less likely to be used when the test is not that of equal protection? Would it not have been better if the Republican Form of Government Guarantee had been used in such cases and, even better, if the long-needed corrective measures had been developed by Congress rather than by the Courts? See Anastaplo, *The Constitution of 1787,* 173–74, 184–85; note 68, above, note 209, below. See also note 236, below.

206. Or does such a provision look less to the powers granted and more to the end or purpose of the powers and rights referred to? See Michael P. Zuckert, "Completing the Constitution: The Thirteenth Amendment," *Constitutional Commentary,* 4: 259, 272–73 (1987). Does Section 5 of the Fourteenth Amendment also serve to assure that power of the General Government with respect to the States which *Barron* v. *Baltimore* denied? See note 92, above. See, on affirmative-action programs, notes 211 and 229, below.

207. See *The Slaughter-House Cases,* 83 U.S. (16 Wall.) 36 (1873); *The Civil Rights Cases,* 109 U.S. 3 (1883).

208. 163 U.S. 537 (1896).

209. 347 U.S. 483 (1954). One scholar has observed: "What finally turned the tide [against racial discrimination in the United States] were a series of legislative enactments: the Civil Rights Act of 1964; the Voting Rights Act of 1965; and the Fair Housing Act of 1968. The struggle against racial discrimination required the conscientious effort of all three branches." Louis Fisher, "The Curious Belief in Judicial Supremacy," *Suffolk University Law Review,* 25: 85, 113–14 (1991). See also Fisher, "The Legislative Veto: Invalidated, It Survives," *Law and Contemporary Problems,* 56: 273 (1993). See also notes 14, 68, and 205, above.

210. History may also be responsible, at least in part, for the extra-constitutional changes, such as with respect to both Congressional acquiescence to judicial review (of Acts of Congress) and the enhancement of Executive Power, that I will consider further in Lecture No. 17 of this Commentary.

211. Consider the implications of the Thirteenth and Fourteenth Amendments: they do limit the General Government, but not with respect to matters that the Framers did not want thus limited. See, for the limited scope of the equal-protection restraints, note 204, above. It is often said that the General Government is constitutionally precluded from affirmative-action programs that recognize racial differentiations. I do not believe that this takes sufficient account of the fifth section of the Fourteenth Amendment. See, for prudential, as distinguished from constitutional, arguments against affirmative-action programs, Shelby Steele, "A Negative Vote on Affirmative Action," *New York Times Magazine,* May 13, 1990, 46. I am not persuaded, however, particularly because it is hard to overestimate the corrective measures that will be needed to save us all from the demoralizing effects of deep-rooted racial prejudices in this Country. See, for a challenging comparison by Leo Strauss of the circumstances of Jews and African-Americans in the United States, Anastaplo, "On Trial," 1057–58; "Slavery and the Constitution," 766. See also Ellis Cose, *The Rage of a*

Privileged Class: Why Are Middle-Class Blacks Angry? Why Should America Care? (New York: Harper Collins, 1994); Jerry Bembry, "Why Are Well-Off Blacks So Unhappy? Here's the Truth," *Chicago Sun-Times Book Review,* Jan. 16, 1994, p. 13; note 134, above, notes 229 and 255, below. See as well my essay on African thought in the 1995 *Great Ideas Today.*

212. See *Pollock* v. *Farmer's Loan & Trust Co.,* 158 U.S. 601 (1895). Compare *Springer* v. *United States,* 102 U.S. 586, 602 (1881): "Our conclusions are: that *direct taxes,* within the meaning of the Constitution, are only capitation taxes as expressed in that instrument, and taxes on real estate; and that the [income] tax of which the plaintiff in error complains is within the category of an excise or duty [permitted by the Constitution]."

213. Dennis J. Mahoney, "Seventeenth Amendment," in *Ency. Am. Const.,* 4: 1665.

214. That had been the way State delegations typically were expected to act in Congress under the Articles of Confederation, where the State legislatures had the power of recall. Would omission from Amendment XVII of the stipulation about each Senator having one vote raise the question whether some of the pre-1787 power of the State legislatures has somehow been revived, even though those legislatures no longer choose the Senators?

215. Deborah L. Rhode, "Nineteenth Amendment," in *Ency. Am. Const.,* 3: 1315.

216. Whether women can ever be, in the political life of the community, other then a "minority" (it would once have been possible for respectable citizens to argue openly) may depend, in part, upon whether most women are naturally better equipped than men to rule their respective households and in turn to be ruled in the political life of a healthy community. (See notes 94 ["the natural modesty of the sex"], 106 and 198, above.) To argue thus is to suggest that the realm of love and that of politics, however much they may depend upon and influence one another, should ultimately be distinguished. See the text at note 260 of this Commentary. See also Plato, *Meno* 71E. Compare Plato, *Republic* 455C sq. See as well Strauss, *The City and Man,* 110f; Anastaplo, *The American Moralist,* 349. Consider the fact that the greatest English monarch may well have been a woman.

A substantial minority of law students today will often mistake the proposed Equal Rights Amendment (of 1972) for the Nineteenth Amendment (of 1920). Does this reflect the fact that we generally regard the right to vote as the key to most, if not to all, of our other rights? See, for suggestions about how supporters of the Equal Rights Amendment could have more effectively used their political power in getting that amendment ratified in the 1970s, Lecture No. 14, Section VII, of this Commentary. (Another instructive error with respect to American history is illustrated by the President's 1993 Fourth of July Message, where the Constitutional Convention of 1787 is mistaken for the Continental Congress of 1776. See *New York Times,* July 5, 1993, sec. 1, p. 7; note 15, above. Still another instructive error is noticed in note 176, above.)

217. See James H. Timberlake, *Prohibition and the Progressive Movement, 1900–1920* (Cambridge: Harvard University Press, 1963), 166; William F. Swindler, "A Dubious Constitutional Experiment," in *Law, Alcohol, and Order: Perspectives on National Prohibition*, David E. Kyvig, ed. (Westport, Conn.: Greenwood Press, 1985), 53–54. (Cited hereafter as Timberlake, Swindler, and Kyvig, respectively.)

218. See Timberlake, 145, 147, 171, 173. But see Swindler, 55: "[The Eighteenth Amendment] was then, and remains to date, the only constitutional attempt to incorporate a sumptuary power into the fundamental law of the land." See the text at note 32 of this Commentary. See also note 30, above.

219. In 1913 alcohol could be referred to as "a narcotic poison." See Timberlake, 170.

220. See ibid., 183. See also Anastaplo, *The Constitutionalist*, 154–57.

221. See Timberlake, 164, 180.

222. See Lecture No. 13, Section III, of this Commentary.

223. See, e.g., Wyoming Statutes, 8-4-103 (1977) (declaring December 10 "Wyoming Day," in recognition of the "action of the Wyoming territorial governor on December 10, 1869, in approving the first [?] law found anywhere in legislative history which extend[ed] the right of suffrage to women"). See also Lecture No. 13, Section V, of this Commentary.

224. See Timberlake, 125.

225. 41 Stat. 305 (1919). See Dennis J. Mahoney, "Volstead Act," in *Ency. Am. Const.*, 4: 1978–79.

226. This formulation did permit the continued use of intoxicating liquors for medicinal, sacramental, and other such purposes. See 41 Stat. 308 (1919); Timberlake, 183.

227. This grace period was intended, in part, to permit holders of stocks of alcohol to dispose of them by sale or otherwise, whether in this Country or abroad. Also, it was suspected by some that the grace period was intended to permit those with sufficient resources to accumulate a substantial supply, perhaps even a lifetime supply, for their personal use.

228. See, e.g., Timberlake, 1–4, 125–27.

229. Ibid., 177. See, for how law-abidingness and the equality principle reinforce one another in the United States, Thomas P. O'Neill, Jr., *Man of the House: The Life and Political Memoirs of Speaker Tip O'Neill* (New York: Random House, 1987), 6–7:

> It was at Harvard University in 1927 that I first decided to go into politics.
>
> No, I wasn't a Harvard man. But I was born and raised in North Cambridge, Massachusetts, a stable, mostly Irish, working-class neighborhood a mile or two from the university. At the age of fourteen, I landed a summer job as a groundskeeper, cutting the grass and trimming the hedges at Harvard. It was tough work, and I was paid seventeen cents an hour.
>
> On a beautiful June day, as I was going about my daily grind, the class of 1927 gathered in a huge canvas tent to celebrate commencement. Inside

I could see hundreds of young men standing around in their white linen suits, laughing and talking. They were also drinking champagne, which was illegal in 1927 because of Prohibition.

I remember that scene like it was yesterday, and I can still feel the anger I felt, almost sixty years ago, as I write these words. It was the illegal champagne that really annoyed me. Who do these people think they are, I said to myself, that the law means nothing to them?

Although I could walk home from my Harvard job in twenty minutes, North Cambridge might just as well have been on the other side of the moon. My own neighborhood was relatively well off by working-class standards, but you didn't have to go far to find pockets of real poverty. Every town had its poorhouse, and in those days, of course, there was no such thing as health insurance or Social Security. When you turned sixty-five, your family had to take care of you, and if they couldn't you were out of luck. . . .

On that commencement day at Harvard, as I watched those privileged, confident Ivy League Yankees who had everything handed to them in life, I made a resolution. Someday, I vowed, I would work to make sure that my own people could go to places like Harvard, where they could avail themselves of the same opportunities that those young college men took for granted.

Domestic tranquillity, as well as simple justice and the general welfare, requires that basic opportunities should be available to everyone in this Country. But does not domestic tranquillity also require repeated consideration of measures, including carefully designed affirmative-action programs, which encourage and permit all of our citizens to make productive use of the opportunities available to them? See Anastaplo, "Slavery and the Constitution," 784–85; note 211, above. See also Sections XI–XIII of Lecture No. 12 of this Commentary. It is unfortunate when it can be plausibly argued, as it is today, that "the record is replete with examples of the myriad ways in which the Reagan administration opposed the affirmative action policy of national law in every area of its responsibility." Norman C. Amaker, *Civil Rights and the Reagan Administration* (Washington, D.C.: The Urban Institute Press, 1988), 158. Also unfortunate is the position taken in Harvey C. Mansfield, "Why Equality Is Ridiculous," *Wall Street Journal*, Sept. 6, 1994, p. A12. Compare note 47, above. See note 211, above.

See, for reservations about what has happened to the office of the Speaker of the House of Representatives, "The Shrinking Speaker" (editorial), *New York Times*, Jan. 8, 1994, p. 14; Letters, *New York Times*, Jan. 23, 1994. For how long will the 1994 elections change this?

230. Timberlake, 177 (quoting *Congressional Record*, 65:5587 [1924]).

231. See note 178, above.

232. See Timberlake, 62. One problem with this argument is that it assumed that the State legislatures could not do by ratifying a constitutional amendment what they could do in prohibiting alcohol in their respective

States. Is there, subject to natural-right limitations and valid divine revelation, any limit upon the "despotic power" of the people to change its institutions? See note 204, above. See, on amending the Constitution, Anastaplo, *The Constitution of 1787*, Lecture No. 14, "The Constitution at Two Hundred," 1053. See, for limitations upon the exercise of the right of revolution, *The Complete Works of Lincoln*, 4: 255, 432f.

233. See, e.g., Swindler, 61; Anastaplo, "Governmental Drug-Testing and the Sense of Community," *Nova Law Review*, 11: 295 (1987). See, for a sampling of positions being taken at this time with respect to the possible decriminalization of some drugs, the letters to the editor published in the December 16, 1993, and December 28, 1993, issues of the *New York Times* (the latter set of letters was in response to a "dialogue" published in the *Times* on December 15, 1993). See also note 103, above.

234. See Timberlake, 228. See also Lecture No. 10, Section V, of this Commentary.

235. Ibid., 184.

236. Dennis J. Mahoney, "Twenty-First Amendment," in *Ency. Am. Const.*, 4: 1928. The decision to rely upon the convention-mode for ratification reflects the malapportionment problems referred to in note 205, above.

237. See Swindler, 56, 57–58, 63. See, on the dubious (originally proslavery and later antibusiness-regulation) "burdens on interstate commerce" doctrine, Anastaplo, *The Constitution of 1787*, 52–53. See, on the influence of slavery upon interpretations of the Constitution, Anastaplo, "Mr. Crosskey, the American Constitution, and the Natures of Things," 247 n. 146, 253 n. 190.

238. Paul L. Murphy, "Societal Morality and Individual Freedom," in Kyvig, 78. Similar complaints about the uses of law may be heard with respect to abortion and assisted-suicide restraints, school-prayers and animal-rights empowerments, and other such efforts.

239. Thus the Ten Commandments legislated, or at least confirmed, the morality among the Israelites of Moses' day. See, on the morality of the Israelites, Anastaplo, "On Trial," 821, 854, 882. See, on the legislation of morality, Blackstone, 1: 120; Anastaplo, *Human Being and Citizen*, 46, 74; note 106, above.

240. Consider the implications of Section 5 of the Northwest Ordinance about what are considered generally accepted legal arrangements that government can properly draw upon. See Robert L. Stone, "Commerce and Community in the Constitution of the United States," in *Law and Philosophy*, 2: 752. See also notes 36 and 68, above. See as well notes 30 and 135, above, note 260, below.

241. See, on the abolition of broadcast television in the United States, Anastaplo, *The American Moralist*, 245–74; the text at note 249 of this Commentary. Compare Sheppard, "American Principles, Prudence, and Practice," 723; Sharp, Book Review, *Law and Philosophy*, 1: 551.

242. See Anastaplo, *The Constitution of 1787*, 92. There is one argument for term limitations for Members of Congress, inspired by considering

what has happened to politicians' schedules, that I have not heard: something is to be said for requiring our more talented political men and women to retire from time to time to more leisurely activities. Whatever term limitations are established should not be designed to keep Members from returning to Congress after they have had time to think properly both about the problems of the Country and about the nature of human existence.

We return to the issue of Presidential term limitations by noticing what the eminently pious Roman Catholic churchman, John Henry Newman, confided to his diary:

> It is not good for a pope to live twenty years. It is an anomaly and bears no good fruit; he becomes a god, has no one to contradict him, does not know facts, and does cruel things without meaning it.

Kenneth L. Woodward, *Making Saints: How the Catholic Church Determines Who Becomes a Saint, Who Doesn't, and Why* (New York: Simon and Schuster, 1990), 363. It may be prudent in our circumstances to continue to have, if We the People are to begin to know the candidates who offer themselves, long campaigning periods for the Presidency (but with much reduced campaign budgets and hence far less use of television by candidates and far more reliance upon printed accounts of campaigns by the electorate). In any event, it can be reassuring to notice, with Charles de Gaulle, "The graveyards are full of indispensable men." *Chicago Tribune,* Sept. 9, 1990, sec. 1, p. 21.

243. Term limitations are periodically suggested for judges, but these proposals usually meet the resistance that proposals for court packing and jurisdiction stripping do—namely, that they threaten the traditional independence of judges.

244. It should be noticed that even if the convention-mode of proposing amendments is resorted to by State legislatures to develop a term-limitations amendment, Congress will still have considerable control over what happens in the preparation and promulgation of any proposed term-limitations amendment. See Anastaplo, "The Constitution at Two Hundred," 1053–60.

Until a term-limitations amendment should be developed, Congress can probably regulate (and even nullify) State-imposed term limitations for Members of Congress. Not only may such State impositions be unconstitutional, but also the States that resort to them are likely to reduce their influence in any Congress where Members from other States face no such limitations. See note 256, below.

245. The original expectation of the Framers of the Constitution seems to have been that residents in the Federal District would remain citizens of the States from which they came, in most cases only temporarily, to serve in the General Government. See, e.g., Dennis J. Mahoney, "District of Columbia," in *Ency. Am. Const.,* 2: 569: "The Framers of the Constitution apparently did not foresee a large permanent population in the district distinct from the population of the surrounding states."

246. The Republican Party is most reluctant to have the District of

Columbia converted into a State because it is so heavily Democratic. State-hood would mean, among other things, two more liberal (probably African-American) Democrats in the Senate. See B. Drummond Ayres, Jr., "District of Columbia is Denied Statehood," *New York Times,* Nov. 22, 1993, p. A5 (reporting a 277–153 adverse vote in the House of Representatives). See also R. Hewitt Pate, "No Statehood for D.C.—Unless We Amend the Con-stitution," *Wall Street Journal,* Dec. 16, 1992, p. A15; Lecture No. 10, Sec-tion 1, and Lecture No. 16, Section I, of this Commentary.

247. The Acting President provision is preceded by a provision desig-nating as President any Vice President who permanently replaces a Presi-dent who is removed from office, dies, or resigns. This designation for-mally confirmed what had been the practice ever since Vice President John Tyler succeeded to the Presidency in 1841 upon the death of William Henry Harrison.

248. The term *Electoral College* is not used in the Constitution of 1787. It is used in the Confederate Constitution of 1861 (art. VII, sec. 2).

249. Leo Bogart, *Preserving the Press* (New York: Columbia University Press, 1991), 47. See also Greta Camille Guest, "Flipping through the Fax," *U.S. Air Magazine,* February 1991, 20: "only 51 percent of American adults read a newspaper each day, down from 73 percent in the 1960s." See as well note 241, above.

250. See Anastaplo, *Human Being and Citizen,* 160–74, *The Constitution of 1787,* 33, 312 n. 41, 317 n. 85, *The American Moralist,* xviii, 290–94, 431–39. See, for the official Iran-Contra investigation and the responses to it, *Final Report of the Independent Counsel for Iran-Contra Matters* (Washington, D.C.: Government Printing Office, 1994); *New York Times,* Jan. 19, 1994, pp. A1, A4–A7, A18, A19; Jan. 23, 1994, sec. 4, p. 4; *Wall Street Journal,* Jan. 19, 1994, pp. A2, A4, A15; Jan. 24, 1994, p. A14; *Washington Times,* Jan. 19, 1994, pp. A1f; *Chicago Tribune,* Jan. 19, 1994, sec. 1, p. 20; Jan. 23, 1994, sec. 4, p. 4. Representative Lee H. Hamilton commented on the *Final Report,* "A small group of Government officials decided they knew what was right for the United States, they kept it secret from Congress, they showed disdain for the law and acted totally in conflict with the Constitution." *New York Times,* Jan. 21, 1994, p. A19. Such clandestine manipulations not only are intrin-sically dubious but also open the way to years of recrimination (including distorted charges). Theodore Draper observed, after the Iran-Contra scan-dal broke in 1986, that "if ever the constitutional democracy of the United States is overthrown we now have a better idea how this is likely to be done." Peter Kornbluh and Malcolm Byrne, "Where the Bodies are Buried," *New York Times,* Jan. 19, 1994, p. A19. See, for my letter to the editor on the questionable Caspar Weinberger indictment, Jaffa, *Original Intent,* 365.

251. The disturbing presumptuousness of Presidents was displayed on a grand scale most recently in how the Bush Administration manipulated matters with respect to the Gulf War by using United Nations Security Council resolutions, by shipping more and more troops to Saudi Arabia after the original emergency consignment to that country, and by issuing

one ultimatum after another to a villainous Saddam Hussein. This manipulation, which included misleading American public opinion, made it very difficult for Congress to do anything in January 1991 but "authorize" an immediate use of massive force, appropriate only for a major war, against a war-weary country of fewer than twenty million people. We see in that episode (whatever it may have temporarily done for the morale of the post-Vietnam American army) a remarkable failure in imagination on our part, including moral imagination, however noble our intentions may have at times been. We also see there, as in the 1950 Korean crisis and the 1994 Haitian crisis, the President of the United States seeking authorization from the United Nations rather than from the American Congress upon preparing to resort to acts of war. This unfortunate Presidential habit, however much a distortion of Constitutional principles it may be, does reflect a lingering awareness that something more than an exercise of Executive will is required to justify action in such circumstances. See Anastaplo, *The American Moralist*, xvi–xix, 225. See also Imanuel Geiss, *July 1914: The Outbreak of the First World War* (London: B. T. Batsford Ltd., 1967); Anastaplo, "On Freedom," 589, 604, 626–29; Lecture No. 13, Section VII, and Lecture No. 15, Section IX, of this Commentary. (Presidential presumptuousness was symbolized for our time by the willingness in 1989 of a former American President to "earn" a one to two million dollar honorarium for speeches in Japan shortly after he left office. Concerns were repeatedly indicated in the Federal Convention of 1787 about the susceptibility of executive officers to improper foreign influence. See the text at notes 31–32 of this Commentary. See also note 99, above.)

Is it not the tendency of Presidential government to encourage plebiscitary democracy? The unreliability of plebiscites is suggested by what the contemporary deference to public-opinion polls does to the exercise of prudence. The current situation in Eastern Europe (including Russia) is instructive here. Consider also this warning from Machiavelli: "[I]f there be no enemy outside, [a republic] will find one at home, as it seems necessarily happens in all great cities." Machiavelli, *Discourses*, II, 20. War may suspend, but it does not eliminate, deep (perhaps even natural) divisions at home. See also ibid., II, 25; Shakespeare, *2 Henry IV*, act 4, sc. 5; note 188, above.

252. See, for exchanges relating to these matters, the sources cited in note 11, above.

253. It may not contribute to proper military morale to have involuntary recruits with diverse privileges keyed to age differences. (I recall the anomaly, as an eighteen-year-old Air Cadet [albeit a volunteer], of not being eligible to vote in the 1944 elections, even while I was being trained to be entrusted with the lives of my air crew. Even so, I do not recall a personal sense of grievance on that occasion.) May the Republican Form of Government Guarantee also bear upon this, especially considering how critical the dedication to some form of equality has always been among us?

See, for arguments for expanding the American electorate even more than it has been in the twentieth century, Vita Wallace, "Give children the vote," *Nation*, Oct. 14, 1991, p. 430. The precocious sixteen-year-old who wrote this article is now eligible to vote—which is, no doubt, as it should be.

254. Edward B. Fiske, "Minorities a Majority in New York," *New York Times*, Mar. 22, 1991, p. B1. See also "Changing Face of America," *Chicago Tribune*, Sept. 29, 1993, sec. 1, p. 1. See, on the "hate-speech" codes designed to minister (however imprudently) to our volatile diversity, Anastaplo, "On Freedom," 540, 555, 562, 707.

255. The most favored balanced-budget amendment proposal today permits Congress to override the amendment's spending limitations by a three-fifths vote in each House. Since this is the vote long required to stop a filibuster in the Senate, this kind of amendment would not be likely to make much difference at this time. (Consider also the implications here of the two-thirds vote required for Congress to override a Presidential veto. Thus, any President who advocates a balanced-budget amendment and is willing to risk his popularity already has enough Constitutional power to do what such an amendment would do.) I have commented at length on our ill-conceived balanced-budget amendment agitation in my Commentary on the Constitution of 1787. Publius' long note in *Federalist* No. 84 (note 14, above) is instructive here. The principal provisions of one 1995 Balanced Budget Amendment proposal may be found in Lecture No. 14, Section IX, of this Commentary.

The kind of questions raised about the effects of budget deficits can also be raised about balance-of-trade problems. Consider, for example, the difficulties that the Japanese face if they continue to supply us abundant tangible goods without so opening their markets as to permit us to compensate them with something other than printed promises. Until the Japanese do this, Japanese capitalists and perhaps even more their workers will continue to subsidize the American standard of living. See, on relations between Japan and the United States, Anastaplo, "On Freedom," 644. See also note 83, above.

See, for sources of future amendment proposals, note 198, above. See also Appendixes I-1 and I-2 of this Commentary. See as well note 229, above. Concerns have shifted from the integrity of the community (including the family) to the integrity of the individual (including transient erotic relations)—with the integrity of such things as the planet, the gene pool, and even our relations with supposed extraterrestrial beings perhaps destined to emerge as vital issues. Constitutional rights are more apt to be advanced for homosexuals, as homosexuals, wherever individualism begins to dominate any way of life. The paramount considerations here, however, should be those of justice for and decent treatment of homosexuals, looking more to political than to constitutional redress of grievances. See, for my suggestions here (which Mr. Jaffa vigorously opposes, at least in public), Jaffa, *Original Intent*, 367, 386 n. 13. See, on justice and friendship, note 260, below. See also notes 68, 133 and 211, above.

256. See, for the turnover rates in the history of the U.S. House of

447

Representatives, Neil Gorsuch and Michael Guzman, "Will the Gentlemen Please Yield? A Defense of the Constitutionality of State-Imposed Term Limitations," *Hofstra Law Review,* 20: 341, 385 (1991). The thirteen lowest House turnover rates between 1790 and 1988 were in 1988 (7.6%), 1968 (9%), 1984 (9.9%), 1956 (10.6%), 1986 (11.5%), 1954 (12.9%), 1970 (12.9%), 1926 (13.6%), 1960 (13.8%), 1962 (15.4%), 1976 (15.4%), 1952 (15.6%), and 1950 (15.8%). The thirteen highest House turnover rates between 1790 and 1988 were in 1842 (76%), 1852, (63.8%), 1816 (63.7%), 1854 (62%), 1862 (61.5%), 1874 (60.6%), 1850 (58.2%), 1848 (57.4%), 1846 (54.7%), 1860 (53.5%), 1844 (51.1%), 1870 (50.6%), and 1838 (50.4%). Is it merely a coincidence that the consistently higher turnover rates were during those decades (leading up to the Civil War) that were least distinguished in the history of the Congress (as well as in the history of the Supreme Court?) for prudent decisions? See the texts at notes 149 and 243 to 244 of this Commentary. See also notes 12 and 68, above.

I recall that when I first became aware of political things, the accepted wisdom was that the South (despite a population smaller than that of the North) dominated Congress because it tended to keep its Members there much longer than did Northern constituencies. Is the complaint today, then, that constituencies outside of the South have learned from Southern examples? See note 244, above. Be that as it may, should lifetime service in the federal bureaucracy be permitted (however efficient it may seem to be) if term limitations are ever imposed upon the legislators who are supposed to oversee the bureaucrats?

257. Still, one does encounter more and more people who resent what they take to be the unseemly, intimidating aspects of such executive agencies as the Internal Revenue Service. I suspect that it would be good for the moral sense of the community if taxes did not "have" to be collected in such a way as to provoke all too many otherwise law-abiding taxpayers to be less candid in dealing with their governments than they are in financial dealings with others. The total amount of money paid in taxes should not be the critical issue here. But however their money is collected, citizens should insist upon being kept informed about precisely how much they are consenting to be taxed. This is an advantage of the personal income tax, however disguised it may be as to its full extent by the corporate income tax. See the texts at notes 5 and 28 of this Commentary.

258. See Anastaplo, *The Constitution of 1787,* 113–15, 316 n. 78. Compare Terry Eastland, "War Powers Resolution Redux," *Wall Street Journal,* Dec. 17, 1993, p. A21. On the other hand, there are observers who consider the Congress as the branch of the General Government that is most in need of curbing: "To help put Congress back in its constitutional place will require significant campaign finance reform with public financing and a Presidential line-item veto. Campaign finance reform is critical to give the President more power to assert the national interest over the special interests that prevail on Capitol Hill. The line-item veto is essential to end the Congressional blackmail contained in lengthy bills the President is forced to sign in order to keep Government functioning." Joseph A. Califano, Jr., "Imperial

Congress," *New York Times Magazine,* Jan. 23, 1994, 41. See also Anastaplo, *The Constitution of 1787,* 312 n. 41. The Califano article begins and ends with a fundamental misconception, that the Founding Fathers intended the Executive Branch to have a "coequal status" with the Congress.

See, as illustrative of the extent to which Cold War follies could lead misinformed American Presidents astray, Mary Jo Clogg and Richard Clogg, eds., *Greece* (Oxford: The World Bibliographical Series, Clio Press, 1980), 17: 107–8 (items 491–94). See also ibid., xv–xvi, 41–43 (items 202, 206, 211), 90–107, 110, 114 (item 517), 168–69 (items 752, 758). See as well James G. Pyrros, "PASOK and the Greek Americans," in Nikolaos A. Stavrou, ed., *Greece under Socialism:* (New Rochelle, N.Y.: Orpheus Publishing Co., 1988), 221, 231; Anastaplo, *Human Being and Citizen,* 3–7, *The Artist as Thinker,* 331–53, *The American Moralist,* 501–15, 611; Jaffa, *Original Intent,* 363f.

The ultimate sources, as well as the limits, of American power are suggested by the following remarks that I made to an August 1986 conference sponsored by the Defense Intelligence College, Washington, D.C.:

> We should be on guard, then, against that cleverness which can be easily mistaken for prudence, thereby lulling us into a general thoughtlessness, whether in the academy or in the councils of state and of war.
>
> For example, thoughtlessness may be seen in the temptation to try to imitate the Russians in the conduct of our own affairs at home as well as abroad. We have heard a number of references, in the course of this Conference on Intelligence and Policy, to how much easier it is for the world to know what Americans are up to than to know what the Russians are up to. All too often these references have had the tone of laments, whereas the state of things reflected here should be cause for celebration. Does not our enduring strength depend upon a freedom that enlists the imagination and energy of an entire people to a degree unprecedented in the annals of mankind for so large a country?
>
> Perhaps the most instructive thing for me this week has been something that many of you must have already been familiar with. I could not help but be intrigued a few days ago by the openness, even the casualness, of the lobby entrance to the Defense Intelligence Agency headquarters out at Bolling Air Force Base—especially as I tried to imagine what the Russian counterpart to that place must look like. The considerably greater strength, now and for the foreseeable future, of the United States seems to me very much the consequence of a sensible and highly productive freedom.
>
> How our freedom can be kept sensible is, of course, a serious question. Much depends upon the moral character, and hence the education, of our people. We should take care lest we depend unduly upon clandestine operations and secret information, a dependence whose horrendous costs should be appreciated as we observe how generations of Russians have crippled themselves.
>
> Indeed, it can be said, the world depends upon us to conduct the informed debate that is needed over the next decade for a sensible guidance

of mankind into the twenty-first century. Not the least of the beneficiaries of our virtues should be the Russians themselves, whom it would be prudent not to regard always or simply as adversaries.

Anastaplo, "Clausewitz and Intelligence: Some Preliminary Observations," *Teaching Political Science,* 16: 81 (1989). See also note 99, above. See, on mobilization North and South during the Civil War, note 66, above. All this bears upon the lessons we teach abroad and how we are regarded thereafter.

259. *Contemporary Quotations,* James B. Simpson, ed. (New York: Thomas Y. Crowell, 1964), 266. See, for the most celebrated Continental European, and indeed a French, attempt to combine individual rights (and hence respect for regionalism?) with the general will, note 60, above. See, on de Gaulle and the United States, Stone, ed., *Essays on the Closing of the American Mind,* 284 n. 50; Dean Rusk, *As I Saw It* (New York: W. W. Norton, 1990), 271.

See, for a distressed Southerner's case for the promotion of constitutional amendments in the service of American regionalism, Donald Davidson, *The Attack on Leviathan: Regionalism and Nationalism in the United States* (Chapel Hill: University of North Carolina Press, 1938), e.g., 120f, 368 ("two great principles, local autonomy and federation"). This provocative book, which is most apt to appeal to antiquarians today, is flavored by such sentiments as the following:

> Under Calhoun's leadership the South therefore abandoned the extreme equalitarian features of early Jeffersonian doctrine. Unfortunately for realistic Southerners, their Northern brethren insisted on a thoroughly romantic application of Jeffersonian equalitarianism, and added to it (as if to parallel the South's paradoxical defense of slavery) their own paradox of a glorified Federal union, which they did not concede would be in the least oppressive to the liberties of white Southerners or specially partial to the "peculiar institutions" of the North. The war that followed was thus a struggle between two kinds of liberalism.

Ibid., 269–70. Earlier it is said:

> If New England encouraged man to believe in an ordered universe, Georgia—and a good deal of the South besides—compelled him to remember that there were snakes in Eden. Nature, so ingratiating and beautiful, which bound the Georgian to his land with a love both possessive and fearful, was a fair but dreadful mistress, unpredictable and uncontrollable as God. The New Englander knew exactly where to find nature harsh and nature yielding, and he could make his arrangements accordingly. But the Georgian never knew. His safest policy was to relax, and he readily developed a great degree of tolerance for irregularity in nature and man. At his lowest level, this quality made him lackadaisical and trifling. In this he differed from the New England Yankee, who became a perfectionist, and then at his worst might turn into zealot, strangely intolerant even while, as idealist, he argued for tolerance.

Davidson, 140–41. "The forebears of the Vermont Yankee had once failed to understand how Southerners could be devoted both to slavery and democracy." Ibid., 133.

Professor Davidson, in turn, evidently failed to understand the ways in which Lincoln's thought was superior to that of all of his adversaries, both North and South. See, e.g, ibid., 216–18, 224, 269, 334, 342. (This superiority may even be seen in Lincoln's meticulous preference for *middle States* over *border States*. See, e.g., *Collected Works of Lincoln*, 4: 428 ["the border States, so called—in fact, the middle States"]. Consider also his distinction between *generality* and *locality* with respect to the distribution of powers by the Constitution. Ibid., 4: 435; note, 60, above.) Lincoln stood for constitutional processes, as illustrated by this statement to Congress on July 4, 1861:

> Our popular government has often been called an experiment. Two points in it, our people have already settled—the successful *establishing*, and the successful *administering* of it. One still remains—its successful *maintenance* against a formidable internal attempt to overthrow it. It is now for them to demonstrate to the world, that those who can fairly carry an election, can also suppress a rebellion—that ballots are the rightful, and peaceful, successors of bullets; and that when ballots have fairly, and constitutionally, decided, there can be no successful appeal, back to bullets; that there can no successful appeal except to ballots themselves, at succeeding elections. Such will be a great lesson of peace; teaching men that what they cannot take by an election, neither can they take it by a war—teaching all, the folly of being the beginners of a war.

Collected Works of Lincoln, 4: 439. See notes 66, 134, and 185, above. See also note 156, above. Underlying and nourishing Lincoln's constitutionalism is a moral sense that more and more white Southerners (truly "realistic Southerners"?) have come to appreciate in recent decades, a moral sense as well as political principles grounded in the Declaration of Independence and reflected in the insistence, "If slavery is not wrong, nothing is wrong." Ibid., 7: 281. See also note 146, above, and the texts at notes 29 and 163 of this Commentary, along with the quotation from Ulysses S. Grant among the epigraphs for this Commentary. See as well Anastaplo, "Slavery and the Constitution," 681–91; notes 156, 178, and 191, above; Lecture No. 1, Section IV (end), of this Commentary. See, on Calhoun and the morality of a race-based system of slavery, ibid., 722; Anastaplo, *The Constitution of 1787*, 332.

See, on the moral sense and its bearing upon the constitutional status of nonpublic schools and their support by public funds, Anastaplo, "The Religion Clauses of the First Amendment," *Memphis State University Law Review*, 11: 151 (1981). See also O'Neill, *Man of the House*, 168–69; note 135, above. I suggest, if only in passing, that both *Pierce v. Society of Sisters*, 268 U.S. 510 (1925), and *Wisconsin v. Yoder*, 406 U.S. 205 (1977), may have been mistaken as matters of constitutional laws, whatever merits the positions there vindicated may have as political decisions in some circumstances.

More defensible, as constitutional-law determinations, are *Reynolds* v. *United States*, 98 U.S. 145 (1879), *West Virginia Board of Education* v. *Barnette*, 319 U.S. 624 (1943), and even the much-criticized case of *Employment Division* v. *Smith*, 494 U.S. 872 (1990). Sensible political accommodations to minority interests (both religious and racial) may be seen in legislation permitting conscientious objection to conscription, providing for affirmative-action programs, and extending public services to parochial-school children. See also the Religious Freedom Restoration Act of 1993; note 68, above. An insistence upon supposed constitutional rights with respect to such matters tends to subvert the moral authority and the sobriety (if not even the useful piety) of the political community and to encourage ever more individualism and hence fragmentation, if not even a well-meaning anarchy, in this Country. Compare Michael W. McConnell, "Free Exercise Revisionism and the *Smith* Decision," *University of Chicago Law Review,* 57: 1109 (1990).

See, on what the equality principle can mean to law-abiding Americans, note 229, above. See, on those moral flaws in human beings (as in associations) which show up early and can do permanent damage both to personal relations and to the cause of a reliable decency in associations, Anastaplo, *The Artist as Thinker,* 181–94, 217, 223–25. See also ibid., 323.

See, on "snakes in Eden," Anastaplo, "Can Beauty 'Hallow Even the Bloodiest Tomahawk'? On 'The Killers,' 'A Good Man Is Hard to Find,' and 'The Silence of the Lambs'," *The Critic,* Winter 1993, 2. See, on the trials of Eden, Anastaplo, "On Trial," 767.

260. What is the relation between an emphasis upon sexual love (promoted by a voracious and violence-prone entertainment industry) and a radical inwardness (or a preoccupation with the right of privacy)? What are the Christian influences here? See notes 149 and 172, above. See, on how republicans put the erotic as well as family ties to public use, Anastaplo, *The Artist as Thinker,* 48–49, 51–56, 366 n. 75, 391 n. 79. See, on the tension between the political and the erotic, Strauss, *The City and Man,* 110f. Several of the essays in my *Artist* book touch upon the proper relation between love and politics, a relation that is often sought for in the remarkable variety of our religious experiences. Love, politics and religion (in part an aspect of politics) are interwoven in a distinctively modern way in the poetry of Robert Burns. The Scottish dialect language may have permitted Burns to speak more intimately of love matters than did the English language of his day. A (perhaps natural) yearning for the extraordinary and even divine may be detected as well in our many fanciful reports about UFOs and the like. See Anastaplo, "Rome, Piety, and Law," 96 n. 274, *The American Moralist,* 345, *Human Being and Citizen,* 214. See also notes 68, 216 and 255, above. See, on the modern Greek language, Kostas Kazazis, "Folk Etymology," in *Law and Philosophy,* 2: 1024. See also the translations by Theodora Vasils and Kimon Friar of poems by Constantine P. Cavafy, ibid., 1: xvii, 2: 1048.

Does capitalism, with its welcome productivity, tend to encourage and legitimate self-centeredness and hedonistic self-love, if not simply selfishness and shamelessness? See, e.g., Aleksandr I. Solzhenitsyn, "To Tame Savage Capitalism," *New York Times*, Nov. 28, 1993, p. E11. Institutionalized love for humanity (that is, organized private charity) attempts to compensate for this tendency in capitalism. See notes 30, 99, 135, and 240, above. See also the text at note 249 of this Commentary.

Does not nature require a community to have some recognized public life? If the properly political is depreciated, then may there not be (by way of "compensation") an exposure to public view of much that should be private (even while the Right to Privacy is acclaimed)? It is prudent to notice, in any event, that the erotic may be critical for philosophy and its millennia-long efforts to get beneath and hence beyond the appearances of things. See Lecture No. 11, Section VII, and Lecture No. 16, Section VI, of this Commentary. See also notes 120 and 141, above. Among the promises held out to us by love is that it (and perhaps only it) can lift us out of the Cave (Plato, *Republic* 514A sq.), that Cave which political life must take seriously. Consider, as illuminating the proper relation between politics and love, what Aristotle has to say about the relation between justice and friendship: "Friendship seems too to hold cities together, and lawgivers seem to care more for it than for justice; for unanimity seems to be something like friendship, and this is what lawgivers aim at most of all, and they expel faction as their worst enemy; and when men are friends they have no need of justice, while even when they are just they need friendship as well, and the truest form of justice is thought to be a friendly quality." *Nicomachean Ethics* 1155a22–28. See also note 147, above. The modern distinction between State and Society (note 135, above) may leave the State making more of Justice (and hence prosperity, if not even peace) and the Society making more of Friendship (and hence self-fulfillment, if not even understanding).

See, for teachings about these matters, Anastaplo, "Lessons for the Student of Law: The Oklahoma Lectures," *Oklahoma City University Law Review*, 19 (1995) (including discussions of *New York Times Co. v. Sullivan*, 376 U.S. 254 [1964], of Plutarch's Timoleon, of Socrates and Plato's *Laws*, of Noah, Ham, and Canaan, and of Edmund Burke's 1774 Bristol Electors speech); also, my discussion of the O. J. Simpson case in volume 26 of the *Loyola University of Chicago Law Journal*. (My 1992 *Oklahoma City University Law Review* article, "On Freedom," has been reprinted in part in James L. Swanson, ed., *First Amendment Law Handbook, 1994–1995* [New York: Clark Boardman Callaghan, 1994], 7–110.) See, on what the Classics and the Bible teach about the status of friendship (including homosexual relations), my exchange with Jon-Henri Damski, *Windy City Times*, Chicago, Illinois, Dec. 8, 1994, p. 15, Dec. 29, 1994, p. 12. (The most reliable form of friendship and the most elevated form of localism may be found in the true philosopher.) See, on the Republic of Letters and the influence that scholars of good will may have upon one another, Patrick T. Conley and John P. Kaminsky, *The Bill of Rights and the States* (with respect to the reading of the First Amendment in Leonard W. Levy's *Legacy of Suppression* [1960]). See, on *Robert's Rules of*

Order and on the rights and duties of majority rule, my article for the 1996 volume of *Great Ideas Today*.

See, for a thoughtful redefinition of several vital issues touched upon in this Commentary, Laurence Berns, "The Relation between Philosophy and Religion: Reflections on Leo Strauss's Suggestion Concerning the Source and Sources of Modern Philosophy," *Interpretation*, 19: 43 (1991). (Compare, on music and the Constitution, Anastaplo, *The Constitutionalist*, 818 [in line 3, "40" should be "50"]. See, on the relation of speculation, including mathematical speculation, both to Constitutional interpretation and to philosophical thought, ibid., 806–8. The human desire to know can be stimulated by such mysteries as "the unseemly irregularity in the occurrence of [prime numbers] and variations in the size of the intervals between them." George P. Loweke, *The Lore of Prime Numbers* [New York: Vantage Press, 1982], 90. See also ibid., vii, 5, 123–24. The puzzles encountered here remind one of what it means *to know*, something readily evident in one's grasp of the usual regularities in mathematics. One can also be reminded here of how imprecise any investigations of the much more unpredictable political matters and the much more irregular constitutional matters must be. It is remarkable, in any event, how precise the measurements made with the aid of relatively crude instruments can be, at least in the physical sciences. Is our natural grasp of the physical world somehow drawn upon here? Consider, moreover, this caution:

> [Edmund Husserl] realized more profoundly than anybody else that the scientific understanding of the world, far from being the perfection of our natural understanding, is derivative from the latter in such a way as to make us oblivious of the very foundations of the scientific understanding: all philosophic understanding must start from our common understanding of the world, from our understanding of the world as sensibly perceived prior to all theorizing.

Leo Strauss, "Philosophy as Rigorous Science and Political Philosophy," 3. See also Larry Arnhart, "Mathematics and the Problem of Intelligibility," in *Law and Philosophy*, 1: 19; Roger D. Masters, "Do Ideas Matter? A Note on Hegel and Modern Biology," ibid., 1: 33; Keith S. Cleveland, "The Usefulness of Old Works of Science," ibid., 1: 43; Gerald Proietti, "The Natural World and the Political World in Thucydides' History," ibid., 1: 184; John Van Doren, "Countersign," ibid., 2: 1064; Anastaplo, *The Constitutionalist*, 806–8, *The Artist as Thinker*, 339–41, *The American Moralist*, 83–102. See, on the political conditions for the study of mathematics and philosophy, note 146, above. See also Lecture No. 9, Sections II and XVI, of this Commentary. See as well notes 130 and 131, above.

Index

Many of the entries in this Index may be usefully supplemented by consulting the parallel entries in the Index for George Anastaplo, *The Constitution of 1787: A Commentary* (1989).

Abolitionism, 137, 139–40, 144, 146–47, 152, 154, 160, 191, 193, 200–201. *See also* Slavery

Abortion, 6, 96, 192, 203, 406 n.68, 415 n.110, 443 n.238

Absolutes, absolutism, ix, 20–21, 41, 54–55, 61, 65, 67–68, 82, 95, 171, 199, 319, 404 n.66, 438 n.204. *See also* Natural right, natural rights

Adams, John, xviii, xx, 105, 107–24, 221, 236, 242, 328, 330–40, 417 nn.122, 123, 421 n.131, 425 nn.136, 137, 138, 141, 426 n.146

Adkins, A. W. H., 425 n.139

Adler, Mortimer J., xviii, 438 n.198

Affirmative action, 181–82, 184, 236, 439 nn.206, 211, 441–42 n.229, 452 n.259. *See also* Justice

Africans, African-Americans, 134, 174, 180, 182–83, 200, 439–40 n.211

Alvis, John, xviii, 404–5 n.66, 420 n.130, 428 n.147

American Revolution, 1–2, 6–7, 41–42, 46, 106, 171, 185, 385 n.1, 397 n. 48, 401 n.60. *See also* Revolution, right of; Slavish doctrine of non-resistance

Anastaplo, George, iii, xvi, xviii, 386–87 n.1, 415 n.106, 418 n.124, 446 n.253, 449 n.258. *See also* Prudence; Revolution, right of

Anastaplo, Sara Prince, xvii, 388 n.12

Animal rights, 235, 443 n.238

Animal sacrifices, 406 n.68

Anti-theological ire, 124, 428 n.149

Aristotle, 61, 108, 121, 123–24, 224, 339, 402 n.63, 417 n.120, 425nn. 139, 141, 427 n.147, 453 n.260. *See also* Philosophy; Plato

Arms, keep and bear, 61, 63, 65, 67, 265, 283, 288, 306, 316, 423 n.134. *See also* Second Amendment

Arnhart, Larry E., xviii, 415 n.106, 426 n.146, 454 n.260

Articles of Confederation, 4–10, 31, 38, 40, 77–78, 99, 130, 168, 171, 387 n.2, 388 n.10, 397 n.52, 420 n.130, 440 n.214

Assemble, right to, 43, 52–53, 60, 62, 67–68, 274, 301, 307, 316, 321, 323

Balanced-budget amendment, 20–21, 37, 91, 206, 226–27, 230–31, 384, 447 n.255. *See also* Constitutional frivolity

Bar Admission Cases (1961), xvi, 230, 387 n.1

Barber, Sotirios A., 393 n.14

Barlow, J. Jackson, 389 n.13

Barron v. *Baltimore* (1833), 74–76, 170, 410 n.90, 439 n.206

Benardete, Seth, 432 n.168

Benson, Egbert, 62–63, 408 n.74

Berns, Gisela N., 420 n.130

Berns, Laurence, xvii, xviii, 386 n.1, 388 n.11, 389 n.13, 415 n.106, 418 n.130, 432 n.168, 453–54, n.260

Berns, Walter, 434 n.176, 440 n.216

455

Bible, ix, 112, 120, 122–23, 130–31, 166–67, 185, 412 n.94, 418–20 n.130, 421 n.131, 424 n.134, 426 n.143, 428 n.149, 435 n.187, 436 n.192, 453 n.260

Bill of attainder, 9, 32, 59, 81, 289, 390 n.14

Bill of Rights, England, 2, 27–28, 40, 53, 61, 63, 88, 240, 387 n.3, 391 n.14, 396 n.45; *text*, 240, 263–68

Bill of Rights, U.S., 2, 4–5, 9, 11–21, 22–23, 28, 30–49, 59, 74–76, 78–79, 84, 86–87, 89, 90–96, 101–2, 107, 132–33, 142, 168, 170, 173, 175, 204–5, 229, 237, 293–97, 315–29, 388 n.10, 389–93 n.14, 397 nn.49, 51, 402–3 n.65, 411 n.92, 415 n.113, 434 n.176; *text*, 243, 375–77

Black, Hugo Lafayette, x, 386 n.1, 403–4 n.60

Blackstone, William, 53, 61, 63, 386 n.1, 390–91 n.14, 395 nn.36, 40, 42, 43, 396 n.47, 397 n.48, 400 n.60, 401 n.61, 402 n.63, 405–6 n.68, 408 n.75, 411 n.94, 412 nn.97, 99, 413 n.103, 413–14 n.105, 414 n.106, 415 n.108, 419 n.130, 422–23 n.134, 424–25 n.135, 425 n.136, 426 n.146, 431 n.156, 434 n.177, 435 nn.186, 188, 438 n.204, 443 n.239

Bloom, Allan, 388 n.12, 420 n.130

Braithwaite, Wendy Ann, 420 n.130

Braithwaite, William T., xviii, 386 n.1, 395 n.36, 412 n.96, 415 n.106

Brann, Eva T. H., xviii, 426–27 n.146

British Constitution, 1–2, 30, 40, 69, 217, 273, 319, 397 n.48, 421 n.130, 423 n.134

Brown v. *Board of Education* (1954), 168, 439 n.209

Buckley v. *Valeo* (1976), 230

Burke, Edmund, x, 386 n.1, 453 n.260

Burns, Robert, 452 n.260

Caesar, Julius, 185, 216, 336

Calhoun, John C., 126, 134, 450–51 n.258. *See also* Slavery

Canadian Charter of Rights, 401 n.61

Cantor, Milton, 389 n.13

Capital punishment, 89, 124, 232, 413 n.103, 422–23 n.134

Censorship, 52–53, 119, 403 n.66

Chance, 8, 86, 123, 154–55, 159, 162–63, 165, 167, 181, 186–87, 214, 223, 225–27, 403 n.65. *See also* Providence

Character of the people, xx, 18–20, 32, 46, 221, 226, 234. *See also* Moral standards, sources; Morality and law

Chase, Salmon P., 157–58, 435 n.185

Child labor, suppression of, 196

Children's rights, 235

Chisholm v. *Georgia* (1793), 102–3, 415 n.115

Christianity, 57, 116–21, 124, 134, 166, 283, 285, 332–33, 335, 338–39, 344, 400 n.60, 407 n.69, 418 n.124, 422 n.132, 426 n.144, 428–29 n.149, 433 n.172, 452 n.260

Churchill, Winston S., 30, 108, 385–86 n.1, 387 n.4, 397 n.48, 420 n.130, 426 n.146

Civil Rights Cases (1883), 183, 184, 439 n.207

Civil War, x, 1–2, 7, 21, 31, 46, 51, 125–34, 135–67, 169, 172–73, 179, 182, 185, 190, 192, 207, 224, 385 n.1, 403 n.66, 426 n.146, 429 n.150, 432 n.168, 434 nn.176, 179, 436 n.191, 437 n.192, 447–48 n.256

Cleveland, Keith S., xvii, 454 n.260

Clovis, 436 n.191

Coby, Patrick, 422 n.132

Cold War follies, xvi, 449 n.258

Collins, Ronald K. L., 394 n.25, 401 n.61, 411 n.93, 431 n.157

Colmo, Christopher A., xviii, 415 n.106

Commander in Chief, 17, 79, 143–44, 156–57, 207, 211, 216, 433 n.176

Commerce, commerce powers, 7–8, 17, 19, 22, 29, 98, 127, 129, 184, 196, 273–74, 297, 303, 424 n.135, 443 nn.237, 246. *See also* Market economy

Common good, xix, 44, 46, 67, 96, 116, 121, 225, 234, 250, 284, 288–89. *See also* Prudence

Common law, 13, 18, 22–24, 26, 29–31, 45–46, 61, 67, 74–76, 78–79, 84, 87–89, 91, 94–96, 103, 131, 175–77, 205, 247, 274, 307–8, 313, 317, 322, 324, 391 n.14, 395 n.36, 396 n.37, 401 n.62, 402 n.63. *See also* Natural right, natural rights

Confederate States of America, 1, 429 n.150; Constitution of 1861, 125–34, 168, 172, 243, 309, 429 nn.151, 153, 154, 430 nn.155, 156; Constitution, *text*, 243, 344–61

Congressional compensation, 34, 50–51, 223–24, 297, 304, 316, 323, 397 n.50. *See also* Twenty-seventh Amendment

Conscience, rights of, 55–57, 82, 115, 136, 258, 283, 298, 306, 317, 319, 321–24, 407 n.69

Conscientious objector, 62–63, 66, 301, 316, 321, 323, 408 n.74, 452 n.259. *See also* Individualism

Constitution of 1787: authoritative Congressional interpretations, 20, 76–77, 83, 90, 105, 406 n.68; craftsmanship, 33–34, 46, 59–60, 69, 92, 389 n.13; mode of interpretation, xx, 8, 18, 38–39, 133; signers of the Constitution, 374–75; *text*, 243, 363–75. *See also* Ratification of the Constitution

Constitutional frivolity, 177, 194, 223–24, 230, 234. *See also* Balanced-budget amendment; Term limitations; Twenty-seventh Amendment

Constitutional numbers, 4–5, 7, 17, 179, 213, 219, 228–29, 310, 327, 365–66, 369–71, 373–74; in Confederate Constitution, 346–49, 351, 354–56, 360, 377–79

Constitutionalism, natural, 6, 9, 35, 169. *See also* Natural right, natural rights

Continental Congress, 3–4, 6, 9, 29–30, 83, 108, 271–80, 440 n.216

Crosskey, William W., 62, 243, 389 n.13, 393 n.14, 397 nn.49, 52, 401 n.61, 403 n.66, 408 n.72, 438 n.198, 443 n.237

Cruel and unusual punishment, 88–89, 282, 289, 301, 306, 317, 321, 324

Davidson, Donald, 450–51 n.259

de Alvarez, Leo Paul S., xvii, 420 n.136

Death, 118–19, 122, 235–36. *See also* Suicide, assisted

Declaration of Independence, xx, 1–2, 4–7, 9–10, 21, 24, 29–31, 43, 62, 65, 68, 101, 106–9, 122–24, 130, 142, 162, 171, 176–78, 224, 234, 237, 240–41, 284, 387 n.2, 388 nn.10, 11, 397 nn.48, 52, 402 n.62, 416–17 n.120, 417 n.122, 418 n.130, 420 n.130, 422 n.131, 424–25 n.135, 427 n.147, 434 n.177, 451 n.259; signers of the Declaration, 280; uses of the divine, 417 n.120; *text*, 276–80.

See also Equality principle; Liberty principle

Declaration of the Rights of Man and the Citizen, 438 n.198; *text*, 398–400 n.60. *See also* Napoleon Bonaparte; Natural right, natural rights

Declaration of war, power of, 17, 32, 193–94, 233, 310, 445–46 n.251. *See also* Persian Gulf War

de Gaulle, Charles, 237, 444 n.242, 450 n.259

Dilliard, Irving, 386 n.1

District of Columbia, 125, 210–11, 218–19, 228, 303, 311, 444 n.245, 444–45 n.246

Donohue, Maurice F. X., 386 n.1

Double jeopardy, 80–81, 306, 412 n.97. *See also* Fifth Amendment

Douglas, Stephen A., 166, 174, 188, 197, 437–38 n.197

Douglass, Frederick, 137–38, 163, 439 n.152

Dramatic arts. *See* Sports

Dred Scott v. *Sandford* (1857), 83, 129, 173–74, 177, 385 n.1, 429 nn.152, 153

Drugs, attempted control of, 72, 196, 198, 202–3, 441 n.219, 443 n.233

Dry, Murray, 415 n.108

Due Process Clauses, 82–83, 88, 173, 176–79, 438 n.204; *text*, 328, 378

Due process of law, 26, 80–83, 88, 173, 176–78, 223, 250–52, 260–62, 264, 282, 287, 300, 306, 317, 321, 324, 399 n.60, 406 n.68, 412 n.99, 438 n.204. *See also* Law of the land

Dumbauld, Edward, 242, 388–89 n.13

Education, 56, 73, 107–24, 221, 225, 234–35, 334, 339–40, 419 n.130, 448 n.258

Eidelberg, Paul, 426 n.144

Eighteenth Amendment, 105, 186, 195–206, 229, 243, 441 nn.217, 218; *text*, 380. *See also* Drugs, attempted control of; Twenty-first Amendment

Eighth Amendment, 76–79, 88–89, 91, 94, 248, 264–65, 282, 289, 301, 306, 317, 321, 324, 326, 411–12 n.94; *text*, 328, 376. *See also* Cruel and unusual punishment

Electoral College, 213–14, 231, 361, 416 n.119, 430 n.155, 445 n.248

Eleventh Amendment, 92–93, 102–4, 107, 168, 174, 294, 304, 308, 358, 398 n.57, 415 n.116; *text*, 102, 377

Ellsworth, Oliver, 19

Emancipation Proclamation, xix, 130, 135–67, 181, 183, 396 n.45, 431 n.157, 432 n.161, 433 nn.173, 175, 181, 435 nn.182, 184, 436–37 n.192; *text*, 143, 146, 148–49, 151–57, 159–63, 243, 362

Employment Division v. *Smith* (1990), 452 n.259

Engeman, Thomas, xviii, 389 n.13

Entitlements, 94, 233–34

Environmental concerns, 235, 447 n.255

Envy, democratic, 336, 432 n.168

Equal Protection Clause, 94, 178–79, 181, 184, 438 n.204, 438–39 n. 205; *text*, 378

Equal Rights Amendment, 51, 203, 223, 228, 440 n.216. *See also* Women, nature of

Equality principle, ix, xix, xx, 5–7, 24, 31, 46, 54, 105–6, 114, 122–24, 130, 132–33, 148, 164, 170–71, 174, 178–79, 186, 189, 192, 205, 210, 221–22, 281, 284, 319, 398 n.60, 409–10 n.83, 422 n.133, 423 n.134, 426 n.144, 437 n.192, 439 nn.205, 211, 441–42 n.229, 446–47 n.253, 450 n.259. *See also* Declaration of Independence; Liberty principle

Erie Railroad Co. v. *Tompkins* (1938), 90–91, 96, 175, 295 n.36, 399 n.60. *See also* Common law; *Swift* v. *Tyson*

Erotic element, 122, 225, 237–38, 447 n.255, 452–53 n.260

Establishment of religion, 36, 52, 56–57, 67, 236, 263, 267–69, 284–86, 291–92, 302, 306, 316, 321, 323, 406–7 n.69, 424 n.135. *See also* First Amendment; Religious liberty

Ex post facto laws, 9, 11, 20–21, 32, 59, 289, 308, 390–91 n.14, 399 n.60

Exclusionary rule, 71–73, 76

Executive, corruption of, 446 n.251

Existence, sweetness of, 425 n.141

Expressly (term), 9–10, 37, 44, 97–100, 127, 286, 306

Family relations, vii, 24, 119, 170, 191, 235, 254, 447 n.255, 452 n.260

Federal (term), 54–55, 133, 344, 346, 351, 430 n.155, 450 n.259

Federal Convention of 1787, 1–10, 11–21, 23, 35, 37–39, 43, 86, 169, 208, 224, 241, 293–97, 336, 387 n.2, 394 nn.15, 27, 440 n.216, 446 n.251

Federalist Papers, 21, 23, 242, 424 n.135, 447 n.255; *Federalist* No. 84, *text* (partial), 389–93 n.14

Fehrenbacher, Don E., xviii, 430 n.156

Female suffrage, 31, 197, 229, 440 n.216, 441 n.223. *See also* Nineteenth Amendment

Fifteenth Amendment, 2, 31, 51, 130, 138, 168–70, 182–87, 191–93, 200, 220, 223, 225–26; *text*, 379

Fifth Amendment, 60, 68, 73, 76–89, 91, 94, 129, 173, 176, 181, 287–89, 300, 316–17, 321, 324–26, 438 n.204; *text*, 80, 328, 376

Filibusters, abuses of, 105, 193–94, 447 n.255. *See also* Supermajorities

Finkelman, Paul, 397 n.49

First Amendment, xix, 36, 41–42, 47–58, 60, 62–63, 67–68, 101–2, 200, 205, 236, 263, 265, 272, 274, 276, 279, 283–85, 288–89, 291–93, 298, 301–2, 306–7, 316, 321, 323, 325, 392 n.14, 399 n.60, 403–4 n.66, 405–6 n.68, 407 n.69, 421 n.134, 431 n.156, 447 n.254; *text*, 52, 327, 375. *See also* Establishment of religion; Freedom of speech or of the press; Religious liberty

Fisher, Louis, 439 n.209

Flaumenhaft, Mera, 421 n.131

Fourteenth Amendment, 2, 24, 31, 44–45, 51, 57, 89, 103–4, 130, 138, 154, 156, 168–70, 172–87, 192–93, 200, 207, 218, 223, 225–26, 405 n.67, 422 n.131, 438 nn.202, 204, 439 nn.206, 211; *text*, 378–79

Fourth Amendment, 59–60, 62, 67–76, 78–79, 82, 94, 207, 282, 288, 301, 307, 317, 321–25, 410 nn.84, 85, 89, 410–11 n.91; *text*, 327–28, 375–76

Franklin, Benjamin, 19, 35, 65, 337, 409 n.80

Freedman, Lawrence Zelic, 395 n.32

Freedom of debate for legislators, 53, 256–58, 265, 289, 413–14 n.105

Freedom of expression, 53–56, 63, 68–69, 128–29, 225, 238

Freedom of speech or of the press, 11–13, 42, 52–58, 60, 63, 67–69, 78, 102, 205, 256–58, 283, 298, 301, 307, 316–17, 319, 321–24, 392 n.14, 399 n.60, 403 n.66, 412 n.99, 424 n.134. *See also* First Amendment

Friar, Kimon, 452 n.260

Frisch, Morton J., 108, 393 n.14, 417 n.121

Fritzsche, Hellmut, 426 n.146

Frugality, virtue of, xx, 283, 288

Fugitive slave provisions, 18, 31, 148, 151–52, 171. *See also* Slavery

Fuller, Timothy, 389 n.13

Garrison, William Lloyd, 165–66, 435 n.186

Gene pool, integrity of, 447 n.255

General warrants, 69–70. *See also* Fourth Amendment

General welfare, 132–33, 344, 349, 442 n.229

Gerry, Elbridge, 13–17, 19, 294–97, 408 n.73

Gertz, Elmer, 420 n.130

Gettysburg Address, xx, 1, 4, 9, 31, 179, 185, 387 n.2, 407 n.69, 430 n.155, 437 n.192. *See also* Lincoln, Abraham

Gibbon, Edward, 339, 425 n.138, 435 n.188, 436 n.191

Gildin, Hilail, 416 n.120, 422 n.132

Gleicher, Jules, xvii, 435 n.188

Glenn, Gary D., 423 n.134

Goldwin, Robert A., 397 n.49, 408 n.79

Gorham, Nathaniel, 13, 87, 294–95, 413 n.101

Gourevitch, Victor, 416 n.120

Grand jury, 76, 80, 307, 318

Grant, Ulysses S., x, 386 n.1, 403 n.66, 431 n.156, 432 n.170, 451 n.259

Great War, 150, 193, 195, 202, 214

Gueguen, John A., 415 n.106

Guest, Greta Camille, 445 n.249

Gun control, 61–64, 68, 124, 196, 398 n.59, 408 nn.78, 79. *See also* Second Amendment

Habeas corpus, writ of, 11–13, 25–26, 32, 59, 83, 184–85, 260, 293, 300, 306, 311, 341, 343–44, 390 n.14, 396 n.42

Haiti crisis (1994), 446 n.251

Hamilton, Alexander, 120, 393 n.14, 394 n.22, 397 n.52

Hate-speech codes, 447 n.254

Hedonism, 45, 115, 225, 418 n.130, 421 n.131, 452–53 n.260

Hemingway, Ernest, 452 n.259

Henry VIII, 240, 256–58, 414 n.105

Henry, Patrick, 28–29, 434 n.176

Herodotus, 395 n.30, 404 n.66

Hiccoughs, remedy for, 113, 337

History, 95, 132, 159, 186, 439 n.210. *See also* Chance; Providence

Hoffman, Daniel N., xvii, 438 n.198

Holland, Kenneth M., 401 n.61

Hollingsworth v. *Virginia* (1798), 103

Holmes, Oliver Wendell, Jr., 114, 431 n.156

Homosexuality, 447 n.255, 453–54 n.260

Houston, Sam, 429 n.150

Human nature, 213, 336. *See also* Women, nature of

Hume, David, 113, 116, 119, 339–40, 425 n.143

Hussein, Saddam, 216, 236, 445–46 n.251

Husserl, Edmund, 454 n.260

Impeachment, 11, 78, 85, 213, 304, 312–13, 316–17, 321–22, 324, 346–47, 390 n.14

Indians, 180, 205, 224, 279, 385 n.1, 434 n.177; Indian thought, xix

Individualism, xviii, 40, 44–45, 61–62, 66, 68–69, 96, 115, 118, 121, 124, 128–29, 225, 421 n.131, 422 n.133, 426 n.144, 428 n.149, 443 n.238, 447 n.255, 452 n.259

Innocent III, 245

Internal improvements, 127, 349

Iran-arms and Contra-aid controversy, 79, 215, 445 n.250

Jaffa, Harry V., x, xviii, 135–36, 140–41, 241, 386 n.1, 388 n.11, 403 n.66, 407 n.69, 416 n.120, 420 n.130, 431 n.158, 432 n.168, 434 n.178, 438 n.197, 447 n.255

Japan, 409 n.83, 446 n.251, 447 n.255

Jefferson, Thomas, ix, xviii, xx, 105, 107–24, 208, 221, 236, 242, 330–40,

Jefferson, Thomas (*continued*)
386 n.1, 395 n.33, 416 n.118, 417
nn.122, 123, 124, 418 nn.126, 128, 129,
421 n.131, 422 nn.132, 133, 134, 424
n.135, 425 nn.136, 137, 138, 139, 140,
141, 142, 143, 426 nn.144, 145, 146,
427–28 n.147, 428 n.148, 450 n.259
Jeremiah, xv
Jesus, 117, 120–21, 166, 333, 413 n.100,
424 n.134, 426 n.144, 433 n.171, 436
n.191. *See also* Jews
Jews, 246, 407–8 n.69, 408 n.79, 433
n.172, 439 n.211, 443 n.239
John I, 23–24, 239, 244, 255, 391 n.14
Johnson, William Samuel, 19, 271
Journalism, 142. *See also* Patner,
Andrew
Judas Iscariot, 166, 412 n.94, 436 n.191
Judges and judicial power, xix, xx, 5, 7,
12, 42, 48–49, 75–77, 305, 444 n.243;
life tenure for judges, 11, 32, 78, 80,
278, 290; misconduct by judges, 13–
15, 45
Judicial review, 16, 20, 42, 44–45, 76, 94,
105, 229, 234, 319, 401 n.61, 408 n.74,
439 n.209, 439 n.210
Jury, trial by, 3, 11, 13–14, 24, 26, 29, 31–
32, 49, 55, 85–87, 91, 248, 264–65, 270,
272, 274–75, 278, 282, 287, 300, 307,
317, 319, 322, 324, 390 n.14, 413 n.101
Jury, trial by, in civil suits, 13–17, 86–88,
282, 288, 294–95, 297, 300, 307, 317–19,
322, 324, 396 n.41
Justice, xx, 46, 144, 162, 164, 205, 225,
288, 419 n.130, 423 n.134, 442 n.229.
See also Affirmative action; Natural
justice; Providence

Kalven, Harry, Jr., 386 n.1, 403–4 n.66
Kaminsky, John P., 387 n.1, 453–54
n.260
Kaplan, Simon, 418 n.130
Kates, Don B., Jr., 61–62, 64, 408 n.70
Kazazis, Christina von Nolcken, 405
n.66
Kazazis, Kostas, 452 n.260
Kurland, Philip B., 402 n.64
Kurosawa, Akira, 409 n.83

La Fayette, Marquis de, 14, 333, 394
n.23

Law of the land, 23–26, 31, 70, 239, 250,
252, 260–61, 282, 287, 300, 396 n.41.
See also Due process of law
Law school curriculum reform, 419–20
n.130, 453 n.260
Laws of nature, 217, 234, 273. *See also*
Nature, natural
Lee, Robert E., x, 385 n.1
Lehrberger, James, 415 n.106
Lerner, Ralph, 402 n.64
Levi, Edward H., iii, xviii, 386–87 n.1,
403–4 n.66. *See also* Bar Admission
Cases; Red Scare; Slavish doctrine of
non-resistance; Sophism
Levy, Leonard W., 3, 4, 387 n.4, 419
n.99, 453–54 n.260
Liberty principle, x, xix, xx, 6, 46, 55,
69, 88, 130, 132–33, 149, 160, 162, 200–
201, 205, 210, 273, 409–10 n.83, 423
n.134, 437 n.192, 449 n.258. *See also*
Declaration of Independence; Equality principle
Licht, Robert A., 389 n.13, 411 n.93
Lincoln, Abraham, xv, xix, 21, 100–101,
108, 112, 124, 126, 130, 133–34, 135–67,
171, 174, 185, 188, 193, 197, 224, 243,
362, 386 n.1, 387 n.2, 396 n.45, 397
n.49, 423–24 n.134, 425 n.140, 426
n.146, 428 n.149, 429 n.153, 430 n.155,
431 n.157, 431–32 n.159, 432 nn.163,
173, 175, 434 nn.176, 177, 178, 179, 435
n.185, 436 n.191, 436–37 n.192, 437
n.196, 443 n.232, 451 n.259. *See also*
Emancipation Proclamation; Gettysburg Address
Lincoln-Douglas Debates, 166, 174, 188,
197, 437–38 n.197
Localism, 9, 232, 450–51 n.259, 453–54 n.260
Locke, John, 61, 123, 339, 415 n.106. *See
also* Declaration of Independence

Machiavelli, Niccolò, 113, 385 n.1, 395
n.30, 421 n.131, 426 n.144, 438 n.201,
446 n.251
MacCormack, John R., 428 n.147
McKenzie, Stanley D., 435 n.188
McPherson, James M., 430 n.155
Madison, James, xvi, 12, 18, 35–37, 40,
61, 93, 95, 126, 208, 241, 293–97, 315–
20, 394 nn.16, 27, 395 n.29, 397 nn.49,
52, 427 n.146

Magna Carta, 2, 23–26, 30–31, 34, 70, 80, 82, 95, 215, 218, 234, 239, 260–61, 319, 387 n.3, 391 n.14, 396 nn.40, 41, 42, 410 n.85, 414 n.105, 422 n.131; *text*, 239, 244–55

Mahoney, Dennis J., 3, 188, 387 n.4, 408 n.80, 440 n.213, 441 n.225, 443 n.236, 444 n.245

Mansfield, Harvey C., Jr., 396 n.47, 422 n.229

Mansfield, Lord, 184–85, 341–44, 435 n.186

Manufactures, promotion of, 19, 127, 129, 309, 349

Marbury v. *Madison* (1803), 42, 401 n.61. See also Judicial review

Market economy, 75, 145, 237, 424 n.135, 447 n.255

Marshall, John, 74, 126, 397 n.52, 401 n.61. See also Crosskey, William W.

Mason, George, 13–21, 294–95, 394 n.21

Masters, Roger D., 454 n.260

Meiklejohn, Alexander, 403–4 n.66

Mexican War, 123, 224, 385 n.1

Meyer, Reinhold, 426 n.143

Middle States, 140, 153–54, 158, 432 n.159; (term) 451 n.259

Military, subject to political control, 11, 17, 32, 150, 278, 293–94, 434 n.179

Militia, well-regulated, 61–65, 95, 187, 283, 301, 306, 316, 321, 323, 408 n.79. See also Second Amendment

Miller, Eugene, 419 n.130

Milton, John, 53, 124, 292, 339, 421 n.131

Moderation, virtue of, xx, 18, 46, 283, 288; Dean Swift, 335

Monopolies, concerns about, 17, 170, 224, 297, 310

Montesquieu, 400 n.60, 405 n.68, 418 n.128, 423 n.134

Moral flaws, early signs of, 452 n.259

Moral standards, sources of, 18, 20, 23, 43–46, 55–57, 72–74, 91, 96, 114–15, 123–24, 137, 140, 144, 148, 158–59, 164, 189, 196–97, 204–5, 225, 232–33, 236–37, 406 n.68, 430 n.156, 434 n.178, 443 n.239, 446 n.251, 449 n.258, 451 n.259

Morality and law, 20, 121, 124, 204–6, 233, 443 nn.238, 239

More, Thomas, 53, 240, 256–58, 405 n.68, 414 n.105

Morris, Gouverneur, 16, 19–20, 120, 395 n.30, 397 n.52, 401 n.60, 402 n.62

Murley, John A., xvii, xviii, 386 n.1, 388 n.12, 389–93 n.14, 413 n.101, 415 n.106

Music and the Constitution, 421 n.131, 453–54 n.260

Myths, useful, 24, 34, 48, 52, 119; not so useful, 117–18, 230, 407 n.78

Napoleon Bonaparte, 110–11, 330–31, 336, 337–38, 401 n.60

Nation (term), 430 n.155

Natural justice, 24, 95–96, 419 n.130

Natural right, natural rights, 2, 14–16, 23, 33, 45–46, 48–49, 94–95, 101–2, 111, 124, 130, 132, 162, 170, 178–79, 205, 236, 269–70, 274, 276, 283, 292, 299, 302, 306, 316, 319, 344, 398–400 n.60, 407 n.69, 414–15 n.106, 416 n.120, 419 n.130, 428 n.149, 438 n.198, 442–43 n.232. See also Common law; Constitutionalism, natural; Nature, natural; Philosophy; Prudence; Revolution, right of

Nature, natural, 5–6, 19, 23, 45–46, 48, 56, 68–69, 85–86, 95, 101, 119, 122–23, 129–30, 132, 135, 137, 161, 164, 171, 179, 207, 218, 225–26, 238, 281, 286, 299, 330, 335, 412 n.94, 413 n.103, 415 n.106, 418 n.130, 424 n.134, 428 n.149, 446 n.251, 450 n.259, 453–54 n.260. See also Human nature; Women, nature of

Necessary and Proper Clause, 10, 17, 38, 97, 181, 222, 297. See also *Expressly* (term)

Neumann, Harry, 416 n.120, 427 n.146

New York Times v. *Sullivan* (1964), 453 n.260

Newman, Roger K., 387 n.1, 403 n.66

Nicgorski, Walter, 422 n.132

Nichols, Mary P., 422 n.132

Nineteenth Amendment, 31, 186, 190–92, 197, 218, 220, 223, 229, 440 nn.215, 216, 441 n.223; *text*, 380

Ninth Amendment, 44–45, 57, 60, 62, 86, 92–98, 100, 102, 128, 132, 234, 313, 322, 324–26, 361, 392 n.14, 413–14 n.105, 414 n.106, 415 n.116, 438 n.204; *text*, 93, 328, 376–77

Northwest Ordinance, 6, 31, 83, 134, 171, 173, 362, 387 n.2, 388 n.10, 420

Northwest Ordinance (*continued*)
n.130, 437 nn.193, 194, 443 n.240. *See also* Thirteenth Amendment

O'Connor, Flannery, 452 n.259
Old as *good*, 132, 420 n.130
O'Neill, Thomas P., Jr., 441–42 n.229
Original intention, 8, 38–39, 133
Otis, James, 28, 71, 271

Paine, Tom, 339
Pangle, Thomas L., 412 n.96, 421 n.131, 425 n.143
Pardoning power, 16, 253–55, 266, 312
Patner, Andrew, xvii, 386 n.1
People, State (terms), 62
People, ultimate authority of, xx, 5, 21, 31–32, 46, 53–55, 92, 100, 276, 281, 298–99, 305, 315, 320–21, 398–99 n.60. *See also* We the People
Pericles, vii, 432 n.168
Perpich v. *Department of Defense* (1990), 187
Persian Gulf War (1990–1991), 17–18, 183, 193, 209–10, 215–16, 227, 233, 445–46 n.251
Petition of Right, 2, 23, 24–26, 65, 67, 82, 240, 387 n.3, 391 n.14; *text*, 240, 259–62
Petition, right of, 52–53, 60, 67–68, 263, 265, 272, 274, 276, 279, 288–89, 301, 307, 316, 321, 323, 404 n.66, 423 n.134. *See also* First Amendment
Philosophy, philosopher-king, 119, 225, 425 n.142, 453–54 n.260. *See also* Aristotle; Plato; Strauss, Leo
Pierce v. *Society of Sisters* (1925), 451 n.259
Piety, xx, 131, 284–85, 288, 386 n.1, 417 n.120, 452 n.259. *See also* Providence
Pinckney, Charles, xvii, 12–13, 16, 20–21, 293–96, 394 n.16
Pinckney, Charles Cotesworth, 295, 394 n.16, 415 n.112
Plato, ix, 96, 108–10, 112–24, 331–33, 335, 337–39, 386 n.1, 405 n.46, 412 n.96, 415 n.111, 416–17 n.120, 417–18 n.124, 418 n.125, 421 n.131, 422 nn.132, 133, 425 nn.135, 140, 142, 426 nn.144, 146, 427–28 n.147, 435 n.188, 440 n.216, 453 n.260

Platt, Michael, 420 n.130
Plebiscitary democracy, 446 n.251
Plessy v. *Ferguson* (1896), 184, 439 n.208
Plutarch, 18, 185, 395 n.30, 426 n.143, 428 n.149, 453 n.260
Poe, Edgar Allan, 417 n.124
Political parties, 104–6, 212, 219–20, 228, 416 n.119, 417 n.122
Pollock v. *Farmer's Loan & Trust Co.* (1895), 187, 440 n.212
Polls, public opinion, 28, 218, 227, 446 n.251
Population control, 236
Powell, Colin L., 183
Powell v. *McCormack* (1969), 401 n.61
Power, Robert C., 389 n.13
Preambles, 10, 36, 102, 128, 130, 190, 397 n.52
Presidency, xix, 207–16; Acting President, 383–84, 445 n.247; Presidential disability, 211–13, 283–84; death of President-elect, 208, 381; Presidential selection, 104–5, 189, 193, 214, 218–20, 228, 232, 377–78; term of office, 131, 380–82. *See also* Veto, line-item
Pritchett, C. Herman, 389 n.13, 405 n.404
Proietti, Gerald, 454 n.260
Proietti, Pamela Werrbach, 415 n.106
Privacy, right of, xix, 19, 40, 44–45, 55, 65–73, 96, 226, 233–35, 438 n.198, 452–53 n.260. *See also* Property
Privileges and immunities, 38, 44, 57, 79, 81–82, 91, 93–94, 175–78, 180, 185, 274, 438 nn.198, 204; *texts* of Privileges and Immunities Clauses, 373, 378
Property, 7, 23–24, 54–55, 68, 73, 80–81, 88, 148, 218, 220–21, 281, 284, 299, 324, 338, 396 n.41, 400 n.60. *See also* Privacy, right of
Providence, xv, 130, 155, 162, 207, 276, 279–80, 284–85, 287, 291, 298, 345, 405–6 n.68, 417 n.120, 418 n.130, 422 n.134, 424–25 n.135, 425 n.141, 426 n.144. *See also* Chance; Piety; Religion and politics; Religious liberty
Prudence, 2, 6, 14, 46, 54–55, 89, 112–13, 124, 131, 137, 139, 141–43, 150, 162, 165–66, 188, 201, 208, 224–26, 230, 232, 235, 256–58, 388 n.12, 405–6

n.68, 413–14 n.105, 424 n.135, 438 n.204, 439 n.211, 444 n.243, 447 n.254, 447–48 n.256, 452 n.259, 453 n.260. *See also* Constitutional frivolity; Constitutionalism, natural

Pursuit of happiness, 114–15, 421 n.131. *See also* Virtue

Pyrros, James G., 449 n.258

Quartering of soldiers, 12, 25, 60, 65, 67, 278, 289, 294, 301, 306, 321, 323. *See also* Third Amendment

Quebec, 272, 275, 278, 430 n.156. *See also* Secession, Southern

Race relations, 147, 169, 182, 220, 439 n.209. *See also* Affirmative action; Fifteenth Amendment; Fourteenth Amendment

Randolph, Edmund, 16–17, 295–97

Ratification of the Constitution (1787–1788), 11–12, 21, 35–37, 39, 51, 93–95, 203, 242, 394 n.27

Rawle, William, 61, 63, 408 n.76

Reagan, Ronald W., 215, 442 n.229, 446 n.251

Reapportionment Cases (1962, 1964), 438–39 n.205

Reasonableness and doing justice, 91. *See also* Simpson, O. J., case of

Rebellion and Reconstruction, 124, 168, 180, 190. *See also* Secession, Southern; Slavery

Red Scare, 54. *See also* Unidentified Flying Objects

Religion and politics, 58, 120, 236, 284, 425 n.138, 438 n.198, 452 n.260. *See also* Abortion; Jefferson, Thomas

Religious Freedom Restoration Act of 1993, 406 n.68, 452 n.259

Religious liberty, 52, 55–58, 60, 67–68, 200, 205, 236, 244–45, 255, 263–64, 267, 275, 283–86, 291–92, 298, 301–2, 306, 316–17, 319, 321–23, 396 n.60, 405–6 n.68, 407 n.69, 451 n. 259. *See also* Establishment of religion; First Amendment; Freedom of expression

Representation in legislatures, adequacy of, 5, 29, 34, 50, 194, 270, 273, 277. *See also* Taxation and representation

Republican government, 8, 11–13, 18–19, 32, 38, 55, 94, 105, 164, 185, 190, 194, 220, 318, 390–91 n.14, 435 n.185, 438 n.199, 438–39 n.205, 446 n.253; *text* of Republican Form of Government Guarantee, 373

Requisitions in lieu of direct taxes, 37–38, 302, 309–10. *See also* Tax powers, revenue bills

Revolution, right of, x, 8, 24, 30, 46, 64, 96–97, 100–102, 106, 123, 132, 225, 234–35, 253–55, 276–77, 281, 298–99, 305–6, 316, 379, 386 n.1, 414 n.105, 443 n.232. *See also* Declaration of Independence; Natural right, natural rights; Slavish doctrine of nonresistance

Reynolds v. *Sims* (1964), 438–39 n.205

Reynolds v. *U.S.* (1879), 452 n.259

Rights, human, ix, 21, 237, 398–400 n.60, 445 n.250, 450 n.259

Robert's Rules of Order, 431 n.156, 453–54 n.260

Rodes, Robert E., Jr., 405 n.68

Rome, ancient, ix, 18, 113, 166–67, 185, 395 n.30, 419 n.130, 437 n.195

Rossum, Ralph A., 411 n.93

Rousseau, Jean-Jacques, 61, 116, 337, 339, 400 n.60, 422 n.132

Rule of law, 7–9, 21, 23, 28, 32, 59, 81–82, 95, 148, 178, 261–62, 264–65, 341–44. *See also* Due process of law

Satan, patron saint of individualism, 124

Schaefer, David L., 422 n.132

Schenck v. *United States* (1919), 431 n.156

Schools, public and "private," 230, 236, 443 n.238, 451–52 n.259

Science and technology, 114, 170, 426 n.146, 454 n.260. *See also* Adams, John; Jefferson, Thomas

Secession, Southern, x, 1, 101, 124–67, 170, 403 n.66, 429 n.150, 434 n.176, 437 n.196, 451 n.259. *See also* Rebellion and Reconstruction; Slavery

Second Amendment, 59–68, 207, 264–65, 283, 288, 301, 306, 316, 321, 323, 325, 327, 408 nn.78, 79, 409–10 n.83, 424 n.134; *text*, 61, 328, 375

Self-incrimination, privilege against, 73, 80–82, 85, 287, 316–17, 321

Separation of powers, 5, 164, 233, 274, 282, 290, 299–300, 318–19, 322–24, 400 n.60, 424 n.135, 449 n.258

Seventeenth Amendment, 186–87, 189–90, 197, 218, 415 n.116, 440 nn.213, 214; *text*, 379–80

Seventh Amendment, 16, 70, 76–79, 86–88, 91, 94, 288, 297, 307, 317, 322, 324, 326, 395 n.36; *text*, 328, 376

Seward, William H., 136, 154, 432 n.161, 433 n.175, 435 n.181

Shakespeare, William, 108, 112, 123, 185, 419–21 n.130, 428 n.149, 435 n.188, 437 n.195, 446 n.251, 453 n.260

Shamelessness, 96, 112, 134, 225

Sharp, Malcolm P., 403–4 n.66, 443 n.241. *See also* Levi, Edward H.

Sheppard, Harrison J., 388 n.12, 443 n.241

Sherman, Roger, 15–16, 66, 295

Silence of the Lambs, The, 452 n.259

Simpson, O. J., case of, 453 n.260. *See also* Reasonableness and doing justice

Sixteenth Amendment, 174, 186–87, 190; *text*, 187, 379

Sixth Amendment, 60, 76–80, 84–86, 91, 94, 275, 282, 287–88, 300, 304, 306–7, 317–18, 322, 324, 326; *text*, 328, 376

Slaughter House Cases (1873), 176–77, 438 n.200, 439 n.207

Slavery, x, xv–xvi, xix, 2, 7, 18, 24, 31, 43, 83, 95, 124, 128–30, 132–34, 135–67, 168–73, 178–82, 184–85, 190, 193, 200–201, 205, 218, 242, 279, 295, 297, 306, 341–62, 364, 368, 373–74, 378–79, 385 n.1, 395 n.29, 400 n.60, 429 n.153, 430 n.156, 432 n.170, 433 n.173, 434 n.179, 436 n.191, 437 nn.192, 195, 196, 443 n.237, 450–51 n.259

Slavish doctrine of non-resistance, 101, 299, 414 n.105. *See also* Revolution, right of

Socrates, ix, 107, 113, 116, 118, 120–21, 123, 333, 386 n.1, 405 n.66, 413 n.100, 416–17 n.120, 418 n.125, 422 n.132, 426 n.144, 453 n.260

Somerset's Case (1792), 184–85, 242–43, 341–44, 435 n.186

Sophism, 115–17, 333

Sorensen, Leonard R., 422 n.132

Soul, immortality of, 118, 333, 425 n.100

Southern character, xvii, 124, 202, 232, 450–51 n.259

Sports, 205, 237

Stamp Act of 1765, ix, 240, 269–71. *See also* Taxation and representation

Standing army, 12, 64, 95, 263–65, 272, 274, 278, 293, 306, 310, 415 n.108, 434 n.176

State action (term), 184–85

States: constitutions, 175, 394 n.25; restraints on States, 8, 55, 317, 322, 324; State Ratification Conventions, 38, 43, 71, 95, 298–314, 397 n.51; States' Rights, 5, 9–10, 37–38, 55, 62, 97, 100, 127, 129–31, 173, 186, 190, 450–51 n.259

Stevens, Richard G., 108, 417 n.121, 426 n.144

Stevens, Thaddeus, 146

Stone, I. F. *See* Patner, Andrew

Stone, Robert L., xvii, xviii, 386 n.1, 388 n.12, 443 n.240

Storing, Herbert J., 415 n.108, 432 n.162

Story, Joseph, 61, 64–67, 98–100, 408 n.79, 415 n.114

Strauss, Leo, ix, 118, 224, 386 n.1, 389 n.13, 414 n.106, 416–17 n.120, 418 n.125, 422 nn.132, 133, 424 nn.135, 142, 427 n.146, 427–28 n.147, 428 n.149, 432 n.168, 439 n.211, 440 n.216, 452 n.260, 453–54 n.260. *See also* Berns, Laurence

Suffrage, universal, 32, 192, 215, 217–18, 222–23, 226, 235, 282, 300

Suicide, assisted, 6, 235, 443 n.238

Sumptuary laws, 18–19, 70, 195–96, 395 n.30, 441 n.218. *See also* Eighteenth Amendment

Supermajorities, 105, 127, 132, 193–94, 206, 296, 303, 310, 447 n.255, 453–54 n.260

Swanson, James L., 386 n.1, 453 n.260

Swift v. Tyson (1842), 14, 395 n.46. *See also* Common law; *Erie Railroad Co. v. Tompkins*

Taking Clause, 74, 83–84, 181, 287, 317, 321, 400 n.60

Tax powers, revenue bills, 7–8, 19, 25, 32, 187, 196, 217, 230, 275, 448 n.257

Taxation and representation, 3, 9, 12, 25,

29, 180, 247, 259–60, 262–63, 265, 269–73, 278, 281, 287, 300, 399 n.60
Television, 205, 214–15, 237, 444 n.242; proposed abolition of, 443 n.241
Temperance, virtue of, xx, 283, 288
Tenth Amendment, 9–10, 37, 60, 62, 92–93, 97–100, 102, 132, 229, 286, 298, 302, 304, 306, 318, 323–24, 326, 328, 361, 415 n.113; *text*, 9, 328, 377. See also *Expressly* (term)
Terkel, Studs, 386 n.1
Term limitations, 208–10, 226–27, 230–32, 281, 286–87, 300, 303, 311–12, 354, 443–44 n.242, 444 nn.243, 244, 447–48 n.256. See also Constitutional frivolity
Texas v. *Johnson* (1989), 41, 230
Third Amendment, 59–60, 65–68, 207, 260–61, 263–65, 272, 274–76, 278, 283, 288–89, 293–94, 301, 306, 316, 321, 323, 325, 408 n.80; *text*, 327, 375
Thirteenth Amendment, 2, 31, 51, 130, 138, 164, 168–76, 181–87, 192–93, 200, 211, 225–26, 229, 362, 397 n.49, 437 nn.192, 193, 195, 439 nn.206, 211; *text*, 378
Thucydides, 435 n.188, 454 n.260
Thurow, Glen E., 389 n.13
Timberlake, James H., 200, 202, 441 n.217
Timoleon, 185, 453 n.260
Titles of nobility, 170, 224, 281, 286, 299, 389–90 n.14
Tobacco, effects of, 196, 199, 205. See also Drugs, attempted control of
Travel, right to, 250
Treason, 11, 32, 53–54, 79, 150, 166, 205, 264–66, 272, 312, 390 n.14, 411–12 n.94, 413 n.99
Trumbull, Lyman, 437 n.193
Twain, Mark, 91, 121, 421 n.131
Twelfth Amendment, 92–93, 104–5, 107–8, 207, 354–55, 398 n.57, 416 n.119; *text*, 377–78
Twentieth Amendment, 199, 207–8; *text*, 380–81
Twenty-eighth Amendment, possible, 384; *text* (partial), 206. See also Constitutional frivolity
Twenty-fifth Amendment, 207, 209, 211–16, 231; *text*, 383–84
Twenty-first Amendment, 34, 105, 186,

196, 199, 201–6, 243, 443 n.236; *text*, 381–82
Twenty-fourth Amendment, 31, 217, 219–21; *text*, 382–83
Twenty-second Amendment, 199, 207–10; *text*, 382
Twenty-seventh Amendment, 17, 27, 34, 36, 38, 50–52, 59, 102, 217, 221, 223–28, 297, 304, 316, 321, 323, 325, 329, 397 n.50, 402 n.64; *text*, 50, 223, 327, 384. See also Constitutional frivolity
Twenty-sixth Amendment, 6, 31, 174, 217–18, 220–23, 229; *text*, 384
Twenty-third Amendment, 207, 210–11, 217–19; *text*, 382
Tyranny, 3, 61, 99, 158, 202–3, 218, 277–79, 283, 331

Unidentified Flying Objects (UFOs), 339, 447 n.255, 452 n.260
Union, perpetual, 3, 7, 9–10, 21, 133, 138–39, 147–48, 182, 430 n.155, 437 n.192; older than the States, 130
Universal Declaration of Human Rights (1948), 190, 438 n.198
University of Chicago, 111, 403 n.66. See also Levi, Edward H.
U.S. v. *Dennis* (1951), 54
U.S. v. *Fisher* (1804), 401 n.61
U.S. v. *Nixon* (1974), 401 n.61

Van Alstyne, William, 402 n.64
Van Doren, John, xviii, xix, 454 n.260
Van Patten, Jonathan K., 388 n.12, 389 n.13, 411 n.94
Vanderslice, Stephen J., xvii, 415 n.106
Vasils, Theodora, 452 n.260
Vaughan, Frederick, 405 n.66
Veto, line-item, 131, 231–32, 349, 429 n.154, 447 n.255
Vice President, selection of, 104–5, 211–14, 231
Vietnam War, 3, 68, 195, 410 n.83, 446 n.251. See also Cold War follies
Virginia Declaration of Rights, xx, 28, 30, 56–57, 88, 241; *text*, 241, 281–83
Virginia Statute of Religious Liberty, 393 n.14, 417 n.122; *text*, 241, 291–92
Virtue, xx, 160, 185, 283, 400–401 n.60, 424 n.135

Voting qualifications and rights, 182–83, 222–23, 439 n.209

War powers, 124, 141, 143–44, 156–59, 161, 164, 200, 222, 232
War Powers Resolution of 1973, 233, 448 n.258
Ward, Artemus, 166–67, 403 n.66, 436 n.191
Washington, George, 4, 14, 35, 37, 49, 126, 163, 208, 215, 336, 374, 394 n.23, 395 n.30, 397 n.52, 407 n.69, 419 n.130
Watergate scandal, 215
We the People, 10, 100, 128, 193, 225–27, 233–34, 238, 286, 344, 363, 391 n.14, 444 n.242
Weisberg, Bernard, xvii, 438 n.198
West, Grace Starry, 422 n.132
West, Thomas G., xviii, 420 n.130, 422 n.132
West Virginia Board of Education v. Barnette (1943), 452 n.259

William and Mary, 27–28, 263–64, 266–68, 336
Williamson, Hugh, 13, 294
Wilson, James, 397 n.52, 411 n.93, 413 n.103
Wisconsin v. Yoder (1977), 451 n.259
Witchcraft, 405–6 n.68
Women, nature of, 412 n.94, 440 n.216; rights, 252

Xenophon, 120, 337, 425 n.143, 432 n.168
Xerxes, x, 395 n.30, 404 n.66

Youngstown Sheet & Tube Co. v. Sawyer (The Steel Seizure Case) (1952), 415 n.110, 433–34 n.176

Zuckert, Michael P., 432 n.168, 439 n.206

George Anastaplo is
Lecturer in the Liberal Arts
at the University of Chicago,
Professor Emeritus of Political Science and of Philosophy
at Rosary College,
and Professor of Law
at Loyola University of Chicago.